MONONGALIA COUNTY, (WEST) VIRGINIA, RECORDS OF THE DISTRICT, SUPERIOR AND COUNTY COURTS

Volume 7: 1808 - 1814

Compiled By Melba Pender Zinn

HERITAGE BOOKS, INC.

Other Heritage Books by the Author

Monongalia County, (West) Virginia, Records of the District, Superior, and County Courts. Volume 1, 1776-1799

Monongalia County, (West) Virginia, Records of the District, Superior, and County Courts. Volume 2, 1800-1808

Monongalia County, (West) Virginia, Records of the District, Superior, and County Courts. Volume 3, 1804-1810

Monongalia County, (West) Virginia, Records of the District, Superior, and County Courts. Volume 4, 1800-1802, 1810

Monongalia County, (West) Virginia, Records of the District, Superior, and County Courts. Volume 5, 1802-1805

Monongalia County, (West) Virginia, Records of the District, Superior, and County Courts. Volume 6, 1805-1808

Published 1994 By

HERITAGE BOOKS, INC.
1540-E Pointer Ridge Place, Bowie, MD 20716
(301) 390-7709

ISBN 0-7884-0138-6

DEDICATED

to my son

JOHN

TABLE OF CONTENTS

PREFACE

In 1776, Monongalia County, (West) Virginia, was formed from a portion of the western part of Augusta County, Virginia, and in 1779 and 1780 small portions of West Augusta were annexed to Monongalia County. At that time, in 1776, Land Commissioners were appointed by the Virginia Assembly to settle land claims, surveys, grants and anything at all that had to do with the claims of the early settlers to land they heretofore had lived on, and where their children were born, and where they had raised crops and dug out a living in the wilderness. Before this time, no deeds, grants, surveys or any sort of ownership was allowed because, before the Revolutionary War, the British King had forbidden all white settlers to enter the western wilderness. Therefore, those that were here, were here illegally and only after the War for Independence were the settlers allowed to make their claims. After the colonies declared their independence, Virginia offered 400 acres free to those settlers that were here before 1773 and could prove they were here by having built a home or raised a crop or had marked their boundary with notches in the trees called "tomahawk rights." An additional 1000 acres could be purchased from the Commonwealth for a small cost per acre, and was called a "Preemption Warrant."

In 1796, the Monongalia County Court records were destroyed by fire. County Clerk, Col. John Evans, stored the records in a small outbuilding on his farm and it was there the records were burned. The only court records preserved for Monongalia County in the period 1776-1796 are those filed in District Court composed of Monongalia [1776], Harrison [1784], Randolph [1787], Ohio [1776], Wood [1798] and other counties as they were formed. Papers from other courts appear at times, usually having to do with action concerning area citizens.

Each name of a person, place or thing is presented as it has been deciphered, with no attempt to change spelling to conform with today's accepted interpretation.

The numeral/letter before each entry is the envelope number in which the documents are filed.

MELBA PENDER ZINN
Route 3, Box 169
Grafton, WV 26354
1994

157a - 1838, Monongalia County Court. Private papers of Nimrod EVANS: EVANS to Charlotte FOSTER, 10 November 1827, to sundry repairs on watch $.87. On 17 April 1828, Thomas P. RAY, one of the executors of EVANS, deceased, received this amount and the receipt was signed by N. WHITESIDE.

On 20 September 1828, Sampson S. FRUM presented a bill for $46 for 4 stacks of hay.

Received 11 February 1807 from William WILLIAMS and Thomas MEREDITH $1, the fee on 2 tracts of land conveyed to them by Jonathan ROWLAND, signed by EVANS.

1821, Deputy Rawley MARTIN for Sheriff John COX served 2 notices on Michael and Jas. KERN $1.

1815, Rawley MARTIN owed $2.25 fees on conveyance of 206 acres of land from D. E. DENT, 512 acres from George KERN and 118 acres from George SMART.

1817, Rawley MARTIN owed $.75 fee on conveyance of 100 acres from Jane TINGLE.

"Nimrod EVANS Presbyterian Church $1000, 1 April 1827 $250, total $1250."

March 1828, to inserting advertisements for sale of property of the deceased and the same for settlement of accounts $2, signed by William THOMPSON.

August 1825, a bill from William PHILIPS for steeling one axe $1. Justice Anthony SMITH.

25 August 1827 - 4 February 1828, a bill from William GUFFY for sundry store merchandise: salt, brandy, cheese, candles, pork, brandy per Agness, turpentine per RAY, $5.14.

1825, a bill from Samuel HANWAY for 65 acre warrant, 1/2 the surveying and recording the same $5.37.

6 March - 3 April 1828, THOMAS P. RAY, executor, charged $20.34 for postage on 2 letters for binding negroes, postage on letters to and from Uniontown, expenses to Uniontown to bind negroes and 3 days services, writing lease for ABLE and 1 day attendance to see land and amount paid to Black Isreal for whiskey.

8 February 1830, Fielding KIGER signed a receipt for $2.43, the balance on an account.

On 11 February 1830, William THOMPSON signed a receipt for $20.96, the balance of an account for 1812, 1815, 1816, and 1817 court fees.

25 March 1828, a bill from Jno. A. DURBINS for a coffin for EVANS $12.

2 March 1830, Harman WATTS signed a receipt for 4 wool hats sold 1824 and 1827 $4.

14 March 1828, Reuben B. TAYLOR presented a bill for one new shoe out of my iron and one 15 foot chain, $2.22 dated 14 and 21 January 1828.

7 September 1825, a list of accounts turned over to John WATTS for collection: Francis COLLINS, Robert FERRELL

(crossed out), Ezra BEALE and George NORRIS.

25 March 1828, receipt signed by John A. DURBINS for $12 on an account.

8 August 1836, William THOMPSON signed a receipt for $.25 for six newspapers, The Mon Chronicle.

March 1823 term of court, Moses BUCK and EVANS owed Ralph BERKSHIRE $.53 for one day attendance as a witness for them against Robbin SMITH.

11 September 1828, William THOMPSON signed a receipt for $1 for making handbills to advertise land on Pappaw Creek.

18 August 1828, Francis BILLINGSLEY signed a receipt for $3.80 for "one half of the following notes bought by us in partnership and collected by you," to wit, John McGEE, _____ BURCHINAL, Job PRICKETT, William G. PAYNE and Joseph ALLEN. 1820, medicine and services for horse. 1821 to cash. 1822 potter's ware. Credited to this account: 5 hoes received of BURCHINAL, cash paid into bank and clerk's notes from 1812-1825. Clerk's notes: R. BERKSHIRE, John LASH, Thomas LAIDLEY, Esther PAINTER, Joseph PARKS and John BROOKOVER.

15 February 1830, R. BERKSHIRE signed a receipt for $3.18 for various services and a note returned on John BROOKOVER.

18 February 1824 and December 1826, John DENT presented a bill for 30 pounds of buckwheat flour and 157 pounds of pork $3.48.

12 June 1828, Jonathan JORDAN signed a receipt for $.16 for ferrying EVANS, servant and horse in 1825.

26 May 1828, David/Daniel MUSGRAVE signed a receipt for $5.62, the amount due to George and David WATSON for fees paid twice including interest.

January 1828, James ARNETT present a bill for $.25 for balance due for butter.

10 November 1820, Elias BRAIN?, treasurer, signed an order for EVANS to pay R. BOGGESS $25 "which will be the balance due from you to the Methodist Church."

16 January 1824 - 30 January 1827, bill from William DERING for $10.62 for mending bridles, reins, collars, saddle bags, girth and 1 dog collar.

22 February 1828, bill from Thomas BROOKE for services and medicine administered.

24 December 1823 - 2 May 1827, bill from Nicholas SCHISLER for $1.12 for repairing shot gun, repairing flute and mending door lock.

25 March 1817 - 11 April 1823, bill from Robert BOGGESS for $22.20 for making one small coffin (25 March 1817), putting ceiling in house and hiring Jno. WATTS, sundry house repairs and repairs on cellar and fixing shop door at the house where WATTS lives $22.20.

November 1827 - February 1828, receipt signed by John H. McGEE for $2.35 for shoe thread and a fine comb.

1828, George DAWSON presented a bill for $4.67 for collecting money and costs in the case of FARMER.

2

14 July 1824 - 9 May 1826, Constable John WATTS present-
ed a bill for $13.87 for execution against Jacob KERN and
James KERN, veal meat, the debt paid to John MALONE for
EVANS, Town Tax for 1827 and 1828, costs for EVANS vs Walter
CARLILE, Francis COLLINS, Alexander ALLEY, Ezra BEELS and
Jacob MILLER, and cost of selling EVANS' real estate by order
of the executors.

January 1828, Robert TOBIN presented a bill for 60
bushels of coal $1.20.

7 January 1827, EVANS signed a receipt to Josiah BOYERS
"for taking up my Negro woman Tansy $5."

19 April 1828, Joseph A. SHACKLEFORD signed a receipt
for $2 for EVANS' "subscription to road across Falling Run."

9 through 25 October 1827, Isaac COOPER presented a bill
for $6.50 balance due on beef account and 175 bushels coal.

1828, Tax Ticket for County Levy, Poor Tax, 3 horses 6
slaves and 537 acres of land $21.48.

4 December 1828, Dudley EVANS signed a receipt for $14,
the amount paid for 1814 and 1815 taxes for Nimrod.

17 October - 18 November 1820, Philip HOLLAND presented
a bill for $9.37 for beef and ferriage from 16 August 1825 to
18 May 1827.

19 April 1828, Purnal HOUSTON signed a receipt for $1.54
for balance due on shingles and straw in 1828.

4 December 1828, Dudley EVANS signed a receipt for $35
for 10 days service in surveying land on Pawpaw Creek and 5
days service in valuing lands in November 1828.

16 November 1825, bill from Dudley EVANS for surveying,
platting and traveling 10 miles at $.05 per mile.

1829, a bill from John HANWAY for surveying some of the
lines of the land sold to SHUMAN and TOOTHMAN and platting
the same.

1 October 1826, a bill from Daniel W. STEWART for $11.71
for balance due on settlement and shaving from 13 October
1826 through 27 February 1828.

June 1828, a bill from James TIBBS for $5 for appraising
the lands of Nimrod under the order of the Court.

1823, Joshua THORN presented a bill for $1.20 for 3
bushels of corn.

15 May 1826, B. F. BLACK presented a bill for $9 for one
and one half boxes of glass.

27 September - 3 November 1827, John THORN presented a
bill for $2.50 for corn meal.

June 1828, Richard WATTS signed a receipt for $5 for 5
days service appraising the lands of the deceased.

April 1822, Alpheus P. WILLSON presented a bill for rent
of a house for one year $160 and other services to the amount
of $290.16 which includes $3.87 paid at ARMSTRONG's on
National Road.

1811 - 1822, John CHISLER owed EVANS $40.57 for wheat, 1
kettle, plowing lot and various court fees.

14 February 1829, Patrick SHEHEN signed a receipt for

$3.50 for balance due on an account dated 23 November 1827.

14 February 1829, Patrick SHEHEN signed a receipt for $2 for digging grave in February 1828.

9 June 1828, Thomas GILL, of the New York Evening Post (formerly the New York Herald), presented a bill for $98.83 the amount of a subscription from 5 November 1805 through 6 January 1827. EVANS paid $80 on the subscription leaving a balance of $18.83 due. Receipt signed by GILL dated 1 May 1829.

1 July 1827, Jacob MADERA presented a bill for $48.75 from 2 March 1804 through 24 November 1827 for cleaning and varnishing bedstead, spade handle, cellar frame, making steps and windows on boarding house, repairing fences, painting Pertishim GITTINGS house, clearing 9 lots, repairing coffee mill and glass stand, making hand railing and putting bottom in chair. EVANS paid $44.92 leaving a balance of $3.83.

15 November 1828, Daniel HALL signed a receipt for $1 for EVANS' subscription on the Cobun Creek Bridge in 1828.

1829, Tax Ticket for Real Estate Taxes for 100, 88, 128, 206 and 61 acres of land $2.94.

1825-1836, fees owing for court services in Harrison County Court and Harrison County Superior Court of Chancery.

17 May 1828, letter signed by Isaac SIFFEN asking EVANS to send information about a parcel of land to The Honorable James WILLIAMS at Fairfield, Pennsylvania.

1828, receipt signed by Peyton DREW, Clerk of the General Court, for probate of EVANS' will.

157a - 1808, Monongalia County Court. "Thomas COURTNEY who is in his 80th year and his wife about 70 has no person to labor for them except one boy and but little property, prays the court to relieve him from County Levy and Poor Rates." June 1808.

157a - 1808, Monongalia County Court. Bond signed by Agnes (x) FRETWELL to be administratrix of the estate of Thomas FRETWELL, deceased, secured by William JOHN and John FAIRFAX, 11 July 1808.

157a - 1808, Monongalia County Court. Bond for Nancy WILFORD, formerly Nancy GARLOW and executrix of Christopher GARLOW, to make a true and perfect inventory of the estate of Christopher GARLOW secured by Joseph WILFORD, Presley MARTIN and Richard HARRISON, 12 August 1808. Justices: William JOHN, Robert FERRELL, Dudley EVANS, James SCOTT, John FAIRFAX, Lemuel JOHN, Benjamin REEDER, Nicholas VANDERVORT, Thomas WILLEY, Simeon EVERLY, John W. DEAN, Frederick HARSH, David MORGAN, Samuel ELLISON, Morgan MORGAN, William JOHNSON, William N. JARRETT, Ralph BARKSHIRE, John NUZUM, Boaz BURROWS, John STEALEY, James E. BEALL, Amos ROBERTS, Augustus WERNINGER, John WAGNER, William WILLEY Jr. and William GEORGE.

157a - 1808, Monongalia County Court. Bond signed by Robert CLARK and James McGREW to be executors for James CLARK Sr., deceased, secured by William TINGLE and Alexander BRANDON, 13 September 1808.

157a - 1808, Monongalia County Court. James (g) CORREY, John BAKER and James WATTS appraised a stray heifer taken up by Levin WATTS at $4, 21 January 1808.

157a - 1808, Monongalia County Court. Henry BARRICKMAN, Joseph JOSEPH and William LAWUS appraised a stray brown mare taken up by Elizabeth CUNNINGHAM at $18, 6 August 1808.

157a - 1808, Monongalia County Court. Levi FREELAND, Samuel BASSNET and Asa DUDLEY appraised a stray mare taken up by John WATSON at $30, 20 August 1808.

157a - 1808, Monongalia County Court. "To the Clerk of Monongalia County, Richmond, 9 August 1808. Sir: The recommendation of persons proposed to be added to the Commission of the Peace for the County of Monongalia has been received, but commissions cannot be issued unless it shall appear that a majority of the acting justices of the said county were present at the time of making the said recommendations; for although the justices of the county had been previously summoned to attend for the purpose of laying a county levy and for other purposes, yet it does not appear that the court signified and entered on their record the intention of making such recommendations, as is positively required by the Act of Assembly passed 21 January 1806, in all those cases where a majority of the justices are not present at the time of making the recommendations. Your extract of the order of court making the recommendation does not state the number of justices present, nor have you transmitted a list of all the justices of the county. Should the fact be that a majority of the acting justices were present at the time of making the recommendations and it shall so appear by your certificates made in conformity with the act aforesaid, the commissions will be made out and forwarded. Otherwise the recommendations must be made again and care taken to conform to the requisites of the law. I am with great respect your obedient servant, William H. CABELL."

157a - 1808, Monongalia County Court. One sorrel horse and one sorrel mare, the property of William CHIPPS, was attached at the suit of John W. DEAN for $18.67 plus cost. In order to retain possession of his property until time of public sale or his debt was paid CHIPPS signed this Delivery Bond secured by John GREEN, 4 July 1808.

157a - 1808, Monongalia County Court. Bond signed by Catherine (x) EVANS to be administratrix of Thomas EVANS, deceased,

5

secured by William TINGLE and Jno. WAGNER, 13 September 1808.

157a - 1808, Monongalia County Court. Bond signed by Horatio MORGAN to serve as Constable for a term of two years secured by James JEFFS and Zackquill MORGAN, 9 August 1808.

157a - 1808, Monongalia County Court. Bond signed by Joseph CAMPBELL to serve as County Coroner secured by Nimrod EVANS, 14 November 1808.

157a - 1808, Monongalia County Court. Sheriff Stephen MORGAN, allowance for services, September 1808. Called court on Alexander BEATY and summoning 10 witnesses. Called court on Henry TEETS and summoning 3 witnesses. Called court on Michael PAUGH and Jos. WISBY. Putting Doctor PRICE in jail and keeping till discharged. Keeping Doctor DOUTY in jail from 14 April till 22nd and fee for the same. Keeping Michael PAUGH in jail from 14 June to 24th and fee for the same. Keeping jail for 12 months, keeping Courthouse and furnishing with wood, attending monthly court, having Courthouse lock mended, and furnishing candles, $104.52. Sheriff was allowed $72 for these services.

157a - 1808, Monongalia County Court. June 1808, Richard COZAD was allowed $3.40 for guarding Michael PAUGH 4 days and traveling and returning 30 miles as guard. William POSTLE was allowed $1 for guarding PAUGH 2 days. Thomas MONTGOMERY was allowed $3.40 for guarding Michael PAUGH 4 days and traveling and returning 30 miles as guard. Constable James MATHENY.

157a - 1808, Monongalia County Court. Bond signed by Thomas (x) LAZEL, Minister of the Methodist Episcopal Church, to perform the Rites of Matrimony secured by Thomas WILSON and William G. PAYNE, 16 November 1808.

157a - 1808, Monongalia County Court. Nimrod EVANS, Clerk of County Court, account for services. To called court on Alexander BEATY, Michael PAUGH, Henry TEETS and Joseph WISBY. Orders drawn on John FAIRFAX, John EVANS and Laurence SNIDER. Examining and certifying commissioner's returns and general allowance, $158.

157a - 1808, Monongalia County Court. "Monongalia County, to wit, Personally appeared before me, Boaz BURROWS, a Justice of the Peace for the County aforesaid David SCOTT and took the oath of Office of Major of the 1st Battalion in the 118th Regiment and the Oath of Fidelity and an oath to support the Constitution of the United States," 11 January 1808.

157a - 1808, Monongalia County Court. "9 January 1808, Capt. James BARKER before me took the Oath of Office and the Oath of Fidelity in the 118th Regiment Virginia." Justice James SCOTT.

157a - 1808, Monongalia County Court. "9 January 1808, Dear Sir: I understand by Sheriff MORGAN that you have taken a certain woman on the county named Penelope HILL and it is certain there is several individuals that has offered to take her and maintain her for what labor she can do and I believe it is our duty not to make anyone a burden on the county that we can shift off in that form, therefore, I think it would be expedient if it can be done to stop that cost," signed by C. HAYMOND and directed to Col. William McCLEERY.

157a - 1807, Monongalia County Court. 14 September 1807, "John RAMSEY, constable, produced in court an account for criminal services amounting to $15.93 which is allowed him and it is ordered that the Sheriff pay the same out of the County Levy of 1806."

157a - 1808, Monongalia County Court. Constable Daniel COX presented an account for services for 1807 and 1808, which was for executing a State Warrant on George SCOTT, Robert SCOTT, Edward McFAGIN, Seth STAFFORD and Joseph JEFFERY. Calling witnesses and attending before the Magistrate, $5.52.

157a - 1808, Monongalia County Court. Constable William BIGGS presented an account for executing a State Warrant on Abraham LAPPINGTON, to taking LAPPINGTON to jail with a guard of two men 30 miles at $.10 per mile. Allowed $3.63.

157a - 1808, Monongalia County Court. "To be sold to the highest bidder on Monday 27 this present month October on the plantation whereon Thomas FRETWELL, deceased, lived all the property belonging to the estate of the above mentioned. The terms of the sale will be made known on the day of sale. All persons having claims against the said estate are requested to come forward with their accounts well authenticated for settlement. Also those indebted to the estate are earnestly requested to come forward and make payment or settle some other way for the situation of the estate will not admit of indulgences, 10 October 1808, Agness FRETWELL, Admin'tx."

157a - 1808, Monongalia County Court. Bond signed Catherine (x) SCOTT and Benjamin HAMILTON, administrators of James SCOTT, deceased, secured by David SCOTT and James SCOTT, 10 October 1808.

157a - 1808, Monongalia County Court. "To Commissioner Alexander BRANDON, for equalizing the land and making the (land) books and examining them and 1 store license, $10.25, 1808."

157a - 1808, Monongalia County Court. "To Commissioner Rawley

MARTIN for equalizing the land and making the (land) books and examining them and 5 store license, $12.25, 1808."

157a - 1807, Monongalia County Court. Rawley SCOTT allowed 50 cents for patroling one night with Joseph ALLEN, August 1807. Joseph ALLEN patroled 9 nights between 9 August and 15 September 1897 and Christian MADERA patroled 5 nights.

157a - 1808, Monongalia County Court. Bond signed by THOMAS (x) EVANS secured by Jacob FOULK, Nicholas MADERA and Thomas McKINLEY dated 11 February 1808. "Whereas on the __ day of this instant, a warrant was issued by Justice Ralph BARKSHIRE against Benjamin EVANS, son of said Thomas EVANS, for the purpose of apprehending said Benjamin to bring him before said Justice to answer a charge of getting a bastard child on the body of Rebecca HAYS and before execution of said warrant and on suggestion that the same could not be executed, the court of said County of Monongalia on motion of the said Thomas EVANS, ordered and directed that said Thomas should take into his care and keeping a female bastard child sworn to the said Benjamin by the said Rebecca so soon as said Thomas should execute a bond agreeable to the tenor thereof conditioned for the maintenance of the said child so long as the said court should direct. Now the condition of this obligation is such that if the above bound Thomas EVANS shall get into his possession the said bastard child and shall take sufficient care of the same by clothing, feeding and tenderly rearing the same until exonerated by the court then the above obligation to be void else to remain in force."

157a - 1808, Monongalia County Court. Bond signed by John WILLETS to act as guardian to Sarah WORLEY and Ann WORLEY, two infant children of Ezekiel WORLEY, deceased, secured by W. TINGLE and Augustus WERNINGER, 8 February 1808.

157a - 1808, Monongalia County Court. Bond signed by George DERING to keep an ordinary at his own house secured by Nimrod EVANS, 14 November 1808.

157a - 1810, Monongalia County Court. To William MARTENY, Esqr. from Noah LINSLY, 22 September 1808. LINSLY said a number of people had requested him to become a candidate in opposition to Mr. JACKSON at the next Congressional Election. He said he would attend next November Court in Randolph County to discuss the matter. On reverse, "Papers finished at May 1810, A. G."

157a - 1808, Monongalia County Court. Bond for Nancy WILFORD, formerly Nancy (x) GARLOW and executrix of Christopher GARLOW, deceased, to make a true and perfect inventory of the estate of Christopher GARLOW secured by Joseph WILFORD, James TARNEY and John THOMPSON, 14 July 1808.

157a - 1809, Monongalia County Court. "A list of notes left with me (N. EVANS) by Michael KERN Jr. as the property of John Barney WHEELER. John CLARK $9, 17 April 1808 due at date. Joseph JANES/JEANES due bill $2, 6 June 1807. John COOPER note $15.25, 26 July 1808, credit $3. Jacob MADERA note $7, 5 March 1808, credit $2. D. F. McCREA $5, 12 March 1808. Charles BYRN account balance $7.97, 2 June 1807. John NICKLIN order $2, 11 July 1807. George HITE account $43.23, 4 October 1808. John NICKLIN order $2, 29 July 1807. Arthur WILSON (in pay of boat) 5 pounds, 1 shilling and 10 pence half penny, $3 on account of ELLIOTT denied by WILSON leaving balance of 4 pounds, 3 shillings and 10 pence." Notes filed are signed by John CLARK, Joseph JEANES, John COOPER witnessed by John SEAMAN, Jacob MADERA, John NICHLIN order for 100# flour and 100# on Monday next (witnessed by Michael KERN), John NICHLIN order on Mathew WILSON for 100# flour, D. F. McRAE and W. N. JARRETT. Notes filed that are not on the above list: note signed by William and James JOLLIFFE to Robert MINNIS dated 28 January 1804 for $60 payable in good corn on or before 25 December next. This note assigned to Jacob FOULK on 20 November 1807. Note signed by Stephen MYARS to WHEELER dated 4 June 1807 for $2.12. A letter written by EVANS to WHEELER on 17 December 1809 expressing EVANS' concern for the health of WHEELER and his family who had moved to Louisiana. EVANS was concerned that WHEELER had "settled too low on the Mississippi to ensure health at all seasons" and said perhaps he should have moved "lower down to Naches on the heights" or near the mouth of the Ohio. EVANS discusses the debts left in his hands and said many denied owing the debt. He said he could not settle with HITE because "I find him a difficult hand to settle with."

157a - 1808, Monongalia County Court. Bond signed by Stephen MORGAN to act as Sheriff secured by William G. PAYNE, John CARTER and John PAYNE, 14 June 1808.

157a - 1808, Monongalia County Court. Bond signed by Stephen MORGAN to be Collector of all taxes imposed by law secured by William G. PAYNE, George HITE, John PAYNE, John C. PAYNE and John FAIRFAX, 27 July 1808.

157a - 1808, Monongalia County Court. Richmond, 8 August 1808, Commission from William H. CABELL for Stephen MORGAN to continue as Sheriff of Monongalia County for two years from date of first qualification "as a difference of construction has prevailed in different counties in the state."

157a - 1808, Monongalia County Court. Arthur WILSON owed N. EVANS $.78 court services, 1808.

157a - 1808, Monongalia County Court. Bond signed by Jordon HALL to be administrator for Henry BARNES, deceased, secured by Augustus WERNINGER, 11 July 1808.

157a - 1808, Monongalia County Court. Re-nomination of Wm. WHITEHAIR to the office of constable signed by Frank HARSH Esqr. who said he would act as security for WHITEHAIR as "there is not the least danger of any misconduct in him," 8 June 1808.

157a - 1807, Monongalia County Court. "Abraham WOODSON has this 31 October 1807, qualified as 2nd Lieutenant in a troop of Cavalry in the 3rd Regiment and 3rd Division of the Virginia Militia before me, Benjamin REEDER."

157a - 1808, Monongalia County Court. "For value received I assign to William POSTALWAITE a judgement recovered by Jacob NUSE against Elihu HORTON for the sum of $120 and costs which was assigned to me by the said Jacob and the clerk will please direct the same to the use of the said William," signed by Jacob FOULK. Directed to William TINGLE, Clerk of the District Court.

157a - 1808, Monongalia County Court. Bond signed by Robert STEWART to act as administrator for Robert STEWART, deceased, secured by Daniel COX and William STEWART, 13 June 1808.

157a - 1808, Monongalia County Court. Peter MEREDITH, Samuel TAYLOR and Moses ROYSE appraised a stray heifer taken up by Andrew COCHRAN at $5, 15 March 1808.

157a - 1808, Monongalia County Court. Bond signed by John GARLOW to act as guardian to Joseph GARLOW, above the age of 14, son of Christopher GARLOW, deceased, secured by Adam SRIVER.

157a - 1808, Monongalia County Court. Bond signed by Presley MARTIN and Robert SCOTT to act as administrators for Jesse MARTIN, deceased, secured by Robert SCOTT, David SCOTT and Charles W. MARTIN, 14 June 1808.

157a - 1808, Monongalia County Court. 28 May 1808, Justices summoned to court on the 2nd Monday in June for the purpose of laying a County Levy and for other purposes.

157a - 1808, Monongalia County Court. William McDANIEL petitioned the court to "inquire of the damages that may be done to any or all persons by his building a water grist mill on his lands on both side of the Tyger Valley River." No date.

157a - 1808, Monongalia County Court. Bond signed by Christian WHITEHAIR to serve as constable for two years secured by Christian BISHOP and Henry BISHOP, 13 June 1808.

157a - 1808, Monongalia County Court. "Elenor DEVELIN personally appeared before me, one of the Justices of Monongalia
County, and made oath she is the same person to whom a
pension of 10 pounds has annually been granted," 2 May 1808.
Signed by Nicholas VANDERVORT who sent a note to the court
that he was in very poor health. This pension was granted to
Elenor by the State.

157a - 1808, Monongalia County Court. Bond signed by Barbary
SNODGRASS and David MUSGRAVE to be administrators of Charles
SNODGRASS, deceased, secured by William SNODGRASS and Robert
SHEARER, 13 June 1808.

157a - 1808, Monongalia County Court. Notice to Sheriff
Stephen MORGAN from Robert SCOTT of intention to pray the
court "to fine you according to law for failing to return a
writ" for $45 and costs in favor of SCOTT against John
FAIRFAX, late Sheriff, put in the hands of Deputy John PAYNE,
which MORGAN failed to return, 25 May 1808.

157a - 1808, Monongalia County Court. Certificate of Appointment for Joseph CAMPBELL to serve as Coroner, 13 September
1808. Signed by Alexander McRAE, Lieutenant Governor.

157a - 1808, Monongalia County Court. "To the Overseers of
the Poor of Monongalia County, The petition of Catherine
BURRELL showeth that at a time when she was young and able to
labor and had abundance of the good things of this life,
being protected by paternal affection, she distributed her
property among her children believing that they would (if
necessary) be able and willing at all times to aid her, but
now so it be that from age and infirmities she is no longer
able to procure for herself a subsistence and is neglected by
her children who either want the ability of affection to
grant her a support, such as infirm old age requires, and
that she is in danger of suffering. Your petitioner, therefore, prays to be allowed a small support from the county for
which she will be ever thankful, 29 November 1808," signed by
Catharine (x) BURRELL. "As it does not appear that the within petitioner is in a suffering condition at the present, and
as in strict justice she ought to be entitled to maintenance
from Smallwood WILSON who hath got a tract of land in which
she is or ought to be entitled to her thirds, I wish to let
the business rest until next court," 29 November 1808, signed
by William McCLEERY.

157a - 1808, Monongalia County Court. Bond signed by Samuel
KENNEDY to serve as constable for two years secured by Boaz
BURROWS and Nicholas MADERA, 11 July 1808.

157a - 1808, Monongalia County Court. Bond signed by Isaac
RIGGS to act as administrator for Simeon RIGGS, deceased,

secured by Asa HARRIS and Robert SHEARER, 12 December 1808. John NICHLIN declined to serve as administrator of the estate of Mr. RIGGS, deceased, because of the "situation of his own affairs", 12 December 1808.

157a - 1808, Monongalia County Court. Bond signed by Thomas BARTLETT to serve as constable for two years secured by Isaac MATHEWS, 13 June 1808.

157a - 1808, Monongalia County Court. To William McDANIEL and Aaron McDANIEL from Adam MINEAR, a notice of intent to ask the court to "summon a jury on the east bank of Tyger Valley River about 60 poles below the mouth of Pleasant Creek to ascertain what damage will accrue to anyone or to the Commonwealth by building a water grist mill and erecting a dam across said river." Notices served on the above by Thomas MEEKS. Justice William GEORGE. No date.

157a - 1807, Monongalia County Court. To Michael KERNS, John DENT and Thomas WILSON for services rendered as Commissioners for building the courthouse and offices as per order of the court: 1800, $20 each; 1801, $15 each; 1802, $10 each; 1803, $2.50 each; 1804, 1805, 1806, 1807, $2 each. 1801, paid to KERNS 400´ plank destroyed in moving old courthouse = $4. To Thomas WILSON, 1800, to cash paid A. HAWTHORN for stamped paper $.75; 1803, to cash paid J. CAMPBELL for _____ tap for conductor $.50 and cash paid to William CROSTON for re-fixing conductor $.50.

157a - 1808, Monongalia County Court. "Summoned in behalf of the Commonwealth by the accusation of George DEIBLER for perjury on the 29th day of March 1808, Elihu HORTON, defendant." Joseph ALLIN, Nicholas CHISLER, Mary DEIBLER, Rebecca THORN, Amelia BANKHART, Frederick SWISHER and Thomas WILSON Esqr. for the Commonwealth. Nicholas VANDERVORT, Sally HENTHORN, Darius PIERPOINT, Noah RIDGWAY, Josiah HOSKINSON, Gertright FULK, William CHIPPS, Ruth BILLS, Catherine RIGEWAY in behalf of HORTON. Constable John COOPER.

ENVELOPE 158 contains executions of some of the cases abstracted before. An EXECUTION is a judicial writ by which an officer is empowered to carry a judgement into effect. (Webster's Collegiate Dictionary). The document names the plaintiff and the defendant, the amount of judgement and to whom awarded, the amount of penalty, court costs and the date of the order. See Volume I, pages 34 and 35 for an example.

158 - 1809, Monongalia County Court. Jonathan HARRIS summoned to answer a Bill in Chancery exhibited against him by John DOWNER, 16 April, 27 May and 4 June 1807. "I promise to make or cause to be made a title to Abraham HARRIS for 300 acres of land adjoining land of Jonathan HARRIS sold to said HARRIS

12

by John DOWNER and extending toward my house on Dunkard Creek only excluding the _____ Camp on said creek adjoining William LANCASTER and my own land and said land is now to remain in and under the claim of $900 to be paid in 7 years in yearly payments unto the said Eaven JENKINS or his order," 1 January 1806. Signed by Even (x) JENKINS and witnessed by Obed MEREDITH and John DOWNER. "I promise to convey unto Jonathan HARRIS or his order 1000 acres of land to include the land adjoining the lands of George SNYDER, Richard TENNET and others on waters of Days Run and Statlers Run, branches of Dunkard Creek, title to be made on or before the second Monday of April next ensuing the date hereof," 1 January 1806. Signed by John DOWNER and witnessed by Abraham HARRIS and Even (x) JENKINS. "I promise to convey unto John DOWNER or his order 500 acres of land where I now live to include the lands that I now hold in my possession, title to be made on or before the second Monday in April next ensuing the date hereof," 1 January 1806. Signed by Jonathan HARIS and witnessed by Abraham HARRAS and Even (x) JENKINS. Summon Alexander CLEGG and Benjamin WHITE Sr. to the house of William G. PAYNE to give their depositions to be heard in evidence in a suit in Chancery John DOWNER, plaintiff, vs Jonathan HARRIS, defendant, 14 June and 26 August 1809. "To Mr. Thomas WILSON, Dear Sir: The bearer, Jonathan HARRIS, and I have settled our dispute he paying all court charges. You'll please to give him a line to the clerk to discharge the suit brought by me against him," 8 December 1809, signed by John DOWNER. HARRIS signed an agreement to dismiss the suit with costs of $8, 9 December 1809.

159 - 1809, Monongalia County Court. Joseph PEARCE summoned to answer a Bill in Chancery (foreclosure on a mortgage) exhibited against him by Isaac POWELL, 7 April 1808. POWELL's complaint: On 11 September 1804, Joseph REED executed his Mortgage Deed to him for a parcel of land and certain personal property for payment of $110 with interest. He said Joseph had not paid the debt and had used the personal property to his own profit. He prayed the court to summon REED to be questioned in the matter. February 1809 term of court, dismissed by order of POWELL.

159 - 1809, Monongalia County Court. Replevin Bond signed by James SCOTT to secure his property which was attached at the suit of Samuel EVERLY and sold at public sale. SCOTT was the highest bidder and signed this bond to ensure he would pay his debt in 12 months. This bond secured by Presley MARTIN on 27 February 1809. (Replevin Bond: a bond to protect or give security for the return to, or recovery by, a person of goods or chattels wrongfully taken or detained upon giving security to try the matter in court and return the goods if defeated in action.)

13

159 - 1809, Monongalia County Court. "John PAYNE personally appeared before me the subscriber, one of the Justices of Monongalia County, and made oath that heretofore previous to the 23rd November 1807, himself and William G. PAYNE advanced at sundry time the sum of 500 pounds and upwards to Jesse PAYNE and for his use upon the consideration that the said Jesse PAYNE would convey to his children certain slaves and other property mentioned in his Bill of Sale to them bearing date the 23rd of November aforesaid," 26 February 1808, signed by B. REEDER. Deed of bargain and sale signed by Jesse PAYNE to Jno C. PAYNE, Polly C. PAYNE, Susanna G. PAYNE, Elisabeth PAYNE, Francis PAYNE, Rhoda PAYNE, William PAYNE and Anna PAYNE, his children, for 500 pounds the following Negroes: Old Vilet, Chany, Young Vilet, Nancy, Peggy, Little William, Moriah, Sarah, Caty, Susannah, Selah and Isaac. Five beds and furniture, one desk and cupboard. The negroes, them and their increase to his children. William GRAHAM, of Green County, Pennsylvania, obtained an attachment against the estate of Jesse PAYNE, deceased, for $40. Attachment Bond signed by GRAHAM to ensure all costs and awards would be paid in case the PAYNE estate prevailed in the suit secured by R. BARKSHIRE, 7 March 1808. "The within attachment levied on one Negro girl named Nancy about 12 years of age now in the possession of Z. MORGAN by me James McVICKER, 7 March 1808." "An agreement this day made and confirmed between John C. PAYNE and Zacquill MORGAN, both of Morgantown, Virginia. The said John C. PAYNE binds himself to let the said MORGAN have his black boy and one black girl, known by the names of Ellick and Nancy for the term of one year and the said MORGAN binds himself to pay unto said PAYNE the sum of $50 in good bar iron, one half to be paid on or before the 15th day of May next ensuing valued at 6 pence per pound. The said MORGAN binds himself to find the two Negroes in good wearing clothes during the said term," 8 January 1808. Signed by PAYNE and MORGAN and witnessed by S. WOODROW. Two notes signed by Jesse PAYNE to William GRAHAM dated 1 October 1807 for $20 payable in good assorted pot metal and due within two months. "We, the jury, find the right of property to be in John C. PAYNE and others." May 1809 term of court, dismissed and judgement for costs.

159 - 1808, Monongalia County Court. Jesse PAYNE summoned to answer Andrew MILLER in a plea of debt for $43 and $10 damage, 31 December 1807. Appearance Bond signed by Jesse PAYNE secured by John C. PAYNE, 20 February 1808. Note signed by PAYNE to MILLER for $43 dated 10 October 1804, due 1 December next and witnessed by John MILLER.

159 - 1809, Monongalia County Court. Re: Thomas MILLER, "A schedule of my whole estate and debts due as follows: A note of $25 on Thomas RUSSELL, I assigned to William TINGLE of which he was entitled to $5 that I owed him, the other $20

14

was intended to pay Philip DODDRIDGE. One claim of Jacob JONES, $5 for making 4 small surveys. 200 acres of land I conveyed to Mrs. Mary BENNETT for the sum of $8 but believe if I could pay her the money that I have a right to redeem the same and I have no other estate," 24 May 1809. There is a list of debts charged to MILLER and Peter FORTNEY by John EVANS Sr., Dudley EVANS and Philip DODDRIDGE for money recovered by suits plus costs, 24 May 1809. MILLER was released from prison after giving his oath as an insolvent debtor.

159 - 1808, Monongalia County Court. Reubin JACO was in jail at the suit of Jacob KETTERMAN and Magdalin BORER, executors of Jacob BORER, deceased, for $40.70 with interest plus costs. Deputy Mathew GAY/GUY for Sheriff Lemuel JOHN, 18 October 1809. "A schedule of the property of Reubin JACO: An account against William THOMAS for $100 for a gold watch paid him toward lands which he hath not conveyed, the contract is lodged in the hands of William GEORGE and I cannot come at it. One note of John BROMWELL for $100. One note for $142 on John BARKER. One note on Richard TRAINER for $93.15. These two last notes have been attached by a man by the name of George HAHN. An account against George KELLER unsettled for the purchase of 100 acres of land which land is in the possession of said KELLER and I suppose the balance to be about $20 or $25. An account against Philip HUFFMAN for $23 and some cents, $5 cost lent George PARSONS, all which above property I hereby transfer to Sheriff Lemuel JOHN," 14 October 1809. Signed by Reubin (x) JACO. "I promise to pay or cause to be paid to Reubin JACO or order $100 cash or the value of it in work in building a house 28´ long 20´ wide and hew the logs, haul them and raise the shell and cover it with joint shingles on or before 1 June next," 16 October 1805, signed by John BROMWELL. Nine month note signed by John BARKER to JACO for $142 dated 20 April 1806 and witnessed by Andrew BARKER. Ten month note signed by Richard TRAINER to JACO for $93.15 dated 14 April 1806 and witnessed by Michael HENRY. On 13 February 1808, JACO escaped from jail and an Arrest Warrant was issued, by Sheriff Stephen MORGAN, to retake him and return him to Debtor's Prison.

159 - 1809, Monongalia County Court. Replevin Bond signed by Amos CHIPPS to secure his property which was attached at the suit of James McVICKER and sold at public sale. CHIPPS was the highest bidder and signed this bond to ensure he would pay his debt in 12 months. This bond secured by William CHIPPS, 11 December 1809. (Replevin Bond: a bond to protect or give security for the return to, or recovery by, a person of goods or chattels wrongfully taken or detained upon giving security to try the matter in court and return the goods if defeated in action.)

159 - 1809, Monongalia County Court. Henry BARRICKMAN sum-

moned to answer a Bill in Chancery exhibited against him by
James WALKER, 3 August 1804. Article of Agreement between
John DOWNER and Henry BARRICKMAN whereby DOWNER was to secure
by title to BARRICKMAN a parcel of land as described in an
entry made by DOWNER for BARRICKMAN with the surveyors of
Monongalia County on 9 September 1802 for which BARRICKMAN
engaged to pay DOWNER $1 per acre for every acre in the lands
as described, signed by both parties and witnessed by Thomas
CHIPPS and Jno BILLS. The survey was made by DOWNER in the
name of BARRICKMAN on which he obtained a patent for 187
acres and BARRICKMAN owed DOWNER $187, of which $100 was to
be paid by a contract or bill delivered within a reasonable
time. DOWNER assigned this $100 contract to WALKER on 4 June
1804 (witnessed by Joshua JONES). The contract was dropped
into the river and lay so long that a great part of it was
destroyed, but so much of it that remains is filed as a part
of this bill. WALKER said BARRICKMAN refused to pay as agreed
and therefore he brings suit. "Henry BARRICKMAN, assignee of
Thomas LAIDLEY, assignee of James MAUREY and John LEWIS,
entered 178 acres part of a Land Warrant of 500 acres #20408
dated 10 November 1783 adjoining lands of Michael KORE,
HANWAY and FORDE, Joseph HUNT, William LANCASTER and Rudolph
SNITHER/SNIDER on Pedlars Run. The above entry was made by
John DOWNER for Henry BARRICKMAN and the survey returned on
the said entry for BARRICKMAN by him," 3 August 1804 and
signed by Samuel HANWAY. March 1809 term of court, dismissed
by order of complainant.

159 - 1809, Monongalia County Court. Caleb TRIBBET/TRIPLET
summoned to answer Davis SHOCKLEY in a plea of assault, 11
October 1806. Bail Bond for TRIBBETT secured by Nicholas
MADERA on 1 April 1809. Appearance Bond for TRIBBET secured
by W. TINGLE on 11 October 1806. May 1809 term, dismissed by
agreement between the parties, TRIPLETT to pay costs.

159 - 1809, Monongalia County Court. James BEALL, plaintiff,
vs Joseph JEANS, defendant. "In Chancery to stay waste" the
court heard evidence and it being proven to the satisfaction
of the court the defendant has for some time in violation of
law and his lease committed waste in the timber of the
plaintiff. The court decreed that JEANS cease from all waste
in cutting timber on the plaintiff's land, that he cut no
timber on the land except for necessary repairs and firewood
and in places least harmful to the land and that he give
security for $400 to the plaintiff that he will keep and
perform this decree, March term 1809.

159 - 1808, Monongalia County Court. Replevin Bond signed by
Sarah BOYLES to secure her property (one two year old colt)
which was attached at the suit of Abel JONES and sold at
public sale. BOYLES was the highest bidder and signed this
bond to ensure she would pay her debt in 12 months. This bond

secured by William BOYLES and Richard HARRISON on 21 May 1808. (Replevin Bond: a bond to protect or give security for the return to, or recovery by, a person of goods or chattels wrongfully taken or detained upon giving security to try the matter in court and return the goods if defeated in action.)

159 - 1810, Monongalia County Court. Robert STEWART complained that Abraham PIXLER owed him $15 and prayed the court to attach so much of his property as to secure the debt, 23 November 1809. One table, the property of PIXLER, was attached at the suit of STEWART, 7 December 1809. Note signed by PIXLER to STEWART for "one bureau of a better quality than John STEWART got of said Robert STEWART as payment for me it being the same now in possession of Robert STEWART," 1 August 1808 and witnessed by P. STEWART and Samuel HARMAN. Attachment Bond signed by Robert STEWART to ensure all costs and awards would be paid in case he be cast in the suit secured by Robert STEWART the oldest, 23 November 1809. John LEWIS summoned as garnishee of Abraham PIXLER, 24 November 1809. Article of Agreement between Abraham PIXLER and John LEWIS whereby PIXLER sold to LEWIS 3 lots in Middletown on the south side of Morgantown Road ($175) to be paid by LEWIS as follows: $57 in hand paid, $15 in a pair of plow irons and pot metal in 4 weeks, $28 to be paid in a horse against 1 April next, $75 against the middle of October next to be paid in a horse at the valuation of two men and when the first $100 is paid, PIXLER to make a clear deed, signed by PIXLER and LEWIS and witnessed by Constable Daniel COX and Daniel STEWART on 19 October 1809. July 1810 term of court, further judgement quashed.

159 - 1806, Monongalia County Court. Jesse MARTIN complained that he rented an improved tract of land to Eleazer/Lazure SMITH for two years beginning March 1803. SMITH was to clear 6 acres and enclose the 6 acres plus __ acres already cleared with a fence and prepare for tillage. SMITH remained on the land until the next August and then sold his crops there growing to John HURLOCK and gave possession of the premises to HURLOCK. HURLOCK knew the terms of the agreement and that SMITH had cleared only about __ acres of land and soon after SMITH left this state. MARTIN prayed the court to summon SMITH and HURLOCK to be questioned in a Court of Equity. HURLOCK's answer: He said he did not rent the land from SMITH and he only bought the crop there growing. He said when SMITH moved out, he was ready to move into the house in order to work and harvest his crop. As SMITH left, he told HURLOCK he turned over possession of the land and house to him and HURLOCK told him "No, I only bought your crop and now you are about to put a trick upon me, for I only come to the house to save my crop" and at that the two parted. MARTIN came to the house and told HURLOCK that by taking possession of the house, he would owe the same rent as SMITH. Sometime

later, MARTIN and HURLOCK met at the house of John SWANK and
MARTIN told him he owed 5 pounds or 50 bushels of Indian Corn
rent per year. HURLOCK told MARTIN that he would not give
that much and moved off the land in January or February and
rented a house from John EVANS of Pennsylvania. MARTIN
attached the property of HURLOCK for 15 pounds or 150 bushels
of corn and stated in his attachment that HURLOCK had rented
the land for 3 years at 50 bushels of corn per year which
attachment was dismissed with costs, 8 October 1804. Deposition signed by Peter (x) SWANK: He was with MARTIN and
HURLOCK at their first meeting and it was agreed between them
that HURLOCK would give up the premises whenever requested, 5
December 1804. Deposition signed by John (x) HUTSON: In 1803
about husking time when HURLOCK was lofting corn (he put the
corn in the loft of a house on the plantation) which he
raised at Simeon EVERLY's on the adjoining plantation, he
heard MARTIN tell HURLOCK he would have to move off the land
in 10 days or pay 5 pounds rent per year. Upon questioning
by both parties, HUTSON said HURLOCK bought the crop from
SMITH, but he (HUTSON) paid for it. He said Nathan MADIN
told him that he rented the same ground from MARTIN for the
same year that MARTIN was charging HURLOCK. He said he
understood that MARTIN had rented the land to SMITH for two
or three years for clearing. HUTSON said his wife and
HURLOCK's mother were sisters. Deposition signed by David
SWANK: He said he was a witness to the lease between MARTIN
and SMITH and the lease was left with him and it was lost.
He said SMITH moved up the Warrior Fork of Dunkard Creek on
land he bought from John ALLY. He said SMITH was his son-in-
law, 5 December 1804. Deposition of Elizabeth HUTSON,
daughter of John HUTSON, heard at the house of Simeon EVERLY
on 2 August 1806: She said she heard MARTIN lease the place
to HURLOCK for three years at 5 pounds per year and HURLOCK
and MARTIN, jointly, was to make a fence from the river near
the mouth of a small drain by a rock to the hill, which fence
was to stand between John SWANK's fence and the fence HURLOCK
lived within. She said she lived with HURLOCK at the time
and it was late fall or the beginning of winter. Deposition
signed by Veachel (x) JACKSON heard at the house of Presley
MARTIN: He said SMITH was living on part of the plantation
belonging to Jesse MARTIN and about August 1803, John HURLOCK
moved to the place and SMITH removed to Pennsylvania. In
January following, he went to MARTIN's in company with
HURLOCK and HURLOCK rented the place for 3 years for 5 pounds
per year or 50 bushels of corn. HURLOCK later denied it and
MARTIN said he would forget the contract if HURLOCK removed
from the land in 10 days. He said HURLOCK "ran away on the
night of the second Tuesday in March 1804 to Col John's Mill
in Pennsylvania," 9 November 1805. Deposition signed by
James (x) MAYFIELD heard at the house of Presley MARTIN: At
the end of May 1804, he was with Nathan MADDAN when he asked
MARTIN to rent the place in dispute. MARTIN said he had

already rented the place to John HURLOCK. He said MADDEN came
from Fort Cumberland about the last of May and left here in
June following and he had no property in this county. He said
when he left here he stole John SWANK's gun, 9 November 1805.
No verdict found.

159 - 1809, Monongalia County Court. Jonathan BRANDON and
Mary his wife, late Mary BIGGS; Joseph SEVERNS and Leah his
wife, late Leah BIGGS; Smith CRANE and Rachel his wife, late
Rachel BIGGS; John SEVERNS and Cittey his wife, late Cittey
BIGGS;   John BIGGS;   William BIGGS;   Margaret BIGGS; James
BIGGS; Jenney BIGGS; Betsy BIGGS; Hannah BIGGS; Thomas BIGGS;
Joseph BIGGS; Beckey BIGGS, heirs and legal representatives
of William BIGGS, deceased, Enoch MOORE and Daniel MOORE
summoned to answer a Bill in Chancery exhibited against them
by Elijah HARDESTY, 10 March 1807. James, Jenney, Betsy,
Hannah, Thomas, Joseph and Beckey were all under age 21.
Bond signed by William BIGGS whereby BIGGS promised to make a
good and sufficient right, agreeable to law, for a tract of
land of 140 acres joining William DAUGHERTY and a tract of
land where Elijah HARDESTY lived to Enoch MOORE dated 16
November 1785. This obligation witnessed by Amos ROBBARTS and
Lawrence CARROL. Enoch MOORE assigned this obligation to
John ROBBARTS on 12 September 1788 which was witnessed by
Ezra HORTON and Thomas BUTLER.   John ROBBARTS assigned the
same to William MORE on 11 October 1790, witnessed by Gervis
TOMPSON and Thomas BUTLER.   Daniel (o) MORE, executor of
William MOORE, deceased, assigned the same to Elijah HARDESTY
on 1 December 1806, witnessed by William SHAHAN and Jesse
BENNETT. William BIGGS died before 1 December 1806 as
HARDESTY accepted this assignment after he died. HARDESTY
said John BIGGS, the son of William, handled the estate and
he could not find a title signed by William. He said when
Enoch MOORE got the bond from William BIGGS for the 140 acres
of land it was in exchange for 150 acres of the same land
where BIGGS lived until his death. He said MOORE made a deed
to BIGGS for the 150 acres, but for some reason it was not
recorded and was now in the hands of John BIGGS.   HARDESTY
prayed the court to compel the defendants to convey the land
to him by deed. May 1809 term, decree of record.

159 - 1809, Monongalia County Court. Absolom MORRIS, guardian to Catherine BURCHINAL, Jeremiah BURCHINAL, Luther
BURCHINAL, Rebecca BURCHINAL and Thomas BURCHINAL, all under
age 21 and heirs of Thomas BURCHINAL, deceased, summoned to
answer a Bill in Chancery exhibited against them by Joseph
MORGAN, 16 April and 26 June 1807. "Not inhabitants of this
Commonwealth." Bond signed by Thomas BURCHINAL, of Springhill, Fayette County, Pennsylvania, to Joseph MORGAN dated 4
October 1802, whereby BURCHINAL promised to make a clear
title, on or before 1 February 1805, to a tract of land in
Monongalia County containing 100 acres known as Crows Tract

and joining lands of George MARTIN and a tract of land known as the Survey Tract, it being one half of the tract which BURCHINAL bought in partnership with Absalom MORRIS from George MARTIN. This bond witnessed by James SCOTT and Betsy (x) GRIFFITH. The land was subject to the dower of _____ BURCHINAL, widow of Thomas. Absalom MORRIS was guardian of the BURCHINAL children for the purpose of this action. MORGAN prayed the court to compel the defendants to convey the land to him by deed. August 1809 term of court, answer of MORRIS filed and rule to show cause.

159 - 1810, Monongalia County Court. Hugh EVANS and James THOMAS summoned to answer a Bill of Injunction exhibited against them by Philip HUFFMAN, 18 December 1802. Complaint of Philip HUFFMAN: He said Michael ANSTINE/AUSTINE, on 1 November 1802, owned the following property, viz, 6 cattle, 28 hogs (young and old), a crop of corn and potatoes in the ground and many other small articles. He said on this day, he purchased all of the above named property for a consider- able consideration and ANSTINE gave him possession and left the county shortly thereafter. A short time later, Hugh EVANS obtained two attachments against the estate of ANSTINE which was levied on part of the goods he purchased from ANSTINE. He prayed the court for an injunction on the attachment. Injunction Bond signed by Philip HUFFMAN to ensure all costs and awards would be paid in case the injunction should be dissolved secured by John GIBBONS and Abel (x) DAVIS, 15 December 1802. James THOMAS´ answer to the complaint of Philip HUFFMAN: He said Michael INESTONE was indebted to him and he "procured an attachment against him and the attachment was levied on one steer or ox, one iron pot and one spider, the property of the said INESTONE, and that he believes the whole of the claim set up to the said property by the said HUFFMAN is founded in fraud and that the steer charged in the said bill, to be taken by this defendant, is not owned by him as purchased from the said INESTONE not being one of the six cattle which he states to have purchased from INESTONE on the first day of November last past but that the said HUFFMAN has acknowledged he purchased the said steer or ox from a certain _____ SMITH since the elopement of the said INESTONE from this county," 17 February 1803. Justice Nathan HALL. Hugh EVANS´ answer to the complaint of Philip HUFFMAN: He said INESTONE was indebted to him and he "procured an attachment against him and the attachment was levied on a quantity of Indian Corn, some potatoes, one iron pot, one steer or ox, and one iron kettle, the property of the said INESTONE, and that he believes the whole of the claim set up to the said goods and chattels of the INESTONE by the said complainant is founded in fraud as he believes that he did not pay him the real value thereof and that he hopes to prove on the final hearing that HUFFMAN acknowledged, since the said INESTONE eloped from this county, that the corn and

potatoes was not his property but was the property of INE-
STONE and that the steer mentioned in the Bill of Complaint
was the property of one SMITH and that he had purchased him
from SMITH since INESTONE left this county," 17 February
1803. Justice Nathan HALL. Deposition of William SMITH
heard at the house of Henry DERING on Saturday 7 July 1804:
He said he was present when HUFFMAN purchased the goods of
ANSTINE and he thought the sale to be a fair one and he saw
HUFFMAN pay ANSTINE and assume some debts for him. Deposition of Abel DAVIS heard at the same time and place: He was
present at the same time and thought the sale a fair one and
the amount paid seemed to satisfy ANSTINE. DAVIS said he
recalled that a rifle ($25), a shot pouch and powder horn, a
pair of shoes, a note HUFFMAN had on ANSTINE ($8 or $9) was
part of the consideration paid to ANSTINE. Deposition of John
HUFFMAN heard at the same time and place: He was present when
the attachment was levied and heard Philip tell them the
property was his and cautioned them not to take it as the
property of ANSTINE. January 1810 term of court, perpetuated
and judgement.

159 - 1809, Monongalia County Court. William THOMAS summoned
to answer Andrew LANTZ in a plea of debt for $60 and $10
damage, 29 May 1809. Note signed by William (x) THOMAS to
LANTZ for $60 dated 8 February 1804, due 1 March next, pay-
able in bar iron at 6 pence per pound delivered at Devault
MOTES at the place where he formerly lived in "Faatt Count_."
Appearance Bond signed by William (x) THOMAS secured by Jacob
MILLER, 4 August 1809.

159 - 1809, Monongalia County Court. William JAMES summoned
to answer Daniel CAPITO, assignee of James WAMSLEY, in a plea
of debt due by account for 7 pounds and 18 shillings ($28.33)
and $20 damage, 20 March and 13 May 1809. "The gross weight
of James WAMSLEY's hogs." A bill for eight hogs weighing
between 152 and 225 pounds signed by William JAMES. Assignment to CAPITO dated 29 November 1808 and witnessed by William ONEIL. Appearance Bond signed by William JAMES secured
by James C. GOFF, 8 August 1809. Justice Joseph WILSON.
November 1809 term of court, judgement confessed and entered
up.

159 - 1809, Monongalia County Court. Benjamin N. JARRETT and
Caleb BENNETT summoned to answer a Bill in Chancery exhibited
against them by Jacob NUSE, 18 August 1801. NUSE's complaint:
He purchased from Benjamin N. JARRETT a tract of land which
descended to Elizabeth JENKINS, one of the heirs of Joshua
JENKINS, deceased, who since married JARRETT and paid the sum
agreed upon for the said land. JARRETT and Caleb BENNETT
showed NUSE the boundaries of the land and he took possession
and JARRETT promised to make a fee simple deed to him. Since
that time he has occupied and improved the tract which is

more fully described in the division plat of Joshua JENKINS. Afterwards JARRETT made a Deed of Conveyance for the same land to Caleb BENNETT which is recorded in the County Clerk's Office. He prayed the court to summon both JARRETT and BENNETT to be questioned in the matter, March 1802. Deposition of George NOOSE, son of Jacob: He said the tract in question was one of eight parcels, it being the parcel allotted to Elizabeth as an heir of Joshua JENKINS, deceased, containing 31 or 32 acres. He said Elizabeth sold this parcel to NOOSE for one sorrel horse ($100). In October 1800, shortly after NOOSE bought the land, he met JARRETT and asked him how he liked his bargain, he said he was well satisfied. NOOSE told JARRETT "that Caleb BENNETT said the hoofs had come off the horse and that you was a fool for giving the land for the horse." Shortly after Jacob NUSE bought the land, Caleb BENNETT came to his father's house and said his father was an heir now as well as himself because as this deponent (NOOSE) there believed, Jacob NOOSE had bought the part which descended to the wife of Benjamin N. JARRETT. This deponent saith that Jacob NOOSE had purchased the land sometime before the deed was made from JARRETT to BENNETT for the same and that BENNETT knew of the sale from JARRETT to NOOSE and at the time NOOSE bought the land, Mrs. JARRETT told NOOSE to take possession of the land, 16 July 1803. Answer of Caleb BENNETT: On 1 October 1799, he purchased from JARRETT, who had married Elizabeth JENKINS, his one full eighth part of the land of Joshua JENKINS, deceased, and paid for the same. He went to the house of NOOSE and informed him he had purchased the land and wished him to allow him (BENNETT) to join fences and NOOSE agreed. Sometime later, Thomas BENNETT's wife informed him that NOOSE had been at their house and said he bought JARRETT's share of the land. Later he met NOOSE on or near the plantation and NOOSE told him he had bought the land. BENNETT told NOOSE he bought and paid for the land long before. NOOSE said JARRETT would pay back his money, but he said since he bought the land he would keep it, 10 July 1802. The court decreed that JARRETT and BENNETT make a deed to NUSE in fee simple and that they be attached until the deed was forthcoming. May 1809 term of court, dismissed by order of the plaintiff.

159a - 1809, Monongalia County Court. Complaint of John DOWNER: On 1 January 1806, Jonathan HARRIS, of Monongalia County who lived on the waters of Sandy Creek near the bridge on Crab Orchard Road, came to him and proposed to barter his land on which he lived with him for a tract of land which DOWNER held on Dunkard Creek as 300 acres. The said tract to be conveyed by HARRIS contained 500 acres. DOWNER gave his obligation to convey the lands on Dunkard Creek agreeable to the contract and paid to HARRIS or for him the sum of $300 in payment of 500 acres and HARRIS gave his obligation whereby he bound himself to convey the 500 acres where he then lived

22

to DOWNER, the deed to be made by 2nd Monday in April next after the date of the obligation which is dated 1 January 1806. HARRIS refused to convey the land, refused to return the $300 and refused to accept a deed for the land sold to him on Dunkard Creek. DOWNER prayed the court to question HARRIS concerning the matter. Answer of Jonathan HARRIS: He was to convey 500 acres of land to John DOWNER on 1 April 1806, when at the same time DOWNER gave him his obligation to convey to him 1000 acres joining lands of George SNIDER, Richard TENANT and others which obligation is dated 1 January 1806. DOWNER was to give $300 boot and he (HARRIS) agreed to take 100 acres of land owned by Evan JENKINS for it if JENKINS would make a title to his son for it (his son having previously purchased of JENKINS 200 acres of land). JENKINS gave his obligation to his son to convey 300 acres which obligation is dated 1 January 1806 and this 100 acres is the $300 DOWNER claims to have paid for HARRIS. He said it was true he refused to make DOWNER a deed for the 500 acres and he told DOWNER he would not take a deed for the 1000 acres, that he "rued" the bargain which it was expressly agreed he could do at anytime within six weeks from the time the writings were signed. He said JENKINS had not made his son a deed for any part of the 300 acres and JENKINS was present at the time of the signing of the contracts and knew he had six weeks to cancel the agreements all around, 14 March 1808. Deposition of Alexander CLEGG heard on 16 September 1809: Sometime after a contract had been made between DOWNER and HARRIS, HARRIS requested that he take the contract and get DOWNER "to give up the bargain." DOWNER refused but then agreed if HARRIS "would make him whole for what he had paid JENKINS, then contract might be void." CLEGG said he was present when DOWNER and HARRIS looked over the land before the contract was made and "I think we were all sober." Deposition of Abraham HARRIS heard on 16 September 1809: DOWNER had notes against Evan JENKINS amounting to $300 and "the bargain was to be null and void on HARRIS paying DOWNER a treat, that DOWNER refused to take the treat and after that went and gave up the notes he had on Evan JENKINS for the $300 in order to charge HARRIS with it as a part of the pay under the contract." He was present when the bargain was made and heard DOWNER and HARRIS agree the if the bargain was cancelled, the "ruer" would make the other a treat and heard HARRIS offer DOWNER 2 gallon of whiskey as a treat, 26 August 1809. December 1809 term of court, "dismissed, agreed by order of the parties, defendant paying all costs and judgement by the court for the costs accordingly."

159a - 1809, Monongalia County Court. William WEBSTER summoned to answer Joseph SEVERNS, assignee of John GRIBBLE, in a plea of debt for $50.80 (due by note dated 8 January 1803, payable 1 December 1807 in good coarse salt at $4 per bushel and good whiskey at $.60 per gallon) and $40 damage, 9 February 1808. Bail Bond for William WEBSTER secured by James WEBSTER, 22 March 1808. Appearance Bond signed by William WEBSTER secured by Gabriel FRICKLE, 2 March 1808. March 1809 term of court, dismissed by order of the plaintiff and judgement for defendant for costs.

159a - 1809, Monongalia County Court. Agnes FRETWELL, administratrix of Thomas FRETWELL, deceased, summoned to answer William FRETWELL, assignee of James GENTRY, in a plea of debt for 154 pounds and 6 shillings ($514.34) due by note, 27 February 1809. There is a summons issued to Agness FRETWELL from each of the creditors as named in the sundry notes listed here, all dated 27 September 1809. Demand note signed by Thomas FRETWELL to James GENTRY for 154 pounds and 6 shillings dated 29 June 1801 and witnessed by Crenshaw FRETWELL and Charles FERGUSON. James (x) GENTRY assigned the note to William FRETWELL, no date. Demand note signed by Thomas FRETWELL and Crenshaw FRETWELL to Richard SNOW for 145 pounds bound by the penal sum of 290 pounds dated 26 November 1801 and witnessed by Lewis DAVIS Jr. Rich'd (x) SNOW assigned this note to William FRETWELL, no date. Demand Note signed by Thomas FRETWELL and William FRETWELL to Thomas AUSTIN for 27 pounds, 7 shillings and 9 pence bound by the penal sum of 54 pounds, 15 shillings and 6 pence dated 20 November 1801 and witnessed by Crenshaw FRETWELL. AUSTIN assigned this note to William FRETWELL on 15 April 1802. Demand Note signed by Thomas FRETWELL to Reuben McCLARY for 114 pounds and 5 shillings bound by the penal sum of 228 pounds, 11 shillings and 2 pence dated 29 November 1801 and witnessed by Crenshaw FRETWELL. McCLARY assigned this note to William FRETWELL, no date. Demand Note signed by Thomas FRETWELL to Samuel GARRISON for 10 pounds, 8 shillings and 8 pence bound by the penal sum of 20 pounds, 17 shillings and 5 pence and witnessed by Crenshaw FRETWELL and Reuben FERGUSON dated 23 November 1801. GARRISON assigned this note to William FRETWELL, no date. Demand Note signed by Thomas FRETWELL to William FRETWELL Jr. for $4000 bound by the penal sum of $10,000 dated 18 November 1802 and witnessed by Elijah WATTS and James DICKENSON. "On the within obligation by balance of the purchase price of 17 slaves purchased of Agnes FRETWELL, administratrix of Thomas FRETWELL, deceased, the 12 November 1808, $3600.30 and one half cent," signed by Attorney Wm. TINGLE, for William FRETWELL and witnessed by James A. WALTON or WATSON. "Rec'd December 12 1808 from Mrs. Agness FRETWELL $115.33 in corn which I have this day purchased from her," signed by TINGLE for William FRETWELL and witnessed by William CHIPPS. Demand Note signed by Thomas FRETWELL to Henry BURK for 76 pounds, 4 shilling and half penny bound in the penal sum of "double the above mentioned sum" dated 17 November 1801 and witnessed by Reuben (x) McCLARY. BURK assigned this note to William FRETWELL, no date. Demand Note signed by Thomas FRETWELL to William FERGUSON for 11 pounds and 5 shillings bound by the penal sum of 22 pounds and 10 shillings dated 25 November 1801 and witnessed by Henry HARRIS. William (x) FARGUSON assigned this note to Crenshaw FRETWELL, no date. Crenshaw FRETWELL assigned his assignment to William FRETWELL Jr., no date.

159a - 1808, Monongalia County Court. Alexander ARTHERS summoned to answer Thomas MONTGOMERY in a plea of assault damage $100, 21 May and 3 September 1808.

159a - 1808, Monongalia County Court. William Jacob STEWART summoned to answer Elihu HORTON in a plea of trespass on the case damage $200, 14 June 1808. Bail Bond for STEWART secured by Benjamin REEDER, no date.

159a - 1808, Monongalia County Court. James COLLINS summoned to answer Reynear HALL, assignee of John HAYMOND, in a plea of debt for $60 due by note dated 28 April 1807 and $20 damage, 1 August 1808. Appearance Bond signed by COLLINS secured by William BALDWIN, 8 October 1808.

159a - 1808, Monongalia County Court. Charles W. MARTIN summoned to answer Samuel EVERLY in a plea of debt for non-payment of a debt, 13 June 1808. Note signed by MARTIN to EVERLY for $15 dated 16 March 1808 and witnessed by John RAMSEY Jr. and Simeon EVERLY. Simon EVERLY, Presley MARTIN, James COLLINS Jr. and John RAMSEY summoned to give evidence, 13 August 1808. August 1808 term of court, judgement for the plaintiff for $15 and $1.14 for the Constable.

159a - 1809, Monongalia County Court. John BROWN summoned to answer Thomas KNIGHT in a plea of trespass on the case damage $100, 18 April 1807. KNIGHT's complaint: In 1806, BROWN rented a mare from him to work in a wagon and promised to tend and care for her with good and proper order and to return her in the same condition. KNIGHT said BROWN so improperly dealt with, managed and treated the mare "that he utterly destroyed and killed" her. BROWN refused to pay him the value of the mare and therefore he brings suit. March 1809 term of court, dismissed being agreed by the parties, plaintiff paying costs except defendant's attorney.

159a - 1809, Monongalia County Court. John BROWN Sr. summoned to answer a presentment against him for failure to keep the road in repair leading from Papaw Creek to Bufflow Creek, 22 November 1808. Richard PRICE and Thomas KNIGHT Sr. summoned to give evidence to the Grand Jury, 22 November 1808. March 1809 term of court, quashed.

159a - 1809, Monongalia County Court. Mary ADAMSON said she was afraid that Charles BURROWS, living with Nicholas B. MADERA in Morgantown, "will do her bodily harm." Nicholas

MADERA summoned to testify in behalf of BURROWS, 13 June 1809. Henry H. WILSON summoned to testify in behalf of Charles BURROWS, 12 June 1809. Appearance Bond for Charles BURROWS, a youth under age being accused on oath of a breach of the peace by Mary ADAMSON, secured by Nicholas B. MADERA, 9 May 1809. Philip SHEETS, John BELL and Roswell MESSENGER summoned to testify in behalf of ADAMSON, 12 June 1809. June 1809 term of court, discharged.

159a - 1809, Monongalia County Court. Notice to Moses Edward McCARTNEY, Nicholas CASEY and Michael KERN Jr. from William McCLEERY, attorney for the Commonwealth, of intent to "apply to the said court to enter up judgement against you for $500, that is to say, against you Edward McCARTEY, Nicholas CASEY and Michael KERN Jr. for the sum of $400 and against you Michael KERN Jr. for the further sum of $100 which several sums were put into your hands respectively as Commissioners appointed by law for the purpose of repairing the State Road from the mouth of Savage Creek," 15 February 1808. "Notice acknowledged by CASEY and KERN ten days before the second day of March Court. McCARTY not an inhabitant in my bailiwick," signed by Deputy John C. PAYNE for Sheriff Stephen MORGAN. "We Edward McCARTY, Michael KERN and William McCLEERY, three of the Commissioners for the State Road do mutually agree that William McCLEERY shall pay $400 public money granted by the Assembly of Virginia for the repairage of the State Road, to Nicholas CASEY whom we agree shall superintend the repairage of said road who is to render satisfactory account to us of the expenditures of said money," 5 April 1797, signed by McCARTY, KERN and McCLEERY. "Rec'd 5 April 1797 of William McCLEERY $400 to be laid out to the best advantage in repairing the State Road and I am to render proper accounts to the above mentioned commissioners for the expenditures of the said money on or before 1 August next," signed by Nicholas CASEY. "Rec'd 20 March 1796 of William McCLEERY $100 which I am to pay for repairage of the State Road and deliver unto the said William McCLEERY a certificate from two of the commissioners appointed by law to repair the road for the disbursement of the said sum that is such a certificate as will pass in the Auditor's Office at or before 1 November next," signed by Michael KERN. March 1809 term of court, "prov'd as to CASEY and KERN and continued."

159a - 1809, Monongalia County Court. Henry HAMILTON, Joseph A. SHACKLEFORD, William MAY and Widow MAY summoned to testify in behalf of George MAY, an orphan boy, in a certain matter pending and undetermined between George MAY and Andrew ARMSTRONG, 16 August 1809.

159a - 1808, Monongalia County Court. John BOUSLOG summoned to answer a presentment against him for failing to keep the road in repair from the Monongahela River at the ford

opposite to Morgantown to Noah RIDGWAY's of which he is Overseer, 4 October 1808. Noah RIDGWAY and Isaac BALDWIN
summoned to testify in behalf of BOUSLOG, 30 November 1808.
Ralph BARKSHIRE summoned to give evidence to the Grand Jury,
23 November 1808.

159a - 1809, Monongalia County Court. John CHIPPS summoned
to answer Alexander CLEGG in a plea for non-payment of a debt
due by protested order, 30 May 1809.   Replevin Bond signed
by CHIPPS to secure his property which was attached at the
suit of CLEGG and sold at public sale. CHIPPS was the highest
bidder and signed this bond to ensure he would pay his debt
in 12 months. This bond secured by Caleb TRIPPETT, 5 August
1809. (Replevin Bond: a bond to protect or give security for
the return to, or recovery by, a person of goods or chattels
wrongfully taken or detained upon giving security to try the
matter in court and return the goods if defeated in action.)
June 1809 term of court, judgement for the plaintiff for $16
debt and $.30 costs.

159a - 1809, Monongalia County Court. Replevin Bond signed by
James SCOTT to secure his property which was attached at the
suit of Samuel EVERLY and sold at public sale. SCOTT was the
highest bidder and signed this bond to ensure he would pay
his debt in 12 months.   This bond secured by Presley MARTIN,
27 February 1809. (Replevin Bond: a bond to protect or give
security for the return to, or recovery by, a person of goods
or chattels wrongfully taken or detained upon giving security
to try the matter in court and return the goods if defeated
in action.)

159a - 1809, Monongalia County Court. Notice to Sheriff
Stephen MORGAN from Clerk John EVANS of intent to move the
court to render judgement against MORGAN in favor of EVANS
for the sum of $1,030.38, the same being the amount of sundry
fee bills due from different individuals as clerk and lodged
in your hands through your deputy, John PAYNE, for collect-
ion, 20 June 1809. List of fees due: 1804, Richard WEAVER &
James TIBBS.   1806, Thomas McFARLAND & John WELTMER, John
MYERS & Ben WILSON, Thomas MARTIN. 1802, John DAVIS & Henry
DERING. 1806, William FRUM, James THOMAS. 1804, Able JONES
& Enoch JONES, Jacob SMITH, James MORGAN, James TIBBS, Robert
HENDERSON, William McLAIN & John McLAIN, William STEVENSON,
Jacob PINDALL (2 notes), John WILLEY.   1802, Joseph MATHENEY
& Nathan MATHENEY. 1804, John PAYNE, Thomas R. CHIPPS, Simeon
ROYCE. 1806, Lewis OTT, James POST, Christian MADERA. 1805,
Sarah BOYLES, Everly BOYLES.   1806, Thomas HAWTHORN, Robert
FERRELL. 1804, George HITE. 1803, James ROBISON, 1804, Reuben
ABRAMS & Daniel MARTIN. 1806, Amos GANDY, Isaac MATHEW, Rob't
PATTON & John EVANS. 1805, George DEIBLER, John DRAGOO, Geo.
WILSON,   Benjamin HARTLEY,   Joseph SUTTON, Benjamin JONES,
George NORRIS,   Thomas SPENCER & Daniel MARTIN, Thomas R.

Jean FRY, Stephen GAPEN & Presley MARTIN, John McFARLAND & Jacob PINDALL, William STAFFORD & James STAFFORD, Joseph WISBY & Abraham WELLS, William POSTLE, B. N. JARRETT, Arthur WILSON. 1806, John SNIDER, James G. WATSON, William CHIPPS, John EDWARDS, David GRAHAM & William G. PAYNE, John CLARK, John SEAMAN, LANHAM & McCREA, David ANDERSON. 1801, Christian WHITEHAIR, Ephraim COOKER, Richard CAIN, John PRIDE, Jean FRY. 1806, James McVICKER, Stephen MYERS, John PAYNE, John HARMAN, Elisha BRIGGS, William SCRIPPS, H. BARRICKMAN & G. PICKENPAUGH, Jean WATTS, Mary & William STEWART, John BASNETT, Samuel HANWAY, John GLASCOCK, Thomas BIRCH, Thomas BURCHINAL, George REINHART, Joshua GOUGH, William JAMES, John JOHNSON, James KNOTTS, Moses WILLIAMS & W. G. PAYNE, Thomas CLEGG Sr. & Jr., Samuel GANDY, Joseph LOUGH, Casper OTT, Abraham WISECUPP, Samuel HARMAN, Walter CAIN, James MORGAN, Benjamin MIDDLETON, John GRUBB, William SYRIS, James GRAY, Jonathan SMITH, William & Edward HILL, Thomas MEEKS, Jacob NOOZ Jr., Jacob MILLER, John CURRANT, Peter HENKINS, Jacob GILMORE, James CURRANT Jr., Thomas KNIGHT, Moses BYARD, Moses CHENY, Robert ABERCRUMBY, Moses ROYCE, George PICKEN-PAUGH, Joseph SUTTON, John FICKLE, Catharine MURALLS, John GRIBBLE, Thomas SEDGWICK, Archibald ANDERSON, Uriah MORGAN, Andrew ARNETT, Leonard CUP Jr., John RENINER, James BOWLBY, John CARPENTER, John MATHEWS, Jeremiah GALLAHER, William BUCKLEW, James STAFFORD, Roger HUNT, Noah FORDE, Kelly & Absalom BRANDON, Zackgill PIERPOINT, Catherine RIDGWAY, James ANDERSON, Ross ALLEY, Peter EVERLY, Reubin JACO, John STOCK-WELL. 1804, Lawrence SNIDER. 1803, Thomas EVANS. 1806, W. G. PAYNE, James BOWLBY, Joseph ALLEN. 1804, Barney JOHNSON. 1805, Jacob JONES Sr., Elizabeth & Ben WHITE, John SULLIVAN, Henry CARATHERS. 1806, Michael CORE, James BEALL, Samuel SWEARINGEN, Samuel EVANS, Thomas EVANS, William WINDSOR & others, William MORRIS, Joseph JEANS, Aaron McDONALD, Amos ROBBARTS, Amos CHIPPS, John MOORE, John BARNES, Thomas LAZEL, William CHIPPS, Nehemiah SQUIRES, John CARTER, James STEEL, John A. BARKSHIRE, Henry BARNES, John NICKLIN, Hugh KELSO, John SMITH, John MATHENY, Sisler DICKERSON, Samuel DEARDORN, William JOHN & others, William THOMAS, Joseph WEAVER, John JOHNSON, John RAVENCROFT, Elizabeth STEWART, James GUTHRIE, Jonathan KERNS, Thomas ADAMSON, Samuel WEST, E. LYNCH & Morgan MORGAN, Abraham GOOSEMAN, Stephen McDADE, Farquer McCREA, John GEAKIN, Jacob NOOS, James WILSON, Ezekiel CHENEY, Samuel HAZLETT, John MURRELL, John BOADLEY, Abraham HUFFMAN, Timothy WARDEN, Abraham OWENS, Richard SMITH, Joseph BRUMAGE, James BURCHINAL, Nancy WEAVER, Thomas LAIDLEY, Thomas McKINLEY. 1800, Simeon EVERLY, John McGEE. 1803, James GOFF. 1806, Thomas MILLER, James BURCHINAL. 1802, John BOUS-LOG, Moses DOOLITTLE Jr, Philip SHIVELY. 1807, W. G. PAYNE. 1806, Reubin FORSTER, Isreal FERREE, Francis COLLINS. 1805, Samuel EVERLY, Thomas BIRD, Joseph SEVERNS, Christian MADERA, Henry HIGHSHOE, David MORGAN. 1800, Arthur WILSON. 1802, Christian CALE, Richard STILES, Valentine KING, John JENKINS,

George KELLER. 1804, John HASTINGS. 1802, Absalom SEVERINS.
1805, Samuel CRAINE, William EVERLY, John HOWELL, James
McKENNION. 1806, Thomas FRETWELL, Barney HANEY, Josiah
WILSON, Enoch & Edward PARISH. 1805, John COOPER, James
CLARK. 1806, William GEORGE, David SCOTT, Larkin CLELLAND,
Owen HARKER, Robert CHOEN, Thomas LAIDLEY, Moses SNIDER,
Aaron M. WADE Jr., MINNIS & DOWNER, William POSTLE, James
WEBSTER. 1804, William SCRIPPS. 1806, M. HANNON & James
STAFFORD, Samuel BALDWIN. 1803, Charles SIMPKINS, Christopher
CALE, John WHIP & Abraham MILEY. 1806, William BAYLES. 1802,
James SCOTT, Nathan HALL. 1805, Michael CORE. 1804, Thomas
DOOLITTLE. 1805, William PRICE. 1803, William CHIPPS, Henry
GRIFFITH, Joseph WILSON. 1805, Jarrett EVANS, John CHIPPS.
1806, Rebecca WILSON. 1803, Samuel GRUBB, George HUFFMAN.
1806, James WEST Sr. 1804, Joseph ROSS, James WEST Jr.,
Nathan SPRINGER, Henry SMITH, Samuel HANWAY. 1802, William
Norris JENKINS, Noah RIDGWAY. 1803, Conrad SHEETS. 1802,
Nicholas MADERA. 1806, Jacob PINDALL & John McFARLAND. 1800,
Morgan MORGAN, John WISBEY Sr. 1801, James POST. 1799, Joseph
HARRISON, Samuel MORTON. 1806, Simeon EVERLY. 1801, Henry
BARRICKMAN, James TIBBS & others, Charles McGILL, John
TAYLOR. 1805, William TRICKETT, Sarah FORSTER (John LANTZ
security). 1806, James E. WATSON, Ross ALLEY, Robert CHOEN,
Owen STANKER, Thomas LAZEL, George SNIDER, Leonard CUP, Jacob
SMITH. 1805, John BOUSLOG. 1806, Thomas EVANS, Jesse MARTIN,
Arthur TRADER Sr., John DOWNER, John B. WHEELER, Richard
NUZUM, Joseph REED, John McGEE, John PIERPOINT, James CAIN &
Samuel PHILIPS, William G. PAYNE for DAVIS heirs, John
McFARLAND, William McDONALD. 1800, James KNOX. 1805, William
STEVENSON. 1803, Joseph HARRISON. 1804, Elias PEARSE. 1806,
Nicholas MADERA, John WILSON, James SCOTT, Thomas McKINLEY,
John MILLER, Henry BARRICKMAN, Levi MORGAN. 1805, Reuben
JACO, Benjamin THORN, Tobias REAM, Jacob SMITH, William
STEVENSON, Robert BOGGESS, Jacob NOOS Sr., and William GREGG.
"Rec'd of John EVANS, late Clerk of Monongalia County, notes
corresponding with the within list and on the persons within
named amounting to $1,033.38 which I hereby engage to collect
and account for agreeable to law," 29 February 1808. Signed
by Deputy John PAYNE for Sheriff Stephen MORGAN.

159a - 1809, Monongalia County Court. "A list of fees due to
Nimrod EVANS, Clerk of Monongalia County, for the year 1807."
Samuel SWEARINGEN, Sarah BOYLES, Nicholas VANDERVORT Jr.,
Nathan GOODWIN, John F. WILSON, Samuel MINOR, Charles
STEWART, John HOULT & C. PRICKETT, R. POTTER & J. W. DEAN,
William KING, George HICKMAN, William GREGG, Mathew GEORGE,
Martin ABEL, William McCLAIN & J. W/M. McCLAIN, George
BAKER, Daniel ANDERSON, Thomas ADAMSON, E. LYNCH (Morgan
MORGAN), Stephen McDADE, Farquer McCREA, James THOMAS, John
ZEGAN, Jacob NOOS Sr., Elisha BRIGGS, John PAYNE, Sarah
BOYLES, Everly BOYLES, William RUSSELL, Joseph JEANS, Lucy
LANHAM, James CURRY, John HANTMAN/HAUTMAN, Arthur WILSON,

John WEST, John SCOTT, Jo REED & John RAMSEY, G. HOLLEBACK &
W. HAYES & C. SNIDER, Abraham WEAVER, Benjamin HAMILTON, John
W. THOMPSON, Francis COLLINS, Robert WOODS, Robert FERRELL,
Adam SIGLER, Richard NUZUM, P. McFEELERS, Samuel HANWAY, John
PIERPOINT, S. PHILLIPS, James CAIN, M. DAVIS, John McFARLAND,
William STEVENSON, John EDWARDS, John CLARK, William CHIPPS,
John SEAMAN, James G. WATSON, William LANHAM, James GUTHRIE,
D. SCOTT & R. SCOTT & P. MARTIN, Thomas EVANS, John GODWIN,
John COZAD, John COOPER, Robert BUTCHER, Robert MEANS, Philip
SHEWMAN, Isaac REED, James BURCHINAL, John F. WILSON, T.
LAIDLEY & C. BYRN, David SCOTT 2nd., Charles McGILL, John
JONES, M. HANNON & James STAFFORD, John TAYLOR, Thomas
MILLER, R. FOSTER, Thomas EVANS, Jesse MARTIN, Richard SMITH,
James THOMAS, Owen HAWKER, George SNIDER, Jacob SMITH, James
JEFFS, Benjamin JONES, George NORRIS, T. SPENCER & D. MARTIN,
Thomas R. CHIPPS, Jean FRY, J. MYERS & B. WILSON, Thomas
MARTIN, Aaron M. WADE & others, Thomas LAIDLEY, Samuel
BALDWIN, John DOWNER, William POSTLE, James WEBSTER, John E.
BILLS, Larkin CLELLAND, Joseph HARRISON, Nicholas MADERA,
Thomas McKINLEY, James SCOTT, John MILLER, Benjamin THORN, S.
REEM & Tobias REEM, Samuel CRANE, William EVERLY, John
HOWELL, Thomas R. CHIPPS, Thomas FRETWELL, Josiah WILSON,
Robert BOGGESS, Arthur TRADER Sr., John DOWNER, John McGEE,
James MORGAN, Lewis OTT, James PORT, Christian MADERA, George
HILL, James ROBISON, R. ABRAMS & Daniel MARTIN, Isaac MATHEW,
Robert PATTON, Benjamin HARTLEY, George DEIBLER, John DRAGOO,
Joseph SUTTON, Jacob HOLLAND, George SNIDER, Daniel WADE,
James WALKER, Samuel GRUBB, John & George WATSON, John
CHRISTIE, David GRUNDY, Jacob WOOLF Sr., Jesse MARTIN, Philip
BARBROWER, Benjamin BROWN, Joseph PICKENPAUGH, David &
William BAYLES, James GOFF, Moses JUSTICES, Henry AMOS, James
SCOTT, Philip ROSS, Duncan F. McCREA, T. LITTLE & Elijah
HAWKINS, Frederick WILHELLAM, Victory ADAMSON, John SHRIOR,
William SNODGRASS Sr., John WELLS, Abraham CONNEGYS, William
HAYMOND, William RAMSEY, Isaac EWING, George ZINN & G. GANTS,
Isaac MARKUS, Henry WATTS, Daniel THOMPSON, Capel HOLLAND,
James CAIN, Cornelius KING, Jonathan MATHEW, Mary SISCO,
Charity FITSORD, George STEWART, Rebecca WILSON, Benjamin
SHAW, Robert WOODS, Nicholas FUNKHOUSER, John JOLLIFFE,
Elisha HOULT, Joseph HOULT, John CHIPPS, James MORRIS, John
SPRINGER, Thomas RUSSELL, Jacob LYMAN, Jacob FEATHERS, Isaac
SADLER, John BRANT, John DAVIS Jr., Amos GANDY, John
DOUGHMAN, Andrew CASTO, William WILSON, Joseph WILSON, John
MANN Sr., James MARSHALL, Joseph TENNANT, George WOOLF,
Henry H. WILSON, James COBURN Jr., William SNODGRASS, William
THOMAS, George MORGAN, Elizabeth FLOYD, Edward PARRISH, James
WEST Sr., Jonathan SMITH, William BILLS, Henry BARRICKMAN,
Hynson COLE, William HART, Ben N. JARRETT, John SHRIOR &
Jacob HAMPTON, William KINKAID, Joshua HART, Samuel CLUTTER,
Reynear HALL, John COOPER, John REED, John SIMMERS, William
RUSSELL, Martin VARNER, William HOLLIFIELD, Bernard BOYLES,
Jonathan HARTLEY, Samuel WILSON, James WILSON, A. GOOSEMAN,

James JOHNSON, Hugh SIDWELL, John JARRETT, Henry BARKER, Alexander CLEGG, Joseph SEVERNS, Elijah HARDESTY, Richard CAIN, Clement MORGAN, Adam WOOLF, Joseph MORGAN, R. POTTER, Thomas KNIGHT, John LYONS, Noah MORRIS, Amos CHIPPS, William BARNETT, John JOHNSON, James CURRANT, Peter TENNANT, Adam BROWN, Jesse PAYNE, Elizabeth JOHNSON, Coverdill COLE, T. HAWKINS & A. HOLLY, George WILSON, Nicholas WEAVER, R. WEAVER & James TIBBS, Robert HENDERSON, Abel JONES & Enoch JONES, S. GAPEN & P. MARTIN, Jarrett EVANS, Peter COOK & A. BRANDON, Jacob PINDALL, John DOWNER, Jo WESBY & A. WELLS, Phillip HUFFMAN and William FRUM. "Rec'd 29 February 1808 of Nimrod EVANS, Clerk of Monongalia County, clerk's notes corresponding with the within list and on the persons within named amounting to $516.06 which I hereby engage to collect and account for agreeable to law," signed by Deputy John PAYNE for Sheriff Stephen MORGAN.

158a - 1809, Monongalia County Court. Thomas EVANS, in his lifetime, placed and bound his son, Thomas EVANS Jr, to George HITE to learn the joiner trade. Thomas Jr. served HITE until within the last year of his apprenticeship and decided to run away. EVANS Sr. said he used every means in his power to prevent him from so doing. EVANS said he went to HITE and informed him and advised HITE to confine him which he neglected to do. On the morning that Thomas Jr. ran away, he immediately went to HITE and told him that Thomas Jr. had set out for Kentucky. He offered HITE his horse to go after him. HITE said the boy must have eloped on a swift running canoe on the river with a full tide and must have been in Pennsylvania before his father informed him that he was gone. He said the road was very deep and muddy when EVANS offered his horse which was on the other side of the river and the river was very full so that there was not the most distant hope of overtaking the boy in any reasonable time with the start he had. HITE said EVANS knew the boy was going to run away and in the contract he agreed to bring the boy back if he did run away or else compensate him for the loss. He said "the only restraint he had upon the boy was the security in the indenture by which EVANS was bound for his son." George HITE obtained judgement for $20.25 plus damages and costs against Thomas EVANS. EVANS prayed for and obtained an injunction against the judgement. Injunction Bond signed by Thomas (x) EVANS to ensure all costs and awards would be paid in case the injunction should be dissolved secured by Josiah (x) HOSKINSON and Jeremiah HOSKINSON, 14 January 1805. Catherine EVANS, executrix of the estate of Thomas EVANS, deceased, vs George HITE: Catherine settled with HITE and the injunction was dissolved 18 October 1809, Catherine EVANS paying all costs.

158a - 1809, Monongalia County Court. Recognizance Bond for William PRICE, yeoman, to keep the peace toward all citizens and especially toward William F. CASEY, yeoman, secured by James GANDY, yeoman, and Micle CONNER, yeoman, 11 March 1809.

158a - 1809, Monongalia County Court. Joshua LOW summoned to answer Nimrod EVANS in a plea of debt for $75 and $50 damage, 22 May 1809. Promissory Note signed by Joshua (x) LOW to Nimrod EVANS for $75, payable 9 June next in good plank delivered to Michael KERNS, 12 June 1806 and witnessed by Thomas R. CHIPPS. November 1809 term of court, judgement.

158a - 1809, Monongalia County Court. Isaac OAKES obtained a judgement against Scott MARTIN and Caleb TRIBETT for $12.50 with costs and obtained an attachment on the same which was levied on one bay mare. The mare was offered at public sale. Replevin Bond signed by Bowers FURBEE, the highest bidder, to ensure he would pay his debt in 12 months. This bond secured by Samuel EVERLY on 11 September 1809. (Replevin Bond: a bond to protect or give security for the return to, or recovery by, a person of goods or chattels wrongfully taken or detained upon giving security to try the matter in court and return the goods if defeated in action.)

158a - 1809, Monongalia County Court. Nathan GOODWIN summoned to answer Henry BARKER in a plea of debt for $74.01 due by purchase of corn, corn meal, flour, dressed deer skins and a gun, 9 March 1807. Bail Bond for GOODWIN secured by William MORRIS, 10 April 1807. April 1809 term of court, dismissed by order of the plaintiff.

158a - 1809, Monongalia County Court. John GREEN obtained an attachment on the property of Thomas PAYNE for $11.50 plus cost. Attachment Bond signed by John GREEN to ensure all costs and awards would be paid in case PAYNE prevailed in the suit secured by Mathew GAY, 6 April 1809. Attachment levied on one sorrel horse. Enos DAUGHERTY summoned to testify in behalf of GREEN, 11 April 1809.

158a - 1809, Monongalia County Court. Benjamin THORN complained that Elihu HORTON "in the open streets of Morgantown took and detained one horse" belonging to him and therefore he brings suit. Order for HORTON to return the horse to THORN dated 9 July 1805. Bond signed by THORN to ensure he would prosecute HORTON secured by Davis SHOCKLEY and Jacob FOULK, 9 July 1805. September 1809 term of court, dismissed by order of the plaintiff.

158a - 1809, Monongalia County Court. Jordon HALL and John PETTYJOHN summoned to answer a Bill of Injunction exhibited against them by John BONER Jr. and John CARREL, 24 January 1809. PETTYJOHN not an inhabitant of this county. Injunction Bond signed by John (x) BONER Jr, to ensure all costs and awards would be paid in case the Injunction should be dissolved secured by Amos (x) BONER and Joseph (x) WISBY Sr., 15 November 1808. BONER and CARROL complained that in 1806 they purchased 200 acres of land ($600) on the east side of the Tyger Valley River from PETTYJOHN Sr., 100 acres for each of them. PETTYJOHN showed them the boundaries, parts marked by trees, but a survey was not run. They paid $230 in part payment and executed their notes for the balance ($370) to be paid by installments and executed a Deed of Trust for the land to Jordon HALL to secure the payments. The Trust Deed was recorded but there was an error in the sum. Instead of $370, it is written "three seventy hundred dollars." After additional sums were paid there should be a balance of about $200. They prayed the court to summon the defendants to be heard in a Court of Equity, 10 October 1808. April 1809 term of court, dismissed by plaintiff's attorney.

159a - 1809, Monongalia County Court. Arrest Warrant issued for "Thomas LAIDLEY who was charged in execution in the jail of the said county by virtue of a former escape from said jail at the suit of Isaac H. WILLIAMS." LAIDLEY escaped from jail, a second time, on the night of 23 July 1809, and all law officers were alerted and instructed to re-take him and "commit him to prison where debtors are usually kept." Deputy Thomas BOWLS for Sheriff Stephen MORGAN.

159a - 1809, Monongalia County Court. Arrest Warrant issued for "John SULIVAN who was charged in execution in the jail of the said county by virtue of a former escape from said jail at the suit of Isaac H. WILLIAMS." SULIVAN escaped from jail, a second time, on the night of 23 July 1809 and all law officers were alerted and instructed to re-take him and "commit him to prison where debtors are usually kept." Deputy Mathew GAY for Sheriff Stephen MORGAN.

159a - 1808, Monongalia County Court. Joseph WISBEY Sr. and Joseph WISBEY Jr. summoned to answer William TINGLE in a plea of debt for $40, 14 November 1808. Appearance Bond signed by Joseph (x) WISBEY Sr. secured by John BONER, Amos BONER and John COOPER, 14 November 1808. WISBEY Jr. not found.

159a - 1809, Monongalia County Court. Escape Warrants for Thomas LAIDLEY and John SULLIVAN at the suit of Isaac H. WILLIAMS, 25 July 1809. (see above)

159a - 1808, Monongalia County Court. George B. HOSKINSON summoned to testify in behalf of John C. PAYNE, plaintiff, vs Evan B. MORGAN, defendant, 11 July 1808.

159a - 1809, Monongalia County Court. Agnes FRETWELL, administratrix for G. FRETWELL, deceased, summoned to answer John WILSON in a plea of debt, __ May 1809. Summons Samuel WILSON for plaintiff. 20 May 1809, judgement for $5.90 & $.75 costs.

159a - 1809, Monongalia County Court. James JEFFS summoned to answer Richard NUZUM in a plea of trespass on the case damage $150, 24 April 1808. "25 July 1801, Due to Richard NUZUM 1108 pounds of good bar iron to be delivered at John NUZUM's Mill on or before 1 March next," signed by James JEFFS and witnessed by John NUZUM. Richard NUZUM assigned this obligation to George BARNS on 27 August 1807. "9 February 1803, Received of the within bill $3 by Richard NUZUM." "Credit by 74# of bar iron at 8 1/2 per pound, 1 November 1803." "Received 15 April 1806 from Richard NUZUM by John NUZUM a note on James JEFFS for 1108# of bar iron with sundry credits thereon upon which I am to bring suit," signed by William TINGLE. March 1809, dismissed, agreed by the parties.

159a - 1809, Monongalia County Court. Jacob PALSBY, Jacob LYMAN and John NUZUM summoned to testify in behalf of Joseph KINCADE concerning a certain Deed of Conveyance to which they are witnesses, 30 October 1809.

159a - 1808, Monongalia County Court. Duncan F. McRAE summoned to answer Jacob FOULK for non-payment of an account, 26 November 1808. Thomas DOOLITTLE and Henry H. WILSON witnesses for McRAE. "No property found in my bailiwick, Jno. COOPER."

159a - 1808, Monongalia County Court. Jesse SPURLAND summoned to answer Jonas FOWLER in a plea of debt for $66 and $10 damage, 3 October and 30 November 1808. "SPURLAND not an inhabitant."

159a - 1808, Monongalia County Court. Adam McGILL obtained an attachment on the property of Benjamin CORNELL for $16 with interest. McGILL signed this Attachment Bond to ensure all costs and awards would be paid in case CORNELL prevailed in the suit secured by Wm. (x) HARTLEY on 14 November 1808. Note signed by Peggy CORNELL to Samuel JACKSON for 4 pounds and 16 shillings in sugar at 9 pence per pound dated 23 March 1808, due 1 May next and witnessed by John JACKSON. JACKSON assigned this note to Adam McGILL on 14 October 1808 which was witnessed by John JACKSON and James CALANGHAN. Two cows and one bay horse, the property of Benjamin CORNELL, was attached at the suit of Adam McGILL. In order to retain possession of his property until time of public sale or his debt was paid Benjamin (x) CORNELL signed this Delivery Bond secured by Philip SHIVELY, 23 November 1808.

159a - 1809, Monongalia County Court. Duncan McRAE, who was charged in execution in the jail of this county at the suit of Isaac DAVIS, assignee of James DUNN, for $10 debt escaped from jail on 2 February 1809. Escape Warrant issued to all law offices to "re-take and return" him to debtor's prison.

34

159a - 1808, Monongalia County Court. Escape Warrant for Bartholomew CLARK who was charged, with John TAYLOR, in execution in the jail bounds at the suit of Hannah STANLEY for $44.40 plus costs. CLARK escaped on 13 November 1808 and a warrant was issued to "re-take and return" him to debtor's prison, 21 November 1808.

159a - 1809, Monongalia County Court. Escape Warrants for Thomas LAIDLEY and John SULLIVAN at the suit of Isaac H. WILLIAMS, 25 July 1809. (see page 33)

159a - 1809, Monongalia County Court. Escape Warrant for William STAFFORD who was charged in execution in the jail bounds at the suit of the Commonwealth "for the sum of $.01 which was adjudged for a fine to him assessed for an assault on the body of Martin CURRANT plus $13.59 costs." STAFFORD escaped on 23 September 1809 and a warrant was issued to "re-take and return" him to debtor's prison, 23 September 1809.

159a - 1809, Monongalia County Court. Escape Warrant for John SULLIVAN and Joseph ALLEN who were charged in execution in the jail bounds at the suit of Benjamin SAYRE for $90 plus cost. They escaped on 13 March 1809 and a warrant was issued to "retake and return" them to debtor's prison, 20 March 1809.

159b - 1809, Monongalia County Court. Edward GALLAGHER, John McGUIRE, William SCRIPPS and the heirs of Thomas BOND summoned to answer a Bill in Chancery exhibited against them by John ZEGAN, 20 October 1806. John CZIGAR's complaint: On 24 September 1788, a survey was made in the name of Charles GALLAGHER for 770 acres of land on the waters of the right fork of Wickware Creek. On 11 June 1792, GALLAGHER executed a Power of Attorney to Doctor Thomas BOND to sell and dispose of the land. On 16 July 1792, BOND sold the land to Edward GALLAGHER, the originals of these documents are filed in the Land Office in Richmond. The copies that are filed here are certified by Charles LEWIS, Register of the Land Office. A grant was issued to Edward GALLAGHER dated 16 August 1792. On 22 August 1792, GALLAGHER made a deed to Doctor Thomas BOND but the deed was never admitted to record. On 24 August 1792, CZIGAR and John McGUIRE purchased the 770 acres from BOND, made a down payment of fully one half of the purchase price and gave their obligation for the balance of the money. McGUIRE not being able to pay full half of the price, passed his notes for the two sums of $88.50 with CZIGAR as security. CZIGAR was compelled to pay one of the notes. BOND, as Power for Edward GALLAGHER, made a deed to CZIGAR and McGUIRE and gave them the deed made by E. GALLAGHER to BOND and these deeds were left in the Office of the Clerk of Monongalia County to be recorded and the fees paid. The last two mentioned documents were destroyed by fire when the Clerk's

Office burned. CZIGAR and McGUIRE, both residing in Alexandria at the time, agreed that the land should be occupied and the taxes paid to ensure their claim would be valid. McGUIRE proposed that CZIGAR should go and settle the land and if he would do so, it was agreed that CZIGAR would have first choice of one half the land that he thought proper to improve. CZIGAR moved upon one part of the land "that country then being in a wild barbarious and inhospitable state" and he resided there ever since and made considerable improvements which rendered that part of the land much more valuable than any other part which still "remains as planted by nature." Sometime later, McGUIRE came to settle on his one half of the land, viewed the land and was much displeased with the quality and situation and told CZIGAR to keep his improved part and sold one half of his one half part to William SCRIPS. They engaged a surveyor and surveyed one fourth for SCRIPS and the other one fourth owned by McGUIRE was to go to CZIGAR for the sum of the note which CZIGAR paid for McGUIRE. McGUIRE moved out of the country without making a deed to CZIGAR for the one fourth part, but SCRIPS lived in the county and claims one part of the land but has not shown any title. BOND died long before and his heirs are unknown and GALLAGHER moved to Kentucky and SCRIPS refused to divide the land and make him a deed. He prayed the court to compel the above named persons or their heirs to make a clear deed and convey the land to him. John EVANS swore that a Deed of Conveyance from Doctor Thomas BOND, as Attorney in fact for Edward GALLAGHER, to John McGUIRE and John ZAGAN was a tract of 770 acres patented to Edward GALLAGHER on 16 July 1792. William SCRIPPS swore he heard McGUIRE say that one half of the 770 acres was the property of John ZEGAN. Jno CREGAN vs William SCRIPPS, Jno McGUIRE, Edward GALLAGHER and the heirs of Doctor Thomas BOND: The court decreed that ZEGAN had a right to the land on which he lived, that he had been compelled to pay $83.50 for McGUIRE in part payment for McGUIRE's half of the land and as security for McGUIRE, will have to pay the other sum of $83.50 a further part due by McGUIRE. The court further decreed that the defendants make a deed to ZEGAN and convey with Special Warranty all their right, title and interest of and into one half of the land. Wm. N. JARRETT was appointed to mark boundaries and lay off the one half on which ZEGAN lived. It was ordered that McGUIRE's one half of the land be exposed to public sale, unless McGUIRE paid the two sums of money heretofore mentioned on or before 1 May 1809, and the money derived from this sale be use to pay the said two sums with interest and costs and the balance, if any, be paid to McGUIRE or his order. It was ordered that the defendants convey to SCRIPPS one fourth of McGUIRE's one half and it was ordered that the defendant, all except SCRIPPS, pay all costs of this suit as well as the costs of carrying this decree into effect and that their bodies be attached until the performance of this

decree was completed.   "Rec´d 13 November 1800 of John ZEGAN
$1.48 in full of his direct tax on one tract of land," signed
by Alexander HAWTHORN, Collector of the Direct Tax. "We
promise to pay on demand to Dr. Thomas BOND $83.50," August
1782, signed by J. McGUIRE and J. ZIGAN.   Deed from Edward
GALLAGHER, Deputy Surveyor of Monongalia County, to Thomas
BOND, of Alexandria, Fairfax County, Virginia, dated 22
August 1792: On 24 September 1788, GALLAGHER surveyed for
himself, as assignee of David ANDERSON, 770 acres of land, a
part of a Treasury Warrant #20599 dated 10 November 1783,
entered 15 September 1788 on the right hand fork of Wickware
Creek adjoining Richard MERRYFIELD, James CURRANT, James
BULLARD/BULLAND and others.   Signed by Edward GALLAGHER and
witnessed by Charles LEE, B. WASHINGTON and Chs. TURNER.
Plat of this survey and plat of the land as divided between
ZEGAN (490 acres), McGUIRE (233 acres) and SCRIPPS (233
acres) dated 18 August 1809. Power of Attorney signed by
GALLAGHER to BOND dated 11 June 1792.

159b - 1809, Monongalia County Court. Peace Bond for John
NEWBROUGH, blacksmith, to keep the peace toward all citizens
and especially toward Charity HALL, widow, secured by William
WHITE, yeoman, and Jonathan COLBOURNE, yeoman, 12 January
1809. On reverse of one of the documents: "I killed HALL and
will kill __ family like snakes." "NEWBURY carries the stamp
of truth. This is NEWBURY´s story to BARKER." Rawley MARTIN
and Susanna SNODGRASS summoned to testify in behalf of
NEWBROUGH, 12 June 1809.   Justice Boaz BURROWS and Constable
George B. HOSKINSON.   Zachariah BARKER summoned to give
evidence to the Grand Jury, 3 June 1809.

159b - 1808,   Monongalia County Court. Notice to Robert
FERRELL Esqr. from Alexander BRANDON of intent to move the
court to render up judgement and execution against him for 7
pounds and 10 shillings with damage and cost amounting to 11
pounds, 14 shillings and 1 penny ($38.98) with interest,
being the sum paid by BRANDON as FERRELL´s security to John
EVANS Jr. and John W. DEAN, executors of Elijah BURROWS, by
virtue of a judgement on 20 December 1806.   John EVANS Jr.
summoned to testify in behalf of BRANDON, 5 March, 4 May, 9
July 1807 and 24 July 1808.

159b - 1807, Monongalia County Court. Notice to George HITE
from Thomas EVANS of intent to take the affidavit of Josiah
HOSKINSON to support a Bill of Injunction that was obtained
on a judgement recovered by HITE against EVANS, 4 December
180_. Affidavit of HOSKINSON heard at the house of W. N.
JARRETT on 8 December 1807: About the time Thomas EVANS Jr.,
the apprentice named in the said bill, was about to elope
from HITE, he came to EVAN´s house and informed him that his
son, Thomas, told him he was about to run away and go to
Kentucky.   He told EVANS Sr. he should warn HITE of Thomas

Jr's. intentions. EVANS Sr. said he would and went away and sometime later returned and told him he had informed HITE of the situation. This happened on Saturday evening and on Sunday morning Thomas Jr. started from his (HOSKINSON) house. On the Monday evening following, he and EVANS Sr. and some other person was at REAS' tavern and HITE was there. EVANS Sr. said his son was gone and asked HITE why he did not stop him. HITE replied, "Dam it! I cared nothing about him, let him go." HITE then added that he had seen him go, he saw him in the ford where when he was starting, he heard hollowing and knowing it to be them, ran down opposite McCRAY's and saw him in the ford. HITE told EVANS Sr. that he had no authority over the boy and he would be ruined in running about and not completing his trade. EVANS said to HITE, "there is my horse, follow him to Kentucky or 1000 miles and retake him." HITE's answered, "I care nothing about him, let him go," 8 December 1807.

159b - 1809, Monongalia County Court. "On the motion of Abraham FULTON it is ordered that Charles BYRN, David MORGAN and James CARROLL be appointed commissioners to assign and lay off the dower of Mary TAYLOR, widow of Wildy TAYLOR, deceased, of the tract of land on which the said Wildy formerly lived and report to September Court," June 1809 term. The commissioners reported that they laid off the widow's dower beginning at a stake between the north end of the old house and the new house...to John SNYDER's line, 9 September 1809.

159b - 1808, Monongalia County Court. William STAFFORD summoned to answer an indictment against him for an assault upon Martin CURRENT, 17 May 1809. Charles McGILL Sr. summoned to give evidence to the Grand Jury, 14 and 22 November 1808. Jonathan HARTLEY summoned to testify in behalf of STAFFORD, 14 August 1809. Jonathan HARTLEY and Reubin BAKER summoned to testify in behalf of STAFFORD, __ March 1809. Samuel WILSON and Joseph ALLEN summoned to testify in behalf of STAFFORD, 14 August 1809. Deputy Thomas BOWLES for Sheriff Stephen MORGAN. "We of the jury find the defendant guilty and amerce him in $.01 damage," Hedgeman TRIPPLETT, foreman.

159b - 1809, Monongalia County Court. Thomas WEST, laborer, summoned to answer an indictment against him for an assault upon James WILSON, yeoman, 22 November 1808 and 11 May 1809. Summons not served because "kept off by force and by running out of the way." Jacob TEWALT, Thomas EWELL and William MILLER summoned to give evidence to the Grand Jury, 24 October 1808. Robert FERRELL, son of James, and James WILSON summoned to give evidence to the Grand Jury, 10 June 1808 and 11 May 1809. James WILSON, Jacob TEWALT, Thomas EWELL and William MILLER summoned to give evidence to the Grand Jury, 23 November 1808. "We the jury find the defendant guilt and amerce him in $.01."

159b – 1809, Monongalia County Court. William STEPHENSON complained that Isaac H. WILLIAMS sued out a writ of execution against his property for $33.56 debt with interest at 5% from 14 August 1805 plus costs. STEPHENSON entered into a bond with Larkin PIERPOINT as his security on 7 September 1805 for the delivery of one horse and two cows which bond was founded on the aforesaid execution. He charged that the judgement was rendered on an account, but that he is informed by his wife that there was a mistake in the settlement of the account. His wife said she was at the Widow PIERPOINT's and at WILLIAMS' own special request, she did board, wash and furnish a room for Betsy/Elizabeth BUCKMAN for 14 months and that Betsy was delivered of a base born child and that she paid the midwife fees for Betsy. She said WILLIAMS promised to pay and settle with her so much as it should be worth. She charged $5 per month, amounting to $70, and WILLIAMS never paid her or gave credit for more than $8 on the said account. STEPHENSON prayed the court for an injunction to stay execution of the judgement until WILLIAMS could be questioned in a Court of Equity, 19 May 1805. WILLIAMS said he furnished Betsy with clothes and money more than sufficient for her support and never promised STEPHENSON's wife to pay for board or any other things. In order to settle the account, he agreed to give an $8 credit and at the time there was no objection by STEPHENSON or his wife. Sworn to by WILLIAMS at Culpepper County in presence of Justice Richard NORRIS on 15 November 1806. November 1809 term of court, dismissed and judgement.

159b – 1809, Monongalia County Court. Order for Jailer Smallwood DEARING to take Andrew SHEPLER and confine him until further notice by the court. SHEPLER was arrested by Justice William BARNES for suspicion of taking and carrying away a shirt ($1.67), the property of Morgan MORGAN. A letter signed by BARNES directed to DEARING concerning a Called Court on Andrew SHEPLER, yeoman. BARNES said he was ignorant in the law and asked if some other justice could do this business for him and stated he would have the witnesses there and if he must do this business, he would need directions, for he wanted to do every thing legal. No date.

159b – 1809, Monongalia County Court. William SCRIPPS summoned to answer John ATKINSON in a plea of trespass on the case damage $40, 23 May 1809. Appearance Bond signed by SCRIPPS secured by Moses DOOLITTLE Jr., 23 May 1809. "This action is brought in trespass on the case for a ____ in the sale of a mare colt." August 1809 term, dismissed by order of the plaintiff.

159b – 1809, Monongalia County Court. David TROWBRIDGE summoned to answer Thomas BUTLER in an action of trover and to show cause why a judgement of damage for wrongfully detaining

two hogs, the property of said BUTLER, should not be had
against him, 28 April 1809. "15 December 1808, Mr. Samuel
TROWBRIDGE, Sir: You are requested to summons Peter MASON and
Mary his wife, Isaac PAUGH, John DEWIT, Rachael BUTLER (later
called BETTY) and William ENGLAND to appear at Becket MINOR's
on Saturday next to give evidence concerning two hogs claimed
by Thomas BUTLER and David TROWBRIDGE..." Signed by David
MORGAN. May 1809 term, judgement for BUTLER. TROWBRIDGE
prayed for and was granted an appeal. John MILLER entered
himself as security for TROWBRIDGE to appeal to June Court
the above judgement in favor of BUTLER, 11 May 1809. "2
March 1809, A Bill of Damages against David STROBRIDGE for
taking, detaining and making use of two hogs, the property of
Thomas BUTLER. The first time I sent three hands, the second
time two hands and the third time three hands and horses each
time for which I charge three shillings per day and ferrage
six times man and horse and four times man only. When we saw
the two hogs of Thomas BUTLER's on our side of Cheat River,
we believe to the best of our 'nollege' that they were worth
$8," signed by Petter MASON and William ENGLAND. Rachel
BETTY, Mary MASON, Isaac PAUGH and William ENGLAND summoned
to testify in behalf of BUTLER, 28 June and 11 July 1809.
Samuel TAYLOR, Burket MINOR, John MASON, Anthoney COZAD,
James GRADY, John GRADY, Michael GRADY and James REED
summoned to testify in behalf of TROWBRIDGE, 13 June and 11
July 1809. Rachel BUTLER's deposition: She said one pig left
home last spring, the other this fall and the least one had a
crooked tail. Deposition of Isaac PAUGH: He helped put the
hogs in a pen and they broke out and they caught them with
dogs. The pigs broke out again and he did not notice it
until he saw it in a pen at Burket MINOR's Mill and several
of the hogs he helped butcher at BUTLER's that fall had
crooked tails. Deposition of William ENGLAND: He helped catch
the largest hog and put it in a pen at BUTLER's. That fall
he helped kill hogs at BUTLER's and several of them had
crooked tails. Deposition of Mary MASON: The smallest hog
was at her house, the last time she saw the hog it was
crossing the river to this side of the falls. BUTLER's black
man said the hog belonged to BUTLER and from the description
she gave BUTLER, he believed the hog to be his. Deposition
of Burket MINOR: BUTLER came to his mill and described his
hogs before he went to see them in the pen. He said the least
one was his hog, but would call his wife or Peter MASON or
some other person to come to view them for they knew his hogs
as well as he did.

Also in this file - - - - "Mr. Isaac BUTLER presents his kind
respects to Mr. SYEAMORE and desires the honor of Mr.
SYEAMORE's company to dinner tomorrow at 2 o'clock Thursday
May 7th 1801." "I expect I will come down this fall." "Mr.
Elijah BUTLER most humble respects attend Miss Eliza CASEY
hoping and humbly requesting of Miss Eliza that she will

honor him by being his partner at the ball on June 12th at
Mr. RIGHTMIRE's." (These three quotes are all written on
one page and each in a different handwriting).

159b - 1809, Monongalia County Court. Samuel PEARCE summoned
to answer Daniel CAPITO in a plea of debt for $42.81 due by
note and $20 damage, 20 March and 31 May 1809. Promissory
Note signed by Samuel PEARCE to Daniel CAPITO for 12 pounds,
16 shillings and 10 pence dated 24 November 1802 and
witnessed by John STALNAKER. November 1809 term judgement
confirmed and entered up.

159b - 1809, Monongalia County Court. Richard POSTLE summoned
to answer John ROBERTS in a plea of debt for $44.18 and $10
damage, 27 April and 31 May 1809. Written Obligation signed
by POSTLE to ROBERTS, of Washington County, Pennsylvania, for
the penal sum of $44.18 dated 27 April 1807 and witnessed by
William HERRING. "Rec'd 20 March 1809 of Jacob FUNK $15.50
of the within in part, William HERRING for John ROBERTS."
November 1809 term, judgement confirmed and entered up.

159b - 1809, Monongalia County Court. Benjamin LAWSON complained that James CLARK owed him $25 and he prayed the court
to attach so much of his property as to satisfy the debt, 2
March 1809. "Summons Peter OSBOURN and David BAYLES as
garnishees." No property found in the hands of either
OSBOURN or BAYLES, 4 March 1809. John GRIBBLE and James
HAMILTON summoned to testify in behalf of LAWSON, 14 March
1809. "1806, Colo. James CLARK to Benjamin LAWSON, dr, to
carpentry work done for him $90.36, credit $65.36, balance
due $25." Attachment Bond signed by LAWSON to ensure all
costs and awards would be paid in case he was cast in the
suit secured by Richard SMITH, 2 March 1809. November 1809
term, dismissed by order of the plaintiff and filed with
November papers.

159b - 1809, Monongalia County Court. John DAVIS, Isaac Hite
WILLIAMS, John B. ARMISTEAD, Henry DERING Jr., late merchants
and co-partners in trade under the firm of John DAVIS and
Company, summoned to answer _____ ROBISON and Asher LEWIS in
a plea of debt for $80 and $20 damage, 20 July 1801. John B.
ARMISTEAD (not an inhabitant) summoned to answer ROBINSON and
LEWIS in a plea of debt for $80 and $20 damage, 27 August
1801. ROBISON and LEWIS complained that Henry DERING Jr.,
for and on behalf of the above named defendants, signed a
Promissory Note dated 26 November 1798, due in 90 days for
$80 for value received "in beef cattle for the use of
Pleasant Furnace whereby and by virtue of an Act of General
Assembly in that case made and provided an action hath
accrued to ROBINSON and LEWIS to demand and receive of the
defendants" the said money. The plaintiffs said the
defendants had not paid the debt or any part of it and there-

fore they bring suit. Joanna CHIPPS, Thomas CHIPPS and William CHIPPS summoned to testify in behalf of Asher LEWIS, plaintiff, against John DAVIS, defendant, 13 May 1802. Joanna, Thomas and William CHIPPS summoned to testify in behalf of ROBISON and LEWIS, 26 July 1802. William McCLEERY, Benjamin REEDER and Samuel HANWAY summoned to testify in behalf of ROBINSON and LEWIS, 13 March 1807. November 1809 term, non-suit.

159b - 1809, Monongalia County Court. Caleb FURBEE summoned to answer Ralph BARKSHIRE in a plea of debt due by note, 20 July 1809. No property found.

159b - 1809, Monongalia County Court. Joseph ONEAL summoned to answer a presentment against him by the Grand Jury for not keeping the road in repair leading from John BRAND's to the Little Falls of the Monongahela River, 21 August 1809. Joseph JENKINS, foreman. Hugh EVANS and Labin PERDEW summoned to give evidence to the Grand Jury, 21 August 1809. November 1809 term quashed (voided).

159b - 1809, Monongalia County Court. James JEFFS summoned to answer Jacob MADERA in a plea of debt for $60.67 and $10 damage, 19 October 1809. Appearance Bond signed by JEFFS secured by James (x) WEST. November 1809 term, dismissed by order of the plaintiff.

159b - 1809, Monongalia County Court. Recognizance Bond for George D. BARNES, wheelright, secured by James BRAND, wheel-right, 9 October 1809. "The condition of this Recognizance Bond is that whereas Polly SOUTHWORTH, single woman, by her examination on oath before Justice W. N. JARRETT declared that on 18 October 1807 at the house of Joseph SOUTHWORTH, she was delivered of a male bastard child which is likely to become chargeable to the county and hath charged the above bound George D. BARNES with having gotten her with child of the said bastard child." Polly (x) SOUTHWORTH signed her sworn statement on 3 October 1809 and on the same day an Arrest Warrant was issued against BARNES. "Summons William HALL and Recene his wife and Anthony CARROL as witnesses for the Commonwealth."

159b - 1809, Monongalia County Court. John WELTNER vs Abraham PIXLER: One month note signed by PIXLER to WELTNER for $12.75 payable in good salt at market price dated 14 November 1809 and witnessed by Francis COLLINS. Three month note signed by PIXLER to WELTNER for $17.79 payable in good rye ($.50 per bushel) and good corn ($.41 per bushel) delivered at PIXLER's Stillhouse dated 14 November 1809 and witnessed by COLLINS. John LEWIS summoned as garnishee, 24 November 1809. No property found. Attachment Bond signed by WELTNER to ensure all costs and awards would be paid in case he should be cast in the suit secured by Lewis JOHN, 24 November 1809. December 1809 term, judgement.

159b - 1809, Monongalia County Court. Arthur WILSON summoned to answer Hugh SIDWELL in a plea of debt due by note, 23 February 1807. One day note signed by WILSON to SIDWELL for $23.25 dated 6 December 1804 and witnessed by Jacob KIGER. Bail Bond for WILSON secured by John CARTER, 14 April 1807. August 1809 term, "We the jury find for the plaintiff the debt in the declaration mentioned with interest at the rate of 6% from 7 December 1804 until paid," Nicholas B. MADERA, foreman.

159b - 1809, Monongalia County Court. Abraham SHREVES summoned to answer Benjamin J. BRICE, assignee of George ICE, in a plea of debt due by note, 17 February 1809. Promissory Note signed by SHREVES to George ICE dated 5 August 1807 for $10 payable in good rye at 3 shillings per bushel delivered at William ICE's on or before 11 September next and witnessed by Abraham ICE and William ICE Jr. Assignment to BRICE signed by George (x) ICE, no date, witnessed by Solomon HOGUE. Appearance Bond signed by Abraham (x) SHREVES secured by William (x) ICE, 21 February 1809. August 1809 term, judgement confirmed and entered up.

159b - 1809, Monongalia County Court. Notice to Thomas MARTIN and Peter FORTNEY from Philip DODDRIDGE of intent to move the court for judgement and execution on a forthcoming bond given by MARTIN and FORTNEY to DODDRIDGE for $30, dated 25 October 1808 and conditioned on the delivery of property, 20 December 1808. Five cows, the property of MARTIN, was attached at the suit of DODDRIDGE for $23.96. In order to retain possession of his property until time for public sale or his debt was paid MARTIN signed this Delivery Bond secured by FORTNEY, 25 October 1808. January 1809 term of court, judgement.

159b - 1808, Monongalia County Court. Charles W. MARTIN summoned to answer Samuel EVERLY in a plea of debt due by note, 18 June 1808. Note signed by MARTIN to EVERLY for $15 dated 16 March 1808 and witnessed by John RAMSEY Jr. and Simon EVERLY. James COLLINS summoned to give evidence, 2 August 1808. John RAMSEY summoned to testify in behalf of EVERLY. Caleb TRIPPETT, Scott MARTIN, James COLLINS Sr. and Henry SMITH summoned to testify in behalf of MARTIN, 12 September 1808. August 1808 term, judgement for the plaintiff for $15 with interest from 19 March 1808 till paid. "The defendant appeals to next court."

159b - 1808, Monongalia County Court. Duncan F. McRA summoned to answer Isaac DAVIS, assignee of James DUNN, in a plea of debt due by note, 11 October 1808.

159b - 1809, Monongalia County Court. W(illiam) STEVENSON summoned to answer Jacob GOOSEMAN in a plea of debt due by note, 31 December 1808. February 1809 term, judgement for the plaintiff for $4.84 debt, $1.02 cost. No property found.

159b - 1809, Monongalia County Court. Thomas MONTGOMERY summoned to answer Zaquill MORGAN in a plea of debt for $13, 17 January 1805. Thomas MONTGOMERY to Zaquil MORGAN, for repairing a still on March 18th 1804 = 3.18.0 ($13). January 1809 term, judgement.

159b - 1808, Monongalia County Court. Order to attach the property of John WADKINS at the suit of Michael CLOUS, 30 November 1808. No property found.

159b - 1809, Monongalia County Court. Charles W. MARTIN summoned to answer Samuel EVERLY in a plea of debt due by note, 13 June 1808. Note signed by MARTIN to EVERLY for $15 dated 16 March 1808 and witnessed by Simeon EVERLY and John RAMSEY Jr. Simon EVERLY, John RAMSEY, Presley MARTIN and James COLLINS summoned to testify in behalf of EVERLY, 12 September, 5 October 1808 and 5 January 1809. Caleb TRIPETT, James COLLINS Sr., Henry SMITH and Scott MARTIN summoned to testify in behalf of MARTIN, 10 October 1808. January 1809 term, judgement affirmed.

159b - 1808, Monongalia County Court. Replevin Bond signed by James MANN to secure his property which was attached at the suit of James COBURN and sold at public sale. MANN was the highest bidder and signed this bond to ensure he would pay his debt in 12 months. This bond secured by Robert GREEN, 20 August 1808. (Replevin Bond: a bond to protect or give security for the return to, or recovery by, a person of goods or chattels wrongfully taken or detained upon giving security to try the matter in court and return the goods if defeated in action.)

159b - 1809, Monongalia County Court. Order for the attachment of the property of Agness FRETWELL, administratrix of Thomas FRETWELL, deceased, to satisfy a judgement in favor of Thomas MONTGOMERY for $20 plus costs, 10 August 1809. No property found, 9 October 1809.

159b - 1809, Monongalia County Court. Under oath, Elizabeth SHOCKLY, a free single woman, swore that "on 19 March last past at the house of Davis SHOCKLEY in Morgan Town she was delivered of a female bastard child which is likely to become chargeable to the county and that Jacob MADERA of the town and county aforesaid, carpenter/joiner, is the father of said child," 14 September 1809. Signed by Elizabeth (x) SHOCKLEY. An Arrest Warrant was issued for apprehending MADERIA on the above mentioned charge by William McCLEERY, Overseer of the

Poor. John W. THOMPSON and Jacob FOULK summoned to testify in behalf of MADERA, 4 September and 8 October 1809. John W. THOMPSON, Simeon WOODROW and Abraham WOODROW summoned to give evidence, 9 May 1809. Recognizance Bond signed by Jacob MADERA secured by Nicholas B. MADERA, 14 September 1809. October 1809 term, judgement.

159b - 1809, Monongalia County Court. Martin CURRANT, yeoman, summoned to answer a indictment against him for an assault on William STAFFORD, 22 November 1808 and 16 May 1809. Charles McGILL Sr. summoned to give evidence, 22 November 1808 and 16 May 1809. August 1809 term, "We the jury assess the defendant to $2" and "We the jury find for the Commonwealth $2," signed by Richard POSTLE, foreman.

159b - 1809, Monongalia County Court. Notice to William and Samuel EVERLY from George SMITH, one of the Overseers of the Poor, of intent to move the court to enter up judgement against them for "the sum of $30 being the amount due on the 10th of September last on a Recognizance Bond entered into by you the said William with you the said Samuel as security on the 12th of September 1804 by order of Monongalia Court to indemnify the said county against the charge of supporting a bastard child begotten by you the said William upon the body of Elizabeth HUTSON," 25 October 1809. November 1809 term, judgement.

159b - 1809, Monongalia County Court. James MANN summoned to answer William and Joseph LOWRY, merchants trading under the firm of William LOWRY and Company, assignee of John PAYNE who was partner to Stephen ROOT, trading under the firm of ROOT and PAYNE, in a plea of debt for $35 and $10 damage, 17 October 1808. Promissory Note from MANN to ROOT and PAYNE for $35 dated 8 December 1803, payable in rye at 3 shillings per bushel to be delivered at Capt. John FAIRFAX's on or before 20 September next. Assignment to LOWRY dated 12 July 1808 and signed by John PAYNE. Appearance Bond signed by James MANN secured by Robert GREEN, 9 November 1808. July 1809 term, dismissed by plaintiff.

159b - 1809, Monongalia County Court. Note from Benjamin HELLEN and Uriah HOOK to James THOMPSON for $1,050 dated 17 December 1805, due 1 September next. "1807, abated as to Uriah HOOK." Bail Bond for HELLEN secured by Abraham and Simeon WOODROW, 8 April 1807. July 1809 term, dismissed by order of the plaintiff and judgement for the defendant.

159b - 1809, Monongalia County Court. Isaac POWELL obtained an attachment on the property of Jeremiah WILSON for $50. Attachment Bond signed by Isaac POWELL, of Washington County, Pennsylvania, secured by John CARTER to ensure all costs and awards would be paid in case he was cast in the suit, 5 July

1809. Bond witnessed by Robert FAUSET and J. Casper (x) MICHAEL. "Summon Henry WEAVER as garnishee and Benjamin WILSON as witness for the plaintiff." "Also summoned Sard WEAVER as garnishee." "Isaac POWELL Sr. enters security for costs," 10 July 1809.

159b - 1809, Monongalia County Court. Two good milch cows, the property of Thomas MARTIN, was attached at the suit of Dudley EVANS for $22. In order to retain possession of his property until time for public sale or his debt was paid MARTIN signed this Delivery Bond secured by Peter FORTNEY, 30 July 1808. January 1809 term, judgement.

159b - 1809, Monongalia County Court. Two good horses, the property of John SULLIVAN, was attached at the suit of Benjamin SAYRE for $18.33 plus cost. In order to retain possession of his property until time for public sale or his debt was paid SULLIVAN signed this Delivery Bond secured by Joseph ALLEN, 29 November 1808. January 1809 term, judgement.

159b - 1809, Monongalia County Court. One horse, the property of Farquer McCREA, executor with William LANHAM of the estate of Barsheba FERGUSON, deceased, was attached at the suit of Christian MADERA, William TINGLE and Abraham GUSEMAN for $20. In order to retain possession of his property until time for public sale or his debt was paid McRA signed this Delivery Bond secured by D. F. McRA, 14 November 1808. January 1809 term, judgement.

159b - 1809, Monongalia County Court. Five cows, the property of Thomas MARTIN, was attached at the suit of Enos DAUGHERTY for $5.97 plus costs. In order to retain possession of his property until time for public sale or his debt was paid MARTIN signed this Delivery Bond secured by Peter FORTNEY, 25 October 1808. January 1809 term, judgement.

159b - 1809, Monongalia County Court. Order for Joseph NEWBURG/NEWBROUGH to give security and keep the peace toward all citizens and especially toward Charity HALL, widow, 30 May 1809. Elizabeth HESS, Otho HENRY, Sophiah HENRY and Sary BARKER summoned to give evidence to the Grand Jury, 3 June 1809. Peace Bond for Joseph NEWBROUGH, blacksmith, secured by Rawley MARTIN, yeoman, and William GAMBLE, stonemason, 1 June 1809. On reverse of one of the documents: "... in cold blood before MARTIN who was not afraid of Joseph. He would rather root her out, he had $80, he wants to spend it to root her out. NEWBURY kicked W. HALL. Mrs. HESS says his general character is bad."

END OF MICROFILM #40

46

159c - 1809, Monongalia County Court. Charles BROWNFIELD and
Richard LEWIS, administrators for Thomas LEWIS, deceased,
complained that William PRICE and his wife Mary PRICE, late
Mary LEWIS, and Thomas BUTLER owed him $65.27 due by note and
therefore he brings suit.   Nine month note signed by Mary
LEWIS and Thomas BUTLER to the administrators for Thomas
LEWIS, deceased, for $65.27 dated 23 September 1805 and
witnessed by Peter CASEY.   Letter of Administration for
Charles BROWNFIELD and Richard LEWIS to be administrators of
the estate of Thomas LEWIS, late of George Township, Fayette
County, Pennsylvania, signed by Alexander McCLEAN, register,
12 March 1805. March 1809 term, judgement confirmed, no plea
being entered.

159c - 1808, Monongalia County Court.   "We the Grand Jury
present Evan MORGAN Overseer of the road leading from George
DORSEY's to Laurel Run Bridge for not keeping the same in
repair for six months last past by the information of Jacob
HOLLAND and Thomas EWELL, two of our own body," 14 November
1808.

159c - 1809, Monongalia County Court. "We the Grand Jury do
present David SCOTT the 3rd, Surveyor of the road from Scotts
Ferry leading up Scotts Mill Run, for not keeping the same in
good repair within two months last past by the information of
Philip SHIVELY and John SNIDER two of our own body," 18 March
1809.   "We the Grand Jury do present the Surveyor of the Road
leading from David SCOTT's Plantation to the forks of Indian
Creek for not keeping the same in good repair within two
months last past by the information of David SCOTT and Joseph
MORGAN two of our own body," 18 March 1809. John BOUSLOG
summoned to testify in behalf of SCOTT, 9 May 1809. May 1809
term, fined.

159c - 1809, Monongalia County Court. Thomas MONTGOMERY summoned to answer Patrick McFEETERS/McFEATERS in a plea of debt
for 23 pounds Pennsylvania currency ($61.33), 21 October and
23 November 1805. Appearance Bond signed by Thos MONTGOMERY
secured by James (x) MURFY, 2 December 1805.   "This action is
brought in debt on two judgements confessed before a Magistrate in Pennsylvania."   Justice Mathew GILEHRIST and Ephraim
DOUGLASS, Prothy., of Fayette County, Pennsylvania. March
1809 term, dismissed by order of the plaintiff.

159c - 1809, Monongalia County Court. William TINGLE summoned
to answer John STEALEY in a plea of debt for $300, 4 Septem-
ber 1809. William TINGLE obtained a judgement, dated 18 March
1808, against James TATE for $75 debt with interest at 6%
from 25 December 1804 plus costs. John STEALY secured Bail

47

Bond for TATE on 13 May 1805. STEALY summoned to show cause, if any he can, why execution should not be had against him as security for TATE, 22 April 1808. TINGLE to STEALEY, an account dated March 1799 through 3 January 1803, for sherry wine, Jamaica Spirits, Hyson Tea, nails, pins, balance on salmon, 3 broken white plates, cups and saucers, shoes, sole leather, hauling wood, salt fish, plank and shoe leather. Total 73 pounds, 2 shillings and 9 pence. Deposition of Caleb FURBEY: About March 1799 he owed TINGLE $14 and TINGLE asked him for the money saying he needed it to send with STEALEY to Baltimore, that STEALEY agreed to purchase liquor for him and to deliver it to him at cost and carriage. He bargained with STEALEY to accept iron instead of cash in behalf of TINGLE and delivered $14 worth of iron at 6/d per pound when iron was selling for 9/d per pound. He also gave STEALEY an order for $8 on _____ SNIDER to induce him to take the iron instead of cash, 5 November 1804. STEALEY in account with TINGLE dated September 1798 through December 1801 for oats, hides, court fees, drafting a Power of Attorney, to Benjamin REEDER for selling Territorial Lands, and many purchases of wines, spirits, brandy and whiskey. Alexander HAWTHORN summoned to testify in behalf of TINGLE, 1 April 1807. Farquire McRAE summoned to testify in behalf of STEALEY, 10 August 1808. Caleb FURBEE summoned to testify in behalf of TINGLE, 29 October 1808. "Mr. McCRAY please let the bearer have 18 gallons whiskey and oblige yours," signed by STEALEY on 8 November 1799. Arbitrators Nimrod EVANS and Alexander HAWTHORN ordered that William pay John $31.52 with interest at 6% from 3 January 1804 plus costs, 17 March 1809. May 1809 term of court, dismissed by order of the plaintiff.

159c - 1809, Monongalia County Court. Thomas POWELL summoned to answer Leonard REAMS in a plea of trespass on the case and $40 damage, 22 July 1809.

159c - 1809, Monongalia County Court. "We the Grand Jury do present Hugh KELSO for not keeping the road in repair on both banks of Cheat River from the crossing of the State Road to his, the said KELSO's, ferry within two months last past by the information of John C. PAYNE and William PRICE," 18 March 1809.

159c - 1809, Monongalia County Court. "We the Grand Jury do present William PRICE for an assault upon the body of William F. CASEY by the information of said CASEY," May 1809. "We the Grand Jury do present William PRICE for an assault upon the body of Elijah BUTLER by the information of said BUTLER," May 1809. Both presentments quashed (voided).

159c - 1809, Monongalia County Court. James MANN summoned to answer Thomas COWSER in a plea of debt for $51.38 and $10 damage, 17 March 1809.

159c - 1810, Monongalia County Court. Elihu HORTON summoned to answer John BOUSLOG in a plea of trespass on the case damage $100, 2 March and 1 April 1805. BOUSLOG swore that Frederick ZIMMERMAN and David SWINDLER were material witnesses for him and he believed they were about to leave the Commonwealth, 10 February 1806. Notice to HORTON of intent to hear the deposition of Fred ZIMMERMAN to be read in evidence, 12 February 1806. On reverse of this notice: William ENGLAND "made oath that on the day of the date of the within notice that he attempted to read the same to Elihu HORTON and did read part of it and followed him for that purpose until HORTON shut a door on him, he would not hear it." Deposition of ZIMMERMAN heard at the house of Henry DERING on 13 February 1806: He saw Mich'l DEVENHOVER, who was then in the employ of BOUSLOG, haul one load of wood from BOUSLOG's place that he said he took to HORTON and DEVENHOVER said he hauled 4 loads of wood to HORTON and HORTON treated him well. ZIMMERMAN said that about three years ago, he hauled a stack of hay to HORTON which he bought of BOUSLOG and last winter he delivered not less than 260 bushels of coal to HORTON drawn on BOUSLOG and hauled 4 loads of wood to HORTON from BOUSLOG's plantation. He said before he was called to give his deposition, HORTON offered him a "good fee if I would clear myself and took out some money which I took to be a bank bill but am not certain." Elihu HORTON to John BOUSLOG, 13 December 1801, to one day hauling hay 1.0.0; 1 hand 0.3.0. November 1802, to 1 stack of hay delivered in town 5.8.0; 4 loads of wood 1.4.0. 1803, to 11 gallons of Bounce $.84 per gallon 3.13.5. November 24, to 3 loads of wood 0.18.0; 75 bushels of coal at $.06 per 1.7.0 and 80 bushels coal 1.8.10. Total 15.12.3. August 1810 term, "We the jury find for the plaintiff $35.60 and damages."

159c - 1808, Monongalia County Court. Isaac COBURN summoned to answer an indictment against him for an assault upon Thomas PILES, 26 March 1808. Moses MANEAR and Daniel FORTNEY summoned to give evidence to the Grand Jury, 16 May, 24 October and 23 November 1808.

159c - 1809, Monongalia County Court. Elizabeth (x) SHOCKLEY, single woman, made oath that on 19 March 1809 at the house of Davis SHOCKLEY, she was delivered of a female bastard child and that Jacob MADERA, joiner, was the father of her child. Recognizance Bond signed by Jacob MADERA secured by Nicholas B. MADERA, 21 April 1809. August 1809 term of court, quashed (voided).

159c - 1809, Monongalia County Court. Nicholas CASEY summoned to answer William PRICE of a plea why he took and detained his property until 10 March 1809. PRICE complained that CASEY took 2 horses, 1 wagon, 1 set of blacksmith tools, 6 beds and foundations, 2 desks, 5 tables, 23 hogs, corn and household and kitchen furniture ($800). Order for CASEY to return to PRICE the property he unjustly detained, 9 March 1809. William PRICE obtained a judgement against Nicholas CASEY for costs. CASEY prayed for and obtained an appeal to the Superior Court. Appeal Bond signed by Nicholas CASEY secured by James CARROLL, 16 August 1809. Lease Agreement signed by CASEY and PRICE dated 25 February 1804, whereby CASEY leased to PRICE, of Allegheny County, Maryland, "that piece or parcel of arable land being part of the tract of land called the Dunkard Bottom lying as follows, to wit, from the mouth of the Mill Run as the fence now runs containing four lots or pieces of ground lying below ANDERSON's and between Cheat River and the mountain" with all appurtenances belonging from 15 March next for five years for the yearly rent of $200. Article of Agreement between CASEY and PRICE dated 25 February 1804 whereby CASEY agreed to build a porch on the front of the dwelling house that was on one of the tracts of leased property and to extend it 10 to 12 feet beyond the house and to build one house as an addition to the present one that will contain one or two rooms on the lower floor and to be two stories high with a passage 12 feet between the old house and new one. He also agreed to build a kitchen behind the passage large enough to be convenient and to have the garret floor in the old house built under the joists with plank as it is not floored at present and to have a good smoke house built in some convenient place and to have part of the barn and stables removed to a more convenient place than it is at present and to have the grain house that now adjoins the barn removed to enlarge the stables and to have the old kitchen converted to a granary. CASEY also agreed to find plank sufficient for all the above improvements and to do all the hauling, find nails, glass, locks and hinges. PRICE agreed to do all the joiner and carpenter work and hewing and all other necessary work at the common prices to be allowed out of the rent. CASEY agreed to have a well dug and walled convenient to the house and kitchen, the cellar walled and garden plowed at his own expense and to have a yard pailed in front of the house. For the true performance of this agreement, the parties bound themselves in the penal sum of $2000. Signed by both parties. Nicholas ASHLY summoned to testify in behalf of CASEY, 14 August 1809. Appeal Bond signed by PRICE secured by Michael BOYLES and John SNIDER Jr., __ March 1809.

159c - 1809, Monongalia County Court. Peace Bond for William GAMBLE, mason, to keep the peace toward all citizens and especially toward Elizabeth his wife, secured by Christian MADERA, mason, and Charles MURRY, yeoman, 15 July 1809. August 1809, dismissed and defendant discharged.

159c - 1808, Monongalia County Court. On 18 March 1808, George SNIDER recovered against Jesse PAYNE and Thomas FRET-

WELL the sum of $118 with interest at 6% on $58 from 1
February 1804 and 6% on $60 from 26 June 1804 plus costs, to
be credited with $30 paid on 24 March 1804. On 7 November
1805, John PAYNE secured Bail Bond for Jesse PAYNE and Thomas
FRETWELL. The debt remained unpaid and John PAYNE was summoned to appear and show cause, if any he can, why execution
should not be had against him, 14 October 1808. John PAYNE
answered and said that SNIDER ought not to have and maintain
his action against him because at the time the execution was
issued against him on 24 September 1808 at the request of
SNIDER, Thomas FRETWELL was dead.

159c - 1809, Monongalia County Court. William TINGLE summoned
to answer Robert HAWTHORN in a plea of debt for $39.93 and
$10 damage, 23 July 1806. Bail Bond for TINGLE secured by
Nimrod EVANS, 31 July 1806. Promissory Note signed by TINGLE
to HAWTHORN for $39.93 dated 3 July 1804, due "at Christmas"
and witnessed by Joseph ROBINETT. August 1809 term, dismissed
by order of the plaintiff and judgement confessed for costs.

159c - 1809, Monongalia County Court. William CHIPPS summoned
to answer Samuel PHILIPS in a plea of debt for $30 and $10
damage, 28 February and 24 April 1806. PHILIPS complained
that William CHIPPS owed him $30 due by note dated 22 January
1805, payable 1 April 1805. Assignment to Phillip COOMBS
dated 11 April 1809 and witnessed by Abraham COX and Zachariah GAPEN Jr. Appearance Bond signed by William CHIPPS
secured by Thos R. CHIPPS, 28 April 1806. James CAIN entered
himself security for costs on 24 December 1805. "Settled the
within CHIPPS, the defendant, for all costs," signed by
Philip COOMBS. August 1809 term, dismissed, agreed, defendant
confessing judgement for costs.

159c - 1809, Monongalia County Court. Notice to William
EVERLY and his security Samuel EVERLY from George SMITH, one
of the Overseers of the Poor, of intent to move the court for
judgement against them for $30, it being the amount of a
Recognizance Bond dated 12 September 1804 to indemnify Monongalia County against the charge of supporting a bastard child
begotten by William on the body of Elizabeth HUTSON, 15 July
1809. August 1809 term judgement.

159c - 1809, Monongalia County Court. Notice to Robert SCOTT
from Attorney William McCLEERY of intent to apply to the
court to enter up judgement against him for $10, it being the
third installment due by Robert, on 9 July 1809, to the Overseers of the Poor for the support of Elizabeth WHITE's
bastard child which the court in their session of January
1808 adjudged Robert to be the father, 22 July 1809.
Stephenson MARINOR summoned to testify in behalf of SCOTT, 15
August 1809. August 1809 term, "he proved by attendance."

159c - 1809, Monongalia County Court. William HOLIFIELD summoned to answer Zadock MORRIS, for the use of Jacob FOULK and Christian MADERA, in a plea of debt for $32 and $20 damage, 4 and 30 November 1808. Note signed by William (x) HOLIFIELD to MORRIS for $32 dated 11 March 1807, due 15 November next, payable in corn, salt or bar iron and witnessed by William DEAN and Sophia DEAN. Assignment to FOULK and MADERA dated 20 November 1807 and witnessed by Abraham WOODROW. August 1809 term, judgement confessed and entered up.

159c - 1809, Monongalia County Court. Valentine JOHNSTON, administrator of James JOHNSTON, deceased, at a court held 11 March 1806 recovered against Isaac SPENCER and William ORSON the sum of $31.79 with interest at 6% from 13 October 1798 until payment for a debt and $12.19 costs. On 9 August 1802, Hugh SIDWELL entered himself bail security for ORSON. On 3 September 1803, Joseph REED entered himself as bail security for SPENCER. The debt remained unpaid and JOHNSTON brought suit. "29 August 1809, Rec'd of H. SIDWELL $73.70 the debt, interest and costs on the judgement of Val JOHNSON, administrator of Jas JOHNSTON, deceased, against said SIDWELL and Joseph REED in the court of Monongalia County."

159c - 1809, Monongalia County Court. Jesse PAYNE summoned to answer Benjamin HARTLEY in a plea of debt due by purchase, 1 November, 9 December 1803 and 3 April 1804. HARTLEY complained that on 23 October 1802, Jesse PAYNE owed him $40, the balance of the price of one horse. "20 May 1809, Rec'd of William G. PAYNE $5 in part of a grey horse," signed by Benjamin HARTLEY and witnessed by Henry CAROTHERS. Thomas ROBINSON, William ROBINSON, William BUCKHANNAN, James STEEL and Isaac REED summoned to testify in behalf of HARTLEY, 9 July, 1 October 1807, 15 February 1808 and 4 August 1809. Abraham CRISS summoned to testify in behalf of PAYNE, 4 May 1807 and 10 November 1808. _____ 180_ term, "We the jury find for the plaintiff $51 in damages."

159c - 1809, Monongalia County Court. Thomas GRAHAM (not found) summoned to answer James STARLING in a plea of debt for $35.65 and $30 damage, 14 March 1808. June 1809 term, dismissed by plaintiff's attorney.

159c - 1809, Monongalia County Court. Samuel BALDWIN and John Anderson BALDWIN summoned to answer Samuel MINOR, assignee of George SNIDER, in a plea of debt for $72 and $60 damage, 14 March 1809. Appearance Bond signed by Samuel (x) BALDWIN and J. A. BALDWIN secured by Elias HOSKINSON and Andrew (x) PARK, 16 March 1809. June 1809 term, dismissed by order of the plaintiff's attorney.

159c - 1808, Monongalia County Court. Zackquill PIERPOINT summoned to answer a presentment against him for failing to keep the road in repair leading from Ices Ferry on Cheat River to Francis TIBBS' to Morgantown of which he is Overseer, 24 October and 22 November 1808. Isaac HAYS and William WALLER summoned to give evidence to the Grand Jury, 24 October and 23 November 1808.

159c - 1809, Monongalia County Court. William FRUM/PHRUM summoned to answer Amos CHIPPS in a plea of covenant damage $1000, 12 January 1808. Appearance Bond signed by William FRUM secured by John W. THOMPSON, 8 March 1809. July 1809 term, dismissed for want of security for costs and judgement for the defendant.

159c - 1809, Monongalia County Court. John JOLLIFFE summoned to answer Jacob FOULK in a plea of trespass damage $1000, 22 March 1806. Jacob FOULK complained that on __ January 1806, John JOLLIFFE assaulted and raped his wife, Gertrude FOULK. Bail Bond for JOLLIFFE secured by John DOWNER, 15 May 1806. Appearance Bond signed by JOLLIFFE secured by Elihu HORTON and James TIBBS, 2 March 1806. August 1809 term of court, agreed, each paying half of the costs.

159c - 1809, Monongalia County Court. On 19 March 1808, John ROBERTS recovered against Jesse PAYNE the sum of 17 pounds, 5 shillings and 4 pence with interest at 6% from 18 May 1804 until paid plus costs. On 7 November 1805, John PAYNE entered himself as bail security for Jesse. John PAYNE summoned to show cause, if any he can, why execution should not be had against him, 28 June 1808. August 1809 term, dismissed agreed.

159c - 1809, Monongalia County Court. In 1808, Ralph BARKSHIRE obtained an attachment on the property of Jacob FOULK, potter. Constable George B. HOSKINSON levied the attachment on a quantity of potter's ware and had the ware in his hands and "being about to remove the said ware in order to sell the same according to law to satisfy the amount of the execution" FOULK came up furiously to where the constable had "collected the ware and making great threats took up some part of the ware and swore he would have it back and that if the constable offered to prevent him from taking it away, he would mash his scull." FOULK "took up an earthen pot and stood in a position to strike the constable while FOULK's family carried off the ware out of the possession of the constable." William McCLEERY, Attorney for the Commonwealth, prayed for the advise of the court that due process of the law may be awarded against FOULK and that FOULK be summoned to answer to the charges against him, 13 August 1808. Benjamin REEDER, Zack MORGAN and Simeon WOODROW summoned to testify in behalf of FOULK, 14 March 1809. August 1809 term, discontinued.

159c - 1809, Monongalia County Court. John ROBERTS vs John
PAYNE. August 1809 term, dismissed agreed. (see page 53)

159c - 1809, Monongalia County Court. Arthur TRADER Jr. summoned to show cause, if any he can, why an information shall
not be filed against him for resisting Deputy John PAYNE and
for "offering and committing great violence and disturbance
of the peace," 25 July, 13 August and 22 November 1808. Ralph
BARKSHIRE obtained an attachment on the property of TRADER.
Deputy PAYNE levied the attachment on 4 horned cattle and
drove them a considerable distance in order to dispose of
them according to law. TRADER and others retook the cattle
out of the possession of the Deputy Sheriff and William
McCLEERY, Attorney for the Commonwealth, prayed the advise of
the court that due process of the law may be awarded against
TRADER and that TRADER be summoned to answer to the charges
against him, 9 August 1808. Ann BROWN, spinster, summoned to
show cause, if any she can, why an information shall not be
filed against her for resisting Deputy John PAYNE and for
"offering and committing great violence and disturbance of
the peace," 25 July, 13 August and 22 November 1808. Deputy
PAYNE swore that Arthur TRADER, Arthur TRADER Jr. and Ann
BROWN retook the cattle with force and arms. August 1809
term, discontinued.

159c - 1809, Monongalia County Court. Jacob NOOS summoned to
answer Anthony CARROLL/Anton CARL in a plea of debt for $100
due by note and $50 damage, 27 October 1804. Note signed by
NOOS to CARL dated 26 April 1803 for $100, due 1 May 1804 and
witnessed by Hannah (x) NUSS. Appearance Bond signed by NOOS
secured by John W. DEAN, 27 October 1804. August 1809 term,
dismissed, agreed.

160 - 1809, Monongalia County Court. Margaret (x) WOTRING,
widow of Abraham WOTRING, deceased, nominated Adam SHAFER to
be administrator of Abraham WOTRING's estate, 5 October 1809.

160 - 1809, Monongalia County Court. "At a court held for
Monongalia County, April 1809 term, Ordered that William
McCLEERY, Abraham WOODROW and Benjamin REEDER be appointed to
settle with Rebecca WILSON, administratrix of William WILSON,
deceased, and report to May Court." Receipts for monies paid
by Rebecca were signed by Robert ROBE for $.50 as one of the
appraisers of the estate on 4 November 1808; Michael KERNS;
Farquer McRA; Charles BYRN;   A. & S. WOODROW; John KERNS/
CARNES and Mary CARNES; E. DAUGHERTY; William GRAY for $.50
as one of the appraisers of the estate; 1805 taxes; and James
WILLIAMS.   County Clerk Nimrod EVANS sued Rebecca for the
amount of court fees for $5.91. He prayed the court to attach
so much of her property as to satisfy the debt. On the
reverse of the attachment order: "We the Grand Jury find
nothing nor have nothing to present," James TIBBS, foreman.

Accounts against the estate presented by James WILLIAMS for 1 horse, 1 pair oxen and salt, a bill from the county for taxes for 1807, 1 county levy, 1 poor levy, 1 horse and 50 acres of land and taxes for 1806.

160 - 1808, Monongalia County Court. 12 September 1808, Ordered that John DENT be allowed $55.50 for services as a commissioner for building the Courthouse and the same be paid out of the levy of 1807.

160 - 1808, Monongalia County Court. 12 September 1808, Ordered that Michael KERNS be allowed $59 for services as a commissioner for building the Courthouse and the same be paid out of the levy of 1807.

160 - 1805, Monongalia County Court. Ordered that Mary McNEELY be allowed $2 per day for four days for the use of her house at November 1804 term and the same be paid out of the levy of 1804, 12 February 1805.

160 - 1808, Monongalia County Court. 12 September 1808, Ordered that Thomas WILSON be allowed $157.25 for services as a commissioner for building the Courthouse, for an order on Russell POTTER, for stamped paper, for the top on the conductor and repairs to the conductor and the same be paid out of the levy of 1807. Credit this order $75.28 the amount drawn by WILSON for wolf scalps.

Also in this file - - - - June Court 1801, Ordered that James SCOTT, late Sheriff, pay the commissioners $15.69 out of the arrears of levies due for the years 1798 and 1799 and that Thomas WILSON, Michael KERNS and John DENT or either of them receive the above sum.

160 - 1817, Monongalia County Court. Correspondence from John B. WHEELER to Clerk Nimrod EVANS dated at New Madrid on 25 February 1810. WHEELER related to EVANS his desire to have a list of debts entered for suit. He said he was surprised that Michael KERNS never gave EVANS his notes, one for $130 and the other for $6. He said, "A. WILSON ought not to dispute ELIOT's account when he had agreed to take it towards the boat." He said, "COOPER has on his hands to collect a due bill on J. JONES for $2 and one on Conrad PIXLER for $2.25 and David SEAMAN is indebted to me 4 bushels rye and $2 for a table. I saw John OLIPHANT at Brownsville as I came and got a box of glass of him, he gave me his word he would pay you the money due me in a short time. I have no note but an account standing on their books at the forge." A list of debts due WHEELER left with EVANS for collection: Christopher STEALEY 2 bushels wheat 0.8.0; _____ SWINDLER 2 1/2 bushels wheat 0.10.0; John TAYLOR 2 bushels wheat 0.8.0; Nathan ASHBY $3.50 lent him 1.1.0; Thomas RUSSEL 2 bushels corn

0.6.0; Mr. MURPHY near GANDY's corn 0.13.6; _____ HARTLEY 1.19.0; _____ MADERA 3 bushels wheat 0.12.0; Mrs EVANS her account 0.12.0; Sigh HOSKINSON 0.8.8; Moses DOOLITTLE cash lent 0.6.0; Ben REEDER's account 2.4.6; David JOHN 1 bushel rye and 1 1/2 bushels wheat 0.9.0; Jno EVANS Jr. 3 bushels rye lent 0.9.9; George HOSKINSON to $1 on MORGAN and to note on WHITE for $5.50 1.19.0; Wm. CRISTY 1 bushel wheat 0.4.0; Charles BYRN's account 2.7.10; Sa'l KENDAY balance on account 0.10.6; Jno CLARK $2 lent 0.12.0; James COLLINS $10. He said he sent a letter by F. SWISHER in July and if any monies were collected and he could safely send it by boat, send it by Capt. John LAVALLE of Madrid.

Correspondence from WHEELER dated 29 January 1811 at Rossville, New Madrid, to EVANS. WHEELER said he and his family had just recovered from "a hard spell of sickness" but were well at the present. He urged EVANS to send what money he had collected and to continue to do his best to collect the debts as he was "very needy." He said he left several accounts with KERNS and named those he had not listed before. Jno DORTON $.50; Bartley CLARK, Joseph REED, Jno TAYLOR and David SEAMAN 1 teakettle. He said these were on his Mill Book with perhaps others. He said James COLLINS owed him 40 bushels of wheat. He received by Mr. OGDEN from Jno and Andrew OLEPHANT 77 1/2 pounds of 10d nails, 1 pair iron traces, 1 log chain, 2 axes, 1 set plow irons and 36 pounds and 225 pounds iron which was sent by Mr. NICHOLSON and Mr. JONES without a bill of prices. He asked Nimrod to send him iron, flour or whiskey or any kind of worked iron that he could turn into some that would be of service to him. "The earthquake which commenced here on 16 December 1811 still continues to shake us a little what is to be the conclusion of this awful scene, time must determine." WHEELER asked Nimrod to write to him soon and said, "Your brother James was in health a few days past."

Correspondence from R. BERKSHIRE dated 15 June 1817 at Philadelphia to EVANS. BERKSHIRE states that he plans to rent the plantation belonging to the heirs of _____ near Carlisle for four years beginning next April which will be about the time "your ward comes of age." He said he hopes to get about $400 per year and have the barn covered by allowing $100 out of the first year's rent in part of the expenses, it will cost about $200 - $250 with new doors. He asked EVANS, as the guardian of one of the heirs, for his agreement to rent the farm. He asked EVANS to direct his reply to Thomas CAROTHERS, Esqr. an Innkeeper at Carlisle. He comments that goods at Philadelphia are uncommonly low and very plenty, money scarce, flour fell to about $10 or $11. "Western chartered paper a little better than it was a short time ago. Western part of Maryland, the W. part of Pa. and Kentucky and Ohio about from 4 - 6 pr ctw dis..." The remaining part of this letter is dark and blurred.

Correspondence from Enoch EVANS dated 10 June 1809 at

Cape Girardean to Nimrod. He said he received the letter sent
by Nimrod with James RAVENSCROFT. He said everything came
safe but the breast chains to the wagon were missing. He
said there were two mistakes in the accounts he sent, the
charge in favor of McVICKER and I. H. WILLIAMS was more
that it ought to be and in the account of CHIPPS. He
complained that since the flour was not available, Nimrod
sent a boat too big for the purpose and he lost $45. Enoch
said if he could not get Billy, if any of Nimrod's would suit
he would take them or he would take Harry in place of Artty.
He said he understood Mrs. JENKINS denied signing a bond but
confessed to Capt. RAMSEY that she did sign it but did'nt
feel she could come down the river at that time. He said it
was her proposal to sign a bond rather than to make a deed as
she was afraid she could not move until next spring. He said
he had not heard from Natches and DAVIS told him he expected
to obtain judgement in May against DUNLOP. He said he wanted
the money by this fall as he planned to purchase "a very fine
place within three or four hundred yards of my house, it is
to be sold by the Sheriff in July next. We have every
prospect of becoming to have a flourishing country, the
Americans immigrate very fast to it. Every thing is dull at
present but appears as would change soon. We are all in good
health. Give my love to Eliza and accept my best wishes for
your welfare."

160 - 1809, Monongalia County Court. Sheriff's Bond for
Stephen MORGAN secured by Thomas McKINLEY, John PAYNE and
William G. PAYNE, 13 June 1809.

160 - 1809, Monongalia County Court. Bond for Adam SHAVER to
act as administrator for Abraham WOODRING, deceased, secured
by Alexander BINGAMAN, John WOODRING and Frederick HARSH, 9
October 1809.

160 - 1796, Monongalia County Court. "I William JARRETT do
swear that my removal to the State of Virginia was with no
intent of evading the laws for preventing the further
importation of slaves nor have brought with me any slaves
with an intention of selling them nor have any of the slaves
which I have brought with me been imported from Africa or any
of the West India Islands since the first day of November
1778. Sworn before me Enoch EVANS this 4th day of November
1796."

160 - 1809, Monongalia County Court. "We the subscribers,
inhabitants of the west side of the Monongahela River,
Monongalia County 118th Regiment are anxious to consolidate
ourselves unto a body of Calvary. Therefore we bind ourselves
by these presents as volunteers under the laws, rules and
regulations of the United States under Captain Rawley MARTIN,
hereafter to be commissioned; Adam PICKENPAUGH, First Lieut-

enant; _____ GEORGE, Second Lieutenant; Richard WELLS,
Cornet. (Signed by) Ezekiel HOSKINSON, James KELLY, John
BARNES, Michael SHIVELY, Curtis HAYES, Jacob SHIVELY, Philip
SHIVELY, Alexander WYATT, Enoch SCOTT, Caleb HURLEY, Joseph
MARTIN, William MARTIN, John W. EVANS, John BARRICKMAN,
George BEIL, Hynson COLE, John LIMING, Moses SNIDER, Samuel
BILLINGSLY, Richard MORRIS, Daniel WADE, George WADE, William
LITTLE, Nimrod DENT, Dudley DENT, James SCOTT, Dugal C. WIL-
FORD, James STONEKING, William WHITE, Samuel BORLLEE?, Thomas
WADE, Weightman FURBY, Enos WEST, Daniel? JACKSON, George
BAREMORE, Enoch EVANS, James MICHAEL, John A. STINESPRING,
Samuel BILLINGSLEY and John FURBEY."

160 - 1809, Monongalia County Court. Bond signed by Sarah
WATSON and Larkin PIERPOINT to act as administrators of John
WATSON, deceased, secured by Nicholas VANDERVORT and Joseph
WEAVER, 13 November 1809.

160 - 1809, Monongalia County Court. One horse, the property
of Jesse GASKINS, was attached at the suit of the executors
of Henry STEPHENS, deceased, for $16.11 with interest at 6%
from 21 January ____ until paid. In order to retain his
property until time for public sale or his debt was paid
Jesse (x) GASKINS signed this Delivery Bond secured by
William MORRIS, 21 January 1809.

160 - 1809, Monongalia County Court. "April 1809 term,
Ordered that elections be held for choosing Overseers of the
Poor of this county on Saturday the 29th instant as follows,
to wit, at Alexander CLEGG's, Richard HARRISON's, Asa HALL's,
Colder HAYMOND's, John PAYNE's, Nicholas VANDERVORT's, John
WILLETT's, Amos ROBERTS', Frederick HARSH's and these
Gentlemen above named be appointed to conduct said election."

160 - 1807, Monongalia County Court. "To Christian MADERA for
patrolling 6 nights in 1807 = $3." MADERA swore before
Justice Augustus WERNINGER that he patrolled 6 nights in 1807
at the summons of Ensign Joseph COLLINS.

160 - 1809, Monongalia County Court. "To Zackquill MORGAN for
patrolling 6 night = $3." MORGAN swore before Justice R.
BARKSHIRE that he patrolled 6 night in 1807 and was ordered
out a Captain by Justice Benjamin REEDER, 15 August 1809.

160 - 1809, Monongalia County Court. Arthur WILSON, William
EVERLY, John NEAL and Robert PATTAN owed Nimrod EVANS various
court fees for a deed of 562 acres of land from Benjamin
REEDER, John DAWSON, Jean SNIDER and Benjamin STEPHEN,
administrator of Adam SIMONSON, deceased.

160 - 1809, Monongalia County Court. "The Worshipful, the
County Court of Monongalia County will please take into con-

sideration the district in which Samuel KENNADY and Rawley MARTIN act as constables will please to add part of the Dunkard District to said KENNADY's and MARTIN's as the latter district is not in proportion with the Dunkard District, the low end of the latter district has about nine or ten miles to attend to justice to take off of that district running with Wade's Road to the Pennsylvania line thence with the said line to the mouth of Jake's Run and with said run to the dividing ridge of Dunkard and Indian Creeks." Signed by Samuel KENNADY. "In BRANDON's list that good: Andrew COCHRAN, Hiram COOPER, James HAMBLETON, Richard JONSTON, Peter MASON, Christin NINE, Marsham RIDGWAY, George RODABAUGH and John SNIDER." "In MARTIN's list: John COX, Jonathan DAVIS, Justine JARRETT, Daniel LEE, Stevenson MARNER, Nathaniel NEEDLES, Roger PARKES, Jacob RICE, Eliab SIMPSON, Jonathan STILES, James TUCKER, James THOMPSON, John TOUTHMAN, George TOUTHMAN, Thomas WILSON."

160 - 1809, Monongalia County Court. "This day came Matthew GEORGE before me and took the oath agreeable to law as Second Lieutenant in the Troop of Cavalry in the Third Regiment and Third Division," 24 June 1809. Signed by Boaz BURROWS.

160 - 1809, Monongalia County Court. Bond signed by John and Frederick SMITH to act as administrators for Jacob SMITH, deceased, secured by William WALLAS and Arthur CUNNINGHAM, 13 February 1809.

160 - 1809, Monongalia County Court. "The Court of Monongalia County will please recommend the following officers in a Rifle Company in the 76th Regiment: John WATSON Captain in the room of Thomas WILSON resigned. Samuel G. WILSON Lieutenant in the room of David BAYLES removed. Francis PIERPOINT Ensign in the room of John WATSON promoted. These are the choices of the company at their last muster but some of the company wish John WELLS to be the Ensign who is the First Sergeant in the company but was down the river at the time of the company's choice," 11 April 1809. Signed by Dudley EVANS, ACC 76th Regiment.

160 - 1809, Monongalia County Court. Bond signed by Alexander BRANDON to serve as constable for a term of two years secured by James WEBSTER and James MATHENY, 12 June 1809.

160 - 1809, Monongalia County Court. "Rawley MARTIN produced a Captain's Commission of Cavalry in the 118th Regiment and was sworn into office," 15 August 1809. Signed by Jas SCOTT.

160 - 1809, Monongalia County Court. "July 1809 term, On the petition of Jacob HOLLAND it is ordered that John NICKLIN, James G. WATSON and John STEVENS be appointed to view and lay out a road from Jacob HOLLAND's to the main road leading from

Clarksburg to Morgan Town Thomas GRIGG's and report to September Court." "Agreeable to the within order, we have laid out a road ____ the lands of Jacob HOLLAND, Widow TRICKETT and Thomas _____ and with the approbation of the aforesaid _____ _____." Signed by the three above named.

160 - 1809, Monongalia County Court. "To Jacob FOULK, 1807, 3 nights patrolling = $1.50." FOULK swore he patrolled 3 nights in 1807 and that he was summoned for that purpose by Captain Zack MORGAN, 15 August 1809.

160 - 1809, Monongalia County Court. Bond signed by Alexander HAWTHORN to act as guardian for ____ ____ secured by Mathew GAY, 13 June 1809.

160 - 1809, Monongalia County Court. Nicholas CHISLER presented a bill for repairing a door lock for the jail for $3 and repairing 2 door locks = $7, 14 August 1809.

160 - 1809, Monongalia County Court. Nicholas MADERA presented a bill for mending the jail and witnessing and to attending = $3, July 1809.

160 - 1809, Monongalia County Court. Nicholas and Jacob MADERA presented a bill for work on jail, shingles and nails and 27 feet of plank = $2.87, 29 July 1809.

160 - 1809, Monongalia County Court. Francis PIERPOINT appeared before Justice Wm. N. JARRETT and took "the oath proscribed by law to act as Ensign in a Company of Riflemen in the ____ Battalion of the 76th Regiment 10th Brigade and 3rd Division of the Militia of this Commonwealth. Also produced his commission from John TYLER, Governor of this State," 5 August 1809.

160 - 1809, Monongalia County Court. "Delinquents for the year 1807 in MARTIN's District. Abell AUGUSTINE, Anthoney ASHER, John ASHER, Henry BARKER, Jacob BASSNETT, Simeon BURGES, Henry BUTTON, Samuel BIRKLER, George BALL, Samuel BALDWIN, John A. BALDWIN, John BATTON, Jacob BIZARD, John BIZARD, Samuel BOYSE, William BOYSE, George BIRD, Adam BALES, Jonah BALDWIN, Ephraim BIGG, Paul BOGG?, Nathan CANFIELD, Benjamin CONNER, Michael CONNER, Bartholomew CLARK, John CAMPBELL, John CANEL, Thomas CANNDAY, William COUS, Jesse CAIN, John COX, John E. DENT, Thomas DENT, Jonathan DAVIS, George DIBLER, John DIGMAN, John DRAGOO, John DAUD 2 entries, Adam SAVER, Daniel FANCHER, Israel FERREE, Henry K. GODDARD, William HOLLIFIELD, Robert HOOD, John HASTINS, Benjamin HILL, John HAVIES, Justice JARRETT, Richard JACKSON, William JOLLIFF Sr., John JOLLIFF, James JOLLIFF, William JONES, James KNOX, Seth STRIGHT, James LINTCH, John LAMPHAR, Daniel LEE, Thomas LEMASTERS, Jacob MUSGRAVE, James MUSGRAVE,

James MILLER, John McGUIRE, John THOMAS, Stephen MENEAR, Michael MARTIN, John McREA, Nathaniel NEEDLES, Isaac PRICE, Roger PARKER, David PERKINS, Andrew ROCK, Jacob RICE, Eliab SIPSON, William SINCLAIR, Samuel SAMPLE, Robert MORRIS, Lowry SNIDER, John SNODGRASS, Henry SMITH, Jonathan STILES, James TUCKER, John THOMAS, Isaac PETRO, Jas. THOMSON, Aaron THOMAS, John TUTHMAN, John THOM, George TOOTHMAN, Alexander TENNANT, Samuel VARNER, Thomas WILSON, Levin WALLS, Mathew WALLS, Samuel WILSON Jr., Thomas WEST, Thomas WILSON, Joseph WISBY, William WATTON/WATSON and Jacob WELDMAN." "Delinquents for the year 1807 in BRANDON's District: Alexander ARTHURS, Richard ADKESON, Ignatius ANDERSON, John ADKESON, James BUCKLEW, Jonathan BUTLER, Amos BIRD, Rachel BERRY, Christopher CUP, Peter COAL/CORK, James COLLINS, John CROSS, Solomon CROSS, James CLARK 2 entries, John CRISTY, William CARR, McClain COOPER, Hiram COOPER, Robert CHOEN, Wm. CRAYCRAFT, Eli DEBERRY, Robert DINWIDDIE, William DAVIS of Wm., Edward DAVIS, Thomas DEMOSS, Charles DIGMAN, Daniel FORTNEY of Peter, Noah FORD, Elisha FORD, Jas. FERREL, Jas. FLYNN, Enoch GREATHOUSE, Elijah GAD, David GRAHAM, Jas. GRADY, Jno. GLENDENNAN, Jas. GRAHAM, Hugh HOSKINSON, Jeremiah HOSKINSON, Jno. HUNT, Reese HASTINGS, William HEBBS, Jno. HOURST, Sam'l HARRISS, Jas. HUNT, Phillip HILL, Sam'l HARRISS of Dan'l, Jas. HAMILTON, Norris W. JINKINS, William JONES, Jno. JOHNSTEIN, Reubin JACO, Joseph JENKINS of John, L___ark KIMMELL, Jno. KRYDER, Henry LEWIS Jr., Jno. LINKHAM/LINKHORN, Henry LAWER, Jno. LITCHFIELD, Fielding LAMPHER, Thos. GRAHAM, Tho. LETHAM, Elisha LEECH, Thos. LUZADDER, Thos. LESTER, Noah LESTER, Adam MORROW, Michael McCARTY, Dan'l MATHENY, Jas. MAYFIELD, William MOYRES 3 entries, Jno. MONTGOMERY, Jas. MONTGOMERY, William MORGAN, Hugh MONTGOMERY, Phillip MARTIN, Peter MASON, Eli MATHEWS, George MOORE, Charles McGEE, William McGEE, Alex. MACKENTOSH, Lawrence McHENRY, Jno. McCARTNEY, Henry MOORE, Jno. MARTIN, Hez'a MAXFIELD, Jas. MORGAN, Christian NINE, Jno ORR, Abr'm PIXLER, Michael PAUGH, Abraham PENROSE, Wm. POSTLE, Jno. PAUGH, Samuel PIERCE, William PATTON, Nathan RIGHT, Jno. RHODES, Daniel RECKMAN, Marsham RIDGWAY, Christian RIDENOVER, Simeon ROYSE, Joseph REED, Jno. RYAN, Lewis RUNNER, George RODEBAUGH, Henry RUMBLE, Jacob SMITH, Jno. SULLIVAN, Henry SMITH, Nicholas STURM, Jno. SNYDER, Coonrod SHEETS, George SHEHAN, Jno. STOCKWELL, William SMITH, Jas. SWOODOUGH, Vincent SANDERS, Andrew SCOTT, William SAYRE, Arthur TRADER Jr., Josiah TRIMBLY, Henry TEETS, Francis TIBBS Jr., Jas. TESEY, Sam'l TANEHILL, Thos. THORN, Asa VANDINE, Robert VANCE, Adam VICTOR, Solomon WALKER, Sam'l WOLFE, Anthony WOODS, Benj. WOODS, Jno. WILSON, Jno. WILSON 2 entries, Benj. WILSON, George WHITEHARE, Jno. WHEELER, Samuel WILLEY, Wm. WOODS, James WALLS of Temperance, Jas. WILSON, Hugh WISBY, Michael WILSON, Jno. YOUNG, William BAZZEL, Hugh HOWEL, Thos. LETHAM, Thomas LEWELLEN Jr., Zac. RHODES, Nimrod SNYDER, Samuel FICKLE, Benj. WILSON, John WOOLF, John McVICKER, Thomas

BRITTON, James WEAVER, Abraham WORKMAN, Benjamin PENROSE and
Robert FERREL Sr." This list of names is crossed out:
William YOUNG, Joshua JONES, Harry GRIFFITH, Jacob NOOSE,
William MILLER, John AUSTIN, William COURTNEY, Jeremiah
CASSAY, Jno. DAVIS, Jesse GASKINS, Jas. HILL, Benjamin JONES,
Benj. JACOBY, Richard LEMASTERS, Davis MUSGRAVE, J. McCARDY,
Jno. MILLER, Jno. STATLER, George WATSON, David WATSON, Jacob
NOOSE and Henery FLOYD. This is another list with the names
crossed out: Jno. EVANS Jr., Simeon EVERLY, Charles BYRN,
George PICKENPAUGH, James SCOTT, Michael CORE, Abraham
SHRIVER, Peter HINKINS, Adam BROWN, Henry TUCKER, Jno.
MILLER, Jno. BEVELIN, Caleb WISEMAN, Charles McGILL,
Zackquill PIERPOINT, Jno. GREEN, Jonathan BRANDON, Alexander
BRANDON, Frederick SMITH, Richard HARRISON, Samuel EVERLY and
George GREENWOOD.

160 - 1809, Monongalia County Court. Bond for Henry HAMILTON
to act as guardian of George MAY, son of George MAY,
deceased, secured by John STEALEY, 17 August 1809.

160 - 1809, Monongalia County Court. "Whereas Abram MUNSEY,
an orphan boy, was bound to me by the court sometime since
and being about to remove down into the State of Ohio and
cannot legally take him with me, therefore, as the boy
desires to be bound to James McVICKER, believing him to be a
_____ man that will treat the boy well, I request Your
Worships to bind the said boy to him during the residue of
his time, he being at this time about 11 years of age," 13
April 1809. Signed by James KNOX. "The boy is 11 years of
age the 20th of June ensuing this date."

160 - 1809, Monongalia County Court. Bond for Zackquill
MORGAN to keep an ordinary at the house of Jacob FOULK in
Morgantown secured by Nicholas MADERA, 10 May 1809.

160 - 1809, Monongalia County Court. "Agreeable to an order
of the court on Saturday 29 April 1809, I superintended the
election held at my house in Monongalia County for to elect
some discreet person for to be Overseer of the Poor in said
county. Benjamin TRIMBLEY nominated for Overseer of the
Poor. Certified by me Amos ROBBARTS." John KRIMMERER Sr.,
Henry LUES, Thomas GAD, Frederick SMITH, Isaac ERWIN, John
KRIMMERER Jr., Tobias REAMES and Dennis JEFFERS.
    Voters for William HAYS: Thos. FLOYD, William THORN,
Henry FOULK, John DARRAH, William KNIGHT, Matthew FLEMING,
and John WEST. Voters for James BARNES: William WOOD, William
BARNS, William HAYS Sr., Thomas FLEMING, Benjamin BROWN and
Israel FERREE. Voters for Asa HALL: James BARNES, Thomas
BARNES, William HAYS Jr., Gilbert GALLION, John STARRITT and
George DAWSON. "This is a true statement of the votes, 29
April 1809. John WEST, clerk, and Asa HALL, superintendent."
    "Agreeable to Squire MORGAN's order, I advertised for an

election to be held at my house to elect an Overseer of the Poor the 29th of April, but there was but one voter appeared, therefore there was none appointed. C. HAYMOND."

"Pursuant to an order of the Worshipful County Court of Monongalia County at the last April session, I have held an election at the said Courthouse for choosing a fit person to serve according to law as Overseer of the Poor for said county in the Middle District and William M. CLARA/McCLARA /McCLEERY was duly elected. Given under my hand and seal this 29th April 1809. John PAYNE."

160 - 1809, Monongalia County Court. Clerk Nimrod EVANS' account for 1809. General allowance = $25, called court on BECK, SHEPARD and McCALL = $3.80 each, examining and certifying commissioner's return = $20, copying, examining and advertising same = $10. Total $65.80. Received of David SCOTT for a fine as surveyor of the road up Scotts Run = $2.50.

160 - 1809, Monongalia County Court. "At a court held for Monongalia County April 1809 term, ordered that Charles BYRN, David MORGAN and James CARROLL be appointed commissioners to assign and lay off the dower of Mary TAYLOR, widow of Wildy TAILOR, deceased, and report to June term next."

160 - 1809, Monongalia County Court. "Commonwealth of Virginia to the Sheriff of Monongalia County, you are hereby commanded to summon the Justices of this county to attend at the Courthouse of said county at October Court next to make allowances and appropriate their levy (agreeable to order of August Court last), 1 September 1809." On reverse: Amos ROBARTS, Ralph BARKSHIRE, Wm. N. JARRETT, Stephen MORGAN, Augustus WERNINGER, Robert FERRELL, John FAIRFAX, Thomas MILLER, Dudley EVANS, James SCOTT, Simeon EVERLY, Benjamin REEDER, Boaz BURROWS, John STEALEY, Nicholas VANDEVORT, David MORGAN, Jacob POLSLEY, Morgan MORGAN, John NUZUM, Samuel MINOR, William BARNS, William WILLEY, William GEORGE and John W. DEAN.

160 - 1809, Monongalia County Court. May 1809 term, ordered that William N. JARRETT and Ralph BARKSHIRE be appointed to settle with John W. DEAN, guardian to William and Nancy BURROWS, heirs of Elijah BURROWS, deceased, and report to July Court next.

160 - 1809, Monongalia County Court. One horse, the property of Elihu HORTON, was attached at the suit of William BUCKHANNON for $4.93 debt plus costs. In order to retain possession of his property until time of public sale or his debt was paid, HORTON signed this Delivery Bond secured by Alexander BRANDON, 12 June 1809.

160 - 1809, Monongalia County Court. "John WATSON personally

appeared before me, Wm. N. JARRETT, one of the Justices of
the Peace and took the oath agreeable to law, to act as a
Captain of a Company of Riflemen in the Battalion of the 76th
Regiment, 10th Brigade and 3rd Division of Militia of this
Commonwealth. Also produced his commission from Jno TYLER,
Governor of the State of Virginia," 5 August 1809.

160 - 1809, Monongalia County Court. Bond signed by Stephen
MASTERS and Zack PIERPOINT to James TIBBS dated 18 March 1809
for $8 debt with interest.

160 - 1809, Monongalia County Court. Bower FURBY obtained a
judgement of $8.03 on a debt dated 12 November 1808 against
William BALDWIN. Appearance Bond signed by BALDWIN secured
by William DEAN dated 29 March 1809.

160 - 1809, Monongalia County Court. Escape Warrant for
Thomas LAIDLEY who was charged in execution in jail at the
suit of Isaac H. WILLIAMS for $280 plus costs. LAIDLEY
escaped on the night of 5 January 1809 and this warrant was
issued to all county official to re-take him and return him
to debtor's prison.

160 - 1809, Monongalia County Court. Samuel TRICKLE obtained
a judgement of $14.42 plus costs against Amos BYRD. Bond
signed by Amos (x) BYRD secured by Edward EVANS, 8 April
1809. Bond witnessed by Rawley MARTIN and Elizabeth MARTIN.

160 - 1809, Monongalia County Court. "The Court will please
to recommend the following persons as officers in the 76th
Regiment which is the choice of the different companies:
James HOARD, Lieut., in the room of Lemuel JOHN removed.
Samuel STEWART, Ensign, in the room of James HOARD promoted.
Jacob SMITH, Captain, in the room of James TIBBS resigned.
William STAFFORD, Lieut., in the room of John DOWNEY,
resigned. Seth STAFFORD, Ensign, in the room of Jacob SMITH
promoted. Archibald WILSON, Lieut., in the Grenadier Company
in the room of James GRAY resigned. James MILLER, Ensign, in
the Grenadier Company in the room of Joseph ALLEN resigned.
James HURRY, Captain, in the room of John COOPER resigned.
Isaac COOPER, Ensign, in the room of James HURRY promoted.
James STEEL, Captain, in the room of Anthony SMITH resigned.
John COROTHERS Jr., Lieut., in the room of James STEEL
promoted. Isaac RIGGS, Ensign, in the room of John COROTHERS
Jr. promoted. James COBURN, Lieut., in the room of Moses
MINEAR removed. David WATSON, Ensign, in the room of James
COBUN promoted. James CURRANT Jr., Lieut., in the room of
Joseph SMITH resigned. Edward KNOTTS, Ensign, in the room of
Jacob HULL resigned, 13 November 1809." Signed by Dudley
EVANS LCC, 76th Regiment.

160 - 1804, Monongalia County Court. Bond for George Robert TINGLE to serve as coroner secured by William TINGLE and Jno STEALEY, 11 June 1804.

160 - 1809, Monongalia County Court. "At a court held for Monongalia County at May 1809 term, it appearing to the court that no elections have been held on the east side of Cheat River for the purpose of choosing Overseers of the Poor, it is therefore ordered that William CONNER, John RODEHEFFER and Samuel POSTLEWAIT be appointed Overseers of the Poor on the east side of Cheat River."

160 - 1809, Monongalia County Court. "At a court held for Monongalia County 12 June 1809, a report of John FAIRFAX, David MORGAN and James E. BEALL, three of the Justices of the Peace for said county before whom a certain Benjamin LEADY was brought charged with being a person of an unsound mind and upon examination the said justices do say that in their said report that the said Benjamin is of an unsound mind and that it is expedient to send him forthwith to the public hospital and therefore they have returned a schedule of the property of the said Benjamin and it is ordered that Robert BEATY, Hugh MORGAN and John MILLER be appointed a committee to take care of the said Benjamin's property as mentioned in the said schedule according to law." In another document in almost the same words as the above it is written, "he should be removed to the public hospital for the maintenance and cure of persons of unsound mind in the City of Williamsburg and having accordingly directed him to be removed by our order bearing date 25 May 1809." Certificate of the estate of Benjamin LEADY which is as follows, to wit, one tract of land containing 162 acres suppose to rent for $40 per year, 1 chest of drawers supposed to be worth $8, 1 chest supposed to be worth $?, 1 cow $15, 1 small seat $?, 1 heifer $8, 1 cow and calf $12, 6 hogs and 11 pigs $15, 3 sheep $6, 1 bedstead and bedding $10, 2 chairs $.75, 1 spinning wheel and reel $2.50, 1 dutch oven and lid $1.50, 4 crocks $.33, 1 churn $.50, 1 iron pot and 1 small iron pot $1, 1 tub $.66, 1 big wheel $1.50, 1 earth disk $?, 1 crock and candlestick $.50, 1 cupboard $1, 2 tin buckets $.75, 1 shovel plow $?, 1 singletree $?, 1 meat ax $1.50, 2 cow chains $.75, 1 lock chain $?, 2 picks $1.50, 1 pitch fork $?, 1 dutch sythe $1, 6 flour barrels $?, 3 straw covers $?, 2 kegs $2.50, 8 straw baskets $2.25, 1 bushel buckwheat $.33, 2 bushels rye $3, 2 tight barrels and 1 keg $1, 2 half barrels $2, 1 loom $2, 1 crock and 1 barrel $.25, 2 augers and 1 taper bit $.37 1/2, 1 mouse trap and 3 candlemolds $.31, 2 pot hooks and 1 curry comb $.33, 1 pair large hinges $1.25, 1 iron wig and 1 dutch anvil $.75, 1 box with sundry old iron $.50, 1 cotter $.66, 1 set of windmill irons and 1 dutch Bible $2, 1 man's saddle and saddle bags and bridle $5, 1 _single and 1 hammer $.66, 1 copper kettle $15, 1 half bushel and 1 basket and 3 pecks

dried apples $.75, 1 skillet $.33, 2 male rings, 1 hoe and 1
ax $1, 1 pair horse gears $3, 11 harrow teeth $1, 1 coffee
mill $2, 2 basins $?, 2 dishes and 5 plates 12 weight $4, 4
knives and 4 forks $.75, 1 lantern, 1 callender and 1 spice
box $?, 1 strainer and 1 pint $?, 1 watering pot, 1 iron
ladle and 1 flesh fork $2, 1 looking glass $1, 1 small
looking glass $.12 1/2, 1 hone, 1 dutch scythe, anvil and 2
chisles $1, 1 pottramel $1.50, 1 pair stillards $1, some
bacon and beef $6, small jug and pitcher $.18, 1 horse $60,
the land supposed to be worth $4 per acre, 1 hammer and
drawing knife $6, 1 hand saw, 1 pair hinges, 1 spike gimlet,
1 scraper, 1 large gouge and 1 small hatchet $2, 1 bottle and
1 bag $.66, 8 lb. tallow $.66 1/2, 2 earthen pots and 1 ten
quart $.33, 1 conkshell $.50, 1 bag and hops $.75, 1 tea
table $4, 1 bedstead and bedding $13.50, 1 copper tea kettle
$1.50, 1 hook $.50, 1 mattock $1, cutting box $1, 1 gun and
shot pouch and powder horn $10.50. "Which is all that has
yet come to our knowledge." Signed by MORGAN, FAIRFAX and
BEALL on 25 May 1809. "Total amount of the property of
Benjamin LEADY except the land = $251.93."

160 - 1809, Monongalia County Court. Bond signed by George
HITE to serve as constable for the term of two years secured
by William TINGLE and Matthew GAY, 19 June 1809.

160 - 1809, Monongalia County Court. "Amount of drafts drawn
on the Sheriff of Monongalia County payable out the Militia
Fines of the 76th Regiment in the year 1808. One order in
favor of Capt. John WEST for furnishing his company with a
drum and fife $7. One order to Charles BYRN for $23 for his
services as clerk for the year 1806. One order to Moses
MINEAR for $5 for making a drum for Capt. John FAIRFAX. One
order to Charles BYRN for $32 for his services as clerk for
the year 1805, One order to Capt. John FAIRFAX for $7 for
furnishing his company with one stand of colors in the year
1805. One order to Charles BYRN for $35 for his services as
clerk in the year 1804. One order to John FAIRFAX for $2.25
for the repairing of a drum and purchase of a fife in the
year 1802. One order to John PAYNE for $2 for his services
as Provost Martial on 12 December 1807. One order to Capt.
John SCOTT for furnishing his company with one stand of
colors in the year 1805, $10. One order to GOOSEMAN for $12
for his services as Fife Major in the year 1807. One order
to Richard PRICE for $20 for his services as Adjutant for the
year 1807."

160 - 1809, Monongalia County Court. One feather bed with 3
quilts, sheets and bedding, 1 coffee mill, 1 coffee pot, 1
skillet, 1 oven, 4 chairs, 1 iron pot, 1 tea kettle, 1
spinning wheel, 1 reel, 1 flat iron, 1 cheese, 1 straw bed
and cover, 1 bedstead, 30 bushels of ears of Indian corn, 3
quilts, 1 meat _____, 2100 pounds of pork, the property of

William HOLLIFIELD, was attached at the suit of Zadock MORRIS for a debt of $32 with interest from 15 November 1807. In order to retain possession of his property until time of public sale or his debt was paid William (x) HOLEYFIELD signed this Delivery Bond secured by William DEAN, 27 December 1809.

160 - 1809, Monongalia County Court. To David SEAMAN for standing guard 2 nights at the jail over Andrew SHEPHARD and was summoned for that purpose by the Sheriff, 10 October 1809.

160 - 1809, Monongalia County Court. Bond signed by Eva (x) WILLHELM to act as administratrix for Peter WILLHELM, deceased, secured by John HAUTMAN, 13 November 1809.

160 - 1807, Monongalia County Court. Bond signed by David SCOTT, dated 4 March 1807, to secure the payment of $350 on a Deed of Trust executed by SCOTT to Enoch JONES secured by Felix SCOTT and witnessed by William WHITE.

160 - 1809, Monongalia County Court. Bond signed by Lemuel JOHN to serve as Sheriff secured by Daniel COX, John EVANS and John EVANS Jr., 11 September 1809.

160 - 1809, Monongalia County Court. "Ordered that John EVANS Jr., Joseph JENKINS and Alexander HAWTHORN be appointed to settle with Agnes FRETWELL, administratrix of Thomas FRETWELL, deceased," July 1809 term. A list of blacksmith work dated 13 June 1808 through 12 December 1808 for sharpening various farm implements, making plows and hoes, and shoeing horses. This account is not identified. George DORSEY signed a receipt whereby he received from Agnes FRETWELL an assignment or transfer on an award made in pursuance of an Arbitration Bond between John STEALEY and Thomas FRETWELL by John OLIPHANT, Jesse EVANS and Andrew OLIPHANT by which it is awarded that STEALEY is to pay FRETWELL $1200, 17 June 1809. A list of various court fees dated 1806 at Orange County and signed by Reynolds CHAPMAN, clerk. A list of various court fees dated January and April 1805 at Charlottesville District Court and signed by John CAN/CON, DC. "1808, Thomas FRETWELL, deceased, in account with John NICHLIN. May 15 to medicine and attendance $4. May 16 to medicine $4." Signed by John NICHLIN on 16 February 1808. There is a list of various court fees dated March through November 1803 at Orange County. Another list of court fees dated March through December 1805 and signed by CHAPMAN. Another list of court fees dated March through November 1804 and signed by CHAPMAN. A list of various court fees dated January through November 1806 at Albermarle County and signed by John NICHOLAS, CC. A list of various court fees dated January through November 1805 at Albermarle County

and signed by NICHOLAS. A list of various court fees dated April through December 1803 at Charlottesville District Court and signed by S. McWILLIAMS. A list of various court fees dated January through October 1804 at Charlottsville District Court and signed by John CARR. A list of various court fees dated January through November 1803 at Albermarle and signed by John NICHOLAS, CC. A list of various court fees dated January through December 1802 at Albermarle and signed by NICKOLAS.

160a - 1809, Monongalia County Court. Deed dated 22 August 1807 between Isaac PRICKET and Polly his wife, of the State of Ohio, to Joshua HICKMAN for 68 acres on Buffalow Lick Run joining John McGEE, William MILLER, John CARPENTER and James MORGAN, signed by Isaac (x) PRICKETT and Polly (x) PRICKETT and witnessed by Clermont County, Ohio, Justice Bernard THOMPSON and Ames THOMPSON. Roger W. WARING, Clerk of Common Pleas, Clermont County, Ohio, certified that THOMPSON was a Justice. Proved in Monongalia County at June 1809 term. Recorded in Deed Book D at page 420. Plat dated May 30, 1792, surveyed for John PRICKETT by virtue of an order of the Court of Monongalia County, 376 acres of land in the said county on the Monongahela River being a tract of land granted to the said PRICKETT as heir at law to Isaac PRICKETT by patent bearing date 25 October 1786 in right of settlement bounded as follows: Beginning at a dogwood on the Big Run, to a Sugar Maple on the Monongahela River, crossing the Big Run by lands of FRANCISCO and GRIMES to a stake on the point of a ridge and crossing the Big Run to the beginning. Signed by Samuel HANWAY, SMC.

160a - 1809, Monongalia County Court. 9 January 1809, William WILSON swore that he was being charged with and compelled to pay taxes on 333 acres of land which he did not own.

160a - 1809, Monongalia County Court. "The County of Monongalia will please to recommend the following persons as officers in a Company of Artillery in the 118th Regiment: Samuel KENADY Captain in the room of George PICKENPAUGH who has resigned. William COLE 1st Lieut in the room of Samuel KENADY promoted. Michael SHIVLEY 2nd Lieut in the room of Matthew GEORGE who refused to serve," 10 July 1809. Signed by James SCOTT. ("forgery by R. S.")

160a - 1809, Monongalia County Court. Isaac MORGAN, William (x) KINCADE and William BAINBRIDGE appraised a one year old stray bull taken up by James MORGAN at $3.03, no date.

160a - 1809, Monongalia County Court. William HAYS, Thomas PINDALL and James BARNES appraised a stray horse taken up by Efram DRAGOO at $25, 20 May 1809.

160a - 1809, Monongalia County Court. Matthew GAY, Marmaduke EVANS and James McVICKER appraised a stray mare taken up by Ezekiel CHENEY at $30, 23 October 1809.

160a - 1809, Monongalia County Court. Samuel POSTLEWAIT, Conrad SHEETS and Martin RIDENOUR appraised 5 stray steers taken up by Nathan ASHBY at $15, 20 December 1809.

160a - 1809, Monongalia County Court. "8 October 1809, To William N. JARRETT for repairing the jail with 1 pair large hinges and hooks $1.25, 6 rivets and 2 staples $.25, 1 cross bar $.58 1/3. Putting the above all on $.25."

160a - 1809, Monongalia County Court. By virtue of a Land Office Treasury Warrant No. 1035 dated 27 December 1794, Dudley EVANS was granted 296 acres, by survey dated 18 April 1807, on the waters of Pappaw Creek and Dunkard Mill Run joining Robert PLEASANTS' survey formerly called GRAY's Flats on the north end and west side and also joining Fleming JONES' survey, John WEBB's survey, Philip ROBERTS' survey and Asa DUDLEY's land, 1 September 1809. (Parchment Document)

160a - 1809, Monongalia County Court. Zackquill MORGAN, William LANHAM and Christian MADERA appraised a stray mare taken up by David SIMMONS/LEMMONS at $10, 16 January 1809.

160a - 1809, Monongalia County Court. William HAMOND, William MILLER and John MILLER appraised a stray steer taken up by Josha HICKMAN at $12, 23 November 1809.

160a - 1809, Monongalia County Court. James NEELY, Matthew GEORGE and James KELLY appraised a stray horse taken up by Joshua LOW at $40, 25 April 1809.

160a - 1809, Monongalia County Court. Charles STEWART, Jacob SMITH and James CAIN appraised a stray horse taken up by James CLELAND at $22, 30 December 1809.

160a - 1809, Monongalia County Court. Adam CAMP, Dannel KNOX and Jeremiah HOSKINSON appraised a stray heifer taken up by Josiah HOSKINSON at $6.50, 17 May 1809.

160a - 1809, Monongalia County Court. Noah RIDGEWAY, Joseph DUNLOP and Jno BOUSLOG appraised a stray cow taken up by Jacob BARRACK at $12 or $13, 4 February 1809.

160a - 1807, Monongalia County Court. December 1807 term, Ordered that John HENTHORN be appointed surveyor of the road in the room of Benjamin JARRETT. "The court will please to appoint either John JACKSON, James EPDEGRAFF or George BAKER in my place," signed by John HENTHORN.

160a - 1802, Monongalia County Court. June 1802 term, Ordered that William BICE be appointed surveyor of the road in the room of Jacob HAMPTON.

160a - 1809, Monongalia County Court. Robert STUART, John WELTNER and John CHIPPS appraised 2 stray white sheep taken up by William JOHN at $2.50, 6 June 1809.

160a - 1809, Monongalia County Court. Noah RIDGEWAY, Joseph DUNLOP and John BOUSLOG appraised a stray horse taken up by Daniel JACKSON at $20, 4 February 1809.

160a - 1805, Monongalia County Court. One black horse, the property of William STEVENSON, was attached at the suit of Fauquer McRAE and William LANHAM, executors of Barsheba FERGUSON, deceased, for $22 plus interest. In order to retain possession of his property until time for public sale or his debt was paid Wm. STEVENSON signed this Delivery Bond secured by William G. PAYNE, 13 March 1805.

160a - 1809, Monongalia County Court. Bond signed by William HILL to serve as constable for the term of two years secured by R. BARKSHIRE and Horatio MORGAN, 13 February 1809.

160a - 1809, Monongalia County Court. "Upon the first day of next January Court for Monongalia County, I shall move said court ____ ____ according to law to impanel a jury to inquire into the propriety of establishing a ferry from my land across the Tyger Valley River to my land in Harrison County near to HILL´s Ferry where I now live," Signed Richard HARRIS by his attorney on 11 December 1809.

160a - 1809, Monongalia County Court. John STATELAR, Abraham (x) SRIVER and Padey (x) CELLEY/CILLEY appraised a stray steer taken up by George SNIDER at $7, 1 February 1809.

160a - 1808, Monongalia County Court. "September 1808 term, Ordered that Dudley EVANS, Thomas BARNES and William WILLEY Jr. be appointed to lay off and assign to Margaret BALLAH, widow of Augustus BALLAH, deceased, her dower of the lands of which said Augustus died, seized and make report to December Court next." A plat showing the land assigned to Margaret taking into view 70 acres conveyed by Thomas PINDELL to Augustus BALLAH and 110 acres out of the old tract of 500 acres bounded as follows, to wit, beginning at a corner of the original survey, crossing Papaw Creek, near Fusby´s Road containing 180 acres assigned to the widow, deduct 6 acres which is to be conveyed to Charles BOYLES leaves the widow 176 acres including all the buildings except the barn which we think is one equal third part of the real estate. Signed by EVANS, BARNES and WILLEY on 17 January 1809. Surveying fee $2.10.

160a - 1809, Monongalia County Court. Bond signed by William BALDWIN to serve as guardian to William BURROWS, above the age of 14, son of Elijah BURROWS, deceased, secured by Levi MORGAN, 10 or 16 February 1809.

160a - 1809, Monongalia County Court. Sheriff Stephen MORGAN's account. June 1809, to sweeping, scouring, furnishing wood and candles for the Courthouse $25, to attending court $25, to attending jail $25, purchasing 2 locks $1.25. "Ordered that the sheriff be allowed $70 of the within account."

160a - 1809, Monongalia County Court. Bond signed by Thomas BALDWIN to serve as constable for the term of two years secured by William BALDWIN and Samuel MINOR, 12 June 1809.

160a - 1809, Monongalia County Court. Bond signed by Daniel COX to serve as constable for the term of two years secured by William TINGLE and Lemuel JOHN, 12 June 1809.

160a - 1809, Monongalia County Court. Delinquents due Nimrod EVANS: Benjamin HARTLEY, Jean FRY, Christian MADERA, Thomas LAIDLEY, Reuben JACO, Archabald ARMSTRONG, Wm. WEBSTER, Thos. MARTIN, David ELENZER & Robert GRAHAM, John LIGHT, Wm. PRICE, David GUNDY, John BRANNON, Arthur TRADER, Thos. MARTIN, Robert FERRELL, Wm. BUCHANAN, Wm. HOLEYFIELD, Thos. BURCHINAL, Thos. ADAMS, John GRIBBLE, John SUMMERS, Henry RUMBLE, John KING, William ROYSE, Jacob NOOSE, Samuel BICE, and E. JOHNSON.

160a - 1809, Monongalia County Court. Bond signed by John RAMSEY, Jr. to serve as constable for two years secured by William RAMSEY and John RAMSEY Sr., 12 June 1809.

160a - 1809, Monongalia County Court. Bond signed by John WEST to serve as constable for a term of two years secured by Lemuel JOHN and James WEST Sr., 12 June 1809.

160a - 1809, Monongalia County Court. Note signed by Thomas R. CHIPPS to Nimrod EVANS dated 22 March 1806 for $100 for rent of property, due 22 March 1807 and witnessed by Jacob FOULK.
    Three months note signed by Faquire (x) McRAE to Nimrod EVANS dated 26 April 1806 for $13 with interest and witnessed by James EVANS.
    Note signed by Matthew GEORGE to Henry BARRICKMAN for $11 dated 26 January 1809, due 1 July next and witnessed by Jehu DAVIS.
    "10 December 1802, Sir, pay Nimrod EVANS 25 shillings which you were in debt to me or sell him cwt," signed by Frederick GIBBLER and directed to Isaac H. WILLIAMS.
    Nine months note signed by Farquire (x) McRAE to EVANS

for $13 with interest from 10 March 1806, dated 20 April 1806 and witnessed by James EVANS.

Note signed by Russell (RO) OLIVER to Nimrod EVANS for $1.87, due 1 June next, payable in linen, dated 18 April 1801 and witnessed by John W. DEAN.

Note signed by James FARNEY to Nimrod EVANS dated 4 April 1809 for $1.75 for recording a deed.

Note signed by Joseph GRATE to Nimrod EVANS dated 1 April 1808 for $45 due in one year with interest and witnessed by Zackquill MORGAN.

Six months note signed by John BOUSLOG to Amelia TANSEY, administratrix of Caleb TANSEY, deceased, dated 1 January 1802 for $14.44. Assignment to EVANS dated 3 _____ 1803.

160a - 1809, Monongalia County Court. Settlement of the Overseers of the Poor 1807. To the amount of tythables for the said year at $.31 1/2 each = $638.75. Amounts following the names entered on this settlement are not identified, only the names are given here. William TANNIHILL, William McCLEERY, Doctor DOUGHERTY, Samuel EVERLY, Mathew FLEMING, Alexander CLAGG, Francis WARMAN, Nicholas VANDERVORT, Robert FORMAN, James WILSON, James DONALDSON, Daniel ANDERSON, Richard HARRISON, William SMITH, John VANDERVORT, and Simeon EVERLY. Disbursements = $594.32. Balance due the county $44.43. "In conformity to the order of the court of December term 1808, the undersigned have examined the accounts of the Overseers of the Poor and find a balance of $44.43 as stated above due to the County, 11 February 1809," signed by Wm. N. JARRETT and Augustus WERNINGER.

Order for William McCLEERY to be allowed $4 for a pair of shoes, 3 yards of linen for a shift and a winter handkerchief for Janey GRUB, one of the poor, and $.33 for paper for last year, 5 September 1808.

Order for Samuel EVERLY to be allowed $25 for keeping, boarding and clothing Elenor KOWAN, one of the poor, 7 September 1807.

Order for William SMITH to be allowed $62.62 for boarding, nourishing, and washing furnished Janey GRUB, one of the poor, 7 September 1807.

Order to pay E. DAUGHERTY for medicine and attendance on Mr. GRUB, 15 October 1808.

Order to pay William TANNYHILL $4 for his services on the board, 2 September 1806.

Order to pay Samuel EVERLY $33 for boarding and clothing Elenor COWEN, one of the poor, 5 September 1808.

Order to pay Samuel G. WILSON $3 for a linsey petticoat and short gown delivered to Janey GRUBB, one of the poor, no date.

Order to pay Robert FOREMAN $12 for maintaining and nursing Ann JONES, one of the poor, no date.

Order to pay William McCLEERY $5.50 for clothing Janney GRUB, one of the poor, no date.

Order to pay Nicholas VANDERVORT $4 for his services on the board, no date.

Order to pay Alexander CLAGG $32, being a part of an order heretofore drawn in favor of Simeon EVERLY for $54.50 for supporting old MURPHY and wife assigned to said CLAGG, the residue afterwards drawn for the use of said CLAGG, 5 September 1808.

Order to pay James DONALDSON $36.66 for keeping, clothing, boarding Thomas WARMAN, one of the poor, 7 September 1807.

Order to pay William SMITH $13.77, the balance due him for boarding, feeding, washing and wine for Janney GRUB, one of the poor, for 9 months at $8 per month ending 5 August 1808, 7 September 1807.

Order to pay Nicholas VANDERVORT $9 for his services settling with the collectors and the court and attending upon taking bond of the present collector, 5 September 1808.

Order to pay Alexander GLEGG, assignee of Simon EVERLY, $22.50, the balance of an order drawn in favor of EVERLY for $54.50 for supporting old MURPHY and wife, two of the poor, 5 September 1808.

Order to pay John VANDERVORT $35, part of $50 allowed by the board for boarding, clothing and nursing William FOREST, one of the poor, ending 27 October next, 5 September 1808.

Order to pay William McCLEERY $10 for his services as clerk to the board for the last year ending this date, 5 September 1808.

Order to pay John Wilson DEAN $30 for 3 years service as clerk to the board at $10 per year from September 1804 and ending September 1807, 6 September 1808.

Order to pay Boaz BURROWS $42 for supporting Mary LANE, one of the poor, for one year ending 9 October next, but as BURROWS never removed Mary to his house and Mathew FLEMING maintained her at his house, the $42 be allowed to FLEMING, 1 September 1806.

Order to pay Doctor Enos DAUGHERTY $15.75 for attendance and medicine for Janey GRUB and other poor, 7 September 1807.

Order to pay William SMITH for supporting Janey GRUB for 10 weeks ending 1 November 1807, no date.

Order to pay William McCLEERY $9 for his services settling with the collector of the poor tax for the years 1804, 1805 and 1806, 6 September 1808.

Order to pay Richard HARRISON $4 for his services as one of the Overseers of the Poor and $1.33 for 2 bushels of wheat furnished Richard JACKSON, one of the poor, 5 September 1808.

Order to pay Francis WARMAN $6.66 for keeping and boarding John CROSS, one of the poor, 7 September 1807.

160a - 1809, Monongalia County Court. "April 1809 term, Ordered that the Justices of the Peace be summoned to attend on the first day of June term next for the purpose of laying a levy, settling with the collector, making allowances and recommending magistrates," April 1809 term.

160a - 1807, Monongalia County Court. Order to pay Thomas MARTIN $7 for 14 days processing, 8 June 1807.

160a - 1809, Monongalia County Court. February 1809 term, Order to summons the Justices of the Peace to attend on first day of March Court next for the purpose of making allowances and settling with the collector. Justices: John FAIRFAX, David MORGAN, William N. JARRETT, Ralph BERKSHIRE, John STEALY, Benjamin REEDER, Samuel MINOR, William BARNES, William WILLEY, William JOHN, Augustus WERNINGER, Boaz BURROWS, Morgan MORGAN, Dudley EVANS and Robert FERREL.

160a - 1809, Monongalia County Court. Order to pay Rawley MARTIN, Commissioner of the Revenue for Equalizing the Lands and taking the list of taxable property and making out the books and examining them, 82 days = $82. 1808, to granting 4 Store License = $1. 1809, to granting 2 Store License = $.50.

160a - 1809, Monongalia County Court. Grand Jury list, March 1809: Rawley EVANS, foreman; Joseph MORGAN, John DRAGOO, John SNYDER Sr., Robert HILL, John BAKER, Christian MADERA, Godfrey GOOSEMAN, David TROWBRIDGE, John MILLER, Daniel KNOX, Philip SHIVELY, David SCOTT, Benjamin WILSON and Alexander WADE. These names are crossed off this list: William POSTLE, John CHISLER, Samuel POSTLE, James CAIN, Anthony KIRKHEART (Kirkheart) John SNYDER Jr., Michael BOYLES and John BRAND.

160a - 1809, Monongalia County Court. William McCLEERY's salary as Attorney for the Commonwealth from September 1808 - September 1809 = $90.

160a - 1809, Monongalia County Court. To Joseph ALLEN for patrolling by a warrant for 5 weeks, 24 hours each = $5, A. WOODROW = $5, Jacob FOULK = $5, and R. CHAFFANT 3 weeks = $3.

160a - 1809, Monongalia County Court. Josiah WILSON petition-ed the court for a re-survey of two tracts of land joining each other, where he then resided, for the purpose of making an inclusive survey of both tracts and taking in the surplus land within the bounds of the survey, 13 February 1809.

160a - 1809, Monongalia County Court. Order to pay George REECE $1 for standing guard at the jail over Andrew SHEPHERD for one night, 10 October 1809.

160a - 1809, Monongalia County Court. Bond signed by William POOR and John LINN to serve as executors of William LINN, deceased, secured by Henry (x) TUCKER, 13 February 1809.

160a - 1809, Monongalia County Court. Bond signed by James METHENEY to serve as constable for the term of two years secured by Alex. BRANDON and James WEBSTER, 12 June 1809.

160a - 1809, Monongalia County Court. Bond signed by John STEVENS to serve as constable for a term of two years secured by Thomas EWELL and Henry COROTHERS, 13 February 1809.

160a - 1809, Monongalia County Court. Bond signed by Rawley MARTIN to serve as constable for a term of two years secured by Rawley SCOTT and Joseph CAMPBELL, 12 June 1809.

160a - 1809, Monongalia County Court. Bond signed by James McVICKER to serve as constable for a term of two years secured by Robert HILL and Marmaduke EVANS, 12 June 1809.

160a - 1809, Monongalia County Court. Bond signed by John BROWN to serve as constable for a term of two years secured by James BROWN and Moses ROYCE, 12 June 1809.

160a - 1809, Monongalia County Court. Bond signed by George B. HOSKINSON to serve as constable for two years secured by Thomas (x) DOOLITTLE and R. BARKSHIRE, 12 June 1809.

160a - 1807, Monongalia County Court. Ralph BARKSHIRE´s Commission as Cornet of a Troop of Cavalry in the 3rd Regiment and 3rd Division of the Virginia Militia, signed by Wm. H. CABELL, Governor, on 3 October 1807. Registered by Sam COLEMAN. Qualified before B. REEDER on 31 October 1807.

160a - 1809, Monongalia County Court. Order to pay William MORRIS $3 for putting up finger boards, July 1807 term. On 2 August 1807, MORRIS assigned this order to John THOMPSON.
  Order to pay Samuel KENNEDY $11.03 for patrolling, June 1807 term.
  Order to pay Rawley SCOTT $.50 for patrolling 1 night, April 1808.
  Order to pay John FOWLER $3 for his service rendered on the public highway, 13 June 1808.
  Order to pay James MATHENEY $9.36 for services, May 1808 term.
  Order to pay William McCLEERY $90 for his services as Attorney for the Commonwealth, 12 September ____.
  Order to pay George HITE and Rebecca DERING, administrators of Henry DERING, deceased, $304.86 out of the 1807 County Levy, it being the balance of money due them for building the Courthouse, 12 September 1808.
  Order to pay Clerk Nimrod EVANS $158 for his services to be paid out of the County Levy of 1807, 12 September 1808.
  Order to pay John COOPER $3.36 for criminal charges, June 1808 term.
  Order to pay Sheriff Stephen MORGAN $72 for his public service, for acting as jailor, for taking care of the Courthouse, for furnishing wood, for putting a lock on the Courthouse door and for furnishing candles - to be paid out of the Levy of 1807, 12 September 1808.

Order to pay William POSTLE $6.67 for bringing the Courthouse bell from Winchester to Morgan Town - to be paid out of the Levy of 1807, 12 September 1808.

Order to pay John BAKER $1.50 for putting up three indexes to be paid out of the 1807 Levy, June 1807 term.

Order to pay George HITE $10 for hanging the Courthouse bell, 12 September 1808.

Order to pay Benjamin REEDER $6.63 for drayage, boxing and carriage of the Courthouse bell from Norfolk to Winchester - to be paid out of the 1807 Levy, 12 September 1808.

Order to pay Abraham and Simon WOODROW $7.37 for irons furnished the hanging of the Courthouse bell - to be paid out of the 1807 County Levy, 12 September 1808.

Order to pay Robert HILL as per amount produced, June 1807 term.

Order to pay John FAIRFAX $70.29 for his services as Sheriff for 1806 and 1807 and for a balance overpaid by him to the County Creditors for his collections of said years, to be paid out of the 1807 County Levy, April 1808 term.

Order to pay Joseph ALLEN $4.60 for patrolling 9 nights, April 1808 term.

Order to pay Samuel KENNEDY $7.58 for criminal charges, June 1807 term.

Wolf Scalps recorded since 7 July 1807 to 22 May 1808.
   4 September 1802, Peter JOHNSON, 1 old.
   11 September 1807, James WALKER, 1 old.
   3 September 1806, Israel COOK, 1 old, proved by William DRAGOO.
   30 December 1807, David PILES, 1 old.
   30 December 1807, Moses JUSTICE, 1 old.
   18 February 1808, Moses JUSTICE, 1 old.
   21 March 1808, Moses JUSTICE, 1 old.
   7 November 1807, Moses JUSTICE, 2 old.
   13 August 1807, Henry AMOS, 1 age unknown.
   3 November 1807, Joseph TENNANT, 1 age unknown.
   3 December 1807, James MARSHALL, 1 age unknown.

On 23 May 1808, Moses (x) JUSTICE signed a receipt that he received the full amount of the 5 scalps turned in by him.

Settlement of the County 1807 Levy. Collections: 2044 tythables at $.50 = $1,022.00. Disbursements: Orders filed herein = $116.20. Delinquents allowed, say 279 at $.50 = $139.50. Wolf scalps listed herein = $25. One order in favor of William WATSON which is said to be lost, but has been discharged by the Sheriff = $.50. Commission on $1,022.00 at 5% after deducting the commission on the amount of delinquents = $44.13. Error not included in above orders = $.70. Balance due the county = $32.97. Total $1,022.00.

160a - 1809, Monongalia County Court. Bond signed by John JONES to serve as constable for a term of two years secured by Dudley EVANS and William GEORGE, 12 June 1809.

160a - 1809, Monongalia County Court. To Alexander BRANDON for equalizing the lands and taking the list of taxable property and in making out the books and examining them = $82. To granting two store licenses in 1809 = $.50 and 2 store licenses in 1808 = $.50.

160a - 1809, Monongalia County Court. To John C. PAYNE, June 1809 term. To 350 feet of plank for repairing jail fence, hauling 25 __ nails and putting up plank = $5.08. $3.72 allowed by court.

160a - 1809, Monongalia County Court. "The petition of the subscribers pray that viewers may be appointed to lay out a road from the Widow WADE´s to Daniel THOMPSON´s on Robinsons Run," not dated. Signed by E. DOUGHERTY, G. GREENWOOD, _____ BUSSEY, Ashbel GUSTIN, Wm. STONE, J. TRIPPLETT, William PAINTER/POINTER, Thomas WADE, Jonth'n TIDROW, Daniel THOMPSON, John THOMPSON, Amos G. THOMPSON, James THOMPSON, Evans WEST, John RAMSEY Jr., Enoch EVANS, Wm. BOYLES, George _____ Sr., Thomas LAZZELL, John LAZZELL, Thomas LAZZELL Jr., Samuel LAZZELL, James LOUGH, Jno SANDERS, Francis BILLINGSLEY, J. SHACKLEFORD, Wm. BILLINGSLEY, Wm. WEBSTER.

160a - 1809, Monongalia County Court. "The petition of Walter KAIN, respectfully represents that he has been blind of one eye from his birth, that his other eye has been failing for several years and at many times he cannot see, scarcely to walk about and besides he is affected with the rheumatism in his knees. But he is usually warned to work on the road and although many of the hands working in the same company are willing to excuse him, some of the hands insist that he shall not be excused and to save any blame to the supervisor, he is induced to petition that an order of court be made that he shall be excused from working the road, Walter KAIN."

160a - 1809, Monongalia County Court. Advertisement, "To Whom It May Concern, Take notice that I do intend to petition the County Court at January term next for the privilege of establishing a ferry across the Monongahela River at the place where the public road now crosses leading through Morgan Town passing my house," 11 December 1809. Signed by Noah RIDGEWAY.

160a - 1808, Monongalia County Court. 5 November 1808, James COBUN Jr. swore into his commission as Ensign of the 76th Regiment of the Militia of Virginia.

160a - 1808, Monongalia County Court. "The court will please to recommend Richard DOWNS as an Ensign in the 76th Regiment in the room of Jacob KRATZER who has removed," 13 December 1808.

160a - 1809, Monongalia County Court. April term 1809, Wm. PRICE was appointed surveyor of the road on the east side of Cheat River at October term 1808. He moved from that district and prayed the court that Martin RIDENOUR, Benjamin THOMAS or Richard POSTLE be appointed in his place. Richard POSTLEWAIT appointed.

160a - 1809, Monongalia County Court. "Deposition of John EVANS for Richard STEPHENS, of Kentucky, for land in Monongalia County." EVANS swore he recalled two deeds whereby Robert CROW conveyed to Richard STEPHENS land in Monongalia County, which deeds were consumed by fire when the county records burned. EVANS recalled that one of the tracts was situated on Buffalow Creek, 12 June 1809.

160a - 1808, Monongalia County Court. Bond signed by John JONES to act as administrator for Robert JONES, deceased, secured by Thomas WILSON and Nimrod EVANS, 10 July 1808.

161 - 1810, Monongalia County Court. Order to pay Thomas WILSON $7.50 for prosecuting the pleas of the Overseers of the Poor against HORTON and others, 5 September 1808.
    Order to pay William SNODGRASS $7.50, the balance of the sum of $30 allowed him by the court for the support of his two sons, James and John, paupers, for a year ending 5 September 1809, 5 June 1810.
    Order to pay William McCLEERY $18 for his services as Clerk to the board for the year 1809, $7 for attending upon the taking of the bond of the Collector of Tax for 1809 and settling with the Collector and with the Commissioners of the Court and 1 day as Overseer attending upon the duties of the board, $2 for a pair of calfskin shoes for Janey/Jenny GRUB, one of the poor, $3 for boarding, washing and clothing William MARTIN, an orphan boy and one of the poor, $.33 for stationary making the whole $30.33, 4 June 1810. 3 October 1810, to 1 quart of wine, nutmeg and muslin = 18 shillings and 6 pence. "Rec'd 22 November 1810 of William McCLEERY $3 for a coffin for Janney/Jenny GRUB, one of the poor," signed by Nicholas B. MADERA.
    Order to pay William SMITH $32, part of $72 allowed him for boarding and nursing Janey GRUB, one of the poor, for 1 year ending this date, $23, a part of the residue assigned to George S. DERING, the remaining $17 assigned to Joseph LOWRY, 4 June 1810. Order to pay these assignments dated 4 June 1810.
    Order to pay William TINGLE $4.06 for clothing furnished Janey GRUB, 4 June 1810.
    Order to pay Jacob BARKER/BANKER $1 for digging a grave for Janey GRUB, 1810.
    Order to pay Doctor Enos DOUGHERTY $28.37 for medicine and attendance upon Janey GRUB, Hattie DODSON and Elizabeth JOHNSTON, three of the poor, 4 June 1810.

Order to pay Margaret STRAYER $3 for nursing an infant child, burying the child and finding a coffin, 5 June 1809.

161 - 1808, Monongalia County Court. Enoch EVANS appointed surveyor of the road in the room of William RAMSEY and that Robert COURTNEY, John COURTNEY, Thomas COURTNEY, Robert COURTNEY (two entries), Abraham COMEGES and hands work under EVANS, September 1808 term. On reverse: William RAMSEY, Abraham COMEGES and George C. SMITH.

161 - 1809, Monongalia County Court. "Thomas PRICHARD to be Overseer of the Road in the place of _____ WATSON, deceased," no date.

161 - 1807, Monongalia County Court. July 1807 Court, Stephen MORGAN appointed Surveyor of the Road in the room of James E. BEALL. On reverse: James E. BEALL to be Surveyor of the Road in the room of Stephen MORGAN.

161 - 1810, Monongalia County Court. Order to pay Henry WRIGHT $30 for the succeeding year for his support as one of the poor, $20 already issued and the remaining $10 to be paid out of the tax of 1809, 5 June 1809.
Order to pay Henry WRIGHT $25, to be put in the hands of Nicholas VANDERVORT, for the support of WRIGHT for the ensuing year, 5 June 1810.

161 - 1809, Monongalia County Court. Order to pay Jacob KAMMERER $2.33 for services on the public highway, October 1809 term.

161 - 1809, Monongalia County Court. April 1809 term, Ordered that Adam BROWN, Abraham SRIVER and John STRATLER be appointed to view and lay out a road from Samuel MINOR's Mill to intersect the County Road near Philip MOORE's on Jacobs Run, a branch of Dunkard Creek, and report to June Court. Ordered that Samuel MINOR, William LANCASTER, Lester DICKISON and Philip MOOR be summoned to attend July next court to show cause, if any they can, why the within road should not be opened.

161 - 1809, Monongalia County Court. The petitioners pray that you appoint viewers to view and lay out a road from David TROWBRIDGE's Mill to intersect the Clarksburg Road between Daniel FORTNEY and John FAIRFAX. If granted appoint Jacob ZINN, _____ _____ and John COZAD. Signed by Charles BYRN and David TROWBRIDGE.

161 - 1807, Monongalia County Court. December 1807 term, Jacob SMITH appointed to be Surveyor of the Road in the room of Reason FOWLER. On reverse: Henery BROCKMAN, Zachariah REED?, and Samuel WILSON.

161 - 1809, Monongalia County Court. William TANNEHILL, Surveyor of the Road leading from MORTON's Mill on Big Sandy Creek to the Sand Spring on the top of Laurel Hill showeth that he with only 11 hands has for several years past worked 8 miles of road over very rough ground and there are 12 hands to work about 2 miles of a road that starts from the Crab Orchard Road near Samuel TANNEHILL's Plantation and inter- sects the road at William TANNEHILL's house. Your petitioner wishes an order to be made dividing the district so that the hands living below him, now working under him, to keep the road in repair from Sandy Creek to his house and the hands belonging to the other district with the residue of the hands between him and the Sand Spring to keep the Cross Road and the Sand Spring Road from his house to the Sand Spring in repair and that William MORTON be appointed Surveyor of the Road from Sandy Creek unto William TANNEHILL's and Daniel BOYCE with his former hands and the hands living next to Laurel Hill to work the Cross Road and the Sand Spring Road. If the court refused TANNEHILL's request, he would not serve any longer by reason of inability of body and prayed MORTON be appointed in his place. Signed by William TANNEHILL, April 1809 term. "Ordered that MORTON be appointed Surveyor of the Road in the room of William TANNEHILL."

161 - 1809, Monongalia County Court. Abraham SHRIVER, Adam BROWN and John STATELER viewed and laid out a road beginning at Samuel MINOR's Mill, through the lands of MINOR a little piece below the mouth of Days Run, thence through the land of Lester DICKISON and Philip MOORE intersecting the County Road on Jakes Run, 17 May 1809.

161 - 1809, Monongalia County Court. A petition was presented to the court objecting to a petition presented by Simeon EVERLY at a former court. The petitioners complained that the road proposed by EVERLY was along the river and almost impassable because of high waters and drift wood that gathered there. They complained that EVERLY mis-represented his petition and prayed the court to void their order to build the road near the river because a better way could be had along the ridge. Signed by Michel HOUSMAN, Thomas (x) HALE, William HALE, Joseph WILLFORD, John GARLOW, Harry SMITH, John (x) SNYDER, Thomas PORTER, Harry STEVENS, John EVANS, Robert DAVIS, Edward PARISH, Andrew ROCK, Weightman DAVIS, Daniel THOMAS, Eleana BRIGHT, Jonathan BRYAN, Thomas MAPEL, Joseph HARRISON, William RUSSELL, George BAREMORE, John FORTNEY, William GRAHAM and James WILSON. These two names are written here, but not as signatures: James MANN and Wm. WILSON. Deposition of John GARLOW: Sometime in the spring of 1806, Simeon EVERLY presented a petition to him to abolish the old road by PARISH's land to lay it out down the river from COLLIN's Mill to Widow EVERLY's, from thence to the mouth of HARRISON's Lane. GARLOW objected to the petition and

observed a better road could be had along the ridge west of the old road. EVERLY said if the petition was granted, his object was to have both ways viewed and the best taken, 13 October 1806. Edward PARISH swore he did not sign the petition for the review of the road from HARRISON's Lane to COLLIN's Mill in consequence of which a road is marked through his lands, 1 July 1809. "Persons named to review the road: John SNIDER, Adam SRIVER, John GARLOW, Joseph HARRISON, Presley MARTIN and Joseph WILLFORD and if the court would give their indulgence there is Harry STEVENS and William GRAHAM of Pennsylvania." Deposition of Richard HARRISON: He saw the order directed to EVERLY, SNIDER and himself to view and mark the said road. He said the order was completed, but SNIDER did not attend, 10 October 1806. James SCOTT, Presley MARTIN, Robert SCOTT, William POSTLE, Jesse BUSSEY (crossed out), John GARLOW, Andrew GARLOW, Adam SHRIVER, John SNYDER, Richard HARRISON, William BOYLES, Waitman DAVIS and Joseph HARRISON were summoned to view the lands of Edward PARISH laid out for a road by James McVICKER, John BAKER, William JOSEPH, John W. DEAN and Hugh SIDWELL and to determine what damage, if any, will be to PARISH by such road. The jurymen ascertained that PARISH would sustain no damage. All the above signed the document.

161 - 1809, Monongalia County Court. 11 August 1809, Hugh MURPHY, Surveyor of the Road from Smallwood WILSON's to Michael KERN's Mill, petitioned the court for the assistance of wheel carriages to improve the road. James Smallwood WILSON and James WEAVER were appointed to value the work and hire of the wheel carriages, 11 August 1809. WILSON and WEAVER valued a wagon and team with the driver belonging to William REED at $2.50 the first day and $2 the second day, They valued a cart, two oxen and driver belonging to George TROUT at $1.25 the first day and $1 the second day, 1809.

161 - 1809, Monongalia County Court. James BUSSEY, Thomas LAZZELL and James BOWLBY were appointed to view and mark a road beginning at Widow WADE's through the lands of Cyrus BILLINGSLEY where Samuel BILLINGSLEY had his corn, nearly a straight course to the fence of Cyrus BILLINGSLEY Jr. to a bridge, still the same course continued to the top of the ridge between Cyrus BILLINGSLEY and Cristopher RAVEN, thence with the ridge to RAVEN's field to the right of the grave-yard, through the lands of RAVEN by a small walnut marked in the fence, nearly the same course to RAVEN's old home, thence a little to the west through RAVEN's improvement to the head of a river, thence with the river down to the lands of James BOLSLEY to Robinsons Run, then through the lands of Thomas LAZZELL to the old road, then with the same to Daniel THOMPSON's, 11 September 1809. Cyrus (x) BILLINGSLEY, Thos. (x) LAZZELL and James BOWLBY signed the return and RAVEN agreed to constructing the road through his lands.

161 - 1809, Monongalia County Court. "The subscribers humbly showeth that they are very much inconvenienced for the want of a road to Morgantown and in a special and particular degree Joseph SHACKLEFORD who is so hemmed in by other lands that he has no public road in any direction to nor from his tanyard or farm." The subscribing petitioners humbly pray that Your Worships will grant them a road leading from the Forge Road at the upper end of George GREENWOOD's land so that it may pass near to SHACKLEFORD's tanyard and to inter- sect the State Road somewhere between Michael KERN's and George DORSEY's field on the north side of said road and to appoint viewers to view and report to the next court, January 1809. Signers: Alexander HAWTHORN, Joseph A. SHACKLEFORD, George GREENWOOD, Robert HAWTHORN, James RANDALL, Godfrey GILMORE, Samuel UPTON, William HALL, Anthoney CARROL, Thomas ROBINSON, John ROBINSON, Jacob NUCE, Lewis WOLF, David SWINDLER, Clayton SWINDLER, Lindsey BOGGESS, George GRISMAN?, Jacob HOLLAND, Neimah POWERS, Peter SWISHER, Samuel ROLSTON and Philip SMELL.

161 - 1809, Monongalia County Court. June 1802 term, order to pay Bartholomew WICKERT $2 for himself and team for road work. 14 August 1805, order to pay WICKERT $1 for use of his team for road work. Presented to court June 1809.

161 - 1806, Monongalia County Court. David PYLES appointed Overseer of the Road in the room of Levi MORRIS, no date. Other men considered: Christopher CORE and John MIARS. June 1806 term, ordered that Levi MORRIS be appointed Surveyor of the Road in the room of Henry BARRACKMAN.

161 - 1809, Monongalia County Court. Ordered that Robert SHAVER be appointed Overseer of the Road from the forks of Indian Creek to Papaw Creek, the same way the road now goes, October 1809. Others considered: Noah RIDGEWAY, John BOUSLOG and Joseph DUNLAP.

161 - 1807, Monongalia County Court. December 1807 term, Ordered that Benjamin THORN be appointed Surveyor of the Road in the room of Forbes BRITTON.

161 - 1809, Monongalia County Court. Ordered that George BARNS be appointed Surveyor of the Road in the room of Benjamin BARNS, no date.

161 - 1809, Monongalia County Court. John COX, Stephen STILES, Andrew CORBLY and Reubin BROWN appointed to view and lay out a road beginning at the State Road near LANE's mill up Dunkard Creek by KELLEY's old improvement and to continue up the right hand fork of the creek to the upper settlement on the creek and report to December Court, no date. "We the subscribers and owners of the land through which the above

mentioned road is laid, we are willing a road should be opened and continued," 2 October 1809. Signed by John RIGHT, Stephen STILES, Peter MYERS, Martin VERNON, Andrew CORBLY and William STILES. The viewers laid out a road through the lands of LANTZ, CORBLY, KNIGHT, STILES, MYERS, COTTON, BROWN, and LONG, 9 December 1808.

161 - 1808, Monongalia County Court. Ordered that Daniel BARRETT be appointed Surveyor of the Road in the room of John BOUSLOG, September 1808 term. Ordered that Noah RIDGWAY be appointed Surveyor of the Road in the room of Daniel BARRETT, no date.

161 - 1808, Monongalia County Court. John BOUSLOG, Surveyor of the road from the west side of the river opposite Morgantown to the mouth of Mill Run, petitioned the court for assistance of wheel carriages to repair the road. Joseph DUNLAP and John SULIVAN valued a wagon, team and driver belonging to Jacob BARRICK at $3.40 per day, 23 September 1808.

161 - 1808, Monongalia County Court. Ordered that David SCOTT III be appointed Surveyor of the Road from the mouth of Scotts Mill Run running up the Willow Lick in the room of George PICKENPAUGH and George HUFFMAN Sr., George HUFFMAN Jr., Philip HUFFMAN, Ezekiel HOSKINSON, John BAXTER, George TUCKER, Enoch JONES and slave, John BALDWIN, Ben CONELL, and John MYERS work under him, September 1808 term. Others considered: John SHIVELY, Enoch JONES and John MIRES.

161 - 1807, Monongalia County Court. July 1807 term, Ordered that Michael MOORE Jr. be appointed Surveyor of the Road in the room of Peter TENNANT. "Appoint Richard TENNANT in the room of Michael MOORE." There is a writing signed by MOORE mentioning the names of Alexander EDY and Geor EDY. This writing is faded and stained, it may suggest that MOORE was already the surveyor of another road.

161 - 1809, Monongalia County Court. Nehemiah POWERS served as Surveyor of the State Road and the Forge Road for more than a year. He returned the names of Godfrey GOOSEMAN, William HALL or Robert HAWTHORN to take his place, no date. GOOSEMAN appointed, October 1809.

161 - 1809, Monongalia County Court. William LANCASTER, Lester DICKINSON and Philip MOORE summoned to show cause, if any they can, why the road as laid out from MINOR's Mill to Jakes Run through their land shall not be established, 27 June 1809.

161 - 1809, Monongalia County Court. 17 June 1809, Jacob KIMMERER's wagon, 2 horses and driver were valued at $1.33,

John RODEHAFFER's wagon, team and driver at $1.33 and Amos
ROBBARTS' wagon, team and driver at $1.33 for work on the
Crab Orchard Road.

161 - 1807, Monongalia County Court. John WAGNER, Surveyor
of the Streets of Morgantown and a road leading to KERN's
Mill petitioned the court for the aid of wheel carriages to
repair a "causey" in the streets and roads. He was given
permission to impress what he needed from persons or their
slaves who were appointed to work on these streets or roads.
John CHISLER and James HURRY were appointed to make valuation
and give the owner a certificate to present to the court for
payment, 29 April 180(4). A team, the property of John
DIGMAN, was value at $3.33 per day, 30 April 1807.

161 - 1809, Monongalia County Court. We Your petitioners
would inform Your Worships that we labor under many difficul-
ities for the want of a road beginning at FURBY's Road on the
ridge leading to PRICE's Mill on Pappaw Creek. Signed by
Thomas KNIGHT Sr., Benjamin BROWN, John PARKER, John CUNNING-
HAM, John PRICE, William GODDARD, Isaac PRICE, Elijah FREE-
LAND, Peter DRAGOO, Peter STRAIGHT, William STRAIGHT, Adam
ICE, William WOOD, Jacob STRAIT, Samuel CONAWAY, John DRAGOO,
John PRICKETT, Andrew DOHEHORTHY, Thomas MARTIN, William
KENNEDY, Dennis BROWN, Henry NEPTUNE, Elisha CLAYTON and
Henry FLOYD, no date.

161 - 1809, Monongalia County Court. Your petitioners labor
under the greatest inconvenience for the want of an outlet or
road to mill, market or _____. We request You will grant them
a gangway or road from Jacob HOLLAND's to the main road leading from Clarksburg to Morgantown near Thomas GRIGGS'.
Signed by Jacob HOLLAND, Benjamin SAYRE, Francis SETH, John
HUFFMAN, Michael TRICKETT, Thomas EWELL, John NICHLIN, James
G. WATSON and John STEVENS, no date.

161 - 1809, Monongalia County Court. Ordered that David
MUSGRAVE, John DICKEY, Fleming JONES and Stephen MORGAN be
appointed to view the ground on oath and make return to the
next December Court, October 1809.

161 - 1809, Monongalia County Court. We Your petitioners
residing on the southwest bank of Cheat River are much
difficulted to get to mill on account of the river hill being
so bad. We have found a much nearer way and much better
ground. Therefore, we pray Your Honors to pass an order for
a review of a road from Jonathan COBURN's to Thomas BUTLER's
Mill and to make a return of the nearest and best way to the
next monthly court. Signed by Thomas BUTLER, Robert BEATY,
Thomas BURCHINAL, Peter DEWIT, Stephen BEATY, Peter MEREDITH,
James COBURN Jr., Jonathan COBURN and James COBURN. James
COBURN, Robert BEATY, Peter MEREDITH and Hugh MORGAN appointed to lay out this road.

161 - 1809, Monongalia County Court. William LANCASTER was
summoned to show cause why a road should not pass through his
land. He answered and said the reviewers did not know the
lay of the land and they did not take the nearest nor the
best way from Samuel MINOR's Mill to Philip MOAR's. He
requested another order to have the road viewed. John
STADLER, Abraham SHRIVER and Adam CORWIN were appointed as
viewers, 10 July 1809.

161 - 1808, Monongalia County Court. George DICKINSON prayed
the court to allow him to alter the road on the opposite side
of the run where his sawmill dam crossed which road would run
through his own land, 13 February 1809.

161 - 1809, Monongalia County Court. Joseph MORGAN build a
mill on Buffalow Creek and the dam overflowed the narrows
where the County Road passed and he prayed the court to allow
him to turn the road a little on the hill and to alter the
road that crosses below the mill and to appoint viewers to
view that part of the road proposed to be altered and report
to September next court, 10 July 1809.

161 - 1809, Monongalia County Court. William BALDWIN served
as Surveyor of the Highway for one year. He returned to the
court the names of John EVANS Jr., John DAVIS or John BAKER
as fit persons to take his place, no date. EVANS appointed.

161 - 1808, Monongalia County Court. September 1808 term,
A report of a road made by Jacob LYMAN and others beginning
at the old road leading to HILL's Ferry near an old high
bridge and from thence to the Tiger Valley River which is
ordered to be established and it is ordered that William BILL
or HILL with the hands under him open and keep in repair the
said road. Ordered that John SPRINGER be appointed Surveyor
of the Road in the room of William BILL/HILL. Others
considered: Henry BARNES.

161 - 1809, Monongalia County Court. Twelve good and lawful
freeholders summoned to attend on the land of John DENT on
Scotts Meadow Run to determine what damage, if any, will
accrue to the public or any private person from the water
grist mill built by DENT on his own land on said run, 25
February 1809. Philip SHIVELY, Benjamin WILSON, John BARKER,
John BRAND, Robert MESSER, Thomas HAMILTON, James ARNETT,
John A. BARKSHIRE, Boaz BURROWS, Mathew GEORGE, David SCOTT
and James BRAND viewed the land and were of the opinion that
no damage would accrue to any person, public or private, 8
March 1809.

161 - 1809, Monongalia County Court. Jacob POLSBY, Joshua
HICKMAN and William HAYMOND were appointed to view a section
of road from Robert RAVEN's to intersect the old road at the

County Line and the report being mislaid, they prayed the court to commission an overseer to open the road for the convenience of the settlement and public in general and the hands belonging to the district from Buffalow Creek to the County Line, under the present overseer, be ordered to cut out the road. Ordered that Peter MILLER be appointed overseer of the said road, no date.

161 - 1808, Monongalia County Court. September 1808 term, Ordered that Joseph ONEAL be appointed Surveyor of the Road from the Little Falls to the road leading to Papaw near James BARNES and that the signers of the petition work under him. ONEAL petition the court for the hands to be allowed to keep the road in repair as the road was already opened. List of hands: John BRAND, James ROBERTSON, George ROBERTSON, Moses TICHENOR, Jonathan TICHENOR, Edwards EVANS Jr., Edward EVANS Sr. and Labin PERDUE.

161 - 1809, Monongalia County Court. "The petition of the people belonging to Philip LYNCH's District beginning at HEWART's Bridge and extending along the State Road as far as the top of the hill beyond Simmeon HURLEY's, also from Henry AMOS's bars down Indian Creek with Dunkard Creek Road till it intersects the State Road and a road leading out of the State Road near the Twelve Mile Tree to the top of the hill beyond William KENNEDY's toward Chunks Run." Signed by John KING, John AMOS, Henry AMOS, Stephen AMOS, Joshua CUNNINGHAM, Simeon HURLY and James WALKER. Overseers considered: William KENNEDY and James ROBERTS. KENNEDY appointed, June 1809.

161 - 1809, Monongalia County Court. "Ordered that James F. WILSON be appointed Surveyor of the Road from James S. WILSON's house to Rock Forge and that Thomas WELLS, Samuel G. WILSON, Thomas HOSKINSON, George HOSKINSON Jr., Joseph JEANS, William BOSLEY, John REED Jr., Peter YEALICK, John HOSKINSON, Augustus WELLS Jr., Thomas PAYNE and John GEANS be hands to work under him," June 1809 term.

161 - 1809, Monongalia County Court. "Ordered that Arthur WILSON be appointed Surveyor of the Road from Deckers Creek to Thomas GRIGGS' in the room of Philip SHUTLEWORTH," June 1809. Others considered: Moses DOOLITTLE and William WILSON.

161 - 1809, Monongalia County Court. Overseers by district:
     John BROWN, Thomas MONTGOMERY, David TROWBRIDGE.
     Thomas BARTLETT, Dunker Bottom District.
     Alexander BRANDON & James MATHENY, Sandy Creek District.
     John WEST & Jasper WATTS, Buffalow District.
     John RAMSEY, Robinsons Run District.
     Horatio MORGAN & John STEVENS, Pricket & White Day Dist.
On bottom of this document: George B. HOSKINSON, John COOPER, Benj. EVANS, Daniel COX, George HITE and James McVICKER.

161 - 1809, Monongalia County Court. Ordered that Richard WELLS be appointed Road Surveyor in the room of Daniel KNOX, no date.

161 - 1809, Monongalia County Court. Ordered that Christian MADERA, Rawley MARTIN and Joseph DUNLAP be appointed to view and lay out a road from the Monongalia (sic) River opposite to KERNS' and DERING's Mill to intersect the County Road leading from Morgantown to Col. James SCOTT's, 13 June 1809.

161 - 1809, Monongalia County Court. 10 June 1809, "I request of you to appoint an Overseer of the Road in my place which was from the mouth of Davis Run to G(e)orge MARTIN/MORTON's house as my order is lost or misplaced so that I cannot find it. I do recommend William WILLEY Esqr., David MORGAN or Samuel BASSNETT. This from Thomas PINDELL (Long)."

161 - 1808, Monongalia County Court. June 1808 term, Ordered that Daniel KNOX be appointed Surveyor of the Road in the room of James BRAND.

161 - 1809, Monongalia County Court. Joseph DUNLAP, R. MARTIN and C. MADERA viewed and laid out a road leading from Morgantown to begin at where a road intersects the river from the house where William SMITH lives and nearly opposite the road from town to the river, then with the meanders of the river and immediately on the bank to a corner tree between William TINGLE and James SCOTT at the mouth of a large gully, then crossing said gully at the mouth to the line between SCOTT and TINGLE and with that line until it intersects said gully or a line tree standing on the bank of the gully, then diverging from the gully and said line to the right hand by marked trees winding from said gully and line again and with said line to the County Road. "We suppose the following companies ought to assist in opening the above road, viz, BARRETS, THOMAS, David SCOTT III, Richard WELLS and the Town Company."

161 - 1808, Monongalia County Court. Andrew ICE and Jean GEORS and driver worked on the road from BARNES' Mill to the mouth of Finch Creek as the request of Thomas BARNES, Overseer. Job HAYHURST & George UNDERWOOD, two honest housekeepers, were appointed to value the work, 15 September 1808.

161 - 1808, Monongalia County Court. April 1808 term, Ordered that James HURRY be appointed Surveyor of the Streets of Morgantown and the road down the river below KERNS' Mill and other roads worked by John WAGGONER in the room of said WAGGONER. John STEALEY to be Surveyor of the Road in the room of James HURRY.

161 - 1809, Monongalia County Court. I recommend Jacob LYMAN

and Andrew BOYD as Overseers of the Road from Samuel SWEARINGEN's to Joseph KINCAID's where Joseph WISBY Sr. formerly lived, signed by John CARPENTER, 14 August 1809.

161 - 1808, Monongalia County Court. June 1808 term, Ordered that Isaac ERVIN be appointed Surveyor of the Road in the room of Leonard CUP. Frederick SMITH, Jacob FEATHERS and Frederick WILHELLEM returned by me, signed Isaac ERVIN.

161 - 1809, Monongalia County Court. Two carts, four horses and their driver, belonging to Andrew ICE, were valued at $7 for 3 days work by Job HAYHURST and George UNDERWOOD. October 1809.

161 - 1809, Monongalia County Court. To James WEVER, William REED and Mereen DUVAL, you are required to appraise the value of such teams per day as may be impressed by James Smallwood WILSON for the purpose of repairing the road, also the value of any timber used in said repairs, 25 October 1808. A wagon and two horses, belonging to Josiah ROBE, were valued at $2 per day for two days hauling stone by the above appraisers. 10 February 1809.

161 - 1807, Monongalia County Court. April 1807 term, Ordered that Mathias FURBEE be appointed Surveyor of the Road from the low gap to Augustus BALLAH's. The hands to work under him are Andrew DAUGHERTY, George FURBEE, John SIMPKINS and Thomas FIDDY. I do return George NELSON and George FURBEE, signed M. FURBEE.

161 - 1808, Monongalia County Court. September 1808 term, Ordered that Joseph ONEEL be appointed Surveyor of the Road from the Little Falls to the road leading to Papaw near James BRANN's and that the signers of the petition work under him. On reverse: Labern PARDU, John EVANS and Edward EVANS Jr.

161 - 1809, Monongalia County Court. Francis BILLINGSLEY and James BOWLBY oversee the road from Widow WADE's to Daniel THOMPSON's, BILLINGSLEY from WADE's to RAVEN's farm and BOWLBY from there to THOMPSON's, October 1809.

161 - 1809, Monongalia County Court. 11 April 1809, We the petitioners and others living on Jacobs Run adjacent laboring under many inconveniences on account of a Mill Road unto Samuel MINOR's Mill. We do pray the court will grant us a road from the aforesaid mill of Samuel MINOR's to intersect the County Road near Philip MOAR's on the aforesaid Jacobs Run. Signed by Alexander CLEGG, Ely MARSHALL, Richard TENNANT, Michael MORE, Goeri EADY, Michael CORE, Joseph TENNANT, Peter TENANT, Peter HAUGHT, Joseph WEAVER, John TENANT, Alexander EDY, Geor EDY, William EDY, Samuel MINOR, Elial LEONG and Elias HOSKINSON.

ENVELOPE 162 contains executions of some of the cases abstracted before. An EXECUTION is a judicial writ by which an officer is empowered to carry a judgement into effect. (Webster's Collegiate Dictionary). The document names the plaintiff and the defendant, the amount of judgement and to whom awarded, the amount of penalty, court costs and the date of the order. See Volume I, pages 34 and 35 for an example.

ENVELOPE 162a contains executions of some of the cases abstracted before. An EXECUTION is a judicial writ by which an officer is empowered to carry a judgement into effect. (Webster's Collegiate Dictionary). The document names the plaintiff and the defendant, the amount of judgement and to whom awarded, the amount of penalty, court costs and the date of the order. See Volume I, pages 34 and 35 for an example.

163 - 1810, Monongalia County Court. September 1803, Jacob PINDALL, son of Edward PINDALL, deceased, vs James, Jemima, Elizabeth and Rachel PINDALL, heirs of Thomas PINDALL, deceased, all summoned on 25 July, 9 and 21 November 1803. Jacob PINDALL complained that on 8 October 1789, he purchased a tract of land containing 136 acres from Thomas PINDALL. Thomas agreed to make a clear title to him by 1 January 1792 or when the last payment was made which he made agreeable to his contract. He complained that neither Thomas, in his lifetime, nor his heirs, James, Elizabeth, Jamima and Rachel PINDALL "yet or either or any of all of them yet have made" him a title. He prayed the court to summons James for himself and as guardian (especially appointed by the court for this purpose) of Jemima, Elizabeth and Rachel to appear and be questioned in the matter, signed William G. PAYNE, attorney for Jacob PINDALL. James answered and said it appeared to be the option of Thomas whether he made title to Jacob on 1 January 1792 or when the last payment was made. He said he did not know of any payments made to Thomas before he died and there were none made to the estate after Thomas died. He said he was ready and willing to convey the property provided Jacob could prove payment had been made as stipulated in the bond. The defendants denied all manner of fraud or unlawful combination and prayed the complaint be dismissed, James EVANS, attorney for the defendants. Jacob PINDALL proved that all payments had been made as of September last. Elizabeth and Rachel PINDALL were not inhabitants of the Commonwealth in November 1803. Conveyance Bond signed by Thos. PINDALL dated 8 October 1789 to Jacob PINDALL for 136 acres joining Phillip PINDALL and witnessed by John DOWNER, John (x) DAWSON and Robert MINNIS. September 1810 term of court, decreed that the heirs of Thomas convey the land to Jacob and pay all cost.

163 - 1810, Monongalia County Court. Stephen FLEAHARTY and Mary FLEAHARTY summoned to answer a Bill in Chancery exhibit-

ed against them by Jacob FULKESON and Catharine FULKESON and Isaac BATTON, 21 July 1810.

163 - 1810, Monongalia County Court. Jeptha MASON summoned to answer Thomas WILSON in a plea of covenant damage $25, 21 March 1810. MASON not an inhabitant.

163 - 1810, Monongalia County Court. Jacob PINDALL, administrator of Thomas PINDALL, deceased, summoned to answer a Bill in Chancery exhibited against him by Joseph LOWRY, 8 November 1810.

163 - 1809, Monongalia County Court. One sorrel horse, the property of Robert GREEN, was attached at the suit of Isaac Hite WILLIAMS for $44.98 debt plus costs. In order to retain possession of his property until time for public sale or his debt was paid GREEN signed this Delivery Bond secured by John C. PAYNE, 3 October 1809.

163 - 1810, Monongalia County Court. Gosham HULL summoned to answer Jonathan HARTLEY, assignee of Francis COLLINS, in a plea of debt for $34 and $10 damage, 29 January 1807. Note signed by HULL to COLLINS dated 28 May 1806, for $34 payable in an assortment of castings at $5 per hundred, due 1 September 1806 and witnessed by Wm GREGG. May 1810 term of court, verdict for the plaintiff.

163 - 1810, Monongalia County Court. Thomas LAIDLEY contracted with Benjamin HIXSON to build a saw mill. HIXSON brought suit for non-payment and obtained a judgement at last May court. LAIDLEY set off from his house at White Day on a raft of boards and expected to arrive at court and hoped to prove he paid HIXSON all that was due per the contract, but was detained on the river and did not arrive until after the suit was determined. He said HIXSON "never did build the mill as engaged in the Article of Agreement" and prayed the court to grant an injunction to stay execution of the judgement until the matter could be heard in a Court of Equity, 18 July 1797. June 1810 term, dissolved as to part and perpetuated as to balance and judgement for the defendant for costs.

163 - 1810, Monongalia County Court. James McCANNON summoned to answer John HEWIT, assignee of John TOLBERT, assignee of James CAIN, assignee of John HOOVER for the use of Francis COLLINS, in a plea of debt for $15 due by note with interest from 15 August 1801. COLLINS obtained a judgement against McKENNON for $34, interest and costs. McKENNON prayed for and obtained an injunction to stay execution of the judgement. Injunction Bond signed by James McKENNON secured by Daniel ANDERSON, __ __ 1805. In 1801, McKENNON agreed to purchase a tract of 100 acres from John HOOVER in Monongalia County adjoining Russell POTTER and others. He took a Conveyance

Bond from HOOVER, paid $118 of the $200 purchase price and gave his bonds for the balance. Each bond was for less than $20 each for the purpose of evading the necessity of paying and procuring stamped paper according to law. McKENNON said HOOVER never had a right to the land, "but that the same is the right and property of Samuel CLARK and his wife, of New Geneva, Pennsylvania." He said before he was informed of the fraud and deception intended by HOOVER, he paid one note of $15 and another of $18. There is a long narrative in which McKENNON accuses HOOVER and the other plaintiffs of fraud, and deception. HIXON said a contract was made 10 June 1788 in which he agreed to build LAIDLEY a sawmill at the mouth of White Day Creek and he completed "the mill in a workman like manner with good and sufficient supporters under that part of the upper frame that extends below the forebay. Also a forebay 4 feet wide and 30 feet long, the floor of which at the end next the wheel to be 4 feet above the floor under the wheel and the end of the said forebay further from the wheel to be sunk 2 feet ____ with wingers at both ends, the sawmill frame to be 45 feet long and 14 wide." LAIDLEY agreed to pay HIXON 31 pounds and 10 shillings, one half cash on the mill being completely finished and the other half in produce at the then market price in the fall following, and 1000 pounds of pork, being a part thereof, delivered at the mouth of Gorges/Georges Creek. He said they bound themselves to each other in the penal sum of 60 pounds for the true performance of the contract. Injunction Bond signed by LAIDLEY to ensure all costs and awards would be paid in case the injunction should be dissolved secured by Robert FERRELL, 16 August 1797. Answer by HIXON to the injunction: The mill was completed and LAIDLEY took possession and rented it out for two years for half the profits which amounted to upwards of 100 pounds. LAIDLEY was obliged to furnish all the material for building, but failed to furnish the materials when needed and he suffered a great loss by being detained in the employment of LAIDLEY nearly 18 months when in fact if he had been supplied with the necessary materials he could have finished in 3 or 4 months. LAIDLEY agreed to pay him for his extra trouble and expense which amounted to much more than the contract stated. HIXON swore the account presented in this case was a true and accurate account of his work and services and prayed the court to deny LAIDLEY's request for an injunction, 11 May 1799. June 1810 term, perpetuated and judgement. "We the jury do find for the plaintiff in damages $45.11," Christopher STEALEY, foreman.

163 - 1810, Monongalia County Court. William N. JARRETT swore that Robert SMITH owed him $33.48 with interest and SMITH had removed himself from the county. JARRETT prayed for and obtained an attachment on SMITH's property. Zaquil MORGAN and Christian MADERA summoned as garnishees, 5 June 1810. Attachment Bond signed by JARRETT to ensure all costs and awards

would be paid in case he was cast in the suit secured by Marmaduke EVANS, 5 June 1810. Attachment levied on 1 saddle, bridle, 1 pair spurs and blanket, 1 pair saddle bags and salt in them, 1 pair hames, 1 back band and 1 horse collar, 7 June 1810. "Summon Mary BENNETT as garnishee and attach 1 umbrella and ____ brown cloth." Demand Note signed by SMITH to JARRETT dated 21 May 1810 for $40.48 with interest.

163 - 1810, Monongalia County Court. Thomas LAIDLEY's complaint: Many years ago he gave his obligation to David BRADFORD for 20 pounds and suit was brought by BRADFORD and a judgement rendered at the last May Court for the full sum plus costs and interest at 5% from 14 March 1787 until paid subject to a credit which was endorsed on the note. The obligation was given by him to BRADFORD as a retaining fee in suits for him against Charles MARTIN and others. LAIDLEY said BRADFORD never managed the suits for him as a lawyer, but received fees from the opposite side. LAIDLEY charged BRADFORD with fraud and confederacy and prayed the court for an injunction to stay execution of the judgement until the matter could be heard in a Court of Equity, 12 June 1810. June 1810 term, judgement for the defendant.

163 - 1810, Monongalia County Court. Article of Agreement signed by John ENGLAND and James (x) THOMAS dated 25 December 1801 in which ENGLAND agreed to leave his property in THOMAS' hands until "18th of this instance" and then ENGLAND agreed to discharge his debt and ____ to THOMAS out of the property that is in THOMAS' hands or other property that shall suit both parties, the property to be at the valuation of two men if the parties could not agree themselves. Also two cows that ____ ENGLAND had at home. Also THOMAS agreed with ENGLAND, by giving a proven security, to take corn at a reasonable cash price, the corn to be paid 25 December 1801. This agreement witnessed by Robert WILSON and John JONES. Received on the within article 6 pounds, 9 shillings and 6 pence on the balance of a mare, signed by John THOMAS. Deposition of Absalom KNOTTS: He was in Morgantown at a September County Court in 1801 where he heard James THOMAS and John ENGLAND enter into an Article of Agreement to the effect that THOMAS was to keep the property that he had in his hands belonging to ENGLAND until ENGLAND should give him good security for payment of the same deducting therefrom the surplus money of the sale of a mare that Constable John JONES sold belonging to ENGLAND at the suit of THOMAS, which money ENGLAND agreed should go toward the debt he owed THOMAS. He understood there was a credit entered on the article. Attorney William N. JARRETT swore he notified ENGLAND of the intent to hear the depositions of sundry witnesses at the home of Henry DERING on 14 April 1806. William THOMAS' deposition: At his father's in April 1802, ENGLAND and THOMAS made a settlement and ENGLAND took up his bond and said he was fully paid and he

was satisfied with the transaction, 14 April 1806. John
ENGLAND obtained a judgement against John JONES for $22.92
and costs. JONES prayed for and obtained an injunction to
stay execution of the judgement until the matter could be
heard in a Court of Equity. Injunction Bond signed by John
JONES to ensure all costs and awards would be paid in case
the injunction should be dissolved secured by Benjamin JONES,
16 August 1804. June 1810 term, judgement.

163 - 1810, Monongalia County Court. James ROBINSON summoned
to answer a Bill of Injunction exhibited against him by
Thomas EVANS to stay proceedings on a judgement at law
obtained by ROBINSON against EVANS, 16 November 1807. EVANS
complained that some time in 17__, he was in partnership with
William BOWNESS and Hedgeman TRIPLETT in surveying of certain
lands of this country. They employed James ROBISON to do the
surveys and they jointly became debtor to him in the sum of
_____ and BOWNESS was to pay the same. ROBISON bought suit
against him (EVANS) for 6 pounds, 14 shillings and 7 1/2
pence. He said an order was drawn on BOWNESS for the amount
and paid to TRIPLETT for ROBINSON, but TRIPLETT did not pay
ROBINSON. Sometime before this action, ROBISON was confined
in jail at the suit of _____ _____ and propositioned EVANS
to release him or assist and contribute in a certain way
towards his enlargement and he (ROBISON) would acquit,
exonerate and discharge him from his responsibility on
account of the judgement aforesaid. EVANS said he consented
to the proposition and considered himself entirely clear of
any further claim and considered the case dead. ROBINSON
renewed the judgement and obtained an attachment on his
property. EVANS prayed the court to summons ROBINSON to be
questioned in a Court of Equity, 12 October 1807. Catherine
EVANS, wife of Thomas, swore she believed the substance of
the facts stated in the bill were true, 12 October 1807.
Injunction BOND signed by Thomas (x) EVANS to ensure all
costs and awards would be paid in case the injunction should
be dissolved secured by Thomas LAIDLEY, 7 November 1807.
ROBINSON's answer to the Bill of Injunction: He never
received anything in payment on the judgement and never drew
any order for the same nor did he draw an order on William
BOWNUSS or any other person either for the judgement or for
the debt or any part of it. If TRIPLETT received any part of
it from BOWNUSS, it was without his knowledge. He said he
was never in jail except one night and the next morning a
certain B. CLARK paid his bail and jail fees and he was
released and the records of the court would prove it. May
1810 term, dismissed, the defendant paying costs at law and
equity except attorney fees.

163 - 1810, Monongalia County Court. Abraham WEAVER was
granted a judgement against William FRUM in the amount of
$16. FRUM complained that the note he gave WEAVER for a side

saddle was valued at $12 and not for $16 and prayed the court for an injunction to stay execution of the judgement until the matter could be heard in a Court of Equity. Injunction Bond signed by William FRUM to ensure all costs and awards would be paid in case the injunction should be dissolved secured by Waitman (x) FURBEE, 18 December 1806. WEAVER's answer to the injunction: He said the saddle was described in the note signed by FRUM and no matter the cost, the saddle as described was the only kind he would accept. James WEAVER's deposition: He wrote the note given by FRUM to WEAVER for a side saddle under the direction of the parties. He read the note to FRUM and he said he understood the contents and signed the note. It was for two steers and the fall before the sale, WEAVER valued them at $14. At the time the note was written there was no price mentioned, but only the saddle as described. After the note was due for sometime, WEAVER called for the saddle and FRUM promised to deliver it and a bridle into the bargain for the trouble WEAVER had been put to, 14 March 1807. William LANHAM's deposition: FRUM told him he had purchased a cow from WEAVER and was to pay WEAVER's sister, Sally, a side saddle with a plush seat for the cow for $12. LANHAM informed FRUM he could furnish such a saddle but not for less than $16. FRUM said he must have the saddle at any note and as WEAVER had been very indulgent to him, he would take the saddle at $16 and if WEAVER would allow him anything it was well, otherwise he should have the saddle and he would leave the pads to WEAVER whether he would allow it or not, but he expected WEAVER would do what was right. He agreed to make the saddle and FRUM agreed to pay the $16, one third in cash, one third in pork or corn and one third in hauling. He made the saddle but could not get his pay from FRUM and he would not let him have the saddle. WEAVER applied to him to get the saddle on FRUM's credit and agreed to pay for it if FRUM did not. He consider it better to stay out of the dispute and would not let WEAVER have the saddle. Since that time WEAVER purchased a quality saddle from him at $16 which was the price of such saddles in this country, 16 March 1807 at the house of W. N. JARRETT in Morgantown. Joseph ALLEN's deposition: About 1803, he went with FRUM to WEAVER to buy a cow, they agreed for a sum at $10 to be paid for in a woman's saddle and WEAVER was to give FRUM $2 besides the cow for the saddle. He understood the saddle was to be worth $12. He and FRUM went to John REED's and when they returned to WEAVER's, FRUM and WEAVER agreed for two steers at $6 each. FRUM then gave WEAVER a man's saddle valued at $10 for the cow and gave his note to WEAVER for a woman's saddle for the two steers and again he understood the saddle was to be worth $12, 8 August 1807 at the house of Henry DERING. June 1810 term, dismissed and judgement.

163 - 1810, Monongalia County Court. James THOMAS summoned to answer a Bill of Injunction exhibited against him by

Philip HUFFMAN, 14 January 1803. THOMAS obtained a judgement against Philip HUFFMAN on 15 December 1802. HUFFMAN's complaint: On 1 November 1802, Michael ANSTINE owned the following goods, viz, 6 head of cattle, 28 young and old hogs, a crop of corn and potatoes in the ground and many other small items. On the same date, HUFFMAN purchased the above mentioned goods and cattle and paid ANSTINE the full purchase price. A short time later, ANSTINE left this county after giving HUFFMAN full possession to the goods. A while later, THOMAS obtained an attachment on the estate of ANSTINE and an Officer of the Court levied the attachment on a part of the goods, viz, 1 steer, 1 iron pot and 1 spider then owned by HUFFMAN. At the time of the attachment, he asserted his claim to the property not withstanding which the property was actually taken by virtue of the attachment. The attachment was returned to court whereupon judgement was entered in favor of THOMAS for 3 pounds, 19 shillings and 9 pence. At the time of the trial, he intended to assert his claim but some of the lawyers were employed by THOMAS and others were absent and he could not engage council. HUFFMAN prayed for and was granted an injunction to stay execution of the judgement until the matter could be heard in a Court of Equity. Injunction Bond signed by HUFFMAN to ensure all costs and awards would be paid in case the injunction should be dissolved secured by John GIBLER and Able (x) DAVIS, 15 December 1802. THOMAS' answer to the injunction: He believed HUFFMAN never paid full price for the goods and cattle and believe the steer that was attached was never the property of ANSTINE as HUFFMAN claimed, February 1803. June 1810 term, injunction perpetuated and judgement.

163 - 1810, Monongalia County Court. William POSTLEWAIT's complaint: He purchased a 400 acre tract of land on Dunkard Creek adjoining George WADE and Thomas WADE from Henry ACTMONGUASH, of "Penelton" County, Jacob BIRD, of Bath County, and Mary WADE, of Monongalia County, (who has since married James BAKER) and they gave him a Title Bond dated 23 August 1796. When the Surveyor of Monongalia County, Samuel HANWAY, surveyed the land it fell short by 12 acres. He gave his bond for 400 pounds and paid all but $51.89 and interest and costs but the grantors never made him a deed. The land was sold for the direct tax and redeemed by him. One of the bonds for the money was assigned to Adam SHROYER who brought suit and recovered a judgement for $51.89 with interest and costs. POSTLEWAIT prayed for and was granted an injunction to stay execution of the judgement until the matter could be heard in a Court of Equity and "for a jury to determine the value of the land that falls short," 6 May 1806. Injunction Bond signed by POSTLEWAIT to ensure all costs and awards would be paid in case the injunction should be dissolved secured by Grafton (x) WHITE, 18 October 1806. Answer to the complaint by ARMONGASH and BIRD: They sold the land by the

tract and not by the acre. They considered the shortage so small as not to be worthy of the consideration of a court. The could not remember whether they sold POSTLEWAIT 400 acres or a tract suppose to contain 400 acres but they intended to think the latter because they were never on the land except one time and knew little about it. They said they were not obliged to make a deed until the last payment had been made and were ready and willing to do so at that time, 5 October 1807 at Pendleton County and signed by Justice Peter HULL Jr. Adam SHROYER's answer to the complaint: He did not know anything about the transaction and the bond was assigned to him for a valuable consideration. When he accepted the assignment he did not know there was a dispute and he prayed the court to discharge the complaint against him, 3 October 1807 at Pendleton County before John HOPKINS. Answer of James BAKER and Mary his wife (daughter of Joseph WADE): Mary learned that a patent was granted to her and others as heirs of Joseph WADE, deceased, for 400 acres and if there had been an overage in the bounds of the survey, nothing would have been demanded. James said he asked POSTLEWAIT to pay Mary's share, it being one third of the whole, and as POSTLEWAIT could not procure the money, it was agreed that BAKER should have 100 acres of the land and he refunded to POSTLEWAIT so much as to make the sum 100 pounds. For sometime afterwards, he occupied and lived on the 100 acres. Later, POSTLEWAIT repurchased the 100 acres and suggested there was a defect of acreage and because of the shortage retained $20 when making payment for which he has never accounted with him, 2 April 1808. Title Bond dated 23 August 1796 from the grantors to POSTLEWAIT for a clear and indisputable deed for 400 acres, it being a tract that belonged to Joseph WADE, deceased. The deed to be made 1 April 1802, that being the last payment due, signed by Jacob (x) BIRD, Henry (x) ARMONGASH, Mary WADE, MarMaget (x) BIRD and Sophiah (x) ARMONGASH and witnessed by Richard WADE, ___al BIRD and Tho. WADE. Deposition of Richard POSTLEWAIT: He remembered when William POSTLEWAIT bought the land and he bought it by the acre at 20 shillings per, 9 July 1810. Order to William N. JARRETT to survey the land in dispute, September term 1806. Plat of survey made by JARRETT on 4 November 1806. The tract contained 384 1/4 acres. Surveyor's fee $5.25 to be included in the costs. July 1810 term, injunction made perpetual.

163 - 1810, Monongalia County Court. Joseph ALLEN, John SULLIVAN, and Rawley SCOTT summoned to answer a Bill in Chancery exhibited against them by Thomas LAIDLEY, 12 October 1809. LAIDLEY's complaint: Benjamin SAYRE obtained a judgement against him to which judgement he prayed for and obtained an appeal. The judgement was affirmed, the execution was paid and on the appeal and execution, John SULLIVAN and Joseph ALLEN became his securities. To secure his securities from any possible damage, he executed a Deed of Trust to

Rawley SCOTT for 489 acres of land. The securities did not pay the debt and he made provisions through John SAYRE, brother of Benjamin SAYRE, for paying the debt and interest. Benjamin SAYRE agreed to settle the same with him. The securities, not having paid the judgement nor any part of it have, under the Trust Deed, proceeded to have the land advertised for sale. LAIDLEY prayed the court to grant him an injunction to stay SCOTT from selling the land until the matter could be heard in a Court of Equity, 10 October 1809. Injunction granted. May 1810 term, dismissed and judgement for the defendants.

163 - 1810, Monongalia County Court. Complaint of Elisha CLAYTON: Some years ago, Jesse CHANEY came to him and asked him to let his daughter, Elizabeth, go and live with him at Westchester, Pennsylvania. He agreed that Elizabeth should go if Jesse would treat her as one of his own children and would bring her back, at his own expense, when and if she wanted to return. She was there for about a year or more when he went for a visit and was greatly surprised to find his daughter greatly abused by Jesse and in tears to come home. He asked Jesse to honor his agreement, but Jesse refused and swore if he did not take her away, he would turn her out of doors. CLAYTON said he was far from home, with little money, and CHANEY owed him a debt of $40. CHANEY agreed to let him have a horse for $80 if the $40 debt could be applied to the purchase price of the horse. The horse was of little value, but since he was so far from home and having no other way to bring his daughter home, he was compelled to consent as Jesse pointedly refused to comply with his agreement and he settled the $40 with him and gave Jesse his note for $40 more at which time Jesse agreed not to assign the note away to anyone but would keep it until he came up and then he would settle the note. Jesse also agreed to pay for his daughter's service, being about one whole year and nine months. CLAYTON complained that CHANEY never paid him one cent for the expense and trouble of bringing his daughter from Westchester nor one cent for her services. He complained that Jesse assigned the $40 away to Pereverie VARNER who brought suit in this court and while the suit was pending, Jesse came to his house and told him he would go to Morgan Town and have the suit dismissed, settle the business with VARNER and pay the costs himself. "By this means he was lulled to sleep and a judgement at law taken against him by complete surprise." An execution was issued on the judgement and he was compelled to give bond on the same. CLAYTON prayed for an injunction to stay execution of the judgement until the matter could be heard in a Court of Equity which motion was overruled, 9 July 1810.

163 - 1810, Monongalia County Court. The complaint of John DAVIS: Enoch JAMES, of Harrison County, recovered a judge-

ment against him for 45 pounds, 3 shillings and 11 pence with
interest from 23 May 1799. He said he paid several sums to
be applied to the execution of the judgement but the credits
were applied to an entirely different deal and now JAMES has
sued for the above amount and obtained judgement. He prayed
the court to grant him an injunction to stay execution of the
judgement until the matter could be heard in a Court of
Equity. Enoch JAMES's answer to the complaint: He remember
receiving from Thomas McKINLY (4.4.0) and from William LANHAM
(8.12.0) and Henry DERING (19.0.4) the sums mentioned in the
complaint for an account that DAVIS owed him. He denied the
payments were taken in discharge of an execution he had
against DAVIS but were taken in part payment of beef and pork
that he sold to DAVIS subsequent to the judgement rendered on
a bond assigned to him on DAVIS by Andrew OLLIPHANT. He prayed the court to dismissed the complaint against him. Harrison County: Enoch JAMES swore the facts as stated were true,
16 March 1802 before Justice John PRUNTY, Notice to John
DAVIS and Henry DERING from Enoch JAMES of intent to hear the
depositions of witnesses at the house of Daniel DAVIS living
on Booths Creek in Harrison County, 28 March 1803. Harrison
County: Isaac JAMES appeared before Justices Daniel DAVISSON
and John HALL and swore he gave DERING Jr. a true copy of the
within notice, 28 March 1803. Notice to DAVIS from JAMES of
intent to hear the depositions of Isaac JAMES and David
DUNHAM at the home of David HEWES in Clarksburg, 13 December
1802. Deposition of Isaac JAMES: In 1799, he heard DAVIS say
he bought 9 beeves and 14 fat hogs from his father, Enoch,
the price to be $5 per hundred all the way around. One half
to be paid in store goods, the other half to be paid in cash
which was to be secured by John DAVIS and William McCLEERY's
bond. Sometime afterward, he called on DAVIS for goods and
DAVIS gave him an order on William LANHAM for two saddles, 1
man's and 1 woman's, but he did not receive them. He
remembered his father receiving two saddles of the same
description. David DUNHAM's deposition: Sometime in the
latter part of 1799. he helped drive some beeves and hogs to
Morgantown for Enoch JAMES who sold them to DAVIS. JAMES
obtained a judgement against John DAVIS and Henry DERING, his
security. DAVIS and DERING prayed for and was granted an
injunction to stay execution of the judgement until the
matter could be heard in a Court of Equity. Injunction Bond
signed by DAVIS to ensure all costs and awards would be paid
in case the injunction should be dissolved secured by
Alexander HAWTHORN, 6 March 1802. 9 July 1810, motion for
injunction and overruled.

END OF MICROFILM #41

163a - 1810, Monongalia County Court. Elizabeth JOHNSON or
JOHNSTON summoned to answer a Bill of Injunction exhibited
against her by Thomas HAWKINS, 13 April 1808. JOHNSON
obtained a judgement against HAWKINS on 17 March 1808 for
$100 plus costs. HAWKINS prayed for and was granted an
injunction to stay proceedings on the judgement until the
matter could be heard in a Court of Equity. Injunction Bond
signed by HAWKINS to ensure all costs and awards would be
paid in case the injunction should be dissolved secured by
Amos HAWLEY, 13 April 1808. HAWKINS' complaint: On 24 July
1804, he gave his note to Elizabeth JOHNSON, "as she called
herself at that time and said she was the wife of Andrew
JOHNSON and had a right as such to assign over a Title Bond,
which had been assigned to Andrew JOHNSON for a part in 57
acres of land on the west side of Cheat River, to Hugh KELSO,
but he thinks she never made the assignment, the said Andrew
JOHNSON at that time being out of the state of Virginia as he
believes and believed she as his wife had a right to assign
the said bond over (which bond he had previously assigned his
part into to the said Andrew JOHNSON who had paid him a part
but not all) and in order to get the bond re-assigned as he
had a chance to sell it to Hugh KELSO he gave the note as
stated to the said Elizabeth in order to remunerate her for
what he had received from said Andrew JOHNSON, at the time
believing it to be fair and that she had a good right to
contract with him and make the assignment as Andrew JOHNSON
had left the state and she was unable to pay him the balance
for the land." He was informed that JOHNSON would not sanc-
tion the bond because he assigned the bond to William PRICE.
He said he believes he is able to prove that Elizabeth was
not the lawful wife of JOHNSON but the lawful wife of KING.
He charged Elizabeth with fraud and prayed for and was
granted an injunction to stay proceedings on the judgement
until the matter could be heard in a Court of Equity, 14
March 1808. JOHNSON's answer to the injunction: About 14
years since she married Joseph KING who, in the fall following, made a journey to Detroit and proposed to return about
May following but never returned nor did she have any information from him since and she does not know what became of
him. Sometime later, she married Andrew JOHNSON who lived
with her sometime and she, being one of the heirs of John
GREE/GREEN, inherited from him part of a tract of land which
land she and JOHNSON sold and with the price of the same made
the payment for 57 acres of the land mentioned in the bill.
When JOHNSON left, he gave her the Title Bond to the 57 acres
so that she and her children might enjoy the profits of the
same and because it had come by her inheritance as aforesaid.
She assigned the Title Bond to Thomas HAWKINS at his request
and obtained his obligation for the same. She said she was

informed and had reason to believe JOHNSON did not assign the Title Bond to William PRICE. She said long before HAWKINS gave his obligation for the land, he must have known she was married to KING because it was well known in the settlement where he lived. She denied all intention of fraud and prayed the injunction be dissolved with costs and damages and that she have the benefit of her judgement and such other relief as may appear to be just and right, 18 July 1809. Notice from JOHNSON to HAWKINS of intent to take the deposition of various witnesses dated 27 January 1810. Emonston MOORE delivered this notice to HAWKINS on 29 January 1810. Deposition of Nicholas CASEY: He received from Thomas HAWKINS one yoke of oxen at $40 and $15 as part payment of the Ferry Lot and HAWKINS told him he got the property of Andrew JOHNSON and said JOHNSON got the property from Thomas MONTGOMERY as part of the pay of his wife's land who is now the plaintiff is this suit. Deposition of Thomas MONTGOMERY: He paid Andrew JOHNSON $20, then $15 and one horse at $57, then $8 which made the first payment which was to be paid by JOHNSON to Thomas HAWKINS for the Ferry Lot and HAWKINS received the horse, the oxen and $40 paid to JOHNSON and by him to HAWKINS, and by said HAWKINS to Nicholas CASEY as part pay of the Ferry Lot. Deposition of James BROWN: It was generally known in the settlement where HAWKINS lived for some years that Elizabeth JOHNSON had been married to a man by the name of KING before she married JOHNSON. Deposition of Peter CASEY: In June 1804, he was called upon by HAWKINS and JOHNSON to settle the accounts between them. Accordingly, he went with Jacob DRAPER to JOHNSON's house and agreeable to the papers left by Andrew JOHNSON with Elizabeth, his wife, and by consent of the parties made a statement of the accounts and Elizabeth gave up a Title Bond assigned to her husband by HAWKINS and took his notes for such money as had been paid by JOHNSON and HAWKINS gave up the claims he had against JOHNSON, 30 January 1810. These depositions heard at the house of John FREELAND on Cheat River before David MORGAN and James E. BEALL on 30 January 1810. Thos HAWKINS agreed to release all errors at law in a judgement obtained against him on 17 March 1808 by Elizabeth JOHNSON for $100 with costs, 13 April 1808, signed by Thos (x) HAWKINS. June 1810 term, perpetuated and judgement.

163a - 1810, Monongalia County Court. Rodham/Rhodam RODGERS summoned to answer a Bill of Injunction exhibited against him by Abraham WELLS and Joseph WISBY, 17 June 1803. Complaint of WELLS: Sometime in 1802, WELLS and RODGERS entered into an agreement concerning the making of fur hats. RODGERS agreed to deliver and did deliver to WELLS fur for three hats and agreed to pay him $2.50 for making each hat and gave him his note for the same. RODGERS requested an instrument in writing to ensure he (WELLS) would make and deliver the 3 hats. He signed the agreement even though he could not read and Joseph

WISBY was his security. Shortly after, WELLS left the foundry
and RODGERS brought suit and obtained judgement for $15 plus
costs and interest from 11 June 1802. WELLS said his property
was under execution for the same. He said the intent of the
original bond was to secure the price of making the fur hats.
He prayed the court to grant an injunction to stay execution
of the judgement until the matter could be heard in a Court
of Equity, 13 June 1805. Injunction Bond signed by Abram
WELLS to ensure all costs and awards would be paid in case
the injunction should be dissolved secure by Joseph (x) WISBY
and James (x) DUNN, 13 June 1803. Deposition of Rodham E.
RODGERS heard at the house of Daniel DAVISSON in Clarksburg
on 21 November 1805: In the fall of 1802, he heard WELLS say
he owed his father 3 raccoon hats naped with beaver and he
would have paid him had RODGERS not brought suit against him.
Notice from ROGERS to WELLS and WISBY of intent to take the
depositions of sundry witnesses at the house of Daniel
DAWSON, tavernkeeper, in Clarksburg, 11 November 1805. Enoch
MOORE's deposition heard before Elias STILLWELL and William
MAULSBY in Clarksburg: In August 1804, he heard WELLS say
that if RODGERS had not brought suit against him, he would
have paid him but now he would "judzel" him out of it. June
1810 term, perpetuated and judgement.

163a - 1810, Monongalia County Court. William STEVENSON, Ann
STEVENSON, Morgan MORGAN, Zadock MORGAN, Levi MORGAN, Uriah
MORGAN, James MORGAN, Zackquil MORGAN, Horatio MORGAN, James
COCHRAN, Temperance COCHRAN, Jacob SCOTT, Catherine SCOTT,
Drucilla MORGAN, and Rachel MORGAN, heirs of Zackquil MORGAN,
deceased, summoned to answer a Bill in Chancery exhibited
against them by John DOWNER, 7 October 1805. DOWNER's
complaint: On 17 March 1786, he purchased Lot #24 in Morgantown from Zackwell MORGAN which was bounded by H. DERING's
lot which was a smith shop on the south and an alley on the
north and east and Water Street (later Front Street) on the
west. He obtained a writing signed and sealed by MORGAN and
Priscilla, his wife. MORGAN died before he could prove the
writing in court and have it recorded. MORGAN died intestate
and the legal title fell to his heirs as named above. The
heirs refused to make title and therefore he brings suit.
Indenture signed by Zack'll MORGAN and Drusilla MORGAN dated
17 March 1786 for Lot #24 and another lot (later Lot #125)
beginning on the river bank at a corner to John DOWNER, being
a part of the land granted to MORGAN by patent dated 7 April
1784, witnessed by James COX and Isaiak BALL. June 1810 term,
the defendants not appearing, the court decreed that the
defendants convey the lots by deed in fee simple to DOWNER
and be attached by their bodies or other property until they
perform this decree.

Also in this file - - - - In Chancery, Peter CLUTTER vs Peter
HAMMON. On 14 September 1802, this court made a decree in

favor of CLUTTER against HAMMON and William ASHFORD, his security. CLUTTER gave security but failed to appear and afterward by a petition to the court, the decree was set aside and CLUTTER filed his answer and the case came to trial and the court decreed that HAMMON pay CLUTTER $83.33 with interest at 6% from 10 April 1800 until paid plus cost.

163a - 1810, Monongalia County Court. Amos PETTYJOHN, William PETTYJOHN, John PETTYJOHN, Abraham PETTYJOHN, Isaac PETTY-JOHN, Richard PETTYJOHN and Mary PETTYJOHN his wife, Thomas PETTYJOHN and Ruth PETTYJOHN his wife, children, heirs and legal representatives of William PETTYJOHN Jr., deceased, summoned to answer a Bill in Chancery exhibited against them by Nathan SPRINGER, 17 April 1808. Right, Title and Interest Deed or Bill of Sale signed by William PETTYJOHN, of West-moreland County, Pennsylvania, to Nathan SPRINGER for his improvement, it being on the waters of Pricketts Creek adjoining William PETTYJOHN, Elias PIERCE and Isaiah PRICKETT and witnessed by Edward HUP/CUP and John SPRINGER dated 31 October 1782. SPRINGER complained that PETTYJOHN did not have a title for the land by virtue of equitable right but by virtue of a Land Office Treasury Warrant and a survey for 300 acres. The survey was to have been assigned to him so that the title could be made to him. The survey was returned to the Land Office in the name of William PETTYJOHN without any assignment and a grant was issued to William for 300 acres as appears by the patent dated 1 July 1791. The grant was delivered to him to have a deed drafted "which the said William engaged to sign, seal and acknowledge but from delay which too often is suffered by the procrastinating turn of man, said William departed this life, the said deed not having been executed and title to the said land has descended to" the above named heirs. He prayed the court to summon the heirs to be questioned in the matter. June 1810 term, the defendants failed to appear and the court decreed the defendants convey to SPRINGER the land in dispute by fee simple with warranty and the defendants be attached by their bodies until they perform this decree.

163a - 1810, Monongalia County Court. James TATE and John STEALEY summoned to answer a Bill in Chancery exhibited against them by Daniel ANDERSON, 27 May and 25 August 1806. ANDERSON's complaint: On 16 August 1805, TATE (James TATE and Co.) gave him a Due Bill for $95 worth of bar iron to be paid by next Christmas at 6 pence per pound to be delivered at Rock Forge. ANDERSON said he was informed that STEALEY was the company or was a partner in the company at the time the Due Bill was given. He said TATE had departed this state and STEALEY was indebted to him (TATE). He prayed the court to restrain STEALEY from paying TATE any money until the matter could be heard in a Court of Equity. STEALEY's answer to the complaint: He was not a partner with TATE and he does not owe any sum to TATE nor have in his possession any money nor property belonging to TATE. He prayed the court to discharge all charges with reasonable costs, 28 September 1807. June 1810 term, dismissed and judgement.

163a - 1810, Monongalia County Court. John WEST's complaint: On 9 October 1804, he gave his obligation to John WEATHERHOLT for 10 barrels of cider, the barrels to go with the cider, which was to be delivered at the mouth of Deckers Creek on or before 1 November next in case the waters would then serve to bring it down from his residence. He said the waters did not rise and were not sufficient for him to convey the cider to the place of delivery. About the time for delivery, WEATHER-HOLT was at his house and said he would trade the note to Capt. John COOPER which he (WEST) believed he did and he called on COOPER to learn if he had the note. COOPER said he and WEATHERHOLT had a disagreement and the note was not traded to him. Later, he learned WEATHERHOLT assigned the note to Jacob BAKER, but BAKER did not call for delivery. He was ready to deliver the cider when waters permitted but could find no agent or anyone with authority to receive it. He asked Michael KERNS Sr., who he believed to be a relative of WEATHERHOLT, if he would accept delivery of the cider and take care of it for WEATHERHOLT and KERNS said he would not. "And then not being able to find..." June 1810 term, dismissed. The remainder of this narrative not found.

163a - 1810, Monongalia County Court. David SCOTT and James NEALEY summoned to testify in behalf of Philip and Michael SHIVELY, defendants, vs the Overseers of the Poor, plaintiffs, 3 February 1810.

163a - 1810, Monongalia County Court. Joseph McDOUGAL summoned to answer a Bill of Injunction exhibited against him by Thomas R. CHIPPS, 25 February 1808. McDOUGAL not an inhabitant of this state. CHIPPS' complaint: Joseph McDOUGAL, one of the securities for himself and Elihu HORTON to Sheriff Russell POTTER for $70, did pay as their security the said sum and brought suit and recovered against him the $70 plus costs. He said McDOUGAL owed him a certain sum of $____ (the paper is folded and the amount hidden) and to HORTON, who as principle was jointly liable, the sum of $23.47 as per account filed. He charged McDOUGAL with fraud in not giving credits in the above amounts and prayed the court to grant him an injunction to stay execution of the judgement until the matter could be heard in a Court of Equity. CHIPPS swore the above was true before Justice Samuel MINORD/MINOR on 10 August 18__. McDOUGAL's answer: He said he paid the $70 as security for CHIPPS and HORTON and brought suit against CHIPPS because HORTON had left the country. He said "$20 was made by virtue of an execution issued on said judgement to his use and that the balance was detained by the Sheriff as his costs attending the sale of property from which said $20 was made. He said that long before HORTON removed himself from Monongalia County, he paid him the amount of the clerk's notes stated in the bill by CHIPPS, which payment was made in hauling. HORTON promised to deliver the same over to CHIPPS, but in violation of his promise _____ _____ HORTON failed to delivered the same over to CHIPPS. After the departure of said HORTON, CHIPPS called on him for payment of the same, he was then compelled to pay the same to CHIPPS which he did in hauling." He said HORTON still owed him a debt of long standing. He prayed the court to dissolve the injunction with reasonable cost, signed by McDOUGAL at Scioto County on 5 March 1808. Alexander CURRANT, Clerk of Common Pleas of Scioto County, Ohio. An account directed to E. HORTON from McDOUGAL for hauling wood from 4 June 1801 through 15 May 1803. Notice to Thomas R. CHIPPS from Joseph McDOUGAL of intent to take the affidavits of sundry witnesses at the house of Robert LUCAS Esqr. in Scioto County, Ohio, 10 May 1808. Richard McDOUGAL swore he delivered a copy of this notice to CHIPPS on 16 May 1808. Richard McDOUGAL's deposition heard at the house of Robert LUCAS Esqr. in Scioto County, Ohio, before Justice Robert LUCAS and Justice Jacob NOEL on 11 June 1808: He said the account as presented was true and correct. Copy of court fees due John EVANS, CMC, from Joseph and Nancy McDOUGAL = $6.20. McDOUGAL's account with E. HORTON : "by lent and sundry other accounts - $37.97, paid on this account $18.50 and 1-16 gallon kettle lent and never returned = $4." June 1810 term of court, dismissed.

163a - 1810, Monongalia County Court. Thomas R. CHIPPS' complaint: He owed $20 to David DAVIS, of Kentucky. DAVIS was passing through Monongalia County and called on him for the debt. He said he had recourse to William CHIPPS who was then indebted to him and William took it upon himself to discharge the debt owing DAVIS. David DAVIS instructed William to pay the debt to John DAVIS, of Morgantown, and the receipt of John, for the whole or any part of the debt, would be good against David. William paid the full debt of $20 to John and received a receipt. David sued and obtained judgement for $20 with interest and cost. Thomas prayed the court to grant an injunction to stay execution of the judgement until the matter could be heard in a Court of Equity, heard before Justice James CLARK, no date. John DAVIS' answer to the injunction: He never had any orders from David DAVIS to receive the sum of $20 from Thomas CHIPPS and William CHIPPS, neither did he receive the said sum from any other person. He received a payment from William CHIPPS on account of a debt due David DAVIS, as agent for a certain company, the price of a mare, which payment was only a part of the debt and he gave William CHIPPS a receipt, 15 March 1806 and heard before Justice Robert FERRELL. David DAVIS' answer heard before Thomas MARSHALL, Clerk of Mason County, Kentucky, 1

February 1806: He did not direct William CHIPPS to pay John DAVIS any money on account of the debt due by Thomas CHIPPS to him, nor was John DAVIS in any wise authorized to receive any money or other thing from William CHIPPS in discharge of the debt due by Thomas CHIPPS. Sometime in 1803, Thomas and William CHIPPS passed by Mrs. WASHINGTON's in Kentucky, which was and still is his residence, and he sold a horse to Thomas CHIPPS for $120 for which he took William's note. William said he did not have sufficient money to bear his expenses home and he (David) loaned him $20 and took his individual note. During the entire dealing there was no conversation between Thomas and William nor was the one in any wise bound for the other. Later, he was in Morgantown and John DAVIS informed him he had received from William CHIPPS about $16 on account of the debt due from William and requested him to permit the payment to pass to the credit of William CHIPPS and as William had some excess pork John needed, John requested that he would permit him to buy the pork to make the entire payment $20 or $30 and he agreed. He never intended the payments to John by William should be applied to the credit of William nor was the name of William mentioned in any manner during the conversation between him and John DAVIS. Affidavit of William CHIPPS heard at Wm. M. JARRETT's tavern in Morgantown on 28 June 1806: Sometime about 1803, he and David DAVIS met at the house of Alexander HAWTHORN. He heard David say "that if he would pay $20 to John DAVIS on account of Thomas CHIPPS, that it would answer him as he had a son then boarding with John DAVIS, that he (William CHIPPS) paid to John DAVIS, in pork, the sum of $20 expressly on account of Thomas R. CHIPPS and took his receipt for the same but has since lost it." June 1810 term, dismissed.

163a - 1810, Monongalia County Court. Francis COLLINS and James McVICKER summoned to answer a Bill in Chancery exhibited against them by Jacob FOULK, 23 February 1805. FOULK's complaint: Sometime in 1805, he had a sealed obligation then due and unpaid on Francis COLLINS for $125 payable in mill stones and grind stones. He and COLLINS made a bet on a horse race soon to be run for $125 and he placed the obligation in the hands of James McVICKER to hold for his part of the bet. Reubin PITCHER and Francis COLLINS were the owners of the horses and he suspected COLLINS, PITCHER and McVICKER were in a conspiracy to defraud him because COLLINS did not deposit anything in McVICKER's hands to hold as his part of the bet and if he (FOULK) won the bet and got possession of the note he left with McVICKER, COLLINS might have an action to recover the said note. He applied to McVICKER, through James THOMPSON, to recover the obligation and advised McVICKER he would not abide by the bet, that it was illegal and sent a written order to give up the obligation but James refused. He prayed the court to summon the defendants to be question in the matter. McVICKER's answer to the complaint:

Sometime last year, Francis COLLINS came to him and informed him that he (COLLINS) had made a bet of a bond on a horse race with FOULK. A few day afterwards, FOULK came to him and brought an obligation for perhaps the sum mentioned in the Bill of Complaint and deposited it with him and instructed him not to give up the obligation to either himself or COLLINS until the race was run and when the race was run to give them up to the party who won. He was not concerned in the bet, he had not the least interest nor was he the gainer or loser in it, but only held the obligations at the request of the parties and delivered them up to COLLINS as instructed by the parties. He knew nothing of it being a sham race or of any fraud in the business. He prayed the court to dismiss the charges against him with reasonable cost, 27 August 1805. Francis COLLINS did not appear and at June 1810 term, the court decreed that COLLINS pay to FOULK $125 with interest at 6% from 1 December 1805 until paid, the sum due as stated in the complaint, plus costs. The complaint dismissed as to the defendant James McVICKER and COLLINS be attached by his body or estate until he performs this decree.

163a - 1810, Monongalia County Court. Stephen McDADE, plaintiff, vs, Richard COUGHLAN and Robert MEANS, defendants. COUGHLAN and MEANS did not appear to answer the complaint and the court decreed that COUGHLIN "do by deed in fee simple convey to McDADE the land in the bill described which lays on the west side of Monongalia (sic) River and bounded by the lands of John SHIVELY, the Richwood Lands now owned by David SCOTT and lands, late the property of Jacob SCOTT, called the Denney Place containing 98 acres," that McDADE have full, quiet and peaceable possession and that COUGHLIN pay all costs, no date.

163a - 1810, Monongalia County Court. Charles CONWAY summoned to answer a Bill of Injunction exhibited against him by John CARTER, 12 July 1809. CARTER's complaint: He said he owed Charles CONWAY $100 with interest from 1 November 1806 and cost due to a judgement obtained by CONWAY in an earlier County Court. He said he paid Daniel SAYRE $2.25 for CONWAY and was to have credit on the judgement, but CONWAY failed to apply the credit. He said he now had a claim of Col. Samuel HANWAY exhibited against him on account of CONWAY for $3 which he has not paid and a credit of $25.10 as of 17 April 1802. He prayed the court to grant him an injunction to stay execution of the judgement until the matter could be heard in a Court of Equity, 10 June 1809. Injunction Bond signed by CARTER to ensure all costs and awards would be paid in case the injunction should be dissolved secured by Levi MORGAN, 8 July 1809. CONWAY's answer to the injunction. He said if CARTER made the above payments and could prove it, he would gladly give credit on the judgement. He said CARTER owed him several small sums and made several small payments on these

several sums and he was indulgent with him "so from the
length of time and the several small payments without being
particular to which have to be applied, a difference arose
concerning the balance due taking the whole into view and
CARTER agreed with him to give all their papers" to Thomas
WILSON who agreed to determine the balance. When all was
done, the two parties agreed on the balance which was due to
CONWAY. He gave CARTER sufficient time to make payment, he
failed to pay as expected and suit was brought, 19 January
1810. "Received of John CARTER $3.06 on account of his
assumpsit for Charles CONWAY," 14 June 1810, signed by Samuel
HANWAY. "Defendant not an inhabitant of this Commonwealth."
June 1810 term, injunction dissolved and judgement.

163a - 1810, Monongalia County Court. George CUNNINGHAM swore
that John PENNINGTON owed him $17 and he believed PENNINGTON
removed from the Commonwealth. He prayed the court to attach
so much of his property as to satisfy the debt, 8 August
1808. "Summon Rebecca DERING, administratrix of Henry DERING,
deceased, as garnishee," Justice Jno WAGNER. CUNNINGHAM
obtained an attachment on the property of PENNINGTON for $17.
Attachment Bond signed by CUNNINGHAM to ensure all costs and
awards would be paid in case he should be cast in the suit
secured by Isaac MATTHEWS, 8 August 1808. Deposition of Capt.
John RAMSEY: In 1803, PENNINGTON was indebted to him for past
due rent and he (RAMSEY) became uneasy and threatened to
distress PENNINGTON. PENNINGTON then gave him a bond on
William PRICE, John RAVENSCRAFT and William ABERNATHY for
about 42 pounds and some odd shillings. Out of this sum, he
was to pay himself the rent in arrears, and to pay CUNNINGHAM
$18 the price of a saddle and bridle. Sometime later, he met
Joseph TIDBALL, of Winchester, at the house of DERING and in
conversation the subject of PENNINGTON came up and TIDBALL
asked him to accept an order in his favor for the amount of a
debt due from PENNINGTON to TIDBALL, either a little over or
under $100. He agreed to accept the order when the salt in
the order should be delivered. Henry DERING was appointed
agent for TIDBALL to receive the salt when delivered by Mr.
PRICE. He said he knew DERING received 19 bushels and 3
pecks of salt. He said DERING brought suit for the balance,
but later compromised with PRICE, who was the principal
obligor, and took a new obligation from PRICE, secured by
Richard PRICE, in favor of TIDBALL. RAMSEY said when he gave
the obligation to DERING, he informed DERING it was subject
to his claim and the claim of CUNNINGHAM, but he never
received "one farthing." DERING promised to give an order on
PRICE in favor of RAMSEY and one in favor of CUNNINGHAM, 10
October 1808. "I promise to pay Francis COLLINS one woman's
saddle and crib bridle, the saddle to have _____ and
sursingel? it being for value received, the saddle to be
paid to COLLINS against Christmas Day 180_," signed by
John PENNINGTON. "August 20, the saddle to be in _____

_____ to the saddle that I got for Thomas WARMAN, George TOBIAS." COLLINS assigned this note to Charles LITTLE, no date and witnessed by James COLLINS. Charles (x) LITTLE assigned the same to George CUNNINGHAM, no date. "Sir, please deliver to Joseph TIDBALL or order 30 bushels of salt of the first that comes into your hands on account of William PRICE, William ABERNATHY and John RAVENSCRAFT´s bond for that article to me for value received," Morgantown, 25 September 1802 and signed by PENNINGTON. "To Liet. John DAVIS, I will deliver the above quantity of salt as soon as there is that much which comes into my hands and out of the above bond 23 bushels of salt when it comes to hand and the balance by 25 December next," signed by John RAMSEY. William PRICE summoned to testify in behalf of CUNNINGHAM, 3 November 1808 and 17 June 1809. William PAINE and John RAMSEY summoned to testify in behalf of PENNINGTON, 7 March 1809. "We the jury find that sufficient property has been delivered to Henry DERING to satisfy the plaintiff´s claim, which property was delivered on account of Defendant PENNINGTON, that said property or the value thereof remains in the hands of the garnishee, Rebecca DERING." June 1810 term, jury verdict and judgement for the plaintiff.

163a - 1810, Monongalia County Court. Petter CLUTTER summoned to answer a Bill of Injunction exhibited against him by Peter HARMAN, 26 October 1802. CLUTTER´s complaint: On 10 April 1798, Peter HARMAN owed him 25 pounds ($83) and HARMAN gave his obligation for the same. He said HARMAN moved from this Commonwealth and left his debt unpaid. He prayed that Edward ELLIOT, Jeremiah HANLEY, William JOHNSTON, John RUNYON, Elijah GADD, Jonathan BUTLER, Joseph FOREMAN, Thomas BURCHINAL, Samuel TAYLOR, James PORT and Edward JONES be summoned to declare what they have in their hands belonging to said HARMAN and that each and every one of them be restrained from paying money or property to HARMAN or anyone for him until the matter could be heard in a Court of Equity. (HARMAN not an inhabitant of this state). HARMAN´s answer: He said it was true he gave CLUTTER a bond as mentioned in the bill for 190 pounds which he agreed to pay to CLUTTER for 377 acres of land, 77 of which was to be deeded on or before 10 May 1802 and a plat of a survey was to be assigned by CLUTTER to HARMAN for 100 acres adjoining on the east side of the aforesaid 77 acres, 25 acres of the 100 the title to be warranted. He said CLUTTER had never assigned over the 100 acres. He said he paid the whole of the said $183. On 14 September 1802, CLUTTER obtained a decree against HARMAN for $18 with interest and costs. HARMAN prayed for and was granted an injunction to stay execution of the decree. Injunction Bond signed by Peter HARMAN to ensure all costs and awards would be paid in case the injunction should be dissolved secured by Joseph REED and Ezekiel CORE, 16 October 1802. Conveyance Bond signed by Peter CLUTTER to Peter HARMAN dated 10 April 1798 whereby CLUTTER promised to convey to HARMAN a 377 acre tract of land where CLUTTER now lives adjoining Michael FLOYD and Joseph FOREMAN. The deed to be made on or before 10 April 1802. CLUTTER was to assign all his right, title and interest in and to a "platt of survey for 100 acres adjoining on the east side of the first parcel and 77 acres, 25 acres of the mentioned 100, the title to be warranted." This agreement dated 10 April 1798 and witnessed by John RUNYON and David SEAMAN.

"The notes I have in my hands of Peter HARMAN's are as follows:"

1 against Edwards ELLIOTT for	4.17.6	
1 mare against said ELLIOTT for	5.18.0	
1 against Jeremiah HANLEY for	2.10.1	
1 against William JOHNSON for	1. 2.0	
1 against John RUNYON for	1.18.1	
1 against Elijah GADD for	1. 0.1	
1 against Jonathan BUTTER/BUTLER	1. 7.8	
1 against Joseph FORMAN for	1.18.5	

The above notes to be paid in iron or castings 1 April next.

1 against Thomas BURCHINAL for	2.16.6	
1 against Samuel TAYLOR for	1. 4.0	
1 against James PORT for	6. 0.0	
to be paid in linen		
1 against said PORT for	6. 0.0	

This is a true account of all the notes I have belonging to Peter HARMAN, 12 March 1802, signed by Edward JONES and directed to Mr. Thos. WILSON.

Christian SYPOLT's affidavit: About 7 years ago, he heard CLUTTER tell HARMAN that he would go with him to town and make him a right to the piece of land and HARMAN refused to go, he said he would not fling away ten shillings and sixpence for it, the land was not worth it. Signed by SYPOLT before Justice Amos ROBBARTS.

William CLUTTER's affidavit: He was present when CLUTTER and HARMAN made the agreement about the plat of survey for a parcel of land and the agreement was that HARMAN was to have the land surveyed at his own expense by John RUNYAN and when so done, CLUTTER was to assign the same to HARMAN. He heard CLUTTER tell HARMAN that he was ready to assign the plat whenever HARMAN would get it, then HARMAN refused to get it and said he would have nothing further to do with it which was about six months after I was chain bearer for RUNYON and carried the chain round the land it being a piece of twenty odd acres joining the tract that CLUTTER sold to HARMAN, 10 October 1803.

Affidavit of Michael FLOYD: In 1800, he heard CLUTTER offer to sign a plat for a piece of land which was in the hands of Mr. RUNYON to which HARMAN refused having anything to do with the plat, 3 October 1803. Signed by Michael S. FLOID.

Affidavit of Elizabeth FLOID: Elizabeth said the same as

Michael. Signed by Elisebeth (x) FLOID on 3 October 1803.

Thomas WARMAN's affidavit: CLUTTER told him he never had assigned over the plat for the land which he had agreed to assign to HARMAN and which plat was for a part of the land, 10 October 1803. Signed by Thomas WARMAN before John McCLAIN.

"I promise to pay or cause to be paid unto Peter CLUTTER or his heirs or assigns the just and full sum of 25 pounds Virginia currency to be paid in horses, cattle, salt or flax at the market price. If we cannot agree, the price to be left to two men chosen by us, said payment to be made on or before 10 April 1800, it being for value received," 10 April 1798, signed by Peter HARMAN and witnessed by John RUNYON and David SEAMAN. "Above payment to be made where CLUTTER now lives."

HARMAN entered his Appearance Bond with William ASHFORD as his security, but having failed to appear for three months, the court took his absence as a confession and decreed that HARMAN and ASHFORD pay CLUTTER the sum aforesaid with costs and his body be attached until he performed this decree, 1810.

163a - 1810, Monongalia County Court. Thomas WARMAN's complaint: In 1805, Stephen WARMAN, for Joshua WARMAN, contracted with Ralph BARKSHIRE to purchase a quantity of nails and he became security for Joshua. The nails were delivered and Joshua found the lot to be different than he ordered and found "fag ends of the iron among the nails, the iron was good for little or nothing." He said he moved to Ohio and BERKSHIRE obtained an attachment and a judgement on a suit against him. He prayed the court to grant an injunction to stay execution of the judgement until the matter could be heard in a Court of Equity, 2 January 180_. BARKSHIRE's answer: In 1805, Stephen WARMAN inquired about a quantity of nails to be sent down the river, but no bargain was made at the time. Sometime later, Thomas by his brother, Stephen, directed him to let Stephen have nails and that he (Thomas) would be bound for payment. He let Stephen have 9 boxes of nails for Thomas, which nails he had purchased from the factory of Alexander and Robert HAWTHORN in boxes which were marked the quantity and quality. The boxes were opened, part by himself and part by Stephen, examined and the weight ascertained to be correct. The nails were packed in the boxes and put into a cart and as each box was weighed and put in the cart, the same was marked and a bill made agreeable unto and delivered to Stephen. A note was written and signed by Stephen for the amount of the nails and the nails were

then taken away by Stephen and as he believes, delivered to
Thomas. Sometime later, Thomas came to him and signed the
note for the nails. After the note became due and remained
unpaid, Thomas came and asked for more time to pay the debt
saying he had not been down the river to sell the nails. At
that time no objection was made on account of the quality of
the nails. He said when nails were purchased to take down
the river often the seller, not being a proper judge, was
persuaded by the buyer that the nails were not of the quality
described on the boxes or perhaps the nails were not those
that were purchased from his store. After he obtained
judgement, Thomas came to him asking for more time to pay the
debt and said he (Thomas) ought not to blame him (BARKSHIRE),
that he did not know all, that he (Thomas) had been injured
by Joshua WARMAN who had sold the nails and had not accounted
with him for them. He agreed to allow Thomas more time upon
giving security which he failed to do and since Thomas lived
in Ohio, he had to take action while Thomas was in this part
of the country, 13 August 1807. Ralph BARKSHIRE obtained a
judgement against Thomas WARMAN for $144.04 with interest at
6% from 10 September 1805 plus costs. WARMAN prayed for and
obtained an injunction to stay execution of the judgement
until the matter could be heard in a Court of Equity.
Injunction Bond signed by Thomas WARMAN to ensure all costs
and awards would be paid in case the injunction should be
dissolved secured by Hedgeman TRIPLETT and David BAYLES, 13
January 1807. Ralph BARKSHIRE obtained a judgement against
Thomas WARMAN for $144.04 with interest at 6% from 10
September 1805 plus costs. WARMAN prayed for and obtained an
injunction to stay execution of the judgement until the
matter could be heard in a Court of Equity. Injunction Bond
signed by Thomas WARMAN to ensure all costs and awards would
be paid in case the injunction should be dissolved secured by
Charles BYRN, 14 March 1809. "Lebanon, Ohio, 17 November
1806. Bill of nails bought of Ralph BERKSHIRE by Stephen &
Thomas WARMAN, 1 box 10d nails, 1 box 6d nails, 7 boxes 8d
nails. I do certify that the above is a true statement of
the nails delivered to me by Stephen and Thomas WARMAN which
I believe to be the same nails they bought from BERKSHIRE,"
signed by Jos. WARMAN. Warren County, Ohio, Joshua WARMAN
swore before Justice Silas HURIN that the bill of nails was a
true bill, 17 November 1806. Notice to BERKSHIRE of intent
to hear the deposition of Joshua WARMAN signed by Thomas
WARMAN and delivered to BERKSHIRE's house and left in the
care of Jacob KYGER who lived with BERKSHIRE, 2 March 1807,
signed by Robert FERRELL. Joshua WARMAN's deposition heard
before Justices Silas HURIN and Matthias CORWIN and Clerk
David SUTTON at the house of Ephraim HATTAWAY in Warren
County, Ohio on 8 March 1807: On 2 March 1806, he received
from Thomas WARMAN 1 box 10 penny nails, 1 box 6 penny nails
and 7 boxes 8 penny nails which were purchased from Ralph
BERKSHIRE of Morgantown by Stephen and Thomas WARMAN for 4

penny, 5 penny, 6 penny and 10 penny nails as he discovered
by the bill accompanying the above nails made out and signed
by BERKSHIRE and had the nails have answered the bill he
would have sold them to very good advantage but when he came
to open the boxes he only found two of the above boxes to
answer the bill signed by BARKSHIRE which caused him to make
a considerable sacrifice in the sale of the nails, he also
found a great many scraps mixed through the nails that was
entirely lost. June 1810 term, perpetuated by agreement.

Nail Advertisement.

To the Public

The contract between Mr. ....
..., of Morgantown, and myself, is
by mutual consent this day ceased to exist, which enables me to advertise that I
will sell nails at my Factory near Morgantown, at the following prices, both by
wholesale and retail, viz.

Wholesale Price.

Flooring Brads at 9 pence per pound.
10 penny Nails at 10 do.   do   do
8 penny do.   at 11 do.   do   do
6 penny do.   at 13 do.   do   do
4 penny do.   at 16 do.   do   do

Retail Price.

Flooring Brads at 10 pence per pound.
10 penny Nails at 11 do   do   do
8 penny do   at 12 do   do   do
4 penny do   at 14 do   do   do

ROBERT HAWTHORN.
Morgantown, May 16, 1805.

N. B. These Nails can also be had
at Mr. Ralph Barkihire's Store in Morgantown, at the above prices.   tf

163b - 1810, Monongalia County Court. Joseph MYERS, William MYERS, Jesse MYERS, John SMITH and Sarah his wife, James MOORE and Pheobe his wife and Ann MYERS, children and heirs of Joseph MYERS, deceased, summoned to answer a Bill in Chancery exhibited against them by Peter COOK, 9 August 1804 and 20 August 1805. Peter COOK's complaint: He married Mary MYERS, daughter of Joseph MYERS, deceased, who died in 1787 leaving his widow, Pheobe MYERS who is deceased and the following children: Joseph, William, Jesse, and Sarah MYERS, Phebe MOORE, Ann MYERS and Mary COOK. COOK said he paid Joseph MYERS 66 pounds and 6 shillings and 8 pence for his one third part of the land and he paid John SMITH the amount herewith filed as a part of this bill. He said the children all agreed that he (COOK) should have the land for 200 pounds of which Joseph MYERS was to receive and has received his one third part of the same, Mary MYERS and Jesse MYERS were to be paid 20 pounds each and the balance to be equally divided between all the children except Joseph MYERS, which left the different children a legacy out of the tract of land of 15 pounds, 12 shillings and 2 and 2/3 pence each. COOK said he paid all the amounts, but the above named defendants refused to make a deed to him and he prayed the court to summon the defendants to be questioned in a Court of Equity. Ann MYERS' answer to the complaint: She never saw the contract made between her mother and others as she lived in Loudoun County at the time and she disputed the different amounts on the account as stated by COOK. She said Mary COOK who married Peter COOK, departed this life without heirs, and she, Ann, claimed her sixth part of the share or dividend of Mary COOK which she is willing to let COOK have at a fair price. She said, for the sake of peace and upon payment, she was willing to convey her claim to COOK but not because of any contract by which she is liable or subject to do so, 5 May 1806. John SMITH's answer: He said it was true his wife agreed to the articles in the contract and that Mary MYERS, afterwards Mary COOK, took a part of the land including the improvement as her full share agreeable to the article and she was in possession of the same when she married COOK. After they married, COOK purchased the land, all except his wife's interest, for 500 pounds to be paid within 5 years from the date of purchase which was in early 1793. He said he and his wife Sarah were ready and willing to convey all their claim as soon as they were paid their full due. He disputed some of the amounts listed by COOK in payment of his inheritance and claimed one-sixth of Mary COOK's estate as did Ann, 5 May 1806. John SMITH affirmed before B. REEDER that his residence was in Loudoun County, 8 May 1806. Indenture dated 13 December 1784 from Thomas CRAFT and Margret his wife, of Loudoun County, to Joseph MYERS, of Monongalia County, for 200 pounds for a tract of land first granted to CRAFT by patent dated 1804, signed by Thomas (TC) CRAFT. Power of Attorney signed by Joseph MYERS dated 29 March 1794 whereby Joseph authorized

John WILLETS to convey a tract of land to COOK, witnessed by
John WORLEY and David SEAMAN. Power of Attorney from Joseph
MIERS and Rachel his wife, John SMITH and Sarah his wife,
Jesse MIERS and Priscilla his wife, and Ann MIERS children
and heirs of Joseph MIERS, deceased, authorizing John WILLETS
to convey a tract of land to COOK, 17 September 1796. Signed
by Jesse MYERS, Priscilla (x) MYERS, Joseph MYERS and Rachel
MYERS and witnessed by William (x) BENSON, John (x) CLALEY?,
Lewis (x) LYIEL, John McCLAIN, John RUNYON and Josiah WOODS.
Power of Attorney signed by James MOORE and Phebe his wife,
of Loudoun County, being son-in-law and daughter of Joseph
MYERS, deceased, of Monongalia County, to John WILLITTS, 18
April 1799 and witnessed by Josiah WOOD and Aaron SMITH.
WILLOTTS was authorized to convey their right, title and
interest in and to a 400 acre tract of land where Joseph
MYERS lived and owned at the time of his death, adjoining
land formerly owned by Robert HARNESS and "on the old path
and waters of Little Sandy Creek" to Peter COOK who was now
in possession. Article of Agreement dated 28 July 1787 by
and between Phebe MYERS widow of Joseph MYERS, deceased,
Joseph MYERS, William MYERS and Jesse MYERS sons of Joseph
MYERS, deceased, and Phebe his widow and Sarah SMITH wife of
John SMITH and Phebe MOORE wife of James MOORE and Ann MYERS
and Mary MYERS, daughters of Joseph MYERS, deceased, and
Phebe his widow. It was agreed that the widow, Phebe, shall
inherit the third of all the estate, real and personal, of
her deceased _____ during her natural life and after her
decease the third shall be the property of her eldest son,
Joseph, who shall maintain his mother during the term of her
life and Jesse MYERS and Mary MYERS shall be paid 20 pounds
each on the sale of the land of Joseph MYERS, deceased. The
remaining part of the estate, exclusive of the above, to be
equally divided between William and Jesse MYERS and Sarah
SMITH, Pheby MOORE, Ann MYERS and Mary MYERS so that each
shall have an equal part. Signed by Sarah SMITH, Pheby MOORE,
Pheby MYERS, Joseph MYERS and Jesse MYERS in the presence of
John SMITH and William MYERS. The court decreed that within
six months after COOK paid to Ann MYERS $81.94 with interest
from 10 December 1808 and all costs of this suit, then Ann
shall by deed with special warranty at COOK's cost, convey to
COOK all her right, title and interest to the land mentioned
in the Bill of Complaint. The same decree was made in regard
to Sarah, both to be performed by 13 August 1810. Additional
decree: Ordered that Joseph MYERS, William MYERS, Jesse
MYERS, and James MOORE and Phebe his wife, absent defendants
against whom publication hath been duly made and they failing
to appear and show cause why the decree against them should
be set aside by appearing and answering the bill, it is
decreed that they convey to COOK all their right, title and
interest in and to the tract of land mentioned in the bill by
deed with special warranty and that they pay COOK his cost of
this suit. Receipt signed by Sarah SMITH, Ann MYERS and

114

Joseph SMITH that COOK paid as decreed and they conveyed the land to him, 10 December 1808. Receipt signed by John PLUMMER that he received for Moses PLUMMER the sum of 2 pounds and 10 shillings and for Ann MYERS the sum of 2 pounds and 5 shillings from Peter COOK, 30 December 1794. Receipt signed by James MOORE to Peter COOK for 15 pounds, 11 shillings and 1 penny in full for all the right, title and interest in the land claimed by himself and wife, 25 April 1797. Receipt from John SMITH to COOK for Sarah's part as one of the children of Joseph MYERS, deceased. Paid by 2 bushels of salt, cash paid your wife, woman's saddle, flax, cash for paper, paid taxes to Sheriff BUTLER, and side saddle for daughter Phebe SMITH = 13.19.0. Receipt signed by Jesse MYERS from COOK for 11 pounds in part pay of his right, title and interest in the land lying in "Monninggaley" County, 5 mo 27th 1792 and witnessed by John PLUMMER. Receipt signed by Jesse MYERS from COOK for 35 pounds in full for all his right, title and interest in the land, 20 day 9th mo 1796 and witnessed by John (x) CALEY. An account for Ann MYERS, daughter of Joseph MYERS, from Peter COOK: to money paid John PLUMMER on 30th of 12th month 1794 as per his _____ on your verbal order, a part of your legacy in the land, 1795 to cash paid by Josiah WOOD for hauling her goods from Loudoun to the Glades, to beef, 1797 to one cow hide, 1798 to upper and sole leather for a pair of shoes per self and Edon her son, first month to 34 lbs. beef, to one sheep paid in the presence of Ben JEFFERIES, to cash paid you by Joseph GREY which he owed me in boot of a horse, amount paid Ann MYERS for land. Total 16.0.6. The amount of her legacy of land = 15.12.2. Overpaid Ann MYERS = 1.8.4. Grant from the Commonwealth to Thomas CRAFT, assignee of Robert HARTNESS, dated 20 July 1784 for 400 acres by survey dated 26 April 1781 lying on the waters of Sandy Creek including his settlement made in 1773 and across the head of Nob Run. There is a list of a part of the estate of Joseph MYERS, deceased, which includes a case of drawers, 4 chains, 1 musket gun, 1 buccaneer gun, 2 iron pots, 1 pot and oven, 1 teakettle, 4 feather beds, 1 arm chair, 1 spinning wheel, sheep shears, steel yards, 4 cover lids, 4 blankets, cloth, linen, shovel and tongs, 5 sheets, saddle bags, a hat, 7 harrow teeth, 2 plows, 4 cows, 1 ox, 2 heifers, 1 bull, 4 steers, 1 swarm bees, 1 crosscut saw, 2 calves, 2 grindstones, bar iron, 2 bed ticks, 2 pair bedsteads, a loom, a goat, 2 great coats, 2 deer hides, 7 files, 12 augers, 9 chisels, smith tools, black horse, bald eagle colt, black mare and colt, 7 sheep, 7 hogs, broad ax, mallings and wedges, drawing knife, mattock, 2 wagons, lock and chain, shovel and saddle. See page 116 for announcement in a local paper from Monongalia County Court, November term, 1805.

Monongalia County ...
... November ... for
Peter Cook, ...
against
Joseph Myers, William Myers,
Jesse Myers, John Smith, and
Sarah his Wife, formerly Sarah
Myers, James More, and Phebe
his Wife, formerly Phebe Myers, and Ann Myers, which a-
foresaid Joseph, William, Jesse,
Sarah, Phebe and Ann were
all children, Heirs and legal
representatives of Joseph Myers, deceased.

Defend-
ants.

In Chancery.

THE Defendants Joseph Myers,
William Myers, Jesse Myers, Jas.
Moore and Phebe his Wife, formerly
Phebe Myers, not having entered their
appearance according to law, and the rules
of this Court, and it appearing to the fat-
isfaction of the court that they are not inhabitants of this commonwealth on motion
of the complainant it is ordered, that the
defendants appear here on the second Monday in March next, to answer the Complainants said bill : and that a copy of
this order be forthwith published for two
months succefsively in the Monongalia
Gazette and that one other copy be post-
ed at the door of the court house of this
county for two months.

Copy Teft.

J. EVANS, c. m c.

Morgantown, November 23, 1805.

All Perſons

WHO are indebted to me are hereby informed that Beef, Pork, or any kind of Grain, will be received in payment at the market price, delivered at Mr. Derings in Morgantown, any time between this and the first of November next. I hope this will be attended to, as after that day I shall proceed to close my accounts, and the money alone will then discharge the claims.

Wm. G. PAYNE.

Morgantown, August 31, 1805. tf

N. B. This request would not be made, but my own situation requires it.

Any pay made to Mr. Henry Dering in Morgantown, in Grain or Meat, will be received at his houſe, on my account, from this time until the 20th of next month, thoſe who do not pay by that time, ſhall be compelled by law.

Wm. G. PAYNE.

Morgantown, November 23, 1805.

ONE DOLLAR REWARD.

LOST near James M'Vicker's Tavern, on the 16th inſt. a ſaddle about half worn. It has been faced with ſcarlet, but the facing is nearly worn off; one of the ſtirrups has but one plate in the bottom, the other has two, one ſteeple and plate is loſt. Any perſon who has foond the ſame and will return it to the ſubſcriber ſhall have the above reward.

JOHN REED

117

163b - 1811, Monongalia County Court. Davis SHOCKLEY and John
SULLIVAN summoned to answer a Bill in Chancery exhibited
against them by Thomas McKINLEY, 15 July 1803. McKINLEY's
complaint: On 21 March 1803, SHOCKLEY mortgaged two feather
beds to him for the purpose of securing 10 pounds and 7
shillings payable on 1 July next which was secured by John
SULLIVAN. He said SHOCKLEY and/or SULLIVAN refused to pay
the debt and therefore he brings suit. Deposition of Fauquer
McRAE heard at his house on 9 November 1805: He heard SHOCKLY
say he owed the debt and would pay it shortly. June 1810
term, decree. Receipt signed by McKINLEY to SHOCKLEY and
SULLIVAN dated 14 November 1811 for $18.86 the balance in
full of a decree from the Monongalia County Court.

163b - 1810, Monongalia County Court. Thomas WILSON summoned
to answer a Bill in Chancery exhibited against him by George
WADE, Aaron WADE, Mary WADE, Elijah WADE, Alexander WADE,
Thomas WADE, Abigal WADE, Sarah WADE, Elisha WADE, Elizabeth
WADE and Hosea WADE, which said Elijah, Alexander, Thomas,
Abigal, Sarah, Elisha, Elizabeth and Hosea are infants under
the age of 21 years, by their next friend Aaron WADE, all the
aforesaid being children, heirs and legal representatives of
Alexander WADE, deceased, 14 November 1803. Complaint of the
WADE heirs: On 20 March 1782, a certificate was granted by
The Board of Commissioners to William ROBISON, assignee of
John MURPHEY, for 400 acres of land on Scotts Mill Run. On 4
April 1786, ROBISON sold the land to Alex. WADE, deceased.
Nathan HALL and Elizabeth HALL, administrators for William
ROBISON, deceased, had the land surveyed for only 306 1/2
acres which survey bears the date of 25 February 1787. Nathan
and Elizabeth HALL assigned the 306 1/2 acre tract to Alexander WADE, deceased, and the grant from the Commonwealth was
issued to Alexander WADE bearing date 19 October 1789. Nevertheless, a certain Thomas WILSON obtained a grant from the
Commonwealth for the same tract, which said grant bears a
much younger date than that which issued to WADE. They hoped
WILSON would convey his claim to them with special warranty,
but he refused and therefore they bring suit. Thos. WILSON's
answer: He said he had a patent from the Commonwealth for 306
1/2 acres which be has reason to believe includes in its
bounds the same land described in the patent to Alex WADE.
He holds the patent as assignee of John ROBISON, heir-at-law
to William ROBISON, deceased, viz, a certificate from the
Commissioners granted to William ROBISON, assignee of John
MURFEY, dated 20 March in the 5th year of the Commonwealth
and entered with the surveyor on 1 May 1781 and the survey
made by virtue of said certificate in the name of William
ROBISON dated 20 February 1787. He believed John ROBISON was
the sole heir of William ROBISON and sold the said land with
others to a certain Hugh MASTERSON as may more full appear by
his obligation dated 24 February 1796 and MASTERSON assigned
the obligation with certain exceptions to Elijah BEALL and

himself (WILSON) on 2 March 1796. About the same date, John was about to leave Monongalia County and go to Kentucky and in compliance with the said obligation did appointed Elijah BEALL, his Attorney in Fact, to convey the said land. Later, BEALL assigned the survey to him by virtue of which he obtained a patent dated 11 July 1798. He said he was absent from home several weeks doing business "in the lower part of this state" and he believed Elijah paid Hugh the balance of the purchase price before he returned home. John ROBISON and Hugh MASTERSON left for Kentucky before he returned home and he has not seen them since. He said he knew nothing of the claim or complaint by the WADE heirs until long after he had purchased and paid for the land. Sometime later, Alexander WADE called on him (speaking through the window of his house) and requested him to convey the land to him. He asked WADE to enter his home and examine the papers and if his claim was valid, he would "let him have the land on terms similar to those granted to others who were situated like him" which was to value the land (not regarding the improvements) and he would take half the valuation and relinquish his right. WADE did not show any papers but offered to pay the fees expended in obtaining a grant, he refused and WADE "made off not well pleased." He never saw WADE again and did not see WADE's title until this suit was brought. He said WADE's heirs never maintained the claim and that he paid all taxes at due times, never had use of the land or profit from it or even saw it except as a traveller going along the road. He believed the WADE heirs and their ancestors had use and occupation of the land. He said if he did not have a legal claim, then it was not in his power to make a deed to WADE and if he did have a legal claim he hopes he can retain the land "as he is an innocent purchaser" and paid a valuable consideration of $1250 for the land besides the fees. He prayed the court to dismiss the case and award him reasonable costs, 19 June 1804. William ROBISON's patent for 306 1/2 acres on waters of Scotts Mill Run adjoining Peter POPINOS and corner to John DENT and adjoining Evan WATKINS and Nicholas HORNER/HARNER, 11 July 1798. Conveyance Bond signed by John (x) ROBISON, of Nelson County, Kentucky, to Hugh MASTERSON, of the same place, for $10,000 dated 24 February 1796. ROBINSON was bound to convey to MASTERSON all of his claim in and to any and all lands of William ROBINSON, deceased, in whatsoever county, either by patent, deed, survey or entry and all and every part or parcel as may be found necessary. Witnessed by Thos. WILSON, J. H. WILLIAMS, Hugh McNEELEY and J. WILLIAMS. At the bottom of this document, MASTERSON assigned all his right, title and interest and claim in and to the above to Elijah BEALL, except two tracts now held by entry, one on the east fork of Booths Creek adjoining the Middle Fork about three miles from the Monongahela River, at a place called RATCLIFF's, containing 400 acres by virtue of a Treasury Warrant No. 17242 dated 23

June 1783 and the other tract by entry containing 300 acres on the east side of the Monongahela River adjoining and above the lands of Thomas MILLER held by virtue of a part of a Pre-emption Warrant No. 200 dated 19 April 1782. Witnessed by John EVANS, Robert TRIPLETT, Andrew HESS and Hedgeman TRIPLETT. Elijah BEALL assigned his right, title, interest and claim into the above to Thomas WILSON, 19 April 1797. Witnessed by Thomas FORSTER, Alexander HAWTHORN and Math'w WILSON. Plat of the land in dispute surveyed by Samuel HANWAY, SMC, dated 10 January 1801. Power of Attorney signed by John (x) ROBISON to Elijah BEALL dated 2 March 1796 and witnessed by J. H. WILLIAMS, Hugh McNEELEY, John WILLEY and Hugh MASTERSON. Certificate from the Land Commissioners to William ROBISON, assignee of John MURPHY, for 400 acres, including his settlement made 1773, dated 1 May 1781 and signed by John P. DUVALL, James NEAL and William HAYMOND. Bond signed by William (WR) ROBINSON to Alexander WADE dated 4 April 1786 for 600 pounds specie, to be calculated at the rate of 7 shillings and 6 pence per Spanish Milled Dollars, whereby ROBINSON promised to survey, return and patent in the name of WADE 400 acres of land in Monongalia County agreeable to a certificate from the Land Commissioners to be paid at the expense of ROBINSON. The patent or deed to be delivered before 1 March next. Witnessed by Basel CRATHER, Theo. PHILIPS and Thomas FREEMAN. Receipt signed by MASTERSON dated 2 March 1796 for $250 in full of his part of the pay due to him for lands sold to Elijah BELL and Thomas WILSON. "In the name of God, Amen, I Alexander WADE of Monongalia County being perfectly in my senses do will and bequeath my property to my dear wife and children as follows. First: the place that I now live on to remain in the hands of my wife during her life or during the time she remains my widow, the children to be raised of the place till the two youngest boys comes of age, Elisha and Hosea, then for my children all to have an equal share, the eldest boys to have their share out of that land up the river as far as it goes, namely Aaron, Elijah, Alexander and Thomas. The rest of my property to be praised and to remain in the hands of my wife for her to sell or keep as she sees fit. Like wise for her to collect all debts due to me and to discharge all just claims against my estate, all to be in the hands of my wife as long as she remains my widow or during her life. There is a mare and one colt and one cow to be charged to George or taken out of his part. Likewise Aaron's mare and saddle to be charged to him or taken out of his part. Likewise the price of Mary's saddle to be taken out of her part. Then for them all to come in for an equal share alike from the eldest to the youngest. Like-wise (I) do leave and desire that Aaron shall be in with his mother to assist her in all of my affairs and do conclude," 20 April 1803. Signed by Alexander WADE and witnessed by William BILLINGSLEY, Jesse BUSSEY and Sias BILLINGSLEY. July 1810 term, decree and judgement for the defendants.

163b - 1810, Monongalia County Court. Jacob FOULK and Christian MADERA summoned to answer a Bill in Chancery exhibited against them by Nicholas MADERA, 1 September 1806. MADERA's complaint: On 11 September 1802, he entered into a contract with FOULK for a lot and improvements for which he was to make payment and receive title. FOULK gave him possession of the lot and a small house and conveyed the lot to him by a Title Deed dated 21 December 1803. The deed was torn and damaged in such a way that it could not be admitted to record. He complained that FOULK did not comply with the Article of Agreement and he (MADERA) did not pay him as agreed because of FOULK's failure to perform and therefore he brings suit. FOULK's answer: He said he never put MADERA in possession of the lot. He said he complied with all the requirements of the agreement and notified MADERA when the materials were ready, but he neglected or refused to proceed with the building. Christian MADERA took the obligation from Nicholas and a deed was made to Christian for the lot. He said he did not want a quarrel with brothers, Nicholas and Christian, and allowed Nicholas to relinquish the contact to Christian. He then received the sums of 3 pounds and 16 shillings and $52 from Nicholas and a note on DUNN and QUICK and gave the notes to the proper person for collection and Nicholas received from him $10 in part of the said notes. He said he re-imbursed Nicholas for the said sums and $50 in pottery ware, a $20 watch and several other sums as shown by receipts. He said Christian paid him in full and satisfied him in stone work, 29 April 1807. Christian MADERA's answer: He knew about the transaction from the beginning but did not know that Nicholas was ever given possession of the lot and house thereon. He did know that Nicholas tore down and carried away a small house that was on the lot. He said he was now in possession of the lot by virtue of a deed given him by FOULK and he paid FOULK for the lot by performing the original contract to FOULK's satisfaction but in a different way, 29 April 1807. Article of Agreement by and between Jacob FOULK and Nicholas MADERA, both of Morgantown, dated 23 December 1802, whereby FOULK promised to pay MADERA $60 in store goods on 1 June and $40 in specie on 1 July and $100 in potter's ware such as Nicholas may chose at the price he sells to the storekeepers on 1 May next. Nicholas promised to build a cellar on FOULK's lot and to find all and every of the materials, work to be laid in good lime mortar, the size of the cellar to be 35 feet in width and 36 feet in length and 6 feet and 6 inches in height and four butmans, each butman sufficient to raise a good chimney. FOULK promised to dig out the cellar as soon as Nicholas was ready to begin work in the spring, so as not to be stopped from work. Nicholas to point the cellar both inside and out and to make 2 courses of range work in the front. Witnessed by Barth. CLARK, G. HITE and Jos/Jon GRATE. Article of Agreement by and between Nicholas MADERA and Jacob FOULK/FULTZ, dated 11 September 1802, whereby Nicholas binds himself to build FOULK a brick house to be 36' x 35', the brick walls to be 24' in height and 14" thick, all the materials to be furnished on the spot ready for building by FOULK by 1 May 1804. The front of the building to be "pincelled" and all to be finished on or before 1 August 1804. Nicholas to furnish his attendant and to find board and diet for himself and hands and the work to be done in a workman like manner for which FOULK is to pay Nicholas one house and lot which FOULK purchased of John EVANS, son of Thomas EVANS, lying and being on Water Street. FOULK to make a good title when the work is perfected and to pay him $25 cash in 12 months after the work is completed. Nicholas to have possession of the lot on or before 20 September 1802, signed by FOULK and MADERA in the presence of William TINGLE and Samuel DOUGHERTY. "Received of Nicholas MADERA 3 pounds and 16 shillings against the lot I sold him adjoining GIBLER and Thomas DOOLITTLE and running down Bimbo Lane to Front Street," 4 September 1805. Signed by FOULK and witnessed by John Wood THOMPSON. Another receipt, dated 8 June 1805, written the same for $52 received from MADERA, signed by FOULK and witnessed by Wm. GEORGE. Between 10 October 1802 and 17 October 1803, Nicholas MADERA received from FOULK 3 pounds, 10 shillings and 4 pence worth of potter's ware. "18 March 1805, received of Nicholas MADERA a note of hand against Jacob DUNN and Martin QUICK for the sum of $50 which I am to collect for said MADERA and if I should trade it for my use, I will deliver MADERA 4000' of plank," signed by FOULK in the presence of Davis SHOCKLEY. "24 January 1805, received of Jacob FOULK 1 pound, 3 shillings and 6 pence on the cash part of our agreement about building of his house," signed by Nicholas MADERA. Indenture dated 21 December 1803, whereby Jacob FOULK and Gertrude his wife conveyed to Christian MADERA, for $120, "a certain lot of ground lying and being in Morgantown described on the General Plat of said town by Number 90 and bound as follows, to wit, beginning at the Monongahela River and running with Bimbo Lane to Front Street and with Front Street to a lot _____esly Joseph RHODES and with the same to the river, thence down the river to the beginning, it being the same lot which FOULK lately purchased from and was conveyed to him by John EVANS with the same reservations which was originally made by Zackquil MORGAN, the proprietor of the said town." Jacob and Gertrude FOULK signatures are torn away. Witnessed by E. DAUGHERTY and Wm. TINGLE. Deposition of Jno. WAGNER: Early in April 1804, Nicholas MADERA was at work for him in daubing a house when WAGNER, FOULK and Christian MADERA happened to gather at the place where Nicholas was working. The two MADERA men and FOULK discussed who was to get the lot and each said it was immaterial who got it and Nicholas told Christian if he would take the contract to build the brick house, and FOULK agreed, he would be willing for FOULK to convey the lot to him (because who ever got it would pay for

it), 28 January 1809.   Deposition of Thomas McKINLY: About a
year ago, he happened at FOULK's shop where Nicholas and
Christian MADERA and FOULK were in dispute concerning the lot
in question. Nicholas said, "damn the lot" that he did not
care anything about it and he said, "pay me for it and take
it."   The three men named a day to meet at Mr. COOPER's and
settle the dispute, 28 January 1809. Deposition of Michael
CLOUSE: Last summer he heard Nicholas say he care nothing
about the lot and he was asked if Nicholas was drunk and he
said, "I cannot say," 28 January 1809. Deposition of Davis
SHOCKLEY: In 1805 or 1806, FOULK told him if Nicholas would
give him an order to _____'s share, for $10 he would convey
the lot to him. He said he did not know when the deed was
made to Christian MADERA but he supposed it was made under
the same proposal and he understood the $10 was the balance
due for the lot. He heard FOULK ask Nicholas how he paid
FOULK for $50 worth of crockery ware and a watch. Nicholas
said he owed for the ware and said he had an account against
the watch. SHOCKLEY said he knew Christian MADERA built a
stone house for FOULK and supposed it was in payment for the
lot, "he heard so from FOULK," 28 January 1809. John COOPER's
deposition: A day was set for FOULK and MADERA to meet with
him and settle the dispute. He said FOULK attended and was
waiting the better part of the day but MADERA did not attend.
John W. THOMSON's deposition: Nicholas was at work at the
smoke house of A. WINEGAR's about 1805.   FOULK came to
Nicholas and told him if he would give him an order for $10
or $11 in stone goods, he would make him a deed for the lot.
He did not know the answer or whether the goods were paid. It
was agreed between FOULK and MADERA that they would abide by
the decision of Arbitrators Samuel HANWAY and Rolley SCOTT.
They were of the opinion that FOULK pay all costs and his
bill be dismissed and that he release Nicholas from the
contract in as much as they considered Nicholas had performed
the contract in full.   Decree: The court decreed that
Christian MADERA, by deed with Special Warranty, convey to
Nicholas MADERA the lot in dispute and subject to the rent
for said lot. That FOULK and Christian MADERA give full
quiet and peaceable possession of the lot to Nicholas and
that they pay all costs.   FOULK prayed for and obtained an
appeal to the Superior Chancery Court at Staunton. FOULK and
Christian MADERA signed this Appeal Bond to ensure they would
prosecute the appeal and pay costs and abide and perform the
decree in this cause in case the decree aforesaid shall not
be reversed, secured by John COOPER on 16 June 1810.

163b - 1810, Monongalia County Court. Complaint of William
JAMES: In May 1809, he owed John BISHOP a debt and BISHOP
brought suit against him before Justice Frederick HARSH and
recovered judgement for $11.50 debt and interest plus costs.
He was unable to pay the judgement at the time and applied to
Justice HARSH to stay execution of the judgement by giving

bond and security according to an Act of Assembly provided for that purpose. Under the direction of Justice HARSH and Constable Christian WHITEHAIR, he entered into a bond payable to WHITEHAIR in May 1809 conditioned for the payment of the said judgement. He paid all costs then due and since the expiration of the Act of Assembly as mentioned above, an execution issued and was levied on his property and the same advertised for sale. WHITEHAIR abandoned the execution and turned it over to the County Clerk with directions to issue an execution against him in favor of WHITEHAIR. He made great effort to procure the money to pay the debt and had enough to satisfy the full amount and called upon WHITEHAIR to settle. WHITEHAIR informed him that the papers were in the hands of Attorney Thomas WILSON. He then called on WILSON with the money to pay the debt and WILSON told him he did not have the papers and while they spoke, he was served a summons from the County Court and threatened to be jailed unless he immediately paid the amount and accumulated costs or give up property. In order to avoid going to jail, he paid the full amount due to BISHOP. He said all documents to prove his claim were in the hands of Justice HARSH and he was away from home at this time. He prayed the Court to summons WHITEHAIR and BISHOP to be questioned in a Court of Equity and to grant him an injunction to stay WHITEHAIR and all others from further proceedings on the judgement, 10 July 1810. Another complaint against John BISHOP and similar complaints against Henry BISHOP and Christian BISHOP are filed and dated the same. 11 August 1810, William JAMES agreed to dismiss all injunctions and pay them in full and WHITEHAIR agreed to pay JAMES $16 in part payment of expenses and costs.

163b - 1810, Monongalia County Court. Zackarah TOLER summoned to answer a Bill in Chancery exhibited against him by Jesse and William PAYNE, 26 August 1807. PAYNE´s complaint: William PAYNE sold 200 acres to TOLER, he having legal right to the 200 acres, but the legal title belonged to Jesse PAYNE. William made a deed to TOLER dated 4 April 1802. TOLER agreed to pay $200 for the land when requested, but they never took a bond or obligation from him to secure the payment. TOLER left the Commonwealth about two years ago and left no personal property. They prayed the court to sell all the land or so much of it as to satisfy the debt with interest and that TOLER be summoned to be question in a Court of Equity, Attorney Mathew GAY for PAYNE. July 1810 term, decree for the plaintiff. See page 125 for **Monongalia Gazette** advertisement.

William G. PAYNE & Jesse PAYNE vs Zachariah TOLER

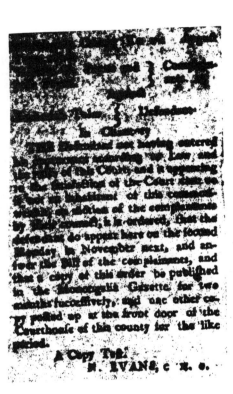

163b - 1810, Monongalia County Court. James STAFFORD summoned to answer a Bill in Chancery exhibited against him by Jane/ Jenney/Janey/Jean FRY, formerly known as Jenney JEFFERIES and by her intermarriage with John McFALL, changed her name and was afterwards called and known as Jenney McFALL and after the death of McFALL, she changed her name by intermarriage with Godfrey FRY, 16 June 1803. FRY's complaint: Godfrey FRY ran away and left Jenney FRY in very indigent circumstances and she understood he married another lady in Pennsylvania and from fear of prosecution ran away again down the Ohio River. STAFFORD agreed by a sealed writing to sell her 30 acres of land to be circumscribed by certain bounds (as she was unable to read, he read or had the obligation read to her) which said writing was destroyed. At the time of the sale, she delivered to STAFFORD a mare and saddle valued by STAFFORD at 30 pounds Virginia currency in full for the consideration, an estimated value of the 30 acres, and she was put in possession of the land where she has continued to live since that time. She said STAFFORD denied he sold her the land and denies that he gave his obligation. She prayed the court to summon STAFFORD to be questioned in a Court of Equity. Daniel COX made oath that he gave James STAFFORD notice cn 18 December 1804 "across Cheat River, the river being fast riding and the ice running so that a boat could not cross," 22 December 1804. STAFFORD's answer: He said there "was not sufficient in law or equity for FRY to have or maintain her action against him" and he prayed the court to quash the judgement and bill. FRY swore that Samuel HARMAN, Benjamin BALDWIN and others were material witnesses for her and they were aged and infirmed and she petitioned the court to take their depositions, 3 January 1804. FRY swore that William CREACRAFT was a material witness for her and he was about to move out of the Commonwealth down the river and prayed the court to take his deposition, 6 November 1804. FRY swore that John RAMSEY and Catherine his wife and George BAKER were material witnesses for her and she prayed the court to hear their depositions, 10 December 1804. George BAKER's deposition: Shortly after STAFFORD bought a mare from Jane McFALL, he was at STAFFORD's place and he showed BAKER the mare and said what a fine mare he had and said he gave a high price, 30 acres of land out toward Lemy JOHNS, 22 December 1804. William CRECRAFT's deposition. Some years ago, he heard STAFFORD say that he bought a horse creature from Jean FRY, alias Jean McFALL, and was to give her 30 acres of land for the horse, 22 December 1804. John RAMSEY's deposition: Sometime in the latter part of 1794, he heard STAFFORD say he bought a mare and saddle from Jean McFALL and he was to give her 30 acres of land and he had marked the land, 22 December 1804. Samuel HARMAN's deposition: After FRY and STAFFORD viewed the land, he heard STAFFORD say they marked off 30 acres or there about. FRY said it must be measured 30 acres, 21 January 1804. Benjamin BALDWIN's

126

deposition: STAFFORD told him about buying the mare and said he paid 29 or 30 acres of land for her, 21 January 1804. Joseph JEFFRY's deposition: He went with FRY and STAFFORD to view the land and afterwards STAFFORD said there was 29 or 30 acres in the bounds and FRY said it must measure 30 acres, 21 January 1804. Richard TIBBS' deposition: Some years ago, he was at FRY's home and was asked to read a bond which he understood was for the conveyance of the 30 acres. While looking at the bond, Michael CAIN, who was in the house, snatched the instrument out of his hands and threw it in the fire saying the bond was more against FRY than for her, 21 January 1804. July 1810 term, bill dismissed and judgement for the defendant.

163b - 1810, Monongalia County Court. James PINDALL, Eliza'th PINDALL, Elizabeth PINDALL, Jeremiah PINDALL, Levi PINDALL, Rachel PINDALL and Jacob PINDALL, (Elizabeth, Jeremiah, Rachel and Levi PINDALL infants by their guardian James PINDALL appointed for that purpose) summoned to answer a Bill in Chancery exhibited against them by John SULLIVAN, 12 July 1804. SULLIVAN's complaint: About 1791, he purchased from Thomas PINDALL a lot of ground bounded on the west by Water Street, by a lot claimed by Jacob FOULK, formerly Asa DUDLEY, on the south, by the Baptist Meeting House and burying ground on the east and by an alley on the north where now and since that time he has resided. He agreed to pay 16 pounds for the 1/2 acre lot. Within the next year, he paid Thomas PINDALL 6 pounds and 11 shillings, a part of the price of the lot. During all this time, he and PINDALL took each others word on the agreement, not having entered into any writing until 30 December 1793 when PINDALL gave his obligation in the penal sum of 50 pounds for the conveyance of the lot and he gave to PINDALL his two obligations in the amount of 8 pounds each, it being the 16 pounds agreed price of the lot. One note was due one year from date and was credited with the above mentioned 6 pounds and 11 shillings. The other 8 pound note was payable two years after date. He learned that Jacob PINDALL has a title to the lot and that he sold the lot to his brother, Edward PINDALL, and Edward sold the lot to Thomas PINDALL, his brother. Thomas PINDALL departed this life, intestate, about the last of 1794 or early 1795 leaving James, Elizabeth, Jeremiah and Rachel PINDALL, his children and heirs all infants and very young and Jacob, Levi and Elizabeth PINDALL heirs of Edward PINDALL, deceased, who departed this life about 1795. He said Jacob PINDALL, as the brother and one of the administrators of Thomas PINDALL and guardian to Thomas' infant children, possessed himself of all the books, patents, deeds and bonds belonging to Thomas' estate, both real and personal, and still remains possessed of them. And Jacob PINDALL, as brother and administrator to Edward PINDALL, possessed himself of all the books, patents, deeds and bonds relative to Edward's estate. He said he had

reason to believe that certain contracts were made whereby
Jacob conveyed the lot to Edward or was bound by writing to
do so and other obligations on other acquaintances given and
discharged as consideration by Edward to Jacob for the lot,
all which came into the hands of Jacob by virtue of his
administrations. He said he hoped to prove that contracts
were made (Jacob being privy to them) whereby Edward conveyed
the lot to Thomas or was bound by writing or otherwise to
convey the lot to Thomas. He said Jacob knew that he purchased the lot long before the death of Thomas and never
raised any objection until after Thomas died and he called
upon him for payment for the amount of the two obligations
well knowing they were for the lot. On 6 May 1801, Jacob
drew upon him, in favor of Waitman FURBEE, for $14 in part of
one of the obligations, which he paid and payment in brick in
further payment of the obligation. If any balance remained
he was ready and willing to pay when he can have a title to
the lot. He said he had improved the lot and made it valuable
and it is a home for him and his "numerous family." He said
he had lived in town a long time and Jacob PINDALL resided
there until lately and Jacob never pretended any claim and
they knew each other very well. He said Jacob had started a
suit in ejectment against him to turn him out of possession
of the lot. He prayed the court to summon the defendants to
be question in a Court of Equity. Jacob PINDALL's answer: He
said he had a title to the lot from Zack'l and Daniel MORGAN
dated 6 September 1785. He said he never sold the lot to his
brother, Edward PINDALL, and did not know the transactions
between Edward and Thomas respecting the lot. He said it was
true that he was one of the administrators to Thomas PINDALL,
deceased, and guardian to James, Elizabeth, Jeremiah and
Rachel PINDALL and he was administrator of Edward PINDALL and
guardian to Levi and Elizabeth and possessed the books,
patents, deeds and bonds of both estates together with his
co-administrator, John McFARLAND and Judith PINDALL. He
denied all knowledge of any contracts and knew nothing of
Thomas selling the lot to SULLIVAN. He said the two
obligation were a part of Thomas' estate and SULLIVAN made
some payment on the notes and gave a draft in favor of
Waitman FURBEE but he does not know the obligations were in
consideration of the lot. He said SULLIVAN had put considerable improvements on the lot and being a poor man with a big
family, he had no wish to turn him out considering the
improvements would be equal to the use of the lot until he
should want it himself. He prayed the court to dismiss the
bill and decree that SULLIVAN deliver peaceable possession of
the lot, 20 December 1804. Conveyance Bond signed by Thomas
PINDALL to SULLIVAN dated 30 December 1793 whereby Thomas is
bound to convey to SULLIVAN the lot adjoining Asa DUDLEY and
the Baptist Church, witnessed by John EVANS and James
COLLINS. The joint answer of James, Elizabeth, Jeremiah and
Rachel PINDALL heirs of THOMAS PINDALL, deceased, and Levi

and Elizabeth PINDALL heirs of Edward PINDALL, deceased, by James PINDALL their guardian: They knew nothing of the sale of the lot because they were all infants under the age of 21 in 1793. They could not understand why Jacob "should suffer his claim to be dormant for upwards of 13 years" and he had not "until lately communicated to any of them any surmise or hint of such claim" although he was in the habit of telling them, and especially James, the condition of the estate. They said Jacob could not have "forgotten the inequity of his claim during the 13 year period because at no time did he reside further than 5 miles from the lot in the possession of SULLIVAN" and at times he lived in the same town and they knew each other. They "repel with indignant distain detraction conferred on their parents by Jacob insisting on their fraudulent alienation of his property and feel confident that an examination of the contrast in character apparent among the brothers no traces of suspicion will remain extant to the prejudice of Thomas and Edward," 14 November 1804. (Thomas and Edward died in the spring or summer of the same year). Deposition of Josiah HOSKINSON: On a day when District Court was held, he and SULLIVAN were at the tavern next to the Courthouse and Jacob PINDALL came in and later SULLIVAN asked PINDALL when he could get a title to the lot. PINDALL said he was going to court that day to administer his brother Tom's estate and as soon as that was done, he would take care to see SULLIVAN should have his title providing the balance was paid. He said he knew SULLIVAN lived on the lot before Thomas' death and that Jacob lived in this county and he believed on his farm west of the river about 4 miles from town. Thomas EVANS' deposition: Sometime after Jacob PINDALL became administrator to Thomas PINDALL, deceased, he heard Jacob say he should have to bring suit against SULLIVAN for the balance due to the estate of his brother Tom. He said he knew Thomas had possession of the lot in his lifetime and in one season he raised a crop of oats and afterwards a crop of buckwheat on it and he heard Tom boast that those two crops were near equal to the price he paid for the lot. This was some years before the death of Thomas and he knew SULLIVAN lived on the lot about 2 years or more before Thomas died. Deposition of William CHIPPS: Before the death of Thomas PINDALL, when Jacob PINDALL was deputy sheriff, he heard him say if he had a lot in Morgantown near the jail, he would build on it and live there, 25 January 1804. "To Mr. John SULLIVAN, 6 May 1802, Dear Sir, please to answer to Waitman FURBEE $14 on note I have against you and Thomas PINDALL and you will oblige me Jacob PINDALL, administrator," executed by John (x) SULLIVAN. June 1810 term, decree and appeal. The court decreed that the legal title to the lot of ground was held by Jacob PINDALL and that no more than an equitable right descended to the other defendants which equity has passed through their ancestors to SULLIVAN which is hereby decreed to him. The court ordered that Jacob PINDALL convey the lot to SULLIVAN and that he pay all costs. Jacob PINDALL prayed for and obtained an appeal to the Superior Chancery District Court at Staunton. Appeal Bond signed by Jacob PINDALL to ensure he would prosecute the appeal and pay all costs and awards secured by Thomas McKINEY, 15 June 1810.

163b - 1810, Monongalia County Court. James TATE's complaint: He was in the business of manufacturing iron and entered into an agreement with John DAVIS whereby DAVIS agreed to give him "3 1/2 tons of pigs for one ton of iron" delivered at DAVIS' Furnace. A short time after, he and DAVIS agreed the iron was not to be delivered unless so directed by DAVIS. DAVIS delivered a quantity of "pigs" and in return a quantity of iron and beef was delivered to DAVIS. DAVIS informed him that "his pigs were of a superior quality and produced more and better iron than any pigs on this side of the mountains." From the described quality of the pigs and that DAVIS was to take the iron made from them at a certain price in payment for the pigs, he was induced to allow DAVIS $53.33 per ton, when in fact good pigs could be procured at other furnaces on this side of the mountain for $42.33 per ton in cash. He said DAVIS' pigs were of very poor quality and produced inferior iron and DAVIS refused the iron made from his own pigs and failed to notify him when to deliver the iron and demanded one ton of good iron. TATE said he knew he did not owe so much, proposed to balance the debt and then pointed out the iron made from DAVIS' pigs and offered the iron to DAVIS in discharged of the debt, DAVIS refused and would not allow the $53 balance to be erased by accepting the iron. DAVIS immediately brought suit and obtained a judgement against him. He said he could not attend the trial and prove his evidence because his wife was ill. He prayed the court to grant him an injunction to stay execution of the judgement until DAVIS could be questioned in a Court of Equity. John DAVIS, for the use of Standish FORDE, obtained a judgement against James TATE for $113.97 plus costs. TATE prayed for and obtained an injunction to stay execution of the judgement until the matter could be heard in a Court of Equity. TATE signed this Injunction Bond to ensure all costs and awards would be paid in case the injunction should be dissolved secured by Jno STEALEY, 6 July 1804. DAVIS' answer to the Bill of Injunction: TATE contracted with him to deliver to his iron forge on Deckers Creek one ton of bar iron in exchange for every three and one half ton of pig iron delivered by DAVIS to Peasant Furnace. The current price of bar iron was 6 pence per pound. If TATE had delivered the iron at the time specified, it would have been equal to that sum to him. Through the default of TATE not delivering the iron as agreed, he was subject to sundry inconveniences and disadvantages. He said TATE agree to weigh off and lay away his (DAVIS') proportion of bar iron when each ton was worked up ready to be delivered whenever he should call for it. He said he often called for a proportion of the bar iron and TATE put him off with promises from week to week. When he did deliver a part of the iron, there would be a proportion still due. He said TATE wanted to be paid in cash which was expressly contrary to the contract. In the trial of this suit, TATE "brought in a discount against him for a quantity of beef which it seems was allowed to him." He said it was unjust as it was delivered on the assumpsit of James GILLISPIE who ran Pleasant Furnace at the time of the delivery of the beef, nearly one year before the contract was entered into and at the time was not charged to his account. He said he asked TATE to make settlement before suit was brought and TATE refused to pay the balance. At that time, he was indebted to Standish FORD, of Philadelphia, and assigned the balance due to FORD agreeable to the contract, 8 August 1804. Affidavit of Andrew WININGS: The pig iron he worked for TATE which was got of DAVIS was the worst he ever worked and would not make merchantable iron. He left the forge on account of the pigs being bad and not fit to make iron. He was at the furnace and knew the pigs to be from DAVIS. He was a refiner of iron by trade and told DAVIS the pigs were not good and DAVIS got angry with him for saying so. He told DAVIS he might make the best market he could of them. In his opinion the pigs were damaged from some mismanagement of the furnace and he had purchased pigs from Mr. SQUIRES and John HAYDE, of Pennsylvania, at $43.33 per ton payable in iron at $6 per pound. He said he never bought pigs at any other place. He said he tried to work DAVIS' pigs at OLIPHANT's and HUSTON's Forge and could not make good iron at either place and he left HUSTON's Forge on account of the pigs would not make good iron, nor could any workmen at those places make good iron from them, 6 October 1804. Robert MINNIS' affidavit: He lived at Mr. DAVIS' Furnace and knew that TATE got pigs of him. DAVIS told him TATE disputed paying him because the pigs did not make good iron. He knew TATE refused to take pigs from others who had them but TATE had promised to take some of the pigs from DAVIS and did take them at $50 per ton. He said some of the iron sent in exchange for the pigs was sent to the blacksmiths who refused working it on account of it being bad. He said he never heard of any complaint from OLIPHANT or others who got several tons of the pigs, but they wanted white pigs and sometimes they would pick them, 6 October 1804. John STEALEY's affidavit: At TATE's request, he went with him to OLIPHANT's Forge to learn if they could make good iron from DAVIS' pigs in order to ascertain if TATE's workmen were doing their duty. OLIPHANT informed them the pigs would not make good iron and said he purchased pigs from DAVIS at $40 per ton payable in bacon, whiskey and other trade and purchased pigs from John RAMSEY at a like price and payable in meat. He said DAVIS told him he had refused TATE's iron, 6 October 1804. June 1810 term, injunction perpetuated and judgement.

131

163c - 1810, Monongalia County Superior Court. Josiah GORDAN, schoolmaster, was arrested and confined in jail on charges of "ravishing" Roda STEPHENSON, 17 January 1810. On same day, the Justices of the County were summoned to appear on Monday 22 January 1810 to hear the case. List of names, possible jurors: Dudley EVANS, Augustus WERNINGER, William N. JARRETT, John STEALEY, John W. DEAN, William JOHN, Thomas MILLER, James BEALL and Nicholas VANDERVORT. Peggy CORNEL, Ledda BUTCHER and Mary MIRES gave bond to ensure they would appear on 22 January 1810 and give "such evidence as they knoweth against said GORDAN." Rhoda STEVENSON, Lydia BUTCHER, Polly MYERS and Peggy COMWELL/CORNWELL gave bond to ensure they would appear in Superior Court on 4 April 1810 to give evidence to the Grand Jury, 24 January 1810. Testimony of Rhoda STEVENSON: She said, "GORDAN came to me he got some ink and put it in a little gourd, put it on the shelf and got a string and tied me, threw me on the floor, then pulled out his cork and put it in mine, he pounded the head as hard as he could, I hollered, children in the house but small, sent the little boys out of the house to catch chickens for him (GORDAN), door was shut a little piece. When tied with string, he (GORDAN) said he was a going to cure my fits, pulled a round stick out of his pocket." Testimony of Peggy CORNWELL: "About a hundred yards from the house heard a noise and went to the house and found prisoner in the very fact, standing up, prisoner went out off the house and returned and wished to make it up and his trousers down and the girls clothes up, very much abused in her private parts, that she never had been regular." Testimony of Lydia BUTCHER: "I found the girl in a bad situation and fresh done she and the parts, it appeared some person had entered the girl's body forcibly, the girls face was bruised, it did not appear that the girl had consented. She can bring water, milch the cow, hoes corn and ____, go errands and home again." Testimony of Polly MYERS: "I found the girl in a bad situation appearing that she had been much abused for more than if been done by her consent, it appeared as if some person had entered her body forcibly, the girl complained of the private parts being very much injured." James WALLS summoned to testify in behalf of GORDAN, 24 January 1810. Matthew GEORGE and Thomas MURPHY summoned to testify in behalf of GORDAN, 22 January 1810. Adam CAMP summoned to testify in behalf of GORDAN, 23 January 1810. No verdict found.

163c - 1810, Monongalia County Court. John LEWIS and Samuel BOWERS summoned to answer the complaint of Michael CROW for the non-payment of a debt due by note, 8 December 1810. No property found by Constable James McVICKER.

163c - 1810, Monongalia County Court. Dunken F. McCRAY summoned to answer William MASTER in a plea of debt due by account, 10 November 1810.

163c - 1810, Monongalia County Court. James N. SCOTT summoned to answer Ephriam BAIN in a plea of debt due by account, 6 March 1810. No property found.

163c - 1810, Monongalia County Court. Anthony LOTT summoned to answer Christopher BIXLER in a plea of debt due by account, 3 September 1810. No property found by Constable John KNOX.

163c - 1810, Monongalia County Court. Joseph REED summoned to answer Joseph CAMPBELL in a plea of debt due by account, 13 September 1810. No property found by Constable G. HITE.

163c - 1810, Monongalia County Court. Isaac PAUGH summoned to answer Michael GRADY in a plea of debt for $40. Warrant for attachment of his property issued 3 February 1810 by Justice David MORGAN.

163c - 1810, Monongalia County Court. Robert WOODS summoned to answer John COOPER in a plea of debt, 15 June 1810. No property found by Constable G. HITE.

163c - 1810, Monongalia County Court. Isaac PRICE Sr. summoned to answer Jesse COMBS in a plea of debt due by a Due Bill, 12 November 1810. No property found by Constable John BROWN. No property found by Constable Aaron BARKER.

163c - 1810, Monongalia County Court. David SCOTT summoned to answer Forbes BRITTON in a plea of debt due by note, 31 December 1810. No property found by Constable G. B. HOSKINSON.

163c - 1811, Monongalia County Court. Duncan F. McCRAY summoned to answer John BURK in a plea of debt due by account, 29 October 1810. November 1810 term, judgement for $2.50 and $.30 costs, Jno STEALEY, foreman. $2 paid on the above judgement, no property found to make the balance, 13 February 1811 by Constable G. HITE.

163c - 1809, Monongalia County Court. William PRICE, yeoman, (not found) summoned to answer an indictment against him for assault and battery on the body of William F. CASEY, 18 March and 16 May 1809. CASEY summoned to give evidence to the Grand Jury, 18 March, 21 August and 17 November 1809. CASEY and Elijah BUTLER (not found) summoned to give evidence to the Grand Jury, 16 May 1809. On reverse of one of the documents, "any other person might prosecute and bring Mr. CASEY as a witness, witness might be an infant or from court, by the information of Benjamin BARTON." "We the Grand Jury find him guilty and amerce him in $50," Charles BYRN, foreman.

163c - 1810, Monongalia County Court. John CRISTY summoned to answer John JOHNSTON in a plea of trespass on the case $100 damage, 4 May 1807. JOHNSTON's complaint: In 1806, he delivered to CRISTY a horse of the value of $100 for which he was to receive another horse of equal value. He said CRISTY had not paid the horse in exchange nor any other thing nor any part thereof and therefore he brings suit. Notice from JOHNSTON to CRISTY of intent to hear the depositions of John POINTS and John LOVELL at the tavern of William N. JARRETT, 7 November 1807. John POYNES' deposition: He knew both parties and knew that JOHNSTON swapped a horse to CHRISTY in consideration of receiving a horse in Pennsylvania that had strayed from CRISTY. JOHNSTON was to pay CRISTY $15 provided he received the horse. They agreed JOHNSTON would go after the horse but he understood JOHNSTON never went after the horse, 14 November 1807. Deposition of John LOVELL: He knew the parties and knew of the deal but did not know the details. He was employed to get his father to go with CHRISTY to Pennsylvania to prove the horse and knew the swap took place in June 1806, 14 November 1807. August 1810 term, dismissed.

163c - 1809, Monongalia County Court. Samuel FRUM, laborer, summoned to answer a presentment against him for assault upon John WATTS, shoemaker, 11 and 17 November 1809. John WATTS summoned to give evidence to the Grand Jury, 17 November 1809. A list of names, possible jurors: David TROWBRIDGE (crossed out), John S. ROBERTS, James CARRELL, William THOMAS, John CHISLER, Archibald LANHAM, Samuel WILSON, James SCOTT, Abraham HESS, Benjamin DOOLITTLE, Thomas DOOLITTLE, John BAKER, John LYNCH, Grafton WHITE, Jacob SMITH, Joseph ONEAL, Henry HAMILTON, Benjamin HAMILTON, William JOSEPH, James CLELAND, John RAMSEY, Edward EVANS, Benjamin SAYRE and James BRAND.

163c - 1810, Monongalia County Court. Notice to Michael and Philip SHIVELY (not found) from George SMITH, one of the Overseers of the Poor, of intent to motion the court to render judgement in favor of the Overseers for $15, "which from your joint and several recognizances appears to be due the said Overseers on 8 February last for the expense of supporting a bastard child begotten by Michael on the body of Catherine TOUTHMAN," 1 and 20 February 1810. John SHIVELY summoned to testify in behalf of the Overseers of the Poor, 18 March 1810. February 1810 term, proved and continued until tomorrow, judgement.

163c - 1810, Monongalia County Court. At a 12 March 1806 court, James WILSON recovered against Benjamin THORN a judgement of $82 and $68.15 and costs for damages in a covenant made between them. Isaac REED secured bail for THORN and neither party had paid the judgement nor had THORN surrendered himself to jail. THORN and REED summoned to show cause, if any they can, why this judgement should not be paid, 22 November 1806. March 1810 term, dismissed and judgement confessed for costs.

163c - 1810, Monongalia County Court. At a court held 11 August 1803, John SNIDER, assignee of William MARTIN, recovered against Thomas LAZELL, Amos SMITH (no inhabitant) and George SMITH $395 debt plus costs. Thomas, Amos and George summoned to show cause, if any they can, why SNIDER should not have execution against them, 27 February 1809. March 1810 term, dismissed, agreed and judgement for the defendants.

163c - 1810, Monongalia County Court. One sorrel mare and one black horse, the property of Enos WEST, was attached at the suit of Ralph BARKSHIRE for $20 debt with interest from 25 December 1808 plus costs. In order to retain possession of his property until time for public sale or his debt was paid WEST signed this Delivery Bond secured by Simion EVERLY, 6 February 1810. March 1810 term, judgement.

163c - 1810, Monongalia County Court. James BROWN and Reubin CHALFANT summoned to answer Joseph ALLEN in a plea of debt for $32 and $10 damage, 10 May 1810.

163c - 1809, Monongalia County Court. Jarrett BALL indicted on charges of assault on Joseph JENKINS Jr. by the information of Alexander HAWTHORN and John WAGNER, "two of our own body," 3 and 22 November 1808, 11 May and 21 August 1809. HAWTHORN and WAGNER summoned to give evidence to the Grand Jury, 22 November 1808, 11 May and 21 August 1809. BALL not found on any of the above dates.

163c - 1809, Monongalia County Court. Benjamin WHITE Jr., mason/laborer, summoned to answer an indictment against him for assault upon John CLARK, yeoman, 17 October and 22 November 1808 and 11 May 1809. WHITE not found on any of the above dates.

163c - 1810, Monongalia County Court. Amos CHIPPS summoned to answer Doctor Adam S. SIMONSON in a plea of debt for $72.03 due by note dated 14 September 1807 and $30 damage, 17 September 1807. Appearance Bond signed by Amos CHIPPS in the presence of Rachel CHIPPS secured by Thomas R. CHIPPS, 23 September 1807. March 1810 term, dismissed by order of the plaintiff's attorney.

163c - 1810, Monongalia County Court. Jacob FOULK prayed for and obtained an attachment on the property of John TAYLOR for $50. Attachment Bond signed by FOULK to ensure all costs and awards would be paid in case he be cast in the suit secured

by John COOPER, 13 January 1810.   Nicholas CHISLER summoned
as garnishee, 13 January 1810. Attachment levied on 7 chairs,
2 dining tables, 1 small table, 1 loom, 1 bowfatt?, bureau,
corn in the loft (the quantity not known), 1 bay horse, 4
hogs, 2 kettles, some kitchen furniture, 3 beds and bedding
and 1 Franklin stove by Constable F. HITE, 13 January 1810.
Davis SHOCKLEY summoned to testify in behalf of FOULK, 14
March 1810. March 1810 term, judgement.

163c - 1810, Monongalia County Court. Henry RUNNER prayed for
an   obtained   an attachment on the property of Charles
EDELBLUTE for $40 debt.   Attachment Bond signed by RUNNER to
ensure all costs and awards would be paid in case he should
be cast in the suit secured by William G. PAYNE, 19 February
1810. Four month note signed by Charles EDELBLUTE to Henry
RUNNER for $40 dated 4 September 1809, payable in bar iron
and witnessed by Robert HAWTHORN. Attachment levied on one
feather bed, 1 coverlet, 1 blanket, 1 sheet, 2 pillows, 2
trunks, 2 flat irons, 4 chairs, 1 table, 1 small bake oven, 1
iron bound barrel, 1 looking glass, 1 water... The remainder
of the list is too dark to read. March 1810 term, judgement.

163c - 1810, Monongalia County Court. Thomas WARMAN summoned
to answer Ralph BARKSHIRE in a plea of debt for $92 and $10
damage, 9 January 1810.   March 1810 term, dismissed by order
of the plaintiff.

163c - 1809, Monongalia County Court. John CHIPPS summoned
to answer Mathew GEORGE, assignee of William G. PAYNE, in a
plea of non-payment of a debt, __ December 1809. No property
found. December 1809 term, judgement for the plaintiff for
$5 debt and $.30 costs.

163c - 1809, Monongalia County Court. Warrant for an attachment on the property of Amos CHIPPS to satisfy George BARNES
in a plea of debt for $24.50, 27 February 1809. BARNES prayed
for an attachment on CHIPPS´ property because he feared
CHIPPS would leave the Commonwealth before he paid his debt.
Three notes signed by Amos CHIPPS to George D. BARNES all
dated 12 January 1809 and payable on or before 1 March 1809.
One note for $4.50 and the other two for $10 each and all
witnessed by C. BARKSHIRE. Attachment levied on one horse by
Constable James McVICKER. Attachment Bond signed by BARNES
to ensure all costs and awards would be paid in case he
should be cast in the suit secured by W. TINGLE, 27 February
1809. Appearance Bond signed by CHIPPS secured by Augustus
WERNINGER in the presence of Amaziah DAVISON, 2 March 1809.

163c - 1810, Monongalia County Court. Joseph GRAHAM (no
inhabitant), assignee of John GUTHREY/GUTHRIE, summoned to
answer a Bill of Injunction exhibited against him by Samuel
BALDWIN, 2 December 1803. BALDWIN said the note was payable

in Pennsylvania currency and not Virginia currency and he believes the note to have been paid in full and "that he is so informed by John E. BILLS," 10 November 1803. On 10 November 1802, GRAHAM obtained a judgement against BALDWIN for 10 pounds ($33.33) with interest at 6% from 29 February 1796. BALDWIN prayed for and obtained an injunction to stay execution of the judgement until the matter could be heard in a Court of Equity. Injunction Bond signed by Samuel (x) BALDWIN to ensure all costs and awards would be paid in case the injunction should be dissolved secured by John Andrews BALDWIN, 18 November 1803. March 1810 term, dismissed by order of the plaintiff, signed by Samuel (x) BALDWIN in the presence of Fielding KYGER. March 1810 term, dismissed, agreed and judgement for the defendant.

163c - 1810, Monongalia County Court. William G. PAYNE summoned to answer Henry CULP, assignee of Jacob SHOWALTER, in a plea of debt for $30 and $10 damage, 2 May 1806. Note signed by PAYNE to SHOWALTER dated 17 July 1804 for $30, payable 15 October next and witnessed by John FUNK. Assignment to CULP dated 28 August 1805 in the presence of John FUNK. Order signed by Henry CULP to pay SHOWALTER the amount of the judgement he obtained against PAYNE, 15 September 1807. "Pay the within to Nimrod EVANS, he having paid me for the same," signed by John SHOWALTER in the presence of French S. GRAY. March 1810, plea waived and judgement and stay of execution.

163c - 1810, Monongalia County Court. William JAMES summoned to answer John BRANNON and Nancy his wife, late Nancy SHERIDEN, in a plea of debt for 20 pounds ($66.66) and $10 damage due by note dated 15 June 1807, 17 July 1809. JAMES signed a note to Nancy SHERIDEN payable nine months after date. Nancy married John BRANNON in 1808. Appearance Bond signed by William JAMES secured by Jas. C. GOFF, 8 August 1809. August 1810 term, dismissed by the plaintiff.

163c - 1810, Monongalia County Court. Samuel GANDY summoned to answer Samuel RICKEY in a plea of debt for $100 and $10 damage due by note dated 11 September 1806 and due two years from date exclusive of interest until due, 20 June 1810. October 1810 term, dismissed and fees paid by GANDY on 19 November 1810.

163c - 1810, Monongalia County Court. David SCOTT summoned to answer John WELLS, assignee of John JENKINS, in a plea of debt for $40.66 and $20 damage, 27 April and 21 July 1808. Note signed by David SCOTT to John JENKINS dated 21 May 1807 for $44.66, payable 1 September next and witnessed by Alexander SCOTT and Alexander JENKINS. Assignment to WELLS not dated. Receipt signed by Wm PAYNE dated 31 May 1810 whereby he received from Maj David SCOTT 7 bushels of corn at 0.2.6 per bushel ($2.91) in part payment of his note to

WELLS. Receipt signed by Wm PAYNE dated 10 July 1810 whereby he received from Maj David SCOTT a cow and calf valued at $11.50 in part payment of his note to WELLS. Receipt signed by Wm PAYNE dated 13 July 1810 whereby he received from Maj David SCOTT 3 bushels of corn at $.42 per bushel and $1.25 in part payment of his note to WELLS. On 14 August 1810, Daniel SCOTT confessed judgement in the presence of Alexander SCOTT.

163c - 1810, Monongalia County Court. Russell POTTER, late Sheriff of Monongalia County, summoned to answer Benjamin WILSON in a plea of trespass on the case damage $67.63, 11 March 1807. "This action is brought in trespass on the case for the sum due as by a list of clerk's fees delivered to E. HORTON, your deputy sheriff, and not accounted for." "A list of fees due the Clerk of Harrison County put in the hands of the Sheriff of Monongalia County to collect: George MARTIN for the use of Robert TRIPLETT $2.98; Benjamin REEDER Esqr. $5.72*; Ryenier HALL $1.88; Elijah HARRYMAN $1.75*; Adin BAYLES $.88; James PETTYJOHN $3.18 and $3.78; Levi MORGAN $1.87; Ralph BARKSHIRE $.40; Martin CURRENT and wife $5.68; William STUART $.40 and $1.21; Henry BARNES $1.75; William MAXSON $1.75; Col David SCOTT $3.56*; Joseph WISBY $3.00* and $1.69*; David BAILS $3.12; Robert FITZGERALD $3.03*; Capt James THOMAS $7.87; Jeremiah ROBEY $1.75*; William MYERS $.92; Jonathan GANDY $.80; Adain MILCHER $1.75*; Caty SAXTON $1.35*; Col David SCOTT $6.06*. Total $67.63." Deputy Elihu HORTON received this list on __ __ 1804 and signed for the same in the presence of James EVANS. (* = bad notes collected by HORTON, total $29.66), September 1805. Appearance Bond signed by Russell POTTER secured by John and Simeon WOODROW, 31 March 1807. August 1810 term verdict and judgement. "We the jury find for the plaintiff $29.40 damage with 6% interest until paid," John CARTER, foreman.

163c - 1810, Monongalia County Court. Elihu HORTON summoned to answer William EVERLY in a plea of trespass on the case damage $50, 24 January and 21 March 1803. William EVERLY complained that Elihu HORTON owed him $50 for bacon. Deposition of Jesse EVERLY heard on 21 March 1806 before Justices John W. DEAN and Simeon EVERLY: In April 1802, he saw William EVERLY deliver to John CHISLER, for the use of Elihu HORTON, 550 pounds of bacon at 6 pence per pound amounting to 13 pounds and 15 shillings. John CHISLER and Enos WEST (not found) summoned to testify in behalf of William EVERLY, __ February 1804, 30 July 1808 and 14 August 1810. Jesse EVERLY, Enos WEST and John CHISLER summoned to testify in behalf of William EVERLY, 6 August 1804 and 5 August 1805. Jesse EVERLY summoned to testify in behalf of William EVERLY, 12 August 1804. __ ____ 18__ term, We the jury find for the plaintiff $45.63 and damages, S. SWEARINGEN, foreman. We the jury find for the defendant, G. DEIBLER, foreman.

163c - 1810, Monongalia County Court. William SNODGRASS summoned to answer John DRAGOO in a plea of trespass on the case damage $100, 12 March 1804. DRAGOO complained that SNODGRASS abused his horse when he (SNODGRASS) rode him to try his gaits in consideration of trade of horse between the two parties. DRAGOO said he warned SNODGRASS not to run or vex the horse as he was difficult to hold. DRAGOO said as soon as SNODGRASS mounted the horse he began to whip and spur the horse and put him to full speed in a rough part of the road, the horse fell and was crippled and rendered useless. DRAGOO said he was put at great expense and trouble in caring for the horse. He said SNODGRASS refused to make compensation for the damage he caused and therefore he brings suit. September 1810 term, judgement for the defendant.

163c - 1810, Monongalia County Court. Thomas FRETWELL summoned to answer Reason HOLLON/HOLLAND in a plea of debt for $85 and $40 damage, 26 March 1808. Note signed by FRETWELL to HOLLON for $85 dated 30 May 1805, payable 25 December next and witnessed by James TATE. HOLLON sued FRETWELL and FRETWELL was summoned to answer the suit. Before final judgement, Thomas FRETWELL died intestate and Agness FRETWELL, widow of Thomas, was appointed administratrix of his estate. Agness FRETWELL summoned to show cause, if any she can, why the suit should not proceed into final judgement, 22 August 1808. August 1810 term, dismissed, agreed.

163c - 1810, Monongalia County Court. Notice to Sarah BAYLES and Richard HARRISON from Able JONES of intent to move the court to render judgement against them on a forthcoming bond dated 19 June 1806 for $40 conditioned for the delivery of property which they have failed to do, 12 July 1810. One sorrel horse, the property of BOYLES, was attached at the suit of JONES. In order to retain possession of her property until time of public sale or her debt was paid BOYLES signed this Delivery Bond secured by Richard HARRISON, 19 June 1806. August 1810 term, judgement.

163c - 1810, Monongalia County Court. Reuben BULLARD summoned to answer James MANN in a plea of assault damage $500, 29 February 1808. Appearance Bond signed by BULLARD secured by Jno STEALEY, 8 March 1808. August 1810 term, non-suit and judgement.

163c - 1810, Monongalia County Court. Jacob FOULK summoned to answer Jesse MARTIN, assignee of Benjamin THORN, in a plea of debt for $198 and $50 damage, 4 March 1805. MARTIN sued FOULK and a summons was served on FOULK. Before the final judgement was rendered, MARTIN died intestate and on 14 June 1808, Presley MARTIN and Robert SCOTT were appointed to administer Jesse MARTIN's estate. FOULK summoned to show cause, if any he can, why MARTIN's administrators should not

proceed with the suit to the final judgement, 24 August 1808.
John W. THOMPSON summoned to testify in behalf of FOULK, 13
July 1810. Thomas McKINLEY summoned to testify in behalf of
FOULK, 29 February 1808 and 12 March 1810. Thomas McKINLEY
and William HOLLIFIELD (not found) summoned to testify in
behalf of FOULK, 9 November 1807, 29 February 1808 and 10
August 1810. Bail Bond for FOULK secured by John TAYLOR, 12
May 1805. Appearance Bond signed by FOULK secured by TAYLOR,
5 March 1805. Note signed by FOULK to THORNE for $198 dated
7 October 1803, payable in good horses on or before 2nd
Monday in October 1804 and witnessed by Charles SNODGRASS.
Assignment to MARTIN dated 30 November 1804 and witnessed by
John COOPER and James JOLLIFFE. "Sirs, please to pay Adam
WILLIS $_2.01 and I will give you credit on the _____ or
notes I sued you on in the County of Monongalia," signed by
Jesse MARTIN and accepted and signed by Jacob FOULK, no date.
"Sir, pay Mr. Frederick GIBBLER $5 worth of potter's ware and
I will give you credit on the note I bought of B. THORN on
what suit is brought and oblige yours," signed by MARTIN on
21 March 1806. "Mr. FULK, pay the bearer Miss WHITE 4
shillings in potter's ware and oblige your most sincere
friend and very humble servant," signed by MARTIN on 9 May
1806. "Mr FULK, if convenient pay William DEEN $3.09 in
potter's ware and I will give you credit on the note I sued
you for in the County Court," signed by MARTIN on 27 March
1806. DEEN received 9 shillings and 6 pence on the note, no
date. "Mr FULK, if convenient pay Thomas EVANS $3 worth of
potter's ware and I will give you credit on the note I sued
you for in the County Court," signed by MARTIN on 31 March
1806. "Mr. FULK, without fail pay Miss N. Eunice BOIDSTONE
$20.06 and I will give you credit on the notes I sued you for
in the County Court," signed by MARTIN on 9 April 1806.
"Received the amount of the within order by me," signed
Eunice BOIDSTONE on 10 April 1806. "And I received $1.50 at
the same time in addition to the above," signed by MARTIN.
"Sir, if on demand you will pay Boaz BURRISS $20 worth of
potter's ware and William BOIDSTONE $3 at the wholesale
proper prices and worth 14 to the dozen and oblige your
friend and very humble servant and I will give you credit on
the note I have sued you for in the County Court," signed by
MARTIN on 12 May 1806. "To Mr. FOULK, potter, please to let
Nancy HARRISON have 9 shillings and 6 pence worth of potter's
ware and this shall be your receipt for the same," signed by
MARTIN on 11 June 1806. "Mr. FULK, let the bearer, Miss
WEST, have 3 shillings worth of potter's ware and I will
credit you as mentioned in my other orders to you," signed by
MARTIN on 27 April 180_. "To Jacob FULK, potter, _____ more
particularly I wish you to pay Miss Jesse EVERLY 10 shillings
worth of potter's ware, then any order I ever sent to you for
or that depends my seed buckwheat. You will therefore pay it
without fail and oblige yours and I will give you credit for
it on the note I sued you for in the County Court," signed by

MARTIN on 30 June 1806. August 1810 term, We the jury find for the defendant, signed by Joshua HART, foreman.

163c - 1810, Monongalia County Court. Henry HENTHORN summoned to answer Thomas COWSER in a plea of debt for 8 pounds, 5 shillings and 2 pence ($22.03) Pennsylvania money and $10 damage, 16 March 1809. "At our settlement, I am indebted to Thomas COWSER or order the sum of 8.5.2 1/2," signed by HENTHORN on 22 April 1808 and witnessed by John SIMPSON. Appearance Bond signed by Henry HENTHORN secured by Jno HENTHORN on 31 March 1809. August 1810 term, plea waived and judgement confessed.

163c - 1810, Monongalia County Court. Charles STEWART summoned to answer James CLELAND in a plea of debt for $80 and $10 damage, 22 April and 31 May 1809. One month note signed by STEWART to CLELAND for $80 dated 22 February 1805, $50 payable in cash and $30 payable in pot metal and witnessed by James KNOX and Daniel COX. Appearance Bond signed by STUART secured by Thomas McKINLEY, 29 July 1809. August 1810 term, "We the jury find for the plaintiff the debt in the declaration mentioned, viz, $80 with interest at 6% from 22 March 1805 until paid with a credit of $30 paid 21 May 1805 and $10 on 10 October 1806 and $4 on 2 July 1807," signed by Joseph ALLEN, foreman.

163c - 1810, Monongalia County Court. Nathan ASHBY summoned to answer William DARLING in a plea of debt for $50 and $10 damage, 3 October 1808. Note signed by ASHBY to DARLING for $50 dated 9 October 1806, due 18 August next, payable in fat cattle and witnessed by Moses ROYSE. Appearance Bond signed by ASHBY secured by Samuel POSTLEWAIT, 29 October 1808. August 1810 term, "We the jury find for the plaintiff $50 the debt in the declaration mentioned with interest at 6% from 18 August 1807 until paid," Joseph ALLEN, foreman.

163c - 1810, Monongalia County Court. Stephen ROOT and John PAYNE summoned to answer Nehemiah CRAVENS in a plea of debt for $32.33 and $10 damage, 15 June 1807. Note signed ROOT and PAYNE to CRAVENS dated 12 February 1803, due October next. It was proven to the court that John PAYNE and Stephen ROOT were partners by the evidence of Samuel HANWAY. ROOT not an inhabitant of this Commonwealth. August 1810 term, "We the jury find for the plaintiff $32.33 the debt in the declaration mentioned with interest at 6% from 15 October 1803 until payment," S. WOODROW, foreman.

163c - 1810, Monongalia County Court. Amos CHIPPS summoned to answer Samuel DAUGHERTY in a plea of debt for $55 and $10 damage, 17 September 1807. Note signed by CHIPPS to DAUGHERTY for $55 dated 4 December 1806, due 1 March next, payable in bar iron at 6 pence per pound delivered in Morgantown and

witnessed by Nathan SPRINGER and Thomas CHIPPS. August 1810
term, plea waived and judgement confessed.

163c - 1810, Monongalia County Court. To Robert SCOTT, "Sir,
take notice that I intend to apply to the Monongalia County
Court on first day of their next April term to enter up
judgement against you for the sum of $10, that being the sum
owed the Overseers of the Poor for the said county on 12
January last past for the support of a bastard child begotten
by you upon the body of Elizabeth WHITE, a single woman, of
the said county," 28 March 1810, signed by William McCLEERY.
April 1810 term, judgement confessed.

163c - 1810, Monongalia County Court. William CHIPPS summoned
to answer a presentment against him for fencing up a road
leading from Little Falls on the "Monongalia" River to the
County Road at John BRAND's, 17 November 1809. Edward EVANS
Sr. and Joseph ONEAL summoned to give evidence to the Grand
Jury, 17 November 1809. John LYNCH and Edward EVANS summoned
to testify in behalf of CHIPPS, 8 December 1809. March 1810
term, "out of court."

163c - 1810, Monongalia County Court. James JEFFS summoned to
answer Reubin CHALFANT, assignee of Christian MADERA who was
assignee of Jacob MADERA, in a plea of debt for $43.13 and
$10 damage, 4 June 1810. Appearance Bond signed by JEFFS
secured by James WILSON, 11 June 1810.

164 - 1810, Monongalia County Court. Thomas MARTIN complained
that, in 1796, he bought a horse from Nester HARDIN for 15
pounds and at the time he paid HARDIN about 6 pounds and 12
shillings leaving a balance of perhaps 8 pounds and 8
shillings. He gave HARDIN his note for the balance and HARDIN
warranted the mare to be sound and healthy. Shortly after
the purchase, he found the mare to be very far gone with the
distemper called "yellow waters." He took her back and asked
HARDIN to cancel the sale and he refused. He ceased to work
her and made a great effort to cure her. He took her to the
best farrier in the neighborhood but she could not be cured
and died of the distemper. He said she had never been "any
profit" to him, nevertheless, HARDIN brought suit and
obtained judgement. The judgement laid dormant for sometime
until HARDIN assigned the judgement to Thomas BIRD and his
property was attached for the amount of the judgement plus
costs. He tried to settle with BIRD, they having dealings as
explained in later depositions. He prayed for and obtained
an injunction to stay execution of the judgement until the
matter could be heard in a Court of Equity. He said, "upon
reflection, he aught not to pay one cent of the judgement,"
12 August 1805. MARTIN prayed for and obtained an injunction
against HARDIN. Injunction Bond signed by MARTIN to ensure
all costs and awards would be paid in case the injunction

should be dissolved secured by Elihu HORTON, 9 September 1805. On January 1809, MARTIN signed another Injunction Bond secured by Peter FORTNEY. Nester HARDIN's answer to the injunction: The horse he sold to MARTIN was low in flesh but in good health. Because he only had the mare a short time, he sold her without warranty and she was fit for work and was used by MARTIN and grew fat. He said MARTIN did not bring the mare back or make any complaint and he (HARDIN) did not sue him for the balance due until he publicly declared he would never pay the same. He said he believed his judgement was obtained by confession from MARTIN and the long delay of payment was from the difficulty of enforcing payment. He continued by referring to judgements and notes mentioned in later depositions (abstracted below), 15 October 1805. George KELLER's deposition: Sometime in the winter of 1796, he attempted to buy a "creature" from Nester HARDAN and after looking at the mare he concluded she was sick and asked one of Mr CARTER's sons about her. He was told not to have anything to do with her and sometime later he asked Mr CONTERAL, who sold the mare to HARDAN, if the mare was sick and CONTERAL said, "he reacond not." Sometime later, he asked HARDAN if he sold the mare and HARDAN said he had sold her for $15. "Either HARDAN or his wife said if MARTIN kept on as he started he would stick in the first mud hole he came to," 4 October 1806. This deposition heard before Justices Nathan HALL and James S. WILSON at the house of James THOMAS. Thomas DEMOSS' deposition heard same time and same place: Sometime in the winter of 1796, HARDIN sent word to him that he bought a mare for him. A few days later, he went to see her and told HARDIN she was not sound and would not give more for her than her skin was worth. HARDIN argued that she was sound and when asked why her legs were swollen, he said "it was pacing meat." DEMOSS told HARDIN he had "packed a great deal of meat and never had a creature to swell." DEMOSS refused to buy her and HARDIN "turned away and swore he would cheat somebody with her." Three or four days later, he saw MARTIN with the mare and later HARDIN said he sold the mare to MARTIN. John KENNEDY's deposition heard at the house of Joseph SUMMERVILLE, in Harrison County, on 16 August 1806: MARTIN brought the mare to him to be bled and half her blood was yellow water and MARTIN left the horse with him to cure. He could not cure her even though he tried "some considerable time." He heard HARDIN tell MARTIN the horse was sound and he said MARTIN lost a crop on account of the horse not being able to work. Peter MERYDETH's deposition: One day he was in the woods near his house and saw a "creature" picking at the side of the Packhorse Road. He was in need of a horse and thought if he could find the owner he might make a bargain with him. On closer inspection, he saw the horse was distempered "which put him out of the thought of purchasing the creature." Later he happened at MARTIN's house, which he often did, and saw the mare and thought she still looked

distempered. He help MARTIN work his corn because MARTIN did
not have the benefit of a horse. He was on the jury when this
case was first tried and he believed the evidence to prove a
fraud, 1 March 1808. Samuel COBB's deposition heard in Randolph County before Justices Lerah OSBORN and Andrew MILLER on
19 October 1805: Sometime in the summer season after MARTIN
purchased a mare from HARDIN, MARTIN came to Sandy Creek to
run a piece of land for Benjamin WILSON and had the horse
with him. John ENGLAND and John PHILIPS were there and they
all heard ENGLAND ask MARTIN if that was the horse he bought
from HARDIN and MARTIN said it was and said the horse was in
good order and to the best of COBB's knowledge, MARTIN had
the horse at Sandy Creek at least three times. "We do certify
that the above witness came to this settlement on Wednesday
evening last from "Caintuck" and tells us that he intends to
leave tomorrow morning, which is given under our hands day
and date above written but said HARDIN knew nothing of him
until sometime on Thursday," signed by OSBORN and MILLER.
Sarah HARDIN's deposition heard in Randolph County at the
dwelling house of Andrew MILLER on 8 February 1806: She "was
very constantly at home" and MARTIN never brought the mare
back. John CASADAY's deposition heard by Justices David
MORGAN and James C. BEALL on 27 September 1806: He saw the
mare after MARTIN owned her and she was in good working order
and six months later he saw her again and she was still in
good order. Deposition of Rachel HANNAWAY heard by Nathan
HALL and James S. WILSON at HALL's house on 5 September 1806:
Sometime in the winter of 1797, she saw the mare and she was
in good order and MARTIN told her "she was a fine mare for he
had rode her with three bushels of grain and she did not mind
it more than if it had been a bird on her back." Charles
BYRN's deposition heard by John W. DEAN and Dudley EVANS at
Henry DERING's tavern on 22 February 1806: In the summer of
1805, MARTIN came to his house and requested him to read a
paper to him, the purport of which was that MARTIN had purchased a judgement against Thomas BIRD from Jeremiah HANLEY.
The judgement was obtained in Monongalia County Court. MARTIN
sent for BIRD with a view of settling the judgement with BIRD
on a judgement BIRD then had in the District Court for costs
against MARTIN. HANDLEY's judgement was for a larger sum than
BIRD's judgement against MARTIN. MARTIN asked BIRD for a note
to secure the difference, BIRD refused and no settlement took
place at that time. This deposition to be evidence in a suit
by injunction wherein Thomas MARTIN is complainant and Thomas
BIRD and Nester HARDIN are defendants. Thomas R. CHIPP's
deposition heard at the same time and place: He saw MARTIN
and BIRD sign the agreement which is lodged in the Clerk's
Office and dated 12 July 1805. In the case of Thomas MARTIN
vs Thomas BIRD and Nester HARDIN, BIRD and HARDIN petitioned
the court to compel MARTIN to give additional security as his
former security (HORTON) was insolvent and "unless he shall
do the same, on or before next term, that his injunction may

stand dissolved as of this day." MARTIN's attorney objected by reason that the plaintiff had not been served with this information and said the plaintiff lived in a remote part of the county. June 1810 term, dismissed as to one part and perpetuated as to balance and each party pay their own costs.

164 - 1810, Monongalia County Court. Abraham GUSEMAN summoned to answer a presentment against him for not keeping the road in repair from Rock Forge to Stephen MASTERS' of which he is Overseer, 28 June 1810. Samuel G. WILSON and Jacob HOLLAND summoned to give evidence to the Grand Jury, 28 June 1810.

Also in this file - - - - "We the Grand Jury do present John STEALEY for keeping his slave sawing on the saw mill at Rock Forge on the Sabbath day within two months last past by the information of James S. WILLIAMS and Samuel G. WILSON, two of our own body," signed by Jas TIBBS, foreman. May 1810 term, dismissed.

164 - 1810, Monongalia County Court. James G. WATSON obtained a judgement of $14.48 and "the defendant (John SHIVELY) not giving bond and security within 60 days agreeable to an act passed 31 January _____ for the Stay of Execution and for other purposes the property being taken and sold on a credit till the rising of the General Assembly of Virginia. Now if the above bound shall well and truly satisfy and pay the sum stated in the condition of this bond, with lawful interest on the same, on or before the rising of the General Assemble of Virginia then this obligation to be void or else to remain in full force," signed by John SHIVELY and secured by George D. BARNES, 4 November 1809. On 1 June 1810, WATSON swore he had not received payment or any part of it.

164 - 1809, Monongalia County Court. Samuel EVANS obtained a judgement against Zachariah BARKER for $6.90. BARKER signed this Stay Bond to stay execution of the judgement until the next Legislature of Virginia, secured by David SCOTT, 25 March 1809.

164 - 1808, Monongalia County Court. One bay mare, the property of John TAYLOR, was attached at the suit of Robert HAWTHORN for $17.50 plus costs. In order to retain possession of his property until time for public sale or his debt was paid TAYLOR signed this Attachment Bond secured by Jacob FOULK, 24 September 1808.

164 - 1808, Monongalia County Court. Robert FERRELL, Esqr. and James WEST Sr. summoned to answer Charity PRICKETT and John HOLT, administrators of the estate of Josiah PRICKETT, deceased, in a plea of non-payment of a debt for $10.55, 10 September 1808. Six month Stay Bond signed by FERRELL to stay execution of the judgement secured by Samuel WEST, 2 October 1808.

145

164 - 1808, Monongalia County Court. Two coats, the property
of William CHIPPS, was attacked at the suit of David SCOTT
for $6.67 plus costs. By virtue of an Act of Assembly passed
10 December 1793 for the relief of insolvent debtors, CHIPPS
signed this bond secured by Amos CHIPPS, 22 July 1808.

164 - 1808, Monongalia County Court. One sorrel mare, the
property of Thomas LAIDLEY, was attached at the suit of Isaac
Hite WILLIAMS. Six month bond signed by LAIDLEY to ensure he
would pay his debt secured by John GARVIN and John PAYNE, 7
May 1808.

164 - 1810, Monongalia County Court. Rachel BILLS swore
before Justice John STEALEY that on "26 July last past at the
house of Ruth BILLS, she was delivered of a female bastard
child and the said bastard child is likely to become
chargeable to the county and that John W. THOMPSON, potter,
did get her with child," 3 August 1810. THOMPSON summoned to
appear and give sufficient security of $100 for his personal
appearance at the next court and then and there to abide by
and perform the order of the court in pursuance of the Act of
the General Assembly entitled "An Act for the Poor and
Declaring Who Shall be Deemed Vagrants," 3 August 1810.

164 - 1810, Monongalia County Court. Peace Warrant for Samuel
HALL, laborer, to keep the peace toward all citizens and
especially toward William HALL, 27 July 1810. August 1810
term, quashed and discharged.

164 - 1810, Monongalia County Court. Matthew GEORGE, assignee
of William GEORGE, assignee of James THOMAS, complained that
John MAN owed him $50 by virtue of a note dated 13 September
1805, payable in good trade on or before 1 May 1806. MANN
summoned on 19 March 1807. Bail Bond for MANN secured by
James CURRANT, 11 May 1807. Appearance Bond signed by John
(x) MAN secured by Jacob HULL and Thomas LEWELLEN in the
presence of William DRAGOO dated 1 May 1807. August 1810
term, dismissed by the plaintiff.

164 - 1810, Monongalia County Court. James FERRELL and Robert
FERRELL summoned to answer Barbara SNODGRASS and David
MUSGRAVE, administrators of Charles SNODGRASS, deceased, in a
plea of debt of 13 pounds and 19 shillings ($46.50) and $10
damage, 29 May and 31 August 1809. Appearance Bond signed by
James FERRELL secured by Adam FAST in the presence of Jacob
FAST, 4 August 1809. Note signed by James FERRELL and Robert
FERRELL to Lurenia WINDSOR or Charles SNODGRASS for 13 pounds
and 19 shillings, it being for goods bought at the venue of
James WINDSOR, deceased, to be paid 25 September 1796 and
witnessed by William SNODGRASS and John HARR. Lurenia WINDSOR
departed this life intestate without having received any part
of the debt leaving the whole business invested in Charles

SNODGRASS. SNODGRASS departed this life in 1807 or 1808 without having received any part of the debt. The administrators of Charles SNODGRASS now bring suit to recover the debt. ____ 1810 term, We the jury find for the plaintiff $46.50 debt with interest at 6% from 26 September 1796 until paid, John CARTER, foreman.

164 - 1810, Monongalia County Court. Felix SCOTT and Presley MARTIN summoned to answer Samuel HARMAN, assignee of James CAIN, in a plea of debt for $57.50 and $10 damage, 28 April and 31 May 1809. Promissory Note signed by SCOTT and MARTIN to James CAIN for $57.50, no date, payable in pot metal and bar iron delivered to JACKSON's or STALEY's Forge on or before 1 January 1809 and witnessed by Lemuel JOHN and William JOHN. Assignment to HARMAN dated 4 November 1808 and witnessed by Thomas CAIN. Bail Bond and Appearance Bond signed by Felix SCOTT and Presley MARTIN secured by Robert C. SCOTT, 25 July 1809. August 1810 term, We the jury find for the plaintiff $7.50 the debt in the declaration mentioned with interest at 6% from 1 January 1809, Joseph ALLEN, foreman.

164 - 1810, Monongalia County Court. Conrad SHEETS/SHEETZ summoned to answer Robert HAWTHORN, assignee of Jacob NUSE Sr., in a plea of debt for $75 and $50 damage, 22 October 1804. HAWTHORN complained that SHEETS owed him $75 by virtue of a writing dated 9 July 1804 and due 7 August 1804. SHEETZ came before the court and swore "he ought not be charged with the debt because the writing is not his deed," 9 April 1805. Bail Bond for SHEETZ secured by Frederick GIBBLER, 12 November 1804. Bail Bond for SHEETZ secured by Jacob NUSE, 1 September 1806. Jacob FULK summoned to testify in behalf of SHEETZ, 11 November 1806 and 10 March 1807. August 1810 term, dismissed.

164 - 1810, Monongalia County Court. Thomas CHIPPS summoned to answer Robert HENDERSON in a plea of trespass on the case, 27 February 1804. "Due Robert HENDERSON $48 of pot metal and him to deliver four fat steers at Pleasant Furnace and me to find a good hand to drive them and the pot metal to be delivered at James GELASKY's (GILLISPEY) old mill," signed by Thomas CHIPPS on 27 December 1802 and witnessed by David STEWART. David STEWART summoned to testify in behalf of HENDERSON, 22 July, 12 November 1805 and 12 August 1807. August 1810 term, abated by the defendant's death (CHIPPS).

164 - 1810, Monongalia County Court. Philip SHIVELY summoned to answer Benjamin BROWNFIELD Sr., assignee of George STREPEY, in a plea of debt for $85 and $10 damage, 11 May and 27 June 1810. Note signed by Philip SHIVELY to STREPEY for $85 dated 4 December 1806, due 1 April next and witnessed by John SHIVELY. Assignment to BROWNFIELD dated 26 November

1808 and witnessed by Samuel MILHOUSE.   Appearance Bond for
Philip SHIVELY secured by John SHIVELY, 27 June 1810.

164 - 1810, Monongalia County Court. Notice to William BOYLES
and John RYON from Thomas GRAYHAM of intent to petition the
court "to enter judgement and accord execution in the name
of" GRAHAM against BOYLES and RYAN "on your forthcoming bond
for the sum of $170 conditioned for the delivery of property"
which they failed to do, 29 May 1810.   Three good horses and
3 milk cows, the property of William BOYLES, was attached at
the suit of GRAYHAM.   In order to retain possession of his
property until time of public sale or his debt was paid
BOYLES signed this Delivery Bond secured by John RYAN and
witnessed by Matthew GAY, 7 December 1807.   August 1810,
judgement.

164 - 1811, Monongalia County Court. Arthur WILSON summoned
to answer James SMITH in a plea of covenant broken damages
$70, 3 July 1806.   James SMITH complained of a breach of
covenant against Arthur WILSON for that whereas WILSON, on 3
January 1806, agreed in writing that he owed SMITH 2 men's
saddles, $10 in cash and 3 "roram hatts" on or before 1 April
next.   SMITH said WILSON had not performed any part of the
agreement and therefore he brings suit, August 1806 term.
Appearance Bond signed by A. WILSON secured by John CARTER,
no date. Note signed by WILSON to SMITH dated 3 January 1806
and witnessed by John (x) HOSKINSON. August 1810 term, judgement for $35 debt, $10.50 interest, $10.29 suit costs, $.63
Sheriff's fee, $1.05 summoning jury and $4.75 to County
Clerk, John COOPER, foreman. "$23 of the within paid by N.
EVANS and the balance and all fees of suit paid to me by
Thomas WILSON," 10 August 1811, signed by James (x) SMITH in
the presence of B. WILSON.

164 - 1808, Monongalia County Court. William STIDGER and
David STIDGER (not inhabitants) summoned to answer a Bill in
Chancery exhibited against them by John STEPHENS, 1 February
1808. John STEPHENS' complaint: On 22 October 1801, he
purchased a 200 acre tract of land lying on Booths Creek from
William STIDGER, late of Monongalia County. STIDGER gave him
a Conveyance Bond conditioned for the conveyance of the land
with general warranty so soon as the balance of the purchase
money should be paid and he immediately took possession. He
extended to STIDGER 8 different notes of same date. Trusting
in the honesty of STIDGER, he made many and great improvements on the land and fully paid 6 of the 8 notes. He said
he was now ready to discharge the last two notes, but STIDGER
conveyed, or in some other way, disposed of the property to
David SIDGER and refused to make him a deed. He prayed the
court to summon William and David STIDGER to be questioned in
a Court of Equity. Conveyance Bond signed by William STIDON
or STIDOR, of Allegheny County, Maryland, to John STEPHENS,

148

of Monongalia County, dated 22 October 1801, for 200 acres of
land on Booths Creek joining lands of Thomas MILLER, William
TINGLE, William ROBE Jr., David SAYERS Jr., Henry BANKS and
William BUCKHANNON it being a part of a larger tract conveyed
by William TINGLE and Janney his wife to STIDGER on 28 August
1799 and duly acknowledged in court at September 1799 term.
The 200 acres to be laid off at the expense of STEPHENS in
the following manner, viz, to begin in the middle of any of
the original survey lines and run toward the middle of the
tract for quantity and including any of the four corners.
The deed to be made upon payment of the balance of the
purchase price and "without fraud or further delay." (1) Note
signed by STEVENS to STIDGER dated 22 October 1801 for 5
pounds in Virginia currency, payable in good merchantable
property delivered to STIDGER's house in Western Port at the
mouth of Georges Creek in Maryland on or before 22 October
1802 and witnessed by J. EVANS Jr. and Robert HAWTHORN. (2)
Note dated, worded, signed and witnessed the same, payable 23
October 1802. Assignment to Jacob PINDELL dated 25 October
1801 and witnessed by David SCOTT and James KNOX. PINDELL
assigned the notes to James JEFF on 12 October 1802 and
witnessed by Thomas LAIDLEY. (3) Note as above dated 20
October 1801, due 20 October 1802. (4) Note as above dated
22 October 1801, due 23 October 1803. #4 note assignment to
PINDELL dated 2 November 1801. #4 note assignment to James
JEFFS dated 21 October 1802 by PINDELL. (5) Note as above
dated 22 October 1801, due 20 October 1803. #5 note
assignment to PINDELL dated 2 November 1801. #5 note
assignment to Thomas EWELL dated 24 December 1803 by PINDELL.
Decree: The court ordered William STIDGER to convey the land
to John STEPHENS with general warranty and ordered David
STIDGER to convey "such title as he may have" in the land at
the same time and that the defendants pay all costs.

Also in this file - "Theophilus MINOR administrators with the
will annexed of Theophilus PHILIPS, deceased, vs John BARRETT
in Chancery." It is ordered and decreed that Theophilius
MINOR, Frances MINOR, Amos MINOR, Philip MINOR, Sarah MINOR,
Samuel MINOR, Matilda MINOR and Stephen MINOR, infants, do as
they severally arrive at the age of 21 years convey all their
several and respective right and title to the 300 acres of
land to John THOMAS and the defendants pay all costs. The
defendants Thomas BARRETT, John BARRETT, _____ WILLIAMS,
Thomas WILLIAMS, _____ BALDON, Elizabeth EVERHART, Adolph
EVERHART, Sarah CRAMER, Baltzer CRAMER, John PHILLIPS,
Theophilus PHILLIPS and Pamelia PHILIPS ordered to convey to
John THOMAS a good deed of all claim to the land which they
now or at any time held as heirs of Theophilus PHILIPS,
deceased. Most of this document is crossed out as if voided.

164 - 1809, Monongalia County Court. Benjamin FREEMAN summoned to answer the complaint of Jacob FOULK for George

HOSKINSON for non-payment of a debt due by note, 15 December 1809. December 1809 term, judgement for the plaintiff for $14.33 debt and $.30 costs, Jno STEALEY, foreman.

164 - 1810, Monongalia County Court. And'w OLIPHANT, assignee of Rese FLESON, obtained a judgement for $10.50 and costs against Zackquill MORGAN. MORGAN signed this bond with Jacob MADERA as security, to ensure the debt and interest would be paid on or before 31 May 1810, 18 March 1810. Bond assigned to Nimrod EVANS by OLIPHANT on 30 October 1810.

164 - 1809, Monongalia County Court. Replevin Bond signed by John PAYNE to secure his property which was attached at the suit of George SNIDER and sold at public sale. PAYNE was the highest bidder and signed this bond to ensure he would pay his debt in 12 months. This bond secured by John C. PAYNE, 12 September 1809. (Replevin Bond: a bond to protect or give security for the return to, or recovery by, a person of goods or chattels wrongfully taken or detained upon giving security to try the matter in court and return the goods if defeated in action.)

164 - 1809, Monongalia County Court. Replevin Bond signed by Isaac MAYFIELD to secure his property which was attached at the suit of William LOWRY and sold at public sale. MAYFIELD was the highest bidder and signed this bond to ensure he would pay his debt in 12 months. This bond secured by Hannah MARTIN, 5 February 1809. In one place the name of Pheobe MARTIN is used instead of Hannah MARTIN and in another place, Charles MARTIN is used instead of Hannah MARTIN. Hannah MARTIN signed the bond. (Replevin Bond: a bond to protect or give security for the return to, or recovery by, a person of goods or chattels wrongfully taken or detained upon giving security to try the matter in court and return the goods if defeated in action.)

164 - 1810, Monongalia County Court. Hester SMITH and William SMITH (not inhabitants), heirs of William Augusta SMITH, deceased, Samuel MERRIFIELD (no inhabitant), John MERRIFIELD, Mary MERRIFIELD, John HAIR/HARE and Elizabeth (MERRIFIELD) HAIR, John SPRINGER and Barsheba (MERRIFIELD) SPRINGER, heirs of Richard MERRIFIELD, deceased, summoned to answer a Bill in Chancery exhibited against them by William and Ann STEVENSON, 18 March and 2 June 1802. William STEVENSON and Ann his wife complained that on 16 May 1788, or sometime before that date, William Augusta SMITH owned title to 400 acres of land on the east side of the Monongahela River on the waters of Pricketts Creek. SMITH sold the land to Richard MERRIFIELD and gave a Conveyance Bond conditioned for the conveyance of the land to MERRIFIELD and gave MERRIFIELD full possession. MERRIFIELD made many and large improvements and resided on the land until his death. Later, MERRIFIELD sold 200 acres of the land

to David PATTERSON and gave his bond conditioned for the conveyance of the 200 acres lying next to the Monongahela River and gave possession to PATTERSON. PATTERSON believed full title belonged to Richard MERRIFIELD and sold 100 acres of the 200 acres to Robert McMULLEN and put McMULLEN in full possession of the 200 acres. With the consent of MERRIFIELD, McMULLEN was given possession of the bond from MERRIFIELD. McMULLEN requested MERRIFIELD to made a deed for the 200 acres to PATTERSON which MERRIFIELD delayed in doing. Suit was brought by McMULLEN against MERRIFIELD to compel him to honor his contract. MERRIFIELD said the title to the land was in the heirs of William Augusta SMITH who was then dead. STEVENSON said there were several depositions taken and a survey was made by order of the court. Before the final decree, Richard MERRIFIELD died and the suit was abated by his death. He said Ann STEVENSON, late Ann PIERPOINT, purchased from David PATTERSON all his right in and to the 200 acres and William STEVENSON purchased all the right and title of McMULLEN. He said William STEVENSON and Ann STEVENSON intermarried and united their claims to the 200 acres. He said he paid all obligations in full, but the above named defendants refused to make title for the various claims. He prayed the court to re-open the suit and summon the defendants to be questioned in the matter. "2 February 1802, This day I assign over all my right and title of 100 acres of land to William STEVENSON, it being for value received. The land lying in PRICKETT's Settlement and the same piece of land that I purchased of David PATTERSON and said PATTERSON bought of Richard MARYFIELD. But I, the said McMULLEN, do not become chargeable to said STEVENSON for any failure of said land so that said STEVENSON has no recovery back on me for any part thereof," signed by Robert (x) McMULLEN in the presence of James PINDELL and Thomas B. CHIPPS. Conveyance Bond signed by Richard MERRIFIELD to David PATTERSON for 200 acres (200 pounds Virginia currency), dated 16 May 1788 and witnessed by Samuel HANWAY and Charles GALLAGHER. Robert McMULLIN's deposition heard before Justices Samuel HANWAY and Dudley EVANS at the house of Hugh McNEELY on 3 April 1802: In 1788, he bought a piece of land from David PATTERSON which PATTERSON purchased from Richard MERRIFIELD. MERRIFIELD showed him the land and pointed out James MORGAN's line saying the land ran into MORGAN's survey and that part would have to be thrown out. He then pointed toward Pricketts Creek and said Robert FERRELL and Thomas LAIDLEY owned an entry there and the land ran into their tract and that part of the land must be thrown out. MERRIFIELD told him the land would run in on him farther than he expected. Later he met MERRIFIELD in Morgantown and asked him if PATTERSON paid for the land and MERRIFIELD said PATTERSON paid all but a trifle, not worth mentioning, and he forgave him because he had paid a long time before the debt became due and he should have the land if he (MERRIFIELD) had none left. Two or three years

later, MERRIFIELD came to him and offered to trade other land
for the land now in dispute and offered either improved land
or woodland for it and to leave the value of the parcels to
uninterested men and each party to pay to the other any
balance on either side which fell due. Order for Monongalia
County Surveyor to survey the land in dispute and return a
plat of the same to August Court next, May Court 1798. Order
for the surveyor to survey the land and return a plat to
November Court dated August Court 1798. Agreeable to this
order, Samuel HANWAY, SMC, by his assistant, Henry BARNES,
returned a survey dated 18 March 1802 of 200 acres where
Robert McMULLIN resided. Notice to the heirs of William A.
SMITH of intent to hear the deposition of Robert McMULLEN.
This notice left with the widow of W. A. SMITH on 22 March
1802 by Christopher TROY. On reverse of one of the documents,
"Mrs. Sarah SMITH, Springhill Township." June 1810 term,
the defendants having failed to appear or answer the Bill of
Complaint, the court decreed their failure was a confession
of guilt and ordered the defendants to convey their right,
title and interest in the disputed land to the plaintiffs and
the complainants "have, hold and enjoy full and quiet
possession" to the 200 acres and the defendants pay all costs
and be attached by their bodies or other proper process until
they perform this decree.

164 - 1810, Monongalia County Court. John CHIPPS summoned to
answer John GREEN in a plea of non-payment of a debt, 22
September 1810. October 1810 term, judgement for the plaintiff for $3.77 due by note and $.30 costs. Order directed to
Constable Jas. McVICKER to attach so much of CHIPPS' property
to satisfy the debt. No property found.

164 - 1810, Monongalia County Court. William N. JARRET swore
that the suit instigated against him by LEE, BROOK and DILLON
"is a transaction he knows nothing about, but by the information of his wife (late Mrs. McNEELY) that Noah LINSLEY,
Philip DODDRIDGE and Jacob KIGER will be material witnesses
for him in the case and therefore cannot safely go to trial
without their testimony," 4 August 1810.

164 - 1810, Monongalia County Court. John STEALY summoned to
answer a presentment against him by the Grand Jury as Overseer of the Street leading by the Widow BENNETT's, 14 April
1810. Larkin PIERPOINT and John SNIDER summoned to give
evidence to the Grand Jury, 7 June 1810.

164 - 1810, Monongalia County Court. Nancy HUGINS/HUGGINS,
widow; John, William, Ginnet, James, Liddy, Benj/Bucy, Rachel
and Sinthey HUGINS, heirs of James HUGANS, deceased, summoned
to answer a Bill in Chancery exhibited against them by John
SMITH, 8 January 1808. The defendants (HUGINS' heirs) were
not inhabitants of this Commonwealth. John SMITH complained

that on 13 April 1804, he purchased 100 acres of land from
James HUGINS. He paid part of the purchase price of $500 and
was given possession of the land. He gave a writing to HUGINS
dated 13 April 1804, signed by both parties and placed in the
hands of John McLAIN, Esqr. James HUGINS died not having
complied with their agreement and the title to the land
descended to his children who are under age of 21 and his
widow who has Right of Dower. HUGINS' heirs are as follows,
viz, Nancy HUGINS, widow; John, William, Ginnet, James,
Leady, Benj/Bucy, Rachel and Sinthey HUGINS. He prayed the
court to summon the above named to be questioned in the
matter and compel the Widow HUGINS to convey her Dower Right
and the right of her children by deed. He said he paid all
the purchase price except a small part not yet due and said
he hoped he would be ready to finish payment at due date.
Widow HUGINS said she was ready to relinquish her Dower Right
and the right of her children whenever SMITH made the last
payment or secured his debt in writing. Article of Agreement
between James HUGINS, of Monongalia County, and John SMITH,
of Pennsylvania, dated 13 April 1804, whereby HUGINS sold to
SMITH 100 acres "where HUGINS now lives." Payment as follows,
viz, $100 in hand 1804, $150 on 1 April 1805, $50 on 1 April
1806, 1807, 1808, 1809 and 1810. SMITH to have full and
peaceable possession and HUGINS to make a good deed at the
time of the last payment, signed by HUGINS and SMITH in the
presence of Mary McLAIN and Stephen McLAIN and written by
John McLAIN. On the reverse of this copy of the Article of
Agreement, a receipt signed by Nancy (x) HUGANS and William
AYERS, administrators of James HUGINS, deceased, to SMITH for
the balance in full of the within sum dated 10 November 1807.
The court decreed that the defendants by their attorney and
guardian, William McCLEERY appointed for that purpose, convey
to the plaintiff all their right, title and interest in and
to the said land, it being the same that James HUGINS
purchased from James DENWOODY on which the plaintiff now
lives, and the plaintiff to have, hold and enjoy full, free
and peaceable possession of the same and that the infant
defendants, so soon as he or she shall arrive to the age of
21 years or within six months after, unless he or she show
good cause to the contrary, do each one for himself or herself by joint deed convey to the plaintiff the land aforesaid. June 1810 term, decree entered.

164 - 1810, Monongalia County Court. Stephen MORGAN summoned
to answer George MORGAN in a plea of debt for $20, "it being
a penalty incurred by Stephen for failing and refusing to
execute a writ which issued from the court in favor of Davis
SHOCKLEY, for the use of George MORGAN, against Jesse PAYNE
for the sum of $14.19 with interest and costs when the writ
was delivered to Sheriff Stephen MORGAN and an offer made by
George MORGAN to show sufficient property of Jesse PAYNE to
satisfy the debt, which penalty is inflicted by the 14th sec-

tion of an act of the General Assembly entitled An Act to Reduce Into One All Acts and Parts of Acts Relating to the Appointment and Duty of Sheriffs and make return on 14th instant how you have executed this warrant," 13 June 1808. Rawley MARTIN summoned to testify in behalf of George MORGAN vs Stephen MORGAN, 13 June 1808. June 1808 term, judgment for $20 as a penalty incurred according to the statute in that case provided. On the same date as the judgement, MORGAN prayed for and was granted an appeal and gave John PAYNE as security. June 1810 term, judgement confirmed.

164 - 1810, Monongalia County Court. William G. PAYNE summoned to answer the complaint of Alexander BOTHWELL for non-payment of a debt due by an overcharge of fees, 17 October 1809. "We have examined the accounts of W. G. PAYNE and Mrs. BOTHWELL (late Mrs. BOYLES) and find from the statement of their accounts as admitted (excepting the rate of fees) a balance of $11.93 due to the late Mrs. BOYLES, but to reduce the fees to what is allowed by law, there will be $19.17 to be added, which would make the sum of $31.10 due Mrs. BOYLES, but as we are uninformed what troubles were attending the suits or whether the charges made by PAYNE are more than ought to have been, we are unwilling as arbitrators to give any opinion," 1 September 1809, signed by William TINGLE and B. REEDER. November 1809 term, judgement for the plaintiff for $19.17 debt and $.51 cost, Augustus WERNINGER, foreman. PAYNE prayed for and was granted an appeal giving Jacob FOULK as security. June 1810 term, judgement affirmed.

164 - 1810, Monongalia County Court. James JOLLIFFE summoned to answer Henry HEINTZMAN in a plea of debt, 13 February 1806. Henry HEINZMAN, assignee of Elijah HARYMAN/HARRIMAN, complained that James JOLLIFFE owed him $65 due by note dated 24 March 1804, payable in six months in pot metal at market price and to be delivered at the mouth of Pawpaw Creek. Note witnessed by Peter DRAGOO. Assignment to HEINZMAN dated 26 November 1805 and witnessed by J. JOLLIFFE. Appearance Bond signed by JOLLIFFE secured by Robert SHEARER, 13 February 1806. Bail Bond for JOLLIFFE secured by Presley MARTIN, March 1806. May 1810 term, judgement for the plaintiff for the debt with interest from 24 September 1804.

164 - 1810, Monongalia County Court. David GRAHAM summoned to answer George HARDEN in a plea of covenant broken damage $150, 31 March and 26 June 1806. Four and one half month note signed by GRAHAM to HARDIN for 95 pounds of good gun powder to be delivered to HARDIN's house dated 17 August 1805 and witnessed by Isabella (x) HARDIN. Appearance Bond signed by GRAHAM secured by John SEAMAN and Jacob FOULK/FULK, 4 July 1806. May 1810 term, judgement for the plaintiff for $47.50 with interest from 14 December 1805, Samuel G. WILSON, foreman.

164 - 1810, Monongalia County Court. Davis SHOCKLEY sued
Ephraim HUNT for slander. HUNT was heard to say, "I (meaning
himself the said HUNT) was never cow skinned by a dam'd horse
thief (meaning thereby that the said SHOCKLEY was a horse
thief and had stolen a horse or horses) and I will take you
back to Kent County in Delaware and I will save my expenses
by it (meaning that he the said HUNT would carry him the said
SHOCKLEY back to the State of Delaware as a horse thief and
felt that by so doing he would receive a reward equal to his
expenses)." August 1810 term, dismissed by the plaintiff's
attorney.

164 - 1810, Monongalia County Court. John HARTMAN/HAUTMAN
summoned to answer John SUMMERS in a plea of slander, 23
January 1807. In December 1806, HARTMAN was heard to say that
SUMMERS, in the company of Jacob WOOLF, broke open his spring
and milk house and broke and destroyed all the crocks and
vessels and used, spilled or carried away the milk and other
property which was in the milk house. HARTMAN swore he heard
SUMMERS threaten to set fire to his (HARTMAN's) fence and
woods when the leaves were dry. Amos ROBERTS, Reubin ASKINS
and Grace WEBSTER summoned to testify in behalf of HARTMAN,
29 June 1810. Isaac BARE's deposition: He heard WOLFE ask
HARTMAN if he judged his son and SUMMERS of doing the
mischief in his milk house. HARTMAN said, "he could not
judge nobody else and that he had judged them and did judge
them." Tobias REAMS' deposition: He heard HARTMAN say "he
judged old Jacob's Indian and John SUMMERS and if he was
before a court he would swear it was them." He did not charge
them with stealing or taking away anything, but said there
were crocks with milk in them that were broken and an iron
pot and a ladle. HARTMAN said the general disposition of
SUMMERS was that he was a bad man and has run away for
stealing, but before that time he was pretty well thought of.
HARTMAN told him (REAMS) that SUMMERS set his fence on fire
and was caught and if he (HARTMAN) had a gun with him, he
would have shot him. He heard HARTMAN had SUMMERS under
warrant for burning his fence. George WOLFE's deposition:
HARTMAN told him he would swear on Bible oath that it was
Jacob WOLFE and John SUMMERS that did the deed in his milk
house. HARTMAN told him he had SUMMERS arrested for burning
his fence and said it was settled on SUMMERS' agreeing to
make HARTMAN 200 rails. Reubin ASKIN's deposition: SUMMERS
lived by him, he was a good neighbor for three or four years.
After the burning of HARTMAN's fence and the mischief in the
milk house, "one said he was a bad man and others believed it
until a majority believed it." He said SUMMERS is a poor man
and HARTMAN pretty well off. HARTMAN was a good neighbor and
honest man and "SUMMERS' character generally was independent
of the charges of burning HARTMAN's fence and doing destruction in his milk house he was guilty of other dishonest and
pilfering action." Deposition by Henry SINES: When he came

into the neighborhood, SUMMERS stood charged with burning the fence and after awhile was charged with destruction in the milk house. For sometime his character was good until it was reported that he was guilty of other bad actions in the neighborhood such as dishonesty and pilfering. He said SUMMERS was a poor man and HARTMAN pretty well off. Deposition of Amos ROBERTS: He said the general character of SUMMERS around the neighborhood was that he was a rogue and dishonest man and he ran away from the country on that account and formerly he knew no bad reports on SUMMERS. "HARTMAN is a man of upright character." Deposition of Grace WEBSTER: She believed that SUMMERS had not been found out until lately, that his character is now bad, supposed to be guilt of pilfering and other bad actions and in consequence thereof, he fled from the country, formerly there were no bad accounts of him. Deposition of Henry WOLFE: HARTMAN told him of the disturbance in his milk house and said he could judge nobody but John SUMMERS and Jacob WOLFE. HARTMAN told him crocks were broken and a ladle bent up and a prop was moved. He said the milk house and spring were as good as common. August 1810 term, "We the jury find for the defendant $.01 in damages," signed by John CARTER, foreman.

164 - 1810, Monongalia County Court. William TINGLE summoned to answer Samuel SWEARINGEN in a plea of trespass on the case damage $100, 25 March 1806. SWEARINGEN's complaint: On 5 October 1800, TINGLE owed him 21 pounds, 17 shillings and 5 pence ($72.94) by virtue of execution in the name of SWEARINGEN against William HOLT and Pat'a CHERRY/CHENEY which execution was $72.94. TINGLE contracted with SWEARINGEN to collect the debt as soon as possible and after deducting $37 for William STIGER's notes, promised to pay the balance to SWEARINGEN or his order so soon as collected. TINGLE collected the debt, but failed to pay SWEARINGEN and therefore he brings suit. James SCOTT summoned to testify in behalf of SWEARINGEN, 15 August 1810. _____ 1810 term, jury sworn, non-suit and judgement for defendant.

164 - 1810, Monongalia County Court. Amos CHIPPS summoned to answer the complaint of William TINGLE for non-payment of a debt due by account, 1 March 1809. Summon Thomas WILSON and Rolley COTT/SCOTT as witnesses. Replevin Bond signed by Amos CHIPPS to secure his property which was attached at the suit of William TINGLE and sold at public sale. CHIPPS was the highest bidder and signed this bond to ensure he would pay his debt in 12 months. This bond secured by William CHIPPS, 20 March 1809. (Replevin Bond: a bond to protect or give security for the return to, or recovery by, a person of goods or chattels wrongfully taken or detained upon giving security to try the matter in court and return the goods if defeated in action.) TINGLE assigned this bond to William LOWRY on 5 September 1809 in the presence of Samuel LOWRY. On 4 June

1810, Joseph LOWRY, one of the firm of William LOWRY and Company, swore, "that no part or parcel of the money specified in the within bond had been paid to him or any person for him and the whole amount remains due." 4 March 1809, CHIPPS "confessed judgement for $5 which judgement is given in favor of TINGLE together with $.72 costs."

164 - 1810, Monongalia County Court. To Christian MADERA from the county, 7 March 1810, mending the criminal room $1.50, mending debtor's room and guard room $1.

To Nicholas CHISLER from the county, 1810, to putting on and making rivets for two locks on the jail door $1.50.

To George HITE from the county, 1810, to making two jail doors $3, to putting in __ sleepers, mending floor and putting in one piece of timber over one of the doors $1.

To Joseph ALLEN from the county, 1810, to mending the roof of the jail with shingles $1.25.

To William N. JARRETT, 10 October 1809, to 6# shingle nails to make jail doors $1; 30 October 1809, to ironing two doors to the jail, putting them up and repairing one door frame $3; 27 January 1810, to taking a door hinge out of the door frame, mending it and putting it in $__; to irons for ironing prisoners in the criminal room $3.__; to two large bolts, 15 inches long and _ inch square to fasten jail door frame $__; to twelve large spikes for spiking flooring plank in the jail $__; to 1 strap and spikes for fastening the jail window frame and putting it on $.50; to one double bolt and padlock for jail window $.75; to irons fixed to fasten on jail lock and support the same and 15 large spikes $1.50; to 6 large spikes to jail door frame $__; to labor done by my Negro man attending the mason when mending the jail walls $1.__; to 100 feet of 1/4 inch plank for jail, doors and floor $__; to my (JARRETT's) services for getting the mason and superintending the work $5. "Deduct the superintending as charged by JARRETT and deduct for ironing the prisoners in criminal room as not being a county charge." (The amount of the charges are torn from the right hand margin of this paper). May 1810 term, charges allowed.

164 - 1810, Monongalia County Court. Daniel KYGER summoned to answer Thomas FRETWELL in a plea of trespass on the case, 22 October 1805. FRETWELL complained that in 1805, KYGER bargained with him to deliver 4 bushels of salt, being then in Morgantown, to his house near the State Road about 14 miles from town. He said he was ready and willing to pay the contract, but was greatly disappointed and under great disadvantage when the salt was not delivered because he had a large quantity of meat to salt which was then on hand. May 1810 term, abated.

164 - 1810, Monongalia County Court. "8 January 1810, on motion of William TINGLE, it is ordered that a jury be

impaneled and sworn by the Sheriff of Monongalia County to
inquire of the necessity and expediency of establishing a
ferry across the Monongalia (sic) River from the lands of the
heirs of Henry DERING, deceased, to the lands of said TINGLE
on the west side of the said river, it appearing to the court
that due and legal notice of this motion has been given and
it is further ordered that said jury and sheriff report to
February Court next." The jury composed of Isaac CAMP, Thomas
DOOLITTLE, William WILSON, Dudley DENT, Zackquill MORGAN,
Marmaduke EVANS, Wm. N. JARRETT, William BALDWIN, John
SCHISLER, Rawley EVANS, John WILSON and James TIBBS returned
their report on 10 February 1810 and recommended the ferry
be established because "such a ferry will be of great public
utility." June 1810, established.

164 - 1810, Monongalia County Court. Sheriff Russell POTTER
prayed for and obtained an injunction against Dudley EVANS by
virtue of the following complaint, to wit, at June term last
past, Lieutenant Colonel Commandant Dudley EVANS procured by
motion, in a summary way against him (POTTER), the sum of $30
supposed to be due and payable out of the Militia Fines for
1802. He said when judgement was rendered, his deputies
"being absent," he did not know what fines they had paid for
that year. He said, "the judgement was awarded in the name of
Dudley EVANS, notwithstanding upon a settlement of Militia
Fines at the Auditor's Office, there appeared to be only
$62.13, a balance due from the county on account of Militia
Fines for 1802 as may appear by the receipt of the Clerk of
Accounts in the Auditor's Office dated 3 June 1805." His
deputies informed him that two orders by Lt. Col. Commandant
William JOHN amounting to $30 each was paid for 1802. POTTER
moved the court to summon EVANS to be questioned in a Court
of Equity, 28 July 1805. Affidavit of John W. DEAN: The
latter end of August or the first of September 1804, Elihu
HORTON and Thomas R. CHIPPS requested him to come to Morgantown to assist them to make out their list of insolvency.
While they were about the business, Jacob PINDELL came into
the house and called on HORTON to settle a militia order he
had. HORTON said he did not know if he had any money in his
hands. CHIPPS said he had no money in his hands and DEAN told
them if they had any money they might as well pay PINDELL as
any other person. They said if they had any money, they would
pay PINDELL and PINDELL went off satisfied, 15 February 1806
at the house of Henry DERING. Affidavit of Jacob PINDELL:
"Sometime last fall, was a year, he let Elihu HORTON, Deputy
Sheriff for Russell POTTER, have an order drawn by the Lt.
Colo. Commandant of Monongalia County in favor of Joseph REED
for $30 payable out of Militia Fines and at that time he owed
taxes to the amount of $24. HORTON agreed to keep the militia
order and settle PINDELL's taxes and settle with him fully
for the order," 22 February 1806. Deposition of William
TINGLE: Within a year last past, he and others called upon

Deputy Elihu HORTON and Deputy Thomas R. CHIPPS to open court. HORTON refused and TINGLE believed his object was to evade a judgement against POTTER in favor of Dudley EVANS upon a motion in regard to militia fines, 12 February 1806. Affidavit of Wm. N. JARRETT: On 20 July 1805, he delivered to HORTON an order drawn by William JOHN for $30 payable out of militia fines and HORTON gave him a receipt as follows, to wit, "Received 20 July 1805 of REED and FORDE by the hand of William N. JARRETT, an order on the Sheriff of Monongalia County for $30 which I agree to pay the amount to said JARRETT," signed by E. HORTON in the presence of Robert JAMES and B. REEDER. Deposition of Thomas WILSON: When he gave POTTER a notice for EVANS to answer his demand for his service as Clerk to the Court Martial from POTTER, Sheriff or Collector of militia fines, which he (WILSON) believes was to March Court 1805, POTTER told him he wished to have the business done here for that he had been or would be notified for the same at Richmond and that he would rather settle the business here than at Richmond and he agreed to acknowledge the notice and by that a fee to the coroner would be saved, 12 February 1806. Affidavit of John EVANS Jr.: At March 1805 Court, Deputy HORTON, under Sheriff Russell POTTER, refused to convene the court and after the court did convene, refused to open court. After being directed to open court, HORTON said, "if the cause then pending would be disposed with, he would open court and act as Deputy Sheriff as formerly." EVANS said the cause then pending in court was a motion made by Dudley EVANS against Russell POTTER for about $30 due to EVANS as Clerk to the Court Marshall. On Wednesday March Court last, EVANS requested HORTON to open court and HORTON said, "he would if Dudley EVANS would agree to continue his motion, he would open court, otherwise he would not." "To the Sheriff of Monongalia County, Sir, Please to pay the bearer, Joseph REED, $30 out of the militia fines for the year 1802," signed by William JOHN, LCC, 76th Regiment on 12 November 1802. REED assigned this order to Francis COLLINS on 5 July 1803 in the presence of William KIRKPATRICK. COLLINS assigned the same to REED and FORDE, of Philadelphia, on 9 July 1803 in the presence of Wm. N. JARRETT. "To the Sheriff of Monongalia County, Virginia, pay Joseph REED, Adjutant of the 76th Regiment and Provost Marshall for said Regiment, $30 for the year 1802," signed by Wm. JOHN, LCC of the 76th Regiment of Militia of Monongalia County, no date. REED assigned this order to Jacob PINDELL on 11 May 1802 in the presence of John McFARLAND. Judgement not found.

164 - 1810, Monongalia County Court. Abel DAVIS summoned to answer James CURRANT Sr. in a plea of debt due by account $50 damage, 11 May 1807. CURRANT complained that DAVIS owed him $38.67 for wares, goods, work, labor and services rendered. DAVIS' account with CURRANT, dated 1805 - 1806, is a long list of sundry merchandise and services including pasture for

2 weeks for horse, pork, bacon, corn, oats, wool hats, cider, wheat, rye, flax, 2 day's work and boarding. Credited to DAVIS in 1806, spinning cotton thread, trousers, knitting stockings and 1 two year old steer, leaving a balance of 4.2.9. Enoch CURRANT summoned to testify in behalf of James CURRANT, 13 August 1810. August 1810 term, "We the jury find for the plaintiff $25.50 in damages, N. WEBB, foreman."

164 - 1810, Monongalia County Court. Arthur WILSON summoned to answer David HANNAH in a plea of debt due by note, 10 February 1810. Note signed by A. WILSON to David HANNAH dated 7 April 1807, payable 1 June next with interest and witnessed by Edw. BOSWELL. Received on the note on 11 July 1807, $7.50 by HANNAH. May 1810 term, judgement.

164 - 1810, Monongalia County Court. John JACKSON complained that Elizabeth LYNCH and Daniel JOHNSON, heirs and legal representatives of Patrick LYNCH, deceased, owed him $37.50 by virtue of 2 notes signed by Patrick LYNCH. He prayed the court to attach so much of their property as to satisfy the debt, 16 April 1806. Note signed by Patrick (x) LYNCH to John JACKSON dated 4 February 1802, due 20 March next, payable by 25 good saw logs 12 feet long to square 18 inches at the top and if the logs are of a larger size, a less number in proportion to the size of the logs to be delivered at the mouth of Big Redstone and witnessed by Israel GREGG and Joseph HOUGH. One other note dated, worded, signed and witnessed the same, due 1 April next. "Water Forge, 3 March 1807, Friend, Mordecai MORGAN, you will please to give James COLLINS credit for $39 on the note COLLINS gave to the widow of Patrick LYNCH for the delivery of 50 saw logs at the mouth of Big Redstone Creek and call on Lawyer WILSON at Morgantown and he will give you credit on the notes that the said Patrick LYNCH gave to myself for the delivery of 50 saw logs several years ago at the mouth of Big Redstone. I have rated the saw logs @ $.75 per log with interest from the time they were to be delivered unto the present. I cannot recollect the length of time they have been due, but when you see the notes you will be able to make out the debt and interest. I shall be at March Court on the first day. If you should have any business at the court, possibly you could meet me at town either the first day of March Court or at the election. Let us try and settle the business of LYNCH, John JACKSON." John JACKSON obtained an attachment on the property of LYNCH for 50 saw logs to the value of $37. JACKSON signed this Attachment Bond to ensure all costs and awards would be paid in case LYNCH prevailed in the suit secured by Thomas BURCHINAL, 16 April 1806. Attachment levied on a quantity of potter's ware, the property of LYNCH. Jacob FOULK summoned as garnishee, 17 April 1806. No verdict found.

164a - 1810, Monongalia County Court. David MORGAN summoned to answer Lewis VANDIVER in a plea of debt, 13 March 1810. Lewis VANDIVER, assignee of Isaac MEANS, complained that David MORGAN owed him $90 by virtue of a note dated 30 October 1807, due 25 December 1808. Note witnessed by Forman SPENCER and Nicholas JEANES. Assignment to VANDIVER dated 18 August 1809. Appearance Bond signed by David MORGAN secured by Jacob FUNK, 13 March 1810. August 1810 term, "We the jury find for the plaintiff $90 with interest at 6% from 25 December 1807 until paid," Augustus WERNINGER, foreman.

164a - 1810, Monongalia County Court. Elisha CLAYTON summoned to answer Peircever VERNON in a plea of debt for $40 due by note, 1 November 1806 and 17 January 1807. Percever VERNON, assignee of Jesse CHENEY, complained that CLAYTON owed him $40 by virtue of a note dated 27 August 1802, due in 12 months. Note witnessed by Jno H. CHENEY and Urith? HEMPHILL. Assignment to VERNON dated 24 April 1806 and witnessed by Thomas HARRISON and John HICKMAN. Appearance Bond signed by CLAYTON secured by David MUSGRAVE, 28 February 1807. Bail Bond for CLAYTON secured by B. REEDER, 11 May 1807. _____ 1810 term, verdict for plaintiff for $40 with interest at 6% from 27 August 1803 until paid.

164a - 1810, Monongalia County Court. John WEST summoned to answer Jacob BAKER, assignee of John WEATHERHOLT, in a plea of covenant damage $50, 3 December 1806. Note signed by WEST to WEATHERHOLT dated 9 October 1804, due 1 November next, payable in 10 barrels of good cider with the barrels, to be delivered at the mouth of Deckers Creek (in case the water serves against the said time) and witnessed by Wm. JARRETT. Assignment to WEST dated 15 January 1805. May 1810 term, verdict for plaintiff for $30 with interest from 1 November 1804 until paid, Thomas GLISSON, foreman.

164a - 1810, Monongalia County Court. James COLLINS summoned to answer John TAYLOR, assignee of Jacob FOULK Jr., in a plea of covenant broken damage $110, 3 March and 24 April 1806. COLLINS not found. Michael KERNS summoned to testify in behalf of TAYLOR, 18 May 1810. Note signed by Jacob FOULK to James COLLINS dated 28 August 1806 for $___ payable in earthen ware. This note is dark and smudged, it looks as if there is water damage. Note signed by COLLINS to Jacob FOULK Jr. dated 28 August 1805, due 1 March 1806, payable in 100 saw logs to be valued by Michael KERNS Jr. at the mouth of Deckers Creek and witnessed by John SCOTT. Assignment to TAYLOR dated 6 January 1806. Appearance Bond signed by COLLINS secured by Horatio MORGAN, 3 May 1806. Bail Bond for COLLINS secured by John CARTER, 14 May 1807. _____ 1810 term, "We the jury find for the defendant," Joseph LOWRY, foreman.

164a - 1810, Monongalia County Court. Joseph BARKER summoned to answer Nathan GOODWIN/GODWIN in a plea of debt due by note, 17 April 1807. Demand note signed by BARKER to GODWIN dated 7 March 1807 for $25.86 with interest and witnessed by Jesper HYATT and Adam? COUGARD/COUGUST. Appearance Bond signed by Joseph (x) BARKER Sr. secured by Joseph BARKER Jr. and Henry BARKER, 28 April 1807. May 1810 term, verdict for the plaintiff for the debt with interest from 7 March 1807 until paid, Thomas GLISSON, foreman.

164a - 1809, Monongalia County Court. Zackquill MORGAN summoned to answer Robert HAWTHORN in a plea of covenant broken damage $150, 1 November 1806 and 17 January 1807. Agreement signed by Zackquell MORGAN to Robert HAWTHORN dated 2 April 1806, for "a good substantial still complete the body of said still to contain 100 gallons," due 15 June next and witnessed by Mathew GAY. "Zaquel MORGAN to Rob't HAWTHORN, to your note for 100 gallon still $100, to your note for $30 worth of iron, to your note for 864 poplar plank $8.64, total $138.64. Credit by my note in your hands $35, by 121# bar iron delivered to William BARKSHIRE $9.64, balance $94." Bail Bond for MORGAN secured by Arthur WILSON, 21 April 1807. March 1809 term, continued.

164a - 1810, Monongalia County Court. James THOMAS summoned to answer Samuel DAVIS in a plea of debt for $24 and $20 damage, 19 June, 27 August 1806, 17 January, 24 March and 16 May 1807. Note signed by James (x) THOMAS to DAVIS dated 5 November 1805 for $24, due 1 December 1805 and witnessed by Andrew COTTREL and John RADCLIFF. Appearance Bond signed by James (x) THOMAS secured by William (x) THOMAS, 16 May 1807. May 1810 term, verdict for the plaintiff for the debt with interest at 6% from 1 December 1805 until paid, A. GUSEMAN, foreman.

164a - 1808, Monongalia County Court. Arthur WILSON and John BOUSLOG summoned to answer Edward EVANS in a plea of debt for $66 and $20 damage, 28 September 1807, 8 March and 5 April 1808. Note signed by WILSON and BOUSLOG to EVANS dated 15 August 1806 for $33 to be paid in good salt at $4 per bushel on or before 15 February 1807 and $33 to be paid in good wheat at 4 shillings and six pence per bushel on 1 September 1807. This note witnessed by Jared EVANS and John LEGGITT. Appearance Bond signed by John BOUSLOG secured by Thomas (x) WELLS, 10 October 1807.

164a - 1810, Monongalia County Court. Nathan MATTHEW summoned to answer James DEWEESE in a plea of debt for $60 and $10 damage, 2 January 1808. Note signed by Nathan MATHEW to DEWEESE dated 13 September 1806 for $60, due 1 April next, payable in good bar iron at market price and witnessed by Susana G. PAYNE. _____ 1810 term, verdict for the plaintiff for the debt with interest at 6% from 1 April 1807 until paid.

164a - 1810, Monongalia County Court. Hedgeman TRIPLETT summoned to answer Robert PATTON Jr., for the use of Nimrod EVANS, in a plea of debt due by note, 3 June 1807. Ninety day note signed by TRIPLETT to PATTON dated 6 June 1798 for 29 pounds, 3 shillings and 7 pence half penny ($97.27). Interest on same from 5 September 1798 to 25 May 1807 $51.06, total $148.33. May 1810 term, judgement confessed.

164a - 1810, Monongalia County Court. Nathanial EWING complained that in April 1799, Nicholas CASEY was indebted to Noah PURCEL the sum of 20 pounds ($66.66) which was due 1 October 1799, PURCEL assigned the debt to EWING on 12 June 1799. The note was accidently destroyed and CASEY acknowledged he owed the debt, but now refused payment and therefore he brings suit. Letter to Thomas WILSON Esqr. from Nathan EWING dated 15 September 1805, "Sir: the note I had on Nicholas CASEY was given to Noah PURCEL for 20 pounds Virginia currency dated in March or April 1799, due 1 October following. Johnston BARKLOW was a witness to the note that was assigned to me 12 June 1799. Jonathan PURCEL can prove the transfer of the note to me, the commission to take the deposition of Jonathan PURCEL must be sent to Vincennis, Knox County, Indiana Territory. Mr WILSON will please to write to me at Vincennis this winter on the subject. Perhaps there is some other person who lives there who can prove something necessary to the recovery of said notes." _____ 18__ term, verdict for the plaintiff for the debt plus interest at 6% from 1 October 1799 until paid, Christian MADERA, foreman.

164a - 1810, Monongalia County Court. Zackquill PIERPOINT summoned to answer William BARRETT, assignee of John STEWART who was assignee of Owen HARKER, in a plea of debt due by note, 28 April 1807. Note signed by Zack PIERPOINT to Owen HAWKER for $50 dated 26 February 1805, due 1 December 1806, payable in grain at market price to be delivered at Kern's Mill and witnessed by John WATSON. Assignment to STEWART dated 9 May 1805 and witnessed by Joseph JENKINS. Assignment to BARRETT dated 12 January 1807. Bail Bond for PIERPOINT secured by Charles McGILL, 11 May 1807. Appearance Bond signed by Zack PIERPOINT secured by Noah RIDGWAY, 28 April 1807. May 1810 term, judgement for the plaintiff for the debt with interest at 6% from 1 December 1806 until paid, Christian MADERA, foreman.

164a - 1810, Monongalia County Court. Thomas McKINLY summoned to answer Rachel BILLS, assignee of John E. BILLS, in a plea of debt due by note, 3 June 1806. Note signed by Thos McKINLY to John E. BILLS dated 16 May 1806 for $50 payable in merchantable produce or trade, it being for sundries consid-

ered as value received. "The said $50 for Ruth the wife of
the said John." Note witnessed by Catran (x) EVANS and
Thomas (x) EVANS and secured by Zackquill MORGAN. Assignment
to Rachel BILLS dated 16 May 1806. Appearance Bond signed by
Thos McKINLY secured by Jacob FOULK, 31 July 1806. May 1810
term, verdict for the plaintiff for the debt with interest at
6% from 16 May 1806 until paid, Nicholas MADERA, foreman.

164a - 1807, Monongalia County Court. John SCOTT summoned to
answer Nathaniel BREADING/BRADING in a plea of debt due by
note, 21 July, 26 September 1806 and 11 January 1807. Note
signed by SCOTT to BREADING dated 1 August 1804 for 8 pounds,
5 shillings and 4 pence half penny, due 1 November next. Bail
Bond for SCOTT secured by Robert WOODS, 11 March 1807.
Appearance Bond signed by Jno SCOTT secured by Hedgeman
TRIPLETT, 20 February 1807.

164a - 1810, Monongalia County Court. Joseph KINCADE summoned
to answer David BAYLES, assignee of Francis COLLINS who was
assignee of Horatio MORGAN, in a plea of debt for $25 and $10
damage, 31 March 1808. Note signed by KINCADE to MORGAN dated
8 April 1807 for $25 payable in pot metal by 13 February 1808
and witnessed by Drusilia (x) MORGAN. Assignment to COLLINS,
not dated, witnessed by Henry ROSS. Assignment to BAYLES
dated __ July 1807, witnessed by Thomas BUTLER. ____ 18__
term, verdict for the plaintiff for the debt with interest
from 3 February 1808 until paid, David SCOTT, foreman.

164a - 1809, Monongalia County Court. James JEFFS summoned
to answer Robert HAWTHORN in a plea of covenant broken damage
$50, 30 January 1808. HAWTHORN complained that on 6 January
1807, by sealed writing, JEFFS promised to deliver to him $30
worth of good bar iron at $150 per ton to be delivered in
Morgantown within 4 months, to wit, 6 May 1808. March 1809
term, continued.

164a - 1810, Monongalia County Court. Jonathan KERNS summoned
to answer Jesse PAYNE, surviving partner of PAYNE and
FRETWELL, for the use of Agness FRETWELL, administratrix of
Thomas FRETWELL, deceased, in a plea of trespass on the case
damage $50, 26 September 1809 and 1 February 1810. May 1810
term, dismissed by the plaintiff.

164a - 1810, Monongalia County Court. Joseph JENKINS Jr. summoned to answer an indictment against him for an assault on
Jarrett BALL by the information of Alexander HAWTHORN and
John WAGNER, two of our own body, 10 and 16 May, 22 November
1808 and 14 April 1810. HAWTHORN and WAGNER summoned to give
evidence to the Grand Jury, 22 November 1808, 16 May, 17 and
21 November 1809. JENKINS not found.

164a - 1810, Monongalia County Court. William FRUM and Frederick GIBLER summoned to answer Mary BENNETT in a plea of debt due by note, 24 December 1805. BENNETT complained that FRUM and GIBLER owed her $30 by virtue of a note dated 23 November 1804 whereby they promised to pay her $30 in good merchantable grain at market price on or before 1 September next. Appearance Bond signed by Wm. FRUM secured by James THOMSON, 25 January 1806. Appearance Bond signed by Frederick GIBLER secured by Wm PAYNE, 24 January 1806. Jane DUNLAP summoned to testify in behalf of BENNETT, 8 July and 29 October 1808. May 1810 term, dismissed by the plaintiff.

164a - 1810, Monongalia County Court. Joseph JEANES summoned to answer John WILSON in a plea of covenant broken damage $220, 8 February 1806. Note signed by JEANES to WILSON dated 5 June 1805 for 200 bushels of good merchantable corn to be delivered at KERN's Mill by 15 February next and witnessed by John B. WHEELER. Appearance Bond signed by Joseph JEANES secured by David SWINDLER, 10 February 1806. Bail Bond for JEANES secured by David SWINDLER, 15 March 1806. Bail Bond for JEANES secured by Thomas ROBISON, 17 December 1807. Upon giving this new security, JEANES was set at liberty. May 1810 term, "We the jury find for the plaintiff $66.67 in damages with interest on the same from 18 January 1806 till payment at 6%," John SANDERS, foreman.

164a - 1810, Monongalia County Court. Thomas LAIDLEY summoned to answer David BRADFORD in a plea of debt for 20 pounds ($66.67) and $10 damage, 28 September 1807. Note signed by LAIDLEY to BRADFORD dated 15 March 1787 for $20. Credited to the debt: 8 pounds of nails at 16/d per pound in March 1787 and 5 pounds worth of horned cattle on 22 November 1793. May 1810 term, plea waived and judgement confessed.

164a - 1811, Monongalia County Court. William STAFFORD summoned to answer John TAYLOR in a plea of assault damage $1000, 29 April 1804. Joseph ALLEN summoned to testify in behalf of TAYLOR, 14 May 1811. James McVICKER summoned to testify in behalf of TAYLOR, 30 April 1811. May 1811 term, verdict and judgement for the plaintiff for $7.87 damage, Matthew GEORGE, foreman.

164a - 1810, Monongalia County Court. William GRAHAM, of Greene County, Pennsylvania, complained that James MANN owed him $240 by virtue of a Bill of Sale dated 26 September 1808 which will be due on 25 December 1809 with interest on $40 from 26 September 1808 and interest on $100 from 25 December 1808. GRAHAM swore he had reason to belive MANN would remove from the Commonwealth before his debt was due. GRAHAM prayed the court to attach so much of his property as to satisfy the debt, 17 March 1809. Attachment levied on one Negro boy, 21 March 1809. Attachment Bond signed by William

GRAHAM to ensure all costs and awards would be paid in case he be cast in the suit secured by Wm. TINGLE, 17 March 1809. May 1810 term, dismissed by the order of the plaintiff and judgement for the defendant for costs.

164a - 1810, Monongalia County Court. At a court held 19 March 1800, Reuben FOSTER recovered against Jonathan DAVIS the sum of $31.63 damages with interest at 6% from 15 November 1804 plus costs which remained unpaid. On 13 May 1805, James MORRIS and John BALDWIN secured bail for DAVIS. MORRIS and BALDWIN summoned to show cause, if any they can, why execution should not be had against them as securities for DAVIS, 31 May 1808. May 1810 term, verdict for the plaintiff for the debt, interest and costs.

164a - 1810, Monongalia County Court. William TINGLE summoned to answer Thomas BRITTON Jr., assignee of Joseph MINOR who was assignee of Isaac MINOR, in a plea of debt for $70 and $20 damage, 3 May 1806. One year note signed by TINGLE to Isaac MINOR for $70 United States currency dated 13 March 1805 and witnessed by G. TINGLE and Thos LAIDLEY. Assignment to Joseph MINOR dated 31 March 1800 and witnessed by Richard KERWOOD/KUWOOD. Assignment to BRITTON Jr. dated 14 April 1806 and witnessed by James EVANS. Credited to the note on 3 March 1806, $24. Bail Bond for TINGLE secured by B. REEDER, 5 May 1806. May 1810 term, plea waived.

164a - 1810, Monongalia County Court. William BAYLES summoned to answer Thomas GRAHAM, assignee of Thomas BRITTON who was assignee of William DAVIS, in a plea of debt for $60 and $10 damage, 17 February 1808. Note signed by William BAYLES to William DAVIS dated 17 August 1807 for $60 worth of bar iron at $8 per hundred, due 25 December next and witnessed by John ROAN. Assignment to BRITTON dated 17 August 1807. Assignment to GRAHAM dated 16 February 1808. Appearance Bond signed by William BAYLES secured by Robert ABERCRUMBY, 7 March 1808. ____ 1810 term, verdict for the plaintiff for the debt with interest from 25 December 1807, Thomas McKINLY, foreman.

164a - 1810, Monongalia County Court. Samuel EVERLY summoned to answer William TINGLE in a plea of covenant damage $150, 14 June 1810. Note signed by EVERLY to TINGLE dated 27 February 1808 for 135 gallons of merchantable whiskey delivered at James COLLINS' on or before 25 December next and witnessed by Rawley SCOTT and George DEIBLER. Appearance Bond signed by EVERLY secured by Nicholas MADERA, 15 June 1810. These papers are torn and dark, the judgement not found.

164a - 1810, Monongalia County Court. William PRICE summoned to answer John RAVENSCRAFT in a plea of debt for 15 pounds, 16 shillings and 10 pence ($52.80), 14 April 1806. Note signed by PRICE to RAVENSCRAFT dated 26 July 1804 for

166

15.16.10 with interest. May 1810 term, verdict for the plaintiff for the debt and interest from 26 July 1804 with a credit of 16 shillings and six pence paid on 24 July 1805, John PAYNE, foreman.

164a - 1810, Monongalia County Court. Simon ROYCE, of Monongalia County, and John McCLEAN, of Addison Township, Somerset County, Pennsylvania, summoned to answer Thomas SPENCER, of Somerset County, in a plea of covenant damage $200, 10 October 1808. On 10 September 1801, ROYCE and/or his security, McCLEAN, promised to procure from the Land Office a patent for the 440 acre plantation on which SPENCER then lived in Addison Township, on or before 10 September 1802. This agreement witnessed by Alexander MORRISON and Peter AUGUSTEIN. May 1810 term, verdict for the plaintiff for $403.58 damages, Reynear HALL, foreman.

164a - 1810, Monongalia County Court. Note signed by Wm. FRUM to Wm. TENNANT for $35 dated 24 February 1806, due 25 December next and witnessed by Catharine (x) CORE. Appearance Bond signed by Wm. FRUM secured by Joseph ALLEN, 8 February 1808. May 1810 term, verdict for the plaintiff for the debt with interest from 25 December 1806, Thomas McKINLY, foreman.

164a - 1810, Monongalia County Court. Samuel MAID indicted on charges of beating his wife, Nacy/Mary MAID, by the information of George B. HOSKINSON and John STEALY. Summon Magruder SELBY, Mary MAID and David NEAL as witnesses for the Common-wealth, 10 April 1810. Appearance Bond signed by Samuel (x) MAID, cooper, secured by Joseph ALLEN, yeoman, 16 April 1810.

164a - 1810, Monongalia County Court. At a court on 18 March 1808, Richard HOLLIDAY recovered against Samuel SMITH $44.30 damages with interest at 6% from 1 December 1802 until paid plus costs. On 12 March 1805, Joseph HARRISON secured Bail Bond for SMITH. The debt remained unpaid and HARRISON summoned to show cause, if any he can, why execution should not be had against him as security for SMITH, 22 April 1808. May 1810 term, verdict for the plaintiff for the debt, David SCOTT, foreman.

164a - 1810, Monongalia County Court. George HOLLENBACK, William HAYES and Moses SNIDER summoned to answer Jesse EVANS, assignee of Asa KELLUM, in a plea of debt for $140 and $10 damage, 10 December 1806. Note signed by HOLLENBACK and HAYES to KELLUM for $140 dated 27 May 1805, due 1 October next and witnessed by Hannah HOLLENBACK, John DRAGOO and James HAYES. Assignment to EVANS dated 1 June 1805 and witnessed by Benjamin JONES, Peter MYERS and Lewis EVANS. Appearance Bond signed by HOLLENBACK secured by James MORGAN and Uriah MORGAN in the presence of James JOLLIFFE, 1 January 1807. Appearance Bond signed by Moses SNIDER secured by

Henry BARRICKMAN, 11 February 1807. Appearance Bond signed by William HAYES secured by J. EVANS Jr, 10 December 1806. "Take notice that apprehending the immediate removal of George HOLLEBACK for whom I am security to you in a note of _____ which is now due, therefore request you to commence suit on said note before the removal of the said HOLLENBACK, William HAYES, Sr., 10 December 1806." May 1810 term, judgement for the plaintiff for the debt with interest from 1 October 1805 with a credit of $65 paid 25 March 1806, $27 paid on 27 January 1806 and $10 paid on 6 June 1806, Thomas GIBSON, foreman.

164a - 1810, Monongalia County Court. James JEFFS summoned to answer Thomas TATE, assignee of John COOPER in a plea of debt for $37.50 and $10 damage, 18 April 1808. Note signed by James JEFFS to John COOPER dated 17 December 1806 for $37.50 payable in merchantable bar iron, hollow ware such as sugar kettles or dutch ovens and hardware on or before 1 November 1807 and witnessed by Thomas McKINLY and Jacob BANKERT. May 1810 term, judgement for the plaintiff for the debt with interest at 6% from 7 November 1807 until paid, David SCOTT, foreman.

END OF MICROFILM #42

MONONGALIA COUNTY RECORDS OF DISTRICT, SUPERIOR AND COUNTY COURTS

164b - 1810, Monongalia County Court. William KENNEDY summoned to answer Noah MORRIS, assignee of Samuel KENNEDY, in a plea of covenant damage $70, 22 April 1807. Seven month note signed by William KENNEDY to Samuel KENNEDY dated 12 April 1803, payable in 160 bushels of good sound merchantable corn to be delivered at William's house and witnessed by Zadock MORRIS. Assignment to Noah MORRIS dated 30 December 1806. Appearance Bond signed by William KENNEDY secured by William JENKINS in the presence of William STEWART, 8 August 1807. August 1810 term, verdict for the plaintiff for the debt plus 6% interest from this date until paid, John CARTER, foreman.

164b - 1810, Monongalia County Court. Thomas MURPHY applied to the court for the return of a black horse wrongfully taken by Samuel WILSON. Bond signed by MURPHY to ensure he would prosecute and perform and satisfy the judgement of the court in case he should be cast in the suit secured by Jonathan (C) KEARNS, 6 February 1806. Order to return to Thomas MURPHY one black horse ($40) which Samuel WILSON took and unjustly detained and summon WILSON to answer MURPHY of the wrongful taking and detaining the horse, 17 February 1806. John PAYNE summoned to testify in behalf of WILSON, 16 August 1810. MURPHY released WILSON of all costs of the suit on 7 February 1806. May 1810 term, verdict and judgement set aside and dismissed.

164b - 1810, Monongalia County Court. George HITE complained that 1 hatter's planking, (kettle and the planks belonging thereto) were stolen from him. He said he had probable cause to believe the items were hidden in the house of Abraham HALE or in Thomas McKINLEY's Hatter's Shop where HALE worked. HITE petitioned the court to issue a Search Warrant and arrest HALE if any evidence was found, 23 December 1810. Appearance Bond for HALE secured by John TAYLOR, 23 December 1810. Paul VEGUS, James REED, John TAYLOR, Thomas HERSEY Sr., George HITE and _____ TAYLOR summoned to give evidence to the Grand Jury, 23 December 1801. "George HITE served execution on the kettle and property of the prisoner which was taken away and found on the Commons." John TAYLOR's testimony: "J. TAYLOR, his son, informed him that they were getting a Search Warrant to search for the kettle and property and that they intended to search deponent's cellar. This deponent went and looked in the cellar and found the kettle being under his porch. He took them out and threw them over the fence." Paul VEGUS' testimony: He heard a person say, "he had the kettle taken away and that if the constable attempted to take it again, he would get a bloody nose or head." _____ BANKERT, Jno W. McKINLY, F. McKINLEY and Jas REED would not testify, "they had nothing." Justices summoned to hold a court for the examination of Abraham HALE, 23 December 1810. 29 December 1810 term, acquitted.

164b - 1810, Monongalia County Court. Abel JONES, James JONES and Josiah JONES summoned to answer Emelia BOYLES in a plea of assault damage $2000, 29 March 1804. The JONES boys said they did not commit an assault on Emelia, but she assaulted them and they were only defending themselves. Hester/Ester SANDERS, Sarah BOYLES and John BOYLES summoned to testify in behalf of Amelia BOYLES, 20 October 1806, 17 April, 3 August and 1 October 1807. August 1810 term, "judgement against Abel and judgement for James and Josiah." "We the jury find that the plaintiff, at the time of the instigation of this suit, was an infant of the age of 19 years and that she is presented here by her guardian or next friend and we find that she prosecuted by the permission of her mother, Sarah BOYLES, in her own name and if the law is for the plaintiff, we find for the plaintiff $30 damages and if for the defendants, then we find for the defendants. We also find that the defendants, James and Josiah JONES, were infants at the instigation of the suit." Abel JONES and Emelie BOYLES came into court and Abel said, "after the verdict found in this case (from which day the plaintiff aforesaid was continued to this day) at the County of Monongalia aforesaid took _____ RICKEY/RICHEY to her husband who is now alive and thus the said plaintiff is under "coverture" and this the said defendant is ready to verify, wherefore he prays judgement of the said verdict and that the same may be arrested." Emelie replied that the judgement aught not to be arrested because on the day of the finding of the verdict she "was and ever since hath been and now is single" and this she is ready to verify and "therefore she prays judgement and her damages by the verdict found."

164b - 1810, Monongalia County Court. Two good horses, the property of John WEST, was attached at the suit of Jacob BAKER, assignee of John WEATHERHOLT, for $30 with interest and costs. In order to retain possession of his property until time of public sale or his debt was paid WEST signed this Delivery Bond secured by James WALKER, 31 May 1810. On 12 July 1810, BAKER gave notice to WEST and WALKER that he intended to petition the court for judgement against them for failure to deliver the property for public sale.

164b - 1810, Monongalia County Court. Samuel MARYFIELD, John MARYFIELD, John SPRINGER and Barsheba his wife, John HARE and Elizabeth his wife and Mary MARYFIELD, heirs and devisees of Richard MARYFIELD, deceased, summoned to answer Isaac MORRIS in a plea of debt for 22 pounds and 10 shillings ($75) and $6.50 all equal to $81.50 and $10 damage due by confessed judgement by Richard MERIFIELD in 1796, 25 March 1807. August 1810 term, dismissed agreed.

164b - 1810, Monongalia County Court. William N. JARRETT summoned to show cause, if any he can, why an information shall not be filed against him for retailing whiskey without having obtained a license for that purpose agreeable to law, 14 April 1810. "We the Grand Jury present Wm. N. JARRETT for retailing whiskey without having obtained a license for that purpose agreeable to law, by the information of James BARKER and John BAKER, two of our own body, within twelve months last past." BARKER and BAKER summoned to give evidence on 7 June 1810. August 1810 term, quashed.

"We the Grand Jury present John COOPER for retailing whiskey without having obtained a license for that purpose agreeable to law, by the information of William WILSON and Abraham HESS, two of our own body, within twelve months last past." "We the Grand Jury present the overseer of the street leading by the Widow BENNET's by the information of John SANDERS and Larkin PIERPOINT, two of our own body, within two months last past." No date on any of these documents.

164b - 1810, Monongalia County Court. George WILL summoned to answer Martin BOWMAN, assignee of William WILL, in a plea of debt for $50 and $30 damage, 22 September 1808. Note signed by Gorg WILL/WILD to William WILL/WILD dated 9 March 1807 for $50, $25 due 1 December next and $25 due 1 May 1807 and witnessed by Frk HARSH. Assignment to BOWMAN dated 4 May 1807 in the presence of Jno GILMORE. George said he aught not be charged with this debt because "the same was obtained by threats and force" and this he could verify. Appearance Bond signed by Gorg WILL secured by Jno WAGNER, 25 October 1808. August 1810 term, verdict for the plaintiff for the debt with interest at 6% from due dates of the two payments.

164b - 1810, Monongalia County Court. Samuel SMITH summoned to answer Jeremiah AXTON in a plea of a breach of covenant damage $100, 24 April, 26 June and 20 December 1806. AXTON complained that SMITH, on 30 September 1803, promised to deliver to him 6500' of good poplar boards on the bank at the mouth of Georges Creek on or before 1 April 1804, "for valued received before that date," which SMITH failed to do and therefore he brings suit. On two summons, SMITH not found and on the third "kept off by force." August 1810 term, dismissed by the plaintiff.

164b - 1810, Monongalia County Court. James PINDLE, Elizabeth PINDLE, Jemima PINDLE and Rachel PINDLE, children and heirs of Thomas PINDLE, deceased, summoned to answer a Bill in Chancery exhibited against them by Jarred EVANS, 6 July, 9 and 21 November 1803. Rachel was not an inhabitant of this county. EVANS' complaint: On 2 May 1795, he purchased a 300 acre tract of land from PINDELL and PINDELL executed a Conveyance Bond to him to convey the land when he made the last payment and he gave to PINDELL his bonds conditioned for

the said payments. He said he made the payments according to
the contracts, but PINDELL nor his heirs ever made a deed to
him and therefore he brings suit. James PINDELL's answer for
himself and guardian to the others (appointed by the court
for that purpose): It was true that PINDELL, in his lifetime,
gave a bond to ONEAL and bound himself to convey to ONEAL a
tract of land when ONEAL would make the last payment in 1799.
He said they were ready and willing to make a good deed if
ONEAL could prove he made payments according to his contract,
1 August 1804. Conveyance Bond signed by Thomas PINDELL dated
2 May 1795 for 240 pounds whereby PINDELL bound himself to
convey to ONEAL a 300 acre parcel of land, with its improvements, on the west side of the "Monnongahalea" River on Big
Indian Creek above the forks of the creek, joining GILMORE?
on the east and John SMITH on the west on or before 1 January
1799 or when last payment is made and witnessed by John
LOGAN, Edward EVANS and Daniel (x) SHEHAN. Bond assigned to
Jared EVANS on 16 May 1795 in the presence of Edward EVANS
and John EVANS. Note signed by ONEAL to PINDEL for 20 pounds
dated 1 May 1795, payable in 1797 in country produce and
witnessed by John LOGAN. "Recovered, 23 December 1797, of
Joseph ONEAL 7 pounds, 6 shillings and 7 pence in part of the
within note," signed by Wm. McCLEERY and Thomas WILSON. Note
signed by ONEAL to PINDLE for 20 pounds dated 2 May 1795,
payable 1 January 1798 in produce and witnessed by John LOGAN
and Edward EVANS. Note signed by _____ _____ (torn away)
to PINDLE for 38 pounds and 10 shillings dated 2 May 1795,
payable 1 January next in produce and witnessed by LOGAN and
EVENS. Assignment to _____ McCLEERY and Thomas WILSON on 17
May 1797, signed by Jacob PINDELL, administrator. "25 November 1795, Received of Joseph ONEEL 23 pounds Virginia money
in part pay for a tract of land that Pall MICKEL now lives
on, formerly the property of James COCHRAN," signed by
PINDELL in the presence of Jarod EVANS. June 1810 term,
decree.

164b - 1810, Monongalia County Court. Richard COUGHLIN and
Robert MEANS summoned to answer a Bill in Chancery exhibited
against them by Stephen McDADE, 22 July and 26 September
1806. McDADE's complaint: On 16 February 1797, COUGHLIN sold
98 acres to Robert MEANS and gave a Conveyance Bond to MEANS
promising to convey the land by 1 November 1798. In payment
of the land, MEANS executed two notes, one for 40 pounds and
the other for 20 pounds totaling $200. The 98 acres was a
part of a larger tract sold by MEANS to John TURNER bounded
by John SHIVAL/SHIVLEY's Richwood land, the place Jacob SCOTT
bought of James DENNEY and other lands which land was, at the
date of the bond, in the possession of COUGHLIN. MEANS failed
to pay as agreed and COUGHLIN assigned the land to McDADE. He
hoped to collect from MEANS but MEANS said he could not raise
the money. COUGHLIN left the country about this time and
McDADE said he could not learn where he lived. McDADE agreed

with MEANS for the land, believing he could obtain a clear title from COUGHLIN, and paid MEANS 80 pounds ($266.33) plus his two obligations and a young horse at 50 pounds and at the same time he obtained COUGHLIN's Conveyance Bond given to MEANS. He said he had not seen COUGHLIN since the time COUGHLIN assigned the land to him and since the departure of COUGHLIN, MEANS pretended to have title to the land and held the land as his own property. He prayed the court to summons COUGHLIN and MEANS to be questioned in a Court of Equity. Robert MEANS' answer: On the date he sold the land to BRANT and TURNER, BRANT assigned his claim and interest to TURNER. TURNER died and his widow married Richard CONKLIN (CONKLIN later died without issue). He procured a title to be made to CONKLIN at which time there remained due to him 10 pounds, part of the purchase price. CONKLIN could not raise the money and proposed to sell the land back to MEANS. MEANS took two notes for the price, which at the same time was assigned to McDADE. The two notes were payable in trade, but McDADE refused to receive trade. He assigned CONKLIN's Bond of Conveyance in discharge of the notes and at the same time received from McDADE a colt valued at $30 only. He said he did not have title nor claim to the land and was ready and willing to surrender possession of the property to McDADE "if it is considered that he have possession." He prayed the court to dismiss the complaint against him with reasonable charges, 8 June 1807. "I certify that there is no land assessed or sold or direct in the name of Richard COUGHLIN or Robert MEANS," signed by Robert HAWTHORN. Conveyance Bond signed by COUGHLIN to MEANS dated 16 February 1797 promising to convey all his right, title and claim into and for a tract of land, it being a part of a larger tract that MEANS sold to John TURNER, now in possession of COUGHLIN and COUGHLIN bound himself to made a clear deed to MEANS and allow MEANS to take possession of the land, without any trouble, on or before 1 November 1798. This bond witnessed by Robert SCOTT and Margary NOX. June 1810 term, the court decreed that the defendants make a good and sufficient deed, at their own cost, to McDADE and that they be attached by their bodies until they performed this decree.

164b - 1810, Monongalia County Court. On Saturday 19 May 1810, John JARRETT recovered against Joseph REED and John RAMSEY the sum of $50 with interest at 6% from 20 July 1805 until paid, plus $10.13 costs and $.21 charges. George CUNNINGHAM secured bail for RAMSEY on 9 March 1807. On 10 March 1807, John EVANS Jr. secured bail for REED. JARRETT said the debt remained unpaid and he prayed the court to summon CUNNINGHAM and EVANS to show cause, if any they can, why execution should not be had against them, 18 July 1810.

164b - 1810, Monongalia County Court. Recognizance Bond for Thomas CAIN, laborer, secured by Anthoney KIRKHART, tanner, 1

December 1810. Lydia BASSET, a single woman, swore before Justice Daniel COX that on 25 November last "she was delivered of a bastard child which is likely to become chargeable to the county and hath charged Thomas CAIN with having gotten her with child of the said bastard child." December 1810 term, "disposed of."

164b - 1810, Monongalia County Court. Jesse MYERS summoned to answer a Bill in Chancery exhibited against him by Mahlon HOUGH, 1 August 1805. About 2 August 1798, HOUGH purchased 200 acres of land for 60 pounds from George SMITH. The land lying and being on Piney Run as shown by a patent granted to Jesse MYERS dated 23 April 1790. On 2nd day 3rd month 1798, MYERS executed his bond to SMITH and by the said bond covenanted and agreed to and with SMITH to warrant and defend the land to SMITH forever. It was understood and agreed that MYERS was to execute a good and sufficient deed of general warrantee to SMITH. On 2 August 1798, SMITH assigned all his right, title and interest in the land to HOUGH. HOUGH said he promptly paid the purchase price, but MYERS, who removed from the county and he does not know where he lives, did not make him a deed and therefore he brings suit. Bond signed by Jesse MYERS, of Sandy Creek Glades, to SMITH dated 2 day 3rd month 1790 whereby MYERS warranted to SMITH a 200 acre tract, formerly belonging to John WITLATCH and John SWEARGIN lying and being in Sandy Creek Glades on waters of Piney Run about 1 1/2 miles east of Piney Grove, joining the land of MEANS he bought of Benjamin FORMAN? on the south and Stephen MASTERSON on the north, signed by Jesse MYERS in the presence of Mary SMITH. Land Grant, by virtue of a Land Office Treasury Warrant #20376 dated 10 November 1783, to Jesse MIERS for 287 acres by survey dated 3 April 1787. February 1810 term, MYERS failed to appear and the court ordered and decreed that he (MYERS), by fee simple, convey the land to HUGH/HOUGH and that MYERS be attached by his body until he performed this decree. A note on reverse of one of the documents, "The land that is within mentioned is improved as belowth, to wit, one house and two stables and twenty ____ barning, apple trees and a little necessary, three fields, one 8 and another 2 and another 1 acre and in reasonable repair. Likewise, I promised to assign a plot good and sufficient of this within land unto George SMITH for value received in order to send to Richmond," signed by Jesse MYERS. At the bottom of this writing, George SMITH signed what appears to be an assignment. This part of the page is too faded to read.

164b - 1810, Monongalia County Court. George GREENWOOD summoned to answer Nicholas RILEY, assignee of Benjamin GREENWOOD, in a plea of debt for $75 due by note, 4 and 23 November 1805. Note signed by George GREENWOOD to Benjamin GREENWOOD dated 4 December 1798 for 22 pounds and 10 shillings and witnessed by Benjan/Beryon GUSTON. Assignment to RILEY dated 28 February 1801 and witnessed by John KENNARD. Bail Bond for George GREENWOOD secured by George DORSEY, 5 April 1806. Appearance Bond signed by Geo GREENWOOD secured by G. DORSEY, 23 November 1805. May 1810 term, verdict and judgement.

164b - 1810, Monongalia County Court. Stephen GAPEN summoned to answer a Bill in Chancery exhibited against him by David SCOTT Jr., 28 June 1810. December 1810 term, judgement for the defendant.

164b - 1810, Monongalia County Court. One sorrel horse, the property William G. PAYNE, was attached at the suit of Alexander BATHWELL for $19.68 with damages and costs. In order to retain possession of his property until time of public sale or his debt was paid PAYNE signed this Delivery Bond secured by Jacob FOULK and Joseph ALLEN, 21 June 1810. On 15 September 1810, BATHWELL gave notice to PAYNE, FOULK and ALLEN of intent to petition the court for judgement against them for failure to deliver the horse for public sale. December 1810 term, judgement for the plaintiff.

164b - 1810, Monongalia County Court. Philip HUFFMAN summoned to answer John LYON, assignee of William HULL/HALL, assignee of Charles HALL/HULL, in a plea of covenant damage $60, 18 April, 4 June and 27 August 1807. Three month note signed by HUFFMAN to Charles HULL dated 27 May 1806 for $25, payable in bar iron, hollow ware, salt or cattle at market price and witnessed by Sam'l PEARSE and Jonathan? ANDERSON. Assignment to William HULL dated 2 June 1806 and witnessed by William BARNS. Assignment to LYON dated _ August 1806 and witnessed by Samuel ROBINSON. Bail Bond for HUFFMAN secured by John C. PAYNE, 20 February 1808. For fear he would be injured in this case, PAYNE took HUFFMAN to jail on 10 December 1808 and Abel DAVIS secured bail for HUFFMAN on 19 December 1808. May 1810 term, judgement for the plaintiff for the debt with 6% interest from 27 August 1806, John REED foreman.

164b - 1810, Monongalia County Court. Anthony WOODS and Robert WOODS summoned to answer Asher LEWIS, assignee of Sennett TRIPLETT, in a plea of debt for $30 and $20 damage, 15 September 1807. Note signed by Anthoney (x) WOODS and Rob't WOODS to Sinett TRIPLET dated 14 March 1807 for $30, due 1 September next, payable in pot metal at market price and witnessed by John THOMPSON and John COOPER. Assignment to LEWIS dated 15 September 1807 and witnessed by Jacob MYERS and Arch'b WILSON. Appearance Bond signed by Robert WOODS secured by Barney HANEY on 15 September 1807 in the presence of Jonathan COBURN. May 1810 term, verdict and judgement.

164b - 1810, Monongalia County Court. Joseph REED and John RAMSEY summoned to answer John JARRETT in a plea of debt due by note, 10 February 1807. Note signed by Joseph REED and John RAMSAY to John JARRETT dated 4 June 1805 for $50, due 20 July 1805 and witnessed by William CRACRAFT and Moses MATHENY. Appearance Bond signed by Joseph REED secured by Charles MAGILL in the presence of John MAGILL, 14 February 1807. Bail Bond for RAMSEY secured by George CUNNINGHAM, 9 March 1807. May 1810 term, judgement for the plaintiff for $50 debt with interest at 6% from 20 July 1805, Christian MADERA, foreman.

164b - 1810, Monongalia County Court. George HITE summoned to answer Nathan NICHOLS in a plea of debt for $25 and $10 damage, 3 November 1806. Note signed by HITE to NICHOLS dated 20 June 1805 for $25, due 1 October next and witnessed by Nimrod EVANS and W. N. JARRETT. Appearance Bond signed by HITE secured by Ben'j HELLEN, 8 November 1806. May 1810 term, judgement for the plaintiff for the debt.

164b - 1810, Monongalia County Court. Elizabeth LINCH complained that James COLLINS refused to perform his covenant. Note signed by James COLLINS to Elizabeth LINCH dated 7 April 1806 for 50 poplar and white oak saw logs to square 16" to be delivered at the mouth of Big Redstone Creek by 1 May if the waters suits and witnessed by Henry ROSS. May 1810 term, judgement for costs confessed.

164b - 1810, Monongalia County Court. Zackquill MORGAN summoned to answer George MORGAN in a plea of debt for $30 and $10 damage, 18 April 1807. Note signed by Zackquill MORGAN to George MORGAN dated 21 September 1803 for $30, due 1 December next, payable in good beef cattle at market price and witnessed by Robert MINNIS. Bail Bond for Zackquill MORGAN secured by F. BRITTON, 11 May 1807. May 1810 term, judgement for costs confessed.

164b - 1810, Monongalia County Court. William PRICE summoned to answer James PEAL, assignee of Charles SNIDER, in a plea of debt due by note, 17 April 1807. Twelve month note signed by William PRICE and James PEAL to Charles SNIDER dated 9 March 1804 for 30 pounds to be paid at Western Port and witnessed by William H. BARNS/BURNS. Assignment to PEAL dated 27 November 1805. May 1810 term, judgement for the plaintiff for the debt with interest at 6% from 9 March 1805.

164b - 1810, Monongalia County Court. John STEALEY summoned to answer James PINDALL, for himself and Elizabeth PINDALL, Jemima PINDALL and Rachel PINDALL, infants under age 21, by James PINDALL their next friend, in a plea of trespass, 16 January 1805. James PINDALL complained that STEALEY entered their property and destroyed 150 fruit trees ($100) and took 10 wagon loads of wood ($10). George R. TINGLE and Robert HILL summoned to testify in behalf of PINDLE, 30 July 1808.

Robert HILL summoned to testify in behalf of PINDLE, 14 April 1810. May 1810 term, "We the jury find for the defendant."

164b - 1810 and 1837, Monongalia County Court. Thomas FIELDS and Ebenezer FIELDS summoned to answer a Bill in Chancery exhibited against them by Mary DAVIS, Susanna DAVIS and Jenny DAVIS, devisees and infants of Ebenezer DAVIS, deceased, by William PRICE their next friend, 3 March 1806. DAVIS' complaint: On 8 December 1792, their father, Ebenezer DAVIS, deceased, purchased from Thomas and Ebenezer FIELDS, heirs of Richard FIELDS, deceased, a certain tract of land... They prayed the court to summons FIELDS to be questioned in a Court of Equity and petitioned the court to compel them to convey the land to them by a deed in fee simple. Conveyance Bond signed by Thomas (T) FIELDS and Ebenezer (x) FIELDS, of Hampshire County, to Ebenezer DAVIS for the sum of 300 pounds current money of Maryland dated 8 December 1792, whereby FIELDS promised to convey land, formerly belonging to Richard FIELDS, on the water of Three Fork Creek. The deed to be made when Ebenezer FIELDS comes of age which will be in 1798. This bond witnessed by Ebenezer DAVIS Jr. and Joseph (x) DAVIS. Will of Ebenezer DAVIS: "I Ebenezer DAVIS, of the County of Allegany and State of Maryland being of sound and disposing mind and memory do make this my last will and testament. Imprimis: Having already advanced my sons Joseph, Levi and Stephen and my daughters Tabitha and Rachel by giving each of them a just and reasonable part of my estate, I hereby give and bequeath them and each of them the sum of 5 shillings. Item: I give and devise to my son, Ebenezer, the land and plantation on which I now live to him and his heirs forever subject to the burdens after mentioned. Item: I give and devise to my three daughters, Mary, Susannah and Jenny, my lands in `Monongahalia´ County, Virginia, to them and their heirs forever equally to be divided between them. Item: I give and bequeath to my loving wife, Sarah, my horse, saddle and bridle, two cows and two calves such as she shall chose from my stock and all my household furniture and stock of sheep. Item: My will and desire is that my said three daughters, Mary, Susannah and Jenny, be maintained and brought up out of the profits of the land bequeathed to them in Virginia and that if these same shall prove deficient, the deficiency shall be made up by my said son, Ebenezer, out of the profits of the plantation herein above devised to him until they arrive respectively at the age of sixteen years complete. Item: My will and desire is that my said wife shall be supported out of the rents and profits of the plantation herein above devised to my son Ebenezer as long as she shall remain my widow. Lastly all the rest and residue of my estate of what nature or kind soever, I devise to be sold for the payment of my just debts and if there should be anything left, I bequeath it to my executors to be applied toward the support of my three younger children, Mary, Susannah and

Jenny, that my son Ebenezer's plantation may not be burdened more than is necessary. And I hereby appoint my said wife Sarah and my son Ebenezer executor and executrix of this my last will and testament and guardians of all my infant children hereby revoking all former wills and testaments by me made. In witness whereof I have hereunto set my hand and affixed my seal this 18th day of November 1793." Signed by Ebenez (x) DAVIS in the presence of P. MURDOCK, John WHETZEL and Susannah BRAIN. A copy of a Land Grant to Richard FIELDS, assignee of Thomas FIELDS, for 400 acres by survey dated 24 October 1786 lying and being in Monongalia on Three Fork Creek Glades, 16 October 1789 and signed by Beverly RANDOLPH. July 1810 term, "decree for plaintiff." "At a court held for Monongalia County on Tuesday 27 March 1837, on motion of William BROWN, it is ordered that the clerk of this court deliver to said BROWN the original title papers filed in a Chancery cause decided in this court between DAVIS against FIELDS upon leaving certified copies thereof."

MONONGALIA GAZETTE

164b - 1810, Monongalia County Court. William TINGLE and George R. TINGLE summoned to answer Augustus WERNINGER, assignee of William CHIPPS, in a plea of debt due by note, 6 November 1807. Two year note signed by Wm TINGLE and George R. TINGLE to William CHIPPS dated 2 October 1805 for $32 and witnessed by Thomas BRITTON Jr. Assignment to WERNINGER dated 10 September 1807 in the presence of Ama. DAVISSON. August 1810 term, judgement for the plaintiff for the debt with 2% interest from 2 October 1807, John A. GUSEMAN, foreman.

164b - 1810, Monongalia County Court. Josiah ROBE summoned to answer Abraham GUSEMAN in a plea of debt for $160 and $10 damage, 3 June 1809. Six month note signed by ROBE to GUSEMAN dated 17 November 1807 for $160 and witnessed by Robert MINNIS and Wm TINGLE. Appearance Bond signed by Josiah ROBE secured by Wm TINGLE, 3 June 1809. August 1810 term, judgement for the plaintiff for the debt with interest at 6% from 17 November 1807 deducting a credit of $93 paid on 28 May 1808, Joseph ALLEN, foreman.

164b - 1810, Monongalia County Court. John GRIBBLE summoned to answer Robert FERREL in a plea of debt for $80.66 and $100 damage, 24 October 1807. Note signed by GRIBBLE to FERREL dated 13 November 1795 for 24 pounds and 4 shillings, payable in salt at market price and witnessed by Thomas CHIPPS. "Received of the within 9 1/2 bushels of salt at 20 shillings per bushel," signed by FERRELL. Appearance Bond signed by GRIBBLE secured by James (x) HAMILTON, 28 October 1807. August 1810 term, judgement for the plaintiff, except 9 pounds and 10 shillings which appears to have been paid, with 5% interest from 13 November 1795 until paid, John A. GUSEMAN, foreman.

164b - 1810, Monongalia County Court. Henry DERING, William TINGLE, John STEALEY, Michael KERNS and Alexander HAWTHORN summoned to answer Robert BOGGESS in a plea of debt, due by work and labor performed by the complainant, damage $100, 10 September 1806. BOGGESS presented a bill to the above defendants for work performed on the "School House." 10 September 1803, to making 3 door frames $4.50, making 10 window frames $15, 4 small window frames $4, 137′ sheeting $7.37. 17 December 1803, to 11 squares of framing $9.16, 43 feet cornice $7.16, 20 feet bor__ $4.16, 62 feet of ba__ board $1.72, nailing on 32 & 1/2 hundred shingles $6.73, totaling $53.82 less nails $.75 leaving a balance of $53.07. On 16 December 1804, Henry DERING, one of the school trustees, directed Thomas WILSON, treasurer, to pay this amount to BOGGESS "when collected out of the school house money." The defendants said they could not pay this order because the subscribers would not pay. August 1810 term, verdict and judgement for the plaintiff for $53.07 damages, S. SWEARINGEN, foreman.

179

164b - 1810, Monongalia County Court. Elihu HORTON was in jail at the suit of Jacob PINDALL and Forbes BRITTON. He petitioned Justices John STEALEY and Ralph BARKSHIRE that he be discharged by the Act of Insolvent Debtors, 24 December 1810. "I have no property either real or personal to deliver up and this is my schedule, E. HORTON."

164b - 1810, Monongalia County Court. One roan horse named Barny, the property of William TINGLE, was attached at the suit of Augustus WERNINGER for $31.66 with interest at 6% from 2 October 1807 plus costs. In order to retain possession of his property until time for public sale or his debt was paid TINGLE signed this Delivery Bond secured by Matthew GAY, 10 September 1810. On reverse: "Delayed by injunction."

164b - 1806, Monongalia County Court. One ton of bar iron, the property of Davis SHOCKLEY, was attached at the suit of Hannah STANLEY for $15.50 plus cost. In order to retain possession of his property until time of public sale or his debt was paid SHOCKLEY signed this Delivery Bond secured by James JEFFS, 28 July 1806. "STANLEY vs SHOCKLEY, Sheriff's fee in the execution $3.71 and commissions and taking bond $3.00, John HOWELL attended 8 days on said suit $4.24." "Rec'd of Davis SHOCKLEY $30 to be appropriated towards the discharge of a forthcoming bond given by said SHOCKLEY with James JEFFS security to the sheriff in favor of Hannah STANLEY," 25 August 1806, signed by N. EVANS.

164b - 1810, Monongalia County Court. John and Susannah McCORMICK summoned to answer Jacob FOULK in a plea of debt for $300 and $10 damages, 10 June 1806. Jacob FOULK's complaint: On 7 July 1804, Susannah HILEY/HILY (now Susannah McCORMICK, wife of John McCORMICK) signed an obligation promising to pay to him $300 which bond is conditioned that HILEY make to FOULK a good general warranty deed for a certain lot in Morgantown adjoining Alex HAWTHORN opposite Baldwin WEAVER and adjoining Henry DERING on Water Street taking in the drain to said street, within six months from written date. In April 1805, Susannah HILEY married John McCORMICK. FOULK said Susannah failed to make the deed as agreed and failed to pay the penal sum as stated in the bond. He prayed the court to question Susannah in the matter. Three hundred dollar penal bond signed by Susannah HIGHLY to Jacob FOULK conditioned on the conveyance of a certain lot in Morgantown. John and James WEST witnessed this bond on 4 July 1804. The document is faded and difficult to read. Appearance Bond signed by John McCORMICK (first signature) and Susannah McCORMICK secured by John McCORMICK (second signature is very different from the first) and Simmeon ROYCE, 11 June 1805. John DOWNER secured bail for McCORMICK, 16 August 1805. ____ 1810 term, judgement for the plaintiff for $128 in damages, Robert BOGGESS, foreman.

164b - 1810, Monongalia County Court. William PRICE and Henry MILLER summoned to answer John ROBERTS in a plea of debt for $22.60 and $10 damage, 3 October and 30 November 1808. ROBERTS complained that PRICE and MILLER owed him $22.60 by virtue of an obligation dated 27 April 1807. "If I am rightly informed, MILLER is not at present an inhabitant," signed by Jno C. PAYNE for Sheriff S. MORGAN. August 1810 term, judgement for the plaintiff for $22.60 to be discharged by the payment of $11.30 with interest at 6% from 20 October 1807, Noah RIDGWAY, foreman.

164b - 1810, Monongalia County Court. Presley MARTIN and Robert SCOTT, administrators of Jesse MARTIN, deceased, summoned to answer David SCOTT 3rd for the use of Nimrod EVANS, in a plea of trespass on the case damage $100, 24 August and 30 November 1808. Note signed by Jesse MARTIN to David SCOTT dated 1 July 1806 for 111 bushels of sound rye at CARN's Mill, due 1 November next and witnessed by Nancy MARTIN. Note assigned to EVANS on 4 September 1806. August 1810 term, judgement for the plaintiff for the debt with $55.50 damages plus interest at 6% from 1 November 1806, John A. GUSEMAN, foreman.

164b - 1810, Monongalia County Court. Recognizance Bond signed by Nancy (x) MADE and Marget (x) MADE secured by Joseph COOMBS, 19 November 1810. The condition of the bond is such that Nancy MAID, wife of John MAID, yeoman, and Marget MAID, spinster, would appear and be examined by the court and in the meantime keep the peace toward all citizens and especially toward Elizabeth DAWSON. December 1810 term, "disposed of."

164b - 1810, Monongalia County Court. Two sorrel horses, the property of Thomas MARTIN, was attached at the suit of Nester HARDING/HARDIN for 8 pounds and 18 shillings debt with interest at 5% from 25 December 1796 plus cost. In order to retain possession of his property until time of public sale or his debt was paid MARTIN signed this Delivery Bond secured by Peter FORTNEY, 12 July 1805. Notice from HARDIN to MARTIN and FORTNEY of intent to petition the court for judgement on a forthcoming bond conditioned on the delivery of property which they failed to do, 18 June 1810. July 1810 term, judgement for the plaintiff for $115.80 debt to be discharged by the payment of $52.90 with interest at 6% from 12 July 1805 plus costs, with damages on the aforesaid sum of $52.90 with interest at 10% from 16 August 1805 until 13 June 1810. Credit this judgement with $20.55 per decree of the court as of 12 July 1805.

164b - 1810, Monongalia County Court. One bay horse, the property of William FRUM, was attached at the suit of Abraham WEAVER. In order to retain possession of his property until time for public sale or his debt was paid FRUM signed this Delivery Bond secured by Joseph ALLEN, 6 November 1806. Notice from WEAVER of intent to petition the court for judgement against FRUM and ALLEN for failure to deliver the horse or pay the debt, 18 June 1810. July 1810 term, judgement for the plaintiff for $44.88 and costs to be discharged by the payment of $23.07 with interest at 6% from 8 November 1806 until payment and the costs with damages on the $23.07 with interest at 10% from 10 November 1806.

164b - 1810, Monongalia County Court. One good race horse, the property of Francis COLLINS, was attached at the suit of James McKENNON for a $14 Bill of Injunction. In order to retain possession of his property until time for public sale or his debt was paid COLLINS signed this Delivery Bond secured by Noah RIDGWAY, 4 July 1810. Notice to COLLINS and RIDGWAY from McKENNON of intent to petition the court for judgement against them for failure to deliver the horse or pay the debt, 15 September 1810. December 1810 term, judgement for the plaintiff.

164b - 1810, Monongalia County Court. William CHIPPS summoned to answer John SEAMAN in a plea of debt for $32 and $20 damage, 28 April 1806. Two month note signed by William CHIPPS to SEAMAN dated 12 August 1805 for $32, $10 to be paid in cash, $10 to be paid in store goods and $12 in bar iron and witnessed by Enoch EVANS and David SCOTT Jr. John BAKER, James McVICKER, Nicholas MADERA, Christian MADERA and John GREEN summoned to testify in behalf of CHIPPS, 14 August 1809. John BAKER and James McVICKER summoned to testify in behalf of CHIPPS, 29 June 1810. Appearance Bond signed by William CHIPPS secured by Thomas R. CHIPPS, 28 April 1806. August 1810 term, judgement for the plaintiff for the debt with interest at 6% from 12 April 1805, John COOPER, foreman.

164c - 1811, Monongalia County Court. Settlement by Robert FERRELL, for George S. DERING vs James SCOTT. One page containing the interest and cost computations on a debt of $280 from 3 May 1805 up to and including 7 September 1811.

164c - 1811, Monongalia County Court. Nicholas MADERA summoned to answer John REED, surviving partner of REED & (Standish) FORDE & Company, merchants, for the use of Josiah BALL in a plea of debt for $79.45 and $40 damage, 17 December 1810. Demand Note signed by MADERA to REED and FORDE dated 9 August 1804 for $79.45. May 1811, judgement confessed.

164c - 1810, Monongalia County Court. One horse and two cows, the property of David GRAHAM, was attached at the suit of George HARDIN for $47.50 with interest at 6% from 14 December 1805 plus costs. Sheriff Lemuel JOHN and Deputy Mathew GAY sold GRAHAM's property at public sale. Bond secured by George

HARDIN, of Fayette County, Pennsylvania, and Zackquill MORGAN to indemnify and save harmless the sheriff and his deputy from all prosecutions and suits that may be brought or exhibited against them for taking and selling the property by virtue of an attachment bond, 13 June 1810.

164c - 1810, Monongalia County Court. Bond signed by William TINGLE and Ralph BARKSHIRE dated 11 December 1810. The condition of the bond is such that whereas Deputy Mathew GAY, by virtue of an execution in favor of William TINGLE against the property of Robert SCOTT, seized a parcel of corn standing on that part of SCOTT's farm occupied by _____ BRITTON and supposed to be paid by BRITTON to SCOTT for rent and whereas it is stated that the corn is claimed by James WALLS, now if TINGLE shall indemnify and save harmless Sheriff Nicholas VANDERVERT and his deputy from all prosecutions and suits that may be brought or exhibited against them for taking and selling the property by virtue of an Attachment Bond, if he exposed the corn for sale.

164c - 1810, Monongalia County Court. One stud horse, the property of Benjamin THORN, was attached at the suit of James WILSON for $150.55. Bond signed by James WILSON and Benjamin (x) FIELDS to indemnify and save harmless Sheriff Lemuel JOHN and his deputy, George S. DERING, from all prosecutions and suits that may be brought or exhibited against them for taking and selling the property by virtue of an Attachment Bond, if he exposed the horse to public sale, 2 May 1810.

164c - 1810, Monongalia County Court. "Jonathan BRANDON, assignee of John GRIBBLE who was assignee of Nathaniel EWING, administrator of Robert EWING, deceased, against George ROBERTS and Samuel PATTERSON. Petition and summons issued 28 January 1805." John GRIBBLE appeared before Justice John FAIRFAX and swore the note given by George ROBERTS, with Samuel PATTERSON as security, to Nathaniel EWING and afterwards assigned to John GRIBBLE and from John GRIBBLE to Jonathan BRANDON Jr., was either mislaid or lost, he believed the amount of the note was $17 and some cents, 8 November 1808. January 1810 term, dismissed, each paying own costs.

164c - 1810, Monongalia County Court. John DAVIS, Francis SETH, John SETH, John HARMAN, John TEMPOLIN, John PAYNE and James MONTGOMERY summoned to answer Thomas R. CHIPPS in a plea of trespass on the case damage $48, 28 July, 5 September and 9 December 1803. Francis and John SETH not found. James MONTGOMERY not an inhabitant. CHIPPS complained that the defendants were indebted to him for labor and work in the amount of $100. August 1810 term, "abated."

164c - 1810, Monongalia County Court. Isaac PRICE Sr. summoned to answer Henry SMITH for non-payment of a debt, 22

November 1810. Summons signed by Jared EVANS in the presence of Joseph BARKER. December 1810 term, judgement & attachment on the property of PRICE. "No property found by me," signed by Aaron BARKER.

164c - 1810, Monongalia County Court. Otho HENRY summoned to answer a presentment against him as Overseer of the Road leading from Indian Creek to DENT's Mill, 14 April 1810. James BARKER and David SCOTT summoned to give evidence to the Grand Jury, 7 June 1810. Aaron BARKER summoned to give evidence to the Grand Jury, 13 August 1810. "We the Grand Jury present the Overseer of the Road leading from Indian Creek by Otho HENRY's to Dent's Mill by the information of David SCOTT and James BARKER, two of our own body, within two months last past." Deputy Geo. S. DERING for Sheriff Lemuel JOHN. August 1810 term, quashed (voided).

Also in this file - "We the Grand Jury present John CARPENTER for committing an assault on the body of Gasper BUNNER on 28 December 1809 by the information of John STEPHENS who was sworn in open court to give testimony." "We the Grand Jury present Gasper BUNNER for committing an assault on the body of John CARPENTER on 28 December 1809 by the information of John STEPHENS who was sworn in open court to give testimony."

164c - 1810, Monongalia County Court. John DAVIS, Francis SETH, John SETH, John HARMAN, John TEMPOLIN, John PAYNE and James MONTGOMERY summoned to answer Thomas R. CHIPPS in a plea of trespass on the case damage $48, 28 July, 5 September and 9 December 1803. (See page 183).

164c - 1810, Monongalia County Court. Andrew MILLER recovered against Jesse PAYNE the sum of $43 debt with interest at 6% from 1 December 1804 plus costs. On 14 April 1808, John C. PAYNE secured bail for Jesse PAYNE. The debt remained unpaid and Jesse did not surrender himself to prison. MILLER prayed the court to summon John C. PAYNE and show cause, if any he can, why execution should not be had against him as security for Jesse, 18 July and 28 September 1810. June 1810 term, judgement for the plaintiff for $51.58 with interest on $43 at 6% from 1 December 1804, Francis COLLINS, foreman.

164c - 1810, Monongalia County Court. Thomas LAIDLEY summoned to answer Isaac Hite WILLIAMS in a plea of debt due by note, 16 March 1810. Order for attachment on LAIDLEY's property dated 10 March 1810. No property found, 20 April 1810.

164c - 1809, Monongalia County Court. On 11 March 1809, William BALDWIN obtained a judgement against Amos CHIPPS for $4.92 plus costs. Bond signed by CHIPPS secured by William CHIPPS to ensure Amos would pay his debt before the rising of the next General Assembly dated 20 March 1809. Assignment of this bond to James McVICKER by BALDWIN dated 18 April 1809 and witnessed by Geo. B. HOSKINSON.

164c - 1810, Monongalia County Court. J. W. RIDDLE obtained an attachment on the property of Charles EDDLEBLUT for $4. The attachment was levied on one feather bed and blanket and several other small articles on which attachment there has been a judgement and an order of sale by the court with $4.94 costs. The property was exposed to public sale and Levi JONES was the highest bidder. Replevin Bond signed by Levi JONES to Henry RUNNER to ensure he would pay his debt within 12 months secured by J. W. RIDDLE/BIDDLE, 23 March 1810. (Replevin Bond: a bond to protect or give security for the return to, or recovery by, a person of goods or chattels wrongfully taken or detained upon giving security to try the matter in court and return the goods if defeated in action.)

164c - 1809, Monongalia County Court. On 1 August 1809, James HURRY obtained a judgement against William CHIPPS for $10.87 plus costs. Bond signed by CHIPPS secured by John CHIPPS to ensure William would pay his debt before the rising of the next General Assembly dated 26 August 1809.

164c - 1809, Monongalia County Court. Amos CHIPPS summoned to answer Abner LORD in a plea of debt due by account, 21 October 1808. LORD obtained an execution against the property of CHIPPS on 27 February 1809 for $16.80 debt plus costs. Bond signed by CHIPPS secured by William CHIPPS to ensure Amos would pay his debt before the rising of the next General Assembly dated 20 March 1809.

164c - 1809, Monongalia County Court. One horse, the property of John C. PAYNE, was attached at the suit of Evan B. MORGAN for $19.05 plus costs. PAYNE's property was sold at public auction and George HITE was the highest bidder at $27.30. Replevin Bond signed by G. HITE to ensure he would pay his debt within 12 months secured by John PAYNE, 23 February 1809. (Replevin Bond: a bond to protect or give security for the return to, or recovery by, a person of goods or chattels wrongfully taken or detained upon giving security to try the matter in court and return the goods if defeated in action.)

164c - 1808, Monongalia County Court. John HINE obtained an attachment on the property of George ARNOLD, of Harrison County, for $27 plus costs. ARNOLD's property could not be sold for 3/4 its value and was returned to him upon his giving this bond with security. Replevin Bond signed by ARNOLD to ensure he would pay his debt within 12 months secured by John PRUNTY, 29 October 1808. (Replevin Bond: a bond to protect or give security for the return to, or recovery by, a person of goods or chattels wrongfully taken or detained upon giving security to try the matter in court and return the goods if defeated in action.)

164c - 1809, Monongalia County Court. David MUSGRAVE obtained a judgement against Zachariah BARKER for $8.50 plus costs. Bond signed by BARKER secured by David SCOTT to ensure BARKER would pay his debt before the rising of the next General Assembly, 25 March 1809. MUSGRAVE assigned this bond to Barbara SNODGRASS on 22 August 1809, witnessed by Nathan MATHENY. SNODGRASS assigned this bond to Ralph BARKSHIRE on 23 August 1809, witnessed by Joseph GRUBEL.

164c - 1808, Monongalia County Court. Three cows, 3 year-lings, 8 old sheep and 1 lamb, the property of James WALKER, was attached at the suit of Thomas CRUMWELL for $57.08 with interest at 6% from 28 March 1804 plus costs. The property was exposed to public sale and the sheep bought 3/4 their value ($9) and the cattle would not sell for 3/4 their value. George HITE was the highest bidder ($35.38). Replevin Bond signed by G. HITE to ensure he would pay his debt within 12 months secured by Rawley MARTIN, 22 April 1808. (Replevin Bond: a bond to protect or give security for the return to, or recovery by, a person of goods or chattels wrongfully taken or detained upon giving security to try the matter in court and return the goods if defeated in action.)

164c - 1810, Monongalia County Court. Two mares, the property of John CARTER, was attached at the suit of Charles CONWAY for $100 with interest at 6% from 1 November 1801. The horses were exposed to public sale but would not sell for 3/4 their value. Replevin Bond signed by John CARTER to ensure he would pay his debt within 12 months secured by John PAYNE, 25 June 1808. (Replevin Bond: a bond to protect or give security for the return to, or recovery by, a person of goods or chattels wrongfully taken or detained upon giving security to try the matter in court and return the goods if defeated in action.) June 1810 term, injunction granted on this bond.

164c - 1809, Monongalia County Court. Joseph BAILEY obtained an execution of $19.50 plus costs against the property of Abraham and Simeon WOODROW on 1 June 1809. Abraham and Simeon signed this Stay of Execution Bond to ensure they would pay their debt before the rising of the next General Assembly secured by John W. THOMPSON, 15 July 1809.

164c - 1809, Monongalia County Court. On 9 September 1809, Ralph BARKSHIRE obtained an execution on the property of John TAYLOR for $5.36. Bond signed by TAYLOR secured by Abraham HALE to ensure he would pay his debt by the rising of the next General Assembly, 7 October 1809.

164c - 1809, Monongalia County Court. Ralph BARKSHIRE obtain-ed an execution against Presley MARTIN for $21.11. Bond signed by MARTIN secured by Robert SCOTT to ensure MARTIN would pay his debt before the rising of the next General Assembly, 23 September 1809.

164c - 1809, Monongalia County Court. Moses MANEAR and George ZINN summoned to answer William LOWRY and Joseph LOWRY and Company, assignee of James COBURN, for non-payment of a debt due by note, 18 June 1809. On 24 June 1809, LOWRY and Company obtained a judgement of $12 with interest from 1 March 1809 against MANEAR and ZINN, his security. Bond signed by Moses MINNEAR secured by John (x) MONTGOMERY to ensure he would pay his debt before the rising of the next General Assembly, 22 August 1809.

164c - 1810, Monongalia County Court. Bowers FURBEE obtained a judgement against William DEAN for $9 with interest. Bond signed by William DEAN secured by William BALDWIN to ensure DEAN would pay his debt before the rising of the next General Assembly, 20 March 1809. The bond assigned to Rebecca DERING on 22 March 1810.

164c - 1809, Monongalia County Court. David SEAMAN obtained a judgement against Thomas FLOYD for $11.30 with interest. Bond signed by FLOYD secured by William SNODGRASS to ensure he would pay his debt before the rising of the next General Assembly, 5 July 1809. The bond assigned to William LOWRY and Company on 2 September 1809, signed by SEAMAN in the presence of Samuel LOWRY.

164c - 1809, Monongalia County Court. On 7 last June, William LOWRY and Company obtained a judgement against Enos WEST for $6 with interest. Bond signed by WEST secured by William EVERLY to ensure he would pay his debt before the rising of the next General Assembly, 25 February 1809.

164c - 1809, Monongalia County Court. 15 July 1809, William LOWRY and Company obtained a judgement against George SCOTT for $9.28 with interest. Bond signed by George (x) SCOTT secured by Caleb WISEMAN to ensure SCOTT would pay his debt before the rising of the next General Assembly, 26 August 1809.

Caleb WISEMAN's signature

164c - 1809, Monongalia County Court. John WEST summoned to answer William CHIPPS, assignee of Philip COOMBS, assignee of John GEFFS, for non-payment of a debt due by note, 19 July 1809. CHIPPS obtained a judgement against WEST for $13 with interest. Bond signed by WEST secured by James (x) LOWE to ensure WEST would pay his debt before the rising of the next General Assembly, 27 September 1809.

164c - 1810, Monongalia County Court. On 8 July 1809, John CAMPBELL (John is crossed out and overwritten with Joseph) obtained a judgement against Peter EVERLY for $11 with interest. Bond signed by EVERLY secured by Nathan MATHENEY to ensure EVERLY would pay his debt before the rising of the next General Assembly, 1 October 1809. CAMPBELL assigned this bond to Mathew GAY on 2 June 1810.

164c - 1811, Monongalia County Court. Thomas LAIDLEY/LEDLEY summoned to answer Benjamin/Banjamon HAYS for non-payment of a debt due by note, 13 April 1810. No property found, 29 March 1811.

164c - 1810, Monongalia County Court. One bobjack horse, one sorrel horse and one roan horse, the property of William FRUM, was attached at the suit of William TENNANT for $35 with interest at 6% from 25 December 1806. In order to retain possession of his property until time of public sale or his debt was paid FRUM signed this Delivery Bond secured by Joseph ALLEN, 25 May 1810.

164c - 1810, Monongalia County Court. Bond for Jesse SPURGEON to serve as executor for James SPURGEON, deceased, secured by Frederick _____ and Alexander BRANDON, 9 July 1810.

Signature of Frederick _____

165 - 1810, Monongalia County Court. Bond signed by William HAYMOND Jr. to serve as guardian to Sarah PEARCE, orphan of Elias PEARCE, deceased, secured by Henry (x) TUCKER, 10 April 1810.

165 - 1810, Monongalia County Court. Bond signed by Rebecca DERING to keep an ordinary at her own house in Morgantown secured by Joseph LOWRY, 13 August 1810.

165 - 1810, Monongalia County Court. Bond signed by William G. LOWMAN, a Minister of the Episcopal Methodist Church, to celebrate the Rites of Matrimony secured by William GEORGE, Jno. A. BARKSHIRE and John SMITH, 9 July 1810.

165 - 1810, Monongalia County Court. Various notes before 1810 that may belong with cases.

1799, Charles (x) LITTLE promised to pay John EVANS $5.

11 February 1797, Robert TRIPLETT signed a note to Samuel FRINEOR? $2, due 25 December 1797, witnessed by Thomas EVANS.

22 July 1799, Caleb TANSEY signed a note to Isaac H. WILLIAMS for 20 pounds in joiner work, my line of business, to discharge a note of Matthias HITE's which is now in the hands of said WILLIAMS assigned to him from John PLUM, and witnessed by Edward TANSEY.

14 March 1805, James MORGAN promised to pay Henry DUNN $15 in cash, witnessed by Zackquil MORGAN. DUNN assigned this note to James DUNN on 19 September 1814 in the presence of James JOHNSTON.

25 April 1804, Levi MORGAN promised to pay Elijah HOUSEMAN $39.50 in pot metal or bar iron to be delivered at or near Morgantown at market price, witnessed by W. R. TINGLE.

1 May 1810, Zackquill MORGAN promised to pay Nicholas CASEY $54 in any merchantable trade, due 60 days after date, and witnessed by Henry ECKEHART.

14 August 1807, M. ANSTINIS promised to pay Izock LINSLY $2.50, due on demand.

4 April 1807, James EVANS promised to pay William LOWRY $4.12.

165 - 1809, Monongalia County Court. A quantity of plank, the property of Samuel SWEARINGEN, was offered at public sale at the suit of Charles MAGILL for $16.12 and would not sell for 3/4 its value. The property was returned to SWEARINGEN upon giving bond with security. Replevin Bond signed by SWEARINGEN to ensure he would pay his debt within 12 months secured by John CARPENTER, 13 January 1809. (Replevin Bond: a bond to protect or give security for the return to, or recovery by, a person of goods or chattels wrongfully taken or detained upon giving security to try the matter in court and return the goods if defeated in action.)

165 - 1809, Monongalia County Court. Mary DUNCAN obtained a judgement for $13.10, bearing date 3 June 1809, against Daniel STEWART. Bond signed by Daniel STEWART to ensure he would pay his debt before the rising of the next General Assembly secured by Charles STEWART in the presence of Arthur STEWART and Daniel COX, 1 August 1809.

165 - 1808, Monongalia County Court. One horse, the property of Levi MORGAN and Uriah MORGAN, was attached at the suit of John STEALEY and Robert MINNIS for $20.48 with 6% interest.

The property was offered at public sale and would not sell for 3/4 its value. The horse was returned to MORGAN upon giving bond with security. Replevin Bond signed by Levi MORGAN and Uriah MORGAN to ensure he would pay his debt within 12 months secured by Zackquill MORGAN, 23 December 1808. (Replevin Bond: a bond to protect or give security for the return to, or recovery by, a person of goods or chattels wrongfully taken or detained upon giving security to try the matter in court and return the goods if defeated in action.)

165 - 1809, Monongalia County Court. Enoch JONES obtained a judgement against William CHIPPS for $30. CHIPPS signed this bond to ensure he would pay his debt before the rising of the next General Assembly secured by Rawley MARTIN in the presence of James ROBISON and Daniel COX, 1 September 1809.

165 - 1810, Monongalia County Court. One large parcel of plank, the property of Alexander HAWTHORN, was attached at the suit of Thomas CARSON Jr. for $94.16 with 6% interest from 30 June 1801. Replevin Bond signed by HAWTHORN to ensure he would pay his debt within 12 months secured by Robert HAWTHORN, 23 May 1810. (Replevin Bond: a bond to protect or give security for the return to, or recovery by, a person of goods or chattels wrongfully taken or detained upon giving security to try the matter in court and return the goods if defeated in action.)

165 - 1809, Monongalia County Court. William TINGLE obtained a judgement against Samuel HARMAN for $5.34, bearing date 25 March 1809. Bond signed by HARMAN to ensure he would pay his debt before the rising of the next General Assembly secured by Joseph HARRISON, 5 April 1809.

165 - 1809, Monongalia County Court. Francis COLLINS summoned to answer Thomas GRAHAM in an action of covenant (for the delivery of 10 feet of grindstone), 2 February 1809. The grindstone was offered at public sale and COLLINS was the highest bidder at $10. Bond signed by COLLINS to ensure his debt would be paid before the rising of the next General Assembly secured by Noah RIDGWAY in the presence of James McVICKER, 1 July 1809.

165 - 1809, Monongalia County Court. Christian WHITEHAIR obtained a judgement against William JAMES on 8 May for $18.61. Bond signed by JAMES to ensure he would pay his debt before the rising of the next General Assembly secured by James C. GOFF in the presence of Elisabeth JORGUSON, 3 May 1809. Another bond dated 8 May 1809 for $2.62 recovered against JAMES signed and witnessed the same. A third bond dated 8 May 1809 for $7.50 recovered against JAMES signed and witnessed the same. A fourth bond dated 8 May 1809 for $6.17 recovered against JAMES signed and witnessed the same.

165 - 1809, Monongalia County Court. David BARKER, assignee of William McBRIDE, recovered a judgement against John WEST and John W. DENT for $31.63 with interest from 20 March 1807. Bond signed by WEST to ensure he would pay his debt before the rising of the next General Assembly secured by Thomas KNIGHT, 16 March 1809.

165 - 1810, Monongalia County Court. Bond signed by Samuel KENNEDY to serve as constable for a term of two years secured by Matthew GEORGE and Noah RIDGWAY, 10 July 1810.

165 - 1810, Monongalia County Court. Bond signed by James COBURN to serve as constable for a term of two years secured by Philip SHIVELY and John McGEE, _ July 1810.

165 - 1810, Monongalia County Court. Demand Note signed by William (x) WALKER to French S. GRAY for $1 dated 29 January 1810.

165 - 1810, Monongalia County Court. Bond signed by Thomas SPENCER to serve as administrator for Reubin ABRAMS, deceased, secured by John SCOTT and Archibald (x) BOYD, 10 May 1810.

165 - 1810, Monongalia County Court. Bond signed by Christian WHITEHAIR to serve as constable for a term of two years secured by Adam SHAFER, 11 June 1810.

165 - 1810, Monongalia County Court. Bond signed by David SCOTT 3rd, the owner of an established ferry across the Monongalia (sic) River at the mouth of Scotts Run, to ensure he would duly keep the ferry according to law and give immediate passage to all public messengers secured by Felix SCOTT, _ April 1810.

165 - 1810, Monongalia County Court. Bond signed by Joseph JENKINS to act as guardian to John WATTS, orphan of John WATTS, deceased, secured by George HITE, 15 May 1810.

165 - 1810, Monongalia County Court. Bond signed by Davis SHOCKLEY to keep an ordinary at his own house in Morgantown secured by Nicholas MADERA, 16 May 1810.

165 - 1810, Monongalia County Court. Bond signed by John KNOX to serve as constable for a term of two years secured by Felix SCOTT and Daniel COX, 10 April 1810.

165 - 1810, Monongalia County Court. Rawley MARTIN presented a bill for equalizing the lands and taking in the taxable property and making out the books and examining and certifying the same $100 and issuing 5 store licenses $1.25, 1810. Allowed June 1810.

165 - 1810, Monongalia County Court. "13 June 1810, This is to certify to the Court of Monongalia County that we relinquish our right of administration on the estate of our brother, Conrad BIXLER, and are fully satisfied that Casper ORTH be admitted to administer the same," signed by _____ _____ and Samuel (x) BIXLER.

165 - 1811, Monongalia County Court. Charles BYRN summoned to answer Thomas SPENCER in a plea of trespass on the case damage $500, 18 August 1810. SPENCER complained that in 1808, he owed one roan mare valued at $100 and under the color of his office as deputy, BYRN took the mare and detained her to be exposed to sale for the sum of $13 which he, SPENCER owed for clerk's fees. BYRN promised SPENCER he would not expose the mare to public sale for two weeks so that SPENCER might have the opportunity to redeem the mare. If at the expiration of two weeks, SPENCER still could not redeem the mare, he (BYRN) would buy her in and return her whenever SPENCER was in a position to pay for her. SPENCER said BYRN made it known to the public that he was to bid in the mare and the bidders and bystanders would not offer more than the $13 that BYRN offered. He said he paid BYRN the money plus costs and demanded the mare, but BYRN refused to restore the mare to him and therefore he brings suit. BYRN said the mare was taken in execution and SPENCER asked him not to sell her for two weeks, but BYRN said he must sell her according to law. The mare was advertised and SPENCER told BYRN to buy her and he would pay him the money. SPENCER requested BYRN to wait two weeks for his money and BYRN said he was willing to sell the mare to SPENCER when he could pay the money. BYRN said SPENCER never tendered the money or called for the mare until some weeks after the time expired for redemption and this he is ready to verify. John COOPER, Robert BOGGESS and Benjamin JENNINGS summoned to testify in behalf of SPENCER, 20 February 1811. _____ ____ term, judgement for the defendant.

165 - 1810, Monongalia County Court. Two horses, the property of Zackquill MORGAN, was attached at the suit of George MORGAN for $30 with interest at 6% from 1 December 1803. In order to retain possession of his property until time of public sale or his debt was paid MORGAN signed this Delivery Bond secured by C. MADERA, 31 May 1810.

165 - 1810, Monongalia County Court. Bond signed by Jasper WYATT to serve as constable for two years secured by Dudley EVANS and William WILLEY Jr., 12 June 1810.

165 - 1810, Monongalia County Court. Bond signed by Nicholas VANDERVORT to serve as sheriff secured by Augustus WERNINGER, Daniel COX, Boaz BURROWS, Alexander HAWTHORN, Mathew GAY and George S. DERING, 10 September 1810.

165 - 1810, Monongalia County Court. To Monongalia County from Christian MADERA: "7 June 1810, to mending gaol at debtor's room, $1.50; to mortar for plastering, $.33. There was an allowance made of $50 to repair the jail. There has orders not been made sufficient to cover that sum yet payable out of the County Levy of 1809, therefore the above $1.83 should be allowed."

165 - 1810, Monongalia County Court. Three hundred bushels of good merchantable Indian Corn, the property of Jesse MARTIN, was attached at the suit of John MOOR for $82.66 plus costs. In order to retain possession of his property until time of public sale or his debt was paid MARTIN signed this Delivery Bond secured by William PRIDE, 27 November 18__.

165 - 1810, Monongalia County Court. John CARTER petitioned the court to condemn a mill seat on his farm at the Great Falls of the Monongahela River and for the establishment of a water grist mill at the same place, the dam to run across the river, 11 June 1810.

165 - 1810, Monongalia County Court. Bond signed by Aaron BARKER to serve as constable for two years secured by Benjamin HAMILTON and Zackquill MORGAN, 13 June 1810.

165 - 1810, Monongalia County Court. James ELLIOTT summoned to answer Frederick GIBLER in a plea of trespass on the case, 19 April 1806. GIBLER complained that on 26 July 1804, ELLIOTT owed him $30 which he, as GIBLER's security, paid to John DAVIS who held an Article of Agreement dated 31 March 1797, by and between Asa DUDLEY and ELLIOTT. ELLIOTT failed to pay the debt and therefore he brings suit. Article of Agreement dated 31 March 1797 by and between Asa DUDLEY and James ELLIOTT and Fred KIBLER (ELLIOTT's security) whereby DUDLEY rented to ELLIOTT a house on Water Street, opposite Nicholas MADERA, for one year beginning 1 March 1797 and ending 1 March 1798 for 9 pounds and leave the house in good repair, signed by DUDLEY, ELLIOTT and Frederick GIBBLER in the presence of Andrew HITE. On reverse of this agreement, "Received from Frederick GIBLER the full amount of the within note," no date, signed by John DAVIS. August 1810 term dismissed for want of prosecution.

165 - 1809, Monongalia County Court. Nimrod EVANS presented a bill for his services in 1809. "General allowance $28. Examining court on GORDON $3.50. Execution Book $8. Deed Book $9. Order Book $3.50. Book and paper for office $12. Acting as clerk to the Commissioners for Establishing Burnt Records 3 years $10."

165 - 1810, Monongalia County Court. "Tuesday 10 April 1810, Ordered that the Justices of this county be summoned to attend at June term next for the purpose of settling with the collector, laying a County Levy, making allowances and etc."

165 - 1810, Monongalia County Court. 7 August 1810, Nicholas MADERA presented a bill for sundry repairs to the Courthouse $16.50; 18 panes of glass, 10x12 at $.17 per light, $3; 21 panes 8x10 at $.10 per, $2.10; 5 pounds of nails $.92; 4 pounds of "whightning" at 10d and oil for putty $.67; 100 of "shinkels" $.50; 15 bannisters by HURRY at $.12 1/2 per $1.87 1/2; 36 feet of plank $.50; blacksmith work by WALKER $1; blacksmith work by WILSON $1.45 1/2.

165 - 1810, Monongalia County Court. Order for review of the lands of Richard PRICE on Paw Paw Creek to erect a dam to work a water grist mill, 13 October 1808. John DENT, Jacob PINDALL, John A. BARKSHIRE, John BRAND, Henry YOUST, Jarret EVANS, John SMITH, Andrew ARNETT, John DICKEN, John CUNNING- HAM, Elisha CLAYTON and Benjamin WILSON viewed the lands of PRICE and determined that no person would be damaged, no obstruction to navigation or to fish passage would occur by erecting a dam 6′ 9″ high from the low water mark, 15 October 1808. Entered February 1810.

165 - 1813, Monongalia County Court. Clerk Nimrod EVANS′ papers, 1798 - 1813.
    A list of notes left by Philip DODDRIDGE for collection, Francis TIBBS $20 due to HOSKINSON on 25 December 1806. Stephen WARMAN $10.17 September 1805. Isaac MATHEW $20 1 September 1805. Zackquill MORGAN $8.
    EVANS to Augustus WERNINGER, 23 April 1803, 1 quire paper and inkpowder $.50; 17 May 1803, 5 yard linen $2.71; 30 July 1804, quart bottle $.25; 20 August 1804, 1 piece Irish Linen $21.67; 22 September 1804, 1 1/2 yards flannel $1; 29 May 1805, 1/2 pound sweet scent James R. TOVANO? $.37; 16 June 1806, 3/4 yard tow linen $.19; 2 May 1807, goods per James McGEE as per bill rendered $22.11; 5 May 1807, goods per McGEE as per bill rendered $.50. Credited to this account: 17 May 1803, by cash overpaid on money lent $.__; 7 February 1803, ditto $10; 22 September 1803, ditto $10; 6 July 1805, hire of blacksmith $.80. Balance $28.76. By my account paid up to 1807, $27.70; by deed to SHROEDER $.75. Balance $.69.
    Michael HOLLOWS, tax of 1807 on 800 acres $.38; received 21 September 1808.

Henry SHOOPS, to tax of 1807 on 100 acres $.12; received 21 September 1808.

Isaac H. WILLIAMS, to tax on 1844 acres for 1807 $2.21; received 21 September 1808.

John SHARK, to tax of 1807 on 305 acres $.48; received September 1808.

Bertrand EWELL, to tax of 1807 on 565 acres $.___; received 21 September 1808.

A list of publications purchased by Nimrod EVANS from William LOWRY and Company: 9 May 1811, Life of Washington $20; Burks Works $12; Currens Speeches $5; Jun(?) Letters $1.12 1/2.

Nimrod EVANS to George HITE: 1 writing desk (1.4.0); 1 cup and table (1.1.0); 1 set steps (0.9.0); 1 ___ bottom bedstead (1.0.0); shelves under stairs (0.4.6); 1 bureau (3.12.0).

Court fees mentioning the names of John LYON, John CLARK, John KENNEDY, Abraham MILEY, Thomas MARTIN, Francis TIBBS, Alexander McCLELAND, William ASHFORD, Ben COPLIN, John McFARLAND, David SAYRE Jr., William ALBIN, George STEWART, Abraham WELLS, Joseph WISBY, James HYDE and many listings of surnames only.

District Court notes, 17 January 1806. On the list are the names of Richard SMITH, Jesse MARTIN, Sam SWEARINGEN, Simeon RICE, John BRANDON, James SCOTT, Matthew GEORGE, Richard POSTLEWAIT and Uriah MORGAN. County Court notes, 17 January 1806. On the list are the names of Joseph MATHENEY, Matthias FURBEE, Jeremiah HANLIN, ___ RIGGS, George RINEHART, Jonathan JANES, Jesse PAYNE, Jacob MYERS, Jacob FOULK Jr., Christopher and Jacob CLUSTER, John FLEMING, John BRUMMAGE, John BROWN, Archibald MOORE, William BICE, George WILSON, J. and Charles SNODGRASS.

A list of fees due Benjamin WILSON, Clerk of Harrison County put in the hands of Deputy John PAYNE for collection: Job CONSTABLE, Henry HAYS, Reuben JACO, William STUART, John ROBERTS, Asa HARRIS, Jacob STORMES, Thomas MAGEE, John POWER, William MAXSON, James PETTYJOHN, James SCOTT, Alexander HAWTHORN, Asa HARRIS, John CARTER, John McVICKER and Adam VANCAMP, April 1808. Jacob NOOSE, George HICKMAN, Nicholas DUNAVIN, Jacob JACOBS, James HAWKINS and James LITTLE, June 1808.

Henry BARRICKMAN to George HITE, computation of interest on a bond due 15 September 1802.

Daniel F. STROTHER presented a bill for serving a petition and summons on Arthur WILSON, $.30, 1806.

Nimrod EVANS presented a bill for serving a petition and summons on Abel DAVIS, $.30, 1806; and a bill for serving a petition and summons on Jesse MARTIN, $.30, 1807.

James EVANS, Esqr. to Augustus WERNINGEN: August 1803, 100 white chapil needles, $.50; 16 December 1803, 3/8 yards of black velvet, $.75; 13 October 1804, 1 "circingle" $1.08; 17 November 1804, 1 pair gloves, $.75; 5 December 1804, 12 yards linen, $10.50; credited by cash paid, $5.25; 12 December 1806, credited by lawyers fee on suit ____ vs Presley MARTIN, $1.25.   Balance $7.06.

John EVANS Sr. to the tax of 1805: to 6 poor levies $2.10; 3 revenues $1.32; 6 horses $.72; 2445 acres land $2.62; 6 poor levies for the year 1804 $2. Received the above tax 13 November 1807.

Nimrod EVANS to tax of 1807: 1 tythable at 81 1/4 cents, 2 blacks at 162 1/2 cents, $3.87 3/4; 2 revenues at 132 cents, 1 horse at 12 cents, __ acres of land for James and Marmaduke EVANS $1.69;   1000 acres of land $.58; 1371 acres for James and Marmaduke EVANS for 1806 $1.69. Total $7.83.   Received 21 September 1808.

John EVANS Sr. to tax of 1807: 2 tythables, 3 black tythes $6.96; 5 revenues at 22 cents and 6 horses at 72 cents, 360 acres at 73 cents,   117 acres at 15 cents,   400 acres at 35 cents, 333 acres at 15 cents, 870 acres at 108 cents $2.46. Total $9.44.   Received 21 September 1808.

A list of fees due Clerk Nimrod EVANS for 1807 and 1808. James BEALL,   Thomas LAIDLEY,   Aaron M. WADE and brother, Samuel BALDWIN,   John SULLIVAN,   William POSTLE,   William GEORGE, David SCOTT son of James,   Lewis OTT, Charles MAGILL, John JONES, Mathew HANNON and James STAFFORD, John TAYLOR, Reuben FORSTER,   John BOUSLOG,   Michael CORE, Thomas EVANS, Jesse MARTIN,   James McVICKER,   Christian MADERA,   George SNIDER, Jacob SMITH, James JEFFS, John WILSON, James SCOTT, Thomas McKINLEY, John MILLER, Reuben JACO, Benjamin THORN, Samuel CRANE, William EVERLY, John HOWELL, Thomas FRETWELL, Josiah WILSON, Robert BOGGESS, Arthur TRADER Sr., John McGEE, Richard NUZUM, Mary BENNETT, John PIERPOINT, Samuel PHILIPS and James CAIN, John McFARLAND, Mary DAVIS, William HARRISON, John EDWARDS, John CLARK, William CHIPPS, Jeremiah AXTON and John CARTER, John SEAMAN, Daniel ANDERSON, Thomas ADAMSON, Eliz. LYNCH and Morgan MORGAN,   Abraham GOOSEMAN, Stephen McDADE, Rachel BILLS, Faquer McCREA, John CREAGEN, Jacob NOOS Sr., Sarah BOYLES, Noah RIDGWAY, Thomas BIRCH, William BAINBRIDGE, James MORGAN, Amos CHIPPS, James BURCHINAL, James DONALDSON, Lucy LANHAM, John HARTMAN, Arthur WILSON, John WEST,   Robert FERRELL,   William GREGG, George HITE, Mathew GEORGE, Robert SCOTT, James WALKER, John and John WATSON, Stepphen MORGAN, Davis SCOTT, Thomas BYRN, Jacob WOOLF, James C. GOFF, Duncan F. McCREA, James BOOTH, John FAIRFAX, John CHIPPS, James MORRIS, Jacob LYMAN, Isaac MATHEWS, John MANN, John RODIHEFFER, James COLLINS Jr., George NORTH and George SMITH,   Edward PARRISH, William HART, Benjamin N. JARRETT, David PILES, Joshua HOSKINSON, George WOOLF, Rynear HALL, John REED,   Joseph ISAACS,   Sydney RALSTON,   John SUMMERS, William RUSSELL, Martin VARNER, William HOLLIFIELD, Jonathan HARTLEY, Samuel WILSON, John JARRETT, Henry BARKER, A. CLEGG, Jo SEVERNS,   Elijah HARDESTY, Abraham HESS, C. COOPER, N. GODWIN,   John LYONS,   Thomas KNIGHT, Noah MORRIS, William BARRETT, James CURRENT, Adam BROWN, William GAD, Elizabeth JOHNSON, Adam SIMONSON, Samuel DAUGHERTY and Coverdill COLE.

Edward EVANS Sr., Thomas HAWKINS, Benjamin HARTLEY, James COLLINS, Richard WEAVER, James TIBBS, Thomas LYMAN, Daniel MARTIN, George NORRIS, Robert HENDERSON, Benjamin JONES, Abel JONES, Enoch JONES, A. GAPEN and P. MARTIN, Ian FRY, Jarrett EVANS, John DOWNER, Philip HUFFMAN, Samuel GRUBB, John MYERS, William FRUM, John GARLOW, Jonathan HARRIS, James WILSON, Thomas BURCHINAL, George GREENWOOD, David CROLL, Joseph ALLEN, Andrew COCHRAN, Anthony COZAD, Jacob LUCAS, John WILSON (Glade), Samuel EVERLY, Charles W. MARTIN, Adam SRIVER, Hedgeman TRIPLETT, Daniel HARTLEY, Noah MORRIS, John SMITH, Richard MERRIFIELD heirs, Caleb WISEMAN, Thomas COURTNEY, Benjamin SAYRE, Phillip SHEETS, John GRIBBLE, William JOLLIFFE Sr., William BALDWIN, Joseph WILFORD, Samuel SHAW, John HARMAN, James DEWEESE, William TENNANT, John PRUKET, Joseph SAPP, Caleb HURLEY, William NORRIS Sr., Henry TUCKER, Joseph FICKLE, Abner MESSENGER, Henry CAROTHERS, George ROBISON, Thomas FLOYD, William MICHAEL, William STILES, Stephen STILES, Richard TENNANT, Levi GANDY, Benjamin MORTON, Abel WILLIAMS, Peter GARDNER, Andrew ICE, David HAYHURST, John BROWN, Joseph SOUTHWORTH, James DEWESE, Joseph HILL, William SHAHAN, Thomas BARTLETT, James MATHENEY, Christopher CORE, Levi FREELAND, Boaz BASNETT, Richard HARRIS, James HAMILTON, William STAFFORD, James TUCKER, Isaac HUFFMAN, George BELL, John JOHNSON, James BRITTON, Laben PUDEU, Abraham BARNES, Hugh KELSO, Catharine EVANS, William and David STEWART, Henry MILLER, John BIGGS, Peter HACKERT, John STEVENS, Jacob ZINN, Lewis ORTH, James STARL-ING, Reason HOLLAND, Joseph and Isaac CAIN, Nathan SPRINGER and S. SWEARINGEN, Thomas HAWKINS, John WILLS, Daniel COX, Thomas MONTGOMERY, John McCLAIN, William GODDARD, Martin BOWMAN, Michael CRONEY, Leonard REEVES, James G. WATSON, Abraham HALE, William JARRETT Sr., Robert HENDERSON and Thomas MARTIN.

1793, John EVANS to Peregrine FORSTER, an account of store items including stockings, pins, twist, silk and whiskey. Credits on the account include butter, soap, recording deeds brought from Philadelphia and swearing FORSTER into office as Deputy Surveyor. Balance 1 pound, 8 shillings and 2 pence half penny.

Nimrod EVANS to Davis SHOCKLEY, 9 May 1810. For ferrying your black boy and horse twice = 0.1.10 and several purchases of veal, beef and pork (all at 3d per pound), and killing one beef at 0.6.0.

Nimrod EVANS to SHOCKLEY, 4 September 1811. For beef and ferrying wife and sisters ___ times.

List of Clerk's notes put into the hands of the Sheriff of Harrison County for collection 1809. William MARTIN, Asher LEWIS, Basil LUCAS, Samuel BOGGESS, Samuel DAVIS, Benj. WILSON, Isaac MORRIS, James SMITH, Mathias HITE, William HACKER, James ARNOLD and Norman RANDALL, 20 May 1810.

To Nimrod EVANS from Thomas WILSON, 27 December 1805. WILSON received 3 bushels of wheat at 4/0 per bushel in part of his fee in the suit of the Commonwealth vs William LANDFIELD.

27 December 1805, EVANS received from Grafton WHITE, the miller, 11 1/4 bushels of wheat to be credited on William LAMPHER's note due to EVANS.

C. BARKSHIRE's receipt for Morgan Town Burrough taxes: 6 town lots, 4 Negroes, 4 horses and 3 tythes = $4.97 1/2 dated 6 July 1813.

"Received of Nimrod EVANS $200 on account of my claim against Henry DERING's estate, J. H. WILLIAMS, 2 February 1813."

"Springhill Furnace, 8 November 1809. I will deliver on your order castings to the amount of $12.39 on account of Arthur TRADER Jr.," signed by Jesse EVANS.

29 October 1805, five month note to EVANS signed by Ann (A) STEVENSON for $13.50 with interest secured by Zack PIERPOINT.

October 1808 - 3 February 1812, Nimrod EVANS to R. BERK-SHIRE, 1 barrel of herring ($5.04), powder, wool hat, hauling brick, hauling wood, corn, tin cups, drab cloth, oats, whiskey, pumps, nails, wool socks, flannel blanket, paper, silk, 1 gallon bottle and loaf of sugar. Credited to this account by cash at sundry times, half of a bill in Washington, cash paid for John STEALEY and gambling money at sundry times.

List of John EVANS' clerk's notes: Charles BOYLES, James and Joseph BARKER, John and Thomas COURTNEY, Aaron HUFFMAN, Joseph HARRISON, Simeon HURLEY, Thomas WRIGHT, William KENNEDY, James LEGGIT, John THOMPSON, John SHUMAN, John SMITH, William WEBSTER and Enoch EVANS, Humphrey B. WILSON, William TINGLE, Richard SMITH, John SNYDER, John LYNCH, Daniel JONES, James WALKER, John MINTON, David SCOTT (Indian Creek), Clement MORGAN, David MUSGRAVE, John TAYLOR, Charles SNODGRASS, James BURCHINAL, Thomas CRANE and John FLEEHARTY.

165 - 1810, Monongalia County Court. Settlement of Overseers of the Poor.

5 September 1808, ordered that Henry WRIGHT and his wife, two of the poor, be allowed $30 for the ensuing year and that Michael CORE be appointed to furnish them with the necessary supplies of provisions to that amount and to be paid out of the poor tax of the year 1809. Directed to Stephen MORGAN, Collector of the Poor Tax, and signed by Wm McCLEERY and Boaz BURROWS.

5 September 1808, ordered that John VANDERVORT be allowed $11 being a part of an order for $46 allowed him for clothing and caring for William FORSTER, one of the poor. $35 of this order being before this time drawn. Directed to Stephen MORGAN and signed by William McCLEERY and N. VANDERVORT.

6 September 1808, Calder HAYMOND allowed $2 attending the business of the poor two days at the board. Signed by Richard HARRISON and N. VANDERVORT.

5 June 1809, Nimrod EVANS allowed $5.12, the cost of a judgement against Wm. G. PAYNE at the suit of the Overseers of the Poor. Signed by Wm. McCLEERY and William HAYS.

5 September 1808, ordered that Richard JACKSON, one of the poor, be allowed $10 for his support and that Richard HARRISON attend to the disbursements. Signed by Wm. McCLEERY and George SMYTH.

5 June 1809, Nicholas VANDERVORT allow $3 for 3 days attending to settle with the Collectors of the Poor Tax for the year 1807 and $2 for attending the board at the same session. Signed by Wm. McCLEERY and William CONNER.

5 June 1809, William WILSON allowed $13 for boarding and clothing Penelopy HILL, one of the poor, four months ending 1 April 1809. Signed by Wm. McCLEERY and N. VANDERVORT.

5 June 1809, Elias HOSKINSON allowed $37.22 for clothing and boarding Mary CAMPBELL, one of the poor, for 8 months starting 7 September 1808 and ending 5 June 1809.

5 June 1809, William CONNER allowed $4 for attending the board at 2 different times. Signed by Wm. McCLEERY and William HAYS.

5 September 1808, William LOWRY allowed $2 for muslin furnished Elenor COWAN, one of the poor, for her to make two shifts.

2 December 1809, Henry WRIGHT allowed $20 for his personal support to be placed in the hands of Nicholas VANDERVORT for the use of WRIGHT.

1804, 1805 and 1806, John WILLITTS allowed $3 for 3 days attending the board. Signed by VANDERVORT and Boaz BURROWS.

5 September 1808, John FAIRFAX allowed $20.36 for his costs in defending two motions in a "do" against him as Collector of the Poor Tax by George WOLFE to be paid out of the poor tax of 1809. FAIRFAX assigned this order to Mathew GAY on 2 November 1808.

No date, William McCLEERY allowed $3 for three days for settling with the Collectors of the Poor Tax of 1807, $2 for attending the board and $.33 for paper.

5 September 1809, William JOSEPH allowed $37.50 for clothing, nursing and boarding John CROSS, one of the poor, for 9 months ending 5 June 1809. Signed by Wm. McCLEERY and George SMITH.

5 September 1808, Elias HOSKINSON allowed $50 for clothing, boarding and nursing Mary CAMPBELL, one of the poor, ending this date. Signed by Wm. McCLEERY and John WILLETS.

5 June 1809, William SMITH allowed $40, a part of an $80 order allowed SMITH for boarding and nursing Jenney GRUB, one of the poor, for 10 months ending this date. The balance of $40 SMITH assigned to Joseph LOWRY.

5 June 1809, Enos DAUGHERTY allowed $38.25 for medicine and attendance on Jenney GRUB and Beckey HAYSE, two of the poor. Signed by Wm. McCLEERY and William HAYS.

5 June 1809, Francis WARMAN allowed $24.45 for boarding

and clothing Thomas WARMAN, one of the poor, for 11 months and 22 days ending this date.

5 June 1809, George Smith allowed $2 for attending the board 2 days.

5 September 1808, George WOLF allowed $47.40 in lieu of two orders to him for supporting Duncan CAMPBELL, one of the poor, for the years 1806 and 1807 at $25 each year, $2.60 being already paid to WOLF.

No date, Joseph LOWRY allowed $40 on account of William SMITH, that being a part of the sum of $40 allowed to SMITH for boarding and nursing Jenney GRUB, one of the poor, for ten months ending 5 June 1809.

5 September 1808, George WOLF allowed $32.30 to pay his costs on two motions which he brought against John FAIRFAX, late Collector of the Poor Tax for 1805. $20.36 issued to Mathew GAY, FAIRFAX's attorney, and the balance of $11.94 to be paid to Thomas WILSON, WOLF's attorney.

21 February 1809, Mary SINCLAIR allowed $.50 for boarding and nursing Rebecca HAYES and her child, "objects of charity and in a suffering condition, which sum shall be passed to your credit in settling your accounts with the Overseers."

No date, Asa HALL allowed $3 for three days attending as an Overseer of the Poor in 1807.

No date, John WILLET allowed $3.17 for attending as an Overseer of the Poor.

5 September 1808, Boaz FLEMING allowed $25 in part of a $45 order which is allowed him for boarding, clothing and nursing Mary LANE, one of the poor, for one year ending 13 October 1808. The order for the balance of $20 not yet issued. Signed by Wm. McCLEERY and Asa HALL.

5 June 1809, William SNODGRASS allowed $22.50 for supporting and clothing James and John SNODGRASS, two of the poor, for 9 months ending this date.

5 June 1809, Samuel EVERLY allowed $26.25 for boarding, clothing and supporting Elenor COWAN, one of the poor, for 9 months ending this date.

5 June 1809, Boaz FLEMING allowed $41.40 for supporting Mary LANE, one of the poor, for 1808 and 1809 and for a coffin and burying cloth. Also $20, a balance due FLEMING being a part of his allowance for supporting LANE, one of the poor, for the year 1807.

5 June 1809, William McCLEERY allowed $7.50 for his services as clerk to the board from 5 September 1808 to 5 June 1809 being 9 months at $10 per year. Signed by Colder HAYMOND and William CONNER.

7 September 1807, James WILLEY allowed $__ for supporting Maryan MURPHY, one of the poor, for one year ending 13 May 1808. Signed by William McCLEERY and William HAYS.

January 1810, The Overseers of Monongalia County, to the poor tax for the year 1809 on 2209 tythables at $.50 each = $1104.50; Collectors commission $50.22; paid the above orders = $795.61; balance due the county = $208.89.

165 - 1810, Monongalia County Court. "April 1810 Muster. There was an election in my company for officers in a Rifle Company, 1st Battalion, 76th Regiment: Sam. G. WILSON, Capt; Godfrey GUSEMAN, 1st Lieut. The Court of Monongalia County will please to recommend the above as officers." "The court will please to recommend Samuel G. WILSON as Captain in a Rifle Company of the 76th Regiment in the room of John WATSON, deceased, and Godfrey GOOSMAN Lieut. in the room of Samuel G. WILSON, promoted," 9 April 1810.

165 - 1810, Monongalia County Court. Bond signed by Lemuel JOHN to serve as sheriff secured by N. VANDERVORT, Mathew GAY and Geo. S. DERING, 11 June 1810. Justices: Robert FERRELL, Dudley EVANS, James SCOTT, John FAIRFAX, Nicholas VANDERVORT, Thomas MILLER, Simon EVERLY, John W. DEAN, Frederick HARSH, David MORGAN, Sam'l MINOR, Morgan MORGAN, William N. JARRETT, Ralph BARKSHIRE, John NUZUM, Boaz BURROWS, John STEALY, James E. BEALL (crossed out), Augustus WERNINGER, Jacob PALSLEY, William GEORGE, William WILEY Jr., John COX, Joseph CAMPBELL, Alexander HAWTHORN, John EVANS Jr., Isaac POWELL, John S. BARNES, John L. ROBERTS, Reynear HALL, Daniel COX, Rawley EVANS, Jerrard EVANS and Charles BYRN.

165 - 1810, Monongalia County Court. "To the Worshipful Court of Monongalia County, the petition of Enoch BALLAH, of Ross County, State of Ohio, showeth to this court that Peggy BALLAH and James BALLAH did obtain Letters of Administration from this court on the estate of Augustus BALLAH, deceased, late of Monongalia County, and have returned an inventory or appraisement of the same which is recorded. Your petitioner is one of the heirs of said estate and prays this court that commissioners may be appointed to adjust and examine the accounts of said administrators (which they may be ordered to produce) and report to next April Court and Your petitioner as in duty bound will pray." Signed by Enoch BALLAH on 13 February 1810. Thomas BARNS, Thomas KNIGHT and William WILLEY appointed as commissioners.

165 - 1810, Monongalia County Court. "To the Worshipful Court of Monongalia County, the petition of Sarah EVERLY, widow and relict of Casper EVERLY, deceased, late of Monongalia County, showeth that her said husband, in his lifetime, had title to 400 acres of land by patent dated 20 September 1783 on which he lived and 100 acres adjoining the same by patent dated 27 August 1783 and that she has never relinquished her dower in said land. Your petitioner prays this court to appoint commissioners who may lay off to Your petitioner her dower in said land as well as any others to which said Casper EVERLY had title and make report to this court," signed Sarah EVERLY by her attorney, F. WILSON. William JOHN, Enoch JONES and John SANDERS appointed as commissioners.

165a - 1810, Monongalia County Court. Settlement of Abraham WOTRING's estate, Adam SHAFER, administrator.

2 April 1810, receipt signed by Margaret (x) WOTRING for $788.95 and 1/2 cents for her part of WOTRING's estate.

2 April 1810, receipt signed by _____ WOTRING for $175.32 and 1/2 cents for his/her part of the estate.

2 April 1810, receipt signed by Daniel WOTRING for $175.32 and 1/2 cents for his part of the estate.

2 April 1810, receipt signed by William WOTRING for $175.32 and 1/2 cents for his part of the estate.

2 April 1810, receipt signed by Alexander WOTRING for $175.32 and 1/2 cents for his part of the estate.

2 April 1810, receipt signed by Jacob WOTRING for $175.32 and 1/2 cents for his part of the estate.

2 April 1810, receipt signed by Nicholas WOTRING for $175.32 and 1/2 cents for his part of the estate.

2 April 1810, receipt signed by _____ WOTRING for $175.32 and 1/2 cents for his part of the estate. All the above receipts witnessed by Christian WHITEHAIR.

17 March 1807, note signed by Abraham WOTRING to Nicholas WOTRING for $161.02, due in nine months and witnessed by _____ _____. 19 March 1810, receipt signed by Nicholas WOTRING for $161.02 debt and interest of $21.73 in full of all demands on the within note.

2 July 1810, receipts for various amounts due from the estate signed by Christian WHITEHAIR, Frederick HARSH and Jacob KITTERMAN.

8 January 1810, receipt signed by Thomas WILSON for $2.50, his fee for attending to the estate.

June 1810 term, Frederick HARSH, Christian WHITEHAIR and Jacob RIDENOUR appointed commissioners to settle with Adam SHAFER, administrator of Abraham WOTRING, deceased.

28 March 1810, receipts for various amounts signed by Frederick HARSH, Jacob WOTRING, Lewis BISHOFF, David STEMPLE, William WOTRING, Nicholas GANER and Christian WHITEHAIR.

165a - 1810, Monongalia County Court. The petition of Godfrey STULL humbly showeth that he is poor and old and unable to labor and has thereto, with much difficulty, raised money to pay the public tax and county levies and poor rates and hopes from his present situation that the court will discharge him from paying any further taxes, 17 June 1810. Allowed June 1810.

165a - 1810, Monongalia County Court. Various fees directed to Clerk Nimrod EVANS, 1810, from James WEST Jr., John CRAVENS, Jonathan TIDEROW, William RUSSEL, William EVERLY, Dudley RAY, William JOLLIFFE (recording the dower of your wife's land) and James MORGAN (for copy of John BONER's will). Various charges directed to Clerk A. EARLE, of Randolph County, from John SANDERS and William HADDIX.

165a - 1810, Monongalia County Court. "I do hereby certify that Henry MILLER was qualified according to law as Captain of the Militia of the 104th Regiment and also Burket MINOR as Ensign of the same Regiment," 3 May 1810, signed by James E. BEALL.

165a - 1810, Monongalia County Court. Bond signed by Philip MARTIN to serve as "a committee" to take care of the estate of Benjamin LEADY/SEADY "who hath been adjudged of unsound mind" secured by James BROWN, 8 January 1810.

165a - 1810, Monongalia County Court. Bond signed by Barbara (x) SNODGRASS to serve as guardian to Elie, Ben___, Margaret, Joseph and Elisha SNODGRASS secured by Nathan MATHENEY and Noah MATHENEY, 8 January 1810.

165a - 1810, Monongalia County Court. December 1809 term, "A list of offices elected for the 104th Regiment of the Virginia Militia in Monongalia County to be recommended so as to be commissioned is as followeth:

James CARROL, Col., in the room of James CLARK, removed.

James McGREW, Major of the 1st Battalion, in the room of John GRIBBLE, resigned.

Jacob FUNK, Major of the 2nd Battalion, in the room of James CARROL, promoted.

Robert CLARK, Capt., in the room of James McGREW.

John TREMBLY, Lieut., in the room of Robert CLARK.

James KING, Ensign.

Nathan ASHBY, Capt., in the room of John RIGHTMIRE, removed.

Aaron GIBBS, Lieut., in the room of Nathan ASHBY.

Thomas ASBY, Ensign, in the room of Joseph WILSON.

Henry MILLER, Capt., in the room of Jacob FUNK, promoted.

Thomas MONTGOMERY, Lieut., in the room of Henry MILLER.

Burket MINARD, Ensign.

Leonard CHIPPS, Capt., in the room of William BRANDON, resigned.

Jacob PAUL, Lieut., in the room of Leonard CUPP.

Henry CALE, Ensign.

John WALLER, Lieut., in Capt. John SEVERN's Company.

Thomas GADD, Ensign."

165a - 1813, Monongalia County Court. Settlement of Augustus BALLAH's estate. Margaret and James BALLAH, administrators.

BALLAH's estate to John WILSON: April 1807, to putting roof on barn (1/2 amount to DOOLITTLE) = $42. January 1806, paid by 19 bushels of rye at 2/6 = $7.92. April 1807, paid by 19 bushels of wheat at 4/0 = $12.17; 9 bushels of rye at 3/2 = $4.50; 1 bushel corn at 2/6 = $.42. 1 1/2 bushels oats at 2/0 = $.34. November 1807, paid by cow = $8. Balance due WILSON = $8.65.

BALLAH's estate to John EVANS: 1793, to cash lent = $5; interest on the same for 15 years = $4.50. 16 November 1805, note = $4; interest on the same $.72. Total $14.22. On 14 December 1808, EVANS swore this amount was correct.

BALLAH's estate to Fleming JONES: October 1800, 1 set handmill irons = $.14; answered to Thomas FIDDY = $.42; paid Isaac EDDY = $.17. 1801, 1 days reaping = $.50; answered to William CARNES = $3; 1/2 day reaping = $.25. 1802, 1 days work = $.50; 1/2 bushel flax seed = $.42; 2 1/2 bushels corn = $1.05. 1803, 4 pounds iron = $.25; 12 pounds salt = $.60. 1804, 2 1/2 bushels rye = $1.25. Total $9.35. On 3 September 1808, JONES swore this amount was correct.

29 September 1808, Thomas LEMASTERS swore BALLAH owed him $14.25.

24 September 1808, James WILEY swore before William WILLEY that BALLAH owed him 7 shillings and 6 pence for flooring plank dated 29 March 1805.

30 May 1809, Thomas BARNES Jr. swore before William BARNES that his account was correct.

10 March 1807, BALLAH's estate to Der_____: making and casing one door = 12 shillings; 4 days work at barn = 1 pound; reaping at 0/4 per day = 8 pence. Total 2 shillings.

26 January 1809, Asa DUDLEY swore before William WILLEY that his account was correct.

28 May 1808, John DAWSON swore before William WILLEY that BALLAH owed him $3.50.

1 February 1809, William STRAIT swore before William BARNS that BALLAH owed him the within account.

13 February 1809, E. BRIGGS swore that BALLAH owed him 5 days plowing in 1806 = $1.50; 1 day harvest work = $.50 and 25 pounds of salt = $1.33 in 1807. Total $3.33.

24 September 1808, Jacob STRAIGHT swore before William WILLEY that BALLAH owed him $2.50.

BALLAH's tax of 1807, 1 tythable 81 1/4 cents, 5 horses 60 cents, 500 acres of land 60 cents, 75 acres 8 cents = $2.09 1/4 cents. Received 14 January 1809.

1 August 1808, BALLAH's estate to Richard PRICE: 15 shillings for work, 6 shillings for a log chain; 1 shilling for leather. Total 1 pound and 2 shillings.

1 August 1808, Mathias DAVIS swore BALLAH owed him $3.59 dated 12 July 1807.

30 August 1808, William CAMPBELL swore before William WILLEY that BALLAH owed him 1 pound, 17 shillings and 6 pence for an old account dated 21 January 1802.

Note signed by Margarett (x) BALLAH, administratrix, to Ralph BARKSHIRE for $7.82 being the balance due BARKSHIRE by her late husband and proved by Jacob BARKSHIRE dated 2 March 1808.

"The appraisement of Augusta BALLAH's estate amounted to $557.03; the amount of the sale bill of said estate $559.39." Certified by Clerk N. EVANS, no date.

No date, BALLAH's estate to John EVANS Jr. $2 for examining the estate.

On the reverse of one of the papers, these words are crossed out, "March the 10 1802: William CAMMEL to 2 bushels of wheat 8 shillings and the 12 Thomas BARNS received 9 bushels and 3 pecks into this mill for Thom MAGINDLY and Jacob BOLSEL of James BALLAH's wheat. 13 March, Jasper WEST to 2 bushels and a half of wheat."

Note signed by Augustus BALLAH to John EVANS for $4 with interest dated 16 November 1805, witnessed by J. CAMPBELL.

30 September 1807, John NICHLIN presented a bill to the estate for medicine and attendance on BALLAH dated 3 August 1805. This account was assigned to "the bearer" by NICHLIN on 25 October 1808.

3 April 1810, John DRAGOO swore before William WILLEY that BALLAH owed him 8 shillings.

25 May 18__, George TUTHMAN swore that BALLAH owed him 22 shillings.

7 January 1809, "Received of John EVANS Jr. $4 for Augusta BALLAH, deceased." Signed by J. CAMPBELL.

19 August 1808, Rebuben SQUIRES swore before William WILLEY that BALLAH owed him 1 pound, 11 shillings and 9 pence.

2 April 1810, receipt signed by Thomas WILSON whereby he received, by note, from James BALLAH $2.50 for his fee "you vs BAYLES," $1.25 for his fee "you by son vs MERIDETH," dated 1803 and $2.50 to administrator of BALLAH's estate dated 1808.

3 April 1810, James BALLAH swore before William WILLEY that BALLAH owed him $5.

No date, BALLAH's estate to E. DAUGHERTY $1 for sundry merchandise dated 5 May 1803.

15 December 1807, George J. BALSER swore before Robert FERRELL that BALLAH owed him 12 shillings for making 1 coat dated 11 September 1807 and 12 shillings and 6 pence for making a great coat and 1 stick of twist dated 19 October 1807.

10 May 1810, Joseph MORGAN swore before William WILLEY that BALLAH owed him $1.19 1/2 cents.

24 September 1808, Jesper WYATT swore before William WILLEY that BALLAH owed him $23.

2 March 1808, Ralph BARKSHIRE swore before William N. JARRETT that BALLAH owed him 2 pounds, 6 shillings and 11 1/2 pence.

15 December 1808, George G. BALTZEL (A. & S. WOODROW & Co.) swore before D. EVANS that BALLAH owed $2.60 for cloth and buttons and 1 shilling for 1 silk handkerchief on an account dated 13 September 1807.

BALLAH's tax for 1806: 1 County Levy at 25 cents, 1 Poor Tax at 12 1/2 cents, 4 horses at 48 cents, 500 acres of land at 60 cents, 75 acres at 8 cents. 30 July 1808, paid.

8 December 1808, Thomas McKINLEY swore that on 7 February 1799, Michael KERNS paid him 15 shillings for Gustavus BALLAH and at the same time, Michael KERNS made oath that he directed Gustavus BALLAH, since the above payment to McKINLEY, to settle the sum of 15 shillings with Fleming JONES.

11 January 1808, BALLAH's estate to Dudley EVANS for 1 bandana handkerchief, 6 1/2 yards calico and 2 yards of broad cloth = 4.5.0 dated August and September 1806. By a bill of 12 shillings dated 20 September 1806. Eight yards of flax and tow linen 1 pound, dated 15 May 1807. Total 2.13.3.

14 December 1808, two week note signed by James BALLAH to John STEALEY for $6.75, payable in good merchantable pork at $3.50 per cwt. and witnessed by Job KYGER.

No date, Thomas BARNES Sr., Thomas KNIGHT Jr. and William WILLEY Sr. appointed a committee to settle with Margaret BALLAH and James BALLAH, administrators of Augustus BALLAH, deceased, on the motion of Enoch BALLAH. Docketed to February 1813 term.

22 February 1809, receipt signed by Jas. HILL for $2.28 1/2 cents for an account due him from Administratrix Margaret BALLAH.

25 November 1809, received of John EVANS Jr. the amount of the within account (2.13.3) and $2.10 for assigning and laying off the dower land to Margaret BALLAH, widow of Augusta BALLAH, deceased. Signed by Dudley EVANS.

Thomas DOOLITTLE and John WILSON presented a bill to the estate for shingles, lath, rafters, a stool, hewing rafters 200 feet at a penny per foot, girders 28 feet long, 7 joist 20 feet long, boards for the gable ends and putting up the gable ends, and for covering a barn in 1807. Total $84 as of 8 May 1807.

3 April 1810, John EVANS Jr. presented a bill dated 21 March 1798 through 22 July 1800 for sundry store goods. On the list are such items as a large dish, calico, combs, salt, cream jug, vest, silk and thread, tea pot, 1 yard of Swansdown, fancy cord, plank, spoons, snuff and Bounce. Total 19.7.0. Cash paid at sundry times reduced the total to 6.12.6 including 2.3.2 interest for 8 years.

165a – 1810, Monongalia County Court. Justices: William JOHN, Robert FERRELL Jr., Dudley EVANS, James SCOTT, Jacob PALSLY Jr., John FAIRFAX, Sheriff Lemuel JOHN, Benjamin ____LES, Nicholas VANDERVORT, Thomas MILLER, Simeon EVERLY, John W. DEAN, Frederick HARSH, David MORGAN, Samuel MINOR, Morgan MORGAN, William N. JARRETT, Ralph BARKSHIRE, John NUZUM, Boaz BURROWS, John STEALY, James E. BELL, Amos ROBERTS, Augustus WERNINGER, William GEORGE, William WILLEY Jr. and William BARNES.

165a – 1810, Monongalia County Court. 2 May 1810, "Thomas MONTGOMERY sworn into the office of a Lieutenant." 24 May 1810, "Jacob FUNK sworn into the office of Major." Signed by David MORGAN.

165a – 1810, Monongalia County Court. Petition to the court to appoint David MUSGRAVE "for want of another constable in our part of the district as there is but one at present and very little dependency can be put in him." Signed by John SNODGRASS, Michael SNODGRASS, William SNODGRASS, William SNODGRASS (two different signatures), Joseph SNODGRASS, James SNODGRASS, Benjamin SNODGRASS, Isaac SNODGRASS, Daniel FLUEHARTY, Nathan SNODGRASS, Thomas FLOYD, Michael FLOYD, Henary FLOYD, Thomas CLAYTON, William MORTON, William WOOD, 7 December 1810. MUSGRAVE appointed.

165a – 1810, Monongalia County Court. 26 May 1810, "Nathan ASHBY sworn into the office of a Captain and Thomas ASHBY sworn into the office of Ensign before me, David MORGAN."

165a - 1810, Monongalia County Court. "The court will please recommend Michael CRIST as Ensign in the 76th Regiment in the room of David WATSON who refused to serve, Zachariah RHODES as Lieutenant in the room of William STAFFORD who refused to serve, John LEWELLEN as Ensign in the room of Seth STAFFORD who refused to serve, (signed) Dudley EVANS, 76th Regiment, 11 June 1810."

165a - 1810, Monongalia County Court. "Elenor DEBLIN personally appeared before me, one of the Justices of the Peace for said county, and made oath that she is the same person to which a pension of 10 pounds annually is granted." "I do certify that the above named Elenor DEBELIN, from her old age and infirmities, is not able to attend court as the law directs in that case made and provided for pensioners." Signed by Nicholas VANDERVORT on 12 February 1810.

165a - 1810, Monongalia County Court. Bond signed by Casper OTT/ORTT to act as administrator for the estate of Conrad PIXLER secured by Daniel COX and John RHODES, 13 June 1810.

165a - 1810, Monongalia County Court. Benjamin SHAW recommended to be guardian to Joseph WEBSTER, a child of 7 years old 18 May 1810, son of William WEBSTER. SHAW was "a relation to the child and with whom the mother to the child left said Joseph" to learn the trade of farming. Signed by Overseers of the Poor John ROTHEN____ and William CONNER, August 1810.

165a - 1810 and 1819, Monongalia County Court. Elenor BATTON for 1810 taxes, 95 acres of land $.14, paid. John STEWART for 1819 taxes on 120 acres of land $.24, paid. On reverse of BATTON's receipt is the name of Elisha SNODGRASS.

165a - 1810, Monongalia County Court. John BOUSLOG, Daniel KNOX and Jeremiah HOSKINSON appraised several sows and one boar taken up by Richard WILES at $16, 31 December 1810.

165a - 1810, Monongalia County Court. James LEMMONS (1799 and 1800), Thomas ADAMSON (1810), John RICKTER (1810), David ADAMSON (1810), John KIMMEL (1809 and 1810), Joseph FOREY (1810) and Adam MANEAR (1810) owed various court fees for the years cited.

165a - 1810, Monongalia County Court. Richard SMITH, Samuel MERRIFIELD and William BAINBRIDGE appraised 2 stray mares taken up by Asa HARRIS at $20, 3 November 1810.

165a - 1810, Monongalia County Court. George SMYTH, John RAMSEY and John HUTSON/HUDSON appraised a stray mare taken up by Enoch JONES at $40, 11 June 1810.

165a - 1810, Monongalia County Court. Bond signed by Nicholas VANDERVORT to serve as sheriff secured by Daniel COX, Boaz BURROWS, Alexander HAWTHORN, Mathew GAY and George S. DERING, 10 September 1810.

165a - 1810, Monongalia County Court. Evan JENKINS, Alexander CLEGG and William LANCASTER appraised a stray bay horse taken up by Solomon CHALFANT at $40, no date.

165a - 1810, Monongalia County Court. James MORRIS, John LANTZ and John BALDWIN appraised a stray mare taken up by Charles DOWD at $27, 24 May 1810.

165a - 1810, Monongalia County Court. William N. JARRETT, George HITE and Fielding KIGER appraised a stray horse taken up by George BAKER at $20, 29 August 1810.

165a - 1810, Monongalia County Court. Nathan ASHBY, John TIMMERMAN and Aaron GIBBS appraised 2 stray steers taken up by William SUDDETH at $17.25 and $17.50, 19 June 1810.

165a - 1809, Monongalia County Court. Alexander BRANDON, Leonard CUPP and Richard BROWN appraised a stray steer taken up by Henry SYNE Sr. at $9, 19 December 1809.

165a - 1810, Monongalia County Court. John STATLER and Jacob MYERS appraised a stray bull taken up by Zacharias PILES at $9, 9 January 1810.

165a - 1810, Monongalia County Court. "It is requested of a number of citizens of Morgantown that the court should appoint some person or persons to regulate weights and measures in the county and as there is a penalty of $30 on each Justice for failing so to do, it is ordered that A. WERNINGER and Doctor E. DAUGHERTY be appointed," 9 January 1810.

165a - 1810, Monongalia County Court. David TROWBRIDGE, Antony COZAD and Jacob FUNK appraised 3 stray steers taken up by Charles BYRNS at $9, 6 April 1810.

165a - 1810, Monongalia County Court. Augustus WELLS, James L. WILSON and Godfrey GOOSEMAN appraised a stray bull taken up by Joseph WILSON at $4, 3 December 1810.

165a - 1812, Monongalia County Court. Re: Military Rifles. Bond ($3000) signed by George BAKER, Frederick HERTZOG and Henry BURRELL, 5 September 1810. "The condition of the above bond is such that if the above bound George BAKER, Frederick HERTZOG and Henry BURRELL, their heirs, executors or administrators, shall well and truly and faithfully make and deliver unto John TYLER or order, Governor of the Common-

wealth of Virginia, one hundred rifles according to the
description and size given and directed by the said John
TYLER, Governor of the State of Virginia, on or before 5
September 1811, then this obligation to be void, otherwise to
remain in full force and virtue." Description of rifles:
"The barrel three feet nine inches long, the calibre the size
of fifty bullets to the pound, the hindsight 15 inches from
the breech of the barrel, the foresight one inch and a
quarter from the muzzle, the barrel heaviest at the breech
tapering a little to the hindsight, then continuing the same
thickness for fifteen inches, from thence a gradual swell to
the muzzle so that the barrel at the muzzle will be nearly as
thick as at the breech, the touch hole made in the barrel
close to the end of the breech pin. The barrel truly bored,
straightened and rifled, then dressed with land and furrow
saws making the land and furrow hollowing of the edges of the
land sharp, the sights to be made low and the bead of the
foresight nicely to fit the notch on the hindsight when
taking aim at any object, the bullet molds to cast round
bullets so that when the necks are cut off it will make no
difference which way they are put in the gun. The lock a
little smaller than the lock of the model presented to the
committee and without wheels. The stock to be one inch
longer in the butt than the model. The ramrod well loaded
with three thimbles and a tail piece, ____ loops. The
rifles are to be brass mounted and stocked with maple. The
rifles or twist in the barrel ought to go 3/4 round in the
whole length." "This is to certify that I have received from
Frederick HERTZOG, a gent from the State of Virginia, fifty
rifles in part of a contract made by him and George BAKER
with said state and entered into on this 5 September 1810,"
signed by N. EVANS, agent, at Morgantown on 9 July 1812.
"Pursuant to a request of the Governor of Virginia, We have
this day preceded to inspect fifty rifles made by Frederick
HERTZOG, of Fayette County, Pennsylvania, in part of a
contract heretofore entered into by George BAKER and the said
Frederick HERTZOG. On inspection we find the barrels of good
quality, averaging about 3 feet nine inches in length, the
caliber averaging about 155 balls to the pound, the lox also
of good quality made with four of the small _illand loxs,
double bridled both inside and out, the stock of plain maple,
the butt pieces, boxes, guard, mussel piece, thimbles, and
tail pipes and side plates all of brass, draw loops of
copper, headed with brass, the wood work generally strong,
but roughly executed, ramrods to each of good hickory well
made with iron sockets and screws, also moulds to each gun
work roughly executed," dated at Morgantown on 8 May 1812.

165a - 1810, Monongalia County Court. On reverse of one of
the above papers dealing with the rifles, there are groups of
names with a check mark at the beginning of the name and a
number such as 26 or 30 at the end. Philip SHIVELY 26 and

George SYPOLT 27.   Robert COURTNEY 26,   Michael COURTNEY 26,
Elisha CLAYTON 27,   James PATTON heirs 28   and Jno CUNNINGHAM
29.   William BODLEY 26,   Driscila BAKER 27,   Jno BARTROWE 29,
H. BRAUCHUYRE 29,   Henry BURUS 30,   Barney BURUS 30   and
Clayrian BRIGHT 30.   Jam TINGLE 26, John THOMPSON 27, George
TURKEYHIZER 29,   Benjamin THORN 30   and   George TUCKER 30.
Peter HAUGHT 26,   Jacob HOLLAND 27,   James HENRY 27,   James
HAYHURST 27,   Nathan HAYS 27,   Justice HECK 27, John HAUT 27,
Philip HILL 27,   John HARTEMAN 28,   Joseph HOWELL 28,   Rynear
HALE 28, Peter HAWKINS 28, Arch HAMILTON 30, Robert HENDERSON
30, Jacob HOLLAND 30,   James HAMILTON 30,   Joshua HART 30 and
Tiftman HILLERA 30.   Jo SNODGRASS 26,   Jo SEXTON 26,   John
STRAIT 27,   Henry SNIDER 28, Alex´d SHAW 28, Philip SHIPLY 28
and Alexander SELBY 30.   Richard B. WALLS 26, James WALLS 26,
Josiah WOODS 28,   John WILLEY 29   and   Augustus WERNINGER 30.
William KINCADE 26,   George KERNS 27,   Absolom KNOTTS 28,
Robert KNOTTS 28,   Thomas KNOTTS 28,   Edward KNOTTS 29   and
Edward KINCADE 30.   James JEFFS 26.   Nathan MATHENEY 26,
Alexander McCLELLAND 27,   Hymas MEEKS 27,   Joseph MARTIN 28,
John MANN 28, Isaac MARCUS 29, Swenson MANENOR 29, James MANS
29 and John McDOUGAL 30.   Mathew ROBINSON 27,   John REEDER 29
and William REED 29.   William CRULL 27.   Thomas PAYNE 27,
John PARKER 27, Adam PICKENPAUG 29,   John POWER 30 and Andrew
PARK 30.   Samuel LEWELLEN 27,   George SlYPOL 27,   William
LITTLE 29   and   Eliu LONG 30.   Christian NUSE 28.   John DUNN
Jr. 28   and   John DAVIS 29.   David ALBRIGHT 28,   Stephen AMOS
29,   George ASHBY 29,   Henry AMOS 29,   Anthony ASHER 29   and
James ARNETT 30.

165a - 1810, Monongalia County Court. One horse and 2 cows,
the property of George WELLS, was attached at the suit of
John WAGNER for $50 with interest from 1 December 1807.   In
order to retain possession of his property until time for
public sale or his debt was paid WELLS signed this Delivery
Bond secured by Jno WAGNER, 5 October 1810.

165a - 1810, Monongalia County Court. Diagram of Monongalia
County Jail, 1810, Morgantown, W.Va. (sic) traced from the
original plans.

165a - 1810, Monongalia County Court. By Deed of Trust dated
10 May 1810, James BROWN, of Harrison County, conveyed to
Nimrod EVANS a tract of land situated in Harrison County on
Tygart Valley River about 2 miles below HILL´s Ferry joining
lands of Jesse NIXON, James BROWN and others, being the same
conveyed by Jesse NIXON to James BROWN by deed containing 50
acres with all the improvements thereon.   EVANS was to sell
the tract for available cash price, within 12 months, to
procure enough money for BROWN to discharge a note he owed to
Reuben CHALFANT for $70 plus any interest that may accrue,
one half payable 1 July 1810 and one half payable 1 May 1811.
EVANS to advertise the land in the Monongalia Gazette for two

211

weeks prior to the sale, if the need arose that the land be sold at public auction. EVANS charged 5% of the selling price for his commission plus reasonable costs. Signed by James (x) BROWN and EVANS in the presence of Mathew GAY, George DERING, Marmaduke EVANS and Joseph ALLEN.

165a - 1810, Monongalia County Court. Sheriff Stephen MORGAN. Settlement with the county to be paid out of the 1809 levy, July 1810.

August 1809, Nicholas MADERA allowed $3 for jail repairs.

August 1809, Nicholas CHISLER allowed $10 for repairs on the locks of the jail.

June 1809, William McCLEERY allowed $90 for his services as attorney for this year.

August 1809, Nicholas and Jacob MADERA allowed $2.87 for repairs on the jail.

June 1809, Reuben CHALFANT allowed $3 for patroling.

September 1809, William REED allowed $2 for a prior order.

June 1809, Charles BYRN allowed $35.47 for a prior order.

June 1809, Abraham WOODROW allowed $5 as per account.

May 1810, William N. JARRETT allowed $12.58 and 2/3 cents for repairs on the jail.

October 1809, William N. JARRETT allowed $2.33 and 1/2 cents for repairs on the jail.

June 1809, John DENT allowed $55.50 for a prior order.

October 1809, John C. PAYNE allowed $3.72 for jail yard repairs.

June 1809, Jacob FOULK allowed $5 for patroling.

June 1809, Sheriff Stephen MORGAN allowed $75 for his public services, his services as jailor, and keeping the Courthouse.

June 1809, Joseph ALLEN allowed $5 as per account.

October 1809, William N. JARRETT allowed $8 for an order granted to Mary McNEELY at February 1804 term of court.

June 1810 term, William N. JARRETT allowed $.50 for jail repairs.

May 1810, George HITE allowed $4 for jail repairs.

May 1810, Joseph ALLEN allowed $1.25 for jail repairs.

October 1809, Benjamin F. REEDER allowed $7.50 as per account.

October 1809, John PAYNE allowed $59.50 for an order granted to Michael KERNS which was unpaid.

14 June 1809, list of wolf scalps recorded since 22 May 1808: David PILES 1 old, 7 young; John STEPHENS 1 young; James W. POSTEN 1 old; Samuel CRAIN 1 old; Benjamin N. JARRETT 2 old.

October 1809, Amos ROBERTS allowed $1.33 for services on the public highway.

March 1809, Thomas MARTIN allowed $7 for a prior order.

14 March 1809, Josiah ROBE allowed $4 for the services of his team working on the public highway.

9 October 1809, Clerk Nimrod EVANS allowed $63 for his services.

June 1810, ordered that Ralph BARKSHIRE, Rawley EVANS and Alexander HAWTHORN be appointed to settle with Sheriff Stephen MORGAN the 1809 County Levy Collection and meet in Morgantown on the first Saturday in July next and report to July Court.

June 1809, Thomas WILSON allowed $97.66 for a prior order.

October 1809, John DIGMAN allowed $3.33 and 1/3 cents for the services of his team for work on the public highway.

1809, number of tythes. All are charged with one tythe unless indicated otherwise in ( ).

John ANDERSON, Samuel BOYD, John BROYTE (crossed out), Andrew BOND (2) (crossed out), Barnabas BOYD, James BELL of Richard, John BUSEY, Henry COLFMAN, Arthur CUNNINGHAM (2). Joseph CRANE, William CRAYCRAFT, Robert CHOEN (crossed out), James CHILDS, William COOK, William CONSTABLE, Hiram COOPER, Joseph DUNWOODY, William DUNWOODY, Caleb DOUTHE___, John DARNELL, Richard DOWNEY (crossed out), Peter EVERLY (crossed out), James EDWARDS, Robert FERRELL Sr., Elisha FORD, William FORD, John GRIBBLE Jr., David GRAHAM, James GRADY, John GRAHAM, William GARDNER, Leonard GARDNER, James GRAHAM, Robert HEWITT, Charles HOUSEMAN (crossed out), Richard HALL, Henry HIGHSHOE (2), Elihu HORTON, Squire HALL (excused), Samuel HARMAN, William HOLBERT, Phillip HARNER (crossed out), Samuel HAWKINS, James HUNT (2), James HUNT (two separate entries), Thomas HOLBERT, Daniel HARRIS, Philip HILL, Philip HILL (two separate entries), Phillip HOFFMAN/HUFFMAN, William JENKINS, Thomas JENKINS, Joseph JEFFERS, Reuben JACO, Zachariah JEANES, Washington KNOX, Thomas KING, Isac KING, John KIRK, Henry LEECH, William LAMBERTH, George SCOTT, James LEMMONS, William LIPSCOMB (2), Elisha LEECH, George LEEK, Willis LOLLER, James LOLLER, Jacob MASON, Henry MILLER, (Germany), Thomas MARTIN, John MILLER (BS), William McGEE, Alexander McENTOSH, Laurence McHENRY, John MARTIN, Hezekiah MAXFIELD, Jeremiah OSTERHAUL, Samuel PIXLER, Jacob PAUL, John PAUGH, Richard POOLE of Samuel, Theophilis PUGH, Samuel PIERCE, Mary PAUGH, William PRICKETT, Jonathan ROBERTS, John RICHER, Josiah ROBE, John ROSS, Joseph REED, Isaac ROMAINE, Lewis RUNNER (2), John RIAN, William SYNES, William STEPHEN-SON, John SEVIER (2), James SEYMOUR (crossed out), John STINEBOUG, Patrick SULLIVAN, John SHAHAN (2), Drake SWINDLER, John SMITH (Rock Forge), Megruda SELBY (crossed out), William SMITH, Adam TEETS, Jacob TEETS, Robert THOMPSON (2), John TIBBS of James, Francis TIBBS Jr., Thomas TANNER, James TROY (2) (crossed out), Arthur TRADER (2), Michael THORN, Caleb WISEMAN Jr., Absalom WARD, Jacob WILYARD, Henry WOLFE, Samuel WOLFE (crossed out), Stephen WOTRING, Benjamin WILSON, James WALLS, Joseph WAITS, Walter WILSON, Joseph YAGER, Peter YALEY, Harmon GREENHOUSE and Samuel TAYLOR Jr. "Return of delinquents to the Overseers of the Poor for the year 1809," assessed by Alexander BRANDON, commissioner, 6 January 1810.

165a - 1810, Monongalia County Court. "A list of delinquents in the County Levy for the year 1809." All are charged with 1 tythe @ $.50 each unless indicated in ( ).

John ATKINSON, Smith ARGO, Zebedie BROWN, George BIRD, Isaac BARNS, John BUTTERS (crossed out), Samuel BUTCHER (crossed out), Pall BOAS, Richard BERY (crossed out), Jacob BIZARD (crossed out), Patrick BOARD, Benjamin BROWN, Able BATSON, Amos BONER, James BONER, Samuel BOYCE, Jonathan BALDWIN (crossed out), Matthias COOK, Caleb CONWAY (crossed out), William CLARK (crossed out), Thomas CONWAY, John DOWNARD, Henry DARLING (2), John DEARLING, John DARROW, Thomas EVANS, Isreal FREE, John FANCHER, John FLEEHARTY, Nehemiah GLOVER, Alexander HART, John HAUGHT Jr., Jeptha HOSKINSON (crossed out), David HELMICK, William HOLIFIELD, William HIGINBOTTOM, William HAYS Jr., John JOLLIFF, Joshua JONES, Isaac JOHNSTON, George HICKMAN, David JENKINS, David JOHN, William JOLLIFF, John KNIGHT (crossed out), William LAMPHER, William LINCH (crossed out), Compton MILLER, David MICHAEL (crossed out), Martin MURPHY (crossed out), William McRA, Subus MANE, Nathaniel NEEDLES (crossed out), Christian NIBURGER, Jacob NOOSE, Isaac PRICE, Mabel PEARSON (crossed out), Peter PATRICK, James PATTERSON, Philip ROBERTS, Elizabeth LEWELLEN (crossed out), David SMITH, William SINCLAIR, Samuel STEWART (crossed out), John STARRETT, Samuel TINGLE (crossed out), George TUCKER (crossed out), George TEADE, Henry THORN, Daniel VARNER, Enoch VINCENT, Jas WILSON (crossed out), Mathew WILSON, Thomas WEST, Samuel WEST, John WELLS (3), John WALTON (crossed out), David WHITE (crossed out), Thomas WADE Jr., John WADKINS, Absolum WARDE, Henry H. WILSON, Joseph WISBY, John YOUST Jr., and William YOUNG, 7 July 1810. John PAYNE collector, 6 January 1810.

165a - 1810, Monongalia County Court. Request to the court for an order signed by John F. COOPER to be placed on the road under James JOHNSON, surveyor of the road from G. R. C. ALLEN's to Cooper's coal bank, no date.

165a - 1810, Monongalia County Court. Request from H. I. PEYTON, Clerk of Chancery Court at Staunton, for a copy of a bill exhibited at the suit of PRICE.

165a - 1810, Monongalia County Court. "Due J. CAMPBELL $3 to be discharged in wheat in 3 months after date," 21 May 1810, signed by Gr. GREENWOOD. "Due J. CAMPBELL $2 payable 2 months after date," 10 April 1810, signed by Fleming JONES. "Due Nimrod EVANS $11.78," 26 July 1810, signed by J. CAMPBELL and witnessed by Dudley EVANS. "For value received, I promise to pay J. CAMPBELL $6.86," 9 April 1810, signed Isaac MATHENY. An account signed by N. EVANS on 26 July 1810 for notes received from Jo. CAMPBELL. Isaac MATHENY $6.86, Samuel BOWEN $4, Francis PIERPOINT $2.38, John STEVENS $3, Joseph ALLEN $3.86, Presley MARTIN $5, Zackquill PIERPOINT $1.80, George

214

GREENWOOD $3, Fleming JONES $2, David MICHAEL $2, James ROBISON $3.36, Boaz BOSWELL $1.33, John BOUSLOG $8.10, Samuel RALSTON $3, Thomas MURPHY $1.25 and Israel FERREE $7.

165a - 1810, Monongalia County Court. Account of Wm. HAYMOND Jr., guardian of Sarah PEARCE. 13 June 1810, received $80.80 for Sarah from Isaac PEARCE. 20 June 1810, received from Joshua HEIMAN a note on Amy PEARCE and Joseph BRUMMAGE, balance due on the same, principal $18.87 with interest $1.24 = $20.11 and a note on Isaac PEARCE and John McGEE, balance due on same, principal $18.30 with interest $1.72 = $20.02 and a note on said HEIMAN for $7.63 and $5 cash = $133.56.

Also in this file - - - The court owed William N. JARRETT for the use of his "Negro man attending the mason when mending the walls of the jail," 7 June 1810. Allowed June 1810.

165a - 1810, Monongalia County Court. Re: William PRICE. "Ordered that the jury meet on the ground of Susan PETERS and John PRICE on __ June next."
"I hereby resign as Overseer of the Road from Rock Forge to Davi_ B. WEAVER's and I recommend Edwin CLEAR or W_____ JOHNSON suitable persons..." (bottom of this document is missing). On reverse, "A. E. THORN."
"Esqr. William PRICE and Morgan BOYERS, Philip COOMBS for west side of the river." Road Commissions appointed, no date.
"James EVANS and Thomas MEREDITH for Road Commissions on the east side of the river," no date.
"Tithables west side 1300, tithables east side 1201," no date.
"James D. WATSON having attended a short distance on the road leading from Smithfield (later Smithtown) to Preston County line, the part altered from the forks of the road leading to FORTNEY's Mill to near corner of WATSON's field all on his own land be established." Comment: Preston County formed 1818.
"Ordered that Sanford SCOTT be appointed Overseer of the forks of the road at James SCOTT's barn to intersect the Grandville Road in Grandville and that David SCOTT work said road," no date.
Grand Jury: Fred ASHBY, foreman. Enoch ROSS, Joshua W. SAER, John ABEL, Shepherd CORNWELL, Isaac CARTWRIGHT, George SWISHER, Leonard SELBY, John HARE, Joseph GRUBB, James DAVIS, Horatio MARTIN, Sanford PICKENPAUGH, Frederick A. DERING (crossed out), Isaac COX, Rawley EVANS, Robert TIBBS, John E. SNIDER, Wm. McCORMICK, John MYERS Jr., James ROBINSON, David CLARK and James KELLY, no date.
Grand Jury: Wm. JOHN, foreman. William ROBISON, Richard HOLLAND, Jacob COSAD, Henry BUNNER, John WELTNER, Thomas LANHAM, James STEEL Jr., Daniel MEDSKER, Joseph MATHIS, Jacob STEWART, Hugh AUSTIN, Jacob CARTRIGHT, John NEELY, Saward NEELY, Frederick DUESENBERY, Saml EVERLY, Stephen S. WILSON,

Draper CALE, Capel HORD, John HAWKINS, Jacob BANIDAND, James
ROBISON and Peter PRICE, no date.
    Grand Jury: William N. JOHN, William F. MARTIN, Joseph N.
STEWART,   John S. STEWART, Benjamin JOSEPH,   Jacob CARTRIGHT,
John HANSEL,   Robert BOWLSBY,   Simon EVERLY,   Archibald
SHUTTLESWORTH, John BARE, John PICKENPAUGH, Cale TANSY, Jared
BOWMAN,   Joseph FETTY, Jesse HENDERSON, Isaac CARTRIGHT, John
HESS, Jeremiah STILLWELL, Joseph GRUBB, Peter PRICE, Jesse
HOLLAND, James KERNS, Capel HOARD and William ROBISON, no
date.

165a - 1810, Monongalia County Court. "I do certify that
Robert TRAVIS´ oxen and sled were employed one day in the
service for which they were hired," signed Rees W. MORRIS,
1810. "I do   certify that Joshua FAST´s oxen and sled were
employed one day in the service for which they were hired,"
1810, signed Rees W. MORRIS.

165a - 1810, Monongalia County Court. "I promise to pay the
administratrix of Henry DERING, deceased, viz, Mrs. Rebecca
DERING, $30 which I assumed to pay for Turner R. WHITLOCK and
which was 'due November 1806," 25 September 1810, signed by
Wm. G. PAYNE.

165a - 1820, Monongalia County Court. Trust Deed to Silas
POWELL from Thomas LAIDLEY dated 2 February 1810 for 314
acres adjoining Nehemiah HARP and the Monongahela River for
$60. If LAIDLEY failed to pay the money, with interest,
before 22 February 1812, Trustee William G. PAYNE, to sell
the land at public sale for ready cash and out of the sale to
pay POWELL $60 with interest plus cost and commissioner fees
and the balance to LAIDLEY.   The deed to be made to the
purchaser in fee simple without recourse to LAIDLEY. Signed
by LAIDLEY in the presence of Samuel HANWAY, John A. GOOSEMAN
and Alexander WILSON.   Proved September 1810 and recorded in
Deed Book E at page 327. "Sold 22 May 1820, Silas POWELL
bought it for $103.50 being the highest bidder. I had
advertised it at Monongalia County Courthouse door for about
six (weeks?) to be sold for ready money," signed by PAYNE.

166 - 1810, Monongalia County Court. Order for William NUZUM,
William GEORGE, Nathan HALL, John JONES and Thomas MURPHY, or
any three of them, to view and lay off a road the nearest and
best way from Peter JOHNSON´s Road at the forks of Wickware
Creek to John NUZUM´s Mill and report to next April Court.
Reply of petitioners to the above order: The petitioners
said the road "which is an almost impracticable part of the
county only for a few individuals and as we are of the
opinion that the said road can be of no great service to the
public in general and we do understand by good information
that attempts will be made to have us open and work the same
when established, which are a lying out of our district, and

we have 11 miles of road to work, which 5 miles of the same
are entirely out of a settlement and never had but a few days
work done upon it and we have but a few in number of men to
work in our own district." The petitioners prayed that if
the road was established that the instigators of the road be
appointed to work and keep it in repair. Signed in April
1810 at Glady Creek by William POWER, John LINN, William
LINN, Samuel LINN, Barney BURNS, Henry TUCKER, William
TUCKER, John POWERS, Robert HENDERSON Sr., George LAKE and
Jeremiah LAKE. GEORGE, NUZUM and JONES returned their report
to court and recommended that the road be opened. Established
April 1810. Abel DAVIS appointed surveyor of the road.

166 - 1810, Monongalia County Court. A cart, oxen and their
driver belonging to Alexander HAWTHORN ($1.75 per day) and a
wagon and 4 horses ($2.75 per day) with their driver belong-
ing to George DORSEY, all impressed by Nehemiah POWERS to
assist in mending the road whereof he is surveyor were valued
by Lindsey BOGGESS and Lewis WOOLF, 24 February 1810. POWERS,
surveyor of the road from KERN's Mill to near Henry CRISS'
and the Forge Road from near Philip SMELL's, was authorized
to impress this equipment on 5 February 1809 and the work was
done sometime in the spring of 1809.

166 - 1810, Monongalia County Court. Francis BILLINGSLEY,
served as Road Surveyor "the time appointed by law" and
petitioned the court to appoint Daniel WADE, Jesse BUSSEY or
Ashiel AUGUSTIN in his place, 12 February 1810. BILLINGSLEY
signed this petition in the presence of Daniel MOORE. WADE
appointed.

166 - 1810, Monongalia County Court. April 1810 term, Samuel
LEMLEY appointed Surveyor of the Road in the room of John
RICH. Others considered: William WILLEY, Jeremiah SNIDER
and David WRIGHT.

166 - 1810, Monongalia County Court. Allen HOLLAND appointed
Surveyor of the Road leading from Smithfield (Smithtown) to
Preston County* by Fishing Road and by Robert FERRELL's and
said HOLLAND's, 1810. A list of unidentified names: John
MALONE, Henry FERRELL (crossed out), Rob't FERRELL, Francis
FERRELL, Enoch FERRELL, Joshua FAST, Adam FAST, Jacob FAST,
John COROTHERS, Robert COROTHERS, Andrew COROTHERS, Allen
HOLLAND, Philip HOLLAND, John HUFFMAN, Philip HUFFMAN, Daniel
HOLLAND, Richard HOLLAND, Andrew KEY, Caleb TARLTON, Silas
STEVENS, Israel STEVENS, William STEVENS, Hezekiah MAXFIELD,
Kinsey MAXFIELD, James MAXFIELD, George REED, Greenbury REED,
Lewis FERRELL (crossed out), Alexander WINDENS and Nathan
STANSBERRY. (#2 list) John WARE, E. COX, R. MORRIS, G.
LEMLEY, Jacob MILLER, Geo WILSON, J. BOYERS, G. D. BARNEY,
Jno SHRIVER, James CHADWICK, Willey THOMAS, J. JEFFS and
Mathew HENRY Jr. (*Preston County formed 1818).

166 - 1810, Monongalia County Court. "We Your petitioners humbly showeth it has long been their desire to have a road beginning at the Round Glade on the Maryland Line near to Charles HOUSEMAN's and known by the name of the Pine Swamps to intersect with the County Line Road at Isack ERVIN's. The principle objects Your petitioners has in view to have the aforesaid road opened is that it would be as much as ten miles nearer to Western Port which is on the common route for the inhabitants of Crab Orchard and Sandy Creek to go to Winchester for salt and other necessaries and to make sale of produce, also to encourage the settling of that large boundary of first quality land called the Pine Swamps which is now inhabited principally by ravens beasts." Signed by Benjamin SHAW, Tobis REEM, Daniel MINNEY, Henry SINES, John WOLF, Reuben ASKINS, Jacob WOLF, Edward _____, Wiliam SINES, Jesse PENROSE, Danel MARTEN, _____ _____, Charles HOUSEMAN, _____ WOLF, William PEARSESON, Isaac ERWINS, _____ _____, Jacob _____, James WEBSTER, Joseph SAVERNS, Robert CONERD, Joh SMITH, June 1810. On reverse: Augusten WOLF, George WOLF, Leonard CUP and Henry MILLER.

218

wil am siner

Jesse Penrose

Danel Marten

Johannus [illegible]

Charles Houseman

Augustein Welf

William Pearceson

Isaac [illegible]

[illegible]

Jacob Peter

[illegible]

Joseph [illegible]

Robert [illegible]

John Smith

166 - 1810, Monongalia County Court. "We the petitioners humbly pray that You appoint viewers to lay out a road from Cornelius KING's to intersect the State Road near or at Kingwood the nearest and best way." Signed by Charles BYRN, Anthoney COZAD, J. ROBERTS, Thos MONTGOMERY, John COSAD, John SNIDER, Jesse TROWBRIDGE and Wm PAYNE, June 1810.

166 - 1810, Monongalia County Court. June 1810, Justice John CHIPPS and James DORAN swore that James STAFFORD, with 2 horses, driver and sled, was employed at working on the highway leading from Stewartstown to Morgantown in the month of December last. They valued the team and driver at $.75 per day, 14 May 1810.

Also in this file - - - - - For killing wolves: Samuel MINOR $6, Dudley EVANS $4, Boaz BURRISS $4, John S. ROBERTS $5, Nick'l VANDERVORT $4, J. POWELL $5, R. HALL $4, Jarad EVANS $4, J. COX $6, William GEORGE $4, J. CAMPBELL $6, J. S. BARNES $6, (two names torn off), Wm. N. JARRETT $12, _____ WERNINGER $4, Charles BYRN $6, Jno NUZUM $6, Simeon EVERLY $4, Jno FAIRFAX $5, Jno EVANS Jr. $_. "The majority of the Justices present is in favor of $4 for wolf scalps for old wolves and half the sum for the young ones under six months of age."

166 - 1810, Monongalia County Court. The petitioners said they labored "under much deficiency by the want of a mill road from Thomas GIBSON's near the mouth of Sandy Creek to REEMS' Mill on Muddy Creek the constancy of this stream in time of low water and the utility of this road with respect to going to Winchester with our produce and to purchase salt and other necessaries would also be great," 6 April 1810. Signed by Alexander BRANDON, Robert GIBSON, Jonathan JENKINS, Jon JENKINS, J. EVERLY, William WALLAR, Samuel WALLAR, John CALE, Thomas GIBSON, James GIBSON, Learey GIBSON, Daniel SEVERNS, John SEVERNS, Nathan METHENEY, John WALER and Benjamin SHAW. William WALLAR, Thomas JENKINS and John JENKINS appointed viewers.

166 - 1810, Monongalia County Court. John BARKER resigned as Surveyor of the Road, having served since August 1808, and recommended William WILSON, George BRAND or John ROGERS to take his place, 3 April 1810.

166 - 1810, Monongalia County Court. Samuel CRANE, J. W. S. ROBERTS and Charles BYRN petitioned the court to appoint viewers to lay out a road from Kingwood by the mouth of Muddy Creek to Crane's Mill. Samuel CRANE, James BROWN and Philip MARTIN appointed as viewers, June 1810.

166 - 1810, Monongalia County Court. "We the petitioners beg Your attention at this time, Your Worships well knows that

the Pine Swamps has lain unsettled as yet and is only a cage
for every kind of vermin which is very injurious to the
neighboring settlements around instead of being settled and
having a number of the best farms in the county in it. We
request Your Honors to grant a review of a road from Mount
Pleasant Crossroads to go through Roaring Creek Gap and in
the nighest way with the most practical ground to the
Maryland Line opposite the Round Glade at the Pine Swamps.
The intention of the road is to have a road from the Pine
Swamps on to the Crab Orchard and crossing Cheat River at
BUTLER's Mill, then to Peter MEREDITH's, then to James
COBWIN/CORBIN's and then to Morgantown. Col. John LYNN
that is Clerk of Aligany (sic) County has promised to have an
order obtained for a road to meet it at the line," April
1810. Signed by John RODHEFFER, Piffer WILLHELM by order,
Dennis JEFFERS, Benjamin JEFFERS, Benjamin TREMBLY, Moses
JUSTIS, Harmin GREATHOUSE, John JOHNSON, Park BUCKLEW, James
METHENY, Benjamin METHENY, Samuel CRANE, Jonathan CRANE,
Isaac MARTIN, Michael HARTMAN, Jacob MARTIN, John ANNON,
Thomas ELDRIDGE by order, Thomas ELDRIDGE and Isaac ROMINE.

166 - 1810, Monongalia County Court. The petitioners prayed
the court for an order to review and lay out a road from
REEM's Ford on Muddy Creek by his mill to intersect the
County Road at Isack ERWIN's it being about 2 miles and an
end of a road that has never been established, so as for the
Surveyor of the Road to work it which is a damage to the
settlement and public, 2 April 1810. Signed by Amos ROBBARTS,
William ROBBARTS, John RODHEFFER, Tobias REEM, Benjamin SHAW,
William PEARCESON, Daniel MINNEY, _____ _____, Isaac
ERWINS, Adam RODAHAFER, Peter MILLAR, Joseph SEVERNS, Samuel
SHAW and Leonard CUPP. Leonard CUPP Sr., Benjamin MIDDLETON
and Daniel MARTIN viewers.

166 - 1810, Monongalia County Court. The petition of a number
of inhabitants of the county "being destitute of a mill only
one which is John NUZUM's and having no road leading to said
mill, Your Petitioners most humbly pray that Your Worships
will order a road to be viewed and laid out from Peter
JOHNSON's Road at the forks of Wickware Creek to the said
NUZUM's Mill the nearest and best way," February 1810. Signed
by Enoch CURRANT, James CURRENT Sr., Martin CURRANT, John
GLENDINING, Stephen POE, William ELLIS, Daniel GRIMSLEY, John
ELLIS, George ELLIS, Peter JOHNSTONE, Abraham JOHNSTONE,
James CURRANT Jr., Robert PETERS, John CURRANT, Aron LUZADDER
Jr., John NUZUM, Thomas NUZUM, Richard NUZUM, Aron LUZADER
Sr., David NORRIS, Leonard CARYL and John HAYMOND. William
NUZUM, William GEORGE, Nathan HALL and John JONES viewers.

166 - 1810, Monongalia County Court. We, the undernamed
petitioners, pray that the district of the road be divided as
follows: from Elkhorns? Creek at Philip SMELL's house to the

bridge at KERN's Mill to compose one district and from the Forge to the State Road and along the State Road to the Glades, the end of the present district, and that a surveyor be appointed to each district, February 1810. Signed by Jno WAGNER, Robert HAWTHORN, George GREENWOOD, Ezekiel CHENEY, Thomas LANHAM, George REDBOUG, John ROBINSON, William STUTLER, Drake SWINDLER, Samuel UPTON, William HALL, David SWINDLER, Isaac SWISHER, Jacob NUSE, Frederick SWISHER, Godfrey GUSMAN, Jacob HOLAND, Philip GORDON, Nemeiah POWRS, and William ROBINGSON. G. GREENWOOD, Jacob HOLLAND and William STUTLER to be placed to the upper end. Robert HAWTHORN to be surveyor of the upper district and George GREENWOOD and Jacob HOLLAND to be allotted to the upper district with all the hands above the cross road. John WAGNER to be surveyor of the lower district and all the hands living below the cross road to work under John WAGNER except the two above mentioned.

166 - 1810, Monongalia County Court. The petition of Thomas BARNES and William HAYES who are surveyors of two several road precincts meeting at BARNES' Mill showeth that Your petitioners are not able to maintain and keep their respective roads in good order without some assistance. Your petitioners therefore pray that for the assistance of the above named BARNES, that William ICE and all his tenants should be put on the road under said BARNES. And for the assistance of the above named HAYES that Henry BATTON, John MERRILL, William KNIGHT, John THORN and Charles STEWART be put on the road under said HAYES. February 1810. "We the under subscribers are of the opinion the above statement is correct." Signed by Asa HALL, John DRAGOO, John JOLLIFFE, William STEWART, William BARNES, Peter DRAGOO Sr., William FLEMING, William McCRAY, Thomas G. WHITLOCK, Reuben WILCUTS, William HAYES Sr., James BARNES, Henry HAYS and Jo S. BARNES. Ordered that William ICE and all the hands that live on his land be added to Thomas BARNES' company. Ordered that Henry BATTON, John MERRILL, John THORN and Charles STEWART be added to the hands working under William HAYES.

166 - 1810, Monongalia County Court. The petitioners of the Upper District of Monongalia County said it would be of public advantage to have a road viewed and laid out beginning at Coal Run and thence through the neighborhood of Benoni and Alexander FLEMING and to intersect the old road at the farm of Nathan FLEMING at the Harrison County line and to appoint Benoni FLEMING, Reubin WILLITT and Alexander FLEMING and their hands to cut out and work the road and exempt them from working any other road, 19 January 1810. Signed by William BARNS, Thomas BARNS Sr., James BARNS, Uz BARNS, Thomas FLEMING, Robert DOWNS, Reuben WILCUTS, Matthis FLEMING, Alexander FLEMING, Peter MILLER, John TANARY?, Boaz FLEMING, William FLEMING, George FLEMING, Lorin? FLEMING, Josias

WILCUTS, Elah HAYHURST and Jo S. BARNS. Asa HALL, Andrew ICE, Jesse ICE and Joshua HART viewers.

166 - 1808, Monongalia County Court. October 1808. Ordered that Thomas STEEL be appointed Road Surveyor in the room of James GREY.

166 - 1806, Monongalia County Court. April 1806. Ordered that Robert HENDERSON be appointed Road Surveyor in the room of William NUZUM. HENDERSON recommended George REES, David MURPHY or William PARKERS/PICKENS to take his place.

166 - 1810, Monongalia County Court. John STAFFORD appointed Road Surveyor in the room of John CHIPPS, April 1808. James DOREN, John FOSTER or Samuel DOREN recommended by STAFFORD to take his place, 1810.

166a - 1810, Monongalia County Court. 14 May 1810, $12 fee paid to Col. William McCLEERY and Nicholas VANDERVORT for prosecuting a suit on behalf of the Overseers of the Poor against Elihu HORTON and James PENDALL, signed by Noah LINSLEY and P. DODDRIDGE.

166a - 1810, Monongalia County Court. 4 June 1810, Samuel EVERLY allowed $32 as part of $35 allowed him for boarding, clothing and nursing Elenor COWAN, one of the poor, for one year ending this date, signed by William McCLEERY and George SMYTH.

166a - 1810, Monongalia County Court. 4 June 1810, Joshua GREGORY allowed at the rate of $42 per year beginning 7 September 1808 or 9 months = $33.75. Signed by William McCLEERY and George SMYTH.

166a - 1809, Monongalia County Court. 5 June 1809, Elias HOSKINSON allowed $50 for nursing, clothing and boarding Mary CAMPBELL, one of the poor, for the year 1809. Signed by William McCLEERY and George SMYTH.

166a - 1810, Monongalia County Court. Joane HAWTHORN allowed $5.71 for boarding, nursing and washing for William MARTIN, an orphan boy, for five weeks and five days, no date. Signed by William McCLEERY and William HAYS.

166a - 1810, Monongalia County Court. 4 June 1810, Rawley MARTIN allowed $1.50 for one day attendance settling with the collector as clerk. Signed by William McCLEERY and N. VANDERVORT.

166a - 1810, Monongalia County Court. To Ralph BARKSHIRE and Rebecca THORN: 3 July - 29 August 1810, for red flannel, calico, muslin and thread furnished by Rebecca THORN for an

orphan boy = 1.15.0.   2 July 1810, 4 quarts of wine for ____
GRUB, one of the poor = 18 shillings.   Receipt signed by
BARKSHIRE for $8.50 in full discharge of this account dated 5
September 1810.

166a - 1810, Monongalia County Court. 4 June 1810, James
MATHENEY allowed $24 for clothing, boarding and nursing a
female bastard child for 11 months ending this date. Signed
by William McCLEERY and George SMYTH.

166a - 1810, Monongalia County Court. 4 June 1810, Benjamin
HILL allowed $40 for boarding and nursing Penelope HILL, one
of the poor. Signed by William McCLEERY and C. HAYMOND.
Archibald WILSON allowed $6.21 for clothes furnished Penelope
HILL, one of the poor. Signed by William McCLEERY.

166a - 1810, Monongalia County Court. 5 June 1810, Cathrine
BURRELL allowed $15 to be paid into the hands of William
McCLEERY for the support of the said Cathrine for the ensuing
year. Signed by William McCLEERY and N. VANDERVORT.

166a - 1810, Monongalia County Court. 24 March 1810, Order
to pay William SAINTCAIR $1 for Rebecca HAYS, who is
seriously ill in child bed. Signed by William McCLEERY and
N. VANDERVORT.

166a - 1810, Monongalia County Court. 5 June 1810, William
SMITH allowed $12.79 for nursing and boarding Hetty/Hatty
DOBSON, one of the poor, for three months and six days
beginning 30 April 1810 and ending 5 August inclusive at $4
per month. Signed by William McCLEERY.

166a - 1810, Monongalia County Court. 4 June 1810, Rebecca
THORN allowed $5 for nursing and boarding Hetty DOBSON, one
of the poor, for five weeks ending this date. Signed by
William McCLEERY and N. VANDERVORT.

166a - 1810, Monongalia County Court. 4 June 1810, Catherine
EVANS allowed $50 for attending upon, nursing, boarding and
assisting in delivering Elizabeth JOHNSTON of two bastard
females and attending upon Elizabeth with her sore breasts
and attending upon said children. Signed by William McCLEERY
and William HAYES. Receipt signed by EVANS, 5 June 1810.

167 - 1808, Monongalia Justice Court. Order to attach the
property of William GAMBLE at the suit of Robert LONG for
$7.45, 25 June 1808. No property found by Con'st S. KENNEDY.

167 - 1808, Monongalia Justice Court. Arthur WILSON summoned
to answer the complaint of Robert BOGGESS, assignee of Jno
COOPER, for non-payment of a debt due by note, 11 January
1808. No property found by Constable James McVICKER.

167 - 1807, Monongalia Justice Court. William DUNWOODS summoned to answer William TINGLE in a plea of debt due by note, 23 November 1807. Signed by J. CLARK. No property found by Constable James KING.

167 - 1808, Monongalia Justice Court. Isaac MAYFIELD summoned to answer the complaint of Presley MARTIN for non-payment of a debt due by note, 15 June 1808. No property found by Constable James McVICKER.

167 - 1808, Monongalia Justice Court. Reubin MATHENY summoned to answer the complaint of David MORGAN for non-payment of a debt due by note, 12 July 1808. No property found by Constable J. STATLER.

167 - 1809, Monongalia Justice Court. Jacob PINDALL summoned to answer the complaint of William CHIPPS for non-payment of a debt due by note, 30 May 1809. No property found by Constable James McVICKER.

167 - 1808, Monongalia Justice Court. Order to attach the property of Charles BOYLES at the suit of Joseph CAMPBELL, assignee of R. SCOTT, for $10, 24 September 1808. No property found by Constable R. MARTIN.

167 - 1810, Monongalia Justice Court. Abraham HALE summoned to answer the complaint of John McCLOUD for non-payment of a debt due by assumpsit, 22 June 1810. No property found by Constable G. HITE.

167 - 1808, Monongalia Justice Court. David PIXLER summoned to answer the complaint of Nicholas RYLAND for non-payment of a debt due by note, 6 February 1808. No property found by Constable R. MARTIN.

167 - 1810, Monongalia Justice Court. Order to attach the property of Alexander SCOTT for $10.50 at the suit of Jacob KYGER, 2 June 1810. No property found by Constable G. HITE.

167 - 1809, Monongalia Justice Court. John CARTER summoned to answer the complaint of William LOWRY and Company for non-payment of a debt due by note, 4 December 1809. No property found by Constable Jno COOPER.

167 - 1810, Monongalia Justice Court. James HILL summoned to answer the complaint of James DAYLY for non-payment of a debt due by note, 8 October 1810. No property found by Constable G. R. HOSKINSON.

167 - 1808, Monongalia Justice Court. Charles MARTIN summoned to answer William LOWRY and Company for non-payment of a debt due by note, 15 September 1808. No property found by Constable G. B. HOSKINSON.

167 - 1808, Monongalia Justice Court. Benjamin WILSON summoned to answer the complaint of John SCOTT for non-payment of a debt due by note, 12 April 1808. No property found by Constable G. B. HOSKINSON.

167 - 1808, Monongalia Justice Court. Arthur WILSON summoned to answer the complaint of Ralph BARKSHIRE for non-payment of a debt due by note, 25 January 1808. No property found by Constable J. COOPER.

167 - 1807, Monongalia Justice Court. Henry BARRICKMAN summoned to answer the complaint of William TINGLE for non-payment of a debt due by clerk's notes, 7 December 1807. No property found by Constable J. COOPER.

167 - 1809, Monongalia Justice Court. John CARTER summoned to answer the complaint of William LOWRY and Company for non-payment of a debt due by note, 4 December 1809. No property found by Constable G. HITE.

167 - 1810, Monongalia Justice Court. John CHIPPS summoned to answer the complaint of James McVICKER for non-payment of a debt due by note, 17 March 1810. No property found by the Constable.

167 - 1810, Monongalia Justice Court. Robert SCOTT summoned to answer the complaint of Archibald WILSON, assignee of John G. _____ for non-payment of a debt due by note, 21 September 1810. No property found by Constable G. B. HOSKINSON.

167 - 1808, Monongalia Justice Court. Order to attach the property of Thomas WEBSTER for $8.69 at the suit of Rebecca DERING, 28 February 1808. No property found by Constable R. MARTIN.

167 - 1809, Monongalia Justice Court. Amos CHIPPS summoned to answer the complaint of George BARNES for non-payment of a debt due by note, __ February 1809. No property found by Constable G. B. HOSKINSON.

167 - 1808, Monongalia Justice Court. William MORRIS summoned to answer the complaint of John STALEY for non-payment of a debt due by account, 9 May 1808. No property found by Constable G. B. HOSKINSON.

167 - 1808, Monongalia Justice Court. John TAYLOR summoned to answer the complaint of Robert HAWTHORN for non-payment of a debt due by note, 15 February 1808. No property found.

167 - 1808, Monongalia Justice Court. Robert FERRELL summoned to answer the complaint of Nimrod EVANS for non payment of a debt due by sheriff's notes, 3 November 1808. No property found.

167 - 1808, Monongalia Justice Court. John JOLLIFF summoned to answer the complaint of John COOPER for non-payment of a debt due by note, 23 January 1808. No property found.

167 - 1808, Monongalia Justice Court. Francis COLLINS summoned to answer the complaint of Jonathan HARTLEY for failing to pay a debt due by acc't, 13 January 1808. No property found.

167 - 1807, Monongalia Justice Court. Benjamin WILSON summoned to answer the complaint of Davis SHOCKLEY for non-payment of a debt due by acc't, 24 December 1807. No property found.

167 - 1809, Monongalia Justice Court. John MILLS summoned to answer the complaint of Joseph CAMPBELL for non-payment of a debt due by account, 16 October 1809. No property found.

167 - 1807, Monongalia Justice Court. Arthur WILSON summoned to answer the complaint of Johnston LOYD for non-payment of a debt due by note, 23 December 1807. No property found by Constable James McVICKER.

167 - 1808, Monongalia Justice Court. William BOWSLEY summoned to answer the complaint of _____ BROCKMIRE for non-payment of a debt due by account, 12 December 1808. Summons Edward McFADDIN as a witness for the plaintiff. No property found by Constable Daniel COX.

167 - 1807, Monongalia Justice Court. Thomas LAIDLEY summoned to answer the complaint of Charley BIRN for non-payment of a debt due by account, 23 November 1807. No property found.

167 - 1810, Monongalia Justice Court. Abraham HALE summoned to answer the complaint of George HITE for non-payment of a debt due by account, 23 March 1810. No property found.

167 - 1808, Monongalia Justice Court. William CRISTEY summoned to answer the complaint of Benjamin WILSON for non-payment of a debt due by note, 16 July 1808.

167 - 1808, Monongalia Justice Court. Order to attach the property of Alexander SCOTT at the suit of Johnson LOYD for $10.65 plus costs, 28 February 1808. No property found.

167 - 1808, Monongalia Justice Court. Duncan McRA summoned to answer the complaint of Jacob LYMAN for non-payment of a debt due by account, 10 _____ 1808. Summons George R. TINGLE and Abraham HALE as witnesses for the plaintiff. No property found by Constable Jno COOPER.

167 - 1810, Monongalia Justice Court. Abraham HALE summoned to answer the complaint of William LOWRY and Company for non-payment of a debt due by account, 6 and 20 January 1810. No

property found by Constable George B. HOSKINSON.

167 - 1807, Monongalia Justice Court. "Amount of Evan B. MORGAN's canoeing me $19.50," 26 January 1807. Signed by John C. PAYNE. PAYNE summoned to answer the complaint of MORGAN for non-payment of a debt due by account, 26 December 1807. Appeal granted.

167 - 1809, Monongalia Justice Court. John CHIPPS summoned to answer the complaint of William CHIPPS for non-payment of a debt due by due bill, 30 May 1809.

167 - 1808, Monongalia Justice Court. Thomas BURCHNELL summoned to answer the complaint of Joseph LOWRY for non-payment of a debt due by note, 13 September 1808. No property found by Constable Jno. COOPER.

167 - 1810, Monongalia Justice Court. Senate TRIPLET summoned to answer the complaint of Daniel SHAHAN for non-payment of a debt due by account, 13 April 1810. No property found by Constable G. HITE.

167 - 1808, Monongalia Justice Court. Order to attach the property of Abraham HUFFMAN at the suit of John BAXTER for 15 shillings plus costs, 24 September 1808. No property found by Constable R. MARTIN.

167 - 1810, Monongalia Justice Court. Abraham HALE summoned to answer the complaint of Zackel MORGAN for non-payment of a debt due by account, 4 May 1810. No property found by Constable George HITE.

167 - 1810, Monongalia Justice Court. Francis TIBBS summoned to answer the complaint of William JARRETT for non-payment of a debt due by account, 11 January 1810. No property found by Constable G. B. HOSKINSON.

167 - 1810, Monongalia Justice Court. Noah RIDGWAY summoned to answer the complaint of Philip SHEETS for non-payment of a debt due by account, 9 April 1810. No property found by Constable G. HITE.

167 - 1809, Monongalia Justice Court. Amos CHIPPS summoned to answer the complaint of Farquire McCRA for non-payment of a debt due by account, 10 January 1809. No property found by Constable G. B. HOSKINSON.

167 - 1810, Monongalia Justice Court. William CHIPPS summoned to answer the complaint of A. J. WOODROW for non-payment of a debt due by note, 8 January 1810. No property found by Constable G. HITE.

167 - 1808, Monongalia Justice Court. Thomas MARTIN summoned to answer the complaint of Philip DODDRIDGE for non-payment of a debt due by note, 11 August 1808. No property found by Constable Jno. COOPER.

167 - 1808, Monongalia Justice Court. Arthur WILSON summoned to answer the complaint of Hedgeman TRIPLETT for non-payment of a debt for money paid as security for him, 9 August 1808. No property found by Constable Jno. COOPER.

167 - 1810, Monongalia Justice Court. William GAMBLE summoned to answer the complaint of William LOWRY and Company for non-payment of a debt due by account ($20 with interest), 13 January 1810. No property found by Constable R. MARTIN.

·167 - 1809, Monongalia Justice Court. William FORD summoned to answer the complaint of James MORRISON for non-payment of a debt due by note, 21 November 1809. No property found by Constable John JONES.

167 - 1809, Monongalia Justice Court. William HOLIFIELD summoned to answer the complaint of John P. WELTNER for non-payment of a debt due by account, 19 January 1809. No property found by Constable Daniel COX.

167 - 1808, Monongalia Justice Court. John WEST summoned to answer the complaint of Jesse MARTIN, for the use of Joseph CAMPBELL, for non-payment of a debt due by note, 15 March 1808. No property found by Constable Jno. COOPER.

167 - 1808, Monongalia Justice Court. Robert FERRELL summoned to answer the complaint of John EVANS for non-payment of a debt due by sheriff's note, 5 November 1808. No property found by Constable G. B. HOSKINSON.

167 - 1808, Monongalia Justice Court. John DOWNER summoned to answer the complaint of John EVANS for non-payment of a debt due by clerk's notes, 6 November 1808. No property found by Constable G. B. HOSKINSON,

167 - 1809, Monongalia Justice Court. John CHIPPS summoned to answer the complaint of Martin BOWMAN, for the use of William CHIPPS, for non-payment of a debt due by note, 30 May 1809. No property found by Constable James McVICKER.

167 - 1807, Monongalia Justice Court. December 1807 term, William CHIPPS appointed Surveyor of the Road in the room of Robert HILL. On reverse: John GREEN, Waitman FURBEE and William PHRUM.

167 - 1808, Monongalia Justice Court. Hannah LEWELLEN summoned to answer the complaint of O. Calihan STEFON for non-

payment of a debt due by account, 23 March 1808. No property found by Constable G. B. HOSKINSON.

167 - 1808, Monongalia Justice Court. Jonathan CARNS summoned to answer the complaint of William STAFFORD for non-payment of a debt due by note, 12 and 16 April 1808. Summons John GARD and Anthony COZAD as witnesses for the defendant. Summons William CREACRAFT and Lemuel JOHN as witnesses for the plaintiff. No property found by Constable G. B. HOSKINSON.

167 - 1808, Monongalia Justice Court. Thomas LAIDLEY summoned to answer the complaint of Philip SHEETS for non-payment of a debt due by account, 25 January 1808. Summons George R. TINGLE as witness for the defendant. No property found by Constable Jno. COOPER.

167 - 1808, Monongalia Justice Court. George HOSKINSON summoned to answer the complaint of Jno. WAGNER for non-payment of a debt due by account, 3 October 1808. No property found by Constable Jno. COOPER.

167 - 1808, Monongalia Justice Court. Farquire McCRAY summoned to answer the complaint of William LOWRY and Company for non-payment of a debt due by note, 25 October 1808. No property found by Constable G. B. HOSKINSON.

167 - 1808, Monongalia Justice Court. Thomas BRITTON summoned to answer the complaint of Jno. WAGNER for non-payment of a debt due by account, 3 December 1808. No property found by Constable Jno. COOPER.

167 - 1808, Monongalia Justice Court. Thomas LAIDLEY summoned to answer the complaint of Thomas MURFEY for non-payment of a debt due by account, 3 September 1808. No property found in Constable G. B. HOSKINSON's district.

167 - 1809, Monongalia Justice Court. James LEGGETT summoned to answer the complaint of Philip SHIVELEY for non-payment of a debt due by note, 18 November 1809. $.60 made and no more property found by Constable R. MARTIN.

167 - 1809, Monongalia Justice Court. James WEST summoned to answer the complaint of F. MAURAY for non-payment of a debt due by note, 2 December 1809. No property found.

167 - 1809, Monongalia Justice Court. John CHIPPS summoned to answer the complaint of William CHIPPS for non-payment of a debt due by due bill, 30 May 1809. No property found in Constable James McVICKER's district.

167 - 1810, Monongalia Justice Court. Benjamin WILSON summoned to answer the complaint of Rebecca DERING for non-payment of a debt due by note, 2 January 1810. No property found in Constable G. B. HOSKINSON's district.

167 - 1810, Monongalia Justice Court. James WEST Jr. summoned to answer the complaint of A. & S. WOODROW for non-payment of a debt due by account, 12 January 1810. No property found in Constable G. HITE's district.

167 - 1808, Monongalia Justice Court. Asa VANDIN summoned to answer the complaint of Philip SHEETS for non-payment of a debt due by note, 2 February 1808. No property found in Constable J. COOPER's district.

167 - 1807, Monongalia Justice Court. David PIXLER summoned to answer the complaint of R. SCOTT for non-payment of a debt due by note, 12 October 1807. No property found in Constable G. B. HOSKINSON's district.

167 - 1810, Monongalia Justice Court. Abraham HALE summoned to answer the complaint of Robert HAWTHORN for non-payment of a debt due by note, 13 February 1810. $3 made, no property found to make the balance, Constable HOSKINSON.

167 - 1808, Monongalia Justice Court. Daniel ANDERSON summoned to answer the complaint of Francis COLLINS for non-payment of a debt due by note, 12 April 1808. Eighteen day note signed by Daniel ANDERSON to Francis COLLINS dated 13 January 1807 for $45 and witnessed by John HAWTHORN. Appeal granted after giving John DOWNEY as security.

167 - 1808, Monongalia Justice Court. Robert FERRELL summoned to answer the complaint of William LOWRY and Company for non-payment of $3.33 debt due by account, 13 June 1808. No property found by Constable Isaac POWELL.

167 - 1810, Monongalia Justice Court. Abraham HALE summoned to answer the complaint of James TUCKER for non-payment of a debt due by an accepted order, 28 July 1810. No property found by Constable G. HITE.

167 - 1808, Monongalia Justice Court. R. PRITCHARD and William CHIPPS summoned to answer the complaint of John TIBBS for non-payment of a debt due by note, 7 March 1808. No property found by Constable James McVICKER.

167 - 1808, Monongalia Justice Court. Richard TIBBS summoned to answer the complaint of William LOWRY and Company for non-payment of a debt due by note, 2 June 1808. No property found by Constable G. B. HOSKINSON.

167 - 1808, Monongalia Justice Court. Samuel EVERLY summoned to answer the complaint of John STALEY for non-payment of a debt due by note, 13 June 1808. Summons Jacob STALEY as witness for the defendant. No property found by Constable James McVICKER.

167 - 1809, Monongalia Justice Court. Jesse PATTEN summoned to answer the complaint of Robert McMULLEN for trover and conversion, 7 January and 7 March 1809. No property found by Constable John RAMSEY.

167 - 1808, Monongalia Justice Court. Peter FOURTNEY summoned to answer the complaint of John REED, assignee of James PINDALL, for non-payment of a debt due by note, 15 September 1808. No property found by Constable Thomas BARTLETT.

167 - 1808, Monongalia Justice Court. Benjamin WILSON summoned to answer the complaint of A. & S. WOODROW for non-payment of a debt due by account, 23 May 1808. No property found by Constable Jno. COOPER.

167 - 1809, Monongalia Justice Court. Thomas BURCHINAL summoned to answer the complaint of Joseph CAMPBELL for non-payment of a debt, under $10, due by note, 18 June 1809. No property found in Alexander BRANDON's district.

167 - 1809, Monongalia Justice Court. Scott MARTIN summoned to answer the complaint of Isaac DEAN in an action of trover, 19 August 1809. Paid $5.50 and all costs.

167 - 1809, Monongalia Justice Court. Samuel FRUM summoned to answer the complaint of John KNOX for non-payment of a debt due by account, 9 September 1809. No property found by Constable G. B. HOSKINSON.

167 - 1808, Monongalia Justice Court. Arthur WILSON summoned to answer the complaint of Sinnett TRIPLETT, assignee of Samuel BOICE, for non-payment of a debt due by note, 15 June 1808. Credited on this note at sundry times $3, 11 pounds of iron $1, 2 meals $.50. Not executed by order of the plaintiff.

167 - 1809, Monongalia Justice Court. John COOPER summoned to answer the complaint of William LOWRY and Company for non-payment of a debt due by note, 9 December 1809. No property found by Constable G. B. HOSKINSON.

167 - 1809, Monongalia Justice Court. William CHIPPS summoned to answer the complaint of John COOPER for non-payment of a debt due by note, 14 August 1809. No property found by Constable George HITE.

167 - 1809, Monongalia Justice Court. Thomas BURCHINAL summoned to answer the complaint of James WALLS for non-payment of a debt due by note, 18 June 1809. No property found in Constable Alexander BRANDON's district.

167 - 1809, Monongalia Justice Court. Duncan F. McRAE summoned to answer the complaint of Amaziah DAVISON for non-payment of a debt due by note, 24 June 1809. No property found in Constable G. B. HOSKINSON's district.

167 - 1810, Monongalia Justice Court. January 1810 term of court, the Justices called to lay a levy for repairing or building a new jail and to settle with the Collectors of the 1809 Levy.

167 - 1810, Monongalia Justice Court. Patrick SULLIVAN summoned to answer the complaint of George HERTZOG for non-payment of a debt due by account, 4 May 1810. No property found in Constable John KNOX's district.

167 - 1809, Monongalia Justice Court. Arthur WILSON summoned to answer the complaint of William STAFFORD, assignee of John GEFFS, for non-payment of a debt due by note, 8 April 1809. No property found by Constable G. B. HOSKINSON.

167 - 1809, Monongalia Justice Court. Reubin JACO summoned to answer the complaint of William LOWRY for non-payment of a debt due by note, 16 March 1809. No property found in Constable John JONES' district.

167 - 1810, Monongalia Justice Court. Thomas LAIDLEY summoned to answer the complaint of Isaac Hite WILLIAMS for non-payment of a debt due by note, 16 March 1810. This debt was settled by the defendant giving the plaintiff a mare.

167 - 1809, Monongalia Justice Court. Arthur WILSON summoned to answer the complaint of Mathew GEORGE for non-payment of a debt due by note, 17 June 1809. No property found.

167 - 1808, Monongalia Justice Court. William HATFIELD summoned to answer the complaint of Jon SNYDER for non-payment of a debt due by note, 25 June 1808. No property found.

167 - 1809, Monongalia Justice Court. Amos ROBERTS summoned to answer the complaint of William LOWRY for trover and conversion, 10 April 1809. LOWRY owned a note for $15 given by Rebecca METHENEY to James G. LAIDLEY who assigned the note to LOWRY. The note came into the hands of ROBERTS who converted it to his own use. No property found by Constable G. B. HOSKINSON.

167 - 1809, Monongalia Justice Court. Charles STUART summoned

to answer the complaint of Elizabeth LIFFLER/SIFFER for non-payment of a debt due by account, 8 December 1809. John and Elizabeth LIFFLER/SIFFER summoned as a witness for the plaintiff. Cristy PIXLER summoned as a witness for the defendant. Judgement for the plaintiff for $20 with costs. The defendant was granted an appeal upon giving William STUART as security.

167 - 1810, Monongalia Justice Court. James SNODGRASS summoned to answer the complaint of James HAYHURST for non-payment of a debt due by account, 26 May 1810. David HAYHURST and William WILLEY summoned as witnesses for the plaintiff. No property found.

167 - 1808, Monongalia Justice Court. Henry FERRELL summoned to answer the complaint of John STEPHENS for non-payment of a debt due by a judgement of 2 pounds and 14 shillings which STEPHENS was awarded against John WEST on 29 November 1806. Execution was put in the hands of FERRELL and he collected the money but failed to pay STEPHENS, 27 February 1808. No property found by Constable Isaac POWELL.

167 - 1808, Monongalia Justice Court. Order to seize the property of Elihu HORTON to sell at public sale to satisfy a a judgement of $4.93 plus costs awarded to William BUCKHANON. Constable John COOPER served an Attachment Warrant on HORTON and HORTON asked to see the warrant and after he had it in his possession he refused to return it to COOPER, 2 June 1808. No property found by Constable Jn. COOPER.

167 - 1808, Monongalia Justice Court. Benjamin CLARK summoned to answer the complaint of William LOWRY for non-payment of a debt due by note, 12 October 1808. No property found by Constable G. B. HOSKINSON.

167 - 1808, Monongalia Justice Court. Simeon ROYCE summoned to answer the complaint of Daniel DAVIDSON for non-payment of a debt due by note, 23 June 1808. No property found by Constable Jno. COOPER.

167 - 1809, Monongalia Justice Court. Arthur WILSON summoned to answer the complaint of William LOWRY and Company for non-payment of a debt due by note, 17 October 1809. No property found by Constable George HITE.

167 - 1808, Monongalia Justice Court. Jonathan CRANE summoned to answer the complaint of John FURMAN, assignee of J. CAMPBELL, for non-payment of a debt due by note, 14 April 1808. No property found by Constable John COOPER.

167 - 1808, Monongalia Justice Court. Jesse PAINE summoned to answer the complaint of Benjamin EVANS for non-payment of

a debt due by note, 23 January 1808. James MAHON and John ALLEN summoned as witnesses for the plaintiff. Thomas FRETWELL summoned as a witness for the defendant. No property found by Constable John COOPER.

167 - 1808, Monongalia Justice Court. William CHIPPS summoned to answer the complaint of John WEST for non-payment of a debt due by account, 15 February 1808. No property found by Constable G. B. HOSKINSON.

167 - 1808, Monongalia Justice Court. Henry H. WILSON summoned to answer the complaint of William LOWRY and Company for non-payment of a debt due by note, 12 October 1808. No property found by Constable G. B. HOSKINSON.

167 - 1808, Monongalia Justice Court. William SANDFORD summoned to answer the complaint of George R. TINGLE for non-payment of a debt due by account, 17 May 1808. No property found by Constable G. B. HOSKINSON.

167 - 1808, Monongalia Justice Court. Benjamin WILSON summoned to answer the complaint of George R. TINGLE for non-payment of a debt due by account, 23 May 1808. No property found by Constable John COOPER.

167 - 1808, Monongalia Justice Court. Arthur WILSON and Hedgeman TRIPLETT summoned to answer the complaint of William REED, assignee of James REED, for non-payment of a debt due by note, 26 March 1808. $6.33 paid, no property found to make the balance, Constable G. B. HOSKINSON.

167 - 1808, Monongalia Justice Court. Joseph REED summoned to answer the complaint of Jno. WAGNER for non-payment of a debt due by account, 12 November 1808. No property found by Constable Jno. COOPER.

167 - 1809, Monongalia Justice Court. R. CLARK summoned to answer the complaint of William LOWRY for non-payment of a debt due by note, 19 January 1809. No property found by Constable G. B. HOSKINSON.

167 - 1808, Monongalia Justice Court. William CHIPPS summoned to answer the complaint of Simion ROYCE for non-payment of a debt due by account, 16 April 1808. Hannah CHIPPS summoned as a witness for the plaintiff. No property found by Constable Daniel COX.

167 - 1809, Monongalia Justice Court. James COLLINS summoned to answer the complaint of James and Thomas WILSON, executors of Andrew _____ for non-payment of a debt due by note, 15 April 1809. No property found by Constable G. B. HOSKINSON.

167 - 1807, Monongalia Justice Court. Order to attach the
property of Robert SHERER at the suit of Robert FERRELL who
was awarded a judgement of $14.61 plus costs on 14 November
1807 which remained unpaid, 26 December 1807. Executed on a
bay mare, blind in the right eye, by Constable John WEST.

167 - 1808, Monongalia Justice Court. Robert THORN summoned
to answer the complaint of Joseph CAMPBELL for non-payment of
a debt due by note, 30 July 1808. No property found by
Constable John COOPER.

167 - 1808, Monongalia Justice Court. William HOLLIFIELD
summoned to answer the complaint of William BILLS for the use
of B. CLARK for non-payment of a debt due by note, 19 July
1808. No property found by Constable John COOPER.

167 - 1807, Monongalia Justice Court. Joseph REED summoned
to answer the complaint of William JARRETT for non-payment of
a debt due by account, 12 November 1807. No property found
by Constable G. B. HOSKINSON.

167 - 1808, Monongalia Justice Court. Arthur WILSON summoned
to answer the complaint of Nicholas MYLAND/TYLAND for non-
payment of a debt due by note, 25 January 1808. No property
found by Constable John COOPER.

167 - 1808, Monongalia Justice Court. Adam SRIVER petitioned
the court for a resurvey of a tract of land where he lived to
rectify the survey courses, 9 August 1808.

167 - 1808, Monongalia Justice Court. Thomas MARTIN summoned
to answer the complaint of John EVANS for non-payment of a
debt due by balance of a clerk's note, 11 August 1808. No
property found by Constable John COOPER.

167 - 1808, Monongalia Justice Court. Thomas MARTIN summoned
to answer the complaint of Enos DAUGHERTY for non-payment of
a debt due by note, 20 August 1808. No property found by
Constable John COOPER.

167 - 1808, Monongalia Justice Court. John WHITE summoned to
answer the complaint of Philip SHEETS for non-payment of a
debt due by account, 6 February 1808. No property found by
Constable John COOPER.

167 - 1808, Monongalia Justice Court. Arthur WILSON summoned
to answer the complaint of Robert BOGGESS for non-payment of
a debt due by note, 11 January 1808. No property found by
Constable James McVICKER.

167 - 1809, Monongalia Justice Court. John TAYLOR summoned
to answer the complaint of William LOWRY for non-payment of a

debt due by note, 9 January 1809. No property found by Constable G. B. HOSKINSON.

167 - 1810, Monongalia Justice Court. Daniel ANDERSON summoned to answer the complaint of William LOWRY and Company for non-payment of a debt due by note, 11 January 1810. No property found by Constable G. B. HOSKINSON.

167 - 1810, Monongalia Justice Court. John WEST summoned to answer the complaint of William TINGLE for non-payment of a debt due by note, 9 March 1810. No property found by Constable Jesse WYATT.

167 - 1810, Monongalia Justice Court. Abner MESSENGER summoned to answer the complaint of R. SCOTT for non-payment of a debt due by account, 4 June 1810. Summons Felix and James SCOTT as witnesses for the plaintiff. No property found by Constable G. HITE.

167 - 1810, Monongalia Justice Court. John SULLIVAN summoned to answer the complaint of William LOWRY and Company for non-payment of a debt due by note, 29 January 1810. $3 paid, no other property found to make the balance, Constable G. B. HOSKINSON.

167 - 1810, Monongalia Justice Court. Robert SCOTT summoned to answer the complaint of Richard PRICE for non-payment of a debt due by note, 2 May 1810. No property found by Constable G. B. HOSKINSON.

167 - 1809, Monongalia Justice Court. William HOLLIFIELD summoned to answer the complaint of Levi MOORE for non-payment of a debt due by account, 24 January 1809. No property found by Constable Daniel COX.

167 - 1807, Monongalia Justice Court. Coverdell COLE summoned to answer the complaint of Jacob MORRIS for non-payment of a debt due by account, 15 September 1807. Appeal granted.

167 - 1810, Monongalia Justice Court. Charles MARTIN summoned to answer the complaint of Farquire McCRAY for non-payment of a debt due by settlement, 18 April 1810. No property found by Constable G. HITE.

167 - 1808, Monongalia Justice Court. Thomas LAIDLEY summoned to answer the complaint of Benjamin SYEARS for non-payment of a debt due by note, 2 February 1808. Note signed by Thomas LAIDLEY to David SEARS dated 2 January 1794 for 5 pounds and 10 shillings worth of plank delivered at the mouth of White Day Creek on or before 1 June 1794 and witnessed by H. DERING Jr. David SAYRS assigned this note to Benjamin SAYRS, no date. Appeal granted upon John SULLIVAN and Thoms EVANS entering as security.

167 - 1809, Monongalia Justice Court. Simeon EVERLY summoned to answer the complaint of Ralph BARKSHIRE for non-payment of a debt due by account, 16 October 1809. No property found by Constable George B. HOSKINSON of the First District.

167 - 1810, Monongalia Justice Court. Darnel/Daniel HARTLEY summoned to answer the complaint of Henry H. WILSON for non-payment of a debt due by account, no date. No property found by Constable G. HITE.

167 - 1809, Monongalia Justice Court. Enos WEST and Simeon EVERLY summoned to answer the complaint of Ralph BARKSHIRE, assignee of Richard HARRISON, for non-payment of a debt due by note, 16 October 1809. No property found in the First District by Constable G. B. HOSKINSON.

167 - 1810, Monongalia Justice Court. John CHIPPS summoned to answer the complaint of Josiah HOSKINSON for non-payment of a debt due by account, 11 April 1810. No property found by Constable G. HITE.

167 - 1810, Monongalia Justice Court. Robert SCOTT summoned to answer the complaint of James SCOTT for the use of William TINGLE for non-payment of a debt due by note, 16 January 1810. No property found by Constable G. HITE.

167 - 1809, Monongalia Justice Court. William GAMBEL summoned to answer the complaint of John COOPER for non-payment of a debt due by note, 30 December 1809. No property found by Constable G. HITE.

167 - 1810, Monongalia Justice Court. Charles MARTIN summoned to answer the complaint of William CHIPPS, assignee of J. CAMMEL, for non-payment of a debt due by due bill, 11 April 1810. No property found by Constable G. HITE.

167 - 1808, Monongalia Justice Court. John DOWNER summoned to answer the complaint of Nimrod EVANS for non-payment of a debt due by note, 5 November 1808. No property found by Constable G. B. HOSKINSON.

167 - 1808, Monongalia Justice Court. John DOWNER summoned to answer the complaint of Zachariah BARKER for non-payment of a debt due by note, 12 April 1808. $2 paid, no property found to make the balance, Constable G. B. HOSKINSON.

167 - 1808, Monongalia Justice Court. John CHIPPS summoned to answer the complaint of Samuel HARMON for non-payment of a debt due by due bill, 3 June 1808. No property found by Constable G. B. HOSKINSON.

167 - 1807, Monongalia Justice Court. James MAHON summoned to answer the complaint of Nicholas MADERA Jr. for non-payment of a debt due by note, 10 December 1807. No property found by Constable John COOPER.

167 - 1807, Monongalia Justice Court. Arthur WILSON summoned to answer the complaint of Abraham and S. WOODROW for non-payment of a debt due by note, 20 December 1807. No property found by Constable John COOPER.

167 - 1808, Monongalia Justice Court. William WALKER summoned to answer the complaint of Enos DAUGHERTY for non-payment of a debt due by account, 3 February 1808. No property found by Constable G. B. HOSKINSON.

167 - 1808, Monongalia Justice Court. Robert HOOD summoned to answer the complaint of P. MARTIN and Robert SCOTT, administrators of J. MARTIN, deceased, for non-payment of a debt due by account, 23 July 1808. Summon Caleb TRIPLET and Scott MARTIN as witnesses for the plaintiff. No property found by Constable Daniel COX.

167 - 1810, Monongalia Justice Court. Larry REX summoned to answer the complaint of William DAVIS for non-payment of a debt due by account, 3 May 1810. No property found by Constable G. HITE.

167 - 1808, Monongalia Justice Court. William HOLLIFIELD summoned to answer the complaint of Nimrod EVANS for non-payment of a debt due by clerk's notes, 26 November 1808. No property found by Constable G. B. HOSKINSON.

167 - 1808, Monongalia Justice Court. Rebecca WILSON, administrator of William WILSON, deceased, summoned to answer the complaint of Christian MADERA for non-payment of a debt due by account, 10 October 1808. No property found by Constable John COOPER.

167 - 1810, Monongalia Justice Court. Thomas LAIDLEY summoned to answer the complaint of Isaac Hite WILLIAMS for non-payment of a debt due by note, 17 March 1810. No property found by Constable G. HITE.

167 - 1808, Monongalia Justice Court. Thomas LAIDLEY summoned to answer the complaint of Paul VIRGUS for non-payment of a debt due by account, 2 February 1808. No property found by Constable G. B. HOSKINSON.

168 - 1800, Monongalia County Court. At March 1798 Court, Overseer of the Poor Calder HAYMOND, by virtue of the Court, was ordered to bind George THOMAS (age seven October 1800)

son of Joseph THOMAS (surviving parent who was out of the county) to be an apprentice (until the age of 21) to Raynear HALL to learn the art of bookkeeping. Indenture dated 6 September 1800 and signed by HAYMOND and HALL and witnessed by Jacob BOLSBY and Jordon HALL.

168 - 1799, Monongalia County Court. At 25 December 1799 Court, Overseer of the Poor Calder HAYMOND, by virtue of a Court Order dated August 1798, bound twins Rachel and Peggy PRAT (age 6 years) to James THOMAS (until the age of 18) to learn the art of spinning and housekeeping. Signed by HAYMOND and James (x) THOMAS and witnessed by Edward HAYMOND and Samuel JONES.

168 - 1801, Monongalia County Court. 19 June 1801, Overseer of the Poor Henry DERING, by virtue of a Court Order dated __ June 1801, bound Thomas McCOY, an orphan boy of the age of 16, to be an apprentice with Peter MESMORE (until age 21) to learn the art of a blacksmith. Signed by DERING and MESMORE in the presence of Alexander HAWTHORN.

168 - 1801, Monongalia County Court. 20 November 1801, by virtue of a Court Order, Overseer of the Poor Calder HAYMOND bound Solomon SNODGRASS (six years old) to James COLLINS (until age 21) to learn the art of a cooper. Signed by HAYMOND and COLLINS in the presence of John and Elisha HOULT.

168 - 1800, Monongalia County Court. 23 June 1800, by virtue of a Court Order, Overseer of the Poor William HAMILTON bound James DENSON/DAWSON, a poor boy of the age of 10 years, to James LEGGET (until age 21) to learn the art of farming. Signed by LEGGITT and HAMILTON.

168 - 1801, Monongalia County Court. 25 November 1801, by virtue of a Court Order, Overseer of the Poor Calder HAYMOND bound Sarah McCALLISTER, a poor orphan girl whose parents are not able to maintain of the age of 8 years, to James FLEMING (until age 18) to learn the art of spinning and housekeeping. Signed by HAYMOND and FLEMING in the presence of James MORGAN and Thomas PRICKETT.

168 - 1801, Monongalia County Court. 2 July 1801, by virtue of a Court Order, Overseer of the Poor William HAMILTON bound Mary DAWSON, a poor girl of the age of ___ to James ROBINSON (until age 18) to learn the art of spinning and sewing. Signed by HAMILTON and ROBINSON.

168 - 1807, Monongalia County Court. 9 June 1807, by virtue of a Court Order, Overseer of the Poor William McCLEERY bound Samuel GRUBB, son of George GRUBB age 9 years, to John WAGNER (until age 21) to learn the art of stocking weaving. Signed by McCLEERY and WAGNER in the presence of Henry DERING.

168 - 1800, Monongalia County Court. 29 October 1800, by virtue of a Court Order dated September 1800, Joseph SNODGRASS, (age 16 on 17 February 1800), was bound to Caleb TANSEY (until age 21) to learn the art of a house carpenter and joiner. Signed by Joseph SNODGRASS; John DENT, guardian; and Caleb TANSEY.

168 - 1803, Monongalia County Court. 1 August 1803, by virtue of a Court Order, John RHOADS (age 17 on 15 September 1803) was bound to Samuel HARMAN to learn the art of candlestick molding. Signed by Overseer of the Poor Nicholas VANDERVORT and HARMAN. Witnesses: Robert ABERCRUMBY and Zack PIERPOINT.

168 - 1800, Monongalia County Court. 5 June 1800, by virtue of a Court Order dated 13 January 1800, Ralph SMITH, "a poor boy whose mother Hannah SMITH is not able to maintain of the age of 6 years last January," bound to David FARQUER (until age 21) to learn the art of a Windsor Chair and spinning wheel maker. Signed by Overseer of the Poor William HAMILTON and David FARQUER in the presence of Wm. TINGLE.

168 - 1809, Monongalia County Court. 1 May 1809, by virtue of a Court Order dated 14 March 1808, Elizabeth JONES (born 19 July 1804) was bound to Patrick McGREW (until age 18) to learn the art of spinning, knitting and sewing. Signed by Overseer of the Poor John WILLITTS and Patrick McGREW in the presence of Robert McGREW and Jane McGREW.

168 - 1804, Monongalia County Court. 22 December 1804, by virtue of a Court Order, Jesse PRIDE (a poor boy of 6 years and 5 months) was bound to Caleb HURLEY (until age 21) to learn the art of farming. Signed by Overseer of the Poor Boaz BURROWS and Caleb HURLEY.

168 - 1805, Monongalia County Court. 10 October 1805, by virtue of a Court Order, Thomas DAWSON, a poor boy of the age of 15 years and 5 months, was bound to Boaz BURROWS (until age 21) to learn the art of farming. Signed by Overseer of the Poor Richard HARRISON and Boaz BURROWS.

168 - 1803, Monongalia County Court. 12 December 1803, by virtue of a Court Order dated November 1803, Nancy RYON (an orphan girl age 12 years) was bound to John SISLER (until age 18) to learn the art of housewifery. Signed by Overseer of the Poor William McCLEERY and John SISLER and Mathew GAY.

168 - 1809, Monongalia County Court. 1 April 1809, by virtue of a Court Order dated January 1807, Mary GREATHOUSE (6 years old on 1 June 1809) was bound to Neal DUGLASS (until age 18) to learn the art of spinning, netting and sewing. Signed by Overseer of the Poor John WILLITS and Neill DOUGLASS in the presence of Rachel FORMAN and Mary FORMAN.

168 - 1810, Monongalia County Court. 11 April 1810, by virtue of a Court Order dated January 1810, Sarah McCALLISTER, age 14, was bound to John WELLS (until age 18) to learn the art of spinning and housewifery. Signed by Overseer of the Poor in the Middle District William McCLEERY and John WELLS.

168 - 1810, Monongalia County Court. __ January 1810, John MADERA (15 years old on 7 November 1807) placed with Zackquill MORGAN, by his father Christian MADERA, to learn the art of a coppersmith. Signed by MADERA and MORGAN in the presence of French S. GREY.

168 - 1810, Monongalia County Court. 11 April 1810, by virtue of a Court Order, Catherine BOGARD (age 12 or 13) bound to William NORRIS (until age 18) to learn the art of reading and weighing in a "cholastick" manner. Signed by Overseer of the Poor Nicholas VANDERVORT and William NORRIS.

168 - 1810, Monongalia County Court. 9 April 1810, by virtue of a Court Order dated 14 August 1809, Mary FOSTER (age 4 years and 2 months on 14 April instant) bound to Thomas McGEE (until age 18) to learn the art of good housewifery. Signed by Overseer of the Poor in the Middle District William McCLEERY and Thomas McGEE.

168 - 1810, Monongalia County Court. 9 April 1810, by virtue of a Court Order dated 14 August 1809, Ephraim FOSTER (age 2 years on 31 March 1810) bound to Thomas McGEE (until age 21) to learn the art of farming. Signed by Overseer of the Poor William McCLEERY and Thomas McGEE.

168 - 1807, Monongalia County Court. 1 January 1807, by virtue of a Court Order dated 8 September 1806, Samuel LYN (age 2 years and 4 months) was bound to Peter OSBORN (until age 21) to learn the art of farming. Signed by Overseer of the Poor of the district east of Laurel Hill William TANNEHILL and Peter OSBORN in the presence of James CLARK and Joseph FICKLE.

168 - 1810, Monongalia County Court. 6 June 1810, by virtue of a Court Order, Catharine CORRELL (age 9 on 10 May 1810) was bound to William JOHN (until age 18) to learn the art of reading and weighing in a "cholestick" manner. Signed by Overseer of the Poor Nicholas VANDERVORT and Wm. JOHN.

168 - 1808, Monongalia County Court. 7 March 1808, by virtue of a Court Order, Lettie BLACK (age 11 on 12 March _____) was bound to Ezekiel McFARLAND (until age 18) to learn the art of reading and weighing in a "cholestick" manner. Signed by Overseer of the Poor N. VANDERVORT and E. McFARLAND.

168 - 1809, Monongalia County Court. 1 May 1809, by virtue of a Court Order dated 14 March 1808, John JONES (age 7 on 8 April 1809) was bound to Robert FORMAN (until age 21) to learn the art of farming. Signed by Overseer of the Poor John WILLITS and Robert FORMAN in the presence of Rachel FORMAN and Jane FORMAN.

168 - 1809, Monongalia County Court. 16 November 1809, by virtue of a Court Order dated November 1809, Buckner S. BARNS (age 2 years on 19 October last) was bound to George D. BARNS to learn the art of a spinning wheel maker. Signed by Overseer of the Poor George SMITH and George D/S BARNS in the presence Thomas SMYTH.

168 - 1806, Monongalia County Court. 15 February 1806, by virtue of a Court Order dated October 1804, Harman WATT by Joseph JENKINS, his guardian, was bound to Benjamin HELLEN (until age 21) to learn the art of a hatter. Signed by Joseph JENKINS and Benj'm. HELLEN.

168 - 1808, Monongalia County Court. 1 January 1808, by virtue of a Court Order, Joseph HEAGER (age 16 next month) was bound to Eli MOORE (until age 21) to learn the art of a blacksmith. Signed by Overseer of the Poor Nicholas VANDERVORT and Eli MOORE.

168 - 1810, Monongalia County Court. 12 February 1810, by virtue of a Court Order dated this day, Samuel CARROL (age 12) was bound to Nehemiah POWER (until age 21) to learn the art of farming. Signed by Overseer of the Poor of the Middle District William McCLEERY and Nehemiah POWER in the presence of Wm. JOHN and Jacob (x) HOLLAND.

168 - 1810, Monongalia County Court. 18 August 1810, by virtue of a Court Order dated August 1810, Joseph WEBSTER (age 7 on 18 of May last) bound to Benjamin SHAW (until age 21) to learn the art of farming. Signed by Overseer of the Poor William CONNER and Benjamin SHAW in the presence of Elizabeth CONNER and Robert CONNER.

168 - 1805, Monongalia County Court. 1 July 1805, by virtue of a Court Order dated May 1805, William SCOTT (an orphan boy age 15 years and 7 months) was bound to George GOLD (until age 21) to learn the art of a cord winder. Signed by Overseer of the Poor William McCLEERY and George GOLD.

168 - 1808, Monongalia County Court. 1 June 1808, by virtue of a Court Order, William FLOWERS (4 years old) was bound to James ROBISON (until age 21) to learn the art of reed making. Signed by Overseer of the Poor Boaz BURROWS and James ROBISON.

END OF MICROFILM #43

Witnesseth ... Witnesseth ... made this first day of January in
the year of our Lord one thousand eight hundred and seven
and in the 31 year of the Independence of the United States
of America between W.m Tonnehill Overseer of the poor
of the District East of the Laurel hill in the County of
Unmogahela of the one part and Betsey Osbourn, said
County of the other part, Witnesseth, that the said William
Tonnehill Overseer of the poor as aforesaid, by virtue of an
order of the Court of the s.d County bearing date the 8.th day
September in the year 1806 hath put, placed and bound, and
by these presents do put, place and bind Samuel Lyn a
poor boy of the age of Two —— years — to be an apprentice
with him the said Betsey Osbourn to dwell from the date of the
presents, until the s.d Samuel Lyn shall arrive to the
age of 21 years, according to the act of the general
Assembly in that case made and provided. By and during
which term term, the s.d Samuel Lyn shall the said

the term aforesaid. and the said further Oldham shaw
teach or cause to be taught to the s'd Samuel [by] reading
writing and common arithmetic ————

And will make over pay unto the s'd [...]
Syn the sum of twelve dollars at [...]
of his afforesaid time. In witness [...]
[...] parties to these presents have set th[eir]
and Seale the day and year first [...]

test

James Clark

Joseph Tuttle.   William [...]

Peter Oldham

Overseers of the
poor

246

169 - 1800, Monongalia County Court. Delinquents in Joseph TRICKET's list for 1800. Acres listed after name.

Joseph ARCHER 364
William ANDERSON 1000
Amos ASHCRAFT 100
James BULLAND 3635
Benjamin BROOK 83
Henry BANKS 4000
Daniel BARTON 311
Jacob BLACKWELL 200
Morris BROWN 34
Jacob BALTZER 200
Susannah BEALL 100
Christian RIDENHOUR 100
Thomas CLAIR 375
Margaret CUNNINGHAM 1275
Henry CROLL 200
Archer CLUTTERFIELD 396
Robert CROW 1129
John CLARK 182
Thomas CHINETH Jr. 400
Samuel CLAIN 500
Henry CORE 50
Edward DAWSON 97
John DAWSON 225
James DENNY 400
Thomas DAVISON 162
David DAVIS 2000
John DOWNER 976
William DAVISON 100
Septimeous CIDWALEDER 160
Lambert FLOWERS 337
Ezekeil FRAZEE 441
Fidelious FOSTER 95
Evan GUINIA 1000
John GARGUS 250
Charles GALLEHER 1750
Frederick WALDEON 404
William WORTH 1000
John WILSON 732
Lidia WADSON 2000
Benjamin WHITSON 125
Christopher WIREMAN 12480
James HENDERSON 500
Jacob HARROW 123

John HEAD 400
John HUNSEEKER 400
Peter HUNT 7 1/2
Samuel HUNT 139
James HOWEL 91 1/2
Thomas JOHNSTON 200
John ICE 400
Christopher YOST 150
Abraham ICE 167
Joseph JENKINS heirs 248
Theophilas PHILIPS 800
Jonathan REECE 400
Lewis RODGERS 240
Joseph RODES 204
Asher ROBBINS 8000
Joshua ROBISON 400
Aaron RICE 232
Robert RETHERFORD 360
William ROACH? 100
George SPARKS 113
Ludowick SWISHER 250
Alexander SMITH 400
Robert & John SMITH 202
George STRADLER 285
John SHIVELY 302
Alexander STERLING 300
Michael SMITH 193
Thomas SEYRS 84
John SPENCER 2731 1/2
James TERNEY 118
Elisha TRIMBLE 100
Bartholomew TARISON 28100
Jacob VANDEGRIFT 564
John VANMETER 600
John & Lemuel PETTIT 437
Barbara GILPIE 255
David GRAY 380
Philip GORDIN 130
John HARROW 172
Justice HARDEN 448
Martin HARDEN 341
William HANNAH 400
George HILY 339

189 - 1800, Monongalia County Court. Alexander BRANDON's return, 1800. Acres listed after name.

William ASHBY 1000
Edward ASKINS 391
George ASHBY 50
Jesse ASHBY 200
Thomas BUTLER Jr. 200
Jarvey BURMINGHAM 400
John BACORN 500
John BARNSTEAD 1250
Ruth BEAL 200
John BARTLETT 205 1/2
John BELL 500
Thomas BAKER 425
Henry BANKS 1000
Daniel, Mary & James BOYLE 300
Samuel CANBY 362
A. CLARKE 782
Peter CLUTTER 277
Hezekiah DAVISON 400
Henry DICE 652
William & Francis DEAKINS 38714
Jacob DUCKMAN 130
Michael EVERHART 100
John DOWNER & JONES 425
William DAUGHERTY 500
Rowland ELICE 148
James EVERINGHAM 100
Samuel FRAZER 400
Abraham FAW 140
Andrew FRIEND 210
Joseph FOX 97
Elijah GRIFFITH 122
David GALWAY 285
Jonas HOGMIRE 165
Enoch HAND 125
Philip HOSE 100
Conrad HOGMIRE 224
Christian HOFFEL &
   Joseph DERICK 378
William HILTON &
   John ORRS 3287
Christopher HAYS 354
John HORSE 628
John HAVENER 400
John HOOKER 2777
Philip JENKINS 400
Benjamin JENKINS 2310
Ezekeil JONES 400
Ezekiel JACOBS 300
Benjamin JININGS 250

Wallace JOHNSTON &
   MORE 12328
John KEELER 200
Mary KERR/KERN 50
Andrew KIRKPATRICK 250
Elias LEATON 137
Bartholomew LONDON 600
Andrew McKEAN 174
Richard MORRIS 447
Joseph MYERS 600
David MORGAN 500
Daniel McCLAIN 250
Henry & James MILLAR 200
George McDONALD 185
Nicholas MUSTILLER 152
Benjamin MUSTILLAR 152
John MAINS 350
Philip MORE 150
John Thompson MASON 1000
Leonard M. DEAKINS 200
Henry NEVEL 200
James PHILIPS 290
Lewis RODGERS 240
Henry RUMBLE 150
Jacob REDEER 537
John SHAY 100
Richard STEPHENS 200
Ludwick SHELL 150
Charles SCOTT 200
James SMITH 157
George STOUT 120
John STOUT 54
William SQUIRES 650
Christian SHAVER 186 1/2
Abraham SEVERNS 650
Andrew STERLING 329
Alexander SCOTT 450
Joseph SWERINGER 400
Peter TROXEL 160
Thomas TALBOT 1 lot
Henry TETRICK 500
Joseph VANMETER 1400
Isaac VANMETER 556
Maran J. WAGONER 30
George WILES 347
William Davis ALEXANDER
   or Davis Alexander
   WILLIAM 7000
Daniel WINDER 222

Abraham WOLINGER 269
William WILES 162
Thomas WOODS 500
Charles Joshua WALLACE &
   John & John MYERS 12328

Jacob WAGGONER 100
Rapheal WALTHEM 150
William WORTH 2000
Amos WORKMAN 100
Ezekiel WORLEY 400

"Virginia, at a Court held for the County of Monongalia 14 September 1801, the within list of delinquents for the year 1800 was returned by W. DEAN and Elihu HORTON, Deputy Sheriff for John T. GOFF, Sheriff, and made oath according to law which is ordered to be certified to the Auditor of Public Accounts. (Signed) John EVANS, Clerk. This and the nine preceding pages copied from return filed in this office. (Signed) Sam'l SHEPARD, Auditor's Office, 15 April 1812."

169 - 1800, Monongalia County Court. Monongalia County Insolvent Lands for 1800. Acres listed after names.

Jacob LUSTY 3400
Philip LEWIS 207
Richard LANGFORD 100
Charles LOSH 400
Abraham LOW 300
John LANCE 43
Cornelius LINCH 3000
Abraham LITTLE 400
David MOORE 100
John NEAL 400
John MITCHEL 1000
Thomas MOORE 2150
William McCLURE 65
James MORRIS 213
John McCLELAND 384
Spencer MARTIN 400
William McDONOLD 100
Samuel MERIFIELD 182
Robert MAXWELL 66 3/4
Benjamin POWELL 150
Daniel MARTIN 272
John PIERPOINT 700
James PATTON 400

Thomas PATTERSON 400
Theophi's PHILIPS 7875
Jonathan REESE 400
Lewis RODGERS 240
Joseph RODES 204
Asher ROBBINS 8000
Joshua ROBISON 400
Aaron RICE 232
Robert RETHERFORD 360
William ROACH 100
George SPARKS
Ludwick SWISHER 250
Alexander SMITH 400
Robert & John SMITH 202
George STRADLER 285
John SHIVELY 302
Alexander STERLING 300
Michael SMITH 193
Thomas SEYRS 84
John SPENCER 2731 1/2
James TERNEY 118
Elisha TRIMBLE 100
Bartholomew TARISON 7875

169 - 1810, Monongalia County Court. "A list of Delinquents for the Revenue of 1810 for Monongalia County." Acres listed after names.

James ARCHER 364
Thomas ARNETT 3400
William ANDERSON 1000
Thomas ANDERSON 200
Benjamin ALTON 350
James BURCHINAL 280

Benjamin BROOKE 83
Elijah BURROWS 400
James BRITTON 19
Henry BANKS 4000
Morris BROWN 34
Sarah BOYLES 215

Jacob BARGDALE 500
John BRYAN 120
Charles BOYLES 313 1/2
Alexander BARE 73
Thomas BROWN/BRAWN 510
James BOOTH 189
Eleanor BATTON 95
John BERDINE 39
Coleby CHEW 214
Jesse CHANEY 200
John CALFLESH 89
John CLARK 92
Thomas R. CHIPPS 176
John DOWNARD 276
James DAVIS 626
David DAVIS 2000
William DAWSON 100
Henry DARROW 465
Benjamin DOOLITTLE 150
Sarah DUHL 100
Jasper EVERLY 800
John ENGLAND 88
Benjamin ESTLE 250
James EDGEL 100
Robert EAST 200
Ledawick ESMINGER 100
George FOULK 496
Tidelus FORISTER 95
John FULLIS 800
Andrew FLEMING 100
Elizabeth FREELAND 110
Standish FORD 1000
Bernard GILISPY 250
Ashbel GUSTICE 92
Evan GWYN 500
Stephen GAPPEN 438
John GOODWIN 100
Charles GALLIGHER 2900
Peter GARDNER 56
James HENDERSON 500
Nelson HARDEN 400
William HANNAH 400
George HIGHLY 339
Allen HULL 208
John HEAD 400
Michael HILDERBRAND 382
James HARTLEY 100
John HOPKINS, etal 52000
James HOWEL 91
Benjamin HENDFORD 450
Jesse HUNT 1000
Barney HANS 86

Martin HESER 100
Lewis HERNS Jr. 50
Charles LASH 400
Abraham LAW 300
Cornelius LYNCH 400
Absalom LITTLE, etal 400
Bartholomew LOTT 71
Joshua LEWMAN 150
Jacob LAVENGOOD 78
Jacob LAROME 400
John LIGHT 204
Joseph MYRES 50
Robert MINNIS 1757
George MAY 90
Richard MERIFIELD 1265
George MOREDOCK 2000
John MITCHELL 1000
Carnaby MARTIN 103
Thomas MALE 2150
William McCLURE 63
Jacob MYRES 120
Daniel MARTIN 272
Robert MAXWELL 66 1/2
Charles McMEEKIN 250
Alexander McGEE 50
William MYERS 600
Jacob MILLER 480
Sampson MATTHEWS 254
Henry MILLER 350
Edward MERCER, etal 200
Charles MORGAN 400
Daniel MORGAN 300
Joseph NEAL 400
William NEWLON 100
Jacob NOOSE 17
William PETTYJOHN 211
James POLLOCK 400
Henry PRATT 322
Elizabeth PRINGLE 2000
Theophilus PHILIPS 3175
Thomas PINDLE 1961
Robert PATTON 772
Elias PEARCE 400
Henry PRUIANCE 383
Francis PATTON 317
Thomas PATTERSON 400
Widow PETTYJOHN 780
Lary PURVIANCE 270
Levi PINDLE 150
James PARKER 400
John W. PATTERSON 185
Jacob PECK 150

John PHILIPS 1000
John QUANDROL 1000
Jonathan ROICE 400
Asher ROBIUS 8100
Joshua ROBISON 400
Thomas REEDER 1968
Jacob RIVER 250
Thomas RUSSELL 50
Simon REEDER 29
David SCOTT 48
Robert SCOTT 545
James SNODGRASS 1 lot & 100
Edward SWISHER 250
Robert SMITH, etal 202
George STOKER 285
William SMILY 1000
John STANLY 118
Timothy SMITH 259
Michael STATLER Jr. 200
David SAYRE 82
John STAG 137
George SPARKS 113
Michael SMITH 203
Thomas SMITH 84
John SPENCER 3262
Joseph SOMMERVILLE 392
Nancy SCOTT 545
Jesse SNIDER 230
John STERN 150
George SHARR 218
William R. SMITH 100
George SWANK 200
Conrod SHAEFFER 802
William SEAMAN, etal 200

Alexander SUTHERLAND 130
James SWANN 7485
John STEWART, etal 202
Nehemiah SQUIRES 100
Rudolph SADLER 72
John SAMPLE 145
Hedgeman TRIPLETT 50
John TAYLOR 25
Jonathan THOMPSON 2000
Israel THOMPSON 48
Elisha TRIMBLE 100
Bartholomew TARRISON 29000
Jacob TUCKING 500
James TIDBALL 1000
Aaron TAYLOR, etal 512
Caleb TARLETON 200
Joseph THOMPSON 477
Jacob VANDAGRIFF 564
Elisha WADE 232
John F. WALDEN 404
William WORTH 1000
Christian WIREMAN 12975
Francis WOLF 318
Brice WORLY 75
Joseph WISBY 90
Lydia WATSON 1200
James WELCH 1000
Nicholas WOODS 410
John WILLY 50
Abraham WISECUP 50
Mary & E. WILLY 141
John WIANS 100
Stephen WEST heirs 2700
Christopher YOST 100

"At a court held for Monongalia County, October term 1810,
George S. DERING, Deputy Sheriff for Lemuel JOHN Sheriff of
this County, produced in Court the within list of delinquents
which was examined and sworn to by the said George S. DERING
and is ordered to be certified." Signed by N. EVANS, CMC.

169 - 1810, Monongalia County Court. Delinquents in BRANDON's
District. Acres listed after name.

William ASHBERY 1233
Edward ASKIN 396
Elizabeth ARNOLD 1/4 of 228
Martha ASBY 1/4 of 228
William AUSTIN 1800
Thomas BAKER 150
Gervies BURNINGHAM 214
John BACKHORN 500

John BURKET 205
Henry BANKS 9500
Ruth BILL 200
Adam BROWN 400
Daniel, Mary &
  James BAILS 300
Elizabeth BEAL 117
William BIGGS 144

John BIGGS, etal 195
William BUCKHANNON 396 3/4
Solomon BURSON 83
Noah BEATTY 276
Abraham BAKER 583
Barton BEEN 339
James BOOTH 6
George BLACKSTONE (0)
Peter BLACK 233
Philip BOYERS 81
Peter BAKER 164 1/4
James BRYON 105
Samuel CANBREY 362
Ann CLARKE 617
Thomas CHIPPS heirs 488
Samuel CLARK 100
Isaac CUSHMAN 410
Moses CURRY Jr. 335
John CHESSLEY 353
Margaret CUNNINGHAM 500
Widow CUNNINGHAM 200
Thomas CLEGG, etal 200
Rebecca CHILDS 1/4 of 228
Amos CHIPPS (0)
Enoch COLVERT &
  Samuel JACKSON 760
Andrew CAMPBELL 120
William CUNNINGHAM &
  William ARMSTRONG 100
Samuel DEADUFF 250
John DIRELING 222
Jacob DOUGHMAN 130
Henry DYER 652
John DOWNER 319
F. & Wm. DEAKINS 18154
William DARLING 160
James DUNWOODY 586
Samuel DARWESS 100
William DAUGHERTY 500
James DEWEESS 160
Lester DICKSON 1000
Peter DRAGOO 128
Jonathan DAVIS 157
Michael EVERHART 100
Rolling ELES 148
David ESTON 600
James EVERINGHAM 50
William EVERLY 100
Benjamin ESTEL 340
Jacob E. HOLT 150
Robert FERRELL 826
Samuel FRASEE 400

Abraham FAW 140
John FIRSEE 131
John FORSYTH 131
Andrew FREND 210
Henry FLOYD 75
William FERGUSON 400
Abraham FULTON 500
Walter FITZGERALD 3000
John FELTAND 240
Jaine FRY 9
Standish FORD 100
Neal GILISPY 100
John GILSPY 622
James GILSPY 392
Ludo GOFF 471
Thomas GETTING 100
Timothy GUARD 400
George G. GOFF 108
John GALLAWAY 500
William HILL 36 1/2
Benjamin HARTLY 89 1/2
Henry HARDESTY 4
James HARTLY 100
William HILTON 700
Conrod HOGMIRE 254
Justice HEX 346
Christian HOFFEE, etal 378
John HORSE 318
Levi HOPKINS 67
James HUGGINS 100
John HAN 200
John HOY 7618
Hazel HUNTS heirs or
  Hunts HAZEL heirs 1 lot
Jacob HAMPTON 110
David HANWAY 200
Joseph HARTLY 324
John HEDLEY 10
James HITE 200
Rodger HUNT
John HADGNER 300
Thomas HEBIN 600
Christopher HAYS 354
Joseph HUSTON 150
Joseph HILL 33 3/4
James HAMILTON 50
Christian HARDING 115
Francis HOFMASTER 150
Charles HOVEROCK 160 1/2
Philip JINKINS 400
Ezekiel JACOBS 300
William JOHNSTON 578

Benjamin JENKINS 4294
Ezekiel JONES & Jno DOWNER 600
Robert JONES 160
Thomas JOHNSTON 5478
John G. JACKSON 400
John JENNEY 1067
John KELLER 200
Mary KINKAID 303
Mary HARR 50
Jacob HUNE 1325
John KALOHN 141
James KNOTS 366
Henry & Jacob KIDDY 100
George KIDDY 160 1/2
Jacob LAWRY 100
Thomas LAIDLEY 7369
Thomas LAIDLEY & Jno HAY 300
James LAWARY 100
Archer LEWIS 200
Thomas LESLY 500
Alexander F. LANHAM 26 1/2
Thomas MARTIN 400
Jacob MINTON 485
Kathan MATHENEY 35
John MORRIS 500
Joseph MOYERS 200
Henry & James MILLER 200
George MAY 1156
John MEANS 350
Thomas S. MASON 1000
Edward McGUIRE 1200
David MOORE heirs 292
Robert MINNIS 653
John MINTHORN 177
Henry MARTIN & John HOY 5000
Samuel MARTIN 400
John MILLER 200
Adam MELCHER 16
David MOORE 100
Philip MOORE 100
Justine MABERRY 100
Christian MILLER 200
John McEVERS 312
John MOORE, Jr. 45
Adam MEANERE 100
John MATHENY 75
Samuel MEREDITH 76
Jacob MACKNER 150
David MINNING 12
Michael, Jacob & Henry
  NICHOLAS 300
George OFFIT 150

John OCLEY 171
James PARKER 400
Thomas PINDALL 300
Ann POSTLE 1/4 of 228
James PHILIPS 290
Hail PECK 600
Jesse PAYNE 1650
Sarah PLUM 200
Joseph PRYOR 750
David PLUNKET &
  David SEWART 500
John PETERS 500
William ROYCE 91
David RITNOUR 1 lot
John RAMSEY, etal 273
Henry RUMBLE 350
John RAVENSCRAFT 118
Thomas RINEHART 608
Jacob RICHARD 573
John RUNNER 50
Simmion RIGGS 100
John ROBERTS 2 lots
John RICHERTY 100
William RUSSELL 56
Thomas RUSSELL 50
Thomas RUCHEL 200
Richard SEVERNS 200
Ludwick STULL 150
Charles SCOTT 200
James SMITH 76 1/2
John STILES 100
Richard STILES 100
George STOUT 126
John STOUT 54
Nicholas SPARY 200
Joseph SWEARINGER 400
A. William SMITH 400
S. William SMITH 2000
Christian SHAVER 186 1/2
John SWAN 3400 (paid)
John SHAY 100
Absolem SEVERNS 600
Christian SHROYER 104
Samuel SNOWDEN 947
Frederick & Abraham
  STEER 204
David STEWART 1015
Henry SPRINKLE 200
William STIGER 76
John SHAVER 200
John SHELL 78
John SAYRE 810

Frederick SPARR Jr. 300	Thomas WOOD 500
Meshack SEXTON 1000	Ezekiel WORLEY 200
Benjamin STODDARD 3600	John WILLIAMS 100
William SMITH 200	John WOODRING 94
Ebenzer STULL 181	Adam WILSON 1 lot
John STARK 305	Jacob WAGGONER 100
Isaac SADDLER 350	Ruplet WALTHAM 150
Jacob SMITH, etal 174	Samuel WILLIAM 187
David SAYRE Sr. 300	Noah WILLIAM 1000
John SAYRE 100	Amos WORKMAN 100
William THOMAS 2000	Levy WALLS 100
Peter TRAXEL 164	Jeremiah WILSON 111 1/2
Hedgeman TRIPLETT 400	Ann WATSON 83
Wildy TAYLOR 190	James WATSON Jr. 384
Zahariah TOLER 200	William WOODS 200
James TATE 514	John WICKWIRE 379
James THOMPSON 90	Benjamin WALKER 71764
David THOMAS 100	William WILLIS 238
John THOMAS 130	Jacob & Frederick
John TRECHELD 2900	WAVELY 100
John TAYLOR 120	Robert WILSON 100
Joseph VANMETER 1400	Josiah WOOD 284
Abraham VANMETER 556	Samuel WARD & Elizabeth
Joseph VANMETER 600	FRIEND 138
Davy Alexander WILLIAM 7000	Andrew WAIGHT 150
Charles WALLIS & John MURE 15483	Valentine WISEMORE &
Abraham WALINGA 269	Elizabeth YOUNG 108

"At a Court held for Monongalia County October 1810 term, Mathew GAY, Deputy Sheriff for Lemuel JOHN, Sheriff of this County, produced in Court the within list of delinquents contained in two sheets and a half which was examined and sworn to by the said Mathew GAY and is ordered to be certified," (signed by) N. EVANS, CMC). "The foregoing eighteen pages is a complete list of all lands and lots returned to this office for non-payment of taxes in the County of Monongalia for the year 1810 and on which the taxes now remain unpaid," (signed) Sam'l SHEPARD, Auditor's Office, 15 September 1812.

169 - 1801, Monongalia County Court. "A list of delinquents returned by John W. DEAN and Elihu HORTON, DS for John T. GOFF, Sheriff for the year 1801 Monongalia County."

Joseph ARCHER 364	Margaret CUNNINGHAM 800
William ANDERSON 1000	Marle CUNNINGHAM 475
James BUTLAND 3635	Henry CROLL 200
Henry BANKS 4000	Thomas CLARE 375
Morris BROWN 34	Arch'b CLUTTERFIELD 396
Charles BRIDINHART 100	Robert CROW 1123
Jonathan BRYAN 120	Henry CON 50
William BIGGS 49	James CARTEY 261

John DOWNER 878
Thomas DAVISSON 162
David DAVIS 2000
William DAVISSON 100
John ENGLAND 15
Robert FERRELL 1530
David FANCHER 300
James FRAZIER 35 1/2
Ezekiel FRAZIER 441
Fidelus FOSTER 95
John FOLLIS 800
Evan GUINEA 1000
Charles GALLAGER 1437
John GURGUS 250
David GRAY 380
Philip GORDON 130
Jonathan GANDY 100
Bernard GILPY 255
Robert GRAHAM 100
Samuel HUNT 7 1/2
John HARROW 172
James HOWEL 91 1/4
Jesse HUNT 1000
Martin HURDIN 341
James HENDERSON 500
William HANNAH 400
Jacob HARROW 123
John HAMILTON 188
John HEAD 400
John HUNSUCKER 400
John JOHNSTON 100
Thomas JOHNSTON 200
John ICE 400
Daniel JOHNSTON 44 1/4
Abraham ICE 187
Jacob LUSTY 3400
Philip LEWIS 207
Charles LASH 400
Abraham LOWE 300
Lucy LANHAM 100
Cornelius LINCH 2600
Abraham LITTLE, etal 400
Richard MERRIFIELD 1265
John MITCHEL 1000
Charity MARTIN 183
Thomas MOLE 350
Thomas MOLE 350
William McCLURE 65
John McCLELLAND 384
Jacob MYRES 120
Daniel MARTIN 272
Robert MAXWELL 68 1/4

Alexander McINTER 370
John NEEL 400
David NORRIS 200
Aaron POWEL 1387
John PHILIPS 200
John PIERPOINT 1100
James POLLOCK 400
Benjamin POWELL 150
James PATTON 400
Thomas PATTESON 400
Sarah PROVINCE 270
Philip ROBERTS 300
Joseph RODES 204
Asher ROBINS 8000
Joshua ROBISON 400
Samuel RUBLE 75
William ROAK 100
Jeremiah SIMPSON 400
Ludwick SWISHER 250
Robert & John SMITH 202
George STATLER 285
John SHIVELEY 302
Joseph SOUTHWORTH 120
Henry STEPHENS 68
Alexander STERLING 300
George SHARKS 113
Michael SMITH 203
John SPENCER 2731 1/2
Phebea SCOTT 400
Nacy SCOTT 545
Elisha TRIMBLE 100
Jacob TUSING 500
Bartholomew TARRISON 4000
Jacob VANDEGRIFT 564
John VANMETER 600
Jacob VANMETER 200
Christopher WIREMAN 13778
John WEBB 400
Frances WOLF 300
Evan WADKINS 300
Brice WORLEY 75
John & Frederick WALDEN
  404
William WORTH 1000
William WORTH (over &
  east of Cheat) 1000
John WADE 52
John WILSON 732
Thomas C. WADE 282
James WALKER 365
Christopher YOST 110

"From Alexander BRANDON's return for year 1801, delinquents continued."

	Example of Amount of tax
William ASHBY 1000	$.82
Edward ASKINS 391	.31
George ASHBEY 50	.06
Jesse ASHBEY 200	.16
Jervis BUORNINGHAM 400	.32
Job BECKHORN 200	.17
John BECKHORN 500	.40
Ruth BEAL 200	.16
John BURKIT 205 1/2	.17
John BELL 500	.60
Henry BANKS 1000	.77
Daniel, Mary & James BAYLES 300	.48
Elijah BEAL 177	.28
Samuel CANLY 362	.28
Samuel CLARKE of James 200	.17
Henry CRISS 185	.25
Ann CLARKE 782	.24
Peter CLUTTER 277	.35
John DARLING 222	.16 1/2
Henry DIRE 652	.50
Francis & William DEACONS 52821	25.12
Francis & William DEACONS 49 lots	1.09
Jacob DUCHMAN 130	.10
John DOWNER, etal 650	.52
William DOUGHERTY 500	.60
Susanah DONALDSON 160	.25
Michael EVERHART 100	.08
Rowland ELLICE 148	.18
John EVANS 100	.16
James EVERINGHAM 100	.08
Henry FLOYD 100	.12
Samuel FRAZER 400	.48
Abraham FAW 140	.11
John FORSHEE 131	.16
Andrew FRIEND 131	.25
Joseph FOX 97	.09
David GALLOWAY 185	.31
Albert GALLATIN 172	.14
Neal GILLISPIE 100	.12
Gabriel GREATHOUSE 400	.64
Henry HARDESTY 98	.15 1/2
Enoch HAND 125	.22
Robert HENDERSON 100	.10
John HOOKER 2777	1.18
Jonas HOGMIRE 224	.20
Philip HOSE 100	.08
Conrod HOGMIRE 224	.22
Christian HOFFEE, etal 378	.30
William HILTON & John ORR 3287	.50

Jno HORSE 318
John HOVER 400
John HOY 203
Eli JOSEPH 135
Edward JONES 133
Philip JENKINS 400
Benjamin JENKINS 4300
Ezekiel JACOBS 300
Benjamin JENNINGS 850
Wallace JOHNSTON & MUIR 12328
John KELLER 200
John KELLEY (Laurel Hill) 336
Mary KERR 50
Andrew KIRKPATRICK 250
Elias LEATON 137
Thomas LAIDLEY 279
Joseph LANE 360
Jacob MINTHORN 436
Andrew McKUION 174
Wm. M. PECK 185
John MORRIS 600
Joseph MIRES 600
David MORGAN 500
Daniel McCLEAN 254
Benjamin MASTELLER 152
Nicholas MASTELLER 152
Philip MOORE 150
John MAINS 350
Thomas L. MASON 1000
Leonard W. DEAKINS 200
Edward MAGUIRE 1200
Martin J. WAGNER 30
Abraham WILLINGER 269
William WILES 509
Thomas WOODS 500
Jacob WAGNER 100
Caphael WALTHAN 150
Amos WORKMAN 100
Alexander SMITH 12000

Christopher HAYS/RAYS 354
Thomas RINEHART 315
Jacob RECKER 537
George ROBERTS 328
Richard STILES 200
Richard STEPHENS 200
Ludwick STULL 150
Charles SCOTT 200
James SMITH 157
John STILES 100
George STOUT 120
John STOUT 54
William SQUIRES 850
Christian SHAVER 186 1/2
John SHAY 100
Absolom SEVERNS 850
Andrew STARLING 329
Alexander SCOTT 450
Joseph SWEARINGEN 400
Benjamin & R. JONES 180
Peter TRAXEL 184
Thomas TALBOT 1 lot
Henry TETRICK 500
Joseph VANMETER 1400
Isaac VANMETER 550
Joshua WALLS 100
Stephen WORKMAN 250
George WORKMAN (0)
George WILES 347
Davy Alexander WILLIAM
Thomas MOORE 711
David MOORE 400
Henry NEVILLE 200
George NORTH 310
James PHILLIPS 290
John RUNYON 200
Lewis ROGERS 240
David RIDENOUR 210
Henry RUMBLE 150

Charles, Joshua & John WALLACE & John MYERS 12328

"Monongalia County, to wit, September 1802 term, personally appeared before the Court John W. DEAN and Elihu HORTON, DS for John T. GOFF, Sheriff, and returned the within list of delinquents for the year 1801 and was allowed by the Court after being sworn according to law. September 14th 1802, sworn to in open court by John W. DEAN and Elihu HORTON," (signed) Jno EVANS, Clerk. "The foregoing ten pages contain a complete list of all lands and lots returned to this office for non-payment of taxes in the County of Monongalia for the year 1801 on which the taxes now remain unpaid," (signed) Sam'l SHEPARD, Auditor's Office, 15 April 1812.

169 - 1805, Monongalia County Court. "Names of delinquents owning land in Monongalia County for the year 1805."

Edward ASKINS 691
Joseph ARCHER 384
Thomas ANDERSON 200
Henry BANKS 13500
Charles BENNET 100
Caleb BENNET 78
Jarvis BURNINGHAM 400
John BACORN 500
Ruth BEAL 200
John BURKET 205 1/2
John BEALL 500
Daniel BOYLES, etal 300
Elijah BEAL 177
Henry BROUGHMIRE 102
James BRANT 105
Mary BATTON 200
Christopher BREDENHARD 1000
Charles BOYLES 313 1/2
Thomas BROWN 518
James BOOTH 189
Isaac CUSHMAN 418
David CRULL 278
Ann CLARKE 782
John CONNER Jr. 100
John CROSS 350
Samuel CLARK 355
Samuel CLARK of James 100
Jarret CLAIRY 1390
John COLDRIN, etal 225
James COPE, etal 100
Widow Joanna CHIPPS 1200
George CRAIGHTON 1036
Jesse CHANEY 200
John COMBS 57
Coleby CHEW 214
Thomas CLARE 375
Henry DYER 652
Jacob DUCHMAN 130
Philip DODDRIDGE 800
Michael EVERHART 100
Rowland ELICE 148
David EASTON 600
John EVANS (Nailor) 100
James ERVINGHAM 100
James EVANS 100
Samuel FRAZER 400
Abraham FAW 140
Jacob FORISIT 131
Andrew FRIEND 210

John FILCE 100
Joseph FOX 97
Neal GILLASPY 100
Charles GALLAHAR 1287
Evan GUINN 1000
Benjamin HINDFORD 450
Ezra HORTON 300
Elihu HORTON 3131
Philip HOSE 100
William HILTON, etal 3487
Christian HOFFEE, etal 378
Christopher HAYES 354
Henry HART 507
John HORSE 318
John HARROW 172
John HOPKINS, etal 52000
Nester HARDEN 400
William HANNAH 400
George HIGHLY 339
John HEARD 400
John HONSUCKER 400
Luke HARMESON 102
Michael HILDERBRAND 382
James HOWELL 91 1/4
Jesse HUNT 1000
Daniel JOHNSTON 77
John HILLER 200
Mary KEER 20
Jacob KUHN 800
Andrew KIRKPATRICK 800
John KALLAHAN 141
Patrick LINCH 140
Elias LAYTON 137
James LOURY 100
Philip LITTLE 200
Levy LINSEY 400
Philip LEWIS 217
Charles LASH 400
Cornelius LINCH 1800
Stokely LITTLE 35
Bartholomew LOTT 71
John LEWIS 100
James LONGALL 100
Jacob LIVENGOOD 78
Jacob LAROME 400
William McGEE 120
Samuel MARTIN 400
John MOR 138 1/2
Philip MORE 100

258

Richard MORRIS 447
John MORRIS 800
Joseph MOYERS 200
George MAY (0)
Benjamin MASTELER 250
Edward McGUIRE 1200
Thomas MOORE 711
Robert MINNIS 3506
John MINTHORN 277
Honore MORAN, etal 3600
Adam MITCHER 6
Justina MABERRY 100
Robert MANLEY 56
William MYERES 800
Alexander MEYE 50
Thomas MAN 850
Henry NEVIL 200
George NORT 310
George OFFIT 150
Amos PETTYJOHN 168
James PARKER 400
David PLUNKET, etal 500
James PHILIPS 290
Kiel PECK 600
Francis PATTON 317
Sarah PROVINCE 270
Lerry PINDALL
John QUANDRALL 1000
James ROSE 100
John RUNYON 500
Henry GUMBLE 150
Jacob RECKER 537
David REAMES 600
William ROBE 915
Allen ROBNET 200
Jonathan REECE 400
James ROBINSON Sr. 166 1/2
Archer ROBINS 8100
Joshua ROBINSON 400
John ROLSTON 825
H. Thomas REEDER 1968 1/2
Richard STEVENS 200
Ludwick STULL 150
Charles SCOTT 200
John STILES 100
Richard STILES 100
George STOUT 120
John STOUT 54
William SQUIRES 203
Nicholas SPERRY 200
A. William SMITH 400
Christian SHAVER 186 1/2

John SWAN (paid) 3400
John SHAY 100
Andrew STERLING Sr. 329
Alexander SCOTT 450
Joseph SWEARINGEN 400
Samuel SNOWDEN 947
Frederick STEER, etal 204
David STEWART 1015
Michael STONEBREAKER, etal
    400
William STIDGER 276
Robert SMITH, etal 202
James SNODGRASS 100
George STADTLER 285
David LUGAR, Jr. 200
John STAGG 137 1/2
John SAYRES 100
George SPARKS 113
Thomas SMITH 84
John SPENCER 3608 1/2
Joseph SOMERVILL 392
Francis STANSBERY 184 1/2
John STEARN 150
George SMAR 118
Conrod SHAFFER 802
John SAVERY 96
James TATE 181
Peter TRAXEL 164
Henry TEDRICK 500
Zachariah TOLER 200
Joseph THOMPSON, etal 2000
Israel THOMPSON 480
Bartholomew TARRISON 2200
Elisha TRIMBLE 100
Jacob TUSING 500
James TIDBALL 1000
Ann TAYLOR, etal 512
Adam TRANGER 200
Joseph VANMETER 1400
Abraham VANMETER 556
Jeremiah WILSON 111 1/2
Thomas WORMAN 130
George WILES 347
D. Alexander WILLIAMS 7000
Martin WAGGONER 30
Charles WALLACE, etal
    15483
Thomas WOODS 500
William WILES 347
William WILES 162
    (2nd entry)
John WILLIAMS 100

Jacob WAGGON 100　　　　　　　Ann WATSON 83
Raphael WALTHAM 150　　　　　William WORTH 1000
Abraham WILLINGER 269　　　　Anthony WILLIAMS 18
Amos WORKMAN 100　　　　　　John YOUNG 50

"The within list of insolvents was produced in Court and
examined with the certificate of John W. DEAN, Gentleman, and
ordered to be certified to the Auditor of Public Accounts,"
(signed) Jno EVANS, Clerk. "Monongalia County, to wit, Personally appeared before me the subscriber, a Justice of the
Peace for the County of Monongalia, John FAIRFAX, Sheriff of
Monongalia County, and returned the within list of insolvents
for the year 1805. Sworn to this 10th day September 1806,"
(signed) John W. DEAN. "The eight foregoing pages is a complete list of all lands and lots returned to this office for
non-payment of taxes in the County of Monongalia for the year
1805 on which the taxes now remain unpaid," (signed) Sam'l
SHEPARD, Auditor's Office, 15 April 1812.

189 - 1806, Monongalia County Court. "A list of delinquents
in the district of Alexander BRANDON, one of the commissioners in Monongalia County for the year 1806."

Edward ASKINS 191　　　　　　　Rebecca CHILES 1/4 of 228
Benjamin AYRES 100　　　　　　　Samuel DEWEES 100
William BIGGS 244　　　　　　　　John DIRLING 222
Thomas BAKER 150　　　　　　　　Henry DICE 652
Jervis BURNINGHAM 400　　　　　Jacob DUCHMAN 130
John BAKORN 500　　　　　　　　F. & William DEAKINS
John BURKETT 205 1/2　　　　　　23524 & 1 lot
John BELL 500　　　　　　　　　　Jonathan DAVIS 157
Henry BANKS 9500　　　　　　　　Rowland ELLICE 148
Daniel, Mary &　　　　　　　　　David EASTON 1000
　James BOYLS 300　　　　　　　John Nailer EVANS 100
Elijah BEAL 177　　　　　　　　　Bertrand EWEL 565
Charles BENNET Jr. 100　　　　　Samuel FRAZEE 400
Noah BEATY 276　　　　　　　　　Abraham FAW 140
James BRYANT 105　　　　　　　　John FORSEE 131
Andrew BYRNS 436　　　　　　　　Andrew FRIEND 210
Francis COLLINS 33　　　　　　　Joseph FOX 97
Samuel CANBERY 316　　　　　　Widow FERGUSON 400
Ann CHARLES 617　　　　　　　　John GALISPIE of Neil 160
John CONNER 100　　　　　　　　Neil GALESPIE 100
Samuel CLARK of James 100　　James GALESPIE 38
Isaac CUSHMAN 418　　　　　　　David HENDRICKSON 100
John CROSBY 350　　　　　　　　Henry HARDESTY 4
Margaret CUNNINGHAM 800　　　Elihu HORTON 2228 1/2
Mark CUNNINGHAM 475　　　　　Philip HOSE 100
Widow CUNNINGHAM 200　　　　William & John HILTON 3487
Henry CRULL 200　　　　　　　　Conrod HOGMIRE 200
Israel & Jasper COPE 100　　　　Christian HOFFE &
Thomas CLEGG, etal 200　　　　　Jos. DIRRICK 378

Christopher HAYS 354
Henry HAZEL 350
Levi HOSKINS 66
John HOYE 12008 1/4
John HOYE & Samuel HANWAY 4719
John HANN 200
Joseph HARTLEY 324
John HEADY 10
James HITE 200
Philip JENKINS 400
Benjamin JENKINS 4310
Ezekiel JACOBS 300
Benjamin JENNINGS 250
Ezekie JONES & John DOWNER 600
Robert JONES 160
John KEELER 200
Mary KERR 5
Andrew KIRKPATRICK 600
John KUHN 1375
John KALAHAN 141
James LOWRY 100
Patrick LINCH 32 1/2
Asher LEWIS 200
Thomas LESLEY 500
Stephens MEREDITH 50
Joseph MOYERS 340
S. Thomas MASON 1000
Edward McQUIRE 1200
Thomas MOORE 313
John MINTHORN 277
Honore MARTIN & Jno HOYE 4000
Samuel MARTIN 200
Justina MAYBERRY 100
Alexander McCLELAND 182
Henry MARTIN 189
Christian MILLER 200
John McIVER 312
William NEIGHBORS 101
Henry NEVEL 200
George NORT 310
Jacob NOOS 118
George OFFET 15
John OAKLEY 171
Russell POTTER 458
James PHILLIPS 290
Kiel PECK 600
James PARKER 400
Thomas RINEHART 540
Jacob RECKER 537
John RUNNER 50
Allen ROBNETT 200
Thomas RUCHEL 200

Christian SAYER 104
Charles STEWART 210
John STEWART 97
Richard STEPHENS 200
Ludwick STULL 150
Charles SCOTT 200
John STILES 100
Richard STILES 100
George STOUT 120
John STOUT 54
Nicholas SPERRY 200
A. William SMITH 400
S. William SMITH 2000
Christian SHAVER 186
Andrew S. STARLING 329
Alexander SCOTT 450
Joseph SWEARINGEN 400
Samuel SNOWDEN 947
Frederick STEER, etal 204
David STEWART 1015
Michael STONEBREAKER &
   Jacob MICHAEL or Michael
   JACOB 400
William STIGER 76
Daniel STOVEY 300
David SIMSON 182
John SHAFFER 200
John SCHELL 78
John SCRIVER 450
Frederick SPARR Jr. 300
John M. T. SCOTT 90
James THOMAS 90
Peter TRAXEL 164
Henry TETRICK 500
Zachariah TOLAR 200
James TATE 514
John TRIMBLE 165
Luke TURMAN 758
David TOMS 100
John TOMS 130
_____ THRECHELD 1800
Joseph VANMETER 1400
Abram VANMETER 556
Joseph VANMETER 600
Thomas WARMAN 130
Alexander Davy WILLIAM
   7000
J. Martin WAGNER 30
Charles WALLACE &
   John MURE 15483
Abraham WALLINGER 269
Thomas WOODS 500

John WILLIAMS 100
Jacob WAGNER 100
Raphael WALTHAM 150
Jeremiah WARAN 187
William WORTH 1000
Davis WEAVER 100
Levi WALLS 100
James WILSON 200

John WATSON 100
William WOODS 200
John WICKWARE 1379
John WINGER 370
Benjamin WALKER 67764
William WILLIS 1146
John YOUNG 50

"At a Court held for Monongalia County September term 1807,
John FAIRFAX produced the within list of delinquents in Court
and made oath that the same is just and true," (signed) N.
EVANS, CMC. "The eight foregoing pages is a complete list of
all lands and lots returned to this office for non-payment of
taxes in the County of Monongalia for the year 1806 and on
which the taxes now remain unpaid," (signed) Sam'l SHEPARD,
Auditor's Office, 15 April 1812.

169 - 1809, Monongalia County Court. "A list of delinquent
land tax for the year 1809 in BRANDON's assessment for Monongalia County." Acres listed after names.

Martha ASHBY 1/4 of 228
William AUSTIN 1800
John ANNON 75
Thomas BAKER 150
Thomas BURCHANALD 150
Jervey BERMINGHAM 400
John BACORN 500
Ruth BEAL 200
John BURKET 205 1/2
John BEAL 500
Thomas BUTLER Sr. 200
Isaac BUTLER 200
Henry BANKS 9500
Daniel, Mary & James BOYLES 300
Elijah BEAL 177
William BIGGS 144
Jesse BAYLES 101
James BRYANT 105
Andrew BYRUS, etal 436
Noah BEATY 276
Barton BEAN 239
Kelly & Absolom BRANNON 331
James BOOTHE 60
George BLACKSTONE (0)
Peter BLACK 233
Samuel CANBY 362
James CLARK Jr. 300
Ann CLARKE 617
John CONER Jr. 100

Samuel CLARKE of James 100
Isaac CUSHMAN 418
John COLDREN 225
John CROSSLEY 350
Margaret CUNNINGHAM 800
Mark CUNNINGHAM 475
Abraham CLUTTER 95
Thomas CLAGG, etal 200
Andrew CAMPBELL 100
John DIRLING 222
Henry DICE 652
Jacob DUCHMAN 130
John DOWNARD 339
Francis & William DEAKINS
   1 lot & 108,604
Samuel DEWEES 100
James DEWEES 160
Lester DICKENSON 100
Michiel EVERHART 100
Rolin ELIS 108
David EASTON 600
John Nailor EVANS 100
Berthand EWEL 565
Robert FERRELL 3 tracts
Samuel FRACER 400
Abraham FAW 140
Andrew FRIEND 210
Joseph FOX 97
Widow FURGURSON 400

Abraham FULTON 8500
Walter FITZGERALD 3000
John FETLAND 240
John GILLISPPIE s/o Neil 560
Neil GILLISPPIE 100
James GILLISPIE 392
Lewdew GOFF 471
George GOUGH 228
Thomas GETTINGS 100
Timothy GARD 400
Samuel HARMAN 1 lot
Henry HARDESTY 4
Daniel HULL 100
John HARRIS 300
James HARTLEY 100
Robert HENDERSON 100
Philip HOSE 100
Christian HOFFEE and
  James DERRICK 378
John HORSE 318
William HOGUE 400
Levi HOPKINS 67
James HUGGANS 100
John HORN 200
John HAYS 11977 1/2
Jacob HAMPTON 110
Mathias HITE 177
Joseph HARTELY 324
John HEADY 10
James HITE 200
John HAGNER 300
Thomas HEBBER 600
Christopher HAYSE 354
Joseph HUSTEN 450
Christian HARDEN 120
Reuben JACO 156
Phillip JENKINS 400
Benjamin JENKINS 4310
Ezekiel JACOBS 300
Benjamin JENNENS 250
Ezekiel JONES & Jno
  DOWNER 600
Robert JONES 160
Benjamin JONES 200
John KELLER 200
Mary KARR 50
Jacob KUHN 1325
John KALLAHAN 141
Leonard KEMMEL 44 1/2
James KNOTTS 366
Thomas LEADLEY 9274 & 1 lot
Thomas LEADLEY & HOY 300

Jacob LOWRY 100
James LOWRY 100
Archer LEWIS 200
Benjamin LEADY 162
Thomas LESSLY 500
Alexander LANHAM
  1/6 of 120
Thomas MARTIN 600
Jacob MENTHORN 238
John MORRIS 749
Joseph MARYES 540
David MORGAN heirs 700
Thomas & David MORGAN 400
George MAY ?
Thomas S. MASON 1000
Edward McGUIRE 1200
Thomas MOORE 711
David MOORE heirs 292
Robert MINNIS 653
John MENTHORN 277
Honore MARTIN & John
  HOYE 3600 or 3/800 &
  1400
Samuel MARTIN 200
Peter MILLER 200
John MILLER 200
Adam MELKER 6
Philip MOORE 100
Justina MAYBERRY 100
Christian MILLER 200
John McIVER 312
John MOORE Jr. (Duck) 45
Adam MANEAR 100
Samuel MEREDITH 78
Henry NEVEL 200
George NORTH 310
George OFFLETT 150
John OAKLEY 171
Andrew & John OLEPHANT 168
James PARKER 400
Thomas PINDALL 300
Ann POSTLE 1/4 of 228
James PHILLIPS 290
Hill PECK 600
Benjamin POWEL 150
Joseph PRYER 750
David PLUNKET &
  David STEWART 500
David REEM 600
Thomas RUCKET 200
William ROYCE 91
Thomas RINEHART 540

George RINEHART 10
Jacob RICHER 537
James ROSE 100
Richard STEPHEN 200
Ludwick STULL 150
Charles SCOTT 200
James SMITH 70 1/2
John STILES 100
Richard STILES 100
George STOUT 120
Nicholas SPERRY 200
William SMITH 400
William S. SMITH 200
Christian SHAVER 186 1/4
John SWAN 3400 (paid)
John SHAY 100
Absolom SEVERNS 600
Christian SEREYER 104
Joseph SWEARINGEN 400
Samuel SNOWDEN 947
Frederick & Abraham STEER 204
David STEWART 1015
Michael & Jacob STONEBREAKER 400
William STIGER 276
David SIMONS 182
John SHAFER 200
John St. CHELL? 78
John SPURGEON 57
William M. JARRET 93
Benjamin STUDDART 5000
John SHRIVER 360
John SMITH 450
William SMITH 200
William WORTH 1000
Levi WALLS 100
Ann WATSON 83

Ebenezer STEEL 181
George STEWART 272
Isaac SADLER 350
John STEWART 126
William TANNEHILL of
    Samuel 124 or 1221
Peter TRAXEL 164
Wildy TAYLOR 270
Henry TETRICK 500
Simon TROY 112
James TATE 513
James THOMPSON 90
John TREMBLE 165
David TOMS 100
Luke TERNAN 6 & 1/2 of
    1505
David TOMS 130
John TRECKALD 1900
Benjamin TOUCHSTONE 400
Joseph VANMETER 800
Abraham VANMETER 556
Joseph VANMETER 600
Davy Alexander WILLIAM
    7000
Charles WALLACE &
    Jno MURE 15483
Abraham WALLENGER 269
William WILES 347
Thomas WOODS 500
John WILLIAMS 100
Adam WILSON 174
Raphal WALTHAM 150
Samuel M. WILLIAMS 187
Amos WORKMAN 100
Jeremiah WILSON 111 1/2

"A list of delinquent lands assessed by Alexander BRANDON,
Commissioner for 1809 in Monongalia County," (signed Jno C.
PAYNE, DS for S. MORGAN SMC.

169 - 1809, Monongalia County Court. "A list of Delinquent
Land Tax for the year 1809 in MARTIN's assessment for Monongalia County." Acres listed after names.

James ARCHER 364
Thomas ARNETT 3400
William ANDERSON 1000
Benjamin BROOK 83
Henry BANKS 4000
Morris BROWN 34
John BRION 120

Alexander BARE 73
James BOOTH 189
John BERDINE 39
Joannah CHIPPS 1200
Colbey CHEW 214
Jesse CHANEY 200
George CRAGEHAD 1036

John CALFLESH 89
John CROSS Jr. 200
James DAVIS 626
Thomas DAWSON 182
David DAVID, Kentucky 2000
William DAWSON 100
John ENGLAND 88
Benjamin ESTILE 250
Thomas EWING 1000
Robert EAST 200
Ezekiel FRACER 400
Fidulas FOSTER 95
John FALLIS 800
Elizabeth FREELAND 100
Thompson FIDDY 190
David GRAY 380
Burnard GUILPY 250
Evan GWYNN 1000
John GOODWIN 100
Charles GALLIGE 2900
Peter GARDNER 56
Nester HARDIN 400
William HANNAH 400
George HIGHLEY 339
John HEAD 400
Luke HARMISON 102
James HARTLEY 100
Samuel HUNT 7 1/2
John HOPKINS, etal 52000
James HOARD 91
Benjamin HINFORD 450
Jesse HUNT 1000
Thomas JEFFS 91
Barney KARNES 86
Martin KEESER 100
Christian KING 341
Benjamin KUGLE 200
Philip LEWIS 207
Charles LASH 400
Abraham LOW 300
Cornelius LINCH 705
Absalom LITTLER, etal 400
Stokeley LITTLE 35
Bartholomew LOW 71
John LYNN 100
Jacob LIVENGOOD 78
Jacob LAROME 400
James LANGWELL 100
Asher LEWIS 2 lots
John LIGHT 204
James MILLER 200
Robert MINNIS 1757

Richard MERIFIELD 1275
John MITCHEL 1000
Thomas MOLE 2150
William McCLURE 63
John McCLELAND 384
Jacob MIERS, farrier 220
Daniel MARTIN 272
Robert MAXWELL 66
Charles McMICKIN 250
Alexander MAGEE 50
William MIERS 600
Philip MICHAEL 30
Jacob MILLER 480
Sampson MATTHEWS 254
Benjamin MIDDLETON 112
Christian MEES 30
Joseph NEAL 400
William NEWTON 100
William PETYJOHN 463
James POLLOCK 400
Henry PRATT 322
Elizabeth PRINGLE 2000
Theophelus PHILIPS 4675
Robert PATTON 210
Henry PURVINCE 363
Francis PATTON 317
Thomas PATTERSON 400
Henry PARTMUS 7
Lary PURVANCE 270
Levi PINDLE 150
Philip PINDLE 200
James PARKER 400
Jacob PEAK 150
Jonathan REECE 400
Asher REUBENS 8100
Joshua ROBESON 400
John ROLSTON 825
Thomas REEDER 1968
Jacob RIVER 250
Benjamin RIDENOUR 192
Edward SWISHER 250
Robert SMITH, etal 202
George STATLER 285
William SMILEY 1000
John STANLEY 116
William SCRIPS 70
Robert STRIGHT 125
David SAYRE 82
John STAG 137
George SPARKES 113
Michael SMITH 203
Thomas SMITH 84

John SPENCER 5208
Nancy SCOTT 545
Joseph SUMMERVILLE 392
Jesse SNIDER 230
John STERN 150
George SMARR 218
George SWANK 200
Conrod SHAFFER 802
John SAVAREY 497
Jona & William SEAMAN 200
Alexander SOTHERLAND 150
James SWAN 78485
George SNIDER, Swamps 150
Rudolph SAULER 7 1/2
Elizabeth STEWART 7 1/2
Jona THOMPSON, etal 2000
James TARNEY 55
Isreal THOMPSON 480
Elisha TRIMBLE 100
Bartholomew TARRISON 29000
Jacob TUCKING 500
James TIDBALL 1000

Ann TAYLOR, etal 512
Jacob VANDERGRIFF 584
Anthony WILLIAMS 18
Abraham WISECOPE 50
James WHEELER 40
Stephen WEST 20078
Christian WIREMAN 12925
Francis WOLF 318
David WATKINS 400
Evan WADKINS 310
Brice WORLY 75
Elisha WADE 232
John F. WALDON 404
William WORTH 1000
Joseph WISBY Sr. 90
Lydia WATSON 1200
Thomas C. WADE 282
John WELCH 290
Nicholas WOODS 410
Christopher YOUST 100
George YOUNG 181

"At a Court held for Monongalia County on Wednesday the 11th
day of October 1809, John PAYNE and John C. PAYNE, deputies
to Sheriff Stephen MORGAN, produced in Court the within list
of delinquents which being examined is ordered to be certified to the Auditor of Public Accounts," (signed) N. EVANS,
CMC. "_____ _____ preceding pages is a complete list of all
lands and lots returned to this office for non-payment of
taxes in the County of Monongalia for the year 1809 and on
which the taxes now remain unpaid," (signed) Sam'l SHEPARD,
Auditor's Office, 15 April 1812.

169 - 1803, Monongalia County Court. "List of delinquent
lands, TRICKETT's District." Acres listed after names.

Joseph ARCHER 364
William ANDERSON 1000
William AUSTIN 5876
William ANDERSON 175
Henry BANKS 4000
Morris BROWN 34
Alexander BEATY 470
Sarah BOYLES 215
Jabish BELL 100
Susannah BELL 100
Adam BROWN 400
Christopher BREDENHART 100
John BRYAN 120
James BROWN 1000
Sarah BARKER 180

Charles BOYLES 313 1/2
James BOOTH 312
Thomas CLAIR 375
Margaret CUNNINGHAM 800
Mark CUNNINGHAM 425
Henry CROLL 200
Archable CLUTERFIELD 396
Robert CROW 1123
Thomas CHEWETH 400
John COMBS 87
Jesse CHANA 200
Thomas DAVISON 162
David DAVIS 2000
John DOWNER 270
Henry DURRO 365

Jno ENGLAND 88
Benjamin ESTLE 250
Christian ERVIN 192
Ezekiel FRAZER 441
Robert FERRELL 1078
Fidelous FOSTER 95
John FOLLIS 800
Andrew FLEMAN 100
James FRAZIER 100
Charles GALLAGHER 2187
David GRAY 380
Philip GORDIN 130
Barney GILPY 253
Robert GRAYHAM 10
James HENDERSON 500
Nester HARDIN 400
William HANNA 400
Jacob HARROW 123
George HAILY 339
John HEAD 400
John HUNSIKER 400
John HUNT 139
Michael HILDERBRAND 382
John HUNE 200
David HANWAY 84
John HARROW 172
James HEWEL 91 1/4
Mathias HITE 420
Benjamin HINEFORD 450
Jesse HUNT 1000
Bartholomew JENKINS 2261
Thomas JOHNSTON 200
John JEE 167
Josiah JENKINS heirs 248
Joshua LOW 391
Philip LEWIS 207
Charles LOSH/LASH 400
Abraham LOW 300
Cornelius LINCH 1400
Absolom LITTLE, etal 400
Stokeley LITTLE 35
Bartholomew LOTT 71
Nicholas WOODS 410
John LYNN 100
Jacob LIVEINGOOD 78
Richard MERIFIELD 1285
John MITCHEL 1000
William MORGAN 400
Thomas MOLE 2150
James MORRIS 213
John McCLELAND 384
Daniel MERCHAND 611

Jacob MYARS 157
David MOORE 100
Daniel MARTIN 272
Robert MAXWELL 88 1/4
Henry MARTIN 400
Charles McMICKEN 250
James MORRIS 45
Thomas MAN 250
Thomas MAN, etal 600
John NEAL 400
Joshua OATLEY 100
William PETTYJOHN 663
James POLLOCK 400
John PEARPOINT 1100
Thomas PATTEN 317
Thomas PATTERSON 400
William PATTEN 97
Sarah PROVENCE 270
James PARKER 400
Sarah PLUM 200
Jonathan REECE 400
Asha ROBINS 8100
Joshua ROBISON 400
Robert RETHERFORD 360
David ROBE 461
John ROLSTON 825
Isaac ROYCE 109
Ludwick SWISHER 250
Robert SMITH, etal 202
William A. SMITH 400
William SMILEY 1000
Rudolph SNYDER 339
John STANLEY 116
Timothy SMITH 259
David SAYRES 200
John STAGG 137
John SAYRS 100
Alexander STERLING 300
George SPARKES 113
Thomas SMITH 84
John SPENCER 5408 1/2
John SAYRE 137
John STERN 150
George SMAR 118
Conrod SHAFFER 802
Elisha TRIMBLE 100
Bartholomew TARRISON 4000
Jacob TUSING 500
James TIDBALL 1000
Ann TAYLOR, etal 512
Jacob VANDERGIFT 564
Jacob VANDERVORT 200

Christopher WIREMAN 12989
Francis WOLF 300
David NORRIS 200
David WADKINS 400
Evan WADKINS 310
Brice WORLEY
John & Frederick WALDEN 404

William WORTH 1000
John WADE 52
Isaac H. WILLIAMS 1844
Moses WILLIAMS 200 & 1 lot
Lidia WATSON 1204
Absolom WILLEYS 100
James WINSER 54
Nicholas WOODS 410

(on same list)

Edward ASKINS 391
Thomas BAKER 150
Thomas BURCHANEL 50
Jerry BURNINGHAM 400
John BECKHORN 500
Ruth BEAL 200
John BURKETT 205 1/2
Joseph BUTLER 390
John BELL 500
Thomas BUTLER Jr. 200
Henry BANKS 5000
Joseph BRANDON 200
Adam BROWN 400
Mary DANIEL & James BOYLES 300
Elijah BEAL 177
Henry BELINGER 50
Samuel CANLEY 362
Christian & Jac. CLESTER 185
Ann CLARKE 782
Samuel CLARKE 100
Tarret CLERY 400
Moses CARY 335
John DIRLING 222
Jonas DAVIS 157
Hezekiah DAVISON 400
Henry DIER 652
John DOWNER & HANWAY 500
John DOWNER 319
Jacob DUCHMAN 130
William DAUGHERTY 500
Susanah DONOLSON 160
JONES & DOWNER 150
Michael EVERHEART 100
Rowland ELIJA 148
John EVANS (Nailor) 100
Jas. EVERINGHAM 50
Jas. ERVIN 50
David EVANS 1000
Edward ELLIOTT 100
Samuel FRAZER 400
Abraham FAW 140

John RUNION 150
John FORSEE 131 1/2
Andrew FRIEND 210
Joseph FOX 97
Neal GELLASPE 100
Jas. GELLASPE 100
Daniel HILL 100
Robert HENDERSON 100
Jonas HOGMIRE 2828
Philip HORSE 100
Conrod HOGMIRE 224
Christian HOFFER &
   Jos. DERICK 378
Christopher HAYS 354
John HORSE 318
William HOG 400
Levi HOPKINS 67
John HOON 200
Philip JENKINS 4310
Ezekel JACOBS 300
Benjamin JENKINS 850
Jno DOWNER & JONES 600
John KELLER 200
Mary KAIR 50
Jacob KUHN 800
John KELCHAN 141
Jacob LEWIS 525
Elias LAYTON 137
Richard LONGFORD 100
Levi LIN 400
James LOURY 100
Andrew McQURE 174
Jacob MINTHORN 438
Richard MORRIS 447
Samuel MARTIN 400
John MORRIS 600
Joseph MYERS 690
David MORGAN 500
Daniel McCLAIN 254
Benjamin MASTITLER 152
John MANIS 350

268

John MYERS 200
Edward McGURE 1200
Thomas MOORE 711
David MORE 400
Alexander McCLELAND 485
John MINTON 277
James MATHUSE 183
Henry NEVEL 200
George NORT 310
David PLUNKETT &
  David STEWART 500
James PHILIPS 290
John RUNION 200
Lewis ROGERS 240
James SHAW 273
Henry RUMBLE 150
Thomas RINEHART 748
Jacob RECKER 537
George ROBERTS 328
David REAMS 600
Richard STEPHENS 200
Charles SCOTT 200
John SCOTT 357
James SMITH 157
John STILES 100
George STOUT 120
John STOUT 54
William SQUIRES 203
Nicholas SPERRY 200
Wm. S. STEPHENS 2000

John SHEY 100
Absalom SERVERNS 650
And'w STAILING Sr. 329
Alexander SCOTT 450
Wm. & Robert JONES 180
Joseph SWEARINGEN 400
Samuel SNOWDEN 947
Frederick & Abraham
  STEER 204
David STEWART 985
Michael STONEBREAKER &
  Jacob MICHAEL 400
Peter TRAXEL 164
Henry TETERICK 500
Thomas TANNEHILL 94
Joseph VANMETER 1400
Isaac VANMETER 556
George WILE 347
Wm. & David ALEXANDER 1000
Matin J. WAGONER 30
Abraham WALLINGER 269
William WILE 509
Thomas WOODS 500
John WILLIAMS 100
Jacob WAGONER 100
Philip WALTON 150
William WORTH 1000
Amos WORKMAN 100
Levi WALLS 100
Stephen WORKMAN 250

"1804, September 11, Elihu HORTON, Deputy Sheriff for Russell
POTTER, made oath that the foregoing is a true list of the
delinquents in Monongalia County," (signed) B. REEDER. "The
foregoing twelve pages is a complete list of all lands and
lots returned to this office for non-payment of taxes in the
County of Monongalia for the year 1803 on which the taxes now
remain unpaid," (signed) Sam'l SHEPARD, Auditor's Office, 10
April 1812.

169 - 1810, Monongalia County Court. "A list of delinquents
in BRANDON's District of the Revenue Tax for 1807." Acres
listed after names.

Richard ADKISON 255
William ASHBY 809 1/2
Edward ASKINS 691
Eliza ARNOLD 1/4 of 228
Thomas BAKER 150
Jervey BURNINGHAM 400
Jno BACORN 500
Jno BURKET 205 1/2

Jno BELL 500
Henry BANKS 9500
Daniel, Mary & James
  BOYLES 300
Elijah BELL 777
James BRYANT 105
Andrew BYRNS, etal 436
Abraham BAKER 583

Barten BEAN 339
Kelly & Absalom BRANNON 331
Jas. BOTH 60
George W. BLACKSTONE (2 tracts)
Mary BROWNFIELD 400
Peter COOK 400
James CLARKE Jr. 350
Samuel CANBEY 362
Ann CLARKE 617
Jno CONNER Jr. 100
Margaret CUNNINGHAM 800
Samuel CLARKE of Jas. 100
Isaac CUSHMAN 418
John COLDREN, etal 225
Jno CROSSLEY 350
Mark CUNNINGHAM 475
Henry CROLL 200
Widow CUNNINGHAM 200
Isreal & Jasper COPE 100
Thomas CLAGG 200
Eliza CHILDES 1/4 of 228
Jno DIRLING 222
Henry DICE 652
Henry DUCHMAN 130
Samuel DEWEES 100
Francis & William DEAKINS
    42 lots & 14479
Jas. DEWEES 160
Lester DICKERSON 1000
Peter DRAGOO 128
Michael EVERHEART 100
Rowland ELLICE 148
David EASTON 600
Jno EVANS (Nailer) 100
Jas. EVINHAM 100
David EVANS 1000
Sam'l FRAZEE 400
Abraham FAW 140
Jno FORSEE 131
Andrew FRIEND 210
Michael FLOYD 250
Joseph FOX 97
Widow FERGUSON 400
Abm. S. FULTON 2 lots
Walter FITZGERALD 3000
Jno GILLISPIE of Neil 695
Neil GILLESPIE 100
Jno S. GOFF 429
Alexander GOFF 215
Ladew GOFF 471
Jno T. GOFF 399
George G. GOFF 228

Henry HARDESTY 41
Daniel HILL 100
Philip HOSE
Wm. HILTON & Jno ORR 6287
Conrod HOGMIRE 254
Christian HOFFEE &
    Joseph DERRICK 378
Levi HOPKINS 67.97
James HUGGANS 100
John HORN? 200
Mathias HITE 177
Jno HAYE/HOYE 12935 3/4
Joseph HARTLEY 324
Jno HEADY 10
James HITE 200
Jno HASTINGS 61 1/2
Jno HAGNER 300
Thomas HIBBEN 600
Christian HOSE/HASE 354
Reuben JACO 156
Philip JENKINS 400
Benjamin JENKINS 4310
Ezekiel JACOBS 300
Benj. JENINGS 250
Robert JONES & Thomas
    WILSON 160
Ezekiel JONES & Jno
    DOWNER 600
Jno KEELER 200
Mary KARR 50
Andrew KIRKPATRICK 196
Jacob KUHN 1375
Jno KALLAHAN 141
Jacob LOWE 525
Richard LANGFORD 100
Jas. LOURY 100
Asher LEWIS 200
Thomas LESSLEY 500
Alexander F. LANGHAM 27
Thomas & David MORGAN 400
Jno MANES 350
Thompson S. MASON 1000
Edward McGUIRE 1200
Robert MINNIS 643
Jno MENTHORN 277
Samuel MARTIN 400
Jno MILLER 200
Adam MELKER 6
Justina MAYBERRY 100
Alexander McCLELAND 182
Adam MANIAR 100
Samuel MERVIN 50

Samuel MEREDITH
Andrew MILLER 300
Christian MILLER 200
Henry NEVEL 200
George NORT 310
George OFFETT 150
Jno OAKLEY 171
Jas. PARKER 400
Thomas PINDALL 300
Russell POTTER 464
Jas. PHILIPS 290
Hill PECK 600
Sarah PLUMB 200
Benjamin POWELL 200
Joseph PRYOR 750
David PLUNKETT &
  David STEWART 500
Simeon ROYCE 304
Henry RUMBLE 150
Thomas RINEHART 543.73
George RINEHART
Jacob RECKER 537
David REEMS 600
Jno RUNNER 50
David ROBE 461
Allen ROBNETT 200
William RUSSELL 56
Thomas RACHEL 200
Coonrod SHEETS 3 lots
Richard STEPHENS 83 3/4
Richard STEPHENS 200
Ludwich STULL 150
Charles SCOTT 200
Jas. SMITH 157
Jno STILES 100
Richard STILES 100
George STOUT 120
Jno STOUT 54
William SQUIRES 203
Nicholas SPERRY 200
William A. SMITH 400
William L. SMITH 200
Christian SHAVER 168 1/2
John SWANN 3400 (crossed out)
Jno SHAY 100
Absalom SEVERNS 400
Christian SAYER 104
Alexander SCOTT 450
Joseph SWEARINGER 400
Samuel SNOWDEN 947
Benjamin WALKER 71764 1/2
Richard WEAVER 100

David STEWART 1012
Frederick & Abram STEER
  204
Michael STONEBREAKER
  & Jacob MICHAEL 400
William STIDGET 272
Daniel STOVER 300
Jno SHAFFER 200
Jno SHELL 78
Jno SAYER 450
Frederick SPARR Jr. 300
Meshack SEXTON Jr. unknown
Jno SCOTT, Morgan Town 90
Benj. STUDDARD 5000
William SMITH 220
Ebenezer STEEL 181
George STEWART 272
Peter TRAXEL 164
Wildy TAYLOR 150
Henry TETRICK 500
Simeon TROY 250
Jas. TATE 658
Jas. THOMPSON 90
Jno TREMBLE 185
Luke TERNAN 758 1/2
David TOMS 100
John TOMS 130
Jno THANKELD 2900
Jno TAYLOR 120
Joseph VANMETER 556
Abraham VANMETER 556
Joseph VANMETER 600
Benjamin WOODS 165
Wm. & Alex. DAY 7000
Charles WALLACE &
  John MURE 15483
Abraham WALLENGER 269
William WILES 347
Thomas WOODS 500
Jno WILLIAMS 100
Jacob WAGNER 100
Raphael WALTHAM 150
Samuel M. WILLIAMS 187
Wm. WORTH 1000
Davis WEAVER 100
Levi WALLS 100
Jeremiah WILSON 111 1/2
Ann WATSON 83
Wm. WOODS 200
Jacob WIVELEY/WISELEY &
  Frederick ? 110
William WILLIS 1146

The foregoing list signed by "Jno C. PAYNE, DS for S. MORGAN, SMC."

(on same list)

"A list of delinquents in MARTIN's District."

Ashbel AGUSTINE 92
Thomas ARNET 3400
James ARCHER 364
William ANDERSON 1000
Andrew BAILES 35
Jeremiah BIGS 100
Benjamin BROOK 83
Elizabeth BURROWS 400
Henry BANKS 4000
Morris BROWN 34
John BRYON 120
James BROWN 1000
Charles BAYLES 313 1/2
Alexander BARE 73
Thomas BROWN 518
Eleazer BIGGS 100
James BOOTH 189
John BASHONE 300
John BERDINE 39
Nathan CANFIELD 15
Bartholomew CLARK 1 lot
John CARREL 100
Thomas CLARE 375
Jo_____ CHIPPS 800
Colby CHEW 214
John COMBS 57
Jesse CHANEY 200
George CRAGHEAD 1036
John CALFLESH 89
Joannah CHIPPS 400
John E. DENT 225
James DAVIS 626
Thomas DAWSON 162
David DAVIS 2000
William DAWSON 100
Able DAVIS 200
John ENGLAND 88
Thomas EWING 1000
James EDGEL 100
Robert EAST 200
Enoch EVANS 255
Ezekiel FRAZER 441
Fidulas FOSTER 95
Standish FORD 1000
John FALLIS 400

Elizabeth FREELAND 100
Thompson FIDDY 237
Mathias FARLEY 154
Elias FLANNIGAN, etal 100
David GRAY 380
Burnard GUILPEY 250
Evan GWYNN 1000
Charles GALLIHER 2900
James HENDERSON 500
Nester HARDEN 400
William HANNAH 400
George HIGHLEY 339
Allen HALL 208
John HEAD 400
John HANSUCKER 400
Luke HARRISON 102
Michael HILDERBRAND 382
James HARTLEY 100
John HOPKINS, etal 52000
James HOWEL 91
Benjamin HINEFORD 450
Jesse HUNT 1000
Philip HILL 85
Michael HOLMES to
   P. & G. HOLLENGER 400
William HART 60
Simon KRANTZER 161
Barney KERNS 86
Martin KEZER 100
Lewis KARNES Jr. 50
Christian KING 341
Levi LENSY 800
Philip LEWIS 207
Charles LASH 400
Abraham LOW/LAW 300
Cornelius LINCH 705
Absolem LITTLE, etal 400
Stokely LITTLE 35
Bartholomew LOTT 71
John LINN 100
Joshua LOWERMAN 150
Jacob LEVENGOOD 18
Jacob LARRANCE 400
James LANGWELL 150
Asher LEWIS 2 lots

James MILLER 200
Morgan MORGAN 88
Robert MINNIS 2412
Richard MERRIFIELD 1265
John MICHAEL 1000
Charity MARTIN 280
Thomas MOLE 2150
William McCLARE 63
Clemont MERRELS 100
John McCLELAND 384
Jacob MIERS 220
Daniel MARTIN 272
Robert MAXWELL 66 1/2
Charles McMICKEN 250
Henry MILEY 100
Alexander MAGEE 50
William MIERS 600
Thomas MARTIN 784
Philip MICHAEL 30
Jesse MARTIN HC 200
Jacob MILLER 400
Sampson MATTHEWS 254
Benjamin MIDDLETON 112
Joseph NEAL 400
William NEWTON 100
William PETTYJOHN 463
James POLLOCK 400
Theophilus PHILIPS 4975
Theophilus PHILIPS heirs 700
Robert PATTON 210
Henry PROVEANCE 363
Francis PATTON 317
Thomas PATTERSON 400
Henry PURTMUS 7
Widow PETTYJOHN 780
Lary PURVEANCE 270
Levi PINDLE 150
Philip PINDLE 200
James PARKER 400
Jonathan REESE 400
Joseph ROADES 204
Asher ROBINS 8100
Joshua ROBISON 400
John RALSTON 825
Thomas REEDER 1968
Jacob RIVER 250
Edward SWISHER 250
Robert SMITH, etal 202
Daniel SCOTT Sr. 48
James SNODGRASS 100
George STATLER 285
William SMILEY 1000

John STANLEY 118
Rudolph SNIDER 339
Timothy SMITH 259
Robert STRAIGHT 120
Michel STRATLER Jr. 200
David SAYR 200
Samuel SMITH 300
John STAG 137
George SPARKS 113
Michael SMITH 203
Thomas SMITH 84
John SPENCER 2731
Joseph SUMMERVILLE 392
John SPENCER 331
Jesse SNIDER 230
John SPENCER 2346
John STERN 154
George SMARR 118
George SWANK 200
Coonrod SHAFFER 802
John SAVERY 496
William K. SMITH 100
Jona. & Wm. SEAMAN 200
Alexander SOTHERLAND 150
James SWAN 7485
George SNIDER, Swamps 150
Rudolph SADLER 7 1/2
Daniel SAYER 220
David SAYER 300
Elizabeth STEWART 7
Jonah THOMPSON, etal 2000
Isreal THOMPSON 480
Elisha TRIMBLE 100
Bartholomew TARRISON 26000
Jacob TUANGER 500
James TIDBALL 996
Ann TAYLOR, etal 512
Samuel WARMAN 155
Joseph WISBY Jr. 90
George WILSON 190
Francis WOLFE 318
David KINS 400
Evan WADKINS 310
Elisha WADE 232
John F. WALDEN 404
William WORTH 1000
Lydia WATSON 1200
Thomas C. WADE 282
Nicholas WOODS 410
Anthony WILLIAMS 18
James WINZER heirs 54
Christopher YOST 100

"At a Court held for Monongalia County September 1808 term, Stephen MORGAN, Sheriff of Monongalia County, produced in Court the within list of delinquents which being examined is ordered to be certified to the Auditor of Public Accounts," (signed) N. EVANS, CMC. "The foregoing fourteen pages is a complete list of all lands and lots returned to this office for non-payment of taxes in the County of Monongalia for the year 1807 and on which the taxes now remain unpaid," (signed) Sam'l SHEPARD, Auditor's Office, 15 April 1812.

169 - 1802, Monongalia County Court. "A list of Delinquents of Revenue for 1802 returned for the examination of the Court of Monongalia County." Acres listed after names.

Joseph ARCHER 364
Josiah LUSTY 1000
William AUSTIN 5976
William ANDERSON 175
Alexander BAYTEY 470
Gilbert BUTLER 71
Henry BANKS 4000
Morris BROWN 34
Susannah BEAL 100
Christopher BUDENHART 100
William BIGS 49
Jona BRYAN 120
Mary CUNNINGHAM 475
Thomas CLARE 375
Mark CUNNINGHAM 800
Archable CLUTTERFIELD 395
Colbey CHEW 214
Robert CROW 1123
Thomas CHINWTH 400
John CLARKE 182
Henry CORE 50
John COMBS 57
James CARTER 261
Jesse CHANEY 200
John DAWSON 225
Thomas DAVISON 162
David DAVIS 100
George NIGH, etal 222
John ENGLAND 88
Barney ESTAL 250
Robert FERRELL 678
Ezekiel KRAZER 441
Fidolus FOSTER 95
John FILLIS 800
Elizabeth FREELAND 100
Thompson FIDEY 190
James FRAZE 100
Evin GUINIEA 1000

Charles GALHEHER 2189
John GARGUS 250
David GRAY 380
Philip GORDIN 130
Barney GILPIE 253
John GIBBEN 200
James HENDERSON 500
John HARROW 172
William HANAHS 400
George HILEY 339
John HEAD 400
John HUNESUCKER 400
John HUNT 200
Samuel HUNT 7.5
James HOWEL 9.25
Abner HARPER 400
Jesse HUNT 1000
Benjamin HINEFORD 450
Bartholomew JENKINS 1087
Thomas JOHNSON 200
John JEE 400
Abraham JEE 167
Jos JENKINS heirs 248
Barberry KERNS 86
Jacob LURTY 3400
Philip LEWIS 207
Charles LASH 400
Abraham LOW 300
Cornelius LINCH 1900
Absalom LITTLE, etal 400
Bartholomew LOTT 71
Nicholas WOODS 410
John LYNN 100
Jeremiah LEACH 145
William MARTIN 312
John MITCHEL 1000
Wm. MORGAN 400
Charity MARTIN 103

Thomas MOLE 2150
Wm. McCLURE 65
John McCLANEN 384
Daniel MARTIN 272
Robert MAXWELL 66 1/2
Henry MARTIN 400
Jacob MERS 50
William MILLER 273
Charles McMEAKIN 250
Henry MILEY 100
John NEAL 400
David NORRISS 224
Joshua OATLEY 100
John PIERPOINT 700
Benjamin POWEL 150
Francis PATTON 317
Sarah PROVENCE 277
Levi PINDAL 150
James PARKER 400
Sarah PLUM 200
James POLLOCK 400
Thomas PATTERSON 400
Widow PETYCHI___ 400
Asher RUBINS 8000
Joshua ROBINSON 400
Daniel ROBE 212
Isaac ROYCE 109
Wharton RUTTER 83 1/2
Nathan SPRINGER 341 1/2
Ludwick SWISER 250
Robert & John SMITH 202
George STATLER 285
John SHIVELEY 302

John STANLEY 116
Thomas SMITH 84
Alexander STARLING 300
George SPARKES 113
John SPENCER 5388.5
William SMITH 35.5
Simon TRAY/TROY 680
Elisha TRIMBLE 100
Bartholomew TARRISON 4000
Jacob TUSING 500
James TIDBALL 1000
William VEACH 100
Jacob VINDEGRIFT 264
Isaac VANCAMP 321
Robert WILSON 130
Elisha WADE 232
Christopher WIREMAN 12972
Francis WOLF 300
James WILSON Sr. 350
Evan WATKINS 310
Brase WORLEY 75
John & Fred'k WALDEN 404
William WORTH 1000
John WADE 52
John WILSON 732
Isaac Hite WILLIAMS 400
Lidia WADSON 1200
James WINSOR 54
James WALKER 365
Reubin WILCUTT 72
Nicholas WOOD 410
John BURKHORN 400

Alexander BRANDON's District on same list.

John ARCHER 365
William ASHBEY 1000
Joseph BUTLER 390
Thomas BAKER 150
Thomas BURCHNAL 50
John BECKEN 500
Ruth BEAL 200
Thomas BATTEN Jr. 200
Henry BANKS 1000
Elijah BEAL 177
Daniel, Mary & James BAYLES 300
Samuel CANBY 362
Ann CLARKE 782
Samuel CLARKE of James 100
John DILAN 222 1/2
Henry DEYER 652

John DOWNER 319
DOWNER & Ezekiel JONES 150
Susannah DELINSON 160
Jacob DUFFMAN 130
William DAUGHERTY 500
John EVANS (N) 100
Michael EVENHART 100
Roland ELLIS 148
James EVERINGHAM 100
David EVANS 1000
Samuel FRAZE 400
Abraham FAW 140
John FERSEE 131
Andrew FRIEND 210
Joseph FOX 97
John FLEMAN 150

James GILLESPIE 354
Neal GILLISPIE 100
David GALLAWAY 185
Gabriel GREATHOUSE 400
Isaac HAYS 61
Daniel HILL 100
Robert HENDERSON 100
Philip HOSE 100
Christian HOFFER &
  Jas. DERRICK 378
William HILTON & John ORR 3287
Christopher HAYS 354
John HORSE 318
John HAVNER 400
William HOGUE 400
Levi HOPKINS 67
Philip JENKINS 400
Benjamin JENKINS 4310
Benjamin JENNINGS 850
Ezekiel JACOBS 300
Ezekiel JONES & John DOWNER 600
John KELLEY 336
Mary KARR 50
Jacob KACKES 800
Andrew KIRKPATRICK 160
Elias LAYTON 137
Thomas LUDLEY 279
James LOWEREY 100
Andrew McKUNE 174
Jacob MINTHORN 436
Wm. McPECK 165
John MORRIS 600
Joseph MYERS 600
David MORGAN 500
Daniel McCLAIN 254
John MANES 350
Edward McGUIRE 1200
Thomas MOORE 711
Alexander McCLANON 285
John MINTHORN 277
Henry NEVEEL 200
George NORT 310
David PLUNKET & Daniel
  STEWART 500

James PHILIPS 290
John RUNER 200
Lewis RODGERS 240
Thomas RINEHART 748
Jacob RICKER 537
George ROBERTS 328
David REEMS 600
Richard STEPHENS 200
Henry STARTSMAN 500
Lodewick STULL 150
Charles SCOTT 200
James SMITH 157
John STILES 100
Richard STILES 100
George STOUT 120
John STOUT 54
Wm. SQUIRES 250
Nichols SPERREY 200
Christopher SHAVER 186 1/2
John SHAY 100
Absalom SEVERNS 650
Andrew STERLING 329
Alexander SCOTT 450
Robert JONES 160
Joseph SWEARINGEN 400
Samuel SNODEN 947
Peter TRAXEL 164
Henry TETRICK 500
Jeremiah TAWNEHILL 87
Joseph VANMUTIN 1400
Isaac VANMETER 558
George WILDS 347
Wm. Daury ALEXANDER 7000
Martin J. WAGONER 30
Abraham WILINGER 269
William WILES 509
Thomas WOODS 500
Wallis Charles Joshua &
  John MYERS 12328
Raphael WALTON 150
Wm. WORTH 1000
Amos WORKMEN 100
Stephen WORKMEN 250

"Virginia, Monongalia County, to wit, September Court 1803.
John W. DEAN and Elihu HORTON, Deputy Sheriffs for Russell
POTTER, Sheriff of Monongalia County, produced in Court the
within list of delinquents for the year 1802 and made oath to
the same according to law which is ordered to be certified
to the Auditor of Public Accounts," (signed) J. EVANS, Clk.
"The eleven foregoing pages is a complete list of all lands

and lots returned to this office for non-payment of taxes in the County of Monongalia for the year 1802 on which the taxes now remain unpaid," (signed) Sam'l SHEPARD, Auditor's Office, 15 April 1812.

170 - 1811, Monongalia Superior Court. John STEALY summoned to answer John HAY/HOYE/HAYES/HOGE in a plea of debt for $550 and $10 damage, 3 March 1810. Two notes signed by STEALEY to HOY dated 21 May 1805 for $275 each, payable in 1 and 2 years and witnessed by Samuel HANWAY and B. REEDER. Appearance Bond signed by STALEY secured by Samuel HANWAY in the presence of S. DERING, 6 March 1810. Bill of Sale ($800) signed by John HAYS to John STALEY for two entries made by HAYS in Sandy Creek Glades adjoining lands purchased by STALEY from HAZEL to be paid by one third in hand and the balance by two equal installments. If any of the land in the survey made by Samuel HANWAY is lost in prior claims, STALEY to have a refund at the rate of $800 for 800 acres for any loss, "as there is a pretended claim for a part known by GRATEHOUSE's claim." STALEY agreed to defend the land, in case suit was brought, at his own expense, 21 May 1805, witnessed by T. R. CHIPPS, Jo SHINN and Samuel HANWAY. Samuel HANWAY surveyed the land and certified the tract contained 720 acres, 4 September 1811.

170 - 1811, Monongalia Superior Court. Order to attach the property of Asa HARRIS equal to $1000 plus costs at the suit of John SAYRE, 30 May 1811. The above to be discharged at the rate of 6% on $200 from 21 June 1804 due 19 March 1805; $150 as follows, to wit, interest as above on $50 from 20 March 1804 due 27 August 1807; $200 with like interest from 20 March 1805 until 27 August 1807; $200 with like interest from 20 March 1806 until 27 August 1807 and costs plus 10% on $450 and cost from 27 August 1807 until 5 August 1809, being adjudged for retaining the execution of the judgement by injunction. Then 6% from that period on $450 until payment. (Yearly interest percentages).

170 - 1811, Monongalia Superior Court. Thomas McKINLEY summoned to answer James MURPHY in a plea of covenant broken, 4 September 1809. MURPHY complained that McKINLEY did not teach him the art of hat making and he was in no way employed in the hat making business but was a laborer not connected to the business. MURPHY said he did not have sufficient wearing apparel during the term and was not allowed schooling as agreed nor did he receive 10 pounds worth of clothing at the end of his term. Indenture dated 25 October 1797 between James MURPHY and Thomas McKINLEY whereby MURPHY placed his son, James MURPHY, as an apprentice to McKINLEY for the term of 11 years and nine months to learn the art of hat making. James (the apprentice) was to behave himself in all things as a good apprentice ought to do and McKINLEY was to teach James

the hat making business, feed him, furnish clothes, washings and lodging, provide 2 years and 3 months schooling (MURPHY to pay for one of the years). At the end of the apprenticeship McKINLEY to furnish James 10 pounds worth of wearing apparel or 10 pounds lawful money of Virginia, signed by James (O) MURPHY Sr., James (x) MURPHY Jr. and Thos. McKINLEY in the presence of Thomas CHIPPS on 30 August 1798. James MURPHY Sr., Jacob FOULK, David LEMAN/SEMAN, John McKINLEY, Nimrod EVANS and William N. JARRETT summoned to testify in behalf of MURPHY Jr., 3 September 1810, 20 February and 15 July 1811. George CLOUS summoned to testify in behalf of MURPHY, 4 September 1811. Paul VEGUS and Abraham HALE summoned to testify in behalf of McKINLEY, 20 August 1810. John TAYLOR summoned to testify in behalf of MURPHY, 6 September 1811. Peter WALKER summoned to testify in behalf of McKINLEY, 19 March 1811. Thomas GLISSON Jr. and William CHIPPS summoned to testify in behalf of McKINLEY, 4 September 1810 and 2 March 1811. Abraham WOODROW and Henry H. WILSON summoned to testify in behalf of McKINLEY, 29 March and 15 July 1811. Benjamin REEDER summoned to testify in behalf of MURPHY, 2 September 1811. James McCLAIN/McCLAUS, of Harrison County, summoned to testify in behalf of MURPHY, 19 June 1811. James McCORLEY, of Harrison County, summoned to testify in behalf of MURPHY, 15 June 1811. Appearance Bond signed by McKINLEY secured by John PAYNE and witnessed by John BARNES and Anthoney COZAD, 25 September 1809. "John McKINLEY personally appeared before me, a Justice of the Peace for Monongalia County, and made oath that at the time James MURPHY was free from his father, he received his freedom dues," signed by J. CAMPBELL, 6 September 1810. Joseph WILLFORD and John SNIDER, two of the jurors in the case of MURPHY and McKINLEY, made oath that they were governed by the belief that McKINLEY had not paid MURPHY his freedom dues, 6 September 1806. McKINLEY came before Justice R. BARKSHIRE and swore that since yesterday's trial with MURPHY, he was able to prove by John COOPER that MURPHY acknowledged that at the time he received the indenture, McKINLEY had fully satisfied him agreeable to the terms. He said at the time of the trial he did not know he could prove the issue by COOPER, 6 September 1810. September 1811 term, "We the jury find for the plaintiff $143 and damages," Fielding KIGER, foreman.

170 - 1811, Monongalia Superior Court. Elijah BUTLER summoned to answer Edward McCARTY and William ARMSTRONG (McCARTY and ARMSTRONG and Company) in a plea of debt for 70.3.4 valued at $233.90 and $10 damage, 10 May and 19 June 1809. The summons not executed, "kept off by force." Demand Note signed by Elijah BUTLER to McCARTY and ARMSTRONG for 70 pounds, 3 shillings and 4 pence dated 9 June 1806 and witnessed by James H. GORDON. September 1811 term, judgement confirmed and entered up.

170 - 1811, Monongalia Superior Court. Noah LESTER summoned to answer James MORGAN, assignee of Zedekiah HAMP, in a plea of covenant broken damage $150, 6 February 1810. February 1811 term, dismissed by the plaintiff's attorney.

170 - 1811, Monongalia Superior Court. Abraham ELIOTT summoned to answer Philip LEWIS in a plea of slander damage $1000, 29 June 1807. ELIOTT was heard to say that LEWIS stole his bacon and sugar. Henry LEWIS and Jacob WOLF summoned to testify in behalf of Philip LEWIS, 26 August 1809. Jacob KISNER, Benjamin TREMBLY, Polly MASON and Susan CRISS summoned to testify in behalf of ELLIOTT, 20 March and 15 July 1811. William BUCKALEW, William MASON, Paul VANDIVER Jr., Henry LEWIS and Jacob WOLF summoned to testify in behalf of Philip LEWIS, 3 September 1810, 20 February and 15 July 1811. Henry LEWIS summoned to testify in behalf of Philip, 20 August 1811. September 1811 term, "We the jury find for the plaintiff $30 in damages," James TIBBS, foreman.

170 - 1811, Monongalia Superior Court. David SCOTT, Dudley EVANS, William JOHN, Justices of Monongalia County, summoned to answer Austin NICKOLS in a plea of trespass on the case damage $1200, 23 August 1802. At a court held for Monongalia County on 12 December 1797, SCOTT, EVANS, JOHN and Thomas CHIPPS, deceased, were present as justices. Robert FERRELL, under commission from Virginia, was sworn to the office of sheriff. The law required that any person accepting the Sheriff's Commission give bond with two or more securities. The above named justices "entirely omitted and neglected to take of the said Robert FERRELL such bond." At a court held 16 September 1797, NICKOLS, assignee of John JACKSON who was assignee of Edward JACKSON, recovered judgement against Daniel SAYRES for $500 with interest at 5% from 4 December 1795 plus costs and $.01 damage. Sheriff FERRELL was ordered to attach SAYRES' property sufficient to satisfy the debt, interest, costs and damage and sell at public sale and have the money available on 1 January 1798. NICKOLS complained that FERRELL collected the money but paid him only a part of it and he brought suit for the balance of $460.08 plus damages against FERRELL. NICKOLS recovered against FERRELL the sum of $460.08 with interest at 5% from 15 May 1798 plus costs until payment. NICKOLS said the debt remained unpaid and because of the neglect of the justices to take FERRELL's bond, he was unable to take advantage of the law and therefore he brings suit to recover the debt, interest, costs and further damages, signed by Noah LINDSEY, attorney for the plaintiff. September 1811 term, abated.

170 - 1811, Monongalia Superior Court. Superior Court of Chancery held in Staunton on 2 April 1811. James BURCHINAL, plaintiff, vs Amos SMITH, George SMITH and William SMITH, defendants. Order to dissolve an injunction awarded to the

plaintiff to stay execution of a judgement recovered against him by the defendants in Monongalia County District Court, 13 July 1810, signed by Henry J. PEYTON, CCC.

170 - 1811, Monongalia Superior Court. John BARRICKMAN and John LEMONS summoned to answer Thomas WILSON and Davis SHOCKLEY in a plea of trespass on the case damage $100, 27 February 1810. "This action is brought in trespass for injury to the lands of the plaintiffs by the defendants." January 1811 term, dismissed by the plaintiff's attorney.

170 - 1811, Monongalia Superior Court. Samuel SWEARINGEN summoned to answer Moses KINCADE, by William KINCADE his next friend, in a plea of slander, 10 January 1810. Moses KINCADE, an infant under the age of 21 by William KINCADE his next friend, complained that Samuel SWEARINGEN, on 5 January 1810, spoke false and slanderous words against him. SWEARINGEN said to William KINCADE, brother to Moses, that Moses swore to a lie in the suit tried by Morgan MORGAN between said SWEAR-INGEN said William KINCADE. SWEARINGEN's answer to the complaint: In August 1809, William KINCADE Jr. obtained from Justice Morgan MORGAN a warrant against him in a plea for 3 1/2 bushels of corn. On 26 August 1809, a trial was held and the question arose as to whether or not Moses KINCADE had previously told SWEARINGEN that he the said SWEARINGEN could not get five yards of coarse country linen from William KINCADE Sr. in pursuance of a contract before that time made between SWEARINGEN and KINCADE Sr. by his son and agent, William KINCADE Jr. and that 2 1/2 bushels of corn advanced before that time by SWEARINGEN for and on account of the five yards of linen must be applied in part payment for 3 1/2 bushels of corn before that time due and owing from SWEAR-INGEN to KINCADE Jr. Moses KINCADE appeared as a witness for William KINCADE Jr. and swore to tell the truth concerning the premises aforesaid. SWEARINGEN said Moses swore falsely in favor of William KINCADE Jr. and against him for the whole value of the 3 1/2 bushels of corn and swore he never told him (SWEARINGEN) that he could not get the linen from KINCADE Sr. Morgan MORGAN, Polly MERRIFIELD, Joshua HICKMAN, Eli B. SWEARINGEN, John STEPHENS and William TRICKETT summoned to testify in behalf of SWEARINGEN, 18 July 1811. James JEFFS, Philip PATTERSON and John BONER summoned to testify in behalf of KINCAID, 20 February and 15 July 1811. James JEFFS, Joseph KINCADE and Philip PATTERSON summoned to testify in behalf of KINCADE, 2 September 1811. S. SWEARINGEN, Morgan MORGAN, Polly MERRIFIELD, Joshua HICKMAN, David JACKSON, Eli SWEAR-INGEN and John STEPHENS summoned to testify in behalf of SWEARINGEN, 16 February 1811. September 1811 term, "We the jury find for the plaintiff $107 in damages," signed by Jno EVANS, foreman.

170 - 1811, Monongalia Superior Court. John STEALEY summoned to answer Joseph SPENCER in a plea of trespass on the case damage $200, 9 May 1810. Demand Note signed by STEALEY to SPENCER dated 23 December 1809 for $100 and witnessed by John SANDERS. September 1811 term, plea waived and judgement with stay of execution.

170 - 1811, Monongalia Superior Court. Bond signed by Rawley SCOTT to served as administrator for William TINGLE, deceased, secured by N. EVANS, Fielding KIGER, E. DAUGHERTY, William N. JARRETT and R. BARKSHIRE, 5 September 1811.

170 - 1811, Monongalia Superior Court. Richard CAIN summoned to answer Roland HANNA, assignee of Marshal ESTES, in a plea of debt for $100 and $10 damage, 10 March 1810. Note signed by Richard CAIN, of "Mohongail" County, to William Marshall ESTES, of Kentucky, dated 11 February 1807 for $100 with interest, due 31 October 1807 and witnessed by Nat CLARK, Isaac TOMLINSON and Marier ESTES. Assignment to HANNA dated 22 October 1807 and witnessed by John CHINN and Samuel SHY. Appearance Bond signed by Richard CAIN secured by James CAIN, 20 March 1810. "Received of Richard CAIN $50, part of a judgement I have against him in Morgan Town, Monongalia County, Va," 20 May 1811, signed by Jesse EVANS. September 1811 term, plea waived and judgement.

170 - 1811, Monongalia Superior Court. James WILSON summoned to answer Pursela/Pensila/Lensela HERRIDAN, an infant under age 21, by her attorney, father and next friend, Thomas HERRIDAN, in a plea of slander damage $1000, 16 August 1808. HERRIDON complained that WILSON was heard to say that she stole cotton. WILSON's answer to the complaint: He said the plaintiff ought not have and maintain her action against him because she did steal as declared and because she was an infant, under age 21, and prosecuted the case by her attorney and not by any guardian. Thomas BYRD, Charlotte BYRNE, Betsy FLOYD and Catherine FIELDS summoned to testify in behalf of WILSON, 6 October 1810. Isaac MATHEWS, Hesekiah MEREFIELD and Barack WADKINS summoned to testify in behalf of HERRIDON, 2 March 1811.

170 - 1811, Monongalia Superior Court. John CLARK summoned to answer Charles HANNEY in a plea of slander, 21 February 1810. CLARK was heard to say that HANEY stole corn out of James COLLINS' Mill. On 16 March 1810, Mathew GEORGE, Deputy for Sheriff Lemuel JOHN, reported that he had served the summons on CLARK and took him in custody, but CLARK escaped. Grafton WHITE, John GIDLEY and Thomas WADE summoned to testify in behalf of HANEY, 2 September 1811. September 1811 term, "We the jury find for the plaintiff $340 in damages," J. EVANS Jr., foreman.

170 - 1811, Monongalia Superior Court. Abraham HALE summoned
to answer George HITE in a plea of assault, 19 March 1810.
HALE said he was defending himself because HITE assaulted him
first. Fielding KIGER summoned to testify in behalf of HITE,
4 September 1811. James TAYLOR, Mrs. TAYLOR or Wm. TAYLOR,
William WALKER and John McKINLEY summoned to testify in
behalf of HITE, 3 September 1811. Bail Bond for HALE secured
by Samuel HANWAY, 25 March 1811. HANWAY swore his estate was
worth $500 after payment of all debts. Appearance Bond signed
by Abraham (x) HALE secured by Samuel HANWAY, 24 March 1810.
September 1811 term, "We the jury find for the plaintiff $.01
in damages," Tho. GLISSON, foreman. Abraham HALE summoned to
answer the complaint of Augustus WERNINGER for non-payment of
a debt due by account, 15 January 1810.   January 1810 term,
judgement confessed for $3.38 debt and $.30 costs. An
attachment was levied on 2 axes and 2 coats on 19 March 1810.
On 5 April 1810, the property was sold at public sale for
$6.01 to satisfy the execution.

170 - 1811, Monongalia Superior Court. On 28 September 1809,
Michael FLOYD, Nathan MATHENEY Jr., Elizabeth TAYLOR and
Elizabeth FLOYD Jr. were summoned to answer the complaint of
Harman GREATHOUSE in a plea of trespass damages $1000. The
summons was served on Michael and Nathan, but not on TAYLOR
and Elizabeth FLOYD for want of time.   TAYLOR and Elizabeth
FLOYD were summoned a second time on 17 January 1810. GREAT-
HOUSE complained that the defendants broke into his house and
stole from his plantation the following items: 9 sheep, 5
hogs,   450 feet of planking, 1 table, 2 bedsteads, 2 spinning
wheels, 1 reel, 1 big wheel,   2 pots, 1 ten gallon kettle, 1
dutch oven, 2 buckets, 1 coffee pot, 1 sugar pot, 1 tin pan,
1 canister, 1 funnel, 1 ladle, 1 flesh fork, 1 melting ladle,
pot trammel, shovel, 2 broad hoes, a grubbing hoe, 1 ax, 1
hay fork, 1 garden hoe, rat trap, hammer, gauge, sifter,
double tree, 4 skeins of woolen yarn, 1 churn and 1 cog all
valued at $500. January 1811 term, dismissed for want of
security for costs.

170 - 1811, Monongalia Superior Court. To the Sheriff of
Harrison County, summons James THOMAS to answer Benjamin and
John COMEGYE in a plea of debt for $1226.28 and $500 damage,
7 March and 30 May 1807. THOMAS not an inhabitant in March
and was not found in May. November 1811 term, dismissed by
the plaintiff's attorney.

170 - 1811, Monongalia Superior Court. Noah RIDGEWAY recovered against Absolom MORRIS $17 plus costs for a certain tres-
pass committed by Absolom. The judgement remained unpaid and
Bail Bond for Absolom was secured by William MORRIS on 15 May
1810. William MORRIS summoned to show cause, if any he can,
why RIDGEWAY should not have execution against him as security for MORRIS, 5 January and 13 June 1811.

170 - 1811, Monongalia Superior Court. "To the Honorable John
BROWN, Judge of the District Chancery Court at Staunton for
the Western District of Virginia." James WALKER's complaint:
On 20 October 1781, he obtained a Pre-emption Land Warrant
#1629 for 1000 acres as an appendage to his settle right
certificate. On 7 January 1782, he entered with the Surveyor
of Monongalia County a tract of 1000 acres joining his settle
right on Prickett's Creek. On 14 February 1782, he had a
survey entered on 210 acres, it being all the waste and
unappropriated lands remaining and not taken by other claims.
Because of the state of war in which the country was involved
soon after the survey, he moved to Pennsylvania for safety.
He learned that the Legislature gave the people instructions
to return their surveys to the Land Office which he was
compelled to do because of lack of money until about the year
1797 when he had his survey lodged in the Office of the
Register, paid the fees and obtained a grant on the survey
dated 21 July 1800. He said he never sold, assigned or
conveyed away the 210 acres to any one and had followed the
law to obtain a title and never knew of any other claim.
During his absence, while in Pennsylvania, Jacob PRICKETT had
a survey made in his own name by virtue of his (WALKER's)
warrant and made an entry of 180 acres of the said 210 acres
which survey was dated 7 November 1788. WALKER said he was
now informed that PRICKETT obtained a grant for the 180 acres
which grant is dated prior to the grant for the same land to
him. PRICKETT sold and conveyed the 180 acres to James
MORGAN who held possession at this time. WALKER said Nathan
SPRINGER obtained a title and had possession of the balance
of the 210 acres, about 30 acres. He said he applied to
PRICKETT, MORGAN and SPRINGER to convey their claim to him,
but they have refused and therefore he brings suit. Answer
of Nathan SPRINGER: He bought William PETTYJOHN's resident
right and he knew that WALKER once had a survey made on the
entry of 210 acres which ran into the lines of PETTYJOHN's
resident right, that sometime later, PETTYJOHN agreed to and
with WALKER to buy a part of the 210 acres for 40 shillings
and added it to the resident tract. By this agreement,
PETTYJOHN was to extend his survey on his resident right and
the purchase from WALKER on a straight line to PRICKETT's
Creek and to cross the creek and extend up the hill from the
creek. He said he had a grant for the land he claimed and
paid WALKER 40 shillings for the same. He understood that
WALKER sold the balance (180 acres) to Thomas PINDALL, now
deceased, who sold the same to Jacob PRICKETT, 26 March 1807.
Jacob PRICKETT's answer: He bought WALKER's right to the 180
acres for which he has a grant of Thomas PINDALL's, deceased,
who he then understood had purchased the same from WALKER.
He paid the purchase price and the land was surveyed for him
as assignee of WALKER and he obtained a grant from the
Commonwealth dated 28 June 1791. He sold and conveyed a part
of the same to James MORGAN and never knew of WALKER's claim

until the instigation of this suit. Signed by Jacob PRICKETT Jr., 1 March 1807. James MORGAN's answer: He bought 53 acres of the land from Jacob PRICKETT Jr., it being a part of the 180 acres as set out in PRICKETT's deposition. He bought 120 acres from Jacob PRICKETT Sr. joining the same and that PRICKETT had a grant for the land when he bought it. He said he understood WALKER claimed a part of the 120 acres but he also understood that about 18 or 20 years ago, WALKER set up a claim to a part of it and he and PRICKETT Sr. referred it to arbitration and it was determined in PRICKETT's favor. He said he purchased the land in 1793 and paid a fair price for it and never knew of any other claim until the instigation of this suit. Signed by MORGAN on 1 March 1807 in the presence of B. REEDER. At Chancery District Court held at Staunton, 1 August 1809 between Jacob WALKER, plaintiff, and James PRICKETT, James MORGAN and Nathan SPRINGER, defendants. Order to try the case at Monongalia Superior Court "to ascertain (1st) whether the plaintiff ever sold or transferred his right in the 210 acres survey in the bill mentioned, or any part thereof, and if any, how much, to Thomas PINDALL. (2nd) Whether he ever sold or transferred his interest in any part of the survey to William PETTYJOHN or to the defendant SPRINGER, if any, how much and return the verdict thereupon to be certified to this court." Chancery District Court, Staunton, "We the jury find (1st) that James WALKER did sell and transfer to Thomas PINDALL 280 acres of land in his bill mentioned, (2nd) we find that he did not sell the balance of 210 to Nathan SPRINGER or William PETTYJOHN." Notice from WALKER to the defendants of intent to hear the deposition of George HALLENBACK and others at the dwelling house of Jonathan WOODS, Esqr., (Licking Township) Muskingum County, Ohio, 1 June 1811. 1 August 1811, Clark HOLLENBACK's deposition: He was now 31 years of age and in 1786, WALKER sold PINDALL a tract of land and PINDALL gave, in part payment, a Negro boy named Josh, a few years older than he was at the time. The tract contained about 400 acres and was WALKER's old home place. He said he remembered the details so well because PINDELL sold his father 200 acres of the same land and the other 200 acres he sold to Edward GUTTRIDGE. He said he lived on the same land for 22 years and during that time he never heard of WALKER selling PINDELL any other land. George HOLLENBACK's deposition heard at the same time and place: In 1786 at May Court in Monongalia County at the house of Thomas PINDELL in Morgan Town, he saw PINDELL deliver to WALKER a Negro boy named Joshua in part payment (60 pounds) of a tract of land in Monongalia County on the east side of Monongahela River adjoining Elias PEARCE and John HOULT containing 400 acres being WALKER's old home place. 200 acres of the same land was sold to him and 200 acres to Edward GUTTRIDGE. He lived on the land about 22 years and never heard of PINDELL buying any other land from WALKER. He remembered the details so well because Jacob PINDELL offered to exchange 800 acres of woods lying on the west side of the Monongahela River for the 400 acres which his brother, Thomas, purchased from WALKER. Signed by George HOLLENBACK. Deposition of Hannah HOLLENBACK heard at the same time and place: She lived in Monongalia County in 1786, a few yards from PINDELL, and knew that Captain Thomas PINDELL, in the spring of the same year, bought a tract of land from WALKER containing 400 acres which was WALKER's old home place. She retold the story much the same as George and Clark HOLLENBACK's deposition and signed her deposition Hannah HOLLENBACK in the presence of Justice Nathan BAKER and Clerk Abel LEWIS of Muskingum County, Ohio. Notice from WALKER to the defendants of intent to hear the deposition of Scilley SIMKINS and others at the Courthouse of Knox County, Ohio, 1 June 1811. 22 July 1811, deposition of Scelley SIMKINS: On 16 January 1811, he was age 83 and in 1786, and before and after he lived in Monongalia County, he was well acquainted with Captain Thomas PINDELL who then lived in the same county with James WALKER Sr. In 1786, he was in company with PINDELL and Jesse MARTIN in Morgantown and PINDELL bragged and told him and MARTIN what a fine bargain he had from WALKER Sr. At the same time and place, he heard PINDELL say that he had bought 400 acres from WALKER Sr, it being his old home place in Monongalia County. He remembered that the land was situated on the east bank of the Monongahela River. He and MARTIN and several others heard PINDELL say that he paid WALKER, in part on the land, a certain Negro boy called Joshua and a certain sum of money which he could not recall the exact sum. SIMKINS said he heard MARTIN say to PINDALL "that if he had done so he, PINDELL, had put it into said WALKER purty deep and had got a fine bargain." Signed by Celley (x) SIMKINS before Justice Sam'l KRATZER and James SMITH, Clerk of Knox County, Ohio. Samuel HANWAY summoned to testify in behalf of PRICKETT, 6 March 1810. Jacob PINDALL summoned to testify in behalf of PRICKET, MORGAN and SPRINGER, 15 July 1811. 22 July 1811, Knox County, Ohio. Deposition of Joseph and Alexander WATKINS heard before Justice Samuel KRATZER: Both swore they were above the age of 33 years and in 1786, WALKER Sr. sold to PINDELL 400 acres of land in Monongalia County, it being WALKER's old home place on the east side of Monongahela River and gave a Negro boy named Joshua in part payment and they had no knowledge of WALKER selling any other land to PINDELL. Signed by KRATZER and James SMITH, Clerk of Knox County. Deposition of Jonathan HORNES: Many years ago John DOWNER, a Deputy Surveyor of Monongalia County, made a survey for him, 11 January 1808. HORNES swore he traveled 17 1/2 miles and crossed one ferry at 6 pence to attend to his deposition heard at DERING's Tavern in Morgantown. John DOWNER's deposition: On 7 November 1788, he surveyed for Jacob PRICKETT, assignee of James WALKER, 180 acres of land, a part of a Pre-emption Warrant of 1000 acres #1629 dated 20 October 1781 which is the same 180 acres for which Jacob PRICKETT Jr. has a grant as assignee of James WALKER bearing date 28 June 1791. He said he was assistant to Surveyor HANWAY and made the survey and Certificate of Survey and recorded it at the request of WALKER and PINDALL, now deceased. Neither WALKER nor PINDALL was present on the ground at the time of the survey, but PINDALL paid the survey fee, paid the chain bearers and found provisions for the crew, heard at the house of Zackqull MORGAN on 11 January 1808. John HOULT's deposition: He was one of the jurors called to settle a dispute between PRICKETT and WALKER because WALKER claimed a part of PRICKETT's resident right and the jury decided in favor of PRICKETT, 7 March 1808. Thomas GRIGGS' deposition: He was acquainted with WALKER who was a justice at the time when they all lived at the fort together. One morning WALKER came to him and insisted he let him have a pair of soles. Leather was scarce at that time and he let WALKER have the soles. WALKER told him if he had "a suit before him, he would decide in his favor, right or wrong," 7 March 1808. Evan MORGAN's deposition: At the time of a "great concourse of people meeting at Morgan Town," Isaac James WALKER received a note from Nathan SPRINGER or William PETTYJOHN for a quit claim for a small quantity of land on Pricketts Creek containing a Mill Seat and this note was on demand because James WALKER demanded payment at the time of receiving it, but it was not discharged, 11 January 1808. Surveyor Samuel HANWAY said he remembered writing a memo at the bottom of the survey that WALKER assigned the said entry to Thomas PINDALL. Dudley EVANS said he was one of the jurors called on to determine the dispute between WALKER and PRICKETT and there is a long narrative concerning how the jury arrived at their verdict in favor of PRICKETT. WALKER's plat for 210 acres adjoining his Settlement Survey on Pricketts Creek, part of Pre-emption Warrant #1629, dated 20 October 1781 and signed by Surveyor of Monongalia County Samuel HANWAY. Jacob PRICKETT Jr., assignee of James WALKER, plat for 180 acres on a branch of Pricketts Creek, dated 7 November 1788, part of Pre-emption Warrant #1629, dated 20 October 1781 and signed by Surveyor of Monongalia County Samuel HANWAY. A list of exhibits which includes the grants, surveys and other legal documents filed in this case. September 1811 term, verdict and judgement for the plaintiff.

170a - 1811, Monongalia Superior Court. David and Joseph BARKER summoned to answer Elizabeth LOWE, administratrix of Robert LOWE, deceased, in a plea of debt for $225 and $10 damage, 20 February and 7 June 1810. 1809, BARKER's account with Mrs. LOWE: July $5 in nails, $5.67 in cash. August $3 in nails and $7 in cash. October $23 in cash. July 30 1808, $43 loaned. Interest to 14 February $14.06. Note signed by David BARKER and Joseph (x) BARKER to Robert LOWE for $225 dated 4 September 1806, payable 8 September 1808 and witnessed by Aaron BARKER and Sarah BARKER. "The use of the within note for the use of Elizabeth LOWE a wife of Robert LOWE." On 30 July 1808, Robert LOWE signed a receipt for $43 paid on the note. Bail Bond for David and Joseph BARKER secured by Zackquill MORGAN, 7 January 1811. Appearance Bond signed by Joseph (x) BARKER secured by Rawley MARTIN, 27 July 1810. Appearance Bond signed by David BARKER secured by Zackquill MORGAN, 7 April 1810. "If BARKER comes forward and pays $50 and gives bond and approved security, Mr. WILSON is authorized to give eight months indulgence," signed by Justice D. DAVISSON Jr.

170a - 1811, Monongalia Superior Court. 5 September 1811, Benjamin JONES surviving partner of Benjamin and Robert JONES vs John MAGEE and James COBURN. "This day came the plaintiff by his attorney and notice of this motion being proved and the defendants being solemnly called came not and it appearing to the Court that the condition of the bond hath not been performed, it is therefore considered by the court that the plaintiff recover of the defendants $445 the penalty of said bond together with his cost, but this judgement is to be discharged by the payment of $220.19 with interest thereon at the rate of 6% per annum from 18 June 1810 until payment." Attachment issued 22 September 1810 which was levied on one bay horse.

170a - 1811, Monongalia Superior Court. Grand Jury, September 1811 term: Dudley EVANS, Jacob PALSLEY, Augustine WELLS, John SULLIVAN, David SCOTT, Jeremiah HOSKINSON, Enoch JONES, David KNOX, John SAUNDERS, William LANHAM, John CHISLER, George HITE, John A. BARKSHIRE (foreman), Henry HAMILTON, Nicholas B. MADERA, George SMITH, Asa HALL, George DORSEY, Godfrey GUSEMAN, Samuel SWEARINGEN, Richard PRICE, George CUNNINGHAM, John REED and Michael CLOUSE.

170a - 1811, Monongalia Superior Court. One black horse, one sorrel horse and _____, the property of William G. PAYNE, was attached at the suit of William LOWRY and Company for $158.60 with interest at the rate of 6% from 18 May 1809, with a credit of $111 paid 31 October 1809 plus costs. In order to retain possession of his property until time of public sale or his debt was paid, William G. PAYNE signed this Delivery Bond secured by Samuel HANWAY, 23 January 1811.

170a - 1811, Monongalia Superior Court. Enoch JONES summoned to answer William and Joseph LOWRY trading under the firm of William LOWRY & Company, merchants, in a plea of debt for $118.45 and $10 damage, 14 February 1811. A form note signed by JONES to LOWRY for $118.45 dated 1 July 1809 and witnessed by Joseph LOWRY. Appearance Bond signed by JONES secured by Robert DAVIS, 20 February 1810. September 1811 term, judgement confessed.

170a - 1811, Monongalia Superior Court. Benjamin MIDDLETON and Mary his wife summoned to answer Samuel CLUTTER and Hester his wife in a plea of slander damage $700, 25 July 1809. In July 1809, Mary was heard to say that Hester swore falsely in the case of Sarah JONES vs Mary MIDDLETON. Benjamin and Mary said that Samuel and Hester ought not have and maintain their action because Mary "is not guilty of the slander" as Samuel and Hester hath complained and because the said "Hester was guilty of swearing to what was false" before Justice Amos ROBERTS. Samuel CRANE summoned to testify in behalf of CLUTTER and wife, 8 September 1811. Joseph SEVERNS, Elizabeth MARTIN, William WORKMAN, John SEVERNS, William WALKER, Sarah JONES and James WEBSTER summoned to testify in behalf of MIDDLETON and wife, 2 March 1811. William WORKMAN summoned to testify in behalf of MIDDLETON, 29 August 1810. William WORKMAN and Cathrine his wife, living 8 miles from Morgantown on Crooked Run, summoned to testify in behalf of MIDDLETON, 19 August 1811. Elizabeth SINES, Mary MARTIN, Elizabeth ROMINE, Andrew WORKMAN, Amos ROBERTS, John JENKINS and William SINES summoned to testify in behalf of CLUTTER, 20 February and 25 August 1811. Joseph SEVERNS, Elizabeth MARTIN, William WORKMAN, John SEVERNS, William WALLER/WALKER, Sarah JONES, James WEBSTER and Daniel MARTIN summoned to testify in behalf of MIDDLETON, 16 July 1811. Daniel MARTIN, Sarah JONES, young Daniel SEVERNS and Katty WORKMAN summoned to testify in behalf of MIDDLETON, 11 March 1811. September 1811 term, "We the jury find for the plaintiff $17 in damages," James BOWLBY, foreman.

170a - 1811, Monongalia Superior Court. John SCOTT summoned to answer John DOWNEY, assignee of Samuel MARTIN, in a plea of covenant damages 900 pounds Pennsylvania money ($2400), 23 April 1810. DOWNEY complained that SCOTT failed to perform his part of the agreement. Article of Agreement between Samuel MARTIN, of Monongalia County, and John SCOTT, of York County, Pennsylvania, dated 1 September 1797. MARTIN agreed to convey in fee simple to SCOTT all his right, title, interest and claim in and to 357 acres, "where he now lived," as soon as he could obtain title from the commissioners. SCOTT, who paid MARTIN 355 pounds, 1 shilling and 9 pence in part payment, agreed to give his bond for 91 pounds, 3 shillings and 3 pence, the remainder of the purchase price, in 50 pound (Pennsylvania money) installments due in full on 1 April 1800. SCOTT also agreed to buy an adjoining tract, if MARTIN could procure it, and pay the same rate per acre as paid for the above. For true performance of this agreement, the parties bound themselves one to the other in the sum of 900 pounds. Signed by both MARTIN and SCOTT in the presence of Samuel WILLITS and John WILLITS. MARTIN assigned this agreement to DOWNEY on 25 June 1801 in the presence of Samuel LEWELLEN. "26 May 1800, Then received of John SCOTT $91.75 in part pay of the land said SCOTT now lives on provided said

MARTIN doth receive a cask of brandy left at Fort Pr_____ by Joseph WOOD rated at $80 which I have received a order for from said WOOD by order of said SCOTT," signed by Samuel MARTIN. Another receipt signed by MARTIN whereby he received brandy rated at $80, dated 25 December 180_. Another receipt signed by MARTIN on 15 May 1800 for 30 pounds which was assigned to Amos ROBERTS by order of the court. Appearance Bond signed by SCOTT secured by John COOPER and Jacob FOULK, 1 May 1810. September 1811 term, plea waived and judgement. SCOTT was granted an injunction to stay execution of the judgement until the matter could be heard in a Court of Equity and signed this bond secured by COOPER and FOULK to ensure all costs and awards would be paid in case the injunction should be dissolved, 4 September 1811.

170a - 1811, Monongalia Superior Court. Rawley MARTIN summoned to answer Michael CONNER in a plea of assault damage $100, 25 August 1810. Michael (x) CONNER assigned his interest in and to a judgement for costs he obtained in Superior Court against MARTIN to Nimrod EVANS on 18 December 1811. John A. BARKSHIRE, Dudley E. DENT and George V. DERING summoned to give evidence to the Grand Jury, 23 January 1810. September 1811 term, dismissed, agreed, judgement confessed for costs by the defendant.

170a - 1811, Monongalia Superior Court. Doctor Thomas BYRNE summoned to answer Joseph LOWRY in a plea of slander damage $5000, 30 April 1810. Joseph LOWRY, former merchant of Monongalia County but now a merchant of Harrison County, complained that Doctor Thomas BYRNE spoke these slanderous words against him, "you are a damned rascal and a damned trifling fellow and a damned cowardly rascal and I can give you a damned floging this minute if you will only turn out." John BYRNE's deposition heard at the house of Thomas MILLER: Sometime in the year 1808 or 1809, he was indebted to Joseph LOWRY and LOWRY agreed that if he would hire him a Negro boy called Harry for a certain length of time (which time he thinks was to expire on 1 April 1810) that he the said LOWRY would let the hire of the boy go in part payment of what he, BYRNE, owed LOWRY, to which he agreed and gave LOWRY his bond for the balance. Sometime after, BYRNE authorized LOWRY to sell the boy to John STEALEY. LOWRY let STEALEY have one of his boys named Peter in place of Harry until Harry's time should expire with LOWRY, at which time he expected LOWRY would give up Harry to STEALEY. He said he wanted LOWRY to keep the boy until the amount of the debt was satisfied but LOWRY said he intended to leave this place and refused to hire him for a longer period of time. Rawley SCOTT summoned to testify in behalf of BYRNE, 1 April 1811. Charles BYRN summoned to testify in behalf of LOWRY, 5 September 1811.

170a - 1811, Monongalia Superior Court. Brooke County. Two beds and bedding, 1 case of drawers, 1 book case, 1 shot gun and a quantity of cooper's stuff, the property of James GRIFFITH and Jno EDIE/EDIR, was attached at the suit of the Trustees of Randolph Academy for $200 to be discharged by the payment of $34.78 1/2 debt plus interest and costs. In order to retain possession of their property until time of public sale or their debt was paid, Jas. GRIFFITH and John EDIE signed this Delivery Bond secured by John HAGEN Jr., 18 June 1810. Deputy John COX for Sheriff William BROWN. September 1811 term, quashed (voided).

170a - 1811, Monongalia Superior Court. William STILES and Anna (Nancy) his wife summoned to answer Jonah BALDWIN and Mary his wife in a plea of slander damage $1000, 12 March 1811. April 1811 term, dismissed, agreed. Deputy Joseph ALLEN for Sheriff Nicholas VANDERVORT.

170a - 1810, Monongalia Superior Court. David GALLOWAY summoned to answer Andrew BOID/BOYD in a plea of covenant broken damage $800, 15 May 1810. Bail Bond for BOYD secured by James TROY, 17 September 1810. Appearance Bond signed by GALLWAY secured by James TROY, 14 July 1810.

170a - 1811, Monongalia Superior Court. Henry BARKER summoned to answer an indictment against him for assault upon Rawley MARTIN, 6 June and 12 October 1810. Rawley MARTIN summoned to give evidence to the Grand Jury, 6 June and 12 October 1810. Indictment: On 4 January 1810, Henry BARKER, laborer, assaulted Rawley MARTIN, yeoman. September 1811 term, not prosecuted.

170a - 1811, Monongalia Superior Court. John RENCHER summoned to answer an indicted against him for an assault on Patrick HANEY, 7 July, 4 November 1809, 5 June and 10 October 1810. RINCHER not an inhabitant of this state. September 1811 term, not prosecuted.

170a - 1811, Monongalia Superior Court. William WOODS summoned to answer an indictment against him, 7 June, 12 November 1809 and 5 June 1810. WOODS not an inhabitant, moved to Pennsylvania. On 10 April 1809, an election was held at the Courthouse of Monongalia County for the election of two delegates to next General Assembly and for the election of one representative of the present district composed of the Counties of Monongalia, Brooke, Ohio, Harrison, Wood and Randolph in the Congress of the United States and for the election of one senator to represent the district. The election was continued from day to day for three days and on 12 April 1809 and during the continuation of the election, William WOODS, laborer, appeared at the Courthouse and voted for two delegates for the General Assembly and for one person to represent the district in the Congress and for one senator. ___ah LINSLEY was a candidate for Congress and objected to WOODS and required WOODS to be polled and to declare by what right he had so to vote and required that he be sworn according to law. He was sworn by Sheriff John PAYNE and said "in his conscience believed himself duly qualified to vote for delegates to serve in General Assembly." The jury was of the opinion that WOODS committed willful and corrupt perjury. Marmaduke EVANS and Zackquill MORGAN were called as witnesses on 7 June 1809, 6 June and 12 October 1810. September 1811 term, not prosecuted.

170a - 1811, Monongalia Superior Court. William GODDARD summoned to answer an indictment against him for an assault on Charles BOYLES, 5 November 1809, 6 June and 12 October 1810. GODDARD not an inhabitant of this state. Indictment: On 14 October 1809, GODDARD assaulted BOYLES, information given by Rawley MARTIN. Rawley MARTIN and Charles BOYLES summoned to give evidence to the Grand Jury, 6 November 1809, 6 June and 12 December 1810. September 1811 term, not prosecuted.

170a - 1810, Monongalia Superior Court. John EVANS recovered a judgement against William HAMBLETON for $8.52 costs in defending an action of covenant brought and prosecuted by HAMBLETON against EVANS. The judgement remained unpaid and EVANS brought suit against HAMBLETON for costs and damages, 8 June 1810.

170a - 1811, Monongalia Superior Court. James SCOTT summoned to answer Robert FERRELL in a plea of trespass on the case damage $500, money due by assumpsit, 17 April 1810. FERRELL complained that on 24 August 1805, SCOTT owed him $318.30 by virtue of a debt SCOTT owed to Alexander and Robert HAWTHORN which FERRELL paid for him, at which time SCOTT promised to repay FERRELL whenever requested. William G. PAYNE summoned to testify in behalf of FERRELL, 1 April 1811. Benjamin REEDER and Isaac POWELL summoned to testify in behalf of SCOTT, 2 March and 15 July 1811. Alexander HAWTHORN, William G. PAYNE and Nimrod EVANS summoned to testify in behalf of FERRELL, 3 September 1811. "Dear Sir: Capt. Robert FERRELL informs me that he has authorized you to receive the money that I am accountable to him. The money I shall pay you against the 15th next month or probably before," signed by James SCOTT, 24 August 1807. Deputy George DERING for Sheriff N. VANDERVORT. September 1811 term, "We the jury find for the plaintiff $280 with legal interest on $250.64 from 3 May 1805, interest on $27.36 from 1 September 1808 until payment," C. BARKSHIRE, foreman.

170a - 1811, Monongalia Superior Court. Rob't FERRELL, Dudley EVANS, Simeon EVERLY, William GEORGE, John FAIRFAX, Jacob PALSLEY, Nicholas VANDERVORT, Augustus WERNINGER, James E.

BELL/BEALL, John STEALEY, Booz BURRIS/BURROWS, Thomas MILLER, William WILLEY, James RICE, James SCOTT, William BARNES, John DEAN, David MORGAN, Samuel MINOR, Morgan MORGAN, John NUZUM, William JARRETT, Frederick HARSH, Ralph BARKSHIRE and John COX, Justices of Monongalia County, summoned to come before the Judges of the Superior Court and answer those things of which they stand charged for failing to do their duty as justices and failing to build or keep in repair a secure jail and hold court, 5 June 1810. Thomas WILSON and Mathew GAY summoned to give evidence to the Grand Jury, 6 June 1810. GAY and WILSON said court had not been held since August 1808 term except for one jury cause in a civil suit, although there were several cases pending and they said the jail was unfit for keeping prisoners, 19 October 1809. GAY said he had practiced law in Monongalia County for several years. Deputy George DERING for Sheriff Lemuel JOHN. September 1811 term, not prosecuted.

Also in this file - - Richard and Joseph HARRISON summoned to give evidence to the Grand Jury in the case of the Commonwealth vs John RENCHER on an indictment of assault and battery, 6 November 1809, 5 June and 12 October 1810.

171 - 1811, Monongalia Superior Court. Robert FERRELL summoned to satisfy Thomas BUTLER $509.34, which BUTLER recovered against him in a previous cause, 30 May and 18 September 1811. FERRELL not found.

171 - 1811, Monongalia Superior Court. Order to attach the property of William THOMAS and Hugh EVANS to satisfy $450 plus cost on a forthcoming bond which George DEARTH, assignee of John FAIRFAX, recovered against them in Superior Court, 25 February 1811.

171 - 1811, Monongalia Superior Court. Wood County. Order to attach the property of John STOKELY to satisfy $344.63 plus cost and interest from 20 May 1803 which Nathaniel BREADING, George HOGUE, Robert BRAND, John MOON, David BREADING, John SOLLIDY? and John PORTER recovered against him in District Court for damages in an action of assumpsit, 29 January 1811. Attachment levied on one Negro man, 1 woman and 2 children, 15 February 1811.

171 - 1811, Monongalia Superior Court. Order to attach the property of William STAFFORD to satisfy $100 with interest from 17 September 1807 plus cost which Jesse EVANS recovered against him in Superior Court, 15 March 1811.

171 - 1811, Monongalia Superior Court. Order to attach the property of Benjamin MIDDLETON and Mary his wife to satisfy $17 and $39.66 plus costs which Samuel CLUTTER and Hester his wife recovered against them for slanderous word spoken, 17 September 1811.

171 - 1811, Monongalia Superior Court. Order to expose to public sale the property of Thomas ROYAL, Hugh MORGAN and John MILLER to satisfy $133.33 with 6% interest from 1 May 1799 plus costs which William HAMBLETON recovered against them by virtue of a Replevin Bond in Superior Court, 11 February 1811. Money made and paid over to plaintiffs by Attorney Mathew GAY.

171 - 1811, Monongalia Superior Court. Thomas LAIDLEY summoned to satisfy Daniel KIGER the sum of $800 with 6% interest from 27 May 1806 plus cost which KIGER recovered against him in Superior Court for a debt, 30 May, 16 July and 18 September 1811. LAIDLEY not found.

171 - 1811, Monongalia Superior Court. Order to expose to public sale the property of Thomas ROYAL, Hugh MORGAN and John MILLER to satisfy $110 with 6% interest from 1 March 1807 plus costs which Charles GLASSCOCK recovered against them by virtue of a Replevin Bond in Superior Court, 11 February 1811. Money made and paid over to plaintiffs by Attorney Mathew GAY. $20 retained for Sheriff's charges.

171 - 1811, Monongalia Superior Court. John RYAN summoned to satisfy Anthoney CARROL the sum of $__.09 plus costs which CARROL recovered against him in Superior Court, 23 May 1811. Money made and paid over to the plaintiff.

171 - 1811, Monongalia Superior Court. Hampshire County. Order to attached the property of David LONG to satisfy Charles GECKQUIN and Henry KUNDE for the use of Henry SHRODER the sum of $1464.50 with 6% interest from 9 January 1806 plus costs which they recovered against him in Superior Court for a debt, 2 June and 17 August 1811.

171 - 1811, Monongalia Superior Court. Order to attach the property of Abraham and Simeon WOODROW to satisfy John FETTY the sum of $10.17 which FETTY recovered against them for costs in a certain action in Superior Court, 30 May 1811. No property found.

171 - 1811, Monongalia Superior Court. Absolom MORRIS summoned to satisfy Noah RIDGEWAY the sum of $17 plus costs which RIDGEWAY recovered against him for trespass, 24 January 1811. MORRIS not an inhabitant.

171 - 1811, Monongalia Superior Court. Order to attach the property of Charles SHIELDS and William KENNEDY to satisfy the sum of $460 which John McFARLAND recovered against him in Superior Court a for debt plus costs, 29 January 1811.

171 - 1811, Monongalia Superior Court. Order to attach the property of Thomas McKINEY to satisfy the sum of $143 and

$30.72 which James MURPHY recovered against him for breach of covenant, 18 September 1811.

171 - 1811, Monongalia Superior Court. Order to attach the property of William G. PAYNE to satisfy the sum of $52 which Thomas BUTLER recovered against him for a debt, 18 September 1811.

171 - 1811, Monongalia Superior Court. Order to attach the property of John SCOTT to satisfy the sum of $280 with 6% interest from 3 May 1805 plus costs which Robert FERRELL recovered against him for damages and costs, 18 September 1811.

171 - 1811, Monongalia Superior Court. Order to attach the property of Enoch JONES to satisfy the sum of $118.45 with 6% interest from 5 July 1809 plus costs which William LOWRY and Joseph LOWRY, merchants, recovered against him for a debt, 18 September 1811. Money made by Deputy George DERING for Sheriff N. VANDERVORT.

171 - 1811, Monongalia Superior Court. William STAFFORD summoned to satisfy Jesse EVANS the sum of $100 with 6% interest from 17 September 1807 plus costs which EVANS recovered against him for debt, 18 September 1811. STAFFORD not found.

171 - 1811, Monongalia Superior Court. Order to attach the property of Arthur TRADER to satisfy the sum of $112 with 6% interest from 1 April 1806 plus costs which Luke WALPOLE recovered against him for breach of covenant, 18 September 1811.

171 - 1811, Monongalia Superior Court. Abraham and Simion WOODROW summoned to satisfy John FETTY the sum of $10.57 which FETTY recovered against him for costs in a previous action, 19 September 1811. Money made by Deputy G. DERING.

171 - 1811, Monongalia Superior Court. Elijah BUTLER summoned to satisfy the sum of $233.90 with 6% interest from 9 June 1806 which Edward McCARTY and William ARMSTRONG, merchants, recovered against him for a debt, 18 September 1811.

171 - 1811, Monongalia Superior Court. Philip (x) LEWIS assigned a judgement he obtained in Superior Court against Abraham ELIOT to Thomas WILSON and Mathew GAY, 3 September 1811. Abraham ELLIOTT summoned to satisfy the sum of $30 and $15.73 which Philip LEWIS recovered against him for slander, 18 September 1811. Money made by Deputy Rawley EVANS.

171 - 1811, Monongalia Superior Court. Persila HERNDON summoned to satisfy the sum of $5.09 which James WILSON recovered against her for costs in a previous action, 18 September 1811. HERRDON not found.

171 - 1811, Monongalia Superior Court. Andrew BOYD summoned to satisfy the sum of $3.92 which David GALLAWAY recovered against him for costs in a previous action, 18 September 1811. This summons was served on one Andrew BOYD who lived near LYMAN, but he was not the one named. The deputy did not have time to serve the summons on the right Andrew BOYD.

171 - 1811, Monongalia Superior Court. William G. PAYNE summoned to satisfy the sum of $150 which William LOWRY and Company recovered against him for debt on a forthcoming bond, 18 September 1811. Money made by Deputy G. DERING.

171 - 1811, Monongalia Superior Court. Samuel SWEARINGEN summoned to satisfy the sum of $20.21 which Moses KINCAID recovered against him for slander, 18 September 1811. No property found.

171 - 1811, Monongalia Superior Court. John CLARK summoned to satisfy the sum of $340 and $16.43 which Charles HANEY recovered against him for slander, 18 September 1811. CLARK not an inhabitant.

171 - 1811, Monongalia Superior Court. Thomas SPENCER summoned to satisfy the sum of $4.90 which Charles BYRN recovered against him for costs in a previous action, 18 September 1811. SPENCER not found.

171 - 1811, Monongalia Superior Court. John STEALEY summoned to satisfy the sum of $550 with 6% interest from 21 May 1806 plus costs which John HAYE/HOYE recovered against him for a debt, 18 September 1811. Bond taken by Deputy George DERING.

172 - 1812, Monongalia Superior Court. Colder HAYMOND summoned to answer William and Joseph LOWRY, merchants, assignee of Simon REEDER who was assignee of Benjamin REEDER, in a plea of debt for $120.72 and $10 damage, 14 February 1811. Bail Bond for HAYMOND secured by George DERING, 28 August 1811. Two years note signed by HAYMOND to Benjamin REEDER dated 11 October 1807 for $120.72 with interest and witnessed by Jacob GUSEMAN. Appearance Bond for HAYMOND secured by Jno STEALEY, 11 March 1811. Assignment to Simon REEDER dated 3 November 1808. Assignment to LOWRY and Company dated 30 March 1809. April 1812 term, "We the jury find for the plaintiff the debt in the declaration mentioned with interest on the same from 11 October 1809," Nath'l HIBB, foreman.

172 - 1812, Monongalia Superior Court. Enoch WARMAN summoned to answer Adam McGILL in a plea of assault, 14 February 1812. July 1812 term, dismissed by order of the plaintiff.

172 - 1811, Monongalia Superior Court. The next three cases or actions are filed as one: DAVIS and COPES and LINDENBERGER

and Company vs Benjamin REEDER, DAVIS and COPES vs Benjamin REEDER, Charles BARING Jr., assignee, vs Benjamin REEDER and DAVIS and COPES and LINDENBERGER and Company vs Benjamin REEDER and the Administrator of Hezekiah REEDER, deceased. There are numerous pages of narratives, correspondences, rules and exceptions filed. The abstracts or quotes given here are representative of those filed. Order to release Benjamin REEDER, a prisoner by virtue of an execution against him at the suit of DAVIS and COPES, assignee of Anthoney RENTZAL, for the sum of $1765.54 debt plus costs, signed by Justices Wm. N. JARRETT and Robert FERRELL, 5 November 1808. "Upon a rule heretofore made, this day came the parties by their counsel and P. DODDRIDGE having yesterday deposited with the clerk of the court $795 subject to the further order of this court in obedience to the order herein made at the last term, James S. WATSON, administrator of Hezekiah REEDER, deceased, is by his consent made a party defendant to this rule and claims the said money so deposited and having by the verdict of a jury and the judgement of this court yesterday in an amiable action against the clerk recovered $500, part thereof, it is ordered that the clerk do pay the said $500 to the administrator and that the rule be made absolute as to $295 the remainder of the money aforesaid and the same to be paid the plaintiffs to be divided between them, pro-rata, according to the amount of their respective demands and that the clerk do thereupon enter full satisfaction of the balance due upon the judgement of REEDER vs BARING referred to in the rule and the respective counsel of the plaintiffs to enter satisfaction for so much on the word of the _____ _____ after deducting therefrom the whole of their costs in the prosecution of the said rule in this court and in the Moorefield Superior Court." "Morgantown, 26 May 1806, Gentleman, In the month of February 1804, my brother Benjamin REEDER transferred to me judgement he had against Charles BARING for certain purposes. Among these purposes, a debt to you was to be satisfied. The judgement against BARING has been affirmed in the Court of Appeals and I am informed the money is in the hands of his bail, Mr. LINSLEY and Mr. DODDRIDGE. If you will take an order on the bail for the money and release my brother from the debt, I am willing at any time to give it to you. Your Ob't Servant, H. REEDER." "Morgantown, 3 July 1806, Gentleman, I have received your two letters. By the last you say Mr. LINSLEY has written to you on this subject. I have shown the letter to my brother who says he supposed LINSLEY wrote in the way he did in order to get some discount made for his own benefit by playing the `yanky' and has forbid my having any thing to say to him on the subject, but to request of you to give me a definitive answer whether you will accept of this mode of payment or not by the 10th of the next month. Proceedings are going against LINSLEY and DODDRIDGE as bail of BARING. Yours, H. REEDER." To COPE & Brothers, Baltimore: "Morgantown, 30 October 1806,

Gentlemen, My brother being absent, I have opened your letter to him of the 16th. I presume he now considers himself as done with the business to which the letter relates. The notes of STEALEY which he offered you had been already given payable at the date he stated and were offered as a loan provided you would accept of them. Therefore any limitation on that score is out of the question and if you take them they must be payment unconditional. For my part, I wish you were paid and if you mean to do anything be pleased to write me at Richmond for which place I shall set out before your letter could reach me here and shall remain during the session of the Legislature for neither the venom of your attorney nor your own ___our can prevent me. And permit me to add that my determination is fixed if it should be for 20 years which is longer than I could affect to live and it should cost me three times the amount of your claim that the unnecessary expense to which you have put me by your unnecessary `risour´ occasioned I suppose by the mean and dastardly disposition of your attorney to oppress and persecute shall be paid from the time the money has been offered to you in your attorney´s hands. With due regard, B. REEDER." "Morgantown, 17 November 1806, Gentlemen: On my return two days ago from Alexandria, I received your letter of the 16th which my brother informs me was opened and answered by him. Knowing well all the circumstances which have led to our correspondences, also knowing that although my brother is bound to pay you, it is a hard case on him and having made you a very fair and generous offer, my fixed determination was to have nothing more to do in the business after my last letter unless something explicit was done. You know of the transfer to me, for your use, but you refuse to accept it. The notes of STEALEY were offered a loan by a Gentlemen who has perhaps more confidence in me than you have and if you had taken them as absolute payment they would have been delivered. Therefore, I am done with the business farther than to apply that part of the money as the fo____ directions of my brother shall advise, and all further correspondence on the subject must be had with himself, he goes in a day or two to Richmond, Your Ob´t Servant, H. REEDER." Statement: REEDER´s judgement vs BARING $4000, damages on appeal $1850. Another judgement obtained in Morgantown District Court now on new trial at Moorefield $950, total $6600. Assignments of the above made by REEDER: to DAVIS and COPES $900, John LAIRD $3000, Nathan JOHNSON $100, BROWN, RANDOLPH and NICHOLAS $500. Interest from 10 February 1804 $1247.50. Salary of Hezekiah REEDER from 1789 inclusive until the summer 1807 at $120 per year is $1020, paid of the above $225, total $6542.50. Difference $57.50 when the judgement is obtained. REEDER, who was charged in execution and committed to jail at the suit of Frederick LINDENBERGER and Company on a judgement issued from the Monongalia County Court on 25 August 1807 for the sum of 247 pounds, 16 shillings and 10 pence ($660.91) Pennsylvania currency with 6% interest plus costs, escaped from jail on 3 November 1808. Arrest Warrant issued to all officials to retake him and return him to debtor's prison, 4 November 1808. Prison Bound Bond signed by REEDER secure by Hedgeman TRIPLETT and Alexander HAWTHORN, 1 November 1808. "Jail broken and taken up on the Escape Warrant this 5th day of November 1808 by me Jno C. PAYNE, DS, for S. MORGAN, SMC." "I have conveyed property and debts to such of my creditors as would receive it. The rest of my estate amounting to 7320 acres of land, I have conveyed in trust to William G. PAYNE to pay my debts all which will appear of record, a true schedule, B. REEDER," November 1808. John LAIRD, of George-town, District of Columbia, Washington County, swore that Robert PATTON Jr. (under the firm of Robert PATTON and Charles SCOTT), of Alexandria, was indebted to him for a previous transaction and they assigned him REEDER's note in the amount of 571 pounds, 16 shillings and 3 pence sterling. REEDER owed them the same amount and they owed LAIRD a larger sum. The note was dated 19 August 1803, made out to LAIRD. After the note remained unpaid until January 1806, LAIRD asked PATTON to pay the debt some other way which he did and the note was returned to PATTON, 5 April 1810. On 12 April 1810, PATTON swore these facts were true. 6 September 1810, REEDER swore that "John LAIRD was informed of the transfer made to H. REEDER of the judgements vs Charles BARING Jr. for the purpose of satisfying a debt due from him the said REEDER to the said LAIRD and that he hath been informed and believes LAIRD, in consequence of said transfer, did not call on his security for the debt he owed LAIRD until sometime in 1806 and he expects proof can be made of the aforesaid facts by the next term." District Court Jurors in the case of REEDER vs BARING, in trover, at September 1801 term: James JENKINS, David MOORE, Henry JACKSON, Thomas McKINLEY, Thomas CHIPPS, Mathew WILSON, John HALL, Josiah HOSKINSON, George BALTZELL, James STAFFORD, George HITE and William HAYMOND who determined that the defendant was guilt and assessed the plaintiff's damages to $1148.34 plus costs. "21 September 1808. Credit this judgement with the debt interest and plaintiff's costs on a judgement recovered at May 1808 term by the defendant as assignee of John HOYE, assignee of Benjamin STODDARD, surviving obligee of FORREST & STODDARD against the plaintiff for a debt of $1909.65, interest $1591.33, costs $43.96, $3544.94. Also with $494.50 part of a judgement recovered by the defendant as assignee of Hanson BRISCO against the plaintiff in the same May 1808 term and off set by and of this Court at September 1808 term which sums amount to $4039.44 the damages and costs in this record." At a January 1810 Hardy County Court, REEDER sued LINDSLEY and DODDRIDGE, bail securities for BARING. District Court Jurors in the case of REEDER vs BARING, in case, at September 1801 term: Henry BARNES, Hugh SIDWELL, John CARTER, John BILLS, Thomas FORSTER, John SCOTT, Joseph SCOTT, Joseph

GRATE, William LANHAM, Christopher STEALEY, James SCOTT and Robert HAWTHORN who determined the defendant was guilty and assessed the plaintiff's damages to $4000 plus costs. September 1811 term, continued and order set aside and rule made absolute.

172 – 1812, Monongalia Superior Court. James KILE, shoemaker, summoned to answer those things of which he stands indicted for an assault on Arthur CHAMBERS, schoolmaster, 28 April 1812. Elizabeth JOHN and Benjamin StCLAIR summoned to testify in behalf of KILE, 26 August 1812. Deputy George DERING for Sheriff N. VANDERVORT. April 1812 term, "We the jury find for the defendant," David SWINDLER, foreman.

172 – 1812, Monongalia Superior Court. "This Indenture made 5 September 1812 between John KIMMERER, of Monongalia County and State of Virginia, of the one part and the members or leading rulers of the Regular Baptist Church holding such principles as the fore knowledge of God in Eternal Election and Perseverance of the Saints through grace and c_____ of the County and State afs'd of the other part witnesseth that for and consideration of the sum of fifteen dollars current money of this State to the said John KIMMER in hand paid at or before the sealing and delivering of these presents the receipt whereof is hereby acknowledged and by these presents do grant, bargain and sell, aline and convey and confirm unto the said members or leading rulers of the aforesaid church or there `suckseeders' a certain lot of ground lying and being in the aforesaid county of Monongalia and situated or binding as followeth, to wit, on the west side of the said John KIMMERS plantation formerly surveyed for a meeting house and burying ground for that church and settlement, the burying ground to be free for any that chooses to bury there and bounded as followeth, to wit, beginning at a poplar in said John KIMMER's line and running thence south fifty east fifteen poles to a white oak, thence with the old line north twenty east thirty eight poles to the beginning containing one acre and three quarters of an acre of land with all the profits and appurtenances thereunto belonging unto the said members or rulers of the said church and their `suckseeders' forever to their only proper use benefit and behalf of them ... and free from all other encumbrances do forever hereafter warrant and defend in witness thereof of the said John KIMMERER hath hereunto set his hand and affixed his seal the day and year above written. Signed, sealed and delivered in the presence of _____ _____ the date before signed." Recorded Book E at page 108. Benjamin TRIMBLY to pay fee.

299

172 - 1812, Monongalia Superior Court. Duncan F. McRAE, laborer, summoned to answer a presentment against him for assault on Jacob FOULK on 4 April 1812, 28 April 1812. Noah LINSLY, Attorney for the Commonwealth. Rawley EVANS and David SEAMAN swore to give evidence and were summoned on 28 April 1812. Moses WELLS summoned to testify in behalf of McRAE, 8 September 1812. Samuel G. WILSON, Abraham WOODROW and Nathaniel WEBB summoned to testify in behalf of McRAE, 25 August 1812. September 1812 term, "We the jury find the defendant guilty and assess his fine to $.01," C. MATTHEW, foreman.

172 - 1812, Monongalia Superior Court. Enos DAUGHERTY summoned to answer Thomas and Abner LORD, for the use of E. PUTNAM, in a plea of debt for $320 with interest at 10% from 1 January 1803, 12 March 1812. Demand note signed by Abner LORD to Robert FOSSETT for $42.16 dated 28 March 1808 and witnessed by Simion POOLS. On 28 October 1808, LORD wrote a letter to E. DAUGHERTY requesting him to pay FAUSET the amount of the note because FAUSET was DAUGHERTY's neighbor and it would be most convenient. Demand Note signed by E. DAUGHERTY to Abner LORD for 4 pounds and 9 pence dated 12 August 1802. "26 October 1807, Sir, please to pay Abraham BIXLER $1 on my account and by so doing you will much oblige your friend, Lemuel JOHN, Enes DOCERTY." "Abner LORD's order in favor of Fauquire McCRAY for $196.20 dated 22 June 1804 to 16 March 1805, $17 part of the order to be paid by a steer delivered to McCRAY by Jonas BENSON in the fall of 1804 ____ ____ on this order. DAUGHERTY is accountable only for the balance of the order." Morgantown, 11 August 1802, note signed by E. DAUGHERTY to Thomas and Abner LORD for $320 with interest from 1 June, due 1 January 1803 and witnessed by T. C. GRIFFITH. April 1812 term, "Please to enter a judgement by confession for $200.67 with interest at 6% from 28 November 1808 until payment, Stay of Execution one year," N. EVANS, Esqr., Clerk of the Superior Court of Monongalia County, 8 April 1812. Signed by E. DAUGHERTY.

172 - 1812, Monongalia Superior Court. LINDENBERGER and Co. vs Benjamin REEDER. Rule of Court. On a judgement against REEDER in 1808, REEDER entered his schedule of insolvency and was released from jail. However, he had due him on a judgement the sum of $666.30. This amount was to be divided among his creditors.

172 - 1812, Monongalia Superior Court. John W. THOMPSON summoned to answer Ruth BILLS in a plea of debt due by account, 15 April 1812. Jacob FULK, Maria THOMPSON, Nicholas MADERA, Sally BILLS, ____ WEBB and George THOMPSON summoned to testify in behalf of John W. THOMPSON, no date. Ruth BILLS' account: 11 June 1807 to ware John BILLS got 0.5.0; 9 August 1808 to ware 0.3.9; to 7 1/2 pounds sugar 0.5.7; 29 August to ware 0.7.4 1/2; 5 November to ware 0.4.3; to ware Sally

300

got 0.3.6; to 2 1/2 bushels potatoes 0.5.0; 3 pint boals
Hiram got 0.1.1 1/2; 4 May 1809 by self 1.4.6; 10 June to
ware 5 pint boals 0.2.3; August to 9 bushels corn @ 3/0 per
1.2.0; 21 September to ware 0.3.9 and 0.2.4; 7 October to
ware by Sally 0.4.7 1/2; to three bushels of wheat 0.12.0;
to 7 pounds flax by Sary 0.5.3; 2 1/2 bushels corn 0.6.3; 4
November to ware by Sarah 0.1.3; 6 March 1810 to ware 0.10.0;
to rent of my house 9 months 6.15.0. Total 12.8.10. 24 April
1812 term, dismissed at plaintiff's costs. "Mrs. BILLS is
in THOMPSON's debt $6.50 which she agrees to be right and she
will pay."

172 - 1812, Monongalia Superior Court. James M. THOMPSON,
house carpenter, summoned to answer an indictment against him
for assault on John LAZELL, 28 April 1812. Thomas LAZELL,
John GIDLEY, Gincy THOMPSON, Daniel THOMPSON, John THOMPSON
and John WALKER summoned to testify in behalf of James M.
THOMPSON, 7 September 1812. Thomas LAZZELL Jr. summoned to
give evidence to the Grand Jury, 28 April 1812. John GIDLEY
and Thomas LAZLE summoned to testify in behalf of THOMPSON, 7
September 1812. September 1812 term, "We the jury find for
the defendant," C. MADERA, foreman.

172 - 1812, Monongalia Superior Court. James G. WATSON,
administrator of Hezekiah REEDER, deceased, complained that
on 7 September 1812, Nimrod EVANS owed him $795 and refused
payment and therefore he brings suit. William N. JARRETT,
Enos DAUGHERTY and George HITE summoned to testify in behalf
of WATSON, 10 September 1812. George HITE's deposition: "Hez.
REED(ER) lived at 96, it might be 95. Question: Did he live
with him in as on wages? He attended store, went to business
over the mountains and hill, etc., farming, etc. He did
attend to twenty acres, tended the farm corn, dug coal, etc.
Mr. WILSON: Considered him as son, seen him attend to corn,
haul wood, work farm ten years ago, did good after that,
attended to his business. Had he any other man to settle his
accounts? Wm. N. G. was to have $240. Hez. REEDER was
attentive to your business, clothing not extra, _____ _____,
attended to the firm and Co. He was ____ the judgement and he
proposed to go into partnership with his brother in January
1807 or 1808, not a Negro slave 18 settled his account books.
I know, kept store after PRINDLE left was fall, attend store,
farm and family mill, labored himself, etc. Doing farm
business, worked hard. If you think him employed by Benj.
REEDER, you will pay him for work time, if not for what it
was worth, they paid for his work." September 1812 term, "We
the jury find for plaintiff $500 in damages," Robert FERAL,
foreman.

172 - 1812, Monongalia Superior Court. Thomas LAZZELL Jr.,
laborer, summoned to answer to those things of which he
stands indicted for assault on Daniel THOMPSON, son of John,

on 15 March 1812, 30 April 1812. James M. THOMPSON summoned to give evidence to the Grand Jury, 28 April 1812. Thomas SMITH, Zaney LAZELL, John WALKER, Samuel BOUSLOG, Waitman FURBEE and James BODLEY summoned to testify in behalf of LAZELL, 4 September 1812. September 1812 term, judgement for the plaintiff. "We the jury find the defendant guilty and amerce him in $.01," Samuel G. WILSON, foreman.

172 - 1812, Monongalia Superior Court. John LAZZELL, laborer, summoned to answer those things of which he stands indicted for an assault on James M. THOMPSON, 28 April 1812. James M. THOMPSON summoned to give evidence to the Grand Jury, 30 April 1812. September 1812 term, "We the jury find for the defendant," William JOHN, foreman.

172 - 1812, Monongalia Superior Court. John GARLOW summoned to answer Joseph WOLFORD and Ann his wife in a plea of trespass damage $500, 26 August 1809. WOLFORD complained that from July 1808 until July 1809, GARLOW, with force and arms, entered their property and carried away hay and other valuable things and therefore they bring suit. Joseph WOLFORD and Ann his wife vs John GARLOW in trespass. WOLFORD said they ought not be prevented from having and maintaining their action against GARLOW because after the death of Christopher GARLOW and before the alleged trespass, viz, on 6 September 1800, GARLOW did, for a valuable consideration, release and quit all his then claim of in and to the land to Ann WOLFORD, widow of Christopher GARLOW, deceased, and after the death of GARLOW and during the time of the alleged trespass, possessed the lands as her dower right. John GARLOW said he was not guilty of the charges mentioned in the declaration because on 2 September 1796, Christopher GARLOW made his last will and testament and devised all his lands to be the property of Ann GARLOW and John GARLOW for the support and education of his younger children until his daughter, Hannah, should arrive at the age of 18 and that which was cut and carried away was his right and this he could verify. Mary CRAWFORD, John ___ard DUGAL, C. WOOLFORD, Daniel WOOLFORD, Lovin GARLOW, John SNIDER Sr., Simeon EVERLY and Henry YOST summoned to testify in behalf of Joseph WOLFORD and wife, 25 August 1810. John RIKS, John BIZERT and Daniel GARLOW summoned to testify in behalf of GARLOW, 13 March 1812. John YOST summoned to testify in behalf of WOLFORD and wife, 3 September 1810. Joseph PICKENPAUGH summoned to testify in behalf of WOLFORD and wife, 5 September 1810. Daniel GARLOW summoned to testify in behalf of GARLOW, 5 _____ 1810. September 1812 term, the undersigned parties met at the house of Widow GARLOW for the purpose of dividing the real and personal property of Christopher GARLOW between Ann GARLOW and John GARLOW, her son, executors. Of the personal property and small grains, John GARLOW to have, viz, 1 cow and calf, 1 white face heifer, 1 small set of irons and plow, 1 old sow and her

pigs, 2 of the killing hogs (the best and the worst), 2 ewes
(the best and the worst), 1 ax, 1 mattock, 1 iron wedge, 2
bee hives (the best and the worst), the fourths of all the
small grain that is now to be thrashed out. John is to help
to thrash out all the small grain and divide it in the bushel
and 1 large stack of hay by PARTMUS´ hay. John is to have the
half of the all intended and is to have two acres of the
small grain next the PROVINCE line for his trouble. John is
further to give the widow, his mother, peaceable possession
and is to move against the first of April next ensuing to the
place that TERANCE improved. John is to have the corn on
said improvement and Ann GARLOW hath to keep all the old
improvement and the remainder of the personal estate and is
to keep all the children and feed, cloth and educate them at
her own expense and is to have all the rest of the real
estate. John is to have 100 acres adjoining said improvement
until the youngest child is of age. Signed by Simeon EVERLY,
Amos SMITH, John SNIDER and Robert HAMILTON on 6 September
1800. On 7 September 1812, the parties agreed to dismiss the
suit, each paying their own costs. Signed by John GARLOW and
Ann WOLFORD.

172 - 1812, Monongalia Superior Court. John THOMPSON, yeoman;
James M. THOMPSON, house carpenter; Daniel THOMPSON, house
carpenter; and John THOMPSON Jr., (son of John Sr., an infant
under age 21) summoned to answer those things of which they
stand indicted for assault on Thomas LAZZELL Jr. on 15 March
1812, 28 April 1812. LAZZELL summoned to give evidence to
the Grand Jury, 30 April 1812. John WALKER summoned to
testify in behalf of THOMPSON and others, 7 September 1812.
September 1812 term, "We the jury find the defendants, Daniel
and John, not guilty," Nathaniel WEBB, foreman.

172 - 1812, Monongalia Superior Court. William JOLLIFF summoned to answer Thomas WILSON in a plea of covenant broken
damages $500, 20 February 1810. Article of Agreement dated 1
November 1800, in which JOLLIFF promised to pay WILSON $1 per
acre for every acre remaining unsold in a certain tract of
land adjoining REEDER and EVANS´ Mill supposed to contain 400
acres, to be paid in cash or country produce delivered to
said mill on or before 1 November 1807 with interest. (Wheat
@ 4 shillings per bushel, rye @ 3 shillings, corn @ 2
shillings and 6 pence, pork @ $4 per hundred, beef @ $3.50
per hundred and all other property at market price). JOLLIFF
promised to clear and put in good fence 35 acres during the
said term of 7 years and agreed not to cut and carry away the
timber except the timber from the 35 acres he was to clear.
JOLLIFF agreed to take good care of the sugar trees and
agreed if the $1 per acre was not paid by the due date, then
the land and all improvements to remain the possession of
WILSON. Agreement signed by JOLLIFFE in the presence of Asa
DUDLEY, Bar´t CLARK and Math WILSON. WILSON said JOLLIFF had

not paid any part of the obligation nor cleared the land and that he did not take care of the sugar trees and other timber, but cut and carried away large quantities of timber and therefore he brings suit. Appearance Bond signed by William JOLLIFFE secured by John JOLLIFFE, 7 May 1810. William HAYS summoned to testify in behalf of WILSON, 15 July 1811. William HAYSE and Joshua HEART summoned to testify in behalf of WILSON, 11 August 1812. Deputies Aaron BARKER and George DERING for Sheriff Lemuel JOHN. September 1812 term, "We the jury assess the plaintiff's damages to $115," Alex. HAWTHORN, foreman.

172 - 1812, Monongalia Superior Court. Basil LUCAS summoned to answer Philip COMBS in a plea of trespass on the case damage $1000, 10 September 1811. September 1812, dismissed.

172 - 1812, Monongalia Superior Court. John DAVIS summoned to answer Thomas WILSON and Davis SHOCKLEY in a plea of trespass damage $100, 20 February 1810. Complaint of WILSON and SHOCKLEY: From January 1809 until January 1810, John DAVIS entered their land and carried away timber to the amount of $100. Samuel HANWAY and Eliab SIMPSON summoned to testify in behalf of WILSON and SHOCKLEY, 13 March and 22 August 1812. September 1812 term, "We the jury find for the plaintiffs damages to $10," A. WOODROW, foreman.

172 - 1812, Monongalia Superior Court. "26 March 1812, Buff-low CREEK, Dear Sir: After by best respects to you my friend, these my lines comes to inquire of you what McCOLEY is a doing in that suit between him and me as I intend to employ you in the suit for me. As I can't come down to see you, according to promise, I want you to write to me by the bearer of this letter as I don't want to come down until the election if you can do without me. S. DERING called at my house and left word that I must come down Friday next to see you about filing a Bill of Injunction. I suppose by that, he must obtained a judgement against me and for this reason I don't like to come to town until I hear from you for I don't know but they have got an execution for my body. As I don't intend they shall get that until I have a chance to turn myself around with DRAGOO. I also want (you) to inform me what chance I have whether bad or good. Let the best or worse come," signed by Jasper WYATT to Mr. Duke GAVENY, Esqr. in Morgantown.

172 - 1812, Monongalia Superior Court. Jacob ZINN, John FAIR-FAX, Thomas BARTLETT, Charles BYRN, Moses MANEAR, William ZINN and James JOHNSTON summoned to answer Peter FOURTNEY in a plea of trespass damage $1000, 13 August and 23 October 1804. David GRIM attended 1 day and travelled 14 1/2 miles, Hunter PILES attended 1 day and travelled 14 1/2 miles, John M. MANEAR attended 1 day and travelled 13 miles, Henry

FORTNEY attended 2 days and travelled 13 miles each time as witnesses on behalf of the plaintiff. May 1805, dismissed as to all but Jacob ZINN. On 18 May 1805, ZINN and FORTNEY agreed to the decision of Arbitrators John STEALY, Thomas FRETWELL, Robert TINGLE, Michael KERNS Sr. and Thomas MILLER. On 18 May 1805, George (x) ZINN authorized Jacob ZINN to sign his name as security and Jacob ZINN signed a bond as George ZINN's Attorney in Fact whereby George secured a bond for Jacob ZINN who agreed to pay whatever the arbitrators awarded and to pay all costs of the action. The bond was also secured by Thomas BIRD. The arbitrators awarded FORTNEY $75 damages and costs, 13 September 1805. September 1807 term, award set aside and case continued until September 1812 when the parties agreed and the case dismissed.

172 - 1812, Monongalia Superior Court. Corporal CAZEY, lessee of John ALLEN, vs Paddy McFAGIN. CAZEY complained that on 1 June 1808, Joseph ALLEN leased a tract of land on Buffalow Creek, a branch of Monongahela River, to him for 10 years from 1 June 1808. On same date, Paddy McFAGIN entered the property and with force and arms ejected him from the land. Delinquent Tax Deed from the Marshall of the Virginia District, Joseph SCOTT, to Joseph ALLEN dated 24 January 1806 for 60 acres ($.17 deeding fee) on Buffaloe Creek assessed in the name of George NORTH and witnessed by Isaac COPLIN and John PRUNTY. Recorded in Book D, Folio 296. Plat for 60 acres on Buffaloe Creek dated 23 March 1812, surveyed by an order of the court dated September 1810, it being a tract of land conveyed by Joseph SCOTT, Marshall of the Virginia District, to Joseph ALLEN by deed dated 24 January 1806, signed by Samuel HANWAY, SMS. Agreement signed by William (x) BAINBRIDGE and Joseph ALLEN dated 14 April 1812 to dismiss their action, each paying their own costs. William ICE and John STRAIT summoned to testify in behalf of BAINBRIDGE, 6 March 1810, 2 March and 16 July 1811.

172a - 1812, Monongalia Superior Court. John EVANS Jr., summoned to answer David JAMISON in a plea of trespass on the case damage $400, 24 May 1811. JAMISON's complaint: He said that EVANS owed him $400 "for work and labor performed by Jacob, a Negro man, the property of said JAMISON and for the purchase price of Jacob who sold for $210." John STEALEY, Augustus WERNINGER, Jacob FOULK, William LANHAM, Elihu HORTON and Philip SHIVELY summoned to testify in behalf JAMISON, 11 August 1812. To Captain John EVANS Jr., 22 August 1802, from JAMISON at Culpepper, "Sir: My man Jacob has prevailed on me to let him visit his wife, I have given into the in____ the more readily in consequence of Mr. STROTHER telling me he thought there was a probability of my selling him to a certain gentleman in your town (whose name I do not now remember). I have always determined to make some sacrifice to get the man and his wife together. I will now do so, provided you can sell him to some one near you so that he can visit his wife. I will take 100 pounds cash. If I cannot get cash and anyone will purchase on a credit of a few months for whom you will become security, I will not refuse on a little higher price, say 8% added to the 100 pounds. This may sound high but when I inform you that Jacob at ditching as the common price here can clear me 40 pounds yearly, you cannot think me extravant, this I aver upon my honor he can do. He is very handy at any common labor. If you can dispose of him as above, you are authorized so to do, I would perfer cash. If you cannot sell him and can get 6 or 8 dollars per month, you may hire him until the spring of the year sometime in March and then send him down. Let me hear soon from you what you do respecting this business. I wish you may be able to accommodate those people as it will not be consistent with my interest to let him pass back and forward to see his wife and I _____ unhappy at the thought of their separating as it appears to distress them. My respects to Mrs. EVANS. Your Disconsolate Friend, D. JAMISON." To Captain EVANS, 15 August 1803, from JAMISON, Culpepper. "Dear Sir: When I received your last favor informing me there was some person within two miles of you who would give 80 pounds for Jacob and considered what a sacrifice I had made to try to accommodate him and found he objected to go to that person, I was so much amazed at his rascally conduct in refusing to give into so reasonable a measure for his benefit, that I really was at a loss what to do or say... I am no longer under any tender consideration, I have done all I can do for his accommodation and am determined to pay no more respect to his feelings. I will sooner lose him altogether than be any longer subservient to his humor..... let me know if the opportunity still exists to sell him, that if he makes any scruples it is his last chance to be accommodated near his wife and children and if he still holds out sell him, I do not care to what distance he is removed. I will send him to Orleans or Natches or any other place. If no such opportunity offers, send him to me in chains and I can dispose of him." JAMISON warned EVANS to have Jacob in such a situation where he could not escape when he was told of this decision and to try to sell him with his consent, but if that was not possible to sell him anyway. To Captain John EVANS Jr. "18 June 1804, Culpepper, Dear Sir: I this day received your favors of the 2nd instant respecting my man Jacob. His behavior has really vexed me so much that I know not what to do nor what to request of you for I suppose you must be as much out of patience as myself. However, your brother and myself has just had a few words of conversation upon the subject and I have come to this determination (as your brother informs me he supposes he may be sold but probably not for cash) if you will sell him for any thing like a tolerable price, I will leave it entirely to yourself to make the best bargain you can at the earliest payment you can

306

obtain. Act for me as you would for yourself. If you sell
upon credit, get the debt well secured, the fact is I am so
much vexed with him that I do not wish to see him. If I can
get shut of him upon tolerable terms, although I have a very
considerable quantity of ditching I wish done and intended
him to do this summer and fall if I could get him without
trouble, you will now understand me, get the most you can and
at the earliest period well secured for payment unless you
think the best price you can get would be too great a
sacrifice. My respects to your lady. Yr. Obliged Friend, D.
JAMISON." To William TINGLE, Esqr. Morgantown, 18 July 1805,
Culpepper, letter from JAMISON concerning Jacob who Capt.
EVANS sold to Philip SHIVELY. JAMISON said Jacob had been
absent from him for about two years before he was sold.
Jacob was hired out at $6 per month and EVANS mis-represented
Jacob for he was not an idle worthless fellow and he had not
received payment for his hire for which he had not made an
accounting and had not paid to JAMISON his master. He said
Jacob had notified him that he was discontent with his new
master and JAMISON told him if he would settle up the money
owed by him and would give for himself so much as SHIVELEY
was to give, he would free him if SHIVELEY would agree to
give up his bargain. He said he never had any intention of
freeing him without compensation. Jacob agreed to the terms
and SHIVELEY agreed to recant his bargain, but JAMISON never
heard another word on the subject. He said he hoped never to
hear from nor to see Jacob again because of his "vile
conduct." To John EVANS Jr., 20 July 1805, from JAMISON in
Culpepper. He expressed his concern for the trouble Jacob
caused EVANS and thanked him for his services. He said he
understood Jacob was sold for $200 payable in one month or
$210 payable in six months. He said he hoped never to see
Jacob again as he had lost much by him and expressed his
sorrow over Jacob's conduct. To Captain John EVANS, 19 May
1806, Culpepper, letter from JAMISON acknowledging receipt of
$200. JAMISON was starting to the "Western Country" and
planned to take a route through Morgantown, but his plans
were changed and he was to take another route. He advised
EVANS that he would leave in a few days and if possible to
send further monies to him by 1 August in care of Samuel
AYRES in Lexington, Kentucky. He sent his respects to Mrs.
EVANS, her brothers and sisters and said George was elected
to the Virginia Assembly. To Col. David JAMISON, Lexington,
Kentucky, 15 June 1806, from EVANS, Walnut Hill. EVANS
acknowledged JAMISON letter of 19 May and advised JAMISON he
had written to Maj'r. James MORRISON, Lexington, Kentucky, to
pay JAMISON $70.50 who had a sum in his hands belonging to
EVANS. He said if JAMISON did not or could not get the money,
to let him know when it would be available. A note written
at the bottom states, "Maj'r. MORRISON informs me he had not
received any money for Capt. EVANS and is in doubt whether
he will." To Thomas WILSON, Esqr, at Morgantown, from D.

JAMISON at Culpepper, 10 July 1811. After giving WILSON his regards and thanking him for beginning the suit against EVANS, he writes that EVANS should have settled the business with him when he was in Morgantown four years ago and expresses his disappointment in EVANS' behavior and said he believes EVANS never intended to do him justice until compelled to do so. He included an account of his dealings with EVANS and said, "About the latter end of September 1802, at the suggestion of Capt. EVANS, by a verbal message by Mr. Daniel STROTHER, I sent Jacob to Capt. EVANS to sell that he might be convenient to his wife (who belonged to Capt. EVANS) with a request that in case he could not sell him for my price that he would hire him in the neighborhood at least that winter at $8 per month which I presumed he might get for him. Jacob stayed there upon hire (to whom I know not) until 27 August 1804, at which time Capt. EVANS informed me he sold him for $210 on six months credit since which time the account shows all he had done. He informed me, before he sold him, that some months he got $6 and some months he got $8, I know not the right of this matter. You must get as much proved as possible. Mr. William TINGLE wrote me once that he had hired him and paid Capt. EVANS for 5 or 6 months, but at what price he did not mention. He further observed in his letter that he knew that he was pretty generally hired until he was sold. Jacob sent me a memo that he worked for Capt. EVANS in harvest 1803 to the amount of $10 and in harvest 1804 to the amount of $11.75. This is Jacob's information. Jacob mentions in the same memo (which by the by came enclosed in Mr. TINGLE's letter) that Capt. EVANS received for him from John STEALEY, Mr. VANIGEN, Mr. FULK, Mr. LANNAM and Mr. HORTON." JAMISON told WILSON to call these men as witnesses and any other he could find to establish his claim. "Mr. JARRETT (a gentleman who kept a house of entertainment when I was in Morgantown) told me he knew of several who had hired Jacob, I hope he will be kind enough to let you know them that they may be summoned." He suggests that WILSON bargain with EVANS in order to get payment without undue costs or trouble and if that is not possible, to use the most rigid measures with him. EVANS' account with JAMISON, 27 August 1804, hire of Jacob from 27 September 1802 until this date at $7 per month = $161; 27 March 1805, sale of Jacob on 6 months credit from 27 August last = $210; 25 March 1806, interest on $210 one year at 6% = $12 and interest on $100 part of hire 19 months = $9.50. Total $393. 25 March 1806, cash received in a letter $200. Balance due $193. September 1812 term, "We the jury find for the defendant."

172a – 1812, Monongalia Superior Court. George DORSEY summoned to answer Davis SHOCKLEY, butcher, in a plea of slander and malicious prosecution damage $1000, 1 September 1810. SHOCKLEY complained that DORSEY obtained a false warrant against him to search his business for one lamb which he charged SHOCKLEY with receiving from a Negro slave. DORSEY's answer to the complaint: He did not obtain the Search Warrant from malice or wickedness, but having lost a lamb over the night before he obtained the Search Warrant. He suspected his own Negro man with having stolen the lamb and when he confronted his man, he told him he had taken the lamb for Davis SHOCKLEY, which was the reason for the warrant and the searching of SHOCKLEY house. Elihu HORTON summoned to testify in behalf of DORSEY, 21 March 1812. Robert SCOTT and Charles BURNS summoned to testify in behalf of DORSEY, 27 March 1812. David SWINDLER and Pernal HOUSTON summoned to testify in behalf of DORSEY, 4 April 1812. James JEFFS and William B. LINDSEY summoned to testify in behalf of SHOCKLEY, 13 March 1812. Zackquil MORGAN and John JOLIFFE summoned to testify in behalf of DORSEY, 7 April 1812. William FRUM summoned to testify in behalf of DORSEY, 8 April 1812. April 1812 term, "We the jury find for the defendant," George PICKENPAUGH, foreman.

172a - 1812, Monongalia Superior Court. John RICH summoned to answer John SHIVELY in a plea of assault damage $1000, 30 May 1810. April 1812 term, execution quashed.

172a - 1812, Monongalia Superior Court. Eight horses and 3 cows, the property of Thomas McKINLEY, was attached at the suit of James MURPHY for $143 plus cost. In order to retain possession of his property until time of public sale or his debt was paid McKINLEY signed this Delivery Bond secured by Waitman FURBY and John W. THOMPSON, 24 September 1811. April 1812 term, "We the jury assess the plaintiff's damages to $40," John W. THOMPSON, foreman.

172a - 1812, Monongalia Superior Court. William McCLEARY and Mathew GAY summoned to answer Farquir McRA, assignee of Nicholas CASEY, in a plea of debt for $100 and $10 damage, 25 March 1811. Obligation signed by McCLEERY and GAY to CASEY dated 10 April 1809 for $100, due 3 October 1810 and witnessed by George S. DERING. Assignment to McRA dated 3 May 1810 and witnessed by D. F. McRA and ____ ECKHART. Bail Bond for McCLEERY and GAY secured by Ralph BARKSHIRE, 25 May 1811. April 1812 term, plea waived and judgement confessed.

172a - 1812, Monongalia Superior Court. Russell POTTER, late Sheriff of Monongalia County; Elihu HORTON; Thomas R. CHIPPS; Henry BATTON; William BIGGS; Joseph SEVERNS and William G. PAYNE summoned to answer William H. CABELL, successor of John PAIGE, late Governor of Virginia, for the use of James ARNOLD, in a plea of debt for $30,000 and $1000 damage, 8 September 1806, 1 August and 25 November 1807. Complaint: On 14 March 1804, the securities named above secure a Sheriff's Bond for POTTER. POTTER appointed Thomas R. CHIPPS as deputy. ARNOLD sued POTTER for breach of the amount of the bond which was $30,000. ARNOLD obtained judgement against the executors of John T. GOFF, deceased, and obtained an attachment on his property for $300 plus damages and costs. The attachment was placed in the hands of Deputy Thomas R. CHIPPS. CHIPPS and POTTER failed to execute the attachment and ARNOLD said the property was carried away and he lost his debt and damages. "And the said James ARNOLD on the 20th day of May 1805 received judgement in the District Court of Monongalia County for $354 damages and costs in an action against James C. GOFF and John S. GOFF, executors of John T. GOFF, deceased." "The Clerk of the Superior Court of Law will dismiss the suit, myself against Russell POTTER and his securities, 18 March 1812." Signed by Jas. ARNOLD and witnessed by F. BRITTON.

Also in this file - - - "Rec'd of Nimrod EVANS the receipt of John CHENWITH for the collection of clerk's notes and to $35.83, 18 March 1812." Signed by George DAVISSON.

172a - 1812, Monongalia Superior Court. One Negro man named Nelson & 2 horses, the property of W. G. PAYNE, was attached at the suit of Henry GRIM for $190 with interest from 15 February 1806 plus costs. In order to retain possession of his property until time of public sale or his debt was paid, PAYNE signed this Delivery Bond secured by John FAIRFAX and Samuel HANWAY, 11 February 1812. April 1812 term, judgement.

172a - 1812, Monongalia Superior Court. Thomas R. CHIPPS and James PINDALL summoned to answer Capt. John GILLISPIE in a plea of debt for $180.84 and $100 damage, 26 April 1808. PINDALL was not an inhabitant, 3 January 1809. To the Sheriff of Harrison County, Capt John GILLISPIE, prosecuted out of the District Court, a writ against CHIPPS and PINDALL in an action of debt, which writ was duly executed, which writ was abated as to CHIPPS by his death. After the execution of the writ and before final judgement, Capt. John GILLISPIE died intestate and on 15 May 1810, Neal GILLISPIE Jr. was appointed his administrator. Neal GILLISPIE continued the action and James PINDALL was summoned to show cause, if any he can, why the said action should not be prosecuted by Neal GILLISPIE Jr., 4 June 1810. Executed on PINDALL 9 June 1810 by Harrison County Sheriff. Note signed by Thomas R. CHIPPS and James PINDALL to Capt. John GILLISPIE for $90.42 dated 16 November 1804, due 1 May 1807 and witnessed by Wm. G. PAYNE and John DAVIS. GILLISPIE assigned this note to Nimrod EVANS on 10 May 1809. Appearance Bond signed by Thomas R. CHIPPS secured by Amos CHIPPS in the presence of J. WOODROW and A. WOODROW, 29 April 1808. April 1812 term, judgement for the plaintiff, GILLISPIE, and appeal granted to PINDALL. James PINDELL against Neal GILLISPIE, administrator of John GILLISPIE, deceased, at a Court of Appeals at the Capitol in Richmond, 5 December 1812. PINDELL appealed to this higher court to recover a judgement granted to GILLISPIE in the Superior Court of Monongalia County on 10 April 1812 for $180.84 with interest at 6% from 16 November 1804 plus costs. Appeal Bond signed by PINDALL to ensure he would prosecute the appeal and pay all awards and costs in case the aforesaid judgement should be affirmed, secured by Forbes BRITTON in the presence of R. SCOTT, DC, 10 April 1812. The transcript was not sent to the Appeals Court in the time allotted by law and the appellant, PINDELL, did not appear and the court dismissed the appeal and PINDELL was ordered to pay cost.

172a - 1812, Monongalia Superior Court. James PINDALL summoned to answer John EVANS Jr., assignee of Rebecca DERING, administratrix of Henry DERING, deceased, in a plea of debt for $171.50 and $10 damage, 19 October 1809. Deputy Mathew GAY for Sheriff Lemuel JOHN. Note signed by PINDALL to DERING for $71.50 with interest dated 29 May 1805. PINDALL paid 13 pounds, 17 shillings and 2 pence of the amount of the note on 6 April 1809. Assignment to EVANS dated 15 April 1809. Appearance Bond signed by PINDALL secured by B. WILSON Jr., 19 October 1809. At a Court of Appeals held at the Capitol, Richmond 5 December 1812. James PINDALL, appellant, against John EVANS Jr., appellee, assignee of Rebecca DERING administratrix of Henry DERING, deceased. EVANS obtained a judgement against PINDALL in the Superior Court of Monongalia County on 19 April 1812 for $163.95 with interest at 6% from 6 April 1809 plus cost. The transcript was not sent to the Appeals Court in the time allotted by law and the appellant, PINDELL, did not appear and the court dismissed the appeal and PINDELL was ordered to pay cost. H. DANCE, clerk. Appeal Bond signed by PINDALL to ensure he would prosecute the appeal and pay all awards and costs in case the aforesaid judgement was affirmed secured by Forbes BRITTON, 10 April 1812.

172a - 1812, Monongalia Superior Court. John FAIRFAX summoned to answer Isaac DRAPER in a plea of debt for $102.50 and $10 damage, 2 March 1811. "Isaac DRAPER lives ____aughton, Post Office Zanesville." Eighteen month note signed by Jonathan COBURN and John FAIRFAX to DRAPER for $102.50 dated 3 April 1809 and witnessed by Richard POSTLE and Peter MERYDETH. List for Magistrates: Benjamin JEFFRIES, John SCOTT, Jonathan BRANDON, Samuel WILLITS, Jno HENTHORN and James TIBBS. ____ 1812 term, plea waived and judgement confessed.

172a - 1812, Monongalia Superior Court. Nimrod EVANS summoned to answer Elihu HORTON, for the use of Thomas FRETWELL, in a plea of debt for $190.50, 13 May 1808. Article of Agreement between Elihu HORTON and Nimrod EVANS dated 12 May 1802 whereby HORTON rented from EVANS a Negro man named Cyrus for 6 months at $10 per month to be paid as follows: one half ($30) in 3 months and one half ($30) at the end of the 6 month period. HORTON agreed to furnish Cyrus with 1 strong linen shirt and 1 pair strong linen trousers or overalls. Signed by HORTON and EVANS in the presence of Alexander HAWTHORN. "Cyrus stayed with HORTON 16 days over the time stated in this agreement. I have received $8, $5 of which is to be placed to the credit of the above 16 days. The clothes stated in the agreement have not been furnished by HORTON, Nimrod EVANS." "May or June 1804, Nimrod EVANS, to a year's rent of my house $100; to cash paid in part of his boy's hire $8; May or June 1805, to a year's rent of my house $100; to three months rent for same house $30; to 3 months rent for 1 room $9. Total $247. Deduct for rent of room $3.50; Deduct for last years rent $50. Balance $193.50." Elihu HORTON, dr, to Nimrod EVANS, 12 August 1812, to hire of my boy from 12 May to 12 August $30; Interest on same 2 years $3.60; hire of same from 12 August 1812 to 28 November $35; Interest on same 1 year $3.15; 1 shirt and 1 pair overalls $3; judgement against _aby SHEAN $24.88; amount of my fee bill against you $132.31; 1805, cash paid you $2 and cash paid Mrs. HORTON $2; 1811, cash lent $1; 1812, cash lent $1.37 1/2. Total $238.31 1/2. EVANS' answer: Sometime in 1807, he attempted to make a settlement with HORTON and HORTON was in his debt about $20. He said he made a statement of the debt along with another $20 debt for repairs that HORTON disputed and gave the statement to HORTON. John EVANS, Marmaduke EVANS and Noah RIDGEWAY summoned to testify in behalf of E. HORTON, 7 September 1812. Noah RIDGEWAY and Thomas McKINLEY summoned to testify in behalf of HORTON, 28 March, 16 July 1811 and 2 April 1812. Daniel SHAHAN summoned to testify in behalf of EVANS, 8 September 1812. Augustus WERNINGER's deposition dated 5 September 1810: He stated that he could not prove HORTON's handwriting, but by next term of court, he would be able to prove the account HORTON owed him. September 1812 term, "We the jury find for the defendant," Charles BYRN, foreman.

172a - 1812, Monongalia Superior Court. Ten tons of bar iron, the property of John STEALY, was attached at the suit of John HOYE for $550 with interest on $275 at 6% from 21 May 1801 until paid plus costs. In order to retain possession of his property until time of public sale or his debt was paid STEALY signed this Delivery Bond secured by Rawley SCOTT, 25 October 1811. September 1812, judgement for the plaintiff.

172a - 1812, Monongalia Superior Court. One bay horse and 1 bureau, the property of George HITE, was attached at the suit of Abraham HALE for $20. In order to retain possession of his property until time for public sale or his debt was paid HITE signed this Delivery Bond secured by George DERING, 27 April 1812. September 1812 term, judgement.

172a - 1812, Monongalia Superior Court. John DOWNER summoned
to answer Jonathan HARRIS in a plea of covenant broken damage
$500, 14 August 1811. Conveyance Bond signed by DOWNER dated
11 April 1805 for $300, due in 9 months, to convey to HARRIS
a 200 acre tract of land on Dunkard Creek adjoining lands of
George SNIDER, Thomas LAIDLEY and Evan JENKINS. Assignment
to Reubin ANSKINS, 23 August 1807, signed by Jonathan HARIS.
ANSKINS refused to accept the assignment after the endorse-
ment by HARIS.   September 1812 term, "We the jury find for
the plaintiff and assess his damages to $400," Wm. JARRETT,
foreman.

172a - 1812, Monongalia Superior Court. "Personally appeared
before me a Justice of the Peace for Monongalia County,
Presley MARTIN and made oath that the child of Richard
MORRISON lies at the point of death with a scald and that the
personal attention of the said Richard was necessary which
was the cause of his not attending the summons to attend this
___ ___ court as a Grand Juror as this deponent believes and
as he was informed by the said Richard," 7 September 1812.
Signed by William N. JARRETT, JP.

172a - 1812, Monongalia Superior Court. William I/J HALL
recovered a judgement of $1635.50 with interest at 6% from 30
January 1799 plus cost against Hedgeman TRIPLETT. On 20
September 1802, Samuel HANWAY secured bail for TRIPLETT.
Samuel HANWAY summoned to show cause, if any he can, why
judgement should not be had against him as TRIPLETT's
security since TRIPLETT refused to pay the debt, 28 August
1810. April 1812, term judgement for the plaintiff.

172a - 1818, Monongalia Superior Court. On 14 January 1811,
the Justices of Monongalia County brought into court their
notice against Stephen MORGAN,   Thomas McKINLEY, John PAYNE
and William G. PAYNE for judgement against MORGAN as 1809
Collector of the Revenue with the others as securities for
the sum of $327.97 it being the sum due and in arrears to the
county as part of the 1809 County Levy, signed by Wm.
McCLEERY, Attorney for the County, 26 December 1810. The
justices won the case and the defendants prayed for and was
granted an appeal to Superior Court. Appeal Bond signed by
Wm. G. PAYNE to ensure he would prosecute the appeal and all
costs and awards would be paid in case the appeal was
dismissed secured by Samuel HANWAY. "Credit this judgement
with $29.83 for vouchers filed." September 1812 term appeal
dismissed and judgement for costs. "$6.11 paid to me by Wm.
G. PAYNE, 5 March 1818," signed by T. P. RAY.

172a - 1812, Monongalia Superior Court. Grand Jury 1812: John
EVANS, foreman; Enoch JONES, George SMITH, Augustus WELLS,
Jonathan BRANDON, William COWNER, Hugh MORGAN, James BEALL,
John EVANS Jr., Robert HILL, James S. WILSON, George DORSEY,

Richard WELLS, Thomas HAMILTON, Jesse SPURGEN, William MILLER, Robert HAWTHORN, Richard HARRISON, Joseph HARRISON, John SHISLER, John A. BARKSHIRE, Thomas DOOLITTLE, John WILSON and John DENT. September 1812 term.

172a - 1812, Monongalia Superior Court. George D. AVERY prayed the court to quash a writ of execution to satisfy a judgement recovered by Sylvester ROBINSON and William ROBINSON which issued from the court on 6 January 1812 against the lands of said AVERY. The motion was overruled by the court and AVERY prayed for and was granted an appeal. Appeal Bond signed by AVERY to ensure he would prosecute and pay all awards and costs in case his appeal should be dismissed secured by Oliver PHELPS and Philip DODDRIDGE, 12 September 1812.

172a - 1812, Monongalia Superior Court. On 24 June 1808, Michael PAUGH was tried in a called court on a charge of felony and sent to further trial. William PRICE and Simeon ROYCE secured his bail. PAUGH was to appear at the next District Court and answer to the charge of man slaughter. PAUGH, PRICE and ROYCE summoned to show cause, if any they can, why a writ of Scire Facias (a writ to obtain judgement or to obtain execution or continuation of a judgement previously entered) should not issue on their recognizance conditioned for the appearance of PAUGH, 28 November 1808 and 5 June 1810. PAUGH not found. Continued to September 1812 term.

172a - 1812, Monongalia Superior Court. Maria HUGGINS was indicted on charges of perjury. On 15 April 1812, before Justice Rawley SCOTT, John W. THOMPSON was summoned to answer Ruth BILLS for non-payment of a debt. BILLS and THOMPSON appeared before Justice Cornelius BARKSHIRE and THOMPSON produced an account containing charges of sundry items which THOMPSON claimed BILLS owed him to be credited to the debt BILLS claimed THOMPSON owed her. One of the charges presented by THOMPSON was 6 pound and 15 shillings for BILLS' renting a house for 9 months at the rate of $30 per year. BILLS claimed she rented the house at $20 per year. Maria HUGGINS appeared as a witness for THOMPSON and swore BILLS rented the house at $30 per year. Ruth BILLS, weaver, prosecutrix. Stephen LUCAS summoned to testify in behalf of HUGGINS, 5 September 1812. Jacob FOULK, Christian MADERA, Davis SHOCKLEY and wife, Nicholas MADERA, Polly ADAMSON and Ruth BILLS summoned to give evidence to the Grand Jury, 9 September 1812. Joseph A. SHACKELFORD, John SULLIVAN, George THOMPSON, John CHIPPS, Elizabeth SHELLS/SPELLS, Susan MADERA, Charlotte WEBB, George DORSEY, George HITE and Jacob MADERA summoned to testify in behalf of HUGGINS, 8 September 1812. Prudence STEALEY and Clary ADAMSON summoned to testify in behalf of HUGGINS, 9 September 1812. Thomas McKINLEY and Rebecca? CHRISTEY sum-

moned to testify in behalf of HUGGINS, 8 September 1812.
September 1812 term, "We the jury find the defendant not
guilty," Jno WAGNER, foreman.

172a - 1812, Monongalia Superior Court. James K. ARCHIBALD,
of Harrison County an infant under age 21 and son of James
ARCHIBALD, yeoman, was indicted on charges of "plundering"
the mail. On 25 March 1812, James was employed by the General
Post Office as a Post Rider on that part of the Post Road
from Washington City by the Fairfax County Courthouse,
Goshen, Middleburg, Paris, Winchester, Romney, Westernport in
Maryland, Gandysville, Clarksburg and Naches to Marietta,
Ohio. Between the Deputy Post Office at Kingwood, attended
by Deputy Postmaster John L. ROBERTS, and Clarksburg with
mail letters to be delivered from Kingwood to Gandysville,
ARCHIBALD detained, delayed and opened the mail. At Gandysville, (Deputy Postmaster Samuel Gandy), ARCHIBALD received
into his possession mail letters to be delivered to Prunty-
town and did detain, delay and unlawfully open the mail.
ARCHIBALD refused to answer the indictment because if any
crime was committed it was against the United States and not
against the Commonwealth of Virginia. To the Sheriff of
Harrison County, Jacob ISRAEL, Nathan DAVIS, Joseph DAVIS,
Simeon MAXWELL and Jesse FITZRANDOLPH summoned to testify in
behalf of ARCHIBALD, 1 September 1812. Reuben JACO, William
SUT/SEET/LUT Jr. summoned to testify in behalf of ARCHIBALD,
1 September 1812. "Joseph NAVELL/NEWELL, Otho GANDY and
Joseph WILLIAMS swore in open court to give evidence to the
Grand Jury now sitting upon this Bill of Indictment." "Josiah
WILLIAMS, age about 11 years old, met prisoner with papers in
his hands put them in his hat except one which he kept in his
hands and cut it or broke it open and after passing deponent
threw it away that this deponent picked up the paper on his
return but does not know what it was written on it deponent
observed to prisoner ___d the name off that deponent
travelled the road aftertimes before but see no papers on the
road side." "Christian RODGERS was walking within about 20
rods of the road where the prisoner passed seen the prisoner
throw away a piece of paper he went and picked it up but
could not tell what was on it." "Elizabeth DAVIS on Wednesday
met the Post Rider and after seeing prisoner who deponent
believes is the prisoner at the bar see a number of papers on
the road side but does not know what they were that she see
the prisoner in jail which is the only reason why she now
thinks the prisoner at the bar is the person she saw." Otho
GANDY on Wednesday 25 March 1812, "prisoner brought the mail
to Samuel GANDY's Postoffice on Monday following went along
the Post Road and found three pieces of post bills and a
number of pieces of paper one bill was endorsed from Washington City to Marietta, Winchester postmark was on one of the
papers. There appeared to be an unusual quantity of papers
in the mail and deponent uncovered no apparent loss of papers

or disorder in the mail." "Joseph NEWELL, Postmaster Clarksburg. The mail came and passed through his office on 25 March 1812 without loss or discovering any defect in the bag. The deponent discovered no disarrangement in the papers or letters in the mail." 7 September 1812, jury called: John A. GUSEMAN, George HITE, Daniel KNOX, Presley MARTIN, Dudley EVANS, William WINDSER, R. MARTIN, M. MORGAN, Abram HESS and F. KIGER. September 1812 term, defendant discharged.

172a - 1812, Monongalia Superior Court. John KIMMER swore that Samuel CRANE threatened his life if he should give evidence for John RHODEFFER in an action of slander now in the Superior Court brought by RHODEFFER against CRANE. KIMMER said he was called as a witness and was afraid to testify against CRANE because of the threat against his life and because CRANE threatened RHODEFFER's life if he obtained a judgement in the above mentioned suit, 7 April 1812. William WALKER summoned to testify in behalf of CRANE, 8 September 1812. Amos ROBERTS, William ROBERTS, Benjamin TRIMBLY, John KIMMER, Adam TEETS and David GRIMES summoned to testify in behalf of CRANE, 3 June 1812. September 1812 term, dismissed.

172a - 1812, Monongalia Superior Court. Jno. W. THOMPSON was indicted on charges of perjury. On 15 April 1812, before Justice Rawley SCOTT, John W. THOMPSON was summoned to answer Ruth BILLS for non-payment of a debt (see page 314). Davis SHOCKLEY and Helen his wife and Jacob FOULK summoned to give evidence to the Grand Jury, 7 September 1812. Elihu HORTON summoned to testify in behalf of THOMPSON, 9 September 1812. Mrs. John CHIPPS, George M. THOMPSON and William HUGGINS summoned to testify in behalf of THOMPSON, 9 September 1812. Christian MADERA, Nicholas MADERA, Polly ADAMSON and Ruth BILLS summoned to give evidence to the Grand Jury, 7 September 1812.

172a - 1812, Monongalia Superior Court. Adam VANCAMP summoned to answer John COOPER in a plea of assault, 2 March 1811. William WHITE and James SCOTT summoned to testify in behalf of Adam VANCAMP, 10 August 1812. James SCOTT and Noah RIDGWAY and wife summoned to testify in behalf of COOPER, 10 August 1812. Daniel KNOX and William WALKER summoned to testify in behalf of COOPER, 7 September 1812. September 1812 term, "We the jury find for the plaintiff $50 in damages," N. WEBB, foreman.

172b - 1811, Monongalia Superior Court. Wood County, 19 March 1811. Notice to John ATKINSON and son, Doctor Daniel LORD, John J. GLOVER, Thomas PEARSELL surviving partner of PEARSELL and PELL and William W. RODMAN & Company from George D. AVERY, a prisoner in the Wood County jail, of intent to petition the court for release from custody upon the various executions charged against him. AVERY gave them notice to produce a certain deed executed by him (by his attorney) to his creditors. Public Notary Henry MEIGS of New York, New York, swore he served this notice on the above named on 2 and 3 April 1811. "We the subscribers, creditors of George D. AVERY, of Wood County, Virginia, agree to accept the (Kanawha County) 50,000 acres of land offered by said AVERY in payment for our respective debts and request Dr. Benjamin BUTLER, of New York, to have a Warrantee Deed drawn expressing each of our names for an undivided share in proportion to our respective claims up to this time. 27 November 1809, New York." Signed by Wm. W. RODMAN for himself and Wm. & S. ROBINSON, John ATKINSON and son, Jeffers JEFFRIES, Daniel LORD for himself and John GELSTON, William and Christ. M. SLOCUM, John J. GLOVER, James J. ROOSEVELT, Gordon MANWARING, Thomas C. PEARSALL for PEARSALL and PELL. Abraham HERRING and son and Doctor Isaac THOMPSON declined to take land for their claims. Notary MEIGS was attested to "By Pierre C. VANWYCK, Esqr., Recorder of the City of New York, in the absence of Dewitt CLINTON, Mayor of the City of New York." MEIGS´ Notary Certificate filed as part of this action.

172b - 1812, Monongalia Superior Court. Alexander STEWART and William STEWART, executors of William STEWART, deceased, who was administrator of John STEWART, deceased, summoned to answer Thomas CORDRAY and Sarah (STEWART) his wife, William STEWART, Elizabeth STEWART, Agnus STEWART, David STEWART, Samuel STEWART for themselves and Mary STEWART (an infant under age 21 by Benjamin REEDER her guardian), the heirs and legal representatives of John STEWART, deceased, in a plea of trespass on the case damage $2000, 23 January 1812. July 1812 term, dismissed by order of the plaintiff.

172b - 1812, Monongalia Superior Court. George HITE summoned to answer Abraham HALE in a plea of trespass damage $1000, 24 March 1810. HALE complained that on 19 March 1810, George HITE seized and carried away goods and chattels and wearing apparel (1 uniform coat, blue cloth faced with red and 1 other broadcloth coat) valued at $1000 from his house and converted them to his own profit and use and therefore he brings suit. Abraham HALE was a private in the Company of Cavalry commanded by Captain Wm. N. JARRETT and attached to the 3rd Regiment in the 3rd Division of the Militia of this Commonwealth and the uniform coat was a part of Abraham´s equipment and as such exempted from execution by law. Deposition of Joseph LOWRY heard at the house of Mrs. R. DERING: Sometime in March 1810, HALE owed him a debt and sold him a horse which later he found was conveyed to HITE by a Bill of Sale. HITE showed him the Bill of Sale which included some other items and HITE said the bill was for the same horse HALE sold to him (LOWRY). Sometime on Saturday afternoon, HALE desired to settle the claim, on which HITE was security for him. On that same evening he made arrange-

ments so as to promise HALE to do it. The next morning, HITE
asked him to settle with HALE and he told HITE he would as
soon as he returned from Harrison County. He settled HITE's
claim as security for HALE and HITE assigned the Bill of Sale
to him and delivered to him 1 bed and bedstead, 1 table, 4
Windsor chairs and 1 table and 1 looking glass, 4 unfinished
hats and perhaps some other articles that may not be recalled
which he told HALE to take home with him, 25 March 1811. HITE
said the action should not be had against him because at the
time of the taking of the goods of Abraham HALE he was a
Constable for Monongalia County and he took the coats in
execution in the name and on behalf of Augustus WERNINGER.
Joseph LOWRY, Mary BENNETT, Ezekial CHANEY, James TAYLOR and
Lucretia TAYLOR summoned to testify in behalf of HALE, 21
February and 16 July 1811. James TAYLOR, Mrs. TAYLOR and
William WALKER summoned to testify in behalf of HITE, 29
March 1811. Wm. N. JARRETT summoned to testify in behalf of
HALE, 9 April 1812. April 1812 term, "We the jury find for
the plaintiff $20 in damage," Jared EVANS, foreman.

172b - 1812, Monongalia Superior Court. James BURCHINAL summoned to answer Amos SMITH in a plea of debt for $323.83 and
$10 damage, 11 October 1809 and 29 January 1810. Note signed
by BURCHINAL to Amos SMYTH for $323.83 with interest dated 15
December 1804 and witnessed by George SMYTH and Samuel SMYTH.
Bail Bond for BURCHINAL secured by Jacob FOULK, 28 May 1810.
FOULK swore that after payment of his debts and those for
which he is security, his estate was worth $400, 28 May 1810.
Acting Jailor, Joseph ALLEN, signed two statements whereby he
received into his custody one James BURCHINAL by Jacob FOULK,
28 April 1812. April 1812 term, "We the jury find for the
plaintiff the debt in the declaration mentioned with interest
from 15 December 1804 with a credit of $220 part of the
within paid 30 March 1805."

172b - 1812, Monongalia Superior Court. John STAFFORD summoned to answer John TIBBS in a plea of assault, 13 July
1812. Jacob HOARD summoned to testify in behalf of TIBBS, 11
August 1812. September 1812 term, "We the jury assess the
plaintiff's damage to $1," John THOMPSON, foreman.

172b - 1812, Monongalia Superior Court. James/Walter CARLISLE
summoned to answer George CROPP in a plea of assault, 19
January 1810. "This is an action of trespass, assault and
battery and false imprisonment for the recovery of damages."
William B. LINSEY, Edmond PRITCHARD, Jacob KYGER and John
STEALEY summoned to testify in behalf of CROP, 20 February
1812. John BUTLER and John EPLY summoned to testify in
behalf of CROP, 16 March 1812. April 1812 term, "We the jury
assess the plaintiff's damages to $150," Augustus WERNINGER,
foreman.

172b - 1812, Monongalia Superior Court. James SCOTT summoned to answer James G. WATSON in a plea of debt to recover money paid by the plaintiff for the defendant, 31 August 1810. April 1812 term, "dismissed by order of the plaintiff's attorney."

172b - 1812, Monongalia Superior Court. Felix SCOTT, Attorney at Law, summoned to answer Richard WELLS, yeoman, in a plea of assault damage $5000, 7 March 1811 and 1 January 1812. Duncan F. McCREA summoned to testify in behalf of SCOTT, 9 April 1812. John WELLS summoned to testify in behalf of Richard WELLS, 9 April 1812. Adam VANCAMP, Laben EVANS, Peter HESS, John SMITH, David SNIDER, Aaron BARKER, Jarrett EVANS and John FISHER summoned to testify in behalf of SCOTT, 6 April 1812. Adam VANCAMP, John EVANS, Rawley MARTIN and John WELLS summoned to testify in behalf of WELLS, 27 August 1812. September 1812 term, "We the jury find for the plaintiff $2 in damages," N. WEBB, foreman.

172b - 1812, Monongalia Superior Court. John W. THOMPSON, potter, summoned to answer an indictment against him for an assault on Jacob FOULK, potter, 2 September 1811 and 4 January 1812. Simion WOODROW and Peter BURRILL summoned to witness for FOULK, 2 September 1811 and 4 January 1812. April 1812 term, judgement confessed by the defendant for costs.

172b - 1812, Monongalia Superior Court. Richard SMITH summoned to answer an indictment against him for a misdemeanor, 4 January 1812. George S. DERING summoned to give evidence to the Grand Jury, 1 June and 12 October 1810. Deputy Sheriff George Small DERING swore that Richard SMITH during the present term of court did request him, DERING, to summon some of his, SMITH's, neighbors and particularly James WEST to be on the jury for a trial in an action of covenant then pending in the Superior Court wherein Asher LEWIS was plaintiff and SMITH was defendant, 19 October 1809. James WEST summoned to testify in behalf of SMITH, 6 April 1812. ____ 1812 term, "We the jury find the defendant not guilty," Dudley EVANS, foreman.

172b - 1812, Monongalia Superior Court. John W. THOMPSON summoned to answer Rachel BILLS in a plea of slander damage $500, 18 August 1810. BILLS' complaint: In May 1810, THOMPSON was heard to say "Rachel was a whore and was common to a number of men and for that reason he the said John could not marry her." THOMPSON's answer to the complaint: In 1808, 1809 and 1810, Rachel BILLS was a whore, etc. and therefore she should not have and maintain her action against him. David CLARK summoned to testify in behalf of THOMPSON, 12 September 1810. CLARK's deposition heard at the house of W. N. JARRETT, Esqr., on 12 September 1810, by JP JARRETT and JP

Thomas MILLER to be used in evidence in the action for a supposed breach of promise on a marriage contract brought by Rachael BILLS, plaintiff, against John W. THOMPSON, defendant: CLARK said he knew that BILLS was "criminally intimate" and had "carnal connections" with men other than THOMPSON about 1 April last year and that the event took place at night on the lot where BILLS lived in the corner next to William LANHAM's house. He refused to reveal the identity of the man and the court asked him if he were to answer the question, "would it tend to incriminate you?" CLARK answered, "It might be so considered, perhaps." William McCLEERY, Esther McCLEERY, Thomas HERSEY, Jacob FOULK, Fielding KIGER, Christian MADERA, Peggy WILLIAMS, John WILLIAMS, John CHISLER, Elizabeth CHISLER, Reuben CHALFANT, John WAGNER, Abigal MESSENGER and Darkey SHOCKLEY summoned to testify in behalf of BILLS, 15 July 1811. April 1812 term, "Abated by the plaintiff's death."

172b - 1812, Monongalia Superior Court. John STEALEY summoned to answer Peter BURRETT in a plea of trespass on the case to recover money due, damage $600, 10 May 1809. Peter BURRETT complained that STEALEY owed him $402.79 for work and labor. Jacob KIGER summoned to bring with him any and all the books in his care containing amounts or settlements between the parties and testify in behalf of BURRETT, 19 March 1810. Adam MAGILL, William JARRETT Sr., George HOSKINSON, Leonard HOSKINSON, John AUSTIN, Samuel WILSON, Godfrey GUSEMAN, William WALKER and Frederick SWITZER summoned to testify in behalf of BURRETT, 19 March 1810. September 1812 term, dismissed, agreed.

172b - 1815, Monongalia Superior Court. Richard PRICE and William PRICE summoned to answer Joseph TIDBALL in a plea of debt for $104 and $10 damage, 20 February 1810. Note signed by Richard and William PRICE to TIDBALL for $104 dated 13 August 1805, payable in good salt at $4 per bushel delivered at DERING's Tavern before 25 November next and witnessed by James EVANS and H. DERING. Appearance Bond signed by Richard PRICE secured by William W. PRICE, 28 February 1810. Appearance Bond signed by William PRICE secured by W. N. JARRETT, 6 March 1810. Nathan ASHBEY summoned to testify in behalf of William PRICE, 25 March 1811. At April 1812 term of Superior Court, TIDBALL obtained a judgement against Richard and William PRICE for $104 with interest at 6% from 25 November 1805 plus costs. PRICE was granted an injunction against the judgement. Richard and William PRICE signed this Injunction Bond secured by William W. PRICE to ensure all costs and awards would be paid in case the injunction should be dissolved, 7 May 1813. "Defendants took benefit of stay law and paid $10.30 costs to N. EVANS on 11 March 1815.

172b - 1812, Monongalia Superior Court. James MURPHY summoned
to answer John MASON, assignee of Elijah HARDESTY, in a plea
of covenant damage $500, 5 April 1811. MASON's complaint: On
10 September 1810, MURPHY agreed with HARDESTY to convey, on
or before 15 February next, his right, title, interest and
claim in and to a 200 acre tract of land on Buffalo River,
where upon the said MURPHY then lived. HARDESTY assigned the
agreement to MASON on 4 February 1811 and MURPHY refused to
convey the property as agreed. Appearance Bond signed by
James (x) MURPHY secured by Robert STEWART, 8 April 1811. "5
March 1812, Dear Sir, I desire you to draw the suit between
me and James MURPHY and also send me the note and title by
Mr. ELLIOT and the suit to be dismissed on my costs from
you," signed by John MASON. "Received 6 April 1812, the
obligation above referred to," signed by Abraham ELLIOT.
State Attorney Noah LINSLEY.

172b - 1812, Monongalia Superior Court. Alexander McCLELAND
summoned to answer John L. ROBERTS in a plea of assault $2000
damage, 14 March 1811. April 1812 term, dismissed, agreed and
judgement for the plaintiff for costs.

172b - 1812, Monongalia Superior Court. One Negro woman
slave named Ann and 1 Mulatto boy slave named Ned and 3
horses, the property of James SCOTT, was attached at the suit
of Robert FERRELL for $280 with interest plus costs. In order
to retain possession of his property until time of public
sale or his debt was paid SCOTT signed this Delivery Bond
secured by Felix SCOTT, 28 September 1811. April 1812 term,
execution quashed.

172b - 1812, Monongalia Superior Court. Thomas CORDRAY summoned to answer William STEWART in a plea of slander damage
$500, 15 August 1809. CORDRAY was heard to say that STEWART
whipped and abused his mother and was a violent and undutiful
son. On 28 March 1812, Thomas CORDRAY swore that Mary STEWART
was a material witness for him and prayed the court to hear
her deposition as she "is now lying very sick and likely to
die." CORDRAY swore that he applied to Deputy Clerk Rawley
SCOTT for a subpoena for Mary STEWART, Elizabeth STEWART,
David SNYDER and Jane TURNER as witness for him and SCOTT
told him the Clerk of the Superior Court "had lately departed
this life and that subpoenas could not issue in consequence"
and he could not get subpoenas for that reason. David
STEWART, Charles BOYLES and James LEASON summoned to testify
in behalf of William STEWART, 20 February 1811 and 10 August
1812. "Notified Charles BOYLES but David STEWART cannot be
found," signed Aaron BARKER. David SNIDER, Mary STEWART and
Elizabeth STEWART summoned to testify in behalf of Thomas
CORDRAY, 22 March 1811 and 2 March 1812. Arbitrators Boaz
BURROWS, Jared EVANS and James BARKER agreed that each party
pay half the costs and the suit be dismissed, 1 April 1812.

172b - 1812, Monongalia Superior Court. James BURCHINAL summoned to answer Joel SMITH in a plea of covenant broken damage $600, 9 May 1808, 21 February and 20 June 1809 and 27 January 1810. SMITH's complaint: By an Article of Agreement entered into by BURCHINAL and SMITH dated 14 June 1803, SMITH promised to convey to BURCHINAL all the remaining part of a tract of land situation on the west side of the Monongahela River on the waters of Robinsons Run for $3 per acre to be discharged at the value of $100 on or before 1 October 1803 and the balance to be paid on or before 1 October 1806 with legal interest and SMITH agreed to make a deed. SMITH said he made a deed to BURCHINAL but BURCHINAL did not pay as agreed. Bail Bond for BURCHINAL secured by Jacob FOULK, 28 May 1810. FOULK swore that after payment of all debts and those of which he stands as security, his estate was worth $600. 9 September 1812, BURCHINAL said he bought of SMYTH 140 acres of land at $3 per acre = $420. He paid $60 before the money was due, a saddle at the same time worth $12 and a cow at the same time worth $12.50. In the fall, he paid $3 before the money was due and $150 when the obligation came due. Interest until 1 November 1807 from the time of the last payment = $13.44 and credit of $40 paid 1 November 1807. Interest from the last payment on the balance then due until 10 September 1812 = $41.29. Balance owing = $183.23. On 9 September 1812, judgement was entered for this amount by BURCHINAL and George SMYTH, agents for Joel SMYTH.

172b - 1812, Monongalia Superior Court. John W. DEAN summoned to answer George SHINN in a plea of debt for $1600 and $10 damage, 24 May 1811. Bond dated 27 June 1808 signed by John W. DEAN whereby DEAN agreed to give SHINN $800 for his right title and interest in and to 333 acres of land whereon DEAN lived, payment to be made as follows: $50 on or before 15 of next month, $184.96 in twelve months and the balance in 18 months. Bond witnessed by Wm. G. PAYNE and Sarah DUGGAN. Receipt signed by SHINN to DEAN for payment of $124 dated 30 July 1808 and witnessed by Peter TENANT. Appearance Bond and Bail Bond for John W. DEAN secured by John DEAN and Isaac DEAN, 27 September 1811. September 1812 term, judgement for the plaintiff.

172b - 1812, Monongalia Superior Court. Order to Lt. Zacquill MORGAN to bring the body of Levi PAGE to Superior Court to face charges of desertion and bounty jumping, 10 September 1812. Lt. MORGAN certified that Levi PAGE, on 1 August 1812, enlisted as a soldier in the 12th Regiment of Infantry in the Army of the United States and as such soldier was detained in his custody and now is delivered to court, 10 September 1812. Deposition of Abraham WOODROW: He was present at the time PAGE enlisted as a soldier under Lt. MORGAN in the Army and at the time he received the bounty from MORGAN he was very much intoxicated with liquor. Sarah SHOCKLEY's deposition:

She met PAGE shortly after his enlistment and knew he was
very intoxicated and took him home with her and put him to
bed and he fell asleep. When he awoke, he did not remember
that he had enlisted. Jacob MOUSER/MANSER said he knew PAGE
had consumed a great deal of drink on the day he enlisted,
before he enlisted and at the time he enlisted and he was
very drunk and was not sober. Thomas McKINLEY said he had
been drinking all day with PAGE before and after he enlisted.
James T. TATTERSON said from the wild conduct of PAGE at the
time he enlisted he must have been drunk or crazy, 10
September 1812.

172b - 1812, Monongalia Superior Court. John STEALEY summoned
to answer Walter JENKINS, surviving partner of W. JENKINS and
Company, in a plea of debt for $370.44 and $50 damage, 18
March 1811. Walter JENKINS and the late Robert RIDDELL,
deceased, constituted the firm of W. JENKINS and Company.
John STEALEY summoned to answer Walter JENKINS in a plea of
debt for $1445 and $1 damage, 18 March 1811. Three day note
signed by STEALEY to JENKINS dated 1 October 1809 at
Baltimore for $370.44 and witnessed by Francis S. JENKINS.
Bond signed by STEALEY to JENKINS for $721 dated 11 September
1810 and witnessed by Augustus WERNINGER and Michael WALTON.
Appearance Bond signed by STEALEY secured by Rawley SCOTT,
20 March 1811. To Nimrod EVANS, Esqr., "16 August 1812,
Baltimore, Dear Sir, Your favor of the 16th June I have duly
received and have complied with your request. You have now
enclosed the account current with my affidavit which is very
explanatory. Likewise that of Mr. WALTON which in my opinion
will settle the business without difficulty. I wish you to
write me the result immediately and when you expect the money
will be collected on this and the other larger judgement. You
will press the business for it is for goods sold 8 years
since and I never wanted money more than at present. I am
surprised that Mr. STEALEY should say he paid $400 but as the
truth is he can only show a receipt for $200. This is getting
over it rather clumsily," signed by JENKINS. To Nimrod EVANS,
Esqr., 27 April 1812, Baltimore, from JENKINS. JENKINS
explained that the receipt produced by STEALEY for "$200
dated 5 October 1809 as a set off against his note dated 4
October 1809 at 3 days after date, it is an error of my own
making which is very fresh on my memory, the $200 was paid on
the 5 October on presenting an account current. The parti-
culars of our whole dealings are stated on the prefixed leaf
and in order to prevent a clashing of the note bearing date
with the receipt, I intended to have dated the note to vary
one day, but through error, dated it one day back in place of
a day ahead." He said he sent STEALEY a current account and
a similar explanation and "I have so good an opinion of his
honesty that he will discover the error he has fallen into
and the judgement be taken for the just sum of $370.44 called
for in the note." He asked that Michael WALTON, of Balti-

more, be questioned if STEALEY presented an objection as WALTON could prove his acknowledgment of the note without any set off. He asked EVANS to inform him if the 500 or 600 barrels of flour had been forwarded to New Orleans, the proceeds or part of which were to liquidate his judgements. He went on to explain that he had given STEALEY the account against STEALEY and SHINN on 5 October 1809 when STEALEY informed him of SHINN's death and as surviving partner he, STEALEY, issued his note for the balance which was $370.44. STEALEY's account dated 13 December 1804 through 28 January 1806 is for merchandise in the amount of 327 pounds, 8 shillings and 5 pence with interest added and a few amounts credited. STEALEY and SHINN in account with JENKINS and COCHRAN is dated 20 October 1806 for merchandise. The bottom of the page is turned up and the amounts are covered. September 1812 term, judgement confessed.

172b - 1812, Monongalia Superior Court. Nimrod EVANS summoned to answer William G. PAYNE in a plea of trespass for the detention of a negro boy named Reuben and $500 damage, 25 February 1811. PAYNE complained that EVANS held and detained 1 Negro boy named Reuben valued at $500. Conveyance Bond signed by Abraham WOODROW to William G. PAYNE for 1 Negro boy named Reuben, about 4 years old, and 1 Negro girl named Clara, about 6 years old, now in Frederick County, Virginia in the possession of WOODROW's wife for $100. This bond witnessed by John A. GUSEMAN and Isaac (x) GUSEMAN dated 18 January 1810. Abraham GUSEMAN, John CHISLER, Abraham HALE and George B. HOSKINSON summoned to testify in behalf of PAYNE, 25 August and 9 September 1812. Abraham WOODROW summoned to testify in behalf of EVANS, 4 September 1812. Appearance Bond signed by Nimrod EVANS secured by John STEALEY, 1 March 1811. September 1812 term, judgement for the plaintiff. "We the jury find the slave in the declaration mentioned of the value of $100."

172b - 1811, Monongalia Superior Court. Lewis OTT sued Jesse PAYNE and Abraham CROSS (the suit was later dropped against CROSS/CRISS) for $60 due by an obligation dated 17 March 1804 which was due 1 June 1804 to be paid in salt at $4 per bushel except $16 which was to be paid in cash. 18 May 1810, a jury consisting of William CHIPPS, Peter BURRITT, James SHANE, James McVICKER, George REES, John DAVIS, James A. WALTON, John CHIPPS, Thomas McKINLEY, Joseph ALLEN, Joseph LOWRY and Jacob FOULK ruled in favor of PAYNE to recover his costs. On 19 May 1810, the verdict was set aside and a new trial granted. On 17 May 1811, another jury was called consisting of Augustus WERNINGER, William CHIPPS, John SULLIVAN, David CAMBLIN, James HURRY, Nicholas B. MADERA, George CROSS, Nicholas CHISLER, David BATZELL, Daniel CHISLER, Richard WALLS and Abraham HALE was of the opinion that PAYNE had not paid his debt as he declared and found for OTT the debt of

$60 with interest at 6% from 1 June 1804. Order to stay execution of a judgement obtained on 16 August 1811 by Jesse PAYNE against Lewis OTT for the costs of an action of debt, OTT having given bond, with security, to prosecute with effect and if the said judgement be affirmed, to pay damages and costs as shall be awarded against him, 28 October 1811. "Jesse PAYNE is not an inhabitant of this Commonwealth." Stay Bond signed by OTT secured by William STEWART, 28 October 1811. STEWART swore that after payment of all debts and those for which he stands security his estate was worth more that the penalty of this bond ($63.33), 28 October 1811.

172b - 1812, Monongalia Superior Court. Phillip DODDRIDGE and Noah LINSLY summoned to show cause, if any they can, why Benjamin REEDER should not have execution against them for damages and costs, 1 July 1808. Benjamin REEDER recovered against Charles BARING Jr. $4000 plus costs which he sustained because BARING was found guilty of slander against REEDER. BARING appealed to the Court of Appeals in Richmond and REEDER recovered $1652.80 against BARING for detaining the execution of the first judgement plus costs. On 19 September 1800, DODDRIDGE of Brooke County, and LINSLY, of Ohio County, appeared before Monongalia County Justice Jonathan DAVIS and secured Bail Bond for BARING. BARING did not pay the debt nor surrender to prison and DODDRIDGE and LINSLY were responsible for the debt. DODDRIDGE and LINSLY said REEDER ought not have and maintain his action against them because "at District Court in 1808, the said Charles by the judgement and consideration of the same court and as assignee of John HOGE, who was assignee of Benjamin STODDARD, surviving obligee of FORREST and STODDARD, recovered of the said Benjamin REEDER the sum of $1909.65 debt with interest" at 6% from 7 November 1794 plus costs. And at the same term, "the said Charles as assignee of Hanson BRISCOE" recovered against REEDER the sum of $1052.09 debt with interest at 6% from 13 October 1807 plus costs. September 1812 term, judgement for the defendants.

172b - 1812, Monongalia Superior Court. Samuel CLUTTER and Hettie/Hester his wife summoned to answer Benjamin MIDDLETON and Mary his wife in a plea of slander damage $400, 15 July 1811. Hester was heard to say that Mary was a whore and dirty hussy. September 1812 term, dismissed, agreed by the parties.

ENVELOPE 173 contains executions of some of the cases abstracted before. An EXECUTION is a judicial writ by which an officer is empowered to carry a judgement into effect. (Webster's Collegiate Dictionary). The document names the plaintiff and the defendant, the amount of judgement and to whom awarded, the amount of penalty, court costs and the date of the order. See Volume I, pages 34 and 35 for an example.

173 - 1812, Monongalia Superior Court. Harrison County. Order to attach the property of John and Andrew DAVISSON to satisfy William DAVISSON $5.64, 13 December 1812.

173 - 1812, Monongalia Superior Court. Ohio County. Order to attach the property of Robert and Ralph GORREL/GARRET to satisfy John McFARLAND $521 with interest at 6% from 12 December 1803, 18 December 1812.

173 - 1812, Monongalia Superior Court. Hampshire County. Order to attach the property of David LONG Jr. and David LONG Sr. to satisfy Paul SANDERS $1049.86, 21 October 1812.

173 - 1812, Monongalia Superior Court. Wood County. Order to attach the property of William and Sylvester ROBINSON to satisfy George D. AVERY $1858.34 with interest at 6% from 31 October 1804, 6 January 1812.

174 - 1813, Monongalia Superior Court. Edward MERCER and James MORGAN leased to Samuel MINOR a 200 acre tract of land on the waters of Maracles Run, a branch of Dunkard Creek, for 10 years from 10 January 1811. On 11 January 1811, MERCER and MORGAN ejected MINOR from the property and they were summoned to answer MINOR for breach of contract. 13 September 1813.

174 - 1813, Monongalia Superior Court. Indenture dated 22 November 1813 whereby David WELLS and Maryan (CAIN) his wife, Walter CAIN and Elizabeth his wife, John CAIN and Elizabeth his wife, Anthony KIRKHART and Jane (CAIN) his wife, Daniel MEDSKER and Rachel (CAIN) his wife, Alexander WALKER and Margaret (CAIN) his wife, Richard CAIN and Hannah his wife, Daniel CAIN and Ann CAIN and the heirs of Samuel CAIN, deceased, all the heirs and legal representatives of Richard CAIN, deceased, conveyed to Thomas CAIN, in consideration of $145, lot #1 in Middletown situated on Main Street and alley with all buildings and improvements. Jane (x) CAIN, John CAIN, Anthony (x) KIRKHART, Richard CAIN, Daniel MEDSKER, Daniel CAIN and Ann (x) CAIN were the only ones to sign this deed. The deed was produced in court and the acknowledgment of John CAIN proved by the oaths of Daniel COX, Lawrence SNIDER and Gasper OTT, witnesses thereto, and acknowledged by Anthony KIRKHART and Jane his wife, Richard CAIN, Daniel MEDSKER, Daniel CAIN and Ann CAIN and ordered to be certified, December 1813 term.

174 - 1814, Monongalia Superior Court. Thomas LAZELL summoned to answer Jane THOMPSON, by James THOMPSON her next friend, in a plea of assault damage $1000, 21 March 1812. July 1813 term, dismissed for want of declaration. On 17 February 1814, James M. THOMPSON paid $2.20 in fees.

174 - 1819, Monongalia Superior Court. At a Court of Appeals held at the Capitol in Richmond on Friday 13 October 1819, Elihu HORTON, William G. PAYNE and James PINDALL, plaintiffs, against Colder HAYMOND, Nicholas VANDERVORT, John WILLITS, William McCLEERY, Richard HARRISON, Asa HALL, Boos BURROWS, Amos ROBERTS and Abraham WOODRING, defendants. The court was of the opinion that a former judgement out of the Superior Court be overruled because the defendants were not Overseers of the Poor of Monongalia County at the time the suit was instigated and the action should exist in their successors and not in them, signed by Clerk H. DANCE. This action was instigated in Superior Court on 18 October 1809 against the Collectors of the 1804 Poor Levy for not accounting to the Overseers of the Poor.

174 - 1813, Monongalia Superior Court. Levi MORAN and David BARKER (not found) summoned to answer John RYAN in a plea of assault damage $500, 23 May 1810. RYAN complained that MORGAN and BARKER entered his plantation, tied him up and destroyed his property including pulling down his house with his family inside. April 1813 term, non-suit and judgement for the defendant for costs.

174 - 1814, Monongalia Superior Court. Samuel and John MERRI-FIELD, John and Bathsehba SPRINGER, John and Elizabeth HARR and Mary MERIFIELD heirs of Richard MERRIFIELD, deceased, summoned to answer David SCOTT in a plea of 200 pounds ($666) and $50 damage, 4 April and 7 June 1803 and 21 March 1804. Zackquil MORGAN, Benjamin REEDER, John SPRINGER and John CARTER summoned to testify in behalf of SCOTT, 17 October 1809, 21 August 1810 and 6 September 1813. James MORGAN summoned to testify in behalf of SCOTT, 25 August 1810. Samuel HANWAY, Morgan MORGAN, John EVANS Sr., Nimrod EVANS and John DOWNER summoned to testify in behalf of MERRIFIELD heirs, 14 August 1812, 17 March and 29 June 1813. Deputy John JOLLIFF for Sheriff Thomas MILLER. At a September 1813 term of court, David SCOTT obtained a judgement against John SPRINGER and John HARE and others for the sum of $137.50 with interest at 5% from 1 December 1798. In the Superior Court of Chancery held at Clarksburg, Harrison County, SPRINGER and HARE obtained an injunction to stay execution of the judge-ment until the case could be heard in a Court of Equity. Injunction Bond signed by SPRINGER and HARR to ensure all costs and awards would be paid in case the injunction should be dissolved secured by Jacob POLSLEY/PALSLEY and Joseph BRUMMAGE in the presence of Thos. P. RAE, 10 November 1813. POLSLEY and BRUMMAGE both swore their estates were worth more than the amount of this bond ($543) after payment of their debts and any securities for which they were liable, 10 November 1813. Conveyance Bond signed by Richard MARRIFIELD to SCOTT dated 6 September 1786 whereby MERRIFIELD promised to deliver to SCOTT 400 acres of land lying between Big Sandy

and Little Sandy as per a certificate and the same to warrant
and defend from all other claims, witnessed by Hugh McNEELY.
The defendants said SCOTT should not have and maintain his
action against them because they "have nothing by descent or
devise from Richard MERRIFIELD, deceased." Grant from the
Commonwealth, as per the Land Commissioners, to Richard
MERRIFIELD for the "ancient composition of two pounds
sterling" a 400 acre tract of land by survey dated 7 December
1785 on Three Fork Creek and Wickwares Creek adjoining lands
of James CURRANT, to include his improvements made in 1776.
By virtue of Pre-emption Warrant #1526 dated 29 September
1781, Richard MERRIFIELD, assignee of David RENSHAW, was
granted 200 acres of land, survey dated 11 June 1785, between
Little Creek and White Day Creek and crossing Laurel Run, 1
July 1791. By virtue of Pre-emption Warrant #1734 dated 3
November 1781, Richard MERRIFIELD (assignee of John PLOM who
was assignee of Morgan MORGAN who was assignee of Bice
BULLOCK) and Rice/Bice BULLOCK was granted 1000 acres, survey
dated 19 February 1788, on Little Creek joining Morgan
MORGAN's settlement right and David FANSHIER's land, 11 April
1793. By virtue of a Certificate in Right of Settlement,
Richard MERRIFIELD, assignee of John MERRIFIELD, was granted
400 acres, surveyed 12 December 1785, in Harrison County at
the head of Otter Creek, 17 October 1789. By virtue of Pre-
emption Warrant #1845 dated 9 December 1781, Richard MERRI-
FIELD was granted 600 acres, surveyed 8 December 1785,
joining his resident right on Three Fork and Wickwares Creek,
9 April 1789. Injunction dissolved 18 October 1814.

END OF MICROFILM #44

174 - 1813, Monongalia Superior Court. John STEALEY summoned
to answer Jesse PAYNE, surviving partner of PAYNE and FRET-
WELL for the use of Agnes FRETWELL, administratrix of Thomas
FRETWELL, deceased, in a plea of debt for $533.03, 6 November
1809. Deposition of Reuben BALLARD, Wilson County, Tennessee,
17 May 1811 before Justice James S. RAWLINGS at the house of
Edward CRULCHER in the Town of Lebanon: He was clerk or
bookkeeper for STEALEY at his forge in July 1807, the time
the account in question was opened. He was still bookkeeper
in January 1808, the last date of the account and he believed
the account was correct. In January 1808 a settlement took
place and a balance of $533.03 remained due to PAYNE and
FRETWELL. STEALEY demanded a credit of $200 for timber cut
and carried off his land. This demand was refused by PAYNE
and FRETWELL and no allowance was made at the time of the
settlement and it was later agreed between the parties to
send the matter to arbitration. William TINGLE and James A.
WATSON summoned to testify on behalf of PAYNE, 2 March, 16
July 1811 and 4 April 1812. April 1813 term, judgement for
defendant.

174 - 1813, Monongalia Superior Court. John STEALEY summoned
to answer Mary CLARK, executrix of Bartholomew CLARK,
deceased, who was assignee of Samuel HANWAY, in a plea of
debt for $1000 and $50 damage, 28 May 1811. Bond signed by
Jno STEALEY to Samuel HANWAY dated 15 August 1808 for the
penal sum of $1000, due 1 November 1810 and witnessed by
Jacob KYGER and Davis SHOCKLEY. Assignment to Bar. CLARK
signed by HANWAY and witnessed by David CLARK, no date. On 5
March 1810, Bartholomew CLARK was confined in jail after
being taken on an escape warrant at the suit of Hannah STANLY
against CLARK and John TAYLOR. In order to be released, he
gave up all his right to this bond and agreed it could be
sold at public sale for the best price (anytime after five
weeks from this date) to raise the amount of STANLY's claim
with costs and the balance to be returned to him. If the
claim should be fully paid before that time, the bond to be
returned to him. "Rec'd 29 March 1810 from M. GAY on account
of Mrs. STANLY's judgement against B. CLARK $35 in bank bills
and I have no further claim on this bond," signed by W.
TINGLE. Appearance Bond signed by Jno STEALEY secured by
Rawley SCOTT, 29 May 1811. John TAYLOR, Robert BOGGESS and
Samuel HANWAY summoned to testify in behalf of CLARK, 2
September 1812. Robert BOGGESS and Samuel HANWAY summoned to
testify in behalf of CLARK, 5 April 1813. STEALEY swore that
Cornelius BARKSHIRE was a material witness for him but he was
now on a journey to Tennessee and was expected to return
soon, 10 September 1812. April 1813 term, plea waived and
judgement confessed allowing just credits.

174 - 1813, Monongalia Superior Court. Samuel CRANE complained that John RODHEIFER slandered him by saying he, CRANE,
committed perjury by "swearing him, RODHEIFER, out of $40."
April 1813 term, judgement for defendant for costs.

174 - 1813, Monongalia Superior Court. John KIMMERER summoned
to answer Samuel CRANE in a plea of slander damage $1000, 13
March 1811. CRANE complained that KIMMERER slandered him by
saying that he, CRANE, "was a man who could not be depended
on when sworn as a witness." April 1813 term, judgement for
costs.

174 - 1813, Monongalia Superior Court. Ann DOUGLASS, demisee
of John MERRICK, deceased, vs Jonathan REES, assignee of Levi
WELLS. As part of a Pre-emption Warrant #1641 dated 20
October 1781, REES, assignee of Levi WELLS, was granted 600
acres by survey dated 5 November 1785 situated on Bushy Fork
of Elk Creek adjoining above his survey. In a petition by Ann
DOUGLASS, the court learned that WELLS made the location of
the Pre-emption Warrant on Glade Run, a branch of Elk Creek.
WELLS wrongfully assigned the land to REES. In 1775, John
MERRICK made a settlement improvement on the east side of
Bushy Fork of Elk Creek which entitled him to 400 acres by
settlement right, to include his settlement, according to an
act passed 1779. John MERRICK died intestate leaving Ann,
his sister, heiress at law and legal representative to whom
the land descended. "After the death of the said John
MERRICK, to wit, on the 27th day of October 1798, a survey of
the said tract of land was duly made for the said Ann
DOUGLASS pursuant to and by virtue of the aforesaid
certificate." The survey was returned to the Register's
Office, but the Commissioner's Certificate was lost. On 8
February 1813, the General Assembly authorized the Register
of the Land Office to issue a duplicate certificate in favor
of the heirs or heir of John MERRICK. In due form of the law,
Ann DOUGLASS was granted a patent for the 400 acres. Ann said
REES' assignment included a great part of her 400 acre patent
and she prayed the court to give notice to the tenants in
possession of the assignment to come before the court "to
show cause, if any they have or can say anything for themselves" why the patent to REES "ought not to be cancelled,
vacated, annulled, disallowed and revoked."

174 - 1813, Monongalia Superior Court. Agnes FRETWELL,
administratrix of Thomas FRETWELL, deceased summoned to
answer John ROBERTS in a plea of debt for $200 and $76
damage, 13 July 1808. Note signed by Thos. FRETWELL and
secured by Jesse PAYNE to John ROBERTS, of Washington County,
Pennsylvania, for $267 dated 5 May 1807, due 5 May 1808 and
witnessed by Jas ROBERTS. Agnes FRETWELL said ROBERTS should
not have and maintain his action against her because Thomas
FRETWELL, in his lifetime, to wit, on 18 October 1802,

obliged himself to pay William FRETWELL Jr. the sum of $4000 (a loan) with interest to be paid on demand. After the death of Thomas, the debt being unsatisfied, William brought suit in the 1809 Monongalia County court against Agnes FRETWELL as administratrix of Thomas, deceased. William prevailed in the suit and recovered against Thomas' estate the debt with 6% interest plus costs to be credited with $3600 paid by Agnes on 12 November 1808 and $15.33 paid by Agnes on 12 December 1808. On 25 November 1801, Thomas signed an obligation promising to pay William FERGUSON 11 pounds and 5 shillings. FERGUSON assigned this obligation to Brenshaw FRETWELL who assigned the same to William FRETWELL and after Thomas died William sued to recover this debt in the March 1809 term of court. William recovered the debt amounting to $37.50 with interest plus costs. On 29 June 1801, Thomas signed an obligation promising to pay James GENTRY 154 pounds and 6 shillings and GENTRY assigned this debt to William FRETWELL. William brought suit to recover the debt amounting to $514.24 at the March 1809 term and recovered the same with interest plus costs. On 26 November 1801, Thomas signed an obligation promising to pay Richard SNOW 145 pounds and SNOW assigned the same to William FRETWELL. After the death of Thomas, William brought suit and recovered the debt $483.33 1/2 with interest plus costs. On 17 September 1801, Thomas signed an obligation promising to pay Henry BUCK/BURK/BANK 76 pounds, 4 shillings and one half penny which Henry assigned to William FRETWELL. After the death of Thomas, William brought suit and recovered $254.01 with interest plus costs. On 29 September 1801, Thomas signed an obligation promising to pay Reuben McCLERY 114 pounds, 5 shillings and 7 pence which Reuben assigned to William FRETWELL. After the death of Thomas, William brought suit and recovered $383.93 with interest plus costs. On 29 November 1801, Thomas signed an obligation promising to pay Samuel GARRISON 10 pounds, 8 shillings and 8 pence which Samuel assigned to Brenshaw FRETWELL who assigned the same to William FRETWELL. After the death of Thomas, William brought suit and recovered $34.79 with interest plus costs. Thomas owed the following debts which were turned over to the Sheriff of Monongalia County who sold Thomas' estate, under distress, for $332.83 1/2 to pay these court fees: to the Clerk of Albermarle County $259.49 1/2 for services. To the Clerk of Orange County $43.42 for services, to the Clerk of Charlottesville $43.80 for services, to the Clerk of Rockingham $6.12 for services. Agnes swore she had administered all the estate of Thomas and did not have anything more to satisfy any debts. Noah LINSLY, attorney for the defendant. James A. WALTHAM, agent for FRETWELL, swore that Elijah WATTS was a material witness for FRETWELL and that WATTS promised to attend court unless prevented by sickness. Elijah WATTS and James DICKERSON summoned to testify in behalf of FRETWELL, 28 June 1810 and 11 June 1812. John PAYNE, William G. PAYNE,

John C. PAYNE and James A. WALTON summoned to testify, 20 August 1810, 12 March and 10 August 1812. April 1813 term, judgement for the defendant.

174 - 1813, Monongalia Superior Court. Richard WELLS summoned to answer Felix SCOTT in a plea of slander damage $1000, 6 July 1811. WELLS was heard to say that SCOTT had "killed and made use of other peoples hogs dishonestly." Jared EVANS, John SMITH, Adam VANCAMP, John FISHER, Joseph DUNLOP, John BOUSLOG, James TIBBS and Samuel HANWAY summoned to testify in behalf of SCOTT, 8 March 1813. Rawley MARTIN and John W. EVANS summoned to testify in behalf of WELLS, 29 March 1813. Deputy John JOLLIFFE for Sheriff Thomas MILLER. April 1813 term, judgement for the plaintiff $24 damage, John GILLMEYER, foreman.

174 - 1813, Monongalia Superior Court. George SMITH vs Agnes FRETWELL. "Valley Furnace, June 20, 1807. On settlement this day with Mr. George SMITH, we find a balance due in favor of Mr. SMITH the sum of $180.36 to be paid in bar iron and castings on or before 20 August next ensuing for value received." Signed by Jesse PAYNE and Thos FRETWELL and witnessed by John JOHNSON. Henry LOUIS summoned to testify in behalf of SMITH, 20 August 1810. Agnes answered this action with the same reasons as in the case described on pages 330 and 331. A list of possible jurors: Purnell HOUSTON, John GARLOW, Richard PRICE, J. FURBY, William BARNES, Moses DOOLITTLE Jr., George SMITH, Patrick KELLY, John MELLET and Hugh MURPHY. April 1813 term, judgement for the defendant.

174 - 1813, Monongalia Superior Court. Nicholas CASEY summoned to answer William PRICE in a plea of covenant broken damage $2000, 23 October 1809. William PRICE complained that Nicholas CASEY failed to keep his promise or covenant dated 21 February 1804 to "have the following improvements put on a place called Dunkard Bottom which the plaintiff (PRICE) leased for five years from the defendant (CASEY)." CASEY promised to build a porch and extend it 10 or 12 feet longer than the house and build one house as an addition to include 2 rooms on the lower floor, 2 stories high with a 12 feet between the two houses. He promised to build a sufficient kitchen at the rear or behind the passage and to have the garret floor in the old house ceiled under the joist with plank as it is not floored at present and to have a good smoke house built in some convenient place. He promised to have part of the barn and stable move to a more convenient place, enlarge the stables and after the new kitchen is built to convert the old kitchen into a granary. He promised to provide planking, hauling, nails, glass, locks, hinges, etc. to do all the improvements. He promised to have a well dug and walled convenient to the house and kitchen, the cellar

walled and garden and yard fenced. To pay the rent, PRICE promised to do all the joiner and carpenter work and hewing. Any other necessary work performed by PRICE would be at common wages. John MASON, Samuel CRANE, John RHODEHEIFFER, Peter MEREDITH, John ROBERTS, John DEBERRY, Nehemiah SQUIRES and Wm WALKER summoned to testify in behalf of PRICE, 16 July 1811. The dispute was turned over to Ralph BARKSHIRE, William JOHNSON and Nicholas VANDERVERT for arbitration. BARKSHIRE did not act as one of the mediators. VANDERVERT and John FAIRFAX, of Monongalia County, William JOHNSON and William ARMSTRONG, of Allegany County, Maryland, signed as arbitrators, 9 October 1811. They determined that CASEY pay all costs and pay to PRICE $440.29. PRICE promised to signed a release to the property upon payment of the award. April 1813 term, award entered and judgement for the plaintiff.

174 - 1813, Monongalia Superior Court. List of jurors: William Haymond, John McGEE, George GREENWOOD, John WAGNER, George FLITE, James RANDLE, John EVANS Jr., Ralph BARKSHIRE, foreman; James TIBBS, John REED, Jacob HOLLON, Thomas HASEL, James HURRY, John HUFFMAN, Francis BILLINGSLEY, Thomas EWEL, Phillip SMELL, Benjamin WILSON, John A. GOOSEMAN, Jacob HOLLON Jr., John EVANS, John BAKER, Phillip SHIVELY and Jacob PINDAL. April 1813.

174 - 1813, Monongalia Superior Court. Case of BARKSHIRE vs HALE: Abraham HALE summoned to answer the complaint of Ralph BARKSHIRE in a plea of debt due by account, 20 March 1810. March 1810 term, Judgement for the plaintiff for $13.92 debt and $.32 cost. Attachment levied on 22 plank and sold to BARKSHIRE for $10 on 9 June 1810. Attachment levied on additional plank on 23 June 1810 to finish paying the debt plus cost and $.25 labor to remove the planks. Case of HALE vs HITE: George HITE summoned to answer Abraham HALE in a plea of trespass on the case $5000 damage, 16 January 1811. HALE complained that HITE entered a false and malicious grievance against him before Justice Ralph BARKSHIRE on 23 December 1810 stating that one hatter's planking, kettle and the plank's belongings had been stolen within 5 days last past and that HITE had reason to believe the property was hidden in the house of John TAYLOR, in the house of Abraham HALE or Thomas McKINLEY's hatter's shop where HALE worked and thereby caused HALE to be arrested. HALE was acquitted after spending time in jail, appearing in court twice, raising bail and security and was put to great expense in his defense. He suffered great injury to his credit, his good name and fame to the damage of $5000. HITE swore that Ralph BARKSHIRE was a material witness for him, 10 September 1812. James TAYLOR and BARKSHIRE summoned to testify in behalf of HITE, 6 April 1813. TAYLOR summoned to testify in behalf of HITE, 31 August 1812. Jacob FOULK, Christian MADERA and William WALKER summoned to testify in behalf of HALE, 2 April 1813.

Robert HAWTHORN, William N. JARRETT, Christian MADERA and Fielding KYGER summoned to testify in behalf of HITE, 27 March 1812. April 1813 term, judgement for the plaintiff for $49.00 in damages.

174 - 1813, Monongalia Superior Court. Agnes FRETWELL, administratrix of Thomas FRETWELL, summoned to answer John HOY in a plea of debt for $100 and $20 damage, 3 March 1810. Note signed by Thos FRETWELL to John HOYE dated 4 September 1806 for $100 due 25 December 1808 and witnessed by Frederick HARSH and Catharine (x) HARSH. Note signed by Thos FRETWELL to John HOYE dated 4 September 1806 for $100 due 25 December 1809 and witnessed by Frek. HARSH. John GREEN, John PAYNE and John C. PAYNE summoned to testify in behalf of HOYE, 10 August 1810, 27 March and 15 July 1811. Elijah WATTS' and James DICKENSON's depositions to be used in evidence in four actions of debt, two wherein John HOYE is plaintiff, one wherein George SMITH is plaintiff and one wherein John ROBERTS is plaintiff vs Agnes FRETWELL. WATTS said he saw Thomas FRETWELL execute his bond to William FRETWELL and Thomas was a merchant in Albermarle County and had a considerable store at one time but had sold out nearly all his goods before he came to the western country. He said Thomas removed his family to the western country before the bond was executed. After Thomas removed to the western country, William FRETWELL, father of Thomas and Granger? FRETWELL, Thomas' brother, collected the accounts of Thomas. At the time the bond was executed, William FRETWELL had four children living and four/some grandchildren, the descendants of a deceased child. WATTS said he lived near William FRETWELL who owned a large plantation and a number of negroes. He estimated William's estate to be worth between $3000 and $4000. He said William usually made 4 hogsheads of tobacco annually and not much wheat and he did not recall that William was in the habit of lending money in the neighborhood. DICKENSON said he witnessed the execution of the bond and a Bill of Sale for negroes but did not know the value of William's estate, sworn on 9 September 1812 before Justice William JOHN. April 1813 term, judgement for the defendant on both notes.

174 - 1813, Monongalia Superior Court. Deed dated 10 September 1812 by and between Zaccheus COPLIN, of Harrison County, and George ASHBY, of Monongalia County, for $350 for 100 acres on the head of Brains Run, a branch of Three Forks, by patent dated 23 August 1799. Signed by COPLIN and witnessed by John FAIRFAX, George BROWN and Henry FORTNEY. Proved in court at June term 1813.

174a - 1814, Monongalia Superior Court. Jacob LUCUS and Josiah PRICKETT summoned to answer Robert FERRELL in a plea of covenant broken damage $3033.33, 29 April 1806. Bail Bond

for LUCUS and PRICKETT secured by Henry BATTON, 15 May 1806.
FERRELL with security, David SAYRE, complained that LUCAS and
his security, PRICKETT, on 25 May 1798, promised in writing
to settle a suit then pending in which FERRELL, as assignee
of David BRADFORD, was the plaintiff and Robinson LUCAS, the
father of Jacob LUCAS, was the defendant. They agreed to
have the dispute settled by arbitrators John EVANS, Frances
WARMAN, Dudley EVANS, Nathan SPRINGER, William HAYMOND,
Joseph JENKINS and David CROLL. The parties agreed that if
FERRELL lost the suit, he would keep them indemnified from
BRADFORD and if LUCUS lost the suit, he would make FERRELL a
clear deed for 66 acres on White Day Creek, the cause of the
suit, agreeable to the plat. James WEST Sr. summoned to
testify in behalf of LUCUS, 18 October 1809 and 20 August
1810. James G. WATSON summoned to testify in behalf of LUCUS
and PRICKETT, 16 September 1807. "Mr. WILSON, When the land
comes to be valued please to call on Richard SMITH, James
JEFFS, Daniel PRICE and oblige your old friend. In that suit
now pending where I am plaintiff and Robinson LUCUS and
others are defendants." Signed by Robert FERRELL. Security
Bond signed by Jacob LUCAS, Josiah PRICKETT and Isaiah
PRICKETT and witnessed by Wm WINSOR, 1 May 1806. The
arbitrators decreed that FERRELL pay his costs and give bond
sufficient to idemnify LUCAS and that LUCAS make a deed to
FERRELL and pay his costs. September 1813 term, "We the jury
find for the plaintiff and assess his damages to $396 with
interest from 4 September 1810 until payment," John PAYNE,
foreman. BATTON surrendered LUCUS to jail on 14 November
1814. Sheriff Thomas MILLER.

Also in this file - - - Case of Mary BENNETT vs George HITE:
Deposition of James TIBBS Jr. Sometime in 1810, HITE directed
his workers to remove 4 or 5 panels of plank fence from
BENNETT's lot and he heard HITE say, in 1809, that he cut
down peach trees which hung over his lot, 17 September 1812.

174a - 1813, Monongalia Superior Court. Grand Jurors 1813:
John FAIRFAX, Thomas PRICHARD, John REED, James TIBBS, Jno
WILSON, David DICKEY, James G. WATSON, Wm SNODGRASS, Frank
BILLINGSLEY, Coverdill COLE, R. HARRISON, Jo JENKINS, John
EVANS, Dan'l COX, Jacob PINDALL, Jno CHISLER, Geo DORSEY,
David GALLAWAY, Augustus WELLS, Wm SHAHAN, John BAKER, John
RODEHAFF__ and William WILSON.

174a - 1813, Monongalia Superior Court. Francis TIBBS Jr.
summoned to answer a presentment against him for an assault
upon Mary TROY, wife of James TROY, yeoman, May, June and
October 1810, 4 January and 28 April 1812 and 20 August 1813.
Hannah TIBBS and Margaret CHAMBERS summoned to testify in
behalf of TIBBS, 6 September 1813. William and Mary BARRET
summoned to give evidence to the Grand Jury, 10 April 1813.
September 1813 term, defendant found guilty and fined $40.

174a - 1813, Monongalia Superior Court. Elisha CLAYTON summoned to answer Joseph KING in a plea of trespass on the case damage $1000, 30 March and 20 April 1813. Note signed by CLAYTON and KING dated 19 April 1813 whereby they settled their dispute and CLAYTON promised to pay KING $40 in trade within one year and CLAYTON to pay his own cost of the suit, witnessed by Noah (x) CLAYTON and Mary M. (x) CLAYTON. "I promise to pay all costs that may accrue in an action of trespass on the case Joseph KING, plaintiff, and Elisha CLAYTON, defendant, by the clerk certifying the same if the said KING should fail to do the same." Signed William SNODGRASS and witnessed by Thos P. RAY. December 1813 term, dismissed.

174a - 1813, Monongalia Superior Court. John FAIRFAX summoned to answer Charles BYRN in a plea of trespass on the case damage $1500, 4 June 1810. BYRN complained that on 1 May 1808, FAIRFAX owed him $1500 for various goods, wares and merchandise. George ASHBEY summoned to testify in behalf of BYRN, 13 March and 10 August 1812. John PAYNE summoned to testify in behalf of BYRN, 13 and 21 March, 10 August 1812 and 19 March 1813. The case was referred to arbitrators Samuel HANWAY, Augustus WERNINGER, Mathew GAY, Alexander HAWTHORN, Rawley SCOTT, James McGEE and Christian MADERA or any three of them. HANWAY, WERNINGER, GAY and MADERA ruled that FAIRFAX pay BYRN $50 on or before 1 June next and that they execute mutual releases of all disputes and "____ally their two years sheriffalty." FAIRFAX was awarded all uncollected outstanding debts relative to their two year sheriffalty and he was charged with all costs of their dispute.

174a - 1815, Monongalia Superior Court. "To the Honorable Dabney? CARR, Judge of the Superior Court of Chancery held at Clarksburg for the 4th District of Virginia." Petitioner David SCOTT 3rd. complained that on 15 March 1813, John SHIVELEY, of Monongalia County, applied to him for a loan of $600 to enable him to pay certain debts. SCOTT loaned SHIVELY the $600, $350 to be paid in salt at the market price by 15 July 1813, $250 in cash by 20 August 1813. SHIVELY executed a Deed of Trust to 104 acres of land lying in Monongalia County to Felix SCOTT as trustee to secure payment of the loan. SCOTT and SHIVELEY made a settlement on 3 November 1813 and SHIVELEY executed his note for $175.75, the unpaid balance, with interest with the Deed of Trust as security. SCOTT complained that SHIVELEY along with Rawley MARTIN, Dudley DENT, Joseph CAMPBELL and Ralph BARKSHIRE were trying to defraud him. In 1815, SHIVELEY made a Deed of Trust to CAMPBELL for the use of MARTIN and DENT to secure them upon a certain contingency upon the 104 acres, they well knowing that the land was bound for the payment of SHIVELEY's debt to him. CAMPBELL sold the land at public auction and BARKSHIRE purchased it for a price well below the real value, BARKSHIRE refused to pay SCOTT and therefore he brings suit.

174a - 1813, Monongalia Superior Court. John STEALEY summoned to answer Thomas MEREDITH in a plea of debt for $979.61, 21 February 1812. Demand Note signed by STEALEY to MEREDITH dated 16 March 1811 for $979.61. Appearance Bond signed by STEALEY secured by Rawley SCOTT, 24 February 1812. James McGEE, attorney for MEREDITH. April 1813 term, judgement confessed and plea waived.

174a - 1813, Monongalia Superior Court. John STEALEY summoned to answer James FERRELL in a plea of $500 debt due by account, 2 July 1812. FERRELL complained that STEALEY, on 24 February 1812, requested him to transport iron nail castings and other goods and merchandise on his (FERRELL's) keel boat from Morgantown to "Cincinate" in the State of Ohio at the rate of $8 per ton. FERRELL said he transported 30 tons and made delivery to STEALEY in March 1812. On 26 March 1812, STEALEY hired FERRELL and his boat to transport goods and merchandise from "Cincinati" to Morgantown at $1.25 per day. FERRELL hired himself and boat for 64 days during which time he worked as a hand on board. FERRELL said STEALEY would not pay his debt and therefore he brings suit. Zacquil MORGAN, Horatio MORGAN, Jacob STEALEY, Cornelius BARKSHIRE, Robert MINNIS and Richard WALLS summoned to testify in behalf of FERRELL, 21 August 1813. R. CHALFANT security for costs.

John Healy Dr. to James Ferrall for freighting a half load
of Iron castings &c — — — — $157-8..

to 97½ Gallons of Whisky Brandy
at 50 cents ff gallon — — — — — — 13-75

4 Pounds of Coffee at 25 Cts ff ℔ — 1-00

half Barrel of Biscuit — — 1-00

And one Dollar for whiskey — 1-00

to Sixty Days work with myself and
Boat at 12½ Cts ff Day — 15-00

Four Days hire of my boat in which
Iron it was sent — — 2-00

3 7
5
2 7
6 4

For steering myself and Boat and one hand
and a Passenger which [?] Boarded
Six Days Detirt morgantown on Cincinnati 12 — 00

NB Started from cincinnati mth april 26th 1819
and arriv'd at Mr Ames Mill May 8 9th —

262 — 75

174a - 1813, Monongalia Superior Court. Henry LEWIS, husband-
man, summoned to answer an indictment against him for assault
on Abraham ELLIOTT, yeoman, 4 January 1812. James BUTLER and
William ELLIOTT summoned to testify in behalf of LEWIS, 17
March and 11 August 1813. September 1813 term, guilty and
fined $10, Davis SHOCKLEY, foreman.

174a - 1813, Monongalia Superior Court. John GRUB summoned to
answer Selee SAYRE in a plea of slander damage $1000, 25 July
1812. GRUB was heard to say that SAYRE was "a dam'd old
thief, a dam'd old liar, a rascal and a villain." James WEST
Jr., Richard SMITH, Stephen FAIRCHILD and James MOFFETT or
MORFIT summoned to testify in behalf of SAYRE, 29 June 1813.
Morgan MORGAN and James MORGAN summoned to testify in behalf
of GRUBB, 31 August 1813. September 1813 term, guilty and
fined $16.66 1/3.

174a - 1813, Monongalia Superior Court. James McVICKER summoned to answer John C. PAYNE in a plea of trover damage
$500, 26 August 1808. John C. PAYNE and Polly C. PAYNE for
themselves and Susanna G. PAYNE, Elizabeth PAYNE, Francis
PAYNE, Rhoda PAYNE, William PAYNE and Anna PAYNE, infants
under the age of 21 (by John C. PAYNE their next friend)
complained of James McVICKER (late a constable in Monongalia
County) in a plea of trover. On 7 March 1808, they were
owners of Nancy, a negro girl valued at $500. They said
McVICKER found her and well knowing Nancy belonged to them,
refused to return her and therefore they bring suit. McVICKER
said Polly C. PAYNE, after she brought suit, married George
KERNS and prayed the court to quash the suit brought by Polly
C. PAYNE. Zacquil MORGAN summoned to testify in behalf of
PAYNE, 5 September 1812 and 6 April 1813. Simeon WOODROW
summoned to testify in behalf of McVICKER, 29 June 1812.
April 1813 term, dismissed, agreed by the parties.

174a - 1813, Monongalia Superior Court. Thomas BUTLER summoned to answer William PRICE in a plea of covenant broken
damage $500, 28 March and 13 June 1811. Constable Philip
MARTIN. PRICE complained that in September 1805, BUTLER
agreed to lease to him a tract of land in Monongalia County
adjoining Nicholas CASEY and Jacob DRAPER on which there was
a mill seat, for a term of 3 years from 15 March next for the
purpose of building a saw mill. During the term, PRICE was
to have the privilege of getting and making use of any timber
on the land to build the saw mill and sawing (walnut only
excepted) and to have all the profits arising from the mill
as compensation for building the mill and BUTLER would pay
one half of the cost of building the mill, from thence to
remain joint partners in all the profits. PRICE agreed to
build the mill on good construction and the framing of good
substance all well put together and at the expiration of the
term to put the land and mill in good repair if any be

necessary. PRICE said BUTLER refused to perform his covenant and therefore he brings suit. Aron ROYSE summoned to testify in behalf of PRICE, 31 August 1812. John FAIRFAX and James E. BEALL summoned to testify in behalf of PRICE, 16 August 1813. BEALL/BELL not an inhabitant of the Commonwealth. Dennis BROWN and Reuben MATHENY summoned to testify in behalf of PRICE, 13 August 1812 and 24 August 1813. September 1813 term, dismissed by order of PRICE's attorney and judgement for BUTLER for costs.

174a - 1813, Monongalia Superior Court. Deed dated 13 April 1813 signed by David SCOTT to Felix SCOTT for a tract of land that David formerly purchased from Felix on the waters of Scotts Meadow Run and near the mouth on the north side adjoining Joseph DUNLAP, James SCOTT, Enoch JONES and Felix SCOTT and the town lots. Deed witnessed by D. SCOTT 3rd., Catherine (x) STONEKING and Wm. JOHN.

174a - 1813, Monongalia Superior Court. On 10 January 1811, Edward MERCER and James MORGAN leased 200 acres of land on the waters of Maricles Run, a branch of Dunkard Creek, to Samuel MINOR for the term of 10 years. On 11 January 1811, John BROOKHAVEN entered into the premises and ejected MINOR off of the land. Deed dated 30 March 1809 signed by Meshack SEXTON and his wife, Hannah SEXTON, to Edward MERCER and James MORGAN for 200 acres on Maricle Run adjoining Alexander CLEGG, the same as purchased by SEXTON for non-payment of the direct tax and deeded to SEXTON by Joseph SCOTT, Marshall of the United States on 26 March 1805. Deed witnessed by William DUHAN, Chesman DRAKE, William YOUNG and David HELMICK. April 1813 term, "We the jury find for the plaintiff (MERCER and MORGAN) the land in the declaration mentioned and assess damage to $.01," A. WOODROW, foreman.

174a - 1813, Monongalia Superior Court. Deed dated 16 September 1812 signed by Mary (x) AGUSTIN, Ashbel AGUSTIN and Sary/Salley AGUSTIN his wife, Amariah AGUSTIN and Als (x) AGUSTIN his wife and Amerce AGUSTIN to William COLE for 2 tracts of ground containing by survey 118 acres on Scotts Mill Run. Deed witnessed by Jas TIBBS, Augustus WERNINGER and Mick'l SHIVELY.

174a - 1813, Monongalia Superior Court. Joseph DUNLAP and William JOHN summoned to answer Parker CAMPBELL, for the use of the Philadelphia Bank at their branch bank in Washington, Pennsylvania, in a plea of debt for $1500 and $100 damage, 24 February 1812. Bail Bond for DUNLAP and JOHN secured by Ralph BARKSHIRE, 22 May 1812. Sixty day note signed by JOHN, DUNLAP and Wm. TINGLE dated 27 February 1810. April 1813 term, judgement for the plaintiff for the debt plus 6% interest from 28 April 1810, Richard WELLS, foreman.

174a - 1813, Monongalia Superior Court. Samuel CRANE sum- moned to answer John RODEHEFFER, merchant, in a plea of slander, 18 April 1810. There is a long narrative in which RODEHEFFER relates the slanderous words spoken by CRANE. RODEHEFFER accused CRANE of saying he was "a dam'd liar, a dam'd rascal and you keep false accounts and false weights" in his business as a store keeper. Most of the witnesses, summoned to testify, either had dealings with the merchant or were witnesses to transactions and are mentioned in this narrative. CRANE swore in open court that he tried to obtain subpoenas, on 21 August last past, to summons his witnesses. He was informed that none could be issued because of the death of the late clerk, 3 September 1811. CRANE swore that he sent a commission to Col. James CLARK, of Cincinati, Ohio, to take the deposition of Thomas GAD to be used in this suit, 9 September 1812. CRANE swore that Thomas ELDRIDGE was a material witness for him, but ELDRIDGE was on public business and could not attend. He swore that Jacob WOOLF, of Cape Jerico, and that Daniel RECKNOR, of Maryland, were material witnesses in this case, 7 April 1812. Jacob PINDALL and William CHIPPS summoned to testify in behalf of CRANE, 2 September 1813. Allegheny County, 19 August 1812, Justice John RIGHTMIRE, of Maryland. Deposition of Daniel RECKNOR: He spoke with John RODHEFFER at John KIMMERER's in the Crab Orchard and RODHEFFER told him he gave $30 for 6 clocks and sold one of the clocks to Samuel CRAIN for $16 and one to John CHIPPS for $16 and another to Jacob WOLF for $16 and another to Fred'r WILEHELLUM for $16. Jacob WOLF Jr. is mentioned as giving his deposition, but it was not found. Eli DEBERRY, Peter MASON, Ann BUCKALUE, Stephen TICHNEL, John ROBERTS, John CHIPPS, Amos ROBERTS, William ROBERTS, Thomas ELDRIDGE, David GRIMES and wife, James GIBSON, John KIMMERER, John KIMMERER Jr., Jacob KIMMERER, Abraham ELLIOTT, Mary MIDDLETON, Elizabeth CRANE, and Samuel CRANE Jr. summoned to testify in behalf of CRANE, 9 July 1812. Jacob KIMMERER, John KIMMERER, James MATHENEY, Jacob KIMMERER Sr., Moses GUSTIN, Joseph SEVERNS and John SEVERNS summoned to testify in behalf of RHODEHEFFER, 15 July 1811. John KIMMERER, John KIMMERER Jr., Jacob KIMMERER, James METHENEY, John HARTMAN, William WALLER, William WALLER Jr., George WOOLF, John SEVERNS and Joseph SEVERNS summoned to testify in behalf of RODHEFFER, 27 March, 10 August 1812 and 29 June 1813. Elihu HORTON summoned to testify in behalf of CRANE, 8 September 1811. April 1813 term, plaintiff awarded $25 damage.

174a - 1813, Monongalia Superior Court. At a court on 18 September 1806, Henry H. WILSON recovered against Davis SHOCKLEY $50 damage and $8.49 for his costs in a suit. The debt remained unpaid and therefore he brings suit. September 1813 term, abated by the death of the plaintiff, WILSON.

343

174a - 1814, Monongalia Superior Court. Abraham ELLIOTT summoned to answer Henry LEWIS in a plea of slander damage $1000, 9 September 1811. ELLIOTT was heard to say that LEWIS stole a cutting box, an iron wedge, a sheet and a bottle of whiskey and "the dam'd thieving son of a bitch cannot go on a plantation without looking for something to steal." William ENGLAND, James BULTEAR/PULTEAN, John BISHOP and Jacob KIMMERER summoned to testify in behalf of LEWIS, 29 June 1813. September 1813 term, verdict and judgement for the plaintiff, damages $185. Henry LEWIS obtained a judgement against Abraham ELLIOTT for $185 at September 1813 term of Superior Court. At a Chancery Court held at Clarksburg, ELLIOTT prayed for and was granted an injunction to stay execution on the judgement. Injunction Bond signed by ELLIOTT to insure all costs and awards would be paid in case the injunction should be dissolved secured by John FAIRFAX, 8 January 1814. FAIRFAX swore that his estate was worth more that the penalty of the Injunction Bond ($400). Injunction dissolved and ELLIOTT signed a release of all errors at law, 8 January 1814.

174a - 1813, Monongalia Superior Court. John BOUSLOG summoned to answer John STEALEY in a plea of debt for $103.30 due on account, 30 March and 13 June 1811. William B. LINDSAY and Catharine TIBBS summoned to testify in behalf of STEALEY, 26 August 1813. Baltzer TIBBS, Aaron HENRY Jr., James DOTSON and Thomas DOOLITTLE summoned to testify in behalf of BOUSLOG, 26 August 1813. James McGEE, attorney for STEALEY. September 1813 term, agreed and judgement for costs.

174a - 1812, Monongalia Superior Court. Stephen TICHINAL summoned to answer David MORGAN in a plea of slander damage $1000, 25 March and 14 June 1812.

174a - 1813, Monongalia Superior Court. Mary BENNETT complained that George HITE, in 1809, cut down a part of several peach trees to the value of $1000 and tore down five panels of plank fence to the value of $1000. James CHANAL, George McNEELY, George HICKMAN, and Jacob BANKARD summoned to testify in behalf of BENNETT, 24 August 1813. Samuel HANWAY and James TIBBS Jr. summoned to testify in behalf of BENNETT, 16 August 1813. William N. JARRETT and Fielding KYGER summoned to testify in behalf of HITE, 6 September 1813. September 1813 term, verdict and judgement for the defendant.

174a - 1813, Monongalia Superior Court. William McCLEERY summoned to answer Aron BARKER in a plea of debt for $120, 14 July 1812. On 15 October 1810, McCLEERY signed a bond for George HITE to BARKER in the amount of $120. September 1813, judgement confessed.

174a - 1813, Monongalia Superior Court. George HITE summoned to answer Aron BARKER in a plea of debt for $120 and $10 damage, 14 July 1812. On 15 October 1810, BARKER hired a negro man named Harry to HITE for one year at $60 and was to furnish Harry with good working clothes and return him as he received him. Agreement signed by HITE and William McCLEERY. September 1813 term, plea waived and judgement confessed.

174b - 1813, Monongalia Superior Court. Settlement of William TINGLE's estate by Rawley SCOTT, administrator. Recorded Book A, page 40. TINGLE was Clerk of the Superior Court and there are many accounts and receipts concerning court proceedings. There are many receipts and accounts concerning TINGLE's personal finances. Only those papers or documents of particular or historical interest are considered here. Estate inventory dated 12 September 1811, signed by appraisers Thomas WILSON, Alexander HAWTHORN, Matthew GAY and James MYERS (amount not given). A list of notes due the estate: Richard JOHNSTON, James COLLINS, Samuel SHAW, Thomas SPENCER, SMITH and PENNYBAKER, Nicholas WEAVER, Frederick REED, Henry H. WILSON, Daniel SHAHAN, William RUSSELL, Henry ENGLAND, Samuel BAKER, John HARMAN, Robert MINIS, Michael CLAUSE, Nathan MATHENY, Samuel G. WILSON, John McCAWLEY. Accounts: Jacob FOULK and POSTLEWAITE and SHIP. Bond signed by TINGLE and SCOTT to Thomas DOOLITTLE dated 25 January 1811 whereby DOOLITTLE purchased from TINGLE Lot #6 in a town established by TINGLE called New Martinsburg in Monongalia County west of the Monongahela River. DOOLITTLE executed his three separate notes in the amount of $30 each and TINGLE promised to give DOOLITTLE a good deed to the lot by 1 June 1813 if the notes were paid promptly and in full. Receipt signed by Thomas (x) DOOLITTLE dated 3 September 1813. Sale Bill dated 2 November 1811 and recorded at September 1813 term of court. Names of individuals not often found in these volumes who were buyers at the estate sale. William WOODS, Edward EVANS, Ale'x BOTHWELL, James WALLS, George PICKENPAUGH, Thomas BODLEY, Hugh SIDWELL, David BALTZELL, Edward MATHEWS, Forbes BRITTON, Michael CLOUSE, Reuben CHALFANT, Thomas PORTOR, Elijah MORRIS, John GRAY, John ARNETT, Joseph ALLEN, A. B. MADERA, James MUSGRAVE, Francis HENRY, William COLE, William FRUM, Joseph CAMPBELL, Robert HILL, Joseph A. SHACKELFORD, John STEEL and James REED. Michael PRICE presented an account against the estate and swore it was correct, 10 September 1811. Note signed by TINGLE to Daniel BARRETT for $11.06 dated 25 January 1811 and witnessed by Samuel G. WILSON. Two notes signed by TINGLE to Noah RIDGEWAY for $210 each dated 13 August 1805. Two notes signed by TINGLE to John HOWELL for $10 and $12 dated 6 January 1811 and witnessed by Eugenius M. WILSON. Note signed by TINGLE to Jacob PALSLY for $23.50 dated 21 January 1811 and witnessed by John H. POLSLEY. Note signed by TINGLE to Joseph SHUTTLESWORTH Jr. for $20 dated 23 January 1811 and witnessed by James TINGLE.

Also in this file. Two horses, the property of Jacob POLSLEY, was attached at the suit of Richard NUZUM for $50 with 6% interest from 15 October 1803 until paid. The horses were exposed to public sale and James MORGAN, the highest bidder signed this bond to insure he would pay the purchase price plus costs within 12 months. Benjamin REEDER signed as his security on 13 April 1808.

ENVELOPE 175 contains executions of some of the cases abstracted before. An EXECUTION is a judicial writ by which an officer is empowered to carry a judgement into effect. (Webster's Collegiate Dictionary). The document names the plaintiff and the defendant, the amount of judgement and to whom awarded, the amount of penalty, court costs and the date of the order. See Volume I, pages 34 and 35 for an example.

END OF MICROFILM #45

Correction: The surname HAUTMAN probably should be HARTMAN.

MONONGALIA COUNTY RECORDS OF DISTRICT AND COUNTY COURTS
Monongalia County, (West) Virginia Personal Property Taxes
Microfilm 10

70a - 1812, "Charles BYRN's Tithable List for 1812."

Persons Name Chargeable with the tax	white males over 16	horses, mares colts, mules	other
John AMBROSE	1	2	
Nathan ASHLEY	3	5	
Daniel ADAMS	1	2	
George ASHLEY	1	2	
John ANDERSON	1	2	
William ALEXANDER	1		
John ADKINSON	1	1	
Ellender ALLEY, widow		1	
John ABDON	1		
Jacob ABDON	1	2	
Andrew ARMSTRONG	1	2	
David ALBRIGHT	1	3	
Reubin ASKINS	2	3	
Martin ABLE	3	3	
Daniel ANDERSON	1	2	
Henry ABDON	1		
Anthony ABLE	1		
Peter ASBURN	3	3	
David ARCHER	1		
Robert ABERCRUMBY	1	1	
William BAKER	1	2	
James BENNET	1	4	
William BAMBRIDGE	1	4	
George D. BARNES	1	7	
(blacks over 16)			1
William BOID	1	2	
Thomas BARTLETT	2	4	
(blacks over 16)			1
William BICE	1	1	
Archabald BOID	1	2	
John BRADLEY	1	3	
William BICE	1	2	
Henry BARNES	2	4	
George BAKER	1	4	
Barney BURNES	1	2	
George BROWN	1	6	
(blacks over 16)			1
(blacks 12-16)			2
Andrew BOID	1	2	
James BRAHAM	1	1	

Charles BYRN	1	2	
(blacks over 16)			1
Edward BOARD	1	1	
Thomas BRAHAM	1	1	
James E. BEALL	1	3	
Robert BEATY	3	6	
Levy BEATY	1	2	
James BROWN	3	6	
Christian BISHOP	2	3	
Mary BENET, widow		2	
(blacks over 16)			1
Alexander BINGAMAN	1	3	
Stephen BOLYARD	2	2	
John BUTLER	1	1	
Moses BEAVER	1	3	
Henry BISHOP	1	2	
Daniel BICE	2	2	
John B. BROWN	1	3	
Jacob BAKER	1	3	
(stud horse)			1
Patrick BURNA	1	2	
Velender BEALL, widow	3	4	
(blacks over 16)			1
James BEALL	1	3	
Thomas BIRCH	1		
Thomas BIRCH, Sr.	1	1	
William BAYLES	1	4	
Benjamin BROWN?	1	3	
William BARRETT	1	2	
George BOMAN	1		
Aaron BEAL	1		
Christopher BARNHART	1	2	
John BISHOP	1	3	
James BOYLON	1	1	
Elisha BIGGS	1	2	
William BENSON	2	2	
Isaac BARB	1	3	
Stephen BICE	1	2	
Alexander BRANDON	1	3	
William BRANDON	1	2	
Richard BRANDON	2	1	
Jonathan BRANDON	1	3	
Philip BIERBOUR	1	1	
Fredrick BIERBOUR	1	1	
John BIERBOUR	1	1	
John BRIGHT	1	1	
Levy BRIGHT	1	2	
William BRIGHT	1	1	
Absalom BRANDON	1	1	
(stud horse)			1
William BUCKLEW	1	5	
George BENSON	1	2	

Thomas BUTLER	1	5	
(blacks over 16)			1
Park BUCKLEW	1	2	
Christina BROCKMIRE, widow	1	4	
Henry BARE	1	2	
Ann BROWN, widow		1	
William BROWN	1	3	
John CAROTHERS	1	3	
Walter CARRE	1	3	
Hiram COOPER	1	1	
William CONSTABLE	1		
Harman CAIN/CAIRN, Exempt		3	
John COSAD	1	2	
Mordica CAMRON	1	1	
Joab CONSTABLE	1		
James CHILES	1	3	
Christian CORE	2	2	
Barbara CROSS, widow	1	2	
Peter CARRICO	3	1	
Robert CALHOON	1	1	
Peter CULBISON, man of color	1		
Martin CURRANT	1	4	
James CURRENT, Sr. &			
Enoch CURRANT	1	4	
John CURRANT	1	3	
James CURRANT, Jr.	1	5	
Samuel CRANE	2	2	
Jonathan CRANE	1	1	
James COBURN, Sr.	2	3	
(blacks over 16)			1
(blacks 12-16)			1
Arthur COBURN	1	1	
John COLLACE	1	1	
James COBURN, Jr.	1	4	
Isaac CRISS	1	2	
John CASADY	1	2	
Henry CRISS	2	2	
Jacob CRISS	1	3	
Francis COLLINS	1	2	
Anthony CARROL	?	3	
David CAMBLEN	3	4	
George CUNNINGHAM	1	3	
John CHIPPS	1	2	
Thomas CANE	1	1	
Daniel COX	1	6	
Richard CANE	1	3	
Anthony CASADE	1	1	
Mathias COOK	1		
Michael CONNER	1	3	
Sarah CONNER, widow	1	3	
John CUP	1	1	
Leonard CUP, Sr.	1	2	

Leonard CUP, Jr.	1	5	
William CONNER	3	5	
John CASTEEL	1	2	
Robert CONNER	1	1	
James CARROL	3	2	
John CONLEY	1		
Samuel CLUTTER	2	4	
Daniel CONNER	1	2	
Christian CALE	2	4	
James CANE	1		
John COLE	1	1	
Robert CHOEN	1	1	
Samuel COSTOLE	1		
Thomas COSTOLE	1		
James CONN	1	2	
Peter COOSIC	1	3	
James CONNER	1		
David CURRY	1	1	
John COLE	1		
James CLELLAND, ferryman		6	
George DORSEY	2	16	
(blacks over 16)			6
(blacks 12-16)			1
Henry DORTON, Sr., man of color	1	3	
Levy DORTON, man of color	1	2	
John DORTON, do	1	1	
Henry DORTON, Jr., do	1		
James DONSON	1	1	
George S. DEARING	1	1	
(blacks 12-16)			1
William DAVY	1	2	
William DEMOSS	1	2	
James DEMOSS	1	2	
Charles DIGMAN	1	1	
William DRAGOO	2	4	
Thomas DRAGOO	1	1	
Able DAVIS	1	3	
Samuel DARNEL	1	2	
James DONELSON	1	4	
Daniel DAVIS	1	2	
William DARNEL	1	2	
Joseph DICKESON	1	1	
John DOWNEY	1	2	
Isaac DAVIS	1	2	
Archabald DEBERRY	1	1	
John DEBERRY	1	2	
Ely DEBERRY	1	1	
Peter DEWIT	2	1	
Neely DOUGLAS	1	3	
Lester DICKESON	1		
Samuel DARBY, Sr.	1	3	

Samuel DARBY, Jr.	1	4	
Thomas EWELL	1	3	
Hugh EVANS	1	2	
William ENGLAND	1		
James EDWARDS	1	1	
John EDWARDS	1	5	
John EPLEY	1	2	
Abraham ELLIOT	1	3	
Isaac ERVIN	1	1	
James ERVIN	1	3	
Thomas ELLRIGE	1	1	
Peter EVERLY, Sr.	1	2	
Peter EVERLY, Jr.	1	1	
Joseph EVERLY	1	1	
Isaac FOREMAN	1	1	
Robert FERRELL	1	2	
Henry FERRELL	1	1	
Robert FERRELL, Sr.	1		
James FERRELL	2	1	
Adam FAST	2	4	
Jacob FAST	1		
Enoch FERRELL	1		
Darniel FORTNEY, Sr.	1	4	
John FORTNEY	1	1	
John FOSTER	2	3	
John FREELAND, ferryman		1	
(stud horse)			1
John FUNK	1	2	
Jacob FUNK	1	2	
(blacks over 16)			1
John FEASTER	2	1	
John FELTON	1	3	
Henry FORTNEY, Sr.	1	2	
Henry FORTNEY, Jr.	1	2	
William FETTY	1	1	
Henry FASTENS	1	1	
William FORD	1	1	
Christian FRUSHOUR	1	3	
Elisha FORD	1	1	
Peter FORTNEY, Sr.	1		
Peter FORTNEY, Jr.	1		
Richard FIELDS	1		
Daniel FORTNEY, Jr.	1	1	
Benjamin FIELDS	2	1	
James FIELDS	1	1	
Alexander FALKNER	1		
John FAIRFAX	2	11	
(blacks over 16)			7
(blacks 12-16)			4
William FAUCET	1	1	
Richard FOREMAN	1	3	
Jacob FEATHERS	2	2	

John FOREMAN	1	5
Mary FOREMAN, widow		2
Samuel FOREMAN	1	3
Joseph FORESYTHE	1	
Benjamin FREELAND	1	1
Joseph FOREMAN	1	3
John FOWLER	2	2
Reason FOWLER	1	3
John FICKLE	1	1
James FLEMING	1	
Patrick FLEMING	1	
Jemimah FUNK, widow		1
Godfrey GOOSEMAN	1	2
Joseph GOOSEMAN	1	
Stephen GILBERT	1	2
Michael GRADY	1	3
Aaron GIBBS	1	1
David GRIM	1	3
James GOFF	2	3
William GRIMES	1	1
James T. GOFF	2	2
Amos GANDY	1	3
Byram GOFF	1	1
Joshua GOFF	1	1
Thomas GOFF	1	2
William GEORGE	1	5
John GLENDENNING	3	3
Samuel GANDY	3	4
George GREENWOOD	1	5
Levy GANDAY	1	
David GALLOWAY	1	4
Abraham GOOSEMAN, Sr.	1	4
(blacks over 16)			1
(stud horse)			1
Daniel GRANT	1	3
John GOOSEMAN	1	
George GRIMES	1	
Thomas GATES	1	
Philip GORDEN	1	2
William GARNER	1	1
Benjamin GLOVER	1	2
John GOOZICK	1	1
James GUTHREY	3	5
Jacob GILMORE	1	1
Amos GLOVER	1	1
David GRIMES	1	
Thomas GIBSON	1	3
Levy GIBSON	1	1
James GIBSON	1	2
Robert GIBSON	1	1
John GRIBBLE, Sr.	1	
John GRIBBLE, Jr.	1	6

William GRIBBLE	1	2	
Joseph GILES	1		
Enoch GREATHOUSE	1	1	
Amos GRIFFITH	1	2	
Hugh GOLLOUGHUR	1		
Jacob HOLLAND, Coburn Creek	1	4	
James HAMELTON	1	2	
James HILL, Sr., man of color	1		
James HILL, Jr., do	1	1	
William HILL do	1	2	
Benjamin HARTLEY	1	1	
Jacob HOLLAND, Joes Run	3	6	
(blacks over 16)			1
John HUFFMAN	1	2	
Asa HARRIS	2	1	
James HILL	1	2	
Benjamin HILL	1	2	
Philip HILL	1		
Elijah HAWKINS	1	1	
Robert HENDERSON	1	2	
William HALL	1	4	
George B. HOSKINSON	1	5	
George HITE	3	2	
(blacks over 16)			1
Frederick HARSH	2	5	
(blacks over 16)			2
Julies HOOD	1	1	
James HOLBERT	1	1	
John HOLBERT	1	1	
William HOLBERT	1	2	
William HEBB	1	1	
Coonrod HOLESTINE	1	4	
Peter HICKART	1	3	
Soloman P. HIRRENGDON	1	1	
James HUNT, Jr.	1	1	
James HUNT, Sr.	1	2	
Thomas HUNT	1		
Michael HILDERBRAND	1	1	
Joseph HILL, man of color	1	1	
Nathan HALL	2	3	
Jacob HULL	1	2	
John HAYMAN	1	2	
Robert HAWTHORN	1	1	
John HENTHORN, ferryman		1	
(blacks over 16)			1
Henry HENTHORN	1	2	
Philip HARNER	1	4	
Owen HAWKER	1	1	
Alexander HAWTHORN	1	2	
(blacks over 16)			1
Leonard HOSKINSON	1		
James HAWK	3		

Abraham HESS	2	4	
Elyhu HORTON	1	1	
Richard HALL	1	4	
Reese HASTINGS	1	2	
William HARTLEY	1	2	
William HAMBRICK	1		
Elijah HARDESTER	1	1	
Michael HARTMAN	1	4	
Charles HOUSEMAN	1	1	
John HARTMAN	2	5	
Samuel HAZELET	1	1	
Daniel HARRADER	1	3	
John HARRADER	1	3	
William HARRISS	1	2	
Jonathan HARRISS	2	3	
Abraham HARRISS	1	2	
James HAMILTON, Laurel Run	1	3	
Isaac HAISE	2	2	
Robert HAMILTON	2	2	
Amos HAWLEY	1	2	
John JACKSON & UPDEGRAFT	1	15	
(blacks 12-16)			1
James JEFFS	1	2	
John JEFFS	1	1	
Barnabas JOHNSTON	1	3	
Richard JONES	1	1	
William N. JARRETT	1	1	
(blacks over 16)			3
(blacks 12-16)			1
Andrew JOHNSTON	1		
Richard JOHNSTON	2	1	
Joseph JINKENS	1		
Luke JACO	1	3	
Mary JINKENS, widow		6	
(blacks over 16)			2
Thomas JACO	1	3	
William JACO	1	1	
Jacob JONES, Jr.	1	2	
John JONES, Constable		3	
Jacob JONES, Sr.	1	1	
William JONES	1	2	
Samuel JONES	1	4	
Benjamin JONES	3	4	
Joseph JINKENS	4	13	
(blacks over 16)			4
Lemuel JOHN	1	5	
Richard JACKSON	1	1	
Margaret JINKENS, widow		4	
(blacks over 16)			1
Joseph JONES	1	6	
Dennis JEFFERIS	1	3	
Thomas JINKENS	1	3	

Benjamin JEFFERIES	3	3	
William JEFFERIS	1	3	
Benjamin JARRETT	1	1	
Benjamin JEFFERIES, Cheat	1	2	
Ural JOHNSTON	1	3	
John JOHNSTON	1		
Evan JINKENS	1	1	
Jonathan JINKENS	1	2	
Thomas JINKENS	1	1	
Moses JUSTICE	1	2	
William KINGCADE, Jr.	1	3	
William KINGCADE, Sr.	2	1	
John KINGCADE	1		
John KIRK	1	2	
Joseph KINGCADE	1	1	
John KIRK	1	2	
Cornelius KING	4	4	
Michael KERNS	1	5	
(blacks 12-16)			1
George KELLER	2	3	
John KELLER	1		
Edward KNOTTS	2	3	
Robert KNOTTS	1	3	
Absalom KNOTTS	1	5	
Hugh KENADY, man of color	1	1	
Samuel KEENER	1	2	
George KEENER	1	4	
Oolery KEENER	1	1	
Jacob KYGER	1	1	
(blacks over 16)			1
Anthony KIRKHART	1	2	
John KIMMER, Sr.	1	2	
Jacob KIMMER	1	4	
John KIMMER	1	4	
William KELLEY	1	3	
Washington KNOW	1		
Loving KIRKMAN	1	1	
John KELLEY, Jr.	1	2	
John KELLEY, Sr.	3	4	
Valentine KING	2	3	
James KING	1	4	
John KING	1	1	
Benjamin KESSINGER	1		
James KINGCADE	1	1	
Hugh KELSO	1	4	
Richard LEASON	1	1	
Gardener LEONARD	1	1	
Daniel LYMAN	1		
Ezabella LYNN, widow	2	4	
John LYNN	1	1	
Henry LEACH	1		
George LAKE	1	1	

Joseph LANE	2		
Alexander LOCKHART	2	7	
(blacks over 16)			2
Henry LANCE	1	2	
William LIPSCOMB	2	3	
(blacks 12-16)			1
Jeremiah LEACH	2	4	
Elisha LEACH	1	2	
Samuel LEWELLEN	1	3	
Thomas LEWELLEN, Jr.	1	2	
Thomas LEWELLEN, Sr.	2	3	
Aaron LUZADDER, Jr.	1	1	
Aaron LUZADDER, Sr.	2	3	
Doctor LEWELLEN	2	5	
Andrew LEWZADDER	1		
George LEGG	1	2	
Robert LUNN	1		
John LYNHHORN	1		
John LEWIS	1		
Henry LEWIS, Jr.	1		
Henry LEWIS, Sr.	1	3	
Philip LEWIS	1		
William LAMBERT	1	3	
William G. LOWMAN		3	
Joseph LAMBERT		2	
Edward LAREW	1		
William LITTLE	1	3	
John LAP	1	3	
James LEMMAN	2	2	
Benjamin LAWSON	2	4	
John LEWELLEN	1	1	
Evan MORGAN	2	2	
Evan S. MORGAN	1	1	
Hesekiah MARFIELD	2	2	
John McCARTY	1		
James MORGAN, Jr.	1	2	
John MALONE	1	2	
Morgan MORGAN	2	7	
(blacks over 16)			1
Jacob MEANS	1		
David MORGAN	1		
John P. MARTIN	1	3	
Isaac MORGAN	1	2	
David MURPHY	1	4	
James MURPHY	1	3	
John MILLER, D. B.	2	6	
David MILLER	1	1	
Henry MILLER, D. B.	1		
John MASON	1	3	
Birket MINOR	1		
Isaac MILLER	1		
Thomas MONTGOMERY	1	3	

Michael MURPHY	2		
Matthew McGINNISS		2	
Peter MEREDITH	2	2	
Philip MARTIN, Constable		4	
Thomas McGEE	1	2	
William MORGAN	1	3	
Abner MESSINGER	1	1	
Rozzell MESSINGER	1		
Jacob MOUSER	3	2	
Hugh MORGAN, D. B.	1	8	
(blacks over 16)			1
David MORGAN, D. B.	1	7	
Thomas MARTIN	2	1	
Isaac MATTHEW	1	1	
Joseph MATTHEW	1	3	
John MINNEAR	1	2	
Isaac MORRIS	1	4	
John MANN	1	1	
Jacob MILLER	1	3	
John MILLER	1	2	
Aaron McDANIEL	1	2	
Thomas MEAKS	1	3	
Samuel MINNEAR	1	2	
Samuel McCAURMIC	1		
Ely MATTHEW	1	1	
Moses MINNEAR	1		
William McGEE	1	3	
Thomas McGEE, Jr.	1		
David MINNEAR	1	2	
William MINNEAR		1	
Absolem MATHENY	1	2	
John MORE	1	3	
Joseph MATHENEY	2	3	
Hugh MURPHY, Deckers Creek	3	4	
Robert MOODY	1	3	
Thomas MUCKLEROY	1	1	
Samuel MAID	1	1	
Ely MORE	2	1	
James MONTGOMERY	1		
James McVICKER, Constable		6	
Stephen McDADE	1	2	
Charles McGILL, Jr.	1	2	
Daniel METZER	1	2	
John McGILL	1	1	
Charles McGILL, Sr.	1	3	
Joseph McGILL	1	2	
Nathan MATTHEW	1	1	
Benjamin MATTHEW	1	2	
James MUFFET	1	1	
Joseph MAYFIELD	1	2	
Epram MATTHEW	1	1	
Peter MASON	1	1	

357

Joshua MASON	1	1	
William MASON, Sr.	1	2	
Daniel MINNEY	1	2	
Jacob MILLER	1	4	
Patrick MAGREW	2	8	
Henry MILLER, blacksmith	1	2	
Joshua MORTON	2	2	
Nancy MIRES, widow		1	
John MIRES	1	3	
William MAXEN	1	2	
Benjamin MIDDLETON	1	2	
Charles MONTOGOMERY	1	2	
William MASON, Jr.	1	2	
Henry MILLER, Muddy Creek	1	4	
(stud horse)			1
Daniel MARTIN	2	3	
James MATHENY, Constable		3	
Nathan MATHENY son of Jas.	1	3	
Timothy MIDDLETON	1	1	
William MICHAEL	1	3	
Nathan MAXEN	1	1	
Peter McKEEVER	1	1	
Matthew McDOOLE	1		
Frances McSHANE	1	1	
(blacks over 16)			1
Joseph MARTIN	1	5	
James MAGREW	1	2	
Daniel McCOLLUM	2	6	
William MORTON	1	5	
Hannah MARTIN, widow		2	
Mathew McCONNEL	1		
James MONTGOMERY	1		
John MONTGOMERY	1		
Robert McMULLEN	3	3	
Robert McSHANE	1		
George NUZUM	1	3	
John NUZUM	1	1	
Thomas NUZUM	1		
William NUZUM	1	2	
James NUZUM	2	2	
Christian NINE	1	2	
George NEAL	1		
Philip NICKLES	1	4	
Michael NOSE	1	2	
David NISS	1	4	
Richard NUZUM	1	1	
Jacob NOOSE, Jr.	1	4	
William NORRIS	1	10	
(blacks over 16)			3
George NORRIS	1	2	
Wheat NEIGHBORS	1	2	
Patrick NEWMAN	1		

John ORR	1	2	
Gasper ORT	1	2	
Nehemiah POWERS	1	2	
Thomas PILES	1	1	
Philip PATTERSON	1	1	
John PATTERSON	1		
Joseph POWELL	1	1	
Stephen POE	1	2	
John POWERS	1	2	
William POWERS	1		
Thomas PRITCHARD	1	3	
(blacks over 16)			1
William PRICE	2	4	
Richard POSTLE	1	3	
John PAUGH	1	1	
James W. POSTON	2	4	
James PAUGH	1		
Theophelis PEW	1	4	
Emanuel PIPHER, Sr.	1	3	
Emanuel PIPHER, Jr.	1	1	
Andrew PIXLER	1	2	
Samuel PIERCE	2	2	
John PARSONS, man of color	1	1	
Hunter PILES	1	2	
Larken PIERPOINT	1	2	
Francis PIERPOINT	1	1	
Edward PRICHARD	1		
John PLUMB	1	1	
Andrew PEW	1	2	
Zackquell PIERPOINT	1	2	
Fredrick PROTZMAN	1		
William PIERSON	1		
Jacob PAUL	1	4	
Jesse PENROSE	1	4	
Abraham PENROSE	1	1	
Samuel POSTLEWRIGHT	2	4	
Samuel PATTERSON	1	3	
Robert PATTERSON	1	2	
Mellon PEW	1		
George QUICK	1	1	
James RANDLE	1	3	
Isaac REED	2	5	
Isaac RIGGS	1	3	
Adley RAY		1	
Henry RUNNER	1	1	
(blacks over 16)			1
William ROBINSON	1	1	
Cyrus RIGGS	1	2	
Thomas ROBINSON	1	2	
John ROBINSON	1	1	
John S. ROBERTS	2	4	
Moses ROYOR	2	8	

George RUBLE	1	1
Jacob RIDENOUR	2	5
John RIDENOUR	1	
Aaron ROYSE	1	1
Levy RUNNER	2	2
John REEDER	1	1
Matthew ROBINSON	1	2
Hesekiah ROYSE	1	5
William ROGERS	1	4
Isaac ROMINE	1	2
Jacob ROMINE	2	1
George RODABAUGH	2	2
John REED	2	5
John ROWEN	1	1
William REED	2	7
Samuel RALSTON	1	1
Catharine RIDGEWAY, widow	1	3
John RYON	1	2
John ROWEN	1	2
Othaniel RODES, ferryman		2
George REASE	2	2
Joseph REED	1	1
Aaron ROISE, blind	1	2
John RODEHEAVER	1	4
Amos ROBERTS	2	4
William ROBERTS	1	1
Augustus E. RECKART	2	6
George RINGER	2	3
Martin RIDENHOUR	1	2
John ROSS	1	2
Benjamin REED	1	
William REED	1	
Shedrick RICE	1	
Zachariah RODES	1	4
Jacob RUBLE	1	3
William RODES	1	1
Charles ROSE	1	2
Benjamin ROGERS	1	
Hopkin ROSE	1	
David SWINGLER	2	2
William SMITH	1	1
Jacob SMELL	1	2
Philip SMELL	2	4
Thomas STEEL	1	2
William SCOTT	1	2
Benjamin SAURES	1	4
Joseph SHOVIAUGH?	1	
Jacob SETH	2	2
Richard W. SMITH	1	7
John STEPHENS	2	2
Simeon STEPHENS	1	
John SRIVER	1	5

Nehemiah SQUIRES	3	3
William SINCLARE	1	
Daniel SHEHAN	2	5
David SEAMAN	1	2
George SNYDER	1	5
Coonrod SHEATS	1	2
John D. SHAVER	1	
David STEMPLE	2	4
Martin STEMPLE	2	3
John STEMPLE	1	4
John SANDERS	1	1
Adam SHAVER	1	3
John SMITH	1	1
John STINEBAUGH	1	3
Nimrod SNYDER	1	1
William K. SMITH	1	2
Henry SNYDER	1	1
John SNYDER, Sandy Creek	1	3
David SIMPSON	1	3
John SIMPSON	1	1
William SHAW	2	1
John SROYERS	1	2
John STOCKWELL	2	2
George SHEHAN	1	2
John SHEHAN	1	
Jesse SNYDER	2	3
John SIGGINS	1	3
Joseph SAVERNS, Jr.	1	
Jacob SMITH	1	3
Joseph A. SHACKLEFORD, Exempt		4
Magruder SELBY	1	2
Rawley SCOTT	2	2
(blacks over 16)			1
Joseph SMITH & mother	1	3
Jonathan SALYARDS	1	1
John SMITH	1	
Jacob SHAVER	2	2
Ann STEPHENSON, widow		3
John SULLAVAN	1	1
Alexander SOMERS	1	1
Drake SWINGLER	1	1
Mary SPURGEON, widow		1
Edmond M. SPURGEON	1	1
Jacob SNYDER	1	2
Fredrick SNYDER	1	1
Adam SWIERS	1	2
John SNYDER	1	2
Hugh SIDWELL	1	4
John STEWARD	1	
William STAFFORD	1	3
John STILLWELL	1	1
Charles STEWARD	3	6

James STAFFORD, ferryman	2		
(blacks over 16)			2
(blacks 12-16)			1
Seth STAFFORD	1	2	
John STAFFORD		3	
Thomas STAFFORD	1	1	
Robert STEWARD	1	2	
Laurance SNYDER	2	1	
Robert STEWARD		2	
Fredrick SMITH	1	5	
Henry SINE	1	1	
Henry SINE, Jr.	1	1	
Samuel SHAVER?	1	5	
John G. SMITH	2	3	
Joseph SAYRES	2	4	
John SCOTT	2	2	
Jonathan SPURGEN	1	4	
John SPURGEN	1	1	
Frederick SHAW	1	4	
Samuel SMITH	1	3	
Jesse SPURGEN	1	2	
Elizabeth SPURGEN, widow		1	
George SMITH	1		
Jacob SMITH	1		
George SYPOLT, Jr.	1	4	
John STAFFORD	1	2	
Thomas SWEATMAN	1	1	
Alexander SHAW	2	2	
William STRAWHEN	1	3	
George SYPOLT, Sr.	1	2	
Christopher SYPOLT	1	2	
Nathan SYPOLT	1	4	
Philip SOMERS	1	2	
Neil SWANEY	1		
Jonathan SMITH	1	2	
Thomas SCOTT	1	1	
Margaret SEVIER, widow		1	
Frederick SWISHER	1	2	
Bartholomew SEVIER	1	2	
Thomas SCOTT	1	1	
Joseph SEVERNS	2	8	
Daniel SEVERNS, Sr.	1	1	
James SWANEY	1		
John SEVERNS	1	4	
Daniel SEVERNS	1	3	
William SINE	1	1	
Andrew STARLING	3	4	
William SIGLER	1	1	
Benjamin SHAW	1	1	
James SEMORE	1	4	
Michael TRICKETT	1	3	
Margaret TRICKETT, widow	1	2	

William TRICKETT	1	2
William TUCKER	1	1
Henry TUCKER	1	2
Samuel TROBRIDGE	1	2
John TIMMERMAN	1	2
Zachariah TURNER	1	1
Samuel TAYLOR	1	2
William TWOMIRE	1	1
Jacob TRICKETT	1	2
(blacks 12-16)			1
Thomas THOMAS	2	5
James THOMAS	1	
William THOMAS	1	
Thomas THORNE	1	1
Samuel TAYLOR	1	2
James TROY	1	1
Richard TIBBS	1	
Francis TIBBS, Sr.	1	1
Catharine TIBBS		1
(blacks over 16)			1
John TIBBS	1	1
Francis TIBBS, Jr.	1	2
Benjamin TRIMLEY	2	2
Jacob TEATS	1	2
Jacob THOMAS	1	3
Arthur TRADER	1	1
Henry TEATS	1	4
Adam TEATS	1	1
John TRIMLEY	1	
Stephen TITCHANEL	1	1
Samuel TAWNEYHILL	1	1
William TAWNEYHILL	2	3
Arthur TRADER	1	
Robert THOMPSON	2	2
Jesse TROWBRIDGE	1	2
David TROWBRIDGE	1	2
Ebenezer VANDAGRIFT	1	3
Nicholas VANDAVERT	4	8
John WAGNER	1	1
Stephen WATKINS	1	1
James WILSON, shoemaker	1	1
Alexander WINDERS	1	1
Timothy WARDEN	1	
James WEST	1	
Archabald WILSON, Constable		2
William WILSON, the 3rd	1	1
George WILSON		2
Walter WILSON	1	2
Stephen WATKINS	2	4
William H. WILSON	1	
James WATKINS	1	1
William WATSON	1	3

Lewis WOOLF	1	4	
(blacks over 16)			1
James WALLS	1		
Augustus WERNERGER	2	2	
(blacks over 16)			1
John WATTS	1	1	
Enoch WARMAN	1		
Jacob WOODRING	1	2	
Michael WILT	4	6	
(stud horse)			1
Christian WHITEHAIR	1	2	
Henry WILES	1	4	
John WHEELER	2	3	
Abraham WOODRING	2	2	
John WOODRING	2	1	
Nicholas WOODRING	1	5	
John WHETSEL	1		
George WHETSAL	1		
Daniel WOODRING	1	3	
Jacob WEAVER	1	3	
James A. WALTON	1	1	
Abraham WOODROW	1	1	
Alexander WATTS	1	2	
Jane WATTS, widow		2	
Elijah WOOD	1	3	
Rebeckah WILSON, widow		1	
(blacks over 16)			1
James WILSON	1	3	
Jacob WOOLF	2	4	
David WATSON	1	2	
Jacob WATSON	1	1	
Clark WILLIAMS	1	1	
Sarah WATSON, widow		4	
(blacks over 16)			1
Richard WISE	1	1	
Joseph WEAVER	1	3	
Elizabeth WOLVERTON		2	
Richard WATTS	1		
(blacks over 16)			1
John WATTS	1	1	
James WEAVER	1	3	
Abraham WEAVER	1		
Samuel WILSON	1	2	
Benjamin WALLS	1		
Francis WARMAN	1	3	
James S. WILSON	2	6	
(blacks over 16)			2
Joseph WILSON	2	2	
(blacks over 16)			1
(blacks 12-16)			1
Augustus WELLS, Sr.	2	3	
Hesekiah WELLS	1		

Thomas D. WELLS	1	
Augustus H. WELLS	1	
Peter WILLHELM	1	1
William WALLER	1	2
Soloman WILLHELM	1	1
Frederick WILLHELM	1	3
Augusteen WOOLF	2	4
(stud horse)			1
John WOOLF	1	1
Jacob WOOLF, Jr.	1	1
John WELLETS	2	6
Josiah WOOD	1	3
John WOOD	1	2
Robert WOODS	2	3
Samuel WELLETS	1	4
John WILSON, Sand Creek	1	5
James WEBSTER	2	6
George WOOLF	2	4
Thomas WILLIAMS	1	
James WILSON	1	1
Joseph WALLER	1	
William WALLER, Jr.	1	1
John WALLER	1	2
Samuel WALLER	1	1
Henry WILYARD, Sr.	2	1
Henry WILLYARD, Jr.	1	2
Jacob WILLYARD	1	
George WILLYARD	1	3
Catharine WARMAN, widow		2
(blacks over 16)			1
Benjamin WILSON	5	
Joseph YAGER	1	2
Jacob ZINN	1	4
(blacks over 16)			1
George ZINN	1	2
William ZINN	1	1
Alexander ZINN	1	2
Michael ZINN	1	2
John ZINN	1	2
Peter ZINN	1	1

"I do certify that I have examined the within list of
tythables and do find the same to be correctly stated,
Given under my hand this 1st day of June 1812."
Chas. BYRN, C. R.

APPENDIX B

70a - 1813, "Charles BYRN's Tithable List for 1813"

Persons Name Chargeable with the tax	white males over 16	horses, mares colts, mules	other
Robert ABERCRUMBY	1	2	
Ellinder ALLEY, widow	1		
Jacob ABDON	1	2	
John ABDON	1		
Richard ADKINSON	1		
John ADKINSON		2	
Andrew ARMSTRONG	1	2	
Thomas ASHBY	1	2	
(stud horse)			1
George ASHBY	1	2	
Nathan ASHBY	1	3	
David ALLBRIGHT	1	2	
Reubin ASKINS	2	4	
Daniel ANDERSON	1	1	
Anthony ABLE	1	1	
Martin ABLE	2	2	
Thomas ADAMS	1	2	
John AMBROSE	1	2	
Peter AUSBUN	3	3	
Jonathan BLANEY	1	1	
John BAKER	1	1	
William BAYLES	1	3	
Andrew BOID	1	4	
James BENNETT	1	3	
William BASSETT	1	2	
Mary BENNETT		2	
(blacks over 16)			1
Francis BILLINGSLEY	1	3	
Cornelius BIRK	1	4	
Timothy BACON	1	1	
John BUTLER	1		
Thomas BIRCH	1		
Izra BEALS	2	2	
James BARNES	1	1	
William BOID		3	
Benjamin BRAIN	1	2	
Joseph BONER	3	2	
Joseph BONER		1	
Park BUCKLEW	1	2	
James BRANDON	1	3	

William BRANDON		2	
Richard BRANDON	2	2	
Jonathan BRANDON	1	3	
Catharine BROCT, widow		3	
Philip BARBOWER	1	1	
Frederick BARBOWER	1	3	
George BENSON	1	2	
Mary BENSON, widow	1	2	
Isaac BARB	1	4	
William BOSWELL	1	3	
Windle BROWN	1	3	
Stephen BICE	1	2	
George BORMAN/BOMAN	1		
Daniel BPYCE	2	1	
Christian BARNHART	1	2	
William BICE		1	
Absolim BRANDON	1	2	
Cristina BROCKMIRE, widow		3	
Henry BARE/BARR	1	3	
George BAKER	1	2	
James BROWN	2	4	
Thomas BURCHENAL	1		
Robert BROWN	1		
James _____?	?	?	
William BAMBRIDGE	1	4	
George D. BARNES	2	4	
Henry BARNES	2	5	
Samuel BICE	2	1	
Barnabus BURNS	1	2	
Thomas BARTLETT	2	4	
(blacks over 16)			1
James BRAHAM	1	1	
Thomas BRAHAM	1	1	
William BUCKLEW	3	5	
William BARLEY	1	1	
George BROWN	2	3	
(blacks 12-16)			2
Samuel BROWN	1	2	
Charles BYRN	1	4	
(blacks over 16)			1
John BRADLEY	1	3	
Jacob BAKER	1	3	
James BELL, Swamps	1	1	
Patrick BURNS	1	2	
Levy BEATY	1	2	
Robert BEATY	2	3	
Stephen BEATY	1	2	
Virlinder BEALL, widow	2	3	
John B. BROWN	1	3	
James BEALL	1	4	
Christian BISHOP	2	4	
Alexander BINGAMON	1	3	

Henry BISHOP	1	2
Moses BEAVERS	1	3
Stephen BOLYARD	1	3
John BISHOP	1	4
James BOLLIAN	1	1
William BENTLEY	1	
Jonathan BLACK	1	2
Elisha BRIGGS	1	2
Thomas BUTLER	1	5
(blacks over 16)			1
James CARROLL	3	4
John CONLEY	1	
John COLLAR	1	1
James COBUN	1	4
(blacks over 16)			2
James CLELAND	1	7
Jane CANE, widow	1	2
Daniel COX	1	5
Thomas CANE	1	2
Richard CANE	1	2
George CUNNINGHAM	1	3
Archabold CASTEEL	3	4
Shederick CASTEEL	1	
Butler CASE	1	
Anthony CARROLL		2
John COROTHERS, Sr.	2	3
John COROTHERS, Jr.	1	1
Walter CANE		2
John CLENDENING	3	4
Mathias COOK	1	1
Jobe CONSTABLE	1	1
Henry CRIST	2	3
Peter CUBINSON, man of color	1	
James CURRANT, Sr.	1	4
John CURRANT	1	4
Martin CURRANT	1	2
James CURRANT, Jr.	2	5
John CZIGAN	1	2
Harman CRIM		2
Mordicci CAMRON	1	
William CONSTABLE	1	1
James COBUN, Jr.	1	3
Isaac CRISS	1	
James CHILES	1	3
Robert CALHOON	1	1
Peter CARRICO	1	2
James CARRICO	1	1
Michael CONNIE	1	3
Jacob CRISS	1	4
Leonard CUP, Sr.	2	2
Samuel CRANE	1	2
Jonathan CRANE		1

Richard CONNER	1	2		
Daniel CONNER	1	2		
Sarah CONNER, widow		2		
Richard CONNER	1	1		
James CONNER	1	2		
Christian CALE	1	4		
Samuel CLUTTER	2	4		
Robert CONNER	1	1		
William CONNER	1	2		
John CASTEEL	1	2		
Leonard CUP, Jr.	1	5		
David CURRY	1	2		
John COLE	1	2		
Robert CHOEN	1	1		
James CONN	1	3		
Samuel COSTOLOE	1			
Thomas COSTOLO	1			
Francis COLLINS	1	2		
Arthur COBUN		1		
John CASSADAY	1	3		
John COSAD	1	3		
Christian CALE	1			
Thomas DUNN		3		
George S. DEARING	1	1		
(blacks over 16)			1	
George DORSEY	2	16		
(blacks over 16)			6	
(blacks 12-16)				1
William DARNEL		2		
John DAVIS	2	4		
Daniel DAVIS	1	2		
James DONSON	1	1		
William DAVY	1	3		
Charles DIGMAN	1	1		
James DEMOSS	1	2		
William DEMOSS	1	2		
William DRAGOO	2	4		
Thomas DRAGOO	1			
Able DAVIS	1	2		
Peter DEWIT	2			
Neal DOUGLAS	1	3		
John DEBERRY	2	3		
Ely DEBERRY		2		
Samuel DARBY, Jr.	1	3		
Samuel DARBY, Sr.	1	3		
Davey DICKEY	1	2		
Leonard DEVALL	1	1		
John DOWNEY	1	3		
James DONELSON	1	4		
Henry DORTON, Jr., colored	1	1		
Henry DORTON, Sr., colored	1	2		
Levy DORTON, man of color	1	2		

Samuel DEBERRY	1		
Rebecca EPLEY, widow	1	2	
Thomas EWELL	1	3	
(blacks 12-16)			1
William ENGLAND	1		
Hugh EVANS	1	3	
James EDWARDS	1	1	
John EDWARDS	1	4	
Thomas ELDRIGE	1	1	
Abraham ELLIOT	2	4	
Isaac ERVIN	1	1	
Peter EVERLY, Jr.		2	
Joseph EVERLY		1	
Peter EVERLY, Sr.	1	3	
Henry EVERLY	1	1	
Abby ERVIN		3	
Jacob FUNK	1	2	
Benjamin FURBY	1	1	
John FOSTER		3	
Daniel FORTNEY, Sr.	1	3	
John FORTNEY	1		
Alexander FALKNER	1		
John FAIRCHILD	1		
Benjamin FREEMAN	1	2	
James FERRELL		2	
Robert FERRELL, Sr.	2	2	
Robert FERRELL, Jr.	1	2	
Adam FAST	2	3	
Jacob FAST	1		
Peter FORTNEY, Sr.	2		
Peter FORTNEY, Jr.	1		
Henry FORTNEY of Peter	1	2	
William FETTY	1	2	
Henry FASTENS	1	2	
Elisha FORD	1	1	
William FORD	1		
Christian FRUSH	2	3	
John FUNK	1	2	
Henry FORTNEY of Dan'l	1	2	
Daniel FORTNEY, Jr.	1	2	
Richard FIELDS	1	1	
Benjamin FIELDS	1	1	
John FIELDS	1		
James FIELDS	1	1	
John FAIRFAX	2	10	
(blacks over 16)			11
(blacks 12-16)			2
Richard FAUCET	1		
John FEASTER	2	1	
John FELTON	1	2	
Jemima FUNK, widow		1	
Jacob FEATHERS	1	2	

Joseph FORMAN	1	4
Richard FOREMAN	1	3
Samuel FORMAN	2	5
Mary FOREMAN, widow		2
John FOREMAN	2	5
Nicholas FRANKHOUSER	1	4
Joseph FORSYTHE	1	
William FAUCET	1	
John FICKLE	1	2
John FOWLER	2	3
Reason FOWLER	1	3
John FREELAND, ferryman		2
Benjamin FREELAND	1	1
David GALLOWAY	1	2
George GREENWOOD	1	2
Abraham GROVES	1	
Abraham GOOSEMAN	1	6
Jacob GOOSEMAN	1	1
Godfrey GOOSEMAN		3
Philip GORDON		1
Jesse GASKINS	1	2
Samuel GANDY	3	4
Levy GANDY	1	
Michael GRADY	2	3
Amos GRADY	1	2
Benjamin GOFF	1	2
Joshua GOFF	1	
Thomas GOFF	1	3
William GEORGE	2	4
David GRIM	1	2
Aaron GIBBS	1	
James C. GOFF	3	4
William GRIMES	1	1
James GOFF	2	3
William GARNER	1	1
Benjamin GLOVER	1	2
John GOOSIC	1	1
David GRAHAM	2	1
Levy GIBSON	1	1
Thomas GIBSON	2	3
Robert GIBSON		1
James GIBSON	1	2
James GUTHRIE	3	4
Jacob GILMER	1	2
Amos GLOVER	1	2
Amos GRIFFITH	1	2
John GRIBBLE, Sr.	1	
John GRIBBLE, Jr.	1	5
William GRIBBLE	1	2
Joseph GEARING	1	3
Peter GOOSIC	1	2
Joseph GILES	1	

Henry HENTHORN		3	
Richard HALL	1	2	
Jacob HOLLAND	1	4	
Robert HAWTHORN	1	2	
(blacks 12-16)			2
William HALL		4	
George B. HOSKINSON	2	5	
Leonard HOSKINSON	1		
Philip HARNER	1	3	
Owen HAWKER	1	1	
William HARTLEY	1	1	
Abraham HESS		3	
Elyhu HORTON	1	2	
Jacob HOLLAND, Joes Run	3	6	
(blacks over 16)			1
John HUFFMAN	1	2	
Elijah HAWKINS	1	1	
Richard HARRISS		2	
Robert HENDERSON, Glady Creek	1	3	
Charles HAMILTON, colored	1		
Philip HILL	1	1	
James HUNT	1	2	
James HUNT	1	2	
Michael HILDERBRAND	1	2	
Joseph HILL, man of color	1	1	
John HAYMOND	1	2	
Jacob HULL/HALL	1	2	
Nathan HALL	2	2	
Thomas HUNT	1		
Coonrod HOLSTINE, widower	1	4	
Peter HECKART, Jr.	1	3	
Peter HECKART, Sr.		1	
Julius HOOD	1	1	
Frederick HARSH	1	7	
(blacks over 16)			2
Thomas HOLBERT	1	2	
William HOLBERT	1	2	
John HOLBERT	1	1	
William HEBB	1	1	
Michael HOLMAN		4	
Abraham HAYSE	1	1	
Jonathan HARRISS	1	3	
William HARRISS	1	2	
John HARRISS	1	3	
Abraham HARRISS	1	3	
John HARTMAN	2	5	
Jacob HARTMAN	1		
John HARRADER	1	3	
Daniel HARRADER	1	2	
Samuel HAZELET	1		
William HATFIELD	1	1	
John HOWELL	1	1	

James HAMILTON/L. HILL	1	2	
Isaac HAYSE	1	3	
Squire HALL	1	2	
Robert HAMILTON	2	2	
John HAWTHORNE		1	
(blacks over 16)			1
George HITE	2	2	
(blacks over 16)			1
Alexander HAWTHORN	1	1	
(blacks over 16)			1
Elijah HARDISTER	1	1	
James HILL, man of color	1		
James HILL, man of color	1		
Benjamin HARTEY	1	2	
William HAMBRICK	1	2	
Amos HAWLEY	2	2	
Joseph JENKINS	2	9	
(blacks over 16)			4
John JENKINS	1	2	
Lemuel JOHN	1	5	
Joseph JENKINS, Jr.	1		
Levy JENKINS	1		
Margaret JENKINS, widow		3	
(blacks over 16)			
William N. JARRETT	2	1	1
(blacks over 16)			3
(blacks 12-16)			1
Richard JONES	1	1	
Rhabian JENKINS	1		
Joseph JONES		2	
Barnabus JOHNSTON	1	3	
Richard JACKSON	1	2	
Richard JOHNSTON	1	1	
Thomas JOHNSTON	1		
Luke JACO	1	2	
Thomas JACO	1	2	
John JONES	1	3	
William JONES	2	2	
Jacob JONES, Sr.	1	1	
Samuel JONES	1	4	
Jacob JONES, Jr.	1	2	
Benjamin JONES	2	4	
John JOSEPH	1	1	
Andrew JOHNSTON	1		
Benjamin JEFFERES	1	2	
Dennis JEFFERIS	1	3	
Jonathan JENKINS	1	2	
Evan JENKINS		1	
John JENKINS	1	2	
Thomas JENKINS	1	1	
John JOHNSTON	1	5	
William JEFFERIS	1	3	

John JACKSON	1	14	
Benjamin JARRETT	1	1	
Mary JENKINS, widow		5	
(blacks over 16)			2
Thomas JENKINS	1		
John JARRETT	1		
James JEFFS	2	2	
John JEFFS	1	1	
Anthony KIRKHART		2	
Jacob KERNS	1	1	
Michael KERNS	1	6	
(blacks over 16)			1
Jacob KYGER	1	2	
John KELLER	1	2	
Joseph KINGCADE	1	2	
John KINGCADE	1		
William KINGCADE, Sr.	2	1	
William KINGCADE, Jr.	1	3	
John KIRK	1	1	
Hugh KELSON		5	
Cornelius KING	1	3	
George KELLER	1		
George KELLER, Sr.	1	2	
Robert KNOTTS	1	2	
Edward KNOTTS	2	3	
Oolery KEENER	1	1	
Samuel KEENER	1	2	
George KEENER	2	6	
Absalom KNOTTS	2	4	
John KIMMER, Sr.	1	2	
Jacob KIMMER	1	4	
John KIMMER, Jr.	1	4	
Jacob KNAVE	1		
John KELLEY	1	2	
William KELLEY	1	4	
John KELLEY, Sr.	2	5	
James KINGCADE	1	2	
Valentine KING	2	2	
James KING	1	3	
Benjamin KESSINGER	1	1	
Washington KNOX	1		
Richard LEASON	1	1	
Gardiner LEONARD	2	2	
Daniel LYMAN	2	1	
Ezabella LYNN, widow	2	3	
John LYNN	1	1	
George LAKE	1	1	
John LIPSCOMB	1		
William LIPSCOMB	1	3	
(blacks over 16)			1
Jeramiah LEACH	3	4	
Elisha LEACH	1	3	

Thomas LEWELLEN	2	3
Thomas LEWELLEN, Jr.		2
Samuel LEWELLEN	1	3
Benjamin LEWELLEN	1	1
Aaron LUZADDER, Sr.	1	3
Moses LUZADDER	1	
Aaron LUZADDER, Jr.	1	1
George LEGG	1	2
Henry LANTS	1	2
John LICKFIELD	1	1
Philip LEWIS	1	
Henry LEWIS, Sr.	1	3
Henry LEWIS, Jr.	1	2
William LAWMAN		3
James LEMMAN	2	2
John LAP	1	4
William LITTLE	1	3
Henry LEACH	1	
Joseph LAMBERT		1
Benjamin LAWSON	2	2
Joshua LAWSON	1	
John LEWELLEN	1	2
Doctor LEWELLEN	2	4
William B. LINDSEY	1	4
Thomas MARTIN	1	1
Hugh MORGAN	1	7
(blacks over 16)			1
Joseph MERRAFIELD	1	1
David MILLER	1	2
Thomas MONTGOMERY	1	5
William MINNEAR		1
Robert MOODY		3
John MORE		3
Moses MINNEAR	1	
John MAID	1	1
Charles MAGILL, Jr.	1	2
Charles MAGILL, Sr.	1	3
John MAGILL		1
Daniel MEDSKER	1	2
James McVICKER	1	4
(stud horse)			1
Joseph MATHINA	1	4
Stephen McDADE	1	2
James MOFFET	1	2
Robert MOFFET	1	
John McKEEVER	1	
Thomas MACKELROY		1
Peter MORAND	1	2
Ely MORE	2	1
Hugh MURPHY, Deckers Creek	2	6
William MURPHY	1	2
Isaac MILLER	1	1

Jobe MAGILL		1	
Evan MORGAN	2	2	
Evan S. MORGAN	1	1	
Hesekiah MARFIELD	2	2	
John MALONE	1	1	
Morgan MORGAN	2	3	
(blacks over 16)			1
James MORGAN		2	
Isaac MORGAN	1	3	
David MORGAN of Mod	1	1	
John P. MARTIN	1	3	
Jacob MIRES	2	2	
Michael MURPHY	1		
Thomas McGEE, Sr.	1	1	
Thomas McGEE, Jr.	1		
John MILLER, D. B.	2	4	
John MASON	1	2	
Jacob MOUSER	3	2	
John MINNEAR	1	3	
Benjamin MATTHEW	2	1	
Nathan MATTHEW	1	1	
Isaac MATTHEW	1	1	
Ely MATTHEW	1	1	
William McGEE	1	3	
Joseph MATTHEW	1	2	
Isaac MARCUS	1	4	
Laurance McHENRY	1	1	
John MANN, Sr.	1	1	
John MANN, Jr.	1	1	
Aaron McDANIEL	1	3	
John MILLER	1	3	
Samuel MINNEAR	1	2	
David MURPHY	1	3	
Hugh MURPHY, D. B.	1	1	
James MURPHY, D. B.	1	3	
Burket MINER	1	1	
Peter MERRADETH	1	2	
Philip MARTIN	1	5	
Henry MILLER, Kingwood	1	1	
John McCLAIN	1	1	
John McCAN	1	1	
Absalem MATHENA	1	2	
Robert McMULLEN	3	4	
David MINNEAR	1	2	
Roswell MESSENGER	1		
Abner MESSENGER	1	1	
William MASON	1	2	
William MORGAN, D. B.	1	2	
David MORGAN, D. B.	2	8	
Willmer MALE, man of color	1		
Willmer MALE, Jr. do	1	1	
William MASON, Sr., Exempt		1	

Joshua MASON	1	1	
Peter MASON	1	2	
Daniel MANNING	1	1	
James MORRIS	1	1	
James MATHENEY	1	3	
Benjamin MATHENEY	1	1	
Nathan MATHENEY	1	4	
Timothy MIDDLETON	1		
Daniel MARTIN	1	2	
Benjamin MIDDLETON	1	1	
William MICHAEL	1	3	
(stud horse)			1
Patrick McGREW	2	6	
William MAXEN	1	3	
John MIRES	1	3	
Ann MIRES		1	
Jacob MILLER	1	4	
Henry MILLER, Sr.	1	5	
Henry MILLER, Jr.	1		
Benjamin MORTON	1	2	
Hannah MORTON		2	
William MORTON	1	5	
Daniel McCOLLUM	2	4	
James McGREW	1	3	
Joseph MARTIN	1	1	
Francis McSHANE	1	1	
(blacks over 16)			1
John McARTHUR	1		
Henry MAY	1	2	
James MARFIELD	1	1	
Thomas MEAKS	1	3	
Edmonson MORE	1	1	
Jacob MILLER, Swamps	1	2	
James NEAL	1	1	
Jacob NUSE	2	5	
George NUZUM	1	2	
John NUZUM	2	1	
Richard NUZUM	1	1	
Thomas NUZUM	1		
William NUZUM	1	1	
James NUZUM	2	2	
Philip NICHLES	1	5	
Michael NOSE	1	1	
James NEDLEY	1		
David NORRIS	1	4	
William NICKLES	1	2	
Christian NINE	1	3	
Wheat NEIGHBORS	1	2	
William NORRIS	1	10	
(blacks over 16)			3
Casper ORTH	1	3	
John ORR	1	3	

John OTT	–	–	
(stud horse)			1
William PRICE	2	4	
Richard POSTLE	1	2	
Thomas PRITCHARD	1	3	
(stud horse)			1
Larkin PIERPOINT		3	
Zackquill PIERPOINT		3	
Francis PIERPOINT		1	
Hunter PILES	1	3	
(blacks over 16)			1
Abraham PEW	1	2	
Thomas PILES	1		
John PATTERSON	1	1	
Joseph POWELL	1	1	
William POWERS		2	
John POWERS	1	2	
Stephen POE	1	2	
James PARSONS		10	
(blacks over 16)			3
Samuel POSTLE	3	3	
John PAUGH	1	1	
James PAUGH	1	1	
Samuel PIERCE	1		
George PIERCE	1		
John PARSON, man of color	1	1	
William PHILIPS	1	2	
James W. POSTON	1	5	
Andrew PITZER	1	3	
Emanuel PEPHER, Sr.	1	5	
Emanuel PEPHER, Jr.	1	2	
Theophelus PUGH	1	4	
William PIERSON	1		
Jesse PENROSE	1	4	
Abraham PENROSE		2	
Jacob PAUL		3	
Robert PATTERSON	1	1	
Samuel PATTERSON	1	3	
John PITTET	1	1	
Nehemiah POWERS	1	2	
George QUICK	1		
Catharine RIDGEWAY, widow	1	3	
John ROWEN	1	1	
John RION	1	3	
Othaniel RODES		2	
John RODES		1	
William ROBINSON	1	2	
Thomas ROBINSON		1	
John ROBINSON		1	
George RADABOUGH	1	2	
James RANDALL	1	2	
George REASE		3	

William REED	2	6
Joseph REED	1	1
John REED	2	6
Isaac REED	2	6
Isaac RIGGS	1	4
Cyrus RIGGS	1	3
Samuel ROLSTON	2	3
Matthew ROBINSON	1	2
Hesekiah ROISE	1	5
William ROGERS	1	3
George RUBLE	1	1
Moses ROYSE	2	6
Henry RUNNER	1	2
Jacob RIDENOUR	1	5
John RIDENOUR	1	
Martin RIDENOUR	1	2
Aaron ROISE		2
(blacks over 16)			1
John ROBERTS	1	1
John RODEHEAVER	1	4
Amos ROBERTS	1	4
William ROBERTS	1	1
Earnest RECKHART	1	5
Isaac ROMINE	1	3
George RINGER	2	4
John ROSS	1	2
William REED	1	
George RUNNETS	1	
Charles ROSE	1	1
John ROSE	1	1
Shedwick ROISE	1	1
Zachariah RHODES	1	4
William RHODES	1	1
Jacob RUBLE	1	3
Benjamin REED	1	
Thomas RUBLE	1	1
Elias RANEY	1	1
Ann STEPHENSON, widow		3
John STAFFORD	1	3
Thomas STAFFORD		1
William STAFFORD		1
Frederick SPATSMAN	1	1
Laurance SNYDER	2	1
Jacob SMITH, Kingwood	1	
Charles STEWART	1	6
Catharine STEWART, widow		2
Hugh SIDWELL	2	7
Seth STAFFORD	1	2
David SEAMAN	1	2
Philip SMELL	1	2
William SMITH, cooper	1	1
William SHAW	3	3

Joseph A. SHACKLEFORD	1	4
Frederick SWISHER	1	2
Drake SWINGLER	1	2
David SWINGLER	2	1
John SULLAVAN	1	1
Jonathan SOLYARDS	1	1
John SMITH	1	
Jacob SETH	1	1
Henry SHAVER	2	4
Magruder SELBY	2	3
Jacob SMITH	1	3
Alexander SOMERS	1	2
Samuel SICKLE	1	
Francis SETH	1	
Jacob SETH	1	1
Richard SMITH	1	2
Jacob SWISHER	1	1
John SHRYVER	2	4
Coonrod SHEATS	1	
John SMITH	3	1
Nehemiah SQUIRES	4	3
John SNYDER, Sandy Creek	1	3
Henry SNYDER	1	2
Kidd W. SMITH		2
David SIMPSON	2	4
John SIMPSON	1	1
William SIMPSON	1	1
John SROYERS	1	3
Nimrod SNYDER	1	1
John SHEHAN	3	
David SHEHAN	1	
George SHEHAN	1	2
Jesse SNYDER	2	2
Frederick SNYDER	1	2
Jacob SNYDER	1	2
William SMITH, D. E.	1	2
John SCOTT	2	3
John STEPHENS	2	2
Martin STEMPLE	2	3
John STEMPLE	1	4
John SANDERS	1	
David STEMPLE	1	6
John STINE	1	3
John SMITH, Germany	1	3
Adam SHAVER	2	4
Tewalt SHAVER	1	1
Benjamin SHAVER	1	1
Jonathan SPURGEN	1	6
Samuel SMITH	1	2
Frederick SMITH	1	5
Alexander SHAW	1	4
Benjamin SHAW	1	

Andrew STARLING	2	4	
Joseph SOVERNS of Dan'l.	2	9	
Daniel SOVERNS, Sr.	1	1	
Mary SYPOLT, widow		2	
Nathan SYPOLT	1	4	
Christopher SYPOLT	1	3	
George SYPOLT	1	4	
William STARLING	1	3	
John SMITH	1	1	
Philip SOMERS	1	1	
Jonathan SMITH	1	3	
Daniel SOVERNS, Jr.	1	3	
John SOVERNS	1	4	
William SINES		2	
Bartholomew SEVIER	1	2	
Samuel SHAW	1	4	
John G. SMITH	1	3	
Frederick SPARR	1	3	
Jesse SPURGEN	1	3	
Elizabeth SPURGEN, widow		1	
Joseph SAYRES	2	4	
Sarah SMITH, widow		3	
Joseph SMITH	1		
Aaron SMITH	1		
William SIGLER	1	1	
Henry SINE, Jr.		2	
Henry SINE, Sr.	1	2	
James SEYMORE		3	
John STAFFORD	1	2	
Neal SWANEY	1	1	
James STAFFORD		2	
(blacks over 16)			2
(blacks 12-16)			1
Jonathan V. SKYHAWK	1		
Thomas SCOTT	2	1	
Thomas SWEATMAN	1		
Rawley SCOTT	2	2	
(blacks over 16)			2
(blacks 12-16)			1
SCOTT & KYGER		15	
(blacks over 16)			3
Jacob SHELL	1	1	
William SIZER, man of color	1	3	
Thomas STEEL	1	3	
Benjamin SAYRES	1	2	
Mary SPURGEN, widow		1	
John SNYDER	1	2	
Samuel SWEARINGEN	1	2	
(blacks over 16)			1
Samuel TAYLOR	1	2	
James TROY	3	2	
Francis TIBBS	1	1	

Margaret TRICKET, widow	1	3	
Michael TRICKET	1	2	
William TRICKET	1	3	
William TUCKER	1	1	
David TROWBRIDGE	2	3	
Zachariah TURNER	1	2	
Lewis TURNER	1		
Samuel TROWBRIDGE	1	2	
Thomas THORN	2	1	
William THORN	1	1	
James THOMAS	1		
Thomas THOMAS	2	5	
Samuel TAYLOR	1	2	
John TIMMERMAN	1	2	
Jacob TETRICK	1	3	
Benjamin TRIMBLY	2	2	
Stephen TITCHANEL	1	3	
Henry TEATS	1	4	
George TURNEY	1	2	
Henry TEATS		1	
John TRIMBLEY	1	1	
Robert THOMPSON	1	2	
Arthur TRADER	1	2	
Francis TIBBS, Sr.	1	1	
Catharine TIBBS		1	
(blacks over 16)			2
Richard TIBBS	1		
Jane TINGLE, widow		1	
Jesse TROWBRIDGE	1	2	
JACKSON & UPDEGRAFT	2	1	
(blacks over 16)			1
Nicholas VANDAVERT	2	6	
Ebenezer VANDAGRIFT	1	4	
David WATSON	1	2	
Sarah WATSON, widow		4	
Joseph WEAVER	1	4	
Richard WISE	1	1	
Elizabeth WOOLVERTON		2	
Benjamin WALLS	1		
Richard WATTS	-	-	
(blacks over 16)			1
Samuel WILSON	1	2	
John WAGNER	1	2	
John WALKER	1	2	
Henry WILLIAMS	2	2	
Joseph WILSON	1	2	
(blacks over 16)			2
Augustus WELLS	2	3	
David B. WEAVER	1		
Edward WILSON	1		
James S. WILSON	2	6	
(blacks 12-18)			1

Alexander WATTS	1	2	
Jane WATTS, widow		1	
Stephen WILSON	1	2	
James & Abraham WEAVER	3	3	
James WILSON, shoemaker	1	1	
James WEST	1	1	
Archey WILSON	1	1	
George WILSON of Wm.		2	
Jeptha WILKINS	1	3	
James WATKINS	1	1	
Rebecca WILSON		1	
(blacks over 16)			1
James WILLIAMS	1	3	
James WALLS	1		
Jacob WATSON	1	2	
Abraham WOODRING	1	4	
John WOODRING	1	2	
Daniel WOODRING	1	3	
Jacob WOODRING	1	2	
John WHEELER	1	2	
Nicholas WOODRING	1	6	
John WHETZEL	1		
George WHETZEL	1		
Christian WHITEHARE	2	2	
Henry WILES	1	4	
George WHITEHARE	1		
Peter WILLHELM	1	2	
Frederick WILLHELM	1	3	
Thomas WILSON	1	1	
James WEBSTER	1	6	
William WALLER, Sr.	1	2	
William WALLER, Jr.		1	
John WALLER	1	2	
Samuel WALLER		1	
Robert WOODS	1	2	
John WOOD	2	3	
Josiah WOOD	1	7	
Samuel WILLETS	1	3	
George WOOLF	1	2	
Jacob WOOLF	1		
Henry WOOLF	1		
Augustine WOOLF	1	4	
(stud horse)			1
Jacob WOOLF	1	4	
John WOOLF		1	
John WILLETTS	2	7	
Benjamin WHEELER	1		
Henry WILLYARD, Jr.	1	2	
Henry WILLYARD, Sr.	1		
George WILLYARD	1	2	
James WALL, Lorrel Hill	2	2	
Joseph WILSON	1		

Enoch WARMAN	1		
Catharine WARMAN, widow		2	
(blacks over 18)			1
Francis WARMAN	1	3	
Thomas WILLIAMS	1	1	
John WILSON	1	4	
Augustus WERNINGER	2	2	
(blacks over 18)			1
(blacks 12-18)			2
Stephen WATKINS	1	2	
William WALKER	1	1	
Elijah WOOD	1	3	
Jacob WEAVER	1	3	
Michael WITTS	1	3	
Joseph YAGER	1	2	
Jacob ZINN	2	6	
(blacks over 16)			1
John ZINN	1	1	
Alexander ZINN	1	2	
William ZINN	1	2	
Michael ZINN	1	2	
Peter ZINN	1	1	
George ZINN	1	2	

"Persons owning or occupying Water Grist Mills, Saw Mills, Furnaces and Forges."

	Yearly Rent Thereof
Thomas BARTLETT, saw mill	30
James BEALL, grist mill	30
Thomas BUTLER, grist mill	50
Samuel CRANE, grist mill	70
John FAIRFAX, grist mill	70
Abraham GOOSEMAN, grist mill	50
Frederick HARSH, saw mill	30
John HARTMAN, grist & saw mill	60
Samuel HASLET, grist & saw mill	70
Andrew JOHNSTON, saw mill	20
Michael KERNS, 1 grist & 2 saw mills	300
Burket MINER, grist mill	40
Hannah MORTON, widow, grist & saw mill	60
John NUZUM, grist mill	100
Emanuel PIPHER, Jr., grist mill	30
Theophilis PUGH, grist mill	30
William PEARSON, grist & saw mill	60
Jacob RUBLE, grist mill	70
Charles STEWART, saw mill	20
Hugh SIDWELL, grist mill	70
Samuel SWEARINGEN, grist mill	70
JACKSON & UPDEGRAFT, grist & saw mill & forge	1500
Nicholas WOODRING, grist mill	60

"I do certify that I have examined the within list of taxable property and do find the same to be correctly stated. Given under my hand this 1st June 1813." Charles BYRN, C. R.

MONONGALIA COUNTY RECORDS OF DISTRICT AND COUNTY COURTS
Monongalia County, (West) Virginia Personal Property Taxes
Microfilm #10

70a - 1813, "Property List for the year 1813 in the district
of Rawley MARTIN, Commissioner of the Revenue." "I Rawley
MARTIN have examined the foregoing list of taxable property
subject to taxation and find the same to be correctly stated.
Given under my hand this 31st day of May 1813."

Rawley MARTIN, C. R.

Persons Name Chargeable with the tax	white males over 16	horses, mares colts, mules	other
Stephen ARCHER	1		
James ARNETT, Jr.	1	4	
Daniel ARNETT	1	2	
Henry AMOS, Jr.	1	2	
Andrew ARNETT	1	5	
Stephen AMOS	1	2	
John AUSTIN	1	3	
Isaac AMMONS	2	4	
Anthony ASHER	1	2	
John ASHER	1	2	
Benjamin ALTON	1	3	
Henry AMOS	3	5	
James ARNETT	1		
Jonathan ARNETT	1	2	
(stud horse)			1
Richard? BONER	1	3	
John BAKER	1	5	
John BERKSHIRE	2	5	
(blacks over 16)			1
William BYERS	1	2	
Jacob BARRICK	1	2	
Wm. BODLEY	1	2	
James BODLEY	1	1	
Samuel BILLINGSLEY	1	3	
Benjamin BALDWIN	1	2	
_____ BAKER	1		
James BOWLESBEE	3	7	
Jesse BUSSEY	1	4	
(blacks over 16)			1
John BUTTERS/BUTTENS	1	1	
Wm. BILLINGSLEY	2	3	
Cirus BILLINGSLEY, Exempt		2	
Nelson BOLING	1	2	
Jacob BOWERS	1	1	
George BAREMORE	1	2	

Levy BATHWELL		2	
George BRAND	1	4	
___sa BRITTAN	1	2	
_____ BARRICKMAN	1	4	
Boaz BASNETT	1	1	
Daniel BARRET	1	4	
(blacks over 16)			1
(blacks 12-16)			2
John BOWSLOG	1	6	
John BRAND, Jr.	1	3	
James BRAND	3	6	
Zebedee BRAWN	1	2	
George BARRICK	1	2	
Reuben BRAWN	1	4	
John BRAWN, D. C.	1	1	
Philip BITOBARGER	1	1	
Lemuel BUCKER	2	2	
George BELL	1	1	
Mog BARNUS	2	3	
Joseph BRUMAGE	1	3	
Joseph BARKER, Jr.	1	1	
Joseph BONER	1	2	
David BARKER	1	2	
(blacks over 16)			1
David BLACK	2	3	
Boaz BURROWS	1	7	
John BARKER	1	3	
James BARKER	1	3	
(blacks over 16)			1
Rober BUCKER	1	2	
Joseph BARKER	2	4	
(blacks over 16)			1
Aron BARKER	1	3	
Zahariah BARKER	1	2	
James BALLAH	1	2	
Charles BAYLES, Jr.	1	3	
Samuel BASNETT	1	2	
James BARKER	2	3	
Benjamin BRAWN	1	2	
John BRAWN	2	3	
Durris BRAWN	1	2	
Peter BRAWN	1	1	
Linzey BOGGIS	2	2	
Benjamin BURTON	1	1	
Thomas BARNES	1	1	
John S. BARNES	1	8	
James BARNES	1	2	
Henry BARNHOUSE	1	2	
Henry BATTON	2	3	
Thomas BARTLETT, Jr.	1	2	
Wm. BARNES	1	1	
(mill)			2

John BRAND	3	5	
John BRAND, blacksmith	2	1	
Joseph BRITTON	2	3	
Abraham BRAWN	1	1	
Adam BRAWN	2	2	
(mills)			2
John BATTON	1	2	
Samuel BERDINE	1	1	
Michael BARR	2	4	
Samuel BALDWIN	1	3	
Richard BLAND	1	2	
Ephram BIGS	1	1	
Noah BIGS	1	2	
John BROOKOVER	2	1	
Charles BOYLES	1	2	
Wm. BALDWIN, Exempt		1	
Richard BERRY	1	2	
Sary BARKER		2	
Ezekiel BURROWS, Exempt		2	
Wm. BAKER	1	1	
Andrew BOYD	1	2	
Jasper BONER	1	2	
Samuel BICE	1	1	
Wm. BICE	1	2	
Joseph BONER	1	2	
Wm. BARNES	1		
Jacob BRUMAGE	1	1	
John BRUMAGE	1	1	
Isaac BRUMAGE	1	3	
James BONER	1	1	
Abraham BARNES	1	2	
Enoch BONER	1	2	
Widow BONER	1	2	
(blacks over 16)			1
Amos BONER	1	2	
John BARNETT	1	2	
Jacob BANKER/BARKER	1		
Cornelius BERKSHIRE	1	3	
Caney BRITE	2	4	
Robert BOGGIS	1		
(blacks over 16)			1
Abraham BAWIN	1	4	
Absolem BARKSHIRE	2	3	
George J. BALTSELL	2		
Daniel BALTSELL	1	1	
Christian BIXLER	1	1	
Samuel BIXLER	1		
William CHIPPS	1	2	
James COLLINS	1	2	
David CAMLIN	1	4	
John CASS	1	1	
John CUNNINGHAM	1	1	

Michael COURTNEY	2	3	
John COURTNEY	1	4	
Robert COURTNEY	1	4	
Robert COURTNEY, Jr.	1	2	
William COURTNEY	1	2	
Joseph CUMMINS	1	2	
Abraham CUMMAGYS	2	6	
(blacks over 16)			2
Caleb CONAWAY	1	1	
John CARTER	1		
Thomas CORDREY	1	7	
(mill)			1
Richard CALE/COLE	1	3	
(blacks over 16)			1
Michael CONNER	1		
Adam CAMP	1	3	
Ezekiel CHANEY	1		
Robert CUNNINGHAM	1	3	
James COLLINS	2	4	
(blacks over 16)			1
(mills)			2
Joseph COMBS	1	2	
Hynson CALE	1	2	
Joseph CALE	1	2	
Wm. CALE	1	4	
Christopher CORE	1	4	
William COLLAN	1	3	
Richard CANNON	1	1	
Abisha CLARK	1	1	
Isaac CAVALT	1	2	
Soloman CHAFFIN	1	3	
Robert CHAFFIN	1	2	
Henry CORATHERS	1	5	
John CARPENTER	1	3	
Samuel CONAWAY	1	2	
John COX	1	3	
Henry CARVER	1	1	
Andrew COLLINS	1	1	
Ezekiel COX	1	2	
Isaac CAMP	1	3	
Michael CARY	1		
Benjamin CHESNEY	1	3	
Moses COX, Exempt	2		
Abraham COX	2	6	
(mill) CLAYTON			1
Elisha CLAYTON	2	3	
Peter CRISS	1	2	
Wm. CAMPBELL	1	1	
Joseph CAMPBELL	1	2	
(blacks over 16)			1
(blacks 12-16)			1
Thomas CONAWAY	1	1	

Jeremiah CONAWAY	1	2	
Michael CORE	2	7	
Alexander CLEGG	2	4	
(blacks 12-16)			2
Richard CHEW	1	3	
Andrew CORBLEY	1	2	
Isaac COEN	1	1	
Jesse CANE	1	1	
John CARTER	1	1	
John COOPER	1		
Elizabeth CUNNINGHAM	1	3	
Ezekiel CUNNINGHAM	1	2	
John CARPENTER, Jr.	1	2	
John CARROLL	1	1	
John CLELLAND	1	3	
James CUNNINGHAM	1	1	
Nicholas CHISLER	1	1	
James CHADWICK	4	1	
John CAMPBELL	1	2	
Widow CLARK	1	2	
Reuben CRAWFORD	1		
Michael CLAUCE	1	1	
John CHISLER	1	1	
Rieuben CHAFFIN	1		
Wm. CRISTY	1		
Henry CULVER	1		
John DAWSON, Jr.	1	2	
George DAWSON	1	1	
Luke DAVIS	1	1	
John DEUSENBERRY	1	5	
John DAVIS	1	4	
Weightman DAVIS	1	2	
Robert DAVIS	2	3	
Robert DAVIS, Jr.	1	2	
John DENT	2	8	
(blacks over 16)			2
(mill)			1
Joseph DUNLOP	1	2	
Enos DOUGHERTY	1	1	
(blacks 12-16)			1
Mary DUNN	1	1	
Philip DIGMAN	1		
Dudley DENT	1	1	
Daniel DAVIS	2	5	
Solomon DAVIS	1	3	
Jehu DAVIS	1		
Thomas DAWSON, Jr.	1	2	
Moses DOOLITTLE	1	2	
John DUNN	1	2	
D. DUNHAM	1	3	
John DAWSON	1	2	
Thomas DAWSON	1	3	

John DANBY	1	2
John DICKEN	1	3
Matthias DAVIS	3	4
Jacob DRAGOO	1	3
Dennis DELANEY	1	1
Henry DAVIS	1	2
Asa DUDLEY	1	2
Samuel DUDLEY	1	3
John DRAGGOO	1	3
John DAVIS	1	2
Ephram DRAGGOO	1	3
Peter DRAGGOO	1	2
Robert DOWNS	1	3
Lary DIEL		1
Robert DARROW	1	4
Samuel DUESENBERRY	1	1
Simon DEAKEN	1	1
Thomas DOOLITTLE	1	1
(mill)			1
Caleb DAVIS	1	1
John DEEN/DUN, Exempt		2
Rebeca DEARING	2	2
(blacks over 16)			1
(blacks 12-16)			1
Dudley EVANS	2	8
(blacks over 16)			3
(blacks 12-16)			1
John EVANS, Jr.	1	10
(blacks over 16)			3
(blacks 12-16)			1
John EVANS	1	11
(blacks over 16)			3
(blacks 12-16)			1
Enoch EVANS	1	3
Jacob EVANS	1	1
John EVANS	1	1
Jarrod EVANS	3	4
(mill)			1
Nimrod EVANS	2	4
(blacks over 16)			5
Marmaduke EVANS	1	
Samuel EVERLY	2	6
Simeon EVERLY	2	7
_____ EASTBURN	1	4
Edward EVANS	2	4
Charles EDILBLUTE?	1	2
David EADY	1	2
Gayon EADY	2	3
Alexander EADY	2	4
Wm. EADY, Exempt		3
Edward EVANS, Jr.	2	3
Thomas EVANS	1	2

Catherine EFAU	2	2	
Rawley EVANS	1	3	
(blacks over 16)			1
Michael FLOYD	1	3	
(blacks over 16)			1
Jacob FAULK	3	1	
John FISHER	2	3	
John FOURTNEY	1	1	
Wm. FRUM	4	7	
Wm. FLEAHARTY	1		
Thomas FLEMING	1	5	
(blacks over 16)			1
George FURBEE	1	2	
Alexander FLEMING	1	2	
Frederick FOX	2	1	
Joel FARMER	2	2	
Elijah FREELAND	1	3	
John FLEAHARTY	1	1	
Samuel FELBY	1	1	
John FORTNER	1	2	
Binona FLEMING	2	2	
Wm. FLEMING	1	1	
Boaz FLEMING	1	2	
Matthew FLEMING	1	2	
Aaron FOSTER	1	3	
John FETTY	1	5	
George FETTY	1	2	
Joseph FETTY	1	2	
Adam FAUVER	1	1	
John FANCHER	1	2	
Robert FAUCET	4	3	
Samuel FRUM	1	1	
Stephen GILBERT	1	3	
George GOULD	1	1	
John L. GILLMEYER	2	2	
Charles GLASCOCK	1		
(mill)			1
Samuel GOODWIN	1	1	
John GIDLEY	1	1	
Richard GRIMES	1	3	
Matthew GAY	1	1	
John GARLOW	1	4	
Andrew GARLOW	1	3	
Thomas GLISSON, Jr.	1		
James GUTTREY	1	5	
Thomas GRIGS	1	2	
John GRUB	1	3	
John GACKINAUR	1	1	
Wm. GRAY	2	4	
Thomas GLISSON	1	4	
(blacks over 16)			1
Thomas GALLION	1		

Nehemiah GLOVER	1	1	
Samuel GLOVER	1	1	
Samuel GRUB	1	1	
John GLASCOCK	1	2	
James GUTTREGE, Exempt		2	
Jeremiah GALLIHUE \	2	2	
Henry GALLIHUE /	1		
Henry GRIFFIN	1	1	
John A. GOOSMAN	1	2	
Robert HILL	3	11	
George HUFFMAN	2	1	
Matthew HANNON	1	1	
Justis HECK	2	2	
David HAYHURST	1	3	
(mill)			1
Joseph HOLT	2	3	
Peter HESS, Jr.	1	1	
Charles HANEY	1	2	
Widow HANEY	1	2	
Patrick HANEY	1	2	
John HOWARD	2	3	
Thomas HAMPSON	1	1	
Caleb HURLEY	1	2	
Wm. HOLEYFIELD	1	1	
Purnel HOUSTON	2	3	
Henry HAMILTON	2	3	
John HOWEL	1	1	
Joseph HARRISON	1	7	
Widow HOGUE	1		
(blacks over 16)			1
Richard HARRISON	1	6	
(blacks over 16)			2
Thomas HALE	1	2	
Peter HARRIS	1	2	
Curtis HAYS	3	4	
Benjamin HAMILTON	1	2	
Joseph HENRY	1	2	
Francis HENRY	1	3	
Ephram HEDLEY	1	1	
Ananias HUDSON	1	2	
Wm. HOSKINSON	1	2	
Balser HESS	1	2	
Rynear HALL	1	4	
Reason HOLLAND	1	3	
Brice HOLLAND	1	3	
Capel HOLLAND	1	3	
(blacks over 16)			1
Archabald HAMILTON	1	2	
James HAYHURST	1	1	
James HENDERSON	1	4	
Peter HINKINS	2	4	
John HANSELL	1	2	

Abraham HUFFMAN	1	1	
Tobias HAUGHT	1	1	
Jourden HALL	2	6	
Peter HAUGHT	2	3	
Thomas HALL	1	3	
Wm. HILLERY	1	2	
Simeon HURLEY	1	2	
Thomas HESS	1	1	
Soloman HOGUE	1	1	
Aran HENRY, Jr.	1	2	
Jeremiah HOSKINSON	3	5	
(mill)			1
Thomas HAMILTON	1	5	
Otho HENRY	2	3	
Wm. HAYNES	1	1	
James HILL	2	5	
Wm. HAYS	1	1	
Asa HALL	2	5	
Wm. HAYS	1	1	
Peter HESS \	1	3	
John HESS /	1	3	
Elias HOSKINSON	2	5	
John HAUGHT, Jr.	1	1	
John HAUGHT	1	2	
George HIXENBAUGH	1	2	
Peter HAUGHT, Exempt		3	
John HOOVER	2	2	
Charles HOOVER	1	3	
John HOLT	1	3	
(blacks over 16)			4
Ralph HOLT	1	2	
Elijah HOLT	1	2	
(blacks over 16)			1
Elisha HOLT	1	2	
John HUDSON	1	1	
John HAMMER	1	1	
Bethel HUMPHREYS	1	1	
John HARE	1	2	
Joshua HICKMAN	2	5	
(blacks over 16)			4
(mill)			1
Wm. HAYMOND	2	8	
(blacks over 16)			2
Joseph HARTLEY	1	2	
Joseph HARTLEY, Jr.	1	2	
Horatio HARTLEY	1	2	
Amos HARTLEY	1	2	
Elijah HARTLEY	1	2	
Edward HARTLEY	1	1	
Asa HARRIS	2	1	
Hiram HENRY	1		
James HOARD	1	5	

Wm. HAREBOLT	1	2	
Samuel HANAWAY	1	1	
Abraham HALL	1		
James HENRY	1	3	
James HURRY	3	2	
Wm. JOSEPH	2	3	
Thomas JENKINS	1	3	
Widow JONES, P. P.	1	2	
Enoch JONES	3	3	
(blacks over 16)			1
(mills)			2
Daniel JACKSON	1	1	
Wm. JOHN	1	6	
(blacks over 16)			1
(blacks 12-16)			1
Vachal JACKSON	1	5	
John JENKINS	1	1	
Benjamin JACOBS	1	2	
Evan JINKENS	1	3	
Nathan JOHNSON	1	3	
Benjamin JENKINSKINS (sic)	1	6	
Lewis JOHN	1	2	
John JOLLIFF	1	1	
Wm. ICE	2	3	
Thomas ICE	1	2	
Abraham ICE	1	1	
John ICE	1	2	
Adam ICE	1	4	
Andrew ICE	3	6	
(mills)			2
George ICE	1	1	
Wm. ICE, Jr.	1	1	
Wm. JOBES	1	3	
John W. JOHNSON	1	5	
Matthew JONES	1	1	
Wm. JONES	1	4	
Wm. JOLLIFF	1	1	
John JOHNSON	2	6	
(blacks over 16)			4
(blacks 12-16)			1
Owin JOHN	1	3	
John KERN, J. C.	1	2	
Benjamin KUGAL	1	2	
Thomas KNIGHT, Jr.	1	1	
Patrick KELLEY	1	3	
Daniel KNOX	2	3	
John KERN	1	3	
Barney KERN, Exempt		2	
Wm. KENNADY	2	3	
Thomas KNIGHT	1	2	
Michael KERN	2	6	
(mill)			1

Samuel KENNADY	1	1	
Samuel KINDLE	1	1	
Samuel KINDLE, Jr.	1	1	
James KINDLE	1	2	
James KELLEY	1	4	
John KNIGHT	1	2	
Samuel KECKLEY	1	2	
John KING	1	2	
John KIRBEY	1	1	
Thomas KING	2	1	
Michael KNIGHT	1	1	
Elizabeth KELSO	2	2	
Fielding KYGER	2	1	
John LEGGET	1	2	
David LOW	1	1	
James LEASON	1	2	
Gabriel LEEP	1		
Thomas LAZZEL	3	7	
Thomas LAZZEL, Jr.	1	2	
John LOUGH	1	2	
Samuel LOUGH	1	2	
Wm. LAWLIS	1		
(mill)			1
James LOUGH	1	1	
John LAUNCE	1	5	
Wm. LANCASTER	1	10	
(mill)			1
Elial LONG	2	3	
John LUNING	1	3	
Joshua LOW	2	3	
(mill)			1
Thomas LADELEY	2	3	
Wm. LINCH	1	2	
John LOUGH, Jr.	1	4	
Joseph LOUGH	1	3	
John LINCH	1	4	
(blacks over 16)			1
John LINCH, Jr.	1	1	
Samuel LEMLEY	1	3	
George LOW	1	1	
Thomas LEMASTERS	1	2	
Isaac LEMASTERS	1	1	
John L. LONG	1	1	
Levy LONG	1	2	
George LAUNCE	1	4	
(blacks over 16)			1
Elial LONG, Jr.	1	1	
Jacob LYMAN	2	3	
Daniel LEE	1	2	
Thomas LANHAM	1	2	
Lucy LANHAM	1	1	
Luis LUNTS	1		

397

Wm. LARRISON	1	2
John LOTT	1	3
Wm. LANHAM	1	2
(blacks over 16)			1
David MICHAEL	1	2
Lewis MORRIS	1	1
Wm. MILLER	1	3
Thomas MEREDITH	1	1
Noah MATHENEY	1	2
Reuben MATHENEY	1	1
John MYERS	1	1
Elias MAGRUDER	1	2
Edward MATTHEW	1	3
Wm. McCANTS	1	
Widow MERRELL		2
John MYERS	1	1
Frederick MYERS	1	3
Noah MORRIS	1	4
Cumpton MILLER	1	
John MYERS, P. R.	2	4
James McCALLASTER	1	3
James MORRIS	2	4
Archabald McCALEB	1	1
Michael MOORE	1	4
Jacob MOORE	1	2
Hezekiah MARSHALL	1	4
Allen MARTIN	3	6
(blacks over 16)			2
Horatio MARTIN	1	1
Jasper MICHAEL	2	3
Wm. MILLER	2	5
Philip MOORE	1	4
John MERRELL	1	3
Adam MYERS	1	2
Jesse MILLET	2	2
John McDOUGAL	1	2
Zackquell MORGAN	1	4
Stephen MORGAN	1	3
Davis MEREDITH	2	3
Peter MILLER	2	6
James MILLER	1	1
Charles MURRY	1	3
Levy MORRIS	1	4
Zadock MORRIS, Exempt		3
Stephenson MORRISON	1	2
Robert MERCER	2	4
Jacob MICHAEL	1	1
John MORRIS	1	2
Wm. MARTIN	1	1
David MUSGRAVE	1	2
David MUSGRAVE, Jr.	1	1
Wm. MORRIS	1	2

Nathan MATHENEY	2	5	
John McCUROY	1	2	
James McGUMMARY	1	1	
Morgan MORGAN	1	2	
Acklis MORGAN	1	3	
George MARTIN	1	2	
Jacob METS	1	3	
Leonard METS	2	3	
Joseph MAGILL	1	1	
Joseph MORGAN	2	4	
(mill)			1
Henry MARTIN	2	2	
(blacks over 16)			2
(blacks 12-16)			1
Zepheniah MARTIN	1	2	
David MORGAN	1	2	
John McRA	1	1	
George McRA	1	2	
Wm. McRA	1	1	
Joseph MERRELL	1	2	
Samuel MINARD	1	2	
(mills)			2
Theophilus MINOR	1	1	
Ely MARSHALL	1	3	
John MYERS	1	3	
(mills)			2
Uriah McDEVIT	1	1	
Lubeus MANE	1	2	
James MARSHALL	1	2	
James MARSHALL, Jr.	1	2	
Thomas MILLER	2	9	
(mill)			1
Jacob MILLER	1	2	
Christian MADERA	1		
Daniel MICHAEL	2	4	
Henry MICHAEL	1	2	
Wm. MICHAEL	1	2	
James MORGAN	1	3	
Horatio MORGAN	1	2	
John MILLER	1	1	
James MANHON	1	1	
Levy MORGAN	1	2	
Joshua MILLER	1	1	
John MILLER	3	2	
John MaGEE	2	4	
Arthur MELLET	1	2	
Wm. MELLET	1	1	
Samuel MERRIFIELD	1	1	
(mill)			1
John MERRIFIELD	1	2	
Wm. MOLLER	1	3	
Jacob MADERA	1		

Isaac MAYFIELD	1	2	
Dunkin McVICKER	2	2	
Joseph McVICKER	1	2	
Robert MINNIS	1	1	
Wm. McCLAAREY	1	2	
(blacks over 16)			1
Nicholas MADERA	1		
Farquire McRA	2	2	
(blacks over 16)			2
Wm. McKINNA	1		
Rawley MARTIN	1	4	
(blacks over 16)			1
Richard MORRIS	1	2	
John NEWBROUGH	1	1	
Nathaniel NEEDELS	1		
Christian NIBARGER	2	3	
Joseph NEWBROUGH	3	4	
Henry NIPTON	1	2	
James NEALEY	2	4	
John ORR	1	3	
Joseph ONEAL	1	4	
George PICKENPAUGH	1	3	
(mill)			1
Henry PRIDE	1	1	
Joseph PICKENPAUGH	1	2	
Edward PARRISH	2	6	
Eleven POINTER	1	1	
Purnel PASWATERS	1	1	
Zachariah PILES	1	4	
Adam PICKENPAUGH	1	3	
Jacob PAWLESBY	2	4	
(mill)			1
Labin PERDUE	1	2	
Wm. POSTLE	2	4	
Job PRICKETT	1	2	
John PARKER	1	2	
Isaac POWEL	2	4	
Richard PRICE	1	5	
(mills)			2
Isaac PRICE	1		
Jacob PINDLE	1	6	
John PITZER	2	3	
Jacob PINDLE, Jr.	1	1	
Caleb PRICE	2	1	
Andrew PARKES	1	4	
Isaiah PRICKETT, Exempt		4	
Jacob PRICKETT	1	1	
Thomas PRICKETT	1	2	
Richard PRICKETT	1	2	
(mill)			1
Isaac PEARCE	1	2	
John PAREPOINT, Exempt		2	

Silas POWEL	1	1
Wm. POINTER	1	2
John PRIDE, Exempt		2
Michael PRICE	1	2
Bazel PORTER	1	2
Wm. G. PAYNE	1	1
(blacks over 16)		3
John ROGERS	1	2
James RENSHAW	1	2
John RAMSEY	1	4
John ROCHESTER	1	2
Wm. RAMSEY	1	4
Frederick RICE	1	
Andrew ROCK	1	2
James ROBISON	1	3
George ROBISON	1	3
Isaac REED	1	1
Isaac RICE	2	3
Robert ROBE	2	2
Noah RIDGWAY	1	1
Alexander RIGS	2	4
John RIGS	1	1
John RAMSEY	3	4
Able RICE	1	2
Wm. RABER	1	3
Christopher RABER, Jr.	1	2
Christopher RABER	1	4
Philip ROBERTS	1	1
Jacob RICE	1	2
Charles RICE	1	
Daniel RICH, Exempt		2
Samuel RIGHT	1	
James ROBISON	1	2
Jonathan ROBERTS	1	2
John ROADS	1	
Felix SCOTT	1	2
George STEWART	1	2
John SHIVELY	2	4
Philip SHIVELY	4	11
James SCOTT, Jr.	1	3
John SMITH	4	5
Joseph SNODGRASS	2	2
Wm. SNODGRASS, Jr.	1	2
Wm SNODGRASS	1	3
Elisha SNODGRASS	1	2
John SNIDER	1	4
David SNIDER	1	5
George SMITH	3	12
Thomas SHAW	1	1
Joseph SAPP, Exempt		1
Samuel SMITH	1	1
Frederick SWISHER	1	4

John SANDERS	2	4
(blacks over 18)			1
Charles SIMPKINS	1	6
Dickson SIMPKINS	1	1
Adam SRIVER	1	4
John SNIDER	3	10
Henry STONE	2	5
Henry SMITH	1	2
Samuel SAMPLE	1	1
John STONE	1	1
James SCOTT	2	4
(blacks over 18)			1
David SCOTT, 3rd.	1	1
Robert SCOTT	1	1
David SCOTT	1	1
John SHADWELL	1	2
(blacks 12-16)			2
John A. STINESPRING	1	
Godfrey STILE, Exempt		3
Thomas SIMPSON	1	
Philip SHORT	1	2
John STILES	1	1
John SULLIVAN	1	1
Wm. SCOTT	1	2
James STEEL, Jr.	1	2
John STEEL	1	3
James STEEL	1	2
(mill)			1
Eliab SIMPSON	1	3
Wm. STILES	1	2
Stephen STILES	1	1
Robert SHEARER	1	2
John SHUMAN	1	2
Peter STRAIGHT	2	4
Samuel STEWART	1	2
John SPRINGER	1	2
Henry SHUMAN	1	1
Robert SIKES	1	
David SMITH	1	1
John SEAMAN	1	
Henry SMITH, J. C.	1	2
Isaac SNODGRASS	1	1
John SUMMAN	3	3
John STRAIGHT	1	1
Joseph SNYDER	1	4
Thomas SCOTT	1	2
Christian SHAVER	1	4
John STRAIGHT	1	2
Wm. STRAIGHT	1	2
Charles STEWART	1	1
Abraham SRIVER	1	2
Charles SHIELDS	1	1

John SHIELDS	1	2	
Benjamin SATTERFIELD	1	2	
Enoch SCOTT	1	2	
David SCOTT, Jr.	1	4	
George SNIDER	1	3	
Jeremiah SNIDER	1	3	
Joseph SUTTON	1	4	
John STATLER, Exempt		4	
Abraham SRIVER	3	7	
Samuel SHULTS	1	1	
John SANTEE	1	2	
Wm. SAMS	1	1	
Robert STEWART, Exempt		2	
Jane SNIDER		2	
Samuel STEWART, J. C.	1	1	
Francis STANSBURY	2	3	
Anthony SMITH	1	5	
Philip SHUTTLESWORTH	1	3	
Archabald SHUTTLESWORTH	1	1	
Daniel STEWART	1	3	
Wm. STEWART	2	3	
Alexander STEWART	1	5	
John STEALEY	2	7	
(blacks over 16)			6
(mills)			4
Davis SHOCKLEY	1	4	
(ferry)			1
Philip J. SHEETS	1		
Soloman SHUFF	1		
John SRIVER	-	-	
(mill)			1
Peter TENNANT	1	4	
(blacks 12-16)			1
Wm. TENNANT	1	2	
Michael TOUTHMAN	2	4	
George TOUTHMAN	2	2	
Crisby TOUTHMAN	2	3	
John TOUTHMAN	1	2	
George TUCKER	2	2	
Daniel THOMPSON	1	2	
Benjamin THOMAS	1	4	
(blacks over 16)			1
(blacks 12-16)			1
Jonathan TEACHENER	1	3	
John TENNANT	1	3	
Leonard TURKEYHIZER	2	3	
Joseph TUTTLE	1	1	
James TIBBS	1	10	
(blacks over 16)			1
Samuel TRICKET	1	2	
George THOMAS	1		
Richard TENNANT	1	3	

Adam TENNANT	1	2	
Joseph TENNANT	1	1	
Tetera TOUTHMAN	2	4	
Richard TENNANT	1	4	
(blacks over 16)			1
Jacob TEWALT	1	2	
Benjamin THORN	1	2	
(blacks 12-16)			1
Aron TEACHENER	1	2	
James THOMPSON	1	2	
Andrew THOMPSON	1	3	
Benjamin THORN, M. R.	1	1	
Joshua THORN	1	2	
Joseph THOMAS	1	1	
John TANEVA	1	1	
John TOUTHMAN	2	2	
Michael TOUTHMAN	1	2	
John THORN	1	3	
Wm. THOMAS	1	3	
John THOMAS	1	1	
Govey TRIPPET	1	2	
John TAYLOR	2	2	
George M. THOMPSON	1		
John W. THOMPSON	1	1	
Jacob VANGUILDER	2	5	
Joseph VARNER, Exempt		2	
Widow VINCENT	2	2	
George UNDERWOOD	2	3	
Samuel UPTON	2	2	
George WATERS	1	2	
William WILSON	2	3	
Benjamin WILSON	2	5	
John WEST	3		
Alexander WADE	1	4	
David WHITE	1	1	
Grafton WHITE	2	6	
Wm. WHITE	1	2	
John WATS	1	1	
Thomas WADE, Jr.	1	1	
James G. WATSON	2	8	
(blacks 12-16)			7
(blacks 12-16)			1
Henry WEAVER	1	3	
Joseph WILFORD	1	6	
Lorance WINKLER	1	2	
Wm. P. WILLEY	1	2	
Daniel WADE	1	2	
(mill)			1
John WELLS	1	3	
Richard WELLS	1	2	
Wm. WILLEY	1	1	
Adam WOLF	1	2	

404

John WILSON	1	3	
James WALKER	1	6	
George WILSON	1	2	
Reuben WILCUT	2	2	
Thomas WELLS	2	4	
Jacob WAGNER	1	1	
Wm. WADKINS	1	3	
James WEST, Jr.	1		
Thomas S. WILSON	1	3	
Josiah WILSON	1	3	
Humphrey B. WILSON	1	2	
George WATSON	1	2	
George WATSON, Jr.	1	3	
John WATSON	1	2	
David WATSON	1	1	
Wm. WILLEY, Jr.	1	3	
James WILLEY	2	3	
Josias WILCUT	1	1	
Wm. WINZER	1	5	
(blacks over 16)			1
Gabriel WILLIAMS	2	4	
Peter WALKER	1	2	
George WISE	1	2	
Robert WALLIS	1	3	
Wm. WILSON	1	3	
James WEST	1	1	
James WILSON	1	2	
James WATTS	1	2	
Stephen WILCOCK	1	3	
Philip WAGNER	1	2	
Thomas WILSON	1	2	
Hezekiah WADE	3	2	
Winmin WADE	1	1	
George WADE, Exempt		1	
George WADE, Jr.	2	2	
Thomas WADE	2	3	
Joseph WADE	1	2	
William WEBSTER	1	2	
Simeon WOODROW	1		
John WAVE	1		
Harvey WHEELER	1	2	
John WILTNER/WILLNER	1	8	
John WILLNER, Jr.	1	4	
Nathaniel WEBB	1		
Thomas WILSON	2	13	
(blacks over 16)			5
Abraham WOODROW	1		
Wm. YOUNG	1	1	
Wm YOUST	1	2	
Peter YOUST	1	4	
Jacob YOUST	1	1	
David YOUST	1	1	

Henry YOUST	1	4
John YOUST	1	1
John YOUST, Jr.	1	2

"List of Store License for the year 1813."

1 May	EVANS & DEARING	$23
1 June	Rynear HALL	$21.17
1 May	Ralph BERKSHIRE	$23
1 May	John L. GILLMEYER	$23
1 May	Augustus WERNINGER	$23
1 May	SCOTT & KYGER	$23

Surname Index

ABDON, 347 367
ABEL, 29 215
ABERCRUMBY, 28 166 241 347
    367
ABERNATHY, 107 108
ABLE, 1 347 367
ABRAMS, 27 30 191
ACTMONGUASH, 95
ADAMS, 71 367
ADAMSON, 25 26 28-30 196 208
    314 316
ADKESON, 61
ADKINSON, 347 367
ADKISON, 269
AGUSTIN, 342
AGUSTINE, 272
ALBIN, 195
ALBRIGHT, 211 347
ALEXANDER, 248 269 276 347
ALLBRIGHT, 367
ALLEN, 2 8 28 35 38 46 64 74 76
    94 96 135 141 147 157 165 167
    175 179 182 188 197 212 214
    235 290 305 318 324 345
ALLEY, 3 28 29 347 367
ALLIN, 12
ALLY, 18
ALTON, 249 387
AMBROSE, 347 367
AMMONS, 387
AMOS, 30 76 86 211 387
ANDERSON, 28 29 37 50 61 72 90
    102 175 196 213 231 237 247
    249 254 258 264 266 272 274
    347 367
ANNON, 221 262
ANSKINS, 313
ANSTINE, 20 21 95
ANSTINIS, 189
ARCHER, 247 249 254 258 264

ARCHER (Continued)
    266 272 274 275 347 387
ARCHIBALD, 315
ARGO, 214
ARMISTEAD, 41
ARMONGASH, 95 96
ARMSTRONG, 3 26 71 252 278 294
    333 347 367
ARNET, 272
ARNETT, 2 28 85 194 211 249 264
    345 387
ARNOLD, 185 197 251 269 309
    310
ARTHERS, 25
ARTHURS, 61
ASBURN, 347
ASBY, 204 251
ASHBERY, 251
ASHBEY, 256 275 320
ASHBY, 55 69 141 204 207 209
    211 215 248 256 262 269 334
    367
ASHCRAFT, 247
ASHER, 60 211 387
ASHFORD, 102 110 195
ASHLEY, 347
ASHLY, 50
ASKIN, 155 251
ASKINS, 155 218 248 256 258 260
    268 269 347 367
ATKINSON, 39 214 316 317
AUGUSTEIN, 167
AUGUSTIN, 217
AUGUSTINE, 60
AUSBUN, 367
AUSTIN, 24 62 215 251 262 266
    274 320 387
AUSTINE, 20
AVERY, 314 316 317 326
AXTON, 171 196

AYERS, 153
AYRES, 260 307
BACKHORN, 251
BACON, 367
BACORN, 248 258 262 269
BAILES, 272
BAILEY, 186
BAILS, 138 251
BAIN, 133
BAINBRIDGE, 68 196 208 305
BAKER, 5 29 38 69 74 76 81 85 95
    96 103 126 134 161 170 171
    182 209-211 248 251 252 260
    262 268 269 275 285 333 335
    345 347 348 367 368 387 389
BAKORN, 260
BALDON, 149
BALDWIN, 25 27 29 30 52 60 64 71
    83 85 126 136 137 158 166 184
    185 187 196 197 209 214 290
    387 389
BALES, 60
BALL, 60 101 135 164
BALLAH, 70 88 201 204-207 388
BALLARD, 329
BALSER, 206
BALTSELL, 389
BALTZEL, 206
BALTZELL, 298 345
BALTZER, 247
BAMBRIDGE, 347 368
BANIDAND, 216
BANK, 331
BANKARD, 344
BANKER, 78 389
BANKERT, 168 169
BANKHART, 12
BANKS, 149 247-249 251 254 256
    258 260 262 264 266 268 269
    272 274 275
BARB, 348 368
BARBOWER, 368
BARBROWER, 30
BARE, 155 216 250 264 272 349
    368
BAREMORE, 58 80 387
BARGDALE, 250
BARING, 296-298 325
BARKER, 6 15 31 32 37 46 60 78
    85 133 145 162 171 184 186
    191 193 196 198 220 238 266

BARKER (Continued)
    286 287 290 304 319 321 327
    344 345 388 389
BARKLOW, 163
BARKSHIRE, 4 8 14 27 28 42 53 54
    58 63 70 75 85 110 111 135 136
    138 162 180 183 186 189 194
    198 201 205-207 213 223 224
    226 238 278 281 287 289 291
    292 309 314 329 333 336 337
    342 389
BARLEY, 368
BARNES, 9 28 39 42 58 62 68 70
    74 85-87 136 138 152 197 201
    205-207 220 222 226 278 292
    298 332 347 367 368 388 389
BARNETT, 31 389
BARNEY, 217
BARNHART, 348 368
BARNHOUSE, 388
BARNS, 34 62 63 82 175 176 201
    205 214 222 223 243
BARNSTEAD, 248
BARNUS, 388
BARR, 368 389
BARRACK, 69
BARRACKMAN, 82
BARRET, 335
BARRETS, 87
BARRETT, 83 149 163 196 345 348
BARRICK, 83 387 388
BARRICKMAN, 5 15 16 28-30 58 71
    168 195 226 280 388
BARTH, 121
BARTLETT, 12 86 197 232 248 304
    347 368 385 388
BARTON, 133 247
BARTROWE, 211
BASHONE, 272
BASNETT, 28 197 388
BASSET, 174
BASSETT, 367
BASSNET, 5
BASSNETT, 60 87
BATHWELL, 175 388
BATSON, 214
BATTEN, 275
BATTON, 60 90 208 222 250 258
    309 335 388 389
BATZELL, 324
BAWIN, 389

BAXTER, 83 228

BAYLES, 29 30 41 59 111 138 139
164 166 206 256 262 272 275
348 367 388

BAYTEY, 274

BAZZEL, 61

BEAL, 248 251 256 258 260 262
268 274 275 348

BEALE, 2

BEALL, 4 16 28 65 66 79 100 118-
120 132 144 196 201 203 247
258 292 313 342 348 368 385

BEALS, 367

BEAN, 262 270

BEATTY, 252

BEATY, 6 65 84 260 262 266 348
368

BEAVERS, 369

BECK, 63

BECKEN, 275

BECKHORN, 256 268

BEELS, 3

BEEN, 252

BEIL, 58

BELINGER, 268

BELL, 26 120 197 207 213 248 256
260 266 268 269 292 342 368
388

BENNET, 112 171 258 260 347

BENNETT, 15 21 22 92 152 165
196 318 335 344 367

BENSON, 114 300 348 368

BENTLEY, 369

BERDINE, 250 264 272 389

BERKSHIRE, 2 56 74 110-112 198
387 389 406

BERMINGHAM, 262

BERRY, 61 389

BERY, 214

BETTY, 40

BEVELIN, 62

BICE, 70 71 195 347 348 368

BIDDLE, 185

BIERBOUR, 348

BIGG, 60

BIGGS, 7 19 197 251 252 254 260
262 272 309 348

BIGS, 272 274 389

BILL, 85 251

BILLINGSLEY, 2 58 77 81 88 120
217 333 335 367 387

BILLINGSLY, 58

BILLS, 12 16 30 137 146 163 164
196 236 298 300 301 314 316
319 320

BINGAMAN, 57

BINGAMON, 368

BIRCH, 28 196 348 367

BIRD, 28 60 61 95 96 142 144 214
305

BIRK, 367

BIRKLER, 60

BIRN, 227

BISHOFF, 203

BISHOP, 10 123 124 344 348 368
369

BITOBARGER, 388

BIXLER, 133 192 300 389

BIZARD, 60 214

BIZERT, 302

BLACK, 3 242 252 262 369 388

BLACKSTONE, 252 262 270

BLACKWELL, 247

BLAND, 389

BLANEY, 367

BOADLEY, 28

BOARD, 214 348

BOAS, 214

BODLEY, 211 302 345 387

BOGARD, 242

BOGG, 60

BOGGESS, 2 29 30 82 179 180 192
196 197 217 224 236 329

BOGGIS, 388 389

BOICE, 232

BOID, 290 347 367

BOIDSTONE, 140

BOLING, 387

BOLLIAN, 369

BOLSBY, 240

BOLSEL, 205

BOLSLEY, 81

BOLYARD, 369

BOMAN, 348 368

BOND, 35-37 93 213

BONER, 32 33 203 214 280 367
387-389

BOOTH, 196 250 252 258 264 266
272

BOOTHE, 262

BORER, 15

BORLLEE, 58

BORMAN, 368
BOSLEY, 86
BOSWELL, 160 215 368
BOTH, 270
BOTHWELL, 154 345
BOUSLOG, 26-29 47 49 69 70 72
    82 83 162 196 208 215 302 332
    344
BOWEN, 214
BOWERS, 132 387
BOWLBY, 28 81 88 288
BOWLES, 38
BOWLESBEE, 387
BOWLS, 33
BOWLSBY, 216
BOWMAN, 171 197 216 229
BOWNESS, 93
BOWNUSS, 93
BOWSLEY, 227
BOWSLOG, 388
BOYCE, 80 214
BOYD, 88 191 213 290 295 389
BOYERS, 3 215 217 252
BOYLE, 248
BOYLES, 16 17 27 29 30 50 70 74
    77 81 139 148 154 170 196 198
    225 249 250 258 262 266 268
    269 291 321 389
BOYLON, 348
BOYLS, 260
BOYSE, 60
BPYCE, 368
BRADFORD, 92 165 335
BRADING, 164
BRADLEY, 347 368
BRAHAM, 347 348 368
BRAIN, 2 178 367
BRAND, 42 74 85-87 134 142 194
    220 292 388 389
BRANDON, 5 7 19 28 31 37 59 61-
    63 74 77 86 183 188 195 204
    209 213 220 232 233 248 251
    256 260 262 264 268 269 275
    311 313 348 367 368
BRANN, 88
BRANNON, 71 137 262 270
BRANT, 30 173 258
BRAUCHUYRE, 211
BRAWN, 250 388 389
BREADING, 164 292
BREDENHARD, 258

BREDENHART, 266
BRICE, 43
BRIDINHART, 254
BRIGGS, 28 29 205 369
BRIGHT, 80 211 348
BRION, 264
BRISCO, 298
BRISCOE, 325
BRITE, 389
BRITTAN, 388
BRITTON, 62 82 133 166 176 179
    180 183 197 230 249 310 311
    345 389
BROCKMAN, 79
BROCKMIRE, 227 349 368
BROCT, 368
BROMWELL, 15
BROOK, 152 247 264 272
BROOKE, 2 249
BROOKHAVEN, 342
BROOKOVER, 2 389
BROOKSHIRE, 2
BROUGHMIRE, 258
BROWN, 25 30 31 54 62 75 79 80
    82-84 86 100 133 135 178 195-
    197 203 209 211 212 214 220
    247 249-251 254 258 264 266
    268 272 274 283 290 297 334
    342 347-349 368
BROWNFIELD, 47 147 270
BROYTE, 213
BRUMAGE, 28 388 389
BRUMMAGE, 195 215 327
BRYAN, 80 250 254 266 274
BRYANT, 260 262 269
BRYON, 252 272
BUCHANAN, 71
BUCK, 2 331
BUCKALEW, 279
BUCKALUE, 343
BUCKER, 388
BUCKHANNAN, 52
BUCKHANNON, 63 149 252
BUCKHANON, 234
BUCKLEW, 28 61 221 348 349 367
    368
BUCKMAN, 39
BUDENHART, 274
BULLAND, 37 247
BULLARD, 37 139
BULLOCK, 328

DEADUFF, 252
DEAKEN, 392
DEAKINS, 248 252 260 262 270
DEAN, 4 5 29 37 52 54 63 64 67 72
    73 81 132 138 144 158 187 201
    207 232 249 254 257 260 276
    292 322
DEARDORN, 28
DEARING, 39 350 370 392 406
DEARLING, 214
DEARTH, 292
DEBELIN, 208
DEBERRY, 61 333 343 350 370
    371
DEBLIN, 208
DEEN, 140 392
DEIBLER, 12 27 30 138 166
DELANEY, 392
DELINSON, 275
DEMOSS, 61 143 350 370
DENNEY, 172
DENNY, 247
DENSON, 240
DENT, 1 2 12 55 58 60 85 119 158
    184 191 194 212 241 272 289
    314 336 391
DENTZ, 13
DENWOODY, 153
DERICK, 248 268
DERING, 2 8 21 27 41 49 75 78 87
    92 98 107 108 117 144 158 179
    180 182-184 187 188 193 198
    201 209 212 215 216 226 231
    237 240 251 277 285 289 291
    292 294 295 299 304 309 311
    312 317 319 320
DERRICK, 263 270 276
DEUSENBERRY, 391
DEVALL, 370
DEVELIN, 11
DEVENHOVER, 49
DEWEES, 260 262 270
DEWEESE, 162 197
DEWESE, 197
DEWIT, 40 84 350 370
DEYER, 275
DIBLER, 60
DICE, 248 260 262 270
DICKEN, 194 392
DICKENSON, 24 262 334
DICKERSON, 28 270 331

DICKESON, 350
DICKEY, 84 335 370
DICKINSON, 83 85
DICKISON, 79 80
DICKSON, 252
DIEL, 392
DIER, 268
DIGMAN, 60 61 84 213 350 370
    391
DILAN, 275
DILLON, 152
DINWIDDIE, 61
DIRE, 256
DIRELING, 252
DIRLING, 260 262 268 270
DIRRICK, 260
DOBSON, 224
DOCERTY, 300
DODDRIDGE, 15 43 152 194 223
    258 296 298 314 325
DODSON, 78
DOHEHORTHY, 84
DONALDSON, 72 73 196 256
DONELSON, 350 370
DONOLSON, 268
DONSON, 350 370
DOODRIDGE, 229
DOOLITTLE, 28 29 34 39 56 75 86
    122 134 158 204 207 250 314
    332 344 345 391 392
DORAN, 220
DOREN, 223
DORSEY, 47 67 82 175 217 287
    308 309 313 314 335 350 370
DORTON, 56 350 370
DOTSON, 344
DOUGHERTY, 72 77 78 122 256
    391
DOUGHMAN, 30 252
DOUGLAS, 350 370
DOUGLASS, 47 241 330
DOUTHE, 213
DOUTY, 6
DOWD, 209
DOWNARD, 214 250 262
DOWNER, 12 13 16 22 23 29-31 53
    89 101 180 197 229 238 247
    248 252 253 255 256 261 263
    266 268 270 275 276 285 313
    327
DOWNEY, 64 213 231 288 350 370

EVENHART, 275
EVENS, 172
EVERHART, 149 248 252 256 258 262
EVERHEART, 268 270
EVERINGHAM, 248 252 256 268 275
EVERLY, 4 13 18 25 27-30 32 43-45 51 58 62 63 72 73 80 81 135 138 140 166 187 188 196 197 200 201 203 207 213 215 216 220 223 232 238 250 252 291 302 303 351 392
EVINHAM, 270
EWEL, 260 262 333
EWELL, 38 47 75 84 149 195 351 371
EWING, 30 163 183 265 272
FAIRCHILD, 341 371
FAIRFAX, 4 6 9 11 45 63 65 66 74 76 79 183 196 199-201 207 220 260 262 291 292 304 310 311 333-336 342 344 351 371 385
FALKNER, 351 371
FALLIS, 265 272
FANCHER, 60 214 255 393
FANSHIER, 328
FARGUSON, 25
FARLEY, 272
FARMER, 2 393
FARNEY, 72
FARQUER, 241
FAST, 146 217 351 371
FASTENS, 351 371
FAUCET, 351 371 372 393
FAULK, 393
FAUSET, 46 300
FAUVER, 393
FAW, 248 252 256 258 260 262 268 270 275
FEASTER, 351 371
FEATHERS, 30 88 351 371
FELBY, 393
FELTAND, 252
FELTON, 351 371
FERAL, 301
FERGUSON, 24 46 70 252 260 270 331
FERREE, 28 60 62 215
FERREL, 61 62 74 179

FERRELL, 1 4 27 30 37 38 63 71 91 104 111 145 146 151 179 182 196 201 206 207 213 217 226 229 231 234 236 252 255 262 267 274 279 291 292 294 296 321 334 335 337 351 371
FERSEE, 275
FETLAND, 263
FETTY, 216 293 294 351 371 393
FICKLE, 28 61 197 242 352 372
FIDDY, 88 204 265 272
FIDEY, 274
FIELDS, 177 178 183 281 351 371
FILCE, 258
FILLIS, 274
FIRSEE, 252
FISHER, 319 332 393
FITSORD, 30
FITZGERALD, 138 252 263 270
FITZRANDOLPH, 315
FLANNIGAN, 272
FLEAHARTY, 89 393
FLEEHARTY, 198 214
FLEMAN, 267 275
FLEMING, 62 72 73 195 200 222 240 250 352 393
FLESON, 150
FLITE, 333
FLOID, 109 110
FLOWERS, 243 247
FLOYD, 30 62 84 109 187 197 207 252 256 270 281 282 393
FLUEHARTY, 207
FLYNN, 61
FOLLIS, 267
FORD, 61 131 213 229 250 252 272 351 371
FORDE, 16 28 130 159 182
FOREMAN, 72 108 109 351 352 372
FOREST, 73
FORESYTHE, 352
FOREY, 208
FORISIT, 258
FORISTER, 250
FORMAN, 72 109 174 241 243 372
FORREST, 298 325
FORSEE, 260 268 270
FORSHEE, 256
FORSTER, 28 29 120 196-198 298

422

HOLLIDAY, 167
HOLLIFIELD, 30 60 67 140 196
    236 237 239
HOLLON, 139 333
HOLLOWS, 194
HOLLY, 31
HOLMAN, 373
HOLMES, 272
HOLSTINE, 373
HOLT, 145 156 252 394 395
HONSUCKER, 258
HOOD, 60 239 353 373
HOOK, 45
HOOKER, 248 256
HOON, 268
HOOVER, 90 91 395
HOPKINS, 96 250 252 258 263 265
    268 270 272 276
HORD, 216
HORN, 263 270
HORNER, 119
HORNES, 285
HORSE, 248 252 257 258 263 268
    276
HORTON, 10 12 19 25 32 49 53 63
    78 103 104 138 143 144 158
    159 180 213 223 234 249 254
    257 258 260 269 276 305 308
    309 311 312 316 327 343 354
    373
HOSE, 248 256 258 260 263 270
    276
HOSKINS, 261
HOSKINSON, 12 31 33 37 38 52 53
    56 58 61 69 75 83 86 88 129
    133 148 150 167 185 194 196
    199 208 214 223 225 226 228-
    239 287 298 320 324 353 373
    394 395
HOUGH, 160 174
HOULT, 29 30 240 284 286
HOURST, 61
HOUSEMAN, 189 213 218
HOUSMAN, 80
HOUSTON, 3 309 332 394
HOVER, 257
HOVEROCK, 252
HOWARD, 394
HOWEL, 61 247 250 272 274 394
HOWELL, 29 30 180 196 211 258
    345 373

HOY, 252 253 257 263 334
HOYE, 261 263 270 277 295 298
    312 334
HUDSON, 208 394 395
HUFFMAN, 15 20 21 28 29 31 83
    84 95 175 197 198 213 228 333
    353 373 394 395
HUGANS, 152 153
HUGGANS, 263 270
HUGGINS, 152 252 314-316
HUGH, 174
HUGINS, 152 153
HULL, 64 90 96 146 175 250 263
    353 373
HUMPHREYS, 395
HUNE, 253 267
HUNESUCKER, 274
HUNSEEKER, 247
HUNSIKER, 267
HUNSUCKER, 255
HUNT, 16 28 61 155 213 247 250
    252 255 258 265 267 272 274
    353 373
HUNTS, 252
HUP, 102
HURDIN, 255
HURIN, 111
HURLEY, 58 86 197 198 241 394
    395
HURLOCK, 17-19
HURLY, 86
HURRY, 64 84 87 185 194 324 333
    396
HUSTEN, 263
HUSTON, 131 252
HUTSON, 18 45 51 208
HYATT, 162
HYDE, 195
ICE, 43 84 87 197 222 223 247 255
    305 396
INESTONE, 20 21
ISAACS, 196
ISRAEL, 315
JACKSON, 8 18 34 58 60 69 70 73
    147 160 199 252 253 279 280
    298 354 374 375 383 385 396
JACO, 15 28 29 61 71 195 196 213
    233 263 270 315 354 374
JACOB, 261
JACOBS, 195 248 252 257 261 263
    270 276 396

KELSON, 375
KEMMEL, 263
KENADY, 68 355
KENDAY, 56
KENNADY, 59 396
KENNARD, 175
KENNEDY, 11 75 76 84 86 143 169
191 195 198 224 293
KERN, 1 2 9 26 81 82 84 165 217
222 248 396
KERNS, 12 28 32 54-56 87 103 161
164 179 206 211 212 216 272
274 305 341 355 375 385
KERR, 248 257 261
KERWOOD, 166
KESSINGER, 355 375
KETTERMAN, 15
KEY, 217
KEZER, 272
KIBLER, 193
KIDDY, 253
KIGER, 1 43 152 209 278 281 282
293 316 320
KILE, 299
KIMMEL, 208
KIMMELL, 61
KIMMER, 299 316 355 375
KIMMERER, 83 299 330 343 344
KIMMERS, 299
KINCADE, 34 68 164 211 280
KINCAID, 88 280 295
KINDLE, 397
KING, 28-30 71 86 99 100 204 213
220 225 265 272 336 355 375
397
KINGCADE, 355 375
KINKAID, 253
KINS, 273
KIRBEY, 397
KIRK, 213 355 375
KIRKHART, 173 326 355 375
KIRKHEART, 74
KIRKMAN, 355
KIRKPATRICK, 159 248 257 258
261 270 276
KISNER, 279
KITTERMAN, 203
KNAVE, 375
KNIGHT, 25 28 31 62 83 84 191
196 201 206 214 222 396 397
KNOTS, 253

KNOTTS, 28 64 92 211 263 355
375
KNOW, 355
KNOX, 29 60 62 69 74 87 133 141
149 191 208 213 232 233 287
316 375 396
KORE, 16
KOWAN, 72
KRANTZER, 272
KRATZER, 77 285
KRAZER, 274
KRIMMERER, 62
KRYDER, 61
KUGAL, 396
KUGLE, 265
KUHN, 258 261 263 268 270
KUNDE, 293
KUWOOD, 166
KYGER, 111 137 157 206 225 318
329 334 344 355 375 382 397
406
LADELEY, 397
LAIDLEY, 2 16 28-30 33 35 64 71
90-93 96 97 146 149 151 165
166 184 188 196 216 227 230
233 237 239 253 257 293 313
LAIRD, 297 298
LAKE, 217 355 375
LAMBERT, 356 376
LAMBERTH, 213
LAMPHAR, 60
LAMPHER, 61 198 214
LANCASTER, 13 16 79 83 85 209
397
LANCE, 249 356
LANDFIELD, 198
LANE, 73 82 200 257 356
LANGFORD, 249 270
LANGHAM, 270
LANGWELL, 265 272
LANHAM, 28-30 46 69 70 94 98
134 196 215 222 253 255 263
287 299 305 320 397 398
LANNAM, 308
LANTS, 375
LANTZ, 21 29 83 209
LAP, 356 376
LAPPINGTON, 7
LAREW, 356
LAROME, 250 258 265
LARRANCE, 272

425

427

MASON (Continued)
343 356-358 377 378
MASTELER, 259
MASTELLER, 257
MASTER, 132
MASTERS, 64 145
MASTERSON, 118-120 174
MASTITLER, 268
MATHENA, 377
MATHENEY, 27 75 188 195 197
203 211 224 253 282 343 357
378 398 399
MATHENY, 6 28 59 61 86 176 186
214 225 253 342 345 357 358
MATHEW, 27 30 162 194
MATHEWS, 12 28 61 196 281 345
MATHINA, 376
MATHIS, 215
MATHUSE, 269
MATTHEW, 162 300 357 377 398
MATTHEWS, 107 250 265 273
MAULSBY, 101
MAURAY, 230
MAUREY, 16
MAXEN, 358 378
MAXFIELD, 61 213 217
MAXSON, 138 195
MAXWELL, 249 250 255 265 267
273 275 315
MAY, 26 62 250 253 259 263 378
MAYBERRY, 261 263 270
MAYFIELD, 18 61 150 225 357 400
MCARTHUR, 378
MCBRIDE, 191
MCCALEB, 398
MCCALL, 63
MCCALLASTER, 398
MCCALLISTER, 240 242
MCCAN, 377
MCCANNON, 90
MCCANTS, 398
MCCARDY, 62
MCCARTEY, 26
MCCARTNEY, 26 61
MCCARTY, 26 61 278 294
MCCAURMIC, 357
MCCAWLEY, 345
MCCLAAREY, 400
MCCLAIN, 29 110 114 197 248 268
276 278 377
MCCLANEN, 275

MCCLANON, 276
MCCLARA, 63
MCCLARE, 273
MCCLARY, 24
MCCLAUS, 278
MCCLEAN, 47 167 257
MCCLEARY, 309
MCCLEERY, 7 11 26 42 44 51 53
54 63 72-75 78 98 142 153 172
198-200 212 223 224 240-243
309 313 320 327 344 345
MCCLELAND, 195 249 261 265
267 269 270 273 321
MCCLELLAND, 211 255
MCCLERY, 331
MCCLOUD, 225
MCCLURE, 249 250 255 265 275
MCCOLEY, 304
MCCOLLUM, 358 378
MCCONNEL, 358
MCCORLEY, 278
MCCORMICK, 180 215
MCCOY, 240
MCCRA, 228
MCCRAY, 38 48 132 133 222 230
237 300
MCCREA, 9 28-30 46 196 319
MCCUROY, 399
MCDADE, 28 29 106 172 173 196
357 376
MCDANIEL, 10 12 357 377
MCDEVIT, 399
MCDONALD, 28 29 248
MCDONOLD, 249
MCDOOLE, 358
MCDOUGAL, 103 104 211 398
MCENTOSH, 213
MCEVERS, 253
MCFADDIN, 227
MCFAGIN, 7 305
MCFALL, 126
MCFARLAND, 27-30 128 159 195
196 242 293 326
MCFEATERS, 47
MCFEELERS, 30
MCFEETERS, 47
MCGEE, 2 28-30 61 68 191 194
196 213 215 242 250 258 333
337 344 357 377
MCGILL, 29 30 34 38 45 62 163
295 357

MCGINNIS, 357
MCGREW, 5 204 241 378
MCGUIRE, 35-37 61 253 259 263 270 276
MCGUMMARY, 399
MCGURE, 269
MCHENRY, 61 213 377
MCINTER, 255
MCIVER, 261 263
MCKEAN, 248
MCKEEVER, 358 376
MCKENNION, 29
MCKENNON, 90 91 182
MCKINEY, 130 293
MCKINLEY, 8 28-30 57 118 140 141 169 196 206 277 278 282 298 309 312-314 323 324 333
MCKINLY, 98 123 163 164 166-169
MCKINNA, 400
MCKUION, 257
MCKUNE, 276
MCLAIN, 27 153
MCMEAKIN, 275
MCMEEKIN, 250
MCMICKEN, 267 273
MCMICKIN, 265
MCMULLEN, 151 152 232 358 377
MCMULLIN, 151 152
MCNEELEY, 119
MCNEELY, 55 151 152 212 328 344
MCPECK, 276
MCQUIRE, 261
MCQURE, 268
MCRA, 43 46 54 214 227 309 399 400
MCRAE, 11 34 48 70 71 118 233 300
MCREA, 61
MCSHANE, 358 378
MCVICKER, 14 15 28 57 61 62 69 75 81 86 105 106 132 136 152 165 182 185 190 195 196 224-227 229-232 236 324 341 357 376 400
MCWILLIAMS, 68
MEAKS, 357 378
MEANERE, 253
MEANS, 30 106 161 172-174 253 356
MEDSKER, 215 326 376

MEEKS, 12 28 211
MEES, 265
MEIGS, 317
MELCHER, 253
MELKER, 263 270
MELLET, 332 399
MENEAR, 61
MENTHORN, 263 270
MERCER, 250 326 342 398
MERCHAND, 267
MEREDITH, 1 10 13 84 215 221 253 261 263 271 333 337 357 398
MEREFIELD, 281
MERIDETH, 206
MERIFIELD, 170 249 250 265 267 327
MERRADETH, 377
MERRAFIELD, 376
MERRELL, 398 399
MERRELS, 273
MERRICK, 330
MERRIFIELD, 150-152 197 208 255 273 280 327 328 399
MERRILL, 222
MERRYFIELD, 37
MERS, 275
MERVIN, 270
MERYDETH, 143 311
MESMORE, 240
MESSENGER, 26 197 237 320 377
MESSER, 85
MESSINGER, 357
METHENEY, 74 220 233 343
METHENY, 221
METS, 399
METZER, 357
MEYE, 259
MIARS, 82
MICHAEL, 46 58 197 214 215 261 265 269 271 273 358 378 398 399
MICKEL, 172
MIDDLETON, 28 221 265 273 288 292 325 343 358 378
MIERS, 114 174 265 273
MILCHER, 138
MILEY, 29 195 273 275
MILLAR, 221 248
MILLER, 3 14 15 21 28-30 38 40 61-65 68 69 74 86 120 132 144

432

PLOM, 328
PLUM, 253 267 275
PLUMB, 271 359
PLUMMER, 115
PLUNKET, 253 259 263 276
PLUNKETT, 269 271
POE, 221 359 379
POINTER, 77 400 401
POINTS, 134
POLLOCK, 250 255 265 267 273 275
POLSBY, 85
POLSLEY, 63 327 345 346
POOLE, 213
POOLS, 300
POOR, 74
POPINOS, 119
PORT, 30 108 109
PORTER, 80 292 401
PORTOR, 345
POST, 27 29
POSTALWAITE, 10
POSTEN, 212
POSTLE, 6 28-30 41 45 61 74 76 78 81 196 253 263 311 359 379 400
POSTLEWAIT, 65 69 78 95 96 141 195
POSTLEWAITE, 345
POSTLEWRIGHT, 359
POSTON, 359 379
POTTER, 29 31 55 90 103 138 158 159 261 269 271 276 309 310
POWEL, 255 263 275 400 401
POWELL, 13 45 46 48 201 216 220 231 234 249 255 271 291 359 379
POWER, 195 211 217 243
POWERS, 82 83 217 359 379
POWRS, 222
POYNES, 134
PRAT, 240
PRATT, 250 265
PRICE, 6 29 31 47-50 61 66 71 78 84 99 100 107 108 133 166 176 177 181 183 184 194 205 214-216 237 287 314 320 332 333 335 341 342 345 359 379 400 401
PRICHARD, 79 335 359
PRICKET, 68 285

PRICKETT, 2 29 68 84 102 145 151 213 240 283-286 334 335 400
PRIDE, 28 193 241 400 401
PRINDLE, 301
PRINGLE, 250 265
PRITCHARD, 231 318 359 379
PROTZMAN, 359
PROVEANCE, 273
PROVENCE, 267 275
PROVINCE, 255 259 303
PRUIANCE, 250
PRUKET, 197
PRUNTY, 98 185 305
PRYER, 263
PRYOR, 253 271
PUDEU, 197
PUGH, 213 379 385
PULTEAN, 344
PURCEL, 163
PURTMUS, 273
PURVANCE, 265
PURVEANCE, 273
PURVIANCE, 250
PURVINCE, 265
PUTNAM, 300
PYLES, 82
QUANDRALL, 259
QUANDROL, 251
QUICK, 121 122 359 379
RABER, 401
RACHEL, 271
RADABOUGH, 379
RADCLIFF, 162
RALSTON, 196 215 273 360
RAMSAY, 176
RAMSEY, 7 25 30 43 44 57 71 77 79 86 107 108 126 131 134 173 175 176 208 232 253 401
RANDALL, 82 197 379
RANDLE, 333 359
RANDOLPH, 178 297
RANEY, 380
RATCLIFFE, 119
RAVEN, 81 85 88
RAVENCROFT, 28
RAVENSCRAFT, 107 108 166 253
RAVENSCROFT, 57
RAWLINGS, 329
RAY, 1 313 336 359
RAYS, 257
REAM, 29

SCOTT (Continued)
168 172 173 175 181-184 186
187 191 195 196 198 201 207
213 215 225-227 231 237-239
243 248 251 253 255 257 259
261 264 266 269 271 273 276
279 281 287-289 291 292 294
298 299 305 309 311 312 314
316 319 321 323 327-329 332
337 342 345 360-362 381 382
401-403 406
SCRIPPS, 28 29 35-37 39
SCRIPS, 36 265
SCRIVER, 261
SEADY, 203
SEAMAN, 9 28 30 55 56 67 109
110 114 154 182 187 196 251
266 273 300 361 380 402
SEARS, 237
SEDGWICK, 28
SEET, 315
SELBY, 167 211 213 215 361 381
SEMAN, 278
SEMORE, 362
SEREYER, 264
SERVERNS, 269
SETH, 84 183 184 360 381
SEVERINS, 29
SEVERN, 204
SEVERNS, 19 23 28 31 196 220
221 248 253 257 264 271 276
288 309 343 362
SEVIER, 213 362 382
SEWART, 253
SEXTON, 211 254 271 342
SEYMORE, 382
SEYMOUR, 213
SEYRS, 247 249
SHACKELFORD, 314 345
SHACKLEFORD, 3 26 77 82 361
381
SHADWELL, 402
SHAEFFER, 251
SHAFER, 54 191 202 203 264
SHAFFER, 259 261 266 267 271
273
SHAHAN, 197 213 228 312 335
345
SHANE, 324
SHARK, 195
SHARKS, 255

SHAVER, 57 82 248 253 257 259
261 264 271 276 361 362 381
402
SHAW, 30 197 208 211 218 220
221 243 269 345 361 362 380-
382 401
SHAY, 248 253 257 259 264 271
276
SHEAN, 312
SHEARER, 11 12 154 402
SHEATS, 361 381
SHEETS, 26 29 61 69 147 197 228
230 231 236 271 403
SHEETZ, 147
SHEHAN, 61 172 361 381
SHEHEN, 3 4
SHELL, 248 253 271
SHELLS, 314
SHEPARD, 63 249 254 257 260
262 266 269 274 277
SHEPHARD, 67
SHEPHERD, 74
SHEPLER, 39
SHERER, 236
SHERIDEN, 137
SHEWMAN, 30
SHEY, 269
SHIELDS, 293 402 403
SHINN, 277 322 324
SHIP, 345
SHIPLY, 211
SHISLER, 314
SHIVAL, 172
SHIVELEY, 230 255 275 307
SHIVELY, 28 34 47 58 74 83 85
103 106 134 145 147 191 210
247 249 305 307 309 333 342
401
SHIVLEY, 68 172
SHOCKLEY, 16 32 44 49 118 122
123 136 153 155 180 191 197
227 280 304 308 309 314 316
320 322 329 341 343 403
SHOCKLY, 44 118
SHOOPS, 195
SHORT, 402
SHOVIAUGH, 360
SHOWALTER, 137
SHREVES, 43
SHRIOR, 30
SHRIVER, 62 80 81 85 217 264

SPURLAND, 34

SQUIRES, 28 131 206 248 251 257 259 269 271 276 333 361 381

SRIVER, 10 70 79 81 197 236 360 402 403

SROYERS, 361 381

STADLER, 85

STADTLER, 259

STAFFORD, 7 28-30 35 38 45 64 126 127 165 196 197 208 220 223 230 233 292 294 298 318 361 362 380 382

STAG, 251 265 273

STAGG, 259 267

STAILING, 269

STALEY, 147 226 232 277

STALNAKER, 41

STANKER, 29

STANLEY, 35 180 265 267 273 275

STANLY, 251 329

STANSBERRY, 217

STANSBERY, 259

STANSBURY, 403

STARK, 254

STARLING, 52 197 257 261 275 362 382

STARRETT, 214

STARRITT, 62

STARTSMAN, 276

STATELAR, 70

STATELER, 80

STATLER, 62 209 225 251 255 265 273 275 403

STEALEY, 4 47 48 55 62 63 65 67 87 91 102 130-133 139 145 146 150 176 179 180 189 198 206 277 281 289 292 295 297 299 305 308 314 318 320 323 324 329 337 344 403

STEALY, 47 48 74 152 167 201 207 277 305 312

STEARN, 259

STEEL, 28 52 64 215 223 264 271 345 360 382 402

STEER, 253 259 261 264 269 271

STEFON, 229

STEMPLE, 203 361 381

STEPHEN, 58 264

STEPHENS, 58 78 148 149 184 212 234 248 255 257 261 269 271 276 280 360 381

STEPHENSON, 39 132 213 361 380

STERLING, 247-249 255 259 267 276

STERN, 251 266 267 273

STEVENS, 59 75 80 81 84 86 149 197 214 217 259

STEVENSON, 27 29 30 44 70 101 132 150 151 198

STEWARD, 361 363

STEWART, 3 10 17 25 28-30 64 69 141 147 163 169 195 197 208 214-216 222 251 253 259 261 263 264 266 269 271 273 276 317 321 325 380 385 401-403

STIDGER, 148 149 259

STIDGET, 271

STIDON, 148

STIDOR, 148

STIGER, 156 253 261 264

STILE, 402

STILES, 28 59 61 82 83 197 253 257 259 261 264 269 271 276 290 402

STILLWELL, 101 216 361

STINE, 381

STINEBAUGH, 361

STINEBOUG, 213

STINESPRING, 58 402

STOCKWELL, 28 61 361

STODDARD, 254 298 325

STOKELY, 292

STOKER, 251

STONE, 77 402

STONEBREAKER, 259 261 264 269 271

STONEKING, 58 342

STORMES, 195

STOUT, 248 253 257 259 261 264 269 271 276

STOVER, 271

STOVEY, 261

STRADLER, 247 249

STRAIGHT, 84 205 273 402

STRAIT, 84 205 211 305

STRATLER, 79 273

STRAWHEN, 362

STRAYER, 79

STREPEY, 147

STRIGHT, 60 265

STROBRIDGE, 40

STROTHER, 195 305 308

STUART, 70 138 141 195 233 234
STUDDARD, 271
STUDDART, 264
STULL, 203 253 254 257 259 261
    264 271 276
STURM, 61
STUTLER, 222
SUDDETH, 209
SULIVAN, 33 83
SULLAVAN, 361 381
SULLIVAN, 28 33 35 46 61 96 118
    127-130 196 213 233 237 287
    314 324 402
SUMMAN, 402
SUMMERS, 71 155 156 196
SUMMERVILLE, 143 266 273
SUT, 315
SUTHERLAND, 251
SUTTON, 27 28 30 111 403
SWAN, 253 259 264 266 273
SWANEY, 362
SWANK, 18 19 251 266 273
SWANN, 251 271
SWEARGIN, 174
SWEARINGEN, 28 29 88 138 156
    179 189 195 197 257 259 261
    264 269 276 280 287 295 382
    385
SWEARINGER, 253 271
SWEATMAN, 362 382
SWERINGER, 248
SWIERS, 361
SWINDLER, 49 55 82 165 213 222
    299 309
SWINGLER, 360 361 381
SWISER, 275
SWISHER, 12 56 82 215 222 247
    249 251 255 265 267 273 362
    381 401
SWITZER, 320
SWOODOUGH, 61
SYEAMORE, 40
SYEARS, 237
SYNE, 209
SYNES, 213
SYPOLT, 109 211 362 382
SYRIS, 28
TAILOR, 63
TALBOT, 248 257
TANARY, 222
TANEHILL, 61

TANEVA, 404
TANNEHILL, 80 242 264 269
TANNER, 213
TANNIHILL, 72
TANNYHILL, 72
TANSEY, 72 189 241
TANSY, 216
TARISON, 247 249
TARLETON, 251
TARLTON, 217
TARNEY, 8 266
TARRISON, 251 255 259 266 267
    273 275
TATE, 47 48 102 103 130 131 139
    168 254 259 261 264 271
TATTERSON, 323
TAWNEHILL, 276
TAWNEYHILL, 363
TAYLOR, 1 10 29 30 35 38 40 55
    56 63 108 109 135 140 145 161
    165 169 186 196 198 213 226
    236 251 254 259 264 266 267
    271 273 278 282 318 329 333
    363 382 383 404
TEACHENER, 403 404
TEADE, 214
TEATS, 363 383
TEDRICK, 259
TEETS, 6 61 213 316
TEMPOLIN, 183 184
TENANT, 23 88 322
TENNANT, 30 31 61 76 83 88 167
    188 197 403 404
TENNET, 13
TERANCE, 303
TERNAN, 264 271
TERNEY, 247 249
TESEY, 61
TETERICK, 269
TETRICK, 248 257 261 264 271
    276 383
TEWALT, 38 404
THANKELD, 271
THOM, 61
THOMAS, 15 20 21 27-30 61 78 80
    87 92 94 95 134 138 143 146
    149 162 217 239 240 254 261
    282 292 363 383 403 404
THOMPSON, 1 2 8 30 45 53 59 68
    75 77 81 88 105 122 140 146
    175 186 198 211 213 251 254